MW01206290

www.KnowledgePublications.com

Harvesting Potatoes on the Ranch of F. H. Badger, near Greeley, Colorado, U. S. A. (See p. 171.)
(Frontispiece.)

DENATURED OR INDUSTRIAL ALCOHOL

A TREATISE ON

THE HISTORY, MANUFACTURE, COMPOSITION, USES, AND
POSSIBILITIES OF INDUSTRIAL ALCOHOL IN THE
VARIOUS COUNTRIES PERMITTING ITS USE,
AND THE LAWS AND REGULATIONS GOVERNING THE SAME,
INCLUDING THE UNITED STATES

WITH CONCISE TABLES, METHODS, AND NOTES FOR

*THE USE OF THE ENGINEER, CHEMIST, MANUFACTURERS
OF ALCOHOL AND ALCOHOL MAKING AND USING
APPARATUS, INCLUDING ALCOHOL MOTORS, ENGINES,
ILLUMINATING LAMPS,
AND HEATING AND COOKING STOVES*

BY

RUFUS FROST HERRICK

CONSULTING CHEMIST AND CHEMICAL ENGINEER

*Member of the American Chemical Society, the Society of Chemical Industry,
and the Society of Arts of the Massachusetts Institute of
Technology, Boston, Mass.*

FIRST EDITION

FIRST THOUSAND

NEW YORK

JOHN WILEY & SONS

LONDON: CHAPMAN & HALL, LIMITED

1907

PREFACE.*

THE enactment of legislation by our Congress, June 7, 1906 (permitting the general use of tax-free domestic alcohol, after it has been suitably denatured, for industrial purposes and for light, heat, and power) immediately created a wide-spread interest and inquiry throughout the United States as to the facts relating to this whole matter. This law takes effect January 1, 1907.

The scarcity of literature treating the subject of Denatured or Industrial Alcohol is so great that there are practically no books concerning it. This book has therefore been prepared for the above reasons and to supply the facts in answer to the inquiries mentioned.

The author had the honor to represent the American Chemical Society and the Society of Chemical Industry, through their New England sections, in favor of Denatured Alcohol, at the so-called "Free Alcohol" Congressional hearings, held at Washington, D. C., February–March, 1906, on the matter of repealing the internal-revenue tax on domestic alcohol after it had been suitably denatured. The testimony given at these hearings was from a great variety of sources and possessed a highly educational value and interesting character, and was afterwards published by our Government. Many important abstracts from such testimony are given in this book under their appropriate subjects.

The author has also availed himself of the large fund of data furnished by the Report of the British Departmental Committee on Industrial Alcohol, presented to both Houses of Parliament by command of His Majesty, March 23, 1905. This report (with the appendices giving portions of the testimony taken before this Committee in England, France,

---

* Since this preface was written, supplementary legislation has been enacted amending and liberalizing the denatured alcohol law. A copy of such legislation is given on page 489.

Germany, and other continental countries) is given in the Appendix to this book. The complete United States Government Rules and Regulations, No. 30, concerning Denatured Alcohol, under the Act of Congress of June 7, 1906, as well as the United States Government tests and methods prescribed for the denaturing materials and the methods for the denaturing of alcohol, are also included in the Appendix to this book. A list of books of reference on industrial alcohol and allied subjects is given in the bibliography on page 493.

There is also a very complete list, on page 494, from the *Patent Review*, New York, of all the important patents relating to improvements in the manufacture of alcohol and in alcohol-distilling apparatus for the past twenty years. Some original work for this book has been done by the author, but the field is so large that it is an impossibility for any one person to cover it. For this reason the assistance of leading experts has been gladly welcomed by him in the various phases and subjects treated in this book.

The furnishing of important public foreign data, through our Department of State from accredited sources as to Denatured Alcohol, has been greatly appreciated by the author, and acknowledgment of the same is hereby duly made, as well as to our Department of Commerce and Labor, for similar aid.

The thanks of the author are cordially extended to Prof. Samuel C. Prescott for collaboration in the material and calculations for Chapter II, to Dr. G. N. Lewis for assistance in preparing the elaboration of the theories connected with the processes of distillation in Chapter III; also to Dr. Augustus H. Gill, Associate Professor of Technical Analysis, for aid in the calculations and data (involved in the combustion of various liquid fuels) in Chapter VII. All of these experts are associated with the Massachusetts Institute of Technology, Boston, Mass.

The author also desires to express his obligation to Mr. Henry J. Williams, Chemical Engineer and Expert on Coals, Boston, Mass., for work done in determining the fuel value of denatured alcohol and the calculations thereon for Chapter VII, as well as to Mr. Frank E. Davis, Mechanical Engineer, Boston, Mass., for data on investigations of the use of alcohol in American types of internal-combustion engines. It is also a pleasure to record the indebtedness of the author to Mr. Leonard V. Goebbels, Mechanical Engineer of The Otto Gas Engine Works, Philadelphia, Pa., for securing the German data relating to alcohol engines and motors, furnished the author through their head company, the Deutz Gas Engine Works of Deutz-Cologne, Germany. The acknowledgements of the author are also due to Dr. H. W. Wiley, Chief of the Division of Chemistry of the U. S. Department of Agriculture, Washington, D. C., for tables and data furnished on the composition of the raw materials used for the manufacture of alcohol and on the methods for its determination. Thanks are also due to other friends of the author who have given him many valuable suggestions used in the preparation of this book.

The effect of the excessive internal revenue tax (of about $2.08 per gallon on alcohol in this country, gradually, from about the year 1860, increased to this sum) has been to prohibit the use of alcohol for industrial purposes. Meanwhile, wood alcohol, being tax free and much cheaper, was introduced for such uses and nearly replaced the better and more desirable, but taxed, ethyl alcohol. As however wood alcohol is at best a poor substitute for the tax-free Denatured Alcohol, we may confidently expect it will in turn replace wood alcohol.

The whole problem of Denatured Alcohol in this country is therefore in a pioneer state of development, and for this reason the alcohol-using apparatus here described is largely of foreign make.

The American manufacturers of internal-combustion engines and motors, as well as of other alcohol-using apparatus, have however begun thorough investigations on the use of alcohol and expect, from results so far obtained, to be able to place upon the market such engines and apparatus adapted to alcohol. The use of alcohol for illuminating purposes has been very highly perfected abroad, and a very promising field for such uses evidently awaits alcohol in this country.

It is the hope and belief of the author that we Americans can solve for this country the problem of Denatured Alcohol in such a successful manner that all the world may secure, from the results we here attain, uses and benefits much greater than those heretofore achieved.

RUFUS FROST HERRICK.

BOSTON, October, 1906.

CONTENTS.

CHAPTER I.

COMPOSITION, HISTORY, AND USE OF DENATURED ALCOHOL.

CHAPTER II.

THE MANUFACTURE OF ALCOHOL.

CHAPTER III.

THE DISTILLATION AND RECTIFICATION OF ALCOHOL.

CHAPTER VII.

THE FUEL VALUE OF ALCOHOL COMPARED WITH THE OTHER USUAL LIQUID FUELS.

CHAPTER VIII.

ALCOHOL AS A SOURCE OF POWER.

CHAPTER IX.

LAWS AND REGULATIONS FOR DENATURED ALCOHOL.

DENATURED OR INDUSTRIAL ALCOHOL.

CHAPTER I.

COMPOSITION, HISTORY, AND USE OF DENATURED ALCOHOL.

Composition of Denatured Alcohol in Foreign Countries. Distilled Spirits Defined. History of Denatured Alcohol in Foreign Countries. History of Tax-free Alcohol in the United States. Use of Denatured or Industrial Alcohol in Foreign Countries. Use of Industrial Alcohol in Cuba. Use of Industrial Alcohol in the United States.

MURRAY's New English Dictionary defines Denature, "2. To alter (anything) so as to change its nature; e.g., to render alcohol unfit for consumption. Hence Denatured, ppl. (a) 1882, Athenæum, 25 Mar., 385/1. A paper on the Denaturation of Alcohol by the action of Wood Spirit. (b) Denaturation, 1882, Chemist and Druggist, XXIV, 5/2. A commission in Germany has reported on the process of denaturalisation of alcohol for manufacturing purposes."

From the above definitions it is seen that we "denature " ordinary alcohol, or deprive it of its nature as a beverage, when we mix with it some substance requisite for this purpose. As to the spelling of the word which signifies such change, philology would indicate the choice of brevity if no shade of meaning were thereby sacrificed. It happens that the shortest word is also the simplest of those which have been used to describe such change.

Between the spellings, Denatured, Denaturalized, Denaturalised, and Denaturized, all of which words have the same meaning when they refer to alcohol, the preference is overwhelmingly in favor of the first. This spelling was also used by the Departmental Committee in their Report on Industrial Alcohol to the British Parliament, March 23, 1905.*

---

* Since the above was written, the United States Regulations and Instructions have been issued, and the word is there spelled Denatured.

Composition of Denatured Alcohol in Foreign Countries.—Denatured alcohol is made by mixing with ordinary alcohol some substances of a poisonous and repugnant character, but which do not detract from the use of such alcohol for industrial purposes. Among the principal substances so used may be mentioned commercial wood alcohol, pyridine partially rectified, bone-oil which contains large amounts of pyridine, benzine, and benzol; and for special purposes, ether, castor-oil, spirits of turpentine, caustic soda, distilled grease from sheeps' wool, and a number of other substances are used as denaturing agents, as will be shown. As a rule the denatured alcohol, as sold for general uses, contains from 90% to 95% of alcohol by volume. Its alcoholic strength therefore conforms to these percentage figures by Tralles' scale. Of such alcohol present a part is usually wood alcohol. The proportion of the latter is governed by the laws in each particular country relative to such denaturing.

The word alcohol is usually understood to mean ethyl alcohol or ordinary grain alcohol, and it is made on the commercial scale by fermenting and distilling processes, in which such raw materials as corn, rye, potatoes, sugar-beets, and molasses are used. The United States Government definition of ethyl alcohol is given as follows:

Distilled Spirits Defined.—Section 3248 of the Revised Statutes defines distilled spirits, spirits, alcohol, and alcoholic spirit, within the true intent and meaning of the act, to be that substance known as ethyl alcohol, hydrated oxide of ethyl, or spirit of wine, which is commonly produced by the fermentation of grain, starch, molasses, or sugar, including all dilutions and mixtures of this substance, and declares that the tax shall attach to this substance, as soon as it is in existence as such, whether it be subsequently separated as pure or impure spirit, or be immediately, or at any subsequent time, transferred into any other substance, either in the process of original production or by any subsequent process.

Ethyl alcohol is also made, commercially, from sawdust by Claassen's recent process, which will be discussed in Chapter V.

Ethyl alcohol must not be confused with wood alcohol, which is not made by fermenting at all, but by destructively distilling (heating) the wood in iron retorts or ovens and then condensing the vapors. It is then refined as described in Chapter V. The alcohol thus obtained is methyl alcohol and is also called, in commerce, wood alcohol. In appearance it is sometimes a pale straw color, sometimes colorless. It is volatile, inflammable, and is a solvent for many resins, gums, etc. It distills unchanged at 66° C. when pure. The valuable disinfectant, formaldehyde, is made from it and also a number of aniline dyes, as the methylene blues, methyl greens, and the methyl violets.

Oil of wintergreen is also made, synthetically, from methyl alcohol. Commercial wood alcohol has a very marked and repugnant odor and taste. The fumes or vapors from it occasion violent headaches, a depressed nervous condition, and often blindness, when prolonged exposure to such vapors has occurred.* Taken internally it nearly always causes blindness or death, and the internal use of wood alcohol is now considered fatal. For this reason it is an admirable substance for denaturing ethyl or ordinary alcohol, being, in fact, one of the best for such a purpose. Specially denatured alcohol, as denatured at the manufactory in foreign countries, will be discussed under Laws and Regulations of these countries.

History of Denatured Alcohol in Foreign Countries.—*Great Britain* was the first country which attempted to denature or methylate ordinary alcohol. The use of methylated (denatured) spirit, duty-free, was first authorized in 1855 by the Act 18 and 19 Vict., C. 38. The present law on the subject is contained in the Spirits Act, 1880, as amended by the Customs and Inland Revenue Act, 1890, and Section 8 of the Finance Act, 1902.† Such denaturing was accomplished by mixing ten per cent of commercial wood alcohol with ordinary alcohol, the resulting mixture being called methylated spirit. The word methyl was taken from the methyl or wood alcohol, and the word spirit is the common designation of the ordinary alcohol. The Standard Distionary defines "Spirit," 9. as "a strong distilled liquor or liquid, especially alcohol, commonly plural—as ardent spirits." Allen's Commercial Organic Analysis, 1898, Vol. I, p. 78, mentions Methylated Spirit of Wine (alcohol) as "a mixture of 90 per cent of rectified spirit (ethyl or ordinary alcohol) with 10 per cent of commercial wood spirit." The acetone and other constituents of the wood naphtha are so difficult to remove that the spirit (so methylated) is considered to be permanently unfitted for drinking purposes and is therefore not subject to duty. The wood spirit and wood naphtha mentioned mean commercial wood alcohol. We note from the U. S. Daily Consular and Trade Reports of the Department of Commerce and Labor, Bureau of Manufactures, Washington, D. C., April 17, 1906, that

---

* See case of Mr. Charles Bedell, a painter permanently blinded by the fumes of wood alcohol, who so testified at the Congressional "Free Alcohol" hearings, at Washington, D. C., February–March, 1906.

† Action has since been taken by Parliament with the result that new and much more liberal regulations have been issued under date of October 1, 1906. These regulations are given in Chapter IX.

the Chancellor of the Exchequer announced in Parliament recently, in response to an inquiry as to whether anything was to be done to free British manufacturers using alcohol in their business from the disadvantages they now suffer compared with their European competitors, that "the matter is now under consideration," and he "hoped to introduce legislation at an early day."

In Germany the use of pure spirits free of tax was first permitted in 1879, modified and liberalized in 1887. The denaturing at the beginning in 1879 was done with wood alcohol. Until 1887 the German Government used what was practically the system employed in England. Later, in order to permit freer general use, the pyridine bases were added, and this was regarded as an advance on the English system. These pyridine bases are exceedingly repugnant to the taste and smell; they belong to the group of alkaloids of which pyridine is the type, and are obtained as "by-products " from the liquid or "coal-tar " portions, which result from the destructive distillation of coal. Other substances are thus obtained, and from them the beautiful aniline or coal-tar dyes, and other coloring materials used in dyeing, are made. The pyridine bases can also be produced by the refining of bone-oil. Bone-oil is commonly made by the destructive distillation of bones. In Germany the "partially rectified " pyridine is the kind used for general denaturing purposes.

France has permitted the use of denatured alcohol, under benefit of a special tax of 37.50 francs per hectolitre, since the law of August 2, 1872. (A hectolitre = 26.4179 U. S. gallons.) This was revised by the consultative committee on May 11, 1881, and modified so as to render the law more efficacious by making it impossible to use any methyl alcohol except that which, being possessed of the characteristic odor of this commercial product, renders any alcohol to which it has been added absolutely unfit for consumption. Such a methyl alcohol is furnished by the commercial wood alcohol.

They used in addition some heavy benzine from the distillation of coal, and some malachite or aniline green dye. This gave a methylated or denatured alcohol of pale-green color, intended for general use. By the law of April 16, 1895, an extra tax of 0.80 franc per hectolitre was added to cover the expense of supervision by the treasury.

The French have also considered the use of an additional denaturing agent, such as the product obtained by Dr. Lang of Switzerland, from the destructive distillation of the grease from sheeps' wool. The substance so obtained is said to be a mixture of several methyl derivatives of very repugnant smell and taste.

Switzerland has permitted untaxed methylated or denatured alcohol since January 31, 1893, by decree of the Federal Council, pursuant to Article 6 of the law relating to spirituous liquors of December 23, 1886, on the proposition of its Department of Finances and Taxes. By a majority of the voting citizens, as well as by a majority of the cantons, the following change in the federal constitution of 1874 has been adopted:

" Art. 32. The Confederation is authorized, by way of legislation, to issue directions relating to the manufacture and sale of distilled liquors.

" *At this legislation those products that are either to be exported or that have undergone a preparation excluding their use as a beverage shall not be subjected to any taxation.*

" The distilling of wine, fruit, and their wastes of fell-wort, of juniper berries, and of similar materials does not, concerning manufacture and taxation, fall under federal legislation."

The choice of methylating substances was left to the federal department of finance, which may require, as an additional guaranty against unlawful employment, that the alcohol intended for relative methylation be diluted with water.

Wood alcohol, pyridine bases, and solvent naphtha were used as denaturing agents in Switzerland.

Belgium granted the use of denatured or methylated alcohol by the law of April 15, 1896, and further liberalized by revisions of June 15, 1896, and July 19, 1896. The minister of finance determines the process of methylation and the nature and the proportion of the materials destined to render the alcohol unfit for human consumption. Methyl or wood alcohol has been used by Belgium as one of the methylating substances. Alcohol has also been specially denatured at the manufactory where it was used.

The Netherlands permitted denatured alcohol since the enactment of the laws of the 7th of July, 1865, and the 14th of September, 1872.

The methylating was done by mixing with wood spirits or commercial wood alcohol, whereby the spirits were made unfit to serve as a beverage. The government also reserved the right to fix the requisite precautions relating to exemption from excise for use of alcohol in vinegar manufactories and in state, provincial, and communal institutions of instructions in the physical sciences.

Italy, by a law under the royal decree of August 29, 1889, concerning the use of untaxed alcohol, gave relief by means of a drawback for spirits used in making vinegar and manufacturing œnolin.

Sweden, by royal decree of October 10, 1890, permitted the denaturing of alcohol free of taxes, and the selling of the same, by circular of this date, relating to the manufacture of alcohol, etc., paragraph 10, mom. 4, and the regulations of July 13, 1887.

Wood alcohol and pyridine bases were prescribed for denaturing agents, and permits were given for special denaturing by manufacturers of varnishes, fulminate and percussion caps, alkaloids, chloroform, iodoform and chloral, tannic acid, vinegar, acetates of lead, and other acetates. Denatured alcohol kept for sale must be mixed with suitable coloring-matter, by special regulation of the chief of the Bureau of Control and Adjustment. Paragraph 24, decree of October 10, 1890, prescribes: 1. Charges for denaturing the alcohol are 3 ore (from January 1, 1895, 2 ore, in accordance with royal circular of June 1, 1894) for each liter of normal strength. 2. When restitution of taxes is made these charges should be included, but charges for denaturing made at distilleries are accounted for by deducting taxes from 94 per cent of the denatured alcohol.

In *Norway*, by royal decree of June 13, 1891, becoming operative January 1, 1892, and by government resolution of June 29, 1894, No. 23, untaxed alcohol, either as methylated (denatured) brandy or when it is found in some other satisfactory manner to be guaranteed against being used for drink, which the government department may allow, is permitted to be relieved of the production tax in the same way as brandy, and the owner of the brandy has to bear the cost of the methylation and the supervision thereof.

Portugal has permitted the use of untaxed alcohol, all the expenses for the methylation, whether it be voluntary (requested by the manufacturer or owner) or obligatory (when decreed for purposes of shipment or on the occasion of a visit), shall be borne by the manufacturer or owners of the liquids to be methylated.

Austria-Hungary has allowed exemption from the consumption tax on methylated alcohol by the Exchequer decree of April 10, 1888. Supplement III to Sections 6, 66–69, and 73 of the law contains the regulations for the spirits destined for use free of duty. Wood alcohol and pyridine bases were prescribed for denaturing agents. Phenolphthalein was prescribed in addition to these two substances by Exchequer decree of August 15, 1889, Govern. Law Gazette, No. 130; Ordinance Gazette, No. 13. The phenolphthalein has the quality that it easily dissolves in alcohol, concentrated, as also diluted, without changing the color of the latter, and when soda-lye or caustic-soda solution is mixed with such alcohol it gives at once an intense-red color, the coloration being said to be noticeable even in as weak a mixture as one of phenolphthalein in ten million of denatured alcohol mixture.

Through the addition of phenolphthalein to the denatured or methyl-ated alcohol, therefore, the controlling officials are put in a position, in a simple manner, at all times to prove whether potable (beverage) spirits have been manufactured from spirits which have been methylated for the common commerce or are blended or not blended with such spirits. And besides this, perhaps, to establish whether or not spirits (alcohol) already methylated by the usual wood alcohol and pyridine bases are presented for methylation. Special denaturing methods were also per-mitted by Austria-Hungary, in which were used vinegar, animal oil, turpentine-oil, ether, shellac solution, mineral oil, and castor-oil soap.

History of Tax-free Alcohol in the United States.—In 1817 the inter-nal-revenue tax on distilled spirits was repealed, and from that time until the outbreak of the Civil War no recourse was had to internal taxes of any kind, though the Treasury suffered periodically from diminished revenues. When, at the breaking out of the Civil War in 1861 it became necessary to resort to every possible means to raise money, a tax was levied on distilled spirits of 20 cents a gallon. As early as 1864 it has been understood Congress wished to relieve the industrial uses of alcohol from taxation, and to tax only that consumed as a beverage, but no way could be devised, as at that time denaturing was not an established fact as it is now. Interest increased in the subject throughout the country, culminating in the passage by our Congress of such legislation as would, by a rebate or repayment of the internal-revenue tax, provide free alco-hol for industrial uses. This law became operative by the tariff act of August 28, 1894, and Section 61 of this law provided for such rebate. No provision was made in this law, Section 61 of this act, for rendering such tax-free alcohol unfit for use as a beverage or denaturing it. Again, Section 61 of this law (the tariff act, August 28, 1894) provided tax-free alcohol under regulations to be prescribed by the Secretary of the Treas-ury, and as such regulations were never formulated, the law was there-fore inoperative. This led to claims from manufacturers, covering some twelve months of the period it was in force, aggregating some $2,500,000, against the government. Suits were brought by these manufacturers for this rebate on alcohol, and these suits were tried in the U. S. Supreme Court and were not allowed.

An act to repeal Section 61 of the law permitting tax-free alcohol for industrial purposes, as explained, was enacted by our Congress and was approved June 3, 1896. In this act of June 3, 1896, Section 2 pro-vided that a Joint Select Committee from the Senate and House of Repre-sentatives was authorized to consider all questions relating to the use of alcohol in the manufactures and arts free of tax, and to report their conclusions to Congress on the first Monday in December, 1896. The Committee were unable to finish the hearings and inquiries at that date, and so stated in their report to Congress, in which they respectfully suggested that the provisions of Section 2 of the act approved June 3, 1896, be continued in force for such purposes. Reports were made by the Senate Finance Committee, January 12, 1895, on the same subject. The Joint Select Committee on alcohol in the manufactures and arts reported on this subject, including hearings, December 17, 1897.

The Joint Select Committee did not recommend exempting alcohol as used in the manufactures and arts from taxation. At this point attention is called to a provision which was incorporated in the so-called Mills bill in October, 1888, as reported by the Senate Committee on Finance, and passed by the Senate, for the untaxed use of alcohol under supervision therein specified. The report on that bill (Senate Report, No. 2332, Fiftieth Congress, First Session) contains, among others, the following reference to this subject: "The heavy tax upon alcohol unnecessarily increases the price of many manufactured products, with no corresponding benefit except the resulting revenue, which is now unnecessary." This provision in the Mills bill, in October, 1888, was deemed by the manufacturers wholly impracticable.

Use of Denatured Alcohol in Foreign Countries.

Use of Methylated Spirits (Denatured Alcohol) in the United Kingdom (British Isles).

COMPARISON OF THE QUANTITY OF SPIRITS, ETC., USED IN MAKING METHYLATED SPIRITS, AND OF THE METHYLATED SPIRITS PRODUCED FOR THE FIVE YEARS ENDING MARCH 31, 1904, IN THE UNITED KINGDOM (BRITISH ISLES).

Year Ending March 31.	Ordinary (Unmineralized) Methylated Spirit for Manu- facturing Purposes.	Mineralized Methylated Spirit for Retail Sale.	Total.
	Gallons.	Gallons.	Gallons.
1900	2,058,450	1,328,162	3,386,612
1901	2,075,514	1,439,243	3,514,757
1902	2,157,127	1,410,603	3,567,730
1903	2,213,580	1,464,672	3,678,252
1904	2,139,784*	1,527,573	3,667,357

* The decrease in 1903-4 is mainly due to the fact that certain firms, e.g., the British Xylonite Company, Nobels, and Leitch and Company, have been allowed the use of duty-free alcohol denatured by other substances than wood naphtha.
    The total quantity so allowed in 1903-4 was 206,452 proof gallons, which would be 125,885 bulk gallons at 64° o.p. 93.5 per cent real alcohol.

Note.—For British method calculating absolute alcohol from strength of spirit, in terms of their standard of "proof" and comparison with United States ditto, see Chapter IV.
    To convert British or Imperial gallons into U. S. gallons multiply by 1.2.

Use of Denatured Alcohol in Germany.

QUANTITIES OF DUTY-FREE SPIRIT ISSUED DURING 1901–1905.

Year.*	Completely Denatured.	Incompletely Denatured.	Undenatured.	Total.
	Gallons.	Gallons.	Gallons.	Gallons.
1901............	17,210,490	7,474,588	744,040	25,429,118
1902............	15,504,038	7,609,668	1,307,394	24,421,100
1903............	19,804,180	7,936,060	391,424	28,131,664
1904............	25,998,865	10,195,553	575,335	36,769,753
1905............	25,889,102	10,353,633	701,134	36,943,869

* From report U. S. Consul-General Alexander M. Thackara, Berlin, Germany.

The use of undenatured duty-free spirit in the preparation of medicinal tinctures and prescriptions was formerly allowed in Germany. This privilege was withdrawn after September 30, 1902. The undenatured alcohol is now only allowed to be used duty-free in certain hospitals, asylums, and public scientific institutions, and for the making of smokeless powders, etc., mainly used in government factories. The sudden increase from 33,820 hectolitres in 1901 to 59,427 hectolitres in 1902 was probably connected with the publication of the intention of the government to disallow the use of pure, duty-free spirits for medicinal purposes, this intention being published a year in advance of the time that it was to take effect.

Use of Denatured Alcohol in France.

TABLE SHOWING THE QUANTITIES OF DENATURED SPIRIT USED IN FRANCE FOR VARIOUS MANUFACTURING PURPOSES DURING THE YEARS 1900–1903.

Manufacture, etc., for which Used.	Gallons* of Pure Alcohol.			
	1900.	1901.	1902.	1903.
Lighting, heating, motor-engines, etc....................	2,764,256	3,366,110	4,999,566	5,764,792†
Varnishes, lacquers, and polishes...	385,264	360,426	312,136	317,834†
Dyeing..........................	3,432	16,346	902	11,704†
Celluloid. etc...................	158,356	111,518	87,186	101,090†
Drugs and chemical preparations. .	100,408	60,852	149,886	613,162
Ether and explosives.............	1,427,206	1,530,848	1,539,912	1,405,338
Scientific purposes..............	8,492	9,438	8,932	11,418
Various.........................	19,294	78,892	88,000	15,818
Total....................	4,866,708	5,534,430	7,186,520	8,241,156

* British or Imperial gallons.
† These spirits, as well as a large proportion of that classed under "chemical preparations" and "explosives," contain 10 per cent of wood naphtha.
Since January 1, 1902, a drawback of 9 francs per hectolitre (about 2½d. per proof gallon) has been allowed on alcohol used for lighting and heating, to compensate for the cost of methylating, and to enable this spirit to compete with petrol in motor-cars, etc.
There was some alteration in the classification of "drugs," "ether," etc., in 1903.

Use of Denatured Alcohol in Switzerland.

QUANTITY OF DENATURED SPIRIT OF ALL KINDS SOLD IN SWITZERLAND DURING 1903.

	Kilograms at 93° to 95°.	Equivalent Gallons at 63° to 66° o.p.
"Absolutely" denatured......	4,758,003	1,284,660*
"Relatively" denatured:		
From monopoly..........	110,980	—
From importations.......	1,567,602	—
	1,678,582	453,217
Total...............	6,436,585	1,737,877

* British or Imperial gallons.

Duty-free Spirit.

Abstract of the Swiss Regulations.—The Alcohol Department are authorized to sell denatured spirits in quantities of not less than 150 liters (33 gallons) at cost price for the following purposes:

(*a*) For cleansing, heating, cooking, lighting, as well as for use in motor-engines;

(*b*) For industrial purposes generally, except the preparation of beverages or of liquid cosmetics and perfumes;

(*c*) For making vinegar;

(*d*) For scientific purposes;

(*e*) For preparing pharmaceutical products which do not contain any alcohol in their finished condition and are not mixed with alcohol when used.

Use of Industrial Alcohol in Italy.

Under date of January 20, 1905, the American Minister in Rome (Mr. Meyer) transmits the following translation of a communication from the Foreign Office and Ministry of Finance of Italy relative to the taxation and consumption of alcohol in that kingdom:

"The taxation imposed in Italy on the manufacture of spirits is 190 lire per 100 liters ($36.67 per 105 quarts) of anhydrous alcohol (pure alcohol), at the temperature of 15.56°, according to the centesimal thermometer (60° F.). Deductions are allowed of 10 per cent upon manufactures of the first category, those in which starch and starchy substances and remains of the manufacture and refining of sugar are used, and of 15 per cent upon manufactures of the second category, distillations of fruits, wines, dregs of pressed grapes, and other remains of wines only.

" Deductions on products of factories provided with meters are allowed of 25 per cent for distillations of fruits, dregs of pressed grapes, and remains of wines, and of 30 per cent for distillations of wines and small wines. The co-operative societies manufacturing articles of the second category enjoy a deduction of 18 per cent, which may rise to 28 per cent if they distill dregs of pressed grapes and other remains mentioned, and 34 per cent if they distill wine only. The last two advantages depend, however, on the condition that the factories are furnished with meters.

"Complete exemption from taxation is not granted, except to spirits derived from wine, dregs of pressed grapes, and other remains from wines when properly adulterated and intended only for lighting, heating, motor power, or other industrial and determined uses; while for spirits obtained from substances not containing wine the taxation is reduced to 15 lire per 100 liters ($2.895 per 105 quarts) of pure alcohol if destined for the above-mentioned purposes. During the financial year 1903–4, for such purposes 17,662 hectolitres (466,277 gallons) of pure alcohol were adulterated, of which 15,077 hectolitres (413,477 gallons) were from substances containing wine and 2585 hectolitres (52,800 gallons) from other substances."

Consul James E. Dunning, of Milan, reports, under date of Monday, August 6, 1906: "There is no demand in Italy, so far as I have been able to discover, for alcohol as fuel for engines, automobiles, etc. Neither is gasoline used for these purposes. Benzine is the principal fuel, and the price in quantities is $16.80 per 100 quarts for German stock, while gasoline is quoted at $23.75 per 100 quarts. I find American benzine is quoted among the dealers in fuel for automobiles at about $16.25 per 100 quarts. Milan dealers tell me that American benzine is imported in exceedingly small quantities, through the port of Venice, but that it is not in favor here. There appears to be no better reason than that no special effort has been made to introduce it here. Most of the benzine used in Italy comes from Germany and Austria, the German stock having a very long lead. The Italian import duty on benzine is $9.50 per hundred kilos, or 220 pounds. Italy has no customs conventions with other countries on oils of this classification, excepting that with the United States, which allows turpentine-oil free entry. The entire manufacture of alcohol is in the way of becoming a government monopoly, on account of the heavy taxation placed upon it and the impossibility of importing any stocks from outside the country under the protective tariff which stands against it. The present price of 95 per cent proof ethyl (grain) alcohol to first hands is 54 cents per quart in large quantities."

Use of Denatured Alcohol in Belgium.

Consul-General G. W. Roosevelt, of Brussels, reports that as denaturing alcohol for fuel is not allowed in Belgium, there is no demand for alcohol as fuel for engines and automobiles. To denature ethyl alcohol, acetonized methylene is specially used, also methylethylketone, but only on a small scale.

Wood (methyl) alcohol 100° is quoted at 75 francs ($14.47) per 100 liters (26.417 gallons); grain (ethyl) alcohol, 90°, at 50 francs ($9.65) per 100 liters. Gasoline for automobiles and motors sells in iron casks (minimum, 100 liters) for 23 francs ($4.44) per 100 liters.

From the British report on industrial alcohol we learn that the quantities of denatured alcohol used during the years 1902-4 in Belgium are as follows:

1902. Gallons at 50°.	1903. Gallons at 50°.	Nine Months of 1904. Gallons at 50°.
769,956.	1,321,584	1,257,146.

Richard Guenther, Consul-General, Frankfort, Germany, March 31, 1905, reports that, according to German papers, there are two industries in Belgium which owe their existence to-day to the fact that denatured alcohol is not subject to any tax in Belgium, namely, the manufacture of ether and of artificial silk, which use more than 2,500,000 gallons * a year. The demand for alcohol by these industries has increased thirteenfold since 1896.

Use of Industrial Alcohol in Spain.

The Report of U. S. Consul-General Benj. H. Ridgely, Barcelona, Spain, January 17, 1905, states that "the organization of a great alcohol trust is the most important recent industrial and commercial development in Spain. The formation of La Sociedad Union Alcoholera Española has just been completed, with home office at Madrid, and a capital of 16,000,000 pesetas, equal nominally to $3,088,000.†

"The basis is the molasses contract entered into with the Sociedad General Azucarera, which owns most of the sugar-mills in Spain. Besides these the combine has already acquired the largest and best situated grain distilleries, and hopes to be able to control also the production of

---

* This probably means the number of gallons in terms of 50°.

† The consul-general estimates the peseta at its gold value, 19.3 cents; the value of the peseta of general currency is about 15 cents.—U. S. Bureau of Statistics.

vinic alcohol. The proposal to form an alcohol trust was, at the outset, regarded with doubts and misgivings by producers of what is known as industrial alcohol when they learned the conditions under which the trust was to be formed; but more than half of all the manufacturers of Spain have now given their adherence, and among them are some of the largest distillers in the country. The director states that the object of the formation of the trust is the acquisition of molasses or dregs from the National Sugar Company on the production of alcohol therefrom on a cheaper scale. The formation of the trust has been favorably welcomed by manufacturers.

"There are 54 industrial alcohol factories, and up to the present 31 of them form part of the Society, the most modern and important establishments being included. The annual production of industrial alcohol is calculated to be 600,000 hectolitres (15,850,200 gallons). We trust that by producing cheaper alcohol the consumption for industrial purposes will increase. The immediate effect of the new alcohol law has been to turn things upside down. Alcohol at present is used almost exclusively for heating, but our purpose is to bring it into general use for light and power."

The above report states, further, that in order to enable the trust to completely control the trade in times such as the present year, when the low price of wine prevents industrial alcohols from competing with vinic alcohol, it has been proposed to invite the distillers of vinic alcohol to join the combine. In any case considerable time must elapse before the trust can hope to be in a position to operate.

Use of Industrial Alcohol in Cuba.

Under date of August 20, 1904, at Havana, Cuba, Mr. H. G. Squiers, the American Minister, writes as follows concerning the use of alcohol motors and pumps in Cuba:

"Matanzas, a city of about 40,000 inhabitants, has water connection in 1700 out of 4000 houses, which use about 100,000 gallons a day. The water-works, operated by an American company incorporated in the State of Delaware, are located a few miles distant from the city, where there are springs giving excellent water in sufficient quantity to supply a city of 100,000 people.

"The alcohol motor-pump, used on Sunday last for the first time, is of German manufacture, and cost complete, with installation, $6000. This motor-pump is a 45-horse-power machine, and is operated at a fuel cost of about 40 cents an hour, or $4 a day of ten hours, pumping 1,000,000 gallons of water. As alcohol is very cheap (10 cents a gallon) the running expenses of these motors are at the minimum. The Germans are selling in Cuba many such motors for electric-lighting and water plants at very low prices. One firm has a contract to put in an alcohol motor-pump at Vento, for use in connection with the Havana water-supply, which is expected to develop 180 horse-power, to cost, with installation, about $25,000, and to pump 1,000,000 gallons an hour, at a fuel cost of $1.60. The same firm has installed an electric-plant alcohol motor of 45 horse-power, which supplies 138 lights (Hersh lamps), at a fuel cost of 5 cents an hour."

Under date of August 6, 1906, Consul-General Frank F. Steinhart, of Havana, reports that "the consumption in motive power is as yet insignificant, as there are but few motors operated by alcohol. Denatured alcohol is used for illuminating purposes in the household to some extent outside of the cities. The molasses obtained as a by-product in the manufacture of cane-sugar in Cuba amounts to thousands of tons. This molasses tests about 50° polarization. If the sugar-factories should set up distilleries to convert this molasses into alcohol, it would resolve the problem of fuel, the most important in sugar industry, by burning alcohol as a spray over the bagasse or spent cane, as is done by the planters of Louisiana with petroleum, and also would furnish low-priced alcohol for industrial purposes."

Quality.—For domestic purposes, as well as for industrial purposes, two kinds of alcohol, of different density, are employed, viz., that called aguardiente, generally 20° to 22° proof, Cartier, or 60° centesimal, and rectified alcohol, 42° Cartier proof, or 90° to 92° centesimal; and as both kinds have the same origin the difference consists only in that the former contains more water and has in solution slight quantities of oily acids, characteristic of the main liquid, while that of 90° proof may be considered practically pure. For denaturalization, alcohol of 90° to 92° proof is generally used.

Proportion of Fusel-oil.—As the alcohol produced and used in Cuba proceeds from the fermentation of molasses or the juices of the sugar-cane, it does not contain any fusel-oil. This substance has never been considered as a problem in hygiene, nor are there any special regulations in regard to it. Spirits, however, when accompanied by the products when first distilled (*mauvais gouts de tête*, as the French say), contain methylic alcohol, and if accompanied by the products of secondary distillation they contain something of fusel-oil; but as these products are easily separated by rectification, alcohol in use in Cuba, such as leaves the distilleries, is practically pure.

Production.—No other prime material is used in the manufacture of alcohol than the products of the sugar-cane. Up to the present time the substance employed to denaturalize alcohol is camphor, at the rate of a gram per liter of alcohol; but the Treasury Department of Cuba has requested the Academy of Science to designate some agent for denaturalization more convenient, and the Academy of Science has suggested that a mixture composed of naphthaline and formaldehyde be used, at the rate of 50 centigrams of each per liter. If the Secretary of the Treasury accepts the proposal of the Academy of Science, the cost of denaturalization of alcohol will be $0.0047 per American gallon. The camphor now employed costs about $0.0135 per American gallon, but as there does not exist any practical means to determine quantitatively the amount of camphor dissolved, and as, moreover, the employees of the Department do not witness the denaturalization, some suppose that the manufacturers put into the alcohol they make for sale a much less quantity of camphor than is ordered by the authorities.

	Per pound.
The present cost of camphor is.	$1.65
" " " " formaldehyde is.	0.25
" " " " naphthaline is	0.90

Denaturalization is tested by the characteristics, such as smell, taste, etc., but in case of litigation or disagreement between parties a sample is sent to the National Laboratory, where the alcohol is examined and analyzed according to the usual chemical process.

The cost of the denaturalized alcohol which is generally sold for public use is from $48 to $50 (Spanish gold) per large pipe, which contains 173 American gallons. The difference depends upon the graduation, generally 40° to 42° Cartier, 90° to 92° centesimal.

It must be taken into account that the graduation or proof is taken in commerce at the temperature of the air (atmosphere), and as the apparatus is graduated at from 15° to 17.5° centigrade, the real strength of the alcohol is about 36° to 40° Cartier. Retailers sell the "garafon" (demijohn), about 4.55 gallons, at $1.60 to $1.70 Spanish silver, while bottles of about the fifth of a gallon in capacity are sold at $0.08 Spanish silver.

Ether, chloroform, smokeless powder, and other explosives, some of which are made from alcohol, are not Cuban industries, and what are consumed there are generally brought from the United States.

Use of Industrial Alcohol in the United States.—In 1838 Augustus Van Horn Webb invented and introduced his "Webb's Camphene Burner." This illuminating lamp used a mixture called "burning fluid," one part of Webb's camphene and four and one-half parts of 95 per cent alcohol.   The use of alcohol for lighting purposes increased to such an extent that during the year 1860, according to the authority of the Hon. David A. Wells, Commissioner of Internal Revenue from 1866 to 1870, in manufacturing this "burning fluid" there were used some 25,000,000 gallons of proof-spirits, equivalent to about 13,157,894 gallons of alcohol of 95 per cent strength, as 1.88 gallons of proof-spirits were required to manufacture each gallon of alcohol used in such "burning fluid."   The imposition of the internal-revenue tax on distilled spirits in 1861, and the fact that camphene rose in price from 35 cents per gallon, prior to the Civil War, to $3.80 in 1864, increased the cost of this " burning fluid " beyond the possibility of using it in competition with kerosene, which was discovered, refined, and put on the market at about this time.   It is interesting to note that about four fifths, or 80 per cent, of the use of industrial alcohol in the United States prior to 1860 was for the "burning fluid " described above.   The small remaining product met the requirements of the druggists and of that used in the arts and manufactures at that time.

As time passed the taxed distilled spirits or alcohol was used by those manufacturers who were obliged to use pure alcohol, but, finally, owing to the excessive internal-revenue tax of $2.08 per gallon on high-proof alcohol, such use was practically prohibited.

Another fact which operated effectively to decrease the use of alcohol was the introduction of wood or methyl alcohol, made by destructively distilling wood in iron retorts or ovens.

Up to the time the present law, permitting denatured alcohol, was passed, such wood alcohol, untaxed, owing to its cheapness, had practically superseded tax-paid ethyl alcohol for industrial uses in the United States.   Wood alcohol, 95 per cent in strength, sells for about 75 cents per gallon, while the taxed alcohol sells in the vicinity of $2.50 per gallon. This law permits tax-free, domestic, denatured alcohol for general purposes after January 1, 1907.   A copy of this law is given in Chapter IX, and a complete copy of the United States Regulations and Instructions concerning Denatured Alcohol is published in the Appendix of this book.

CHAPTER II.

THE MANUFACTURE OF ALCOHOL.

The Raw Materials Used. The Preparation of the Raw Materials for Fermentation. The Composition of the Raw Materials Used. Malting. The Fermentation. Theoretical *versus* Practical Yields of Alcohol. The Micro-organisms. The Use of Moulds in Saccharification. The Fermentation Period. Wild and "Disease" Yeasts. The Control of the Fermentation Operations: (a) The Control of the Yeast; (b) The Estimation of the Fermentable Matter; (c) The Estimation of the Yield in Alcohol from the Fermented Mash. The Conditions Favorable to Alcoholic Fermentation.

In practice on the commercial scale, the manufacture of alcohol is conveniently considered under the five following heads or processes:

1. The preparation of the raw materials.
2. The transformation of the starch into a fermentable sugar (saccharification).
3. The conversion of this sugar, or other sugars present in the sweet wort or mash, by fermentation into alcohol and carbon dioxide.
4. The extraction of the alcohol by distillation.
5. The rectification of the alcohol.

In some instances 4 and 5 are combined in one process, as will be shown in Chapter III.

The Raw Materials Used.—The raw materials usually employed in the manufacture of alcohol are corn, rye, barley, rice, (white) potatoes, sweet potatoes, and molasses. Barley is not used as a direct source of alcohol, but serves to make the malt used in the saccharification process. Sugar-cane molasses is largely used as a source of alcohol, while beet molasses is not employed for this purpose to any great extent, but is used as an ingredient of cattle-feed.

The Preparation of the Raw Materials.—The impurities of all sorts should be removed from the raw materials before they are put into process. Such impurities are dust, dirt, stones, grain accidentally present, etc. Without such purification treatment the distilling apparatus will

17

be liable to become filthy and subject to injury, and a noxious influence be exerted upon the different chemical operations. There will also result a less yield and an inferior quality of alcohol. The treatment respecting the barley, to be used in the production of the malt for saccharification and in the preparation of the yeast cultures, should be particularly careful, otherwise the impurities accompanying the barley will cause mouldiness during the malting, which will prevent the best results from the distillery.

The preparation of potatoes or other tubers requires the employment of a washing apparatus, while the grains are cleaned and separated by the aid of "sorters" or sieves. Some potato-washing machines are supplied with a circular wire cage or barrel, into which the potatoes are fed for conducting them into the washing-machine proper. This removes a large amount of adhering and extraneous dirt and foreign matters. In Fig. 1 is shown a potato-washing machine and elevator as used in the German industrial alcohol distilleries. The manipulation of this machine is clearly indicated by the cut. It is supplied by power, using a fast-and-loose pulley. The capacity of this German potato-washing machine and elevator is from 1000 to 3000 kilograms per hour (from 2200 to 6600 pounds).

After the potatoes have been thoroughly washed they are conveyed, by means of the automatic elevator shown at the right of Fig. 1, to a high-pressure mash-cooker and mashing apparatus. By this apparatus, which is shown in Fig. 2, page 20, the potatoes are converted into a condition of gelatinization which practically liquefies the starch. The liquor thus made is strained and passed through cooling-pipes to the fermenting-vats, where it is fermented for about thirty hours, and is then conveyed to a patent still. Potatoes in Germany contain 20 per cent of starch on an average, and are therefore better for a source of alcohol than the potatoes in this country, which contain on an average about 17.5 per cent of starch, as is shown by the table on page 28. In using sweet potatoes, their preparation for fermentation purposes can be accomplished in the manner as given for white potatoes, or in tropical climates the conversion of the starch into glucose is effected by hydrolyzing with sulphuric or hydrochloric acid, the reaction being complete when no further test for starch is given by the iodine test. By this method (Gustav Wassmuss') there are used about 5.5 kilos of 20 per cent hydrochloric acid for 100 kilos (220 pounds) starch in the form of potatoes, or for 100 kilos sweet potatoes, containing 17 per cent starch, 0.935 kilo 20 per cent hydrochloric acid, or an equivalent amount of sulphuric acid. After cooling this mash is neutralized with soda and

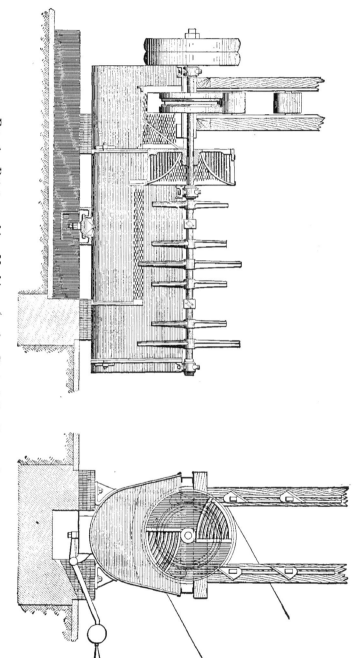

FIG. 1.—Potato-washing Machine, showing Part of the Potato-elevator.

then manipulated, as with any other mash. The chemical changes brought about by this acid treatment are similar to those produced by malting (either floor or pneumatic malting) in grain.

These mash-cookers have a capacity in the largest sizes of about 6000 liters (1584 gallons), corresponding to a charge of 1300 kilograms (2860 pounds) of grains and of about 4000 kilograms (8800 pounds) of white or sweet potatoes. In the case of the grains the time for the

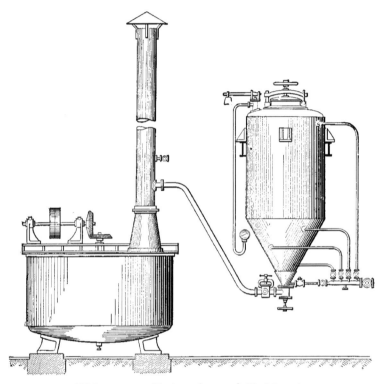

FIG. 2.—High-pressure Mash-cooker and Mashing Apparatus.

cooking and mashing is from 2 to 2½ hours, while for potatoes only about 1 hour is required. This cooker can also be furnished with a power-stirrer. After the charge is cooked it is forced, under steam-pressure from the cooker, into the power-macerator shown at the left of Fig. 2, where it is cooled to the requisite temperature for the mash.

As already intimated, the raw materials must first undergo a preliminary treatment before fermentation is practicable. Where cane-sugar molasses is used it is first diluted with about 3 parts of water. Such molasses usually has a density of about 41.5° Beaumé and weighs about 11.75 pounds to the gallon. It is a base molasses, generally called "black-strap," and is supposed to contain a total of 50 per cent sugars, sucrose and invert. The diluted molasses is best treated by steam to destroy some of the germs present, after which it is cooled and the yeast

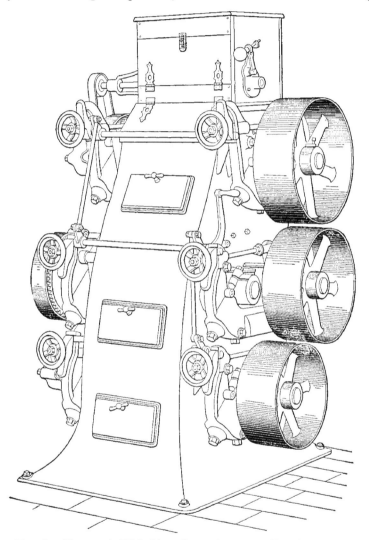

FIG. 3.—Three-pair High Six-roller Mill for Grinding Corn-meal.

for the fermentation is added. The use of beet-sugar molasses is practically analogous to that of cane-sugar molasses for the manufacture of alcohol, and the preparatory treatment is therefore quite similar, except that the reaction must be adjusted to a faintly acid one. In the preparation of whole sugar-beets abroad for fermentation it has been found most advantageous to express the juice by a roller-press and to ferment it. If grains or corn are employed, it is finely ground in a mill of the type shown in Fig. 3, and is then treated with hot water and steam, under pressure, in a special apparatus, to gelatinize and liquefy the starch. The treatment of this liquefied starch, after cooling, with malt,

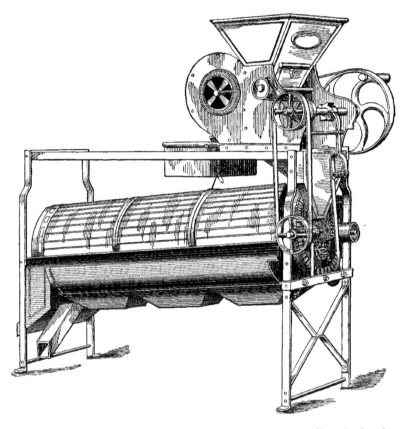

FIG. 4.—Grain-sorter or Power-sieve; runs by power as well as by hand. Built by Vennuleth & Ellenberger, Darmstadt, Germany.

completes the transformation to sugar. It may be mentioned that two important points of advantage result from such grinding: 1. A greater speed of conversion; 2. More thorough conversion.

In the use of corn about 15%–20% solids is used, that is, a mixture of corn and water in the cooker is so prepared, and then the steam blown in for the cooking. In describing the grinding-mill shown in Fig. 3, it may be said that such mills are made in four sizes: 7×14-inch rolls, capacity 30–45 bushels per hour; 7×18-inch rolls, cap. 40–60 bu. per hour; 9×18-inch rolls, cap. 50–75 bu. per hour; and 9×24-inch rolls, cap. 65–100 bu. per hour. This is the most modern grinding-machine now in use in distilleries.

Referring to the preliminary treatment of the grains for fermentation purposes, mentioned on pages 17–18, for the purpose of cleansing them

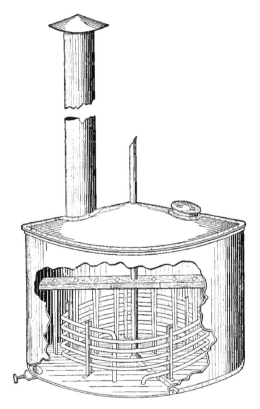

FIG. 5.—Steel Mash-tub. Built by Hoffman-Ahlers Co., Cincinnati, Ohio.

from adhering dirt and foreign substances by means of a power-sieve or "sorter," attention is called to the kind of machine which is used, as shown in Fig. 4, page 22.

For the purpose of preparing raw materials for fermentation by mashing, a steel mash-tub is sometimes used and is shown in Fig. 5. This type of cooker is preferred by most whiskey distillers, as it is an open mash-tub, and lower temperature is obtained than in some other forms of mash-cookers, the claim being that extremely high temperatures of other kinds of cookers injure the flavor of the whiskey. In making

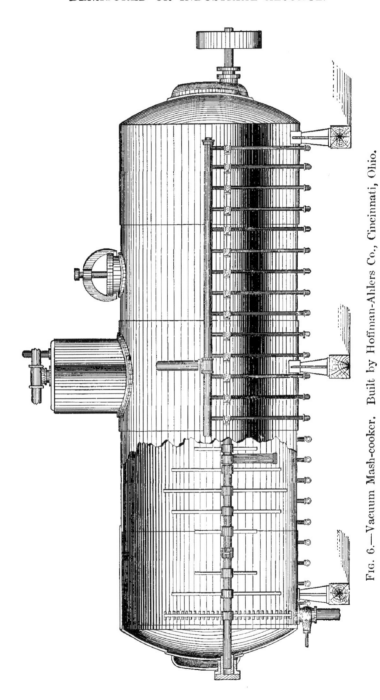

FIG. 6.—Vacuum Mash-cooker. Built by Hoffman-Ahlers Co., Cincinnati, Ohio.

alcohol for denatured alcohol, however, the question of flavor is eliminated and the higher temperature suitable for larger yields can be employed. These steel mash-tubs are made in any size from 6 ft. in diameter to 20 ft., and are supplied with a perforated steam inlet-pipe for heating, and

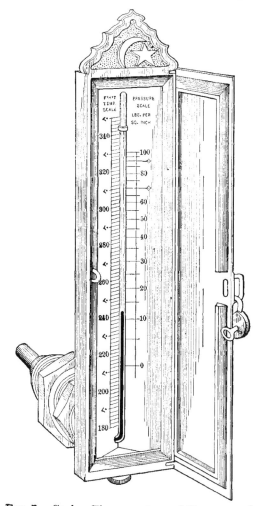

FIG. 7.—Cooker Thermometer and Pressure-scale.

with copper cooling-coils and a power-rake to keep the mash uniformly stirred.

Another type of mashing apparatus is that shown in Fig. 6, page 24, the vacuum mash-cooker. This type is not used by breweries, but by alcohol distillers, and a better yield is produced by using these cylindrical cookers, which are made to stand a pressure of 100 pounds, the mash being thus heated to about 312° F., thereby producing a better conversion and larger yield of alcohol than is the case by using the open mash-tub, where it is not possible to get over 212° F. The cooling is effected by means of a vacuum pump, which draws off the hot vapors and cools the mash to the proper temperature in not more than twenty minutes. These cookers are made in sizes ranging from 50 bushels to 250 bushels each, and are supplied with a revolving

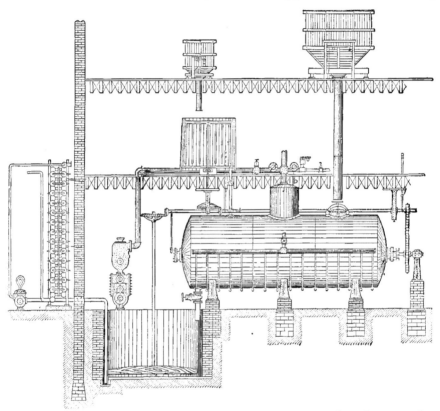

Fig. 8.—Vacuum Mash-cooker and Pump: Small Grain-masher; Double Pipe-cooler for Mash and Slop; Drop-tub and Hopper-scales. Built by The Vulcan Copper Works Co., Cincinnati, Ohio.

power-rake, the steam being introduced by means of a number of small inlets in the bottom by a steam manifold pipe.

In order to control the temperature in these mash-cookers which we have just described, a thermometer is used of the type shown in the accompanying Fig. 7. The thermometer is permanently fitted in the mash apparatus, the screw-thread fastening it, while the glass bulb containing the mercury passes through the side of the vessel and is exposed to the temperatures of the hot vapors during the cooking. As of further interest in the matter of the cooking of the mash and the details of manipulation of the same, an apparatus for this purpose made by The Vulcan Copper Works Co., of Cincinnati, Ohio, is shown in Fig. 8, page 26. This is called the vacuum mash-cooker and pump, and consists of a small grain-masher, a double pipe-cooler for mash and slop, a drop-tub and hopper-scales. In explanation of this cut it may be stated that this is the equipment necessary for the "mashing" department of a modern distillery. The large boiler-shaped apparatus on the first floor represents the vacuum-cooker, for cooking the mash in its preparation for the fermenting-tubs.

The tank containing the rake, on the floor above, is for preparing the "small grain," ready for its conveyance into the cooker, at the proper time, with the meal that has gone through the cooking process. Hopper-scales for weighing the meal are shown on the third floor. After the mash has been properly cooked and partially cooled, it is conveyed to the "drop-tub," from which it is pumped through the double pipe-cooler to the left of the wall to the fermenting-vats. The yeast is next added, fermentation takes place, and the fermented liquor, or "beer," is in readiness for distillation through the continuous still, to be described in Chapter III. In the cut an end view only of the double pipe-cooler is shown. The length and height is governed by the amount of mash to be cooled in a given time, and varies from 500 feet to 5000 feet in length.

The mash is pumped through a 3-inch copper tube, which is enclosed in a 5-inch iron tube. While the hot mash is being pumped through the copper tube in one direction, cold water is circulating in the opposite direction. The mash imparts its heat to the water, while the water is cooling the mash to the proper temperature for the fermenting-vats. Fig. 9 represents a floating thermometer, used for taking the temperature of the mash. The water heated by such cooling of the hot-mash liquor can be utilized to save fuel, in the cooking of additional mash and other purposes.

FIG. 9.—Floating Thermometer.

The Composition of the Raw Materials Used.*—We give on page 28 a table showing the average composition of the various raw materials we have considered for the manufacture of alcohol.

---

* See Bulletins U. S. Dept. of Agric. 9, 45, 58.

TABLE FURNISHED BY THE UNITED STATES DEPARTMENT OF AGRICULTURE, BUREAU OF CHEMISTRY, WASHINGTON, D. C.

	Corn.	Rye.	Barley.	White Potatoes.	Sweet Potatoes.	Molasses (Beet).	Molasses (Cane).
Water..............	9.3	8.9	6.5	76.5	69.0	19.3	20
Ash...............	1.5	2.1	2.9	0.9	1.1	11.7	6
Protein............	10.7	11.6	11.5	2.1	2.1	—	—
Fat...............	5.5	1.8	2.7	—	1.0	—	—
Fibre.............	1.4	1.5	3.8	0.7	2.6	—	—
Pentosans.........	6.5	7.6	7.2	—	—	—	—
Sugars.............	2.2	7.6	7.0	—	6.0	Sugars, Cane and Invert 49.7	Sugars, Cane and Invert 60
Starch............				{ 17.5	17.1	Non-sugars, Organic Substances	Non-sugars, Organic Substances
and	} 62.9	58.9	58.4	{			
Nitrogen-free extract.				{ 2.3	1.1	19.3	14.0

In the above table the figures given under Nitrogen-free extract represent, beside the starch, the amounts of gum, resins, etc., but as these are not present in any appreciable quantity in cereals, the Nitrogen-free-extract figures may practically be taken as starch.

Although the content of starch in rice is extremely high, something like 76 per cent, it may be stated that rice is at present too expensive a material for the making of alcohol in this country. The cost of rice, therefore, prohibits its consideration as a competing material with corn, notwithstanding the considerable excess of its starch content over that of corn.

Malting.—Malt is the name given to barley (or other grain) which has been moistened, kept at a moderate warmth, and thus allowed to germinate under artificial conditions, with the result that the acrospire and rootlets develop, the cells produce a large amount of diastase, and the starch is thereby changed to maltose. There appear to be two well-marked periods of diastase secretion, one occurring on about the second day of growth, the other somewhat later. The most rapid action takes place with malt which has reached the second period, which may be in from three to eight days. Further growth of the grain is stopped by heat, but care is taken not to heat strongly enough to destroy the enzyme itself. The product thus prepared may retain its power of saccharification for a long time, and is therefore of great use in bringing about the conversion of the soluble starch to sugar.

In order to prepare the malt for the conversion process just described it is first crushed through a machine shown in Fig. 10 on page 29. This machine has a capacity up to 2000 kilograms (4400 pounds) of malt per hour.

After crushing, the malt is best treated with water in a special macerating machine. This produces a fluid of milk-like consistency in which the diastase is largely dissolved in consequence of the extremely fine state of division. Under these conditions the saccharifying power of the diastase is very largely increased. This apparatus is therefore of much importance in large modern alcohol distilleries on account of the service it can render and the economy it can effect.

As stated, the ordinary raw materials for the preparation of alcohol

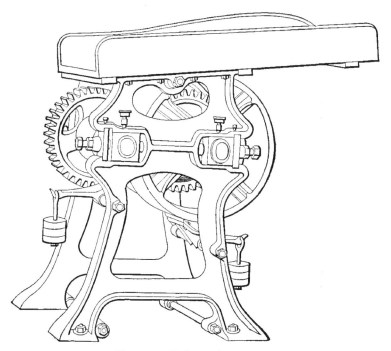

FIG. 10.—Malt-crusher.

are the grains and such other vegetable products as contain a large amount of stored-up starch or sugar, or some substance which can be readily converted into sugar. Most important of the raw materials are corn, rye, barley, rice, white potatoes, sweet potatoes, sugar-beets, and cane-molasses; wheat is not widely used for this purpose and beet-molasses is largely used as an ingredient for cattle feed.

The very high percentage of starch which can be readily converted to fermentable sugar, together with the keeping qualities and case of transportation, make the grains the most important sources of alcohol, although there are many facts which show conclusively the high value of the other raw materials mentioned.

The next process in the manufacture of alcohol is

The Fermentation.—Fermentation is the name commonly applied to certain physiological chemical processes in which a transformation of an organic substance is effected through the agency of micro-organisms. Before considering the fermentation we call attention to a modern fermenting-house as designed by George Stade, of Berlin, Germany. It will be seen that the design permits of the filtration of the air, which is a matter of great advantage and importance, as by this simple expedient much greater freedom from foreign germs hurtful to the process of

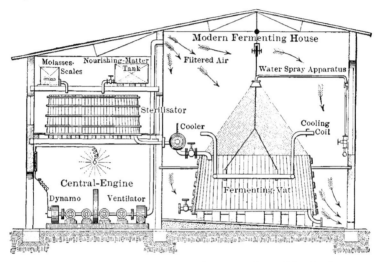

Fig. 11.—Modern Fermenting-house as planned by Stade.

fermentation is assured. Strict cleanliness in carrying out the fermentation processes is absolutely necessary.

On page 31 we show a modern fermenting-house as designed by The Vulcan Copper Works Co., of Cincinnati, Ohio. The cut shows the details and the pipes for conveying the mash and the yeast. (See Fig. 12.)

In continuation of the description of the fermenting-house shown in Fig. 12, it may be stated that the combination of apparatus here presented represents a practical working arrangement of the *yeasting and fermenting appliances* for a grain or molasses distillery. Malt and rye meal which is supplied in proper proportions from the meal floor above is conducted into the tubs through the meal-spouts attached to a movable hopper-truck. This meal is "mashed" or mixed with water at a certain temperature. It stands for a fixed period, during which a lactic-acid souring takes place, which souring is needed for effective yeast production, as will be explained under control of the yeast. The mash

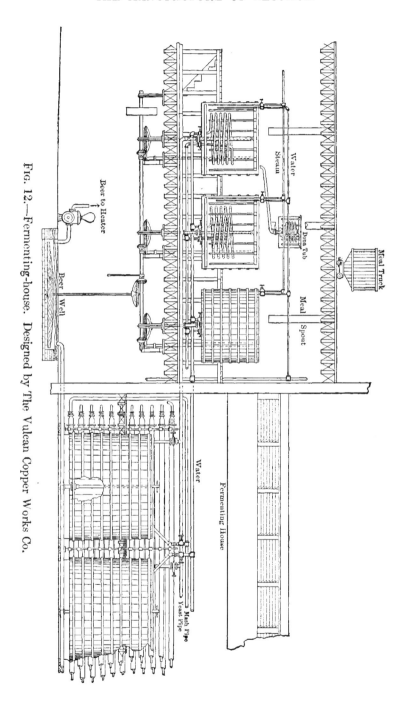

FIG. 12.—Fermenting-house. Designed by The Vulcan Copper Works Co.

is then reduced in temperature by means of cooling water circulating through the coils and by stirring. The yeast in the dona or culture tub, which has been previously built up from a mother-yeast, is now added to the mash in the yeast-tubs. During the following ten- or twelve-hour period the entire mass becomes impregnated with yeast-cells, and is at a proper time conducted into the fermenting-vats. The fermentation period requires ordinarily seventy-two hours, at the end of which the product now technically known as "beer" is emptied into the beer-well. From the beer-well the beer or alcoholic liquor is pumped to the distilling apparatus, where the distilling operation begins.

As before stated, fermentation is the name commonly applied to certain physiological chemical processes in which a transformation of an organic substance is effected through the agency of micro-organisms.

The most familiar example of such a chemical change is the one by which sugars are split into alcohol and carbon dioxide, as in the manufacture of cider, wine, or beer, hence the term fermentation is frequently but erroneously limited to this process.

It is now recognized, however, that this is only one of a large number of such possible changes, others equally familiar being the souring of milk and the turning from cider or wine to vinegar. These different kinds of fermentations vary as the substances acted upon and the organism causing the change vary. It may be stated, however, that each kind of change has its specific organism or race of organisms which can excite the fermentation. Of course, many organisms differing but slightly in character may give rise to fermentation essentially alike.

The carbohydrates are the organic materials yielding the largest amount of definite products, hence, according to some writers, carbohydrates only are recognized as materials for fermentation processes. There seems to the author no reason for such a limitation, however, inasmuch as the mechanism of the process is probably essentially similar in all classes of organic matter affected. Hence he would define *fermentation* as the *change induced in organic matter through the agency, direct or indirect, of micro-organisms or their enzymes.*

The fermenting-vats used vary in size according to circumstances. In Fig. 13, page 33, is shown the largest fermenting-vat in the world, built by Geo. Stade, Berlin, Germany, for a spirit and rum refinery in Mexico. The capacity of this vat is stated to be 54,000 gallons.

In this country the fermenting-vats are made in capacities ranging from 25 bushels to 1000 bushels, figuring 45 gallons of mash to each bushel. In Fig. 14, page 34, is shown the improved manner of operating the valve in the bottom, which discharges the mash.

Theoretical versus Practical Yields of Alcohol.—In the manufacture of alcohol a knowledge of the theoretical yield is of great importance.

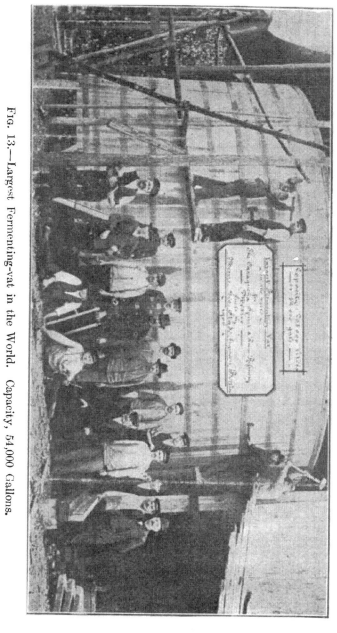

FIG. 13.—Largest Fermenting-vat in the World. Capacity, 54,000 Gallons.

The formation of alcohol depends, as has already been hinted, on the power of yeast to decompose sugars. The monosaccharids or sugars having the general formula $C_6H_{12}O_6$ are most readily broken up, the characteristic chemical equation being $\underset{180}{C_6H_{12}O_6} = \underset{92}{2C_2H_5OH} + \underset{88}{2CO_2}$.   It is thus evident that almost exactly one half the sugar should be transformed into alcohol while the rest is evolved as carbon-dioxide gas. Among the monosaccharids are included dextrose and levulose. Next to the monosaccharids the disaccharids or $C_{12}H_{22}O_{11}$ sugars are most

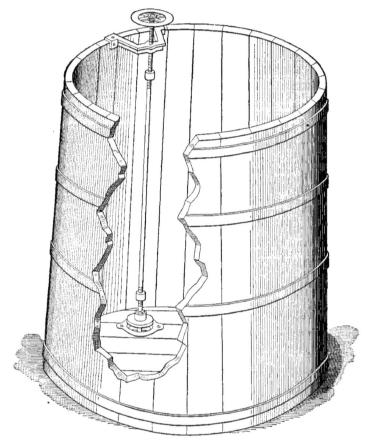

Fig. 14.—Fermenting-vat with Improved Valve. Built by Hoffman-Ahlers Co.

readily fermentable.   Of these maltose and cane-sugar are the most important.   The more complex carbohydrates, polysaccharids, are fermentable only when they have first undergone hydrolysis, which converts them into sugars of the simpler types.   This conversion may be brought about by the action of acids, especially mineral acids, or by certain substances, enzymes, the so-called soluble ferments, secreted by living cells, which bring about a similar transformation as in malting. The latter method is the better for spirit production. The conversion of starch to soluble starch may also be brought about by use of steam under pressure, and the process of transforming starch to sugar practically may thereby be much simplified. For this purpose a temperature of 145°–160° C. is employed. The starch thus acted upon is readily changed to the fermentable sugar by malt.

This process of hydrolysis is by no means as simple as would appear from the statement just made, but involves very deep-seated chemical changes, in which the starch is transformed through a series of steps into products partaking more and more strongly of the qualities of sugar as the action goes on. These intermediate bodies may be numerous. A few of them are characterized by fairly definite chemical reactions, and so may be recognized. The general name *dextrins* or *malto-dextrins* is given to them. These intermediate products are formed and then still further split up by the enzymes, so that in the process of malting, a process essentially that of germination, the starch is gradually changed to the sugar maltose. During germination much more of the enzymes causing the conversion is secreted by the cells than is actually required to convert the starch, so that ordinary malt always contains an excess of enzyme which is ready to react upon more starch. This fact is made use of in fermentation industries, when starchy materials such as corn-flakes are added to the mash.

Theoretical versus Practical Yields of Alcohol.—To determine the approximate amount of alcohol which may be obtained from a given weight of starch it is then necessary to consider the hydrolytic change as well as the fermentation one.

Regarding the formula of starch as $C_6H_{10}O_5$, which is actually far too simple, the change to sugar may be expressed as follows:

$$C_6H_{10}O_5 + H_2O = C_6H_{12}O_6.$$
$$\underbrace{72+10+80}_{162} \quad 18 \quad 180$$

That is, in the conversion, the starch takes up one ninth its own weight of water or nine tons of starch would make ten tons of fermentable sugar. Applying now our first equation

$$C_6H_{12}O_6 = 2CO_2 + 2C_2H_5OH$$
$$180 \qquad 88 \qquad 92$$
$$180 : 92 :: 10 : x = 5.111$$

or nine tons of starch would theoretically give a little more than five

(5.111) tons of alcohol, hence 56.78% by weight of absolute alcohol is the theoretical yield from starch.

The theoretical yield which may be computed in this way is, however, never obtained in practice, because of the losses due to evaporation and to imperfect fermentation. It should be possible, however, to get 90% of the theoretical yield, and this is constantly done in well-managed whiskey houses.

This yield should certainly be possible then, when conditions can be made most suitable for yield, and where questions of flavor, etc., do not have to be considered as in the case of denatured alcohol. Allowing for a loss of 10%, we have practically neutralized the gain in weight through hydrolysis, and a fair means of estimating the possible yield in alcohol would be to regard it as 50% of the weight of the available starch.

In case the raw material contains cane-sugar instead of starch, as in the beet-juice or molasses, a yield of 50% would hardly be expected, as the gain in hydrolysis is only about half that when starch is used.

This is shown by the two chemical equations involved by theory as follows:

$$\underset{342}{\underset{\text{Cane-sugar.}}{C_{12}H_{22}O_{11}}} + H_2O = \underset{360}{\underset{\text{Invert-sugar.}}{2C_6H_{12}O_6,}}$$

and theoretically therefore 100 parts by weight of cane-sugar will give 105.26 parts by weight of invert-sugars; and from

$$\underset{180}{\underset{\text{Invert-sugar.}}{C_6H_{12}O_6}} = \underset{92}{\underset{\text{Alcohol.}}{2C_2H_5OH}} + \underset{88}{\underset{\text{Carbon Dioxide.}}{2CO_2,}}$$

whereby we find that $180 : 92 :: 105.26 : x$ or 53.80, from which it is seen that 100 parts of cane-sugar by weight will give a theoretical yield of 53.80 parts of alcohol by weight. If we assume 90% of the theoretical yield of alcohol in the case of sugar we should have a yield of about 48.42 per cent, but in practice such yield usually averages about 45 per cent.

The theoretical yields may be thus tabulated: *

$C_6H_{12}O_6$, dextrose, levulose, glucose, and grape-sugar, 51.11% absolute alcohol
$C_{12}H_{22}O_{11}$, sucrose or cane-sugar, and maltose........ 53.80%   "   "
$C_6H_{10}O_5$, starch................................. 56.78%   "   "

---

* See researches of Pasteur: Maercker's Handbuch der Spiritusfabrikation, 1898; Maercker-Delbrück's Handbuch der Spiritusfabrikation, 1903.

In case the raw material contains cane-sugar instead of starch, as in beet-juice or molasses, however, no special process of hydrolysis needs to be introduced, as the yeast itself secretes an inverting ferment which will bring about the transformation.

Theoretical versus Practical Yields of Alcohol from Corn.—In calculating the theoretical yield of absolute alcohol from corn, the table given on page 28 is used. By this table it is seen that the average composition of corn shows a content of 2.2 of sugars and 62.9 of starch. The weight of a bushel of corn is 56 pounds, and the calculation is given as follows:

$$2.2\% \text{ sugar } = 1.232 \text{ lbs. sugar}$$
$$62.9\% \text{ starch} = 35.224 \text{ lbs. starch}$$
$$1.232 \times 0.5380 \text{ (alcohol from sugar)} = 0.6628 \text{ lbs. absolute alcohol}$$
$$35.224 \times 0.5678 \text{ (alcohol from starch)} = 20.0000 \text{ " " "}$$

$$1 \text{ bushel of corn yields by theory...} 20.6628 \text{ " " "}$$

Yield in practice from 1 bushel corn $\begin{cases} = 5 \text{ U. S. proof gallons alcohol} \\ = 2\frac{1}{2} \text{ gallons absolute alcohol} \end{cases}$

$$2.5 \times 6.61 \text{ (weight 1 gallon absolute alcohol) } = 16.53 \text{ lbs. absolute alcohol}$$

$\dfrac{16.53}{20.66} = 80\%$ of the theoretical yield of absolute alcohol is obtained, in practice, from corn

Theoretical versus Practical Yields of Alcohol from Rye.

$$\text{Rye, 56 pounds to a bushel}$$
$$7.6\% \text{ sugar } = 4.256 \text{ lbs.}$$
$$58.9\% \text{ starch} = 32.98 \text{ lbs.}$$
$$4.25 \times 0.538 \text{ (alcohol from sugar)} = 0.2289 \text{ lbs. absolute alcohol}$$
$$32.98 \times 0.5678 \text{ (alcohol from starch)} = 18.7300 \text{ " " "}$$

$$\overline{18.9589 \text{ " " "}}$$

1 bushel rye yields in practice 4.77 gallons U. S. proof spirits
$$= 2.38 \text{ gallons 200 U. S. proof or absolute alcohol}$$
$$= 2.38 \times 6.61 = 15.73 \text{ lbs. absolute alcohol}$$

$\dfrac{15.73}{18.95} = 83\%$ of the theoretical yield of absolute alcohol is obtained, in practice, from rye

Rye is not used, however, for making industrial alcohol. This is on account of its high price, about 68 cents per bushel, and the relatively small amount available for this purpose in comparison with corn, molasses, or potatoes. According to the report of the Department of Agriculture for 1905 the crop of rye in the U. S. gave a total yield of 27,616,045 bushels.

Theoretical versus Practical Yields of Alcohol from Cane Molasses.—If we take the base molasses, or black-strap as it is called, which is used for making alcohol, and which is largely obtained from the Southern States, Cuba, and Porto Rico, we find the average total sugar content is supposed to be 50 per cent, ranging from 32 to 38 per cent sucrose and 12 to 18 per cent of invert-sugars, or an average of 35 per cent sucrose and 15 per cent of invert-sugars. Such molasses weighs, on an average, 11.75 pounds per gallon. The content per gallon on above figures will be 4.11 pounds sucrose and 1.76 pounds of invert-sugars.

$$4.11 \text{ lbs. sucrose} \times 0.538 = 2.21 \text{ lbs. absolute alcohol}$$
$$1.76 \text{ lbs. invert} \times 51.11 = 0.899 \text{ '' '' ''}$$

$$\left. \text{Yield of absolute alcohol per} \atop \text{gallon of such molasses} \right\} = 3.009 \text{ '' '' ''}$$

The actual yield, in practice, is as high as 0.85 U. S. proof gallon of alcohol per such gallon of molasses, which yield is equal to 0.425 gallon absolute alcohol, and $0.425 \times 6.61 = 2.81$ lbs. alcohol, divided by 3.1 gives 90 per cent of the theoretical yield obtained, in practice, from such molasses.

Theoretical versus Practical Yields of Alcohol from Potatoes.—A bushel of potatoes weighs about 60 pounds. In the last campaign in Germany the yield of alcohol was about one gallon of absolute alcohol to 1.26 bushels of potatoes, or about 26.45 gallons per ton of 2000 pounds.

This represents $26.45 \times 6.61 = 174.8$ lbs. absolute alcohol per ton of 2000 lbs. The average content of starch in the German potatoes is about 20 per cent. One ton of potatoes, 2000 lbs. $\times 0.20 = 400$ lbs. starch and $400 \times 0.5678 = 227.12$ lbs. absolute alcohol, by theory from a ton (2000 lbs.), showing the actual yield to be about 77 per cent of the theoretical yield of absolute alcohol in the case of German potatoes.

Theoretical versus Practical Yields of Alcohol from Sweet Potatoes.— From the preceding table the per cent of sugar is shown to be 6 per cent, and starch 17 per cent, in the average sweet potatoes. (The table does not state whether this is the Southern sweet or the dryer, more Northern Virginia one.) A bushel of sweet potatoes weighs 54 pounds.

$$6\% \text{ of } 54 \text{ lbs.} = 3.24 \text{ lbs. sugar}$$
$$17\% \text{ of } 54 \text{ lbs.} = 9.18 \text{ lbs. starch}$$
$$3.24 \times 0.5380 = 1.74 \text{ lbs. absolute alcohol}$$
$$9.18 \times 0.5678 = 5.21 \text{ '' '' ''}$$

$$\text{Yield from one bushel sweet potatoes} = 6.95 \text{ '' '' ''}$$

Actual yield in practice from figures furnished by M. S. Durot, manager of a large sweet-potato distillery in Isle de Terceira, Azores, was 10 to 12 liters absolute alcohol per 100 kilograms of sweet potatoes.

A liter = 1.056 United States quarts.

A kilogram = 2.20 lbs. avoirdupois.

This mean yield = 11.62 quarts of absolute alcohol from 220 lbs., or $\frac{11.62}{4} \times 6.61 = 19.17$ lbs., or from 54 lbs. (1 bushel) of sweet potatoes the actual yield of absolute alcohol is 4.70 lbs., or about 68 per cent of the theoretical yield.

Theoretical versus Practical Yields of Alcohol from Sugar-beets.—In this country sugar-beets are not used in the manufacture of alcohol. E. Hourier's Manuel de la Distillation, 1901, revised by Albert Larbalétrier, gives the yield from 2000 kilograms of sugar-beets of 1 hectolitre of 90 per cent alcohol (26.41 gallons), which is equal to about 157 lbs. of absolute alcohol. These beets were Silesian beets and contained from 10 to 11 per cent of sugar. In 2000 kilograms (1 kilo = 2.20 pounds) there are 4400 pounds, and $10\frac{1}{2}$ per cent of this = 462 pounds of sugar, which by theory will yield $462 \times 0.538 = 248$ lbs. absolute alcohol. The actual yield is therefore $\frac{157}{248}$ = about 64 per cent of the theoretical yield.

Let us now further consider the micro-organisms or their enzymes.

The Micro-organisms.—The micro-organisms capable of bringing about such changes may be grouped as three classes of lower fungi,—bacteria, yeasts, and moulds. Of these the bacteria occupy the lowest position, being in some respects the simplest, as indeed they are the smallest, plants known. They are characterized by their method of division by splitting or fission, their small size and lack of coloring matter, and to some extent by remarkable vitality and chemical energy under certain conditions. They attack not merely the carbohydrates, but proteids, and to some extent fats and other organic bodies. Frequently acids are produced as a result of their action, especially upon carbohydrates. They do not produce alcohol.

The fermentation products from the proteids are very variable, some of them, as the toxins of the pathogenic bacteria, being extremely poisonous. Ethyl alcohol is rarely if ever produced, although some higher alcohols are developed in small amounts.

The yeasts and moulds belong to a somewhat more highly organized group of plants, but are also colorless. A strict classification of the "mould" is difficult, since many organisms belonging to different botanical groups are here lumped together under a convenient name, but one really without taxonomic value. The moulds show great variability in form and in fermentation power, but comparatively few of them are of great practical importance. Some may be utilized to convert starch to sugar, as will be mentioned later, and some may, under certain conditions, give rise to a more or less vigorous alcoholic fermentation.

The organisms of special interest to the alcohol producer are the *yeasts*, or *saccharomycetes*, a sub-group of the ascomycetous fungi. Of these there are many kinds which are imperfectly classified into species, varieties, and races. In addition to the yeasts certain other fungi have the power of bringing about alcoholic fermentation to a limited degree, but the yeasts are the most important alcohol producers. Yeast consists of small oval or rounded cells, reproducing by budding rather than direct fission, and forming spores under certain restricted conditions. Their most striking characteristic, however, is the power to attack sugars, especially of the $C_6H_{12}O_6$ and $C_{12}H_{22}O_{11}$ types, and split them into alcohol and carbon dioxide. Upon this property the industries involving alcoholic fermentation depend. These are therefore the organisms of chief importance in this work.

While the phenomenon which we call fermentation has been known for hundreds of years, it is only within the last century that definite knowledge regarding it has been gained. As yeast is a microscopic organism its study was dependent upon the development of the microscope, and although some of the earlier microscopists may have seen yeast, it was not until the instrument had reached a fairly high state of perfection that the organism was systematically studied.

In 1822 Persoon gave to yeast the systematic name mycoderma. In 1837 Kützing elaborated a theory of fermentation which was essentially correct, inasmuch as he assumed the yeast to be the cause of the fermentation rather than merely a product. The organism was regarded as a plant at about this time by Cagniard Latour, Schwann, and Meyen, as well as by Kützing, and it is to Meyen that we are indebted for the botanical name Saccharomyces, which has ever since been retained.

In the early forties important contributions to the chemistry and biology of yeast were made by Mitscherlich, as he doubtless was the first to observe that yeast secretes invertin, and he also made observations on the development of the cells by budding and the multiplication of yeast.

The controversy as to spontaneous generation kept the knowledge of these subjects in check for many years, but the real relation of yeast, as a specific ferment to the alcoholic fermentation, was again made evident from the remarkable work of Pasteur as outlined in his "Studies on Beer and Studies on Wine."

These Studies, no doubt, supplied the impetus which led Hansen to his investigation, which culminated in the Hansen methods of pure yeast cultivation and their application to practical fermentation. Of the latter work mention need be made only of E. Buchner, who was the first to demonstrate that by crushing yeast-cells and submitting them to high pressure an extract may be obtained which is capable of fermenting sugar to alcohol and carbon dioxide as a result of the intracellular enzymes which are thus liberated.

The manner in which yeast brings about the decomposition of the sugar has been a subject of much study and speculation for many years. One of the early theories supposed that the sugar was actually taken in as food by the yeast, and the alcohol and carbon dioxide excreted as waste products. Liebig held that the sugar was mechanically decomposed as a result of molecular motion, and that the yeast was not an exciting cause, but rather a product of the change. This view was somewhat modified in his later years, but he never accepted the true physiological explanation of the phenomenon.

Pasteur at one time held the opinion that fermentation is life without air, and that the activity of the yeast in decomposing sugar was due to its shattering the molecules of sugar in order to obtain the oxygen. That this theory was erroneous Pasteur himself later proved.

Traube, in 1858, explained fermentation as due not to the yeast-cell itself but to certain substances elaborated or secreted by the cells— *the enzymes*—which act like digestive juices upon the sugar and break it into the simpler molecules of alcohol and carbon dioxide. This theory, though long rejected, has in recent years been shown to be correct, and at the present time it is believed that all fermentation processes are the results of enzyme action.

This merely introduces an intermediary between the organism and the change, for only *living* cells are capable of producing the enzymes which thus react upon the sugar. However if we have actively developing and vigorous yeast-cells it is possible, as Buchner has shown, to obtain the enzymes in solution capable of bringing about the change even if the organic cells themselves are not present. Such solutions of the enzymes are obtained generally by crushing the cells and subjecting them to heavy pressure, when the liquid containing the enzymes may be recovered as a yellowish opalescent solution of strong fermenting power.

The fact that the enzymes can be obtained only by breaking the cells seems to indicate that fermentation as carried on in the usual way is an intracellular process, and that the enzyme zymase differs from most other enzymes in its inability to permeate the walls of the cell and thus get into the sugar solution.

The yeasts present a number of different types or "species," most im-

portant of which we may group into beer yeasts, those which are employed in the beer- or ale-brewing industries and generally regarded as

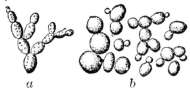

of species Saccharomyces cerevisiæ, the
wine yeasts occurring in nature on the
skins of fruits and of use in wine-making. S. ellipsoideus is the name given
to them. Distillery yeasts are not so
pronounced in type as the foregoing,
but culture yeasts generally of the S.
cerevisiæ type.

FIG. 15.—Shows Sprouting Yeast-
cells (*Saccharomyces cerevisiæ*). (*a*,
after Lürssen; *b*, after Hansen.)

Use of Moulds in Saccharification.—Many moulds, especially those
belonging to the Mucoreæ, secrete diastatic enzymes in abundance, and
can therefore bring about readily the transformation of starch to sugar.
This property was first commented upon by Gayon and Dubourg in
1886, who studied *Mucor circinelloides*, and found that this power is not
possessed by the normal mycelium, but only when the fungus is developing in aggregations of gemmæ, or buds. Since this time numerous observations have been made by Calmette, Eijkmann, and Wehmer.

"Chinese yeast" owes its activity to the combined action of the
mucors, which bring about saccharification, and yeasts which ferment
the sugar thus formed. Suggestions to utilize these fungi in spirit manufacture have been made by some authors. As a result, the so-called
amylomyces process has been developed, a process which depends on
the saccharification of the starch by the mould, other micro-organisms
having been eliminated by sterilization. During this part of the process
germ-free air is forced into the mash, and the material is thoroughly
mixed by mechanical agitators. When thoroughly converted the air-
supply is cut off, yeast added, and the alcoholic fermentation proceeds
rapidly.

Some alcohol is formed by the action of the moulds during the saccharifying process. The details of procedure differ somewhat in different
works. At Seclin, near Lille, the process has been in operation for several
years. Corn, the material employed, is mixed with twice its weight of
water and steamed for three hours under a pressure of $3\frac{1}{2}$ to 4 atmospheres,
then mixed in a mashing-tank with a weight of green malt equivalent to
1% of the weight of the corn used and sufficient cold water to reduce the
temperature to 70° C. After thorough mixture by an hour's stirring the
whole mass is transferred to an autoclave, sterilized at 120° C., and then
forced into a closed cylindrical metal fermenting-tun. The steam is
then shut off and sterilized air is forced into the tank so as to keep the
mash under pressure during the cooling, which is effected by cold water

flowing down over the outside of the tank. When cooled to about 38° C. a pure culture of spore-bearing Amylomyces is introduced and the mash kept in motion by a stirrer, air being gently forced in at the same time. During the next twenty-four hours the development of the fungus proceeds rapidly and is accompanied and followed by a strong converting action. A small amount of pure culture yeast is then added and a period of twenty-four hours is allowed for its increase. At the end of this time the air-supply is cut off and both species of organisms work together during the next three days.

A patent on a similar process, but in which the addition of yeast was omitted, the moulds doing all the work, was taken out in 1898.

This process has been employed in a simpler form at Antwerp. In this case the mash, after mixing with malt, is run directly into the fermenting-tun, where it is boiled a short time by steam, then cooled and aerated, and then inoculated with Amylomyces. When the mash no longer gives a starch reaction with iodine the yeast is added.

It is claimed for the Amylomyces process that it gives increased yields of alcohol over the other methods. At Seclin a yield of 66.2 liters of absolute alcohol for each 100 kilos of starch is reported. No data are at hand to determine if this increased output is balanced by increased expense in operation. The question is still receiving much study especially by European investigators.

The Fermentation Period.—The time required to bring about complete fermentation of sugar to alcohol and carbon dioxide is greatly dependent upon the temperature, since a change of a few degrees in the temperature range may make an enormous difference in the rate of activity of the yeast.

Owing to the law in this country preventing the recharging of fermenting-vats in distilleries oftener than once in seventy-two hours it has sometimes been supposed that this length of time was necessary to bring about the change. With temperatures approaching the optimum for yeast, however, this is not the case. While a fermentation carried on with a temperature of 18°–22° C. might require seventy-two hours for complete splitting of the sugar, at higher temperatures the time may be much shortened, and with a vigorous race of yeast thirty-six hours at 26°–27°, or even less than this time might suffice. It is even probable that twenty-four hours with proper temperature and other conditions might be most economical.

Wild and " Disease " Yeasts.—Wild and "disease" yeasts are those occurring in nature without cultivation and capable sometimes of pro-

ducing bad fermentation, hence the application of the term "disease."
For classification see Klöcher's admirable work on Fermentation
Organisms.

In the preparation of spirits the character of the yeast is in many
ways not as important as in brewing or wine-making, since in these processes the development of flavor, turbidity, etc., are of importance, and
the yeast may have a strong bearing on these matters. For fermentations
in the preparation of denatured alcohol, the desired yeast is one which
ferments vigorously and quickly, and will maintain these qualities under
conditions not rigidly fixed and for many generations. Numerous races
of distillery yeast have been developed by the different laboratories,
stations, and spirit establishments.

THE CONTROL OF THE FERMENTATION OPERATIONS.

(a) The Control of the Yeast.—One of the most important factors
contributing to a successful fermentation, and hence the largest yield of
alcohol in the manufacture of denatured alcohol, is a suitable and
properly developed yeast culture. Different races of yeast differ
widely in their ability to attack different kinds of materials, and
a yeast that will ferment a grain mash with rapidity and a high
yield in alcohol may give quite unfavorable results when used with
molasses.

Having obtained a good culture, however, the question arises as to
how it may be kept in good condition and propagated for successive
fermentations.

In most distillery operations no attempt is made to keep the yeast
a pure culture in the technical sense, but the fermentation is started by
introducing into the prepared mash a certain amount of the yeast from
a previous fermentation. This must be in active condition for good
results. This method has the merit of being easy to apply, and so long
as the yeast does not become badly contaminated by other organisms it
gives satisfactory results. If, however, bacteria or other fungi gain the
upper hand, it may be necessary to build up a culture afresh, starting
with a single cell, such a yeast being prepared in a separate room, in a
perfectly cleanly manner, so as to avoid as far as possible the presence of
dust laden with germs, or to use some other method, such as washing the
yeast with an antiseptic solution or heating to a low pasteurizing temperature for a few minutes. The latter methods cannot be recommended
without reservation, as the yeast itself may be seriously damaged unless

great care is taken and one knows exactly how much the yeast can stand.

The method of preparing a pure yeast from a single cell is a long and somewhat painstaking process. A description of it may be found in the various books on fermentation organisms. It has the advantage that the culture thus prepared is free from invading organisms, but is, of course, practically useless unless the material to be fermented is sterile. For ordinary fermentation operations the extra care and apparatus involved probably are not repaid by a markedly higher yield.

Effront has perfected a process in which fluorides, which have a strong germicidal action on bacteria, but are not harmful to the yeast, are introduced. This method has given good results in European practice, but has not been of sufficient advantage in this country to warrant its introduction on a large scale. Abroad it is possible to buy pure yeast cultures at the government stations where it is prepared, but in this country it is customary for the distiller to prepare his own yeast, and for this purpose the so-called jug-yeast method is employed.

The introduction of a small amount of lactic acid, either by producing it in the mash by fermentation or by the addition of the prepared acid, has also been used with good success, and probably because of the selective antiseptic action of the acid.

(b) **The Estimation of the Fermentable Matter.**—In most fermentation operations the percentage of sugar, or fermentable material, is determined, not by the polariscope, but by a form of hydrometer known as the saccharometer. Like other hydrometers, its use depends on the fact that the greater the specific gravity of a liquid the more buoyant force it exerts upon solid bodies thrust into it. The saccharometer consists of a spindle with elongated bulb, weighted at one end by means of mercury and provided with a stem or slender, graduated shaft on which a scale is made. The Balling hydrometer is provided with a thermometer-bulb, which gives the temperature-correction scale at once. When plunged into a solution it maintains an upright position, and sinks to a greater or less depth, according to the density of the solution. In taking readings, the level of the liquid, i.e., the bottom of the meniscus, is the mark which should be noted rather than the slightly raised line on the stem, due to capillary attraction. As the thermometer-bulb gives the temperature correction at once, no table is required for making corrections. Based on the results obtained in this way, we have instruments known as hydrometers, which give direct readings, and which are undoubtedly accurate enough for practical work. These are of many kinds, according to the use to which they are to be put, but all are alike in theory, depending on the fact that, as liquids vary in density, their power to support or buoy up solids also varies. The practical value 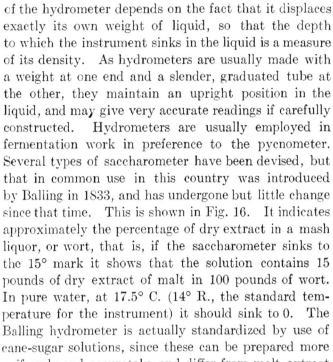 of the hydrometer depends on the fact that it displaces exactly its own weight of liquid, so that the depth to which the instrument sinks in the liquid is a measure of its density. As hydrometers are usually made with a weight at one end and a slender, graduated tube at the other, they maintain an upright position in the liquid, and may give very accurate readings if carefully constructed. Hydrometers are usually employed in fermentation work in preference to the pycnometer. Several types of saccharometer have been devised, but that in common use in this country was introduced by Balling in 1833, and has undergone but little change since that time. This is shown in Fig. 16. It indicates approximately the percentage of dry extract in a mash liquor, or wort, that is, if the saccharometer sinks to the 15° mark it shows that the solution contains 15 pounds of dry extract of malt in 100 pounds of wort. In pure water, at 17.5° C. (14° R., the standard temperature for the instrument) it should sink to 0. The Balling hydrometer is actually standardized by use of cane-sugar solutions, since these can be prepared more

FIG. 16. — The uniformly and accurately, and differ from malt extract Balling Hydrom- only to a negligible extent. If solutions warmer than eter. 14° R. are used, the indication is too low, because of the less density of the liquid and vice versa. These variations being constant for constant temperature variations, the instrument is generally provided with a table of corrections for other temperatures than 14° R., so that the trouble of bringing to this point may be avoided. In order to give accurate readings the saccharometer must be handled with care, kept perfectly clean, and lowered into the solution to be tested, and the solution should be free from foam or gas. Kaiser's saccharometer is based upon exactly the same data, but differs in the manner of making the scale. The table on page **47** gives the relation between specific gravity and per cent extract by Balling.

For specific gravities between those here given, the Balling reading may be estimated by interpolation, or recourse may be had to the complete table as found in works on hydrometric measurements. Another form of hydrometer is that of Brix, which is so arranged that if floated in a watery solution of sugar its scale directly indicates the percentage of sugar present in such solution. Correction has to be made in accordance with the temperature as indicated by the tables furnished with this instrument.

TABLE SHOWING THE RELATION BETWEEN SPECIFIC GRAVITY AND PER CENT EXTRACT BY BALLING.

Specific Gravity.	Per Cent Balling.	Specific Gravity.	Per Cent Balling.
1.000	0.000	1.009	2.250
1.001	0.250	1.010	2.500
1.002	0.500	1.020	5.000
1.003	0.750	1.030	7.463
1.004	1.000	1.040	9.901
1.005	1.250	1.050	12.285
1.006	1.500	1.060	14.666
1.007	1.750	1.070	17.000
1.008	2.000	1.080	19.272

(c) **The Estimation of the Yield in Alcohol from the Fermented Mash.**—To determine the amount of alcohol in a mixture of alcohol and water, another kind of hydrometer known as the Tralles alcoholometer is used. It gives distinct readings of the percentage of absolute alcohol, by volume, in the solution at 12.5° R. (15.6° C.). The scale is graded from 0 to 100, showing 0° in distilled water and 100° in absolute alcohol of specific gravity 0.07939 at the temperature mentioned. The temperature corrections may be very much larger than with the saccharometer. As the greater the amount of alcohol present the less dense the solution, a higher temperature causes the readings to be too high, and a lower temperature too low. Generally each alcoholometer is provided with a table of corrections. The Tralles alcoholometer is shown in Fig. 17, page 48, and the hydrometer-jar used with it.

In testing the alcoholic wash solution the alcohol should be obtained by distillation. Since alcohol has a lower boiling-point than water, it will therefore be driven off in the form of alcohol-vapor when a solution containing it is heated to the necessary degree (boiling-point). By condensing the vapor thus driven off, it may be recovered in the form of alcohol, mixed with a small amount of water. Repeated distillation gives a still purer alcohol, until about 90 or 95 per cent strength is reached. To prepare absolute alcohol, quicklime, anhydrous copper sulphate, and metallic sodium are employed. For the distillation, in determining the amount of alcohol formed in a fermentation at least a half-liter should be used, and larger amounts, up to 2 or 3 liters, are probably preferable.

The distillation is carried out in a glass or metal flask, and the alcoholic vapors are condensed in a tube, or worm, surrounded by cold running water, and collected in a receiver. A German laboratory apparatus

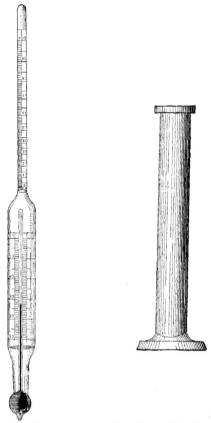

Fig. 17.—Tralles' Spirit Hydrometer, with Glass Cylinder or Hydrometer-jar.
(Illustrations furnished by the Emil Grenier Co., New York City.)

for this purpose is shown in Fig. 18. A specially made small alcohol hydrometer and jar is shown at the left of this cut. The heat is supplied by burning denatured alcohol.

Practically all the alcohol will be contained in an amount of the distillate equal to two fifths of the alcoholic solution taken. This is then accurately made up to the original volume and the specific gravity determined by the pycnometer.

The Pycnometer.—The pycnometer is an instrument used for determining the specific gravity of a liquid. Having determined this with accuracy, the quantity of sugar, alcohol, etc., may be discovered by referring to the tables which have been devised. Various forms of pycnometers are in use. In fermentation work the instrument is used at a standard temperature of 15°, and water at the same temperature is taken as a standard. To determine the specific gravity of a liquid, the instrument is weighed dry, and then again, after filling with the distilled water, and cooling to 15°. Weighing should be carried out to three places of decimals. The difference in weights obtained

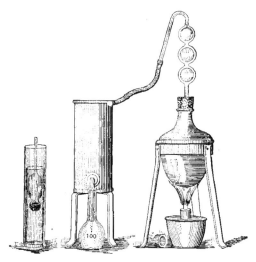

FIG. 18.—German Laboratory Apparatus for the Estimation of Alcohol in the Wash Liquor.

will give the weight of the water. The weight of the solution, the specific gravity of which is desired, is then found in the same way.

$$\frac{\text{Wt. of solution}}{\text{Wt. of water}} = \text{sp. gravity.}$$

The temperature must be carefully noted and either a correction applied or the solution brought to some standard temperature, as variations in temperature give considerable variation in specific gravity. In obtaining the per cent of alcohol the tables given in Chapter IV, pp. 127–141, are used. These tables were adopted by the Association of Official Agricultural Chemists, as published November 14–16, 1901, in Bull. No. 65, Bureau of Chemistry, U. S. Department of Agriculture. A small variation in estimating the per cent of alcohol in the wash means quite an amount when figured on the yearly production of the alcohol of the distillery, and hence there is need of the greatest accuracy possible in such attempted control of the operations. While distillers in this country ordinarily figure yields in terms of gallons of proof spirit per bushel of grain or gallon of molasses it is often convenient for the chemist to express such yields by a decimal system. Such a table is referred to above. The United States Alcohol Tables from the Gauger's Manual are given on pp. 143–145.

Conditions Favorable to Alcoholic Fermentation.—*The factors* to be considered in determining for alcoholic fermentation are *character of the must, temperature, acidity, and light.* For favorable results it is desirable to have these conditions as constant as practicable, since the fermentation organisms are all more or less sensitive to variations in their physical and chemical environments.

Alcoholic fermentation will proceed most vigorously and generally with best results in mashes containing 10–15% of solids of which 65–70% is fermentable. In other words, a content in fermentable sugar of from 7.5 to 10% offers the most suitable opportunity for activity. Much stronger solutions may be fermented, but it is the opinion of expert practical men that there is no appreciable gain by the use of heavier mashes.

Temperature plays a most important part in fermentation. Although capable of enduring and working under a considerable range of temperature and it is in proximity to temperatures of 75°-80° that the best results are obtained, as this is generally most stimulating to yeast fermentation, and any temperature above 85° is almost certain to be dangerous.

Lower temperatures are not necessarily injurious, but retard the fermentative processes.

Light.—As in all fermentations, darkness or a weak diffused light is far better than intense light.

Acidity.—A medium mildly acid with organic acids seems to be the most readily attacked. Alkalis are harmful to yeasts.

Cleanliness.—Filtered air is of great advantage. By this simple expedient much greater freedom from foreign germs hurtful to the process of fermentation is avoided. Strict cleanliness in carrying out the fermentation processes is absolutely necessary.

It is believed that the inclusion of the following paper will prove of interest.

THE FERMENTATION OF CANE MOLASSES AND ITS BEARING ON THE ESTIMATION OF THE SUGARS PRESENT.*

By Dr. George Harker.

The question of the determination of the sugars, and more especially of the saccharose, in cane-molasses is one which has caused much discussion. On account of the large proportion of reducing sugars present in cane-molasses it is recognized that no reliance can be placed on the saccharose figure obtained by direct polarization, since the reducing sugars present also affect the polarization. For exact determination recourse is generally had to the Clerget method, which is not affected by the presence of reducing sugars. In this method, after obtaining the figure for direct polarization, the solution is inverted with acid and the polarization again made. The reducing sugars are not affected by the acid, and the difference in the two polarizations is taken to be due to the production of invert-sugar from the saccharose originally present. From this difference the saccharose is calculated.

Fresh interest has been aroused recently by Remy (Bull. Assoc. Chim. Sucr. Dist., 1904, 21, 1002), who has opposed the Clerget method, on the ground that the polarization of the levulose present in the molasses is not, as assumed, the same in neutral as in acid solutions. Lindet, however (Bull. Assoc. Chim. Sucr. Dist., 1905, 22, 574), has shown that the error can only be a very slight one.

An important paper dealing with the whole question of the determination of saccharose in cane-molasses has been published recently by H. and L. Pellet (Bull. Assoc. Chim. Sucr. Dist., 1905, 22, 744-752). Numerous experiments have been made by the authors with different molasses, in which the reducing-sugars present before and after inversion with acids were determined by means of Fehling's solution. The saccharose was thus calculated by a method independent of the optical properties of the sugars, and in all cases was found to be in very close agreement with the Clerget figure for the same sample. The authors consider that the accuracy of the Clerget method is beyond question.

Now when cane-molasses is fermented, the quantity of alcohol produced is generally much less than that which is indicated by calculation from the figures of analysis for the saccharose and reducing-sugars in the molasses; and it is evident that the yield of alcohol has an important bearing on the question of the determination of the sugars. In this con-

---

* Jour. Soc. Chem. Ind., No. 17, Vol. XXV, Sept. 15, 1906. Sydney (Australia) Section.

nection an account of some experiments undertaken by the author on the fermentation of cane-molasses may be of interest, as they seem to cast some doubt on the methods of analysis for the sugars present.

To account for the low yield of alcohol obtained from the fermentation of molasses several explanations have been given. Of these, apart from bacterial losses, the most important seem to be the presence of organic acids and the possible presence in the molasses of sugars fermentable only with difficulty.

Lafar has shown (Z. Spiritusind, 1895, 18, 238) that free organic acids hinder fermentation.

Bau (Z. Spiritusind, 1894, 17, 366) has discussed the resistance of beet-molasses to fermentation and concludes that it is chiefly due to the presence of sugars fermentable only with difficulty. Boiling with sulphuric acid not only removes volatile acids, but also inverts such sugars as raffinose, fermentable only with difficulty, and so increases the yield.

The majority of the experiments, of which an account is given in this paper, were performed upon a sample of molasses which had the following composition:

Saccharose (Clerget)	41.52
Reducing-sugars	9.26
Other organic matter	11.66
Ash	11.50
Water	26.06
	100.00
Brix	75.1
Specific gravity	1.3832
Total sugar as reducing-sugar	52.94(43.68 + 9.26)
Polarization direct	38.80

After inversion with acids, 55.12 per cent of reducing-bodies, estimated by Fehling's solution, were present; subtracting from this the 9.26 per cent present before inversion, and, following Pellet, calculating the saccharose from the difference, the figure 43.57 was obtained, which seemed to show that the Clerget figure was, if anything, lower than the the truth. It was only as the investigation proceeded that a contrary opinion was formed.

In all the fermentation experiments, whether saccharose or molasses was employed, the solutions were always made so as to contain 10 grms. of sugar, calculated as reducing-sugar, in every 100 c.c. of solution. By this means a comparison of results was rendered very easy. The volume of solution fermented was in all cases 500 c.c. The solutions were placed in bottles previously cleaned, sterilized, and dried. The mouth of each bottle was closed by a plug of cotton-wool and the bottles were then placed in a water-bath, which was kept at a temperature of 310° C. by means of a thermostat. The yeast employed for most of the experiments was pure culture yeast and was obtained fresh for each set of inoculations. In a few experiments ordinary brewery yeast was used.

The attenuation of the solution on fermentation was taken as a basis for calculating the yield of alcohol. The attenuation is the figure (multiplied by 1000) giving the difference in the specific gravity of the solution before and after fermentation. When 16 or 20 solutions were fermented in one operation, as was often the case, it would be difficult to estimate the alcohol in each by distillation on account of the time occupied. The yield of alcohol could be calculated with close approximation by means of the following formula:

$$\frac{\text{Attenuation} \times 100}{47.5}.$$

At the end of a number of experiments the alcohol was removed by distillation and the yield so obtained compared with that calculated from the attenuation. The distillations were conducted with great care, a long fractionating column being used. According to Pasteur, 100 grms. of reducing-sugar produces on fermentation 48.47 grms. alcohol, and as each solution of 500 c.c. contained 50 grms. of sugar calculated as reducing-sugars the maximum yield of alcohol obtainable was 24.235 grms.

The following table gives a comparison of some of the yields of alcohol actually obtained by distillation, with the yields calculated from the attentuation figures:

Material Fermented.	Attenuation Obtained.	Percentage Yield Calculated from Attenuation.	Alcohol Produced.	Percentage Yield Calculated from Alcohol Produced.
Saccharoses.....	43.0	90.5	22.01	90.8
Molasses........	39.3	82.7	19.90	82.1
"	39.3	82.7	19.81	81.75

In the case of the cane-sugar the yield actually obtained was slightly above, while with molasses it was somewhat below, that calculated from attenuation, and this was observed in other cases; but by adding 0.5 per cent to the yield calculated in the case of the saccharose solutions and by subtracting 0.5 per cent in the case of molasses, figures were obtained which were in good agreement with the percentage yields of alcohol obtainable by actual distillation. Accordingly in calculating the yields from the attenuation figures these corrections were applied.

Fermentation of the Molasses.—As the total sugar by analysis in the molasses was 52.94 per cent, each solution for fermentation (500 c.c.) contained 94.45 grms. of molasses. When the molasses was fermented in simple aqueous solution without any previous treatment the attenuation obtained was 38.3, corresponding to a yield of 80.1 per cent by calculation. The yield of alcohol was not increased to a material extent by boiling the solution to sterilize it, nor by adding sulphuric acid before fermentation. The addition of Pasteur's mineral nutrient increased the attenuation to 39.3, corresponding to a calculated yield of 82.2 per cent. In a few experiments the sugar in the molasses solutions was completely inverted by treating with excess of sulphuric acid (10 grms. per 500 c.c.) at 70° C. After this treatment the acid was nearly neutralized with sodium carbonate, mineral nutrient matter was added, and the solution fermented. Although no sugar was destroyed during inversion the yield of alcohol was very little increased—attenuation 39.5. In all cases in which the molasses was fermented the fermentation was vigorous.

Although treatment with sulphuric acid may improve the yield from beet-molasses, it was of very little value here, and consequently the explanation given by Bau to account for the difficulty of fermenting beet-molasses cannot be applied to the cane-molasses under consideration. Further, as after the acid treatment all the sugar was present as reducing-sugar, the low yield obtained under ordinary circumstances cannot be due to incomplete inversion of the saccahrose, as has been asserted. The maximum attenuation obtained, viz., 39.5, corresponded to a percentage yield of 82.7, so that even under the best conditions the yield of alcohol was very low.

To whatever treatment the molasses solutions were subjected before fermentation, there was always a small quantity of some substance present in the spent wash which, although unfermentable, reduced Fehling's solution. The quantity of this, although small, was constant, and amounted to about 2.46 per cent on the weight of molasses taken. In calculating the possible yield of alcohol obtainable from a given molasses, it is always taken that the reducing-sugars given by analysis are completely fermentable; but if we assume that the substance left in the spent wash, which reduces Fehling's solution, is present in the original molasses and is not formed during the fermentation, a correction must be applied to the analysis figures if we wish to know the amount of fermentable reducing-sugar. Thus, in the molasses under consideration, of the 9.26 per cent of reducing-bodies present, only 6.80 can be considered as fermentable sugars; the total sugar calculated as reducing-sugar falls to $(52.94 - 2.46) = 50.48$ per cent, and the percentage yield of alcohol obtainable becomes $\dfrac{50.48 \times 100}{52.94} = 95.3$ per cent of that originally calculated as the maximum possible.

The yield of alcohol of 82.7 per cent actually obtained was calculated on the basis of 52.94 per cent of fermentable sugar, but this is still considerably less than 95.3 per cent, and if, after making the allowance for the reducing substance in the spent wash, the figures of analysis for saccharose and fermentable reducing-sugars are correct, then the low yield of alcohol can only be explained by the harmful effect on the fermentation of bodies either present in the original molasses or produced during the course of the fermentation.

Defecation of the Molasses before Fermentation.—A few preliminary experiments were made in order to determine the effect of removing organic matter by means of lead salts. To solutions of molasses not too concentrated basic lead acetate was added to precipitate organic matter. After filtering off the precipitate, the excess of lead was removed by sulphuretted hydrogen, and after boiling to remove this gas, the solutions were made nearly neutral and were fermented. Before fermentation a sample was taken for the determination of saccharose and reducing-sugars present, and the percentage yield of alcohol was calculated from these figures. Although the solutions fermented rapidly the yield of alcohol was not improved. To avoid the accumulation of acetic acid in the solution, resulting from the employment of basic lead acetate, normal lead nitrate and lime were also used to precipitate the organic matter, but the yield of alcohol was not raised.

Fermentation of Saccharose in Pure Nutrient Solutions and in Solutions of Spent Wash.—To determine with more certainty whether or not the presence of the non-sugar bodies in the molasses exerts a deterrent effect on the fermentation, as is constantly asserted, experiments were made in which saccharose was fermented in solutions of spent wash. For purposes of comparison cane-sugar was also fermented in pure nutrient solutions under similar conditions. In these latter cases the solutions contained 47.5 grms. of pure cane-sugar, equal to 50 grms. of reducing-sugars in each 500 c.c. and in addition the nutrient materials necessary for the growth of the yeast-cells. Pasteur's nutrient mixture was found the best of several tried, but when used by itself the fermentation of the cane-sugar took several days to complete, while in the case of a molasses solution, or of a solution of cane-sugar in spent wash, the fermentation was always finished in forty-eight hours. However, by the addition to every solution of 2 grms. of a nitrogenous yeast food sold under the name of "levurogene," which itself contained no fermentable material, the time taken over the fermentation was reduced to two or three days.

The fermentation of saccharose in the pure nutrient solutions did not proceed so regularly as was expected. In many cases the attenuation reached the figure 45.5, corresponding to a yield of alcohol of 96.3 per cent; a considerable number varied between 45 and 45.5, but sometimes with poor fermentations the attenuation was as low as 43. The principal aim, however, was not to obtain a theoretical yield of alcohol, but to find out how much alcohol was produced when cane-sugar was fermented under conditions approaching as closely as possible to those employed during the experiments on the fermentation of molasses. The experiments showed that under these conditions from a definite weight of cane-sugar the alcohol obtained was about 96 per cent of the quantity obtained by Pasteur.

In the case of the fermentation of cane-sugar in solutions of spent wash, the solutions were prepared by evaporating the alcohol from solutions of molasses which had been completely fermented, care being taken that the solutions were not being too strongly heated. In many cases the solutions had been allowed to stand several days after all fermentation was finished before the alcohol was removed; 47.5 grms. of saccharose were then dissolved in the solution, nutrient matter and yeast added, and the volume made up to 500 c.c. In this way a known amount of sugar was fermented in the presence of all the non-sugar bodies contained in the molasses, with the exception, perhaps, of the most volatile organic acids. The quantity of these removed could only have been very small, as the acidity of the solution of spent wash did not alter to any extent during the removal of the alcohol. Many experiments were made; the fermentation was always more vigorous and the results obtained more regular than with saccharose in nutrient solutions. The addition of Pasteur's nutrient improved the yield slightly, but no gain resulted from the addition of "levurogene," as the spent wash itself contained sufficient nitrogenous food for the growth of the yeast-cells.

The experiments proved conclusively that the yield of alcohol obtained is just as large when saccharose is fermented in solutions of spent wash as when fermented in pure nutrient solutions, and that consequently the non-sugar bodies present in the spent wash exercise no harmful influence on the fermentation.

In some cases the attenuation was as low as 43 or 44, but in most it varied from 45 to 45.5. In one or two cases the calculated figures were checked by actual distillation of the alcohol, when it was found, as for saccharose in nutrient solution, that the yield by distillation was slightly higher than the calculated. A yield of at least 96 per cent of the maximum (taking Pasteur's figures) was obtained.

These results gave rise to a strong belief that the low yields obtained in the case of the molasses were due to the fact that the percentage of sugars present in the molasses is much less than that shown by analysis. It might be said, however, that in the case of molasses the bodies originally present, whatever they may be, which exercise a harmful influence on the fermentation, are themselves altered during the course of the fermentation, and that consequently, although pure sugar gives a theoretical yield of alcohol when fermented in spent wash, it might not do so if fermented in the original molasses.

Experiments already described had shown that a solution containing 47.5 grms. of cane-sugar in 500 c.c. gave an attenuation of 45.5, and one containing 94.45 grms. of molasses in 500 c.c. an attenuation of 39.5. Hence, if the fermentation of saccharose proceeds as well in molasses solutions as in pure nutrient solutions, 23.75 grms. of cane-sugar and 37.22 grms. of molasses in 500 c.c. should give an attenuation of 41.5.

The average figure for seven separate determinations was 41.3, giving further evidence that on fermentation the sugar in a molasses solution is completely converted into alcohol.

Assuming that this is the case, the amount of fermentable sugar present can be calculated. On the basis of 52.94 per cent of fermentable reducing-sugar, it was found that the best results obtained from the fermentation of the molasses gave a yield of 82.7 per cent of alcohol; when pure saccharose was fermented in spent wash under similar conditions the yield of alcohol was 96 per cent, or, in other words, only a small proportion of the sugar was not converted into alcohol. Assuming that this slight loss of sugar takes place also in the case of the molasses, we may consider that

$$\frac{82.7 \times 100 \times 52.94}{96} = 45.63$$

is the percentage of fermentable sugar, in terms of reducing-sugar, present in the molasses. This quantity is 86.2 per cent of the amount given by analysis.

Determination of Ratio of Carbon Dioxide to Alcohol on Fermentation of the Molasses.—In order to determine whether the fermentation of the molasses was normal, the ratio of the carbon dioxide to alcohol was obtained.   The ratio was also determined for pure nutrient solutions of saccharose.

The solutions for fermentation were prepared as previously described, and out of each 500 c.c., 50 c.c. were removed for the estimation of the carbon dioxide.   The remainder, to act as a check, was placed in a bottle and fermented under the same conditions as the smaller quantity.   The 50 c.c. were placed in a small flask, which was immersed in water kept at 31° C.   The carbon dioxide was estimated from the loss of weight sustained by the flask and attached drying apparatus. In the first experiments on molasses and saccharose the gas which escaped was absorbed in potash bulbs to ensure that the loss was due to carbon dioxide, but this precaution was found unnecessary.   A current of dry air removed the last of the carbon dioxide from the apparatus.

RESULTS.

Material.	Attenuation.	Grams Carbon Dioxide.	Grams Alcohol.	Ratio Alcohol to Carbon Dioxide.
Saccharose......	44.0	2.325	2.257	0.971
"	45.5	2.34	2.336	0.998
Molasses........	39.3	2.02	1.993	0.986
"	39.3	2.00	1.993	0.996

Each 50 c.c. of solution contained 5 grms. of sugar in terms of reducing-sugar, it being understood that in the case of molasses the solutions were always made up on the assumption that the analysis figures were correct, and that the content of the molasses in fermentable sugar was 52.94 per cent.   Pasteur gives for the fermentation of 5 grms. of reducing-sugar: carbon dioxide, 2.338 grms.; alcohol, 2.424 grms.; ratio: carbon dioxide to alcohol = 1:1.037.

The fermentations of the nutrient saccharose solutions were never so good as those obtained by Pasteur, hence the ratios of carbon dioxide to alcohol were lower.   It is interesting to note, however, that the ratios with molasses were quite as high as those obtained from the nutrient saccharose solutions.

Inversion of Sugar in Molasses by Means of Invertase.—Although all the evidence derived from the fermentation experiments seemed to indicate the presence of less sugar than was given by analysis, the quantity of reducing-bodies produced by inversion with acids supported the analysis figures.   Consequently it was of importance to determine if possible the amount of reducing-bodies produced in molasses by the action of invertase.

The invertase was prepared by mixing a weighed quantity of fresh yeast with water and keeping it at a temperature of 60° C. for some time. The solutions for inversion were made so as to contain 10 grms. of sugar calculated as reducing-sugar per 100 c.c., and generally 200 c.c. were inverted in each experiment. The temperature of inversion was between 55° C. and 60° C. Saccharose either in aqueous solution or dissolved in spent wash was inverted rapidly and completely.

Turning now to molasses, the action of invertase was found to be much slower. In solutions of saccharose in spent wash 98 per cent of the sugar added was inverted in twenty-four hours, while forty-eight hours were required for the maximum inversion in molasses. If the figures of analysis for saccharose and reducing-sugars are correct, there should have been present, after inversion with invertase, 10 grms. of reducing-sugars in each 100 c.c. of solution, but the quantity obtained actually was only 86 to 87 per cent of this.

Now it has already been shown that the quantity of alcohol obtained on the fermentation of the molasses accounts for about 86 per cent of the sugar indicated by analysis, and this quantity should all be present after inversion with invertase; but to this must be added the unfermentable reducing substance found in the spent wash after fermentation of a molasses solution. Although this does not contribute to the production of alcohol, it is present in the solution. Its amount was found to be 2.46 per cent, calculated on the molasses, or 4.65 per cent of the total sugar, in terms of reducing-sugar. Hence, after inversion with invertase, at least 91 per cent of the sugar indicated by analysis would be expected. The amount found in the experiments was not more than 86 to 87 per cent. When the solutions, after inversion with invertase, were fermented, the yield of alcohol obtained was some 2 or 3 per cent lower than usual, so that evidently a little fermentable sugar had been destroyed through the prolonged inversion. The amount of the loss was easily calculated by subsequent fermentation, and allowing for it, the total quantity of reducing-bodies after inversion was found to be about 90 per cent (9 grms. per 100 c.c.) of that indicated by the analysis. Of this 4.65 per cent is unfermentable, and the quantity of fermentable sugar in the molasses, in terms of reducing-sugar, becomes 45.18 per cent. The figure obtained before from consideration of the alcohol produced from the molasses was 45.63 per cent, and although both these figures are only approximations, the agreement between them made it clear that when the molasses was treated with invertase just that quantity of reducing-sugar was formed which was necessary to produce the quantity of alcohol obtained when the molasses was fermented. Consequently a considerable portion of what analysis indicated as saccharose was not inverted by invertase, and was in reality not that substance.

Although the action of invertase on molasses took a longer time than when cane-sugar was inverted in a solution of spent wash, the results obtained were fairly concordant. This was also found in the case of another molasses treated in a similar way, though with one particular sample no results of value could be obtained, as the action of invertase speedily came to an end, there being evidently something present which inhibited the action of the enzyme. The experiments with invertase confirmed in a striking manner the results obtained earlier in the investigation, and left no room for doubt that the analysis figure for saccharose was considerably too high.

The quantity of reducing-bodies produced by the action of acids was very much greater than by that of invertase, but on subsequent fermentation the yield of alcohol—allowing for the slight destruction of fermentable sugar during inversion with invertase—was no greater. Hence the reducing-bodies produced by acids and not by invertase were not fermentable sugars, and were therefore not derived from saccharose.

H. and L. Pellet, in the paper referred to above, laid great stress on the close agreement of the figures for saccharose in cane-molasses obtained by the Clerget method, and by calculation from the reducing-bodies present before and after inversion with acids. Thus for the molasses under consideration we have:

Saccharose (Clerget).	Reducing-bodies after Inversion.	Reducing-bodies before Inversion.	Difference.	Saccharose calculated.
41.52	55.12	9.26	45.86	43.57

The authors mentioned obtained a much closer agreement for the molasses examined by them, and they regard it as a complete confirmation of the accuracy of Clerget's process, but since a considerable proportion of the reducing-bodies obtained by inversion with acids are not fermentable sugars, no figure for saccharose of any value can be deduced from them.

The conclusion of the investigation was, therefore, that the possible yield of alcohol from cane-molasses indicated by analysis is considerably higher than that which can be obtained by fermentation, and that this is due to the fact that the analytical figures overstate the amount of fermentable sugars actually present.

By making use of the figures obtained in some of the experiments it becomes possible to apply a correction to the ordinary analysis. Thus for the molasses under consideration, the quantity of fermentable reducing-sugar being 6.80 instead of 9.26, the figure for saccharose can be obtained by first subtracting this from the total fermentable sugar, expressed in terms of reducing-sugar. For this two figures were arrived at, viz., 45.63 and 45.18. Taking the mean of these, viz., 45.41, and subtracting 6.80, we obtain 38.61 as the figure for saccharose expressed in terms of reducing-sugars; whence saccharose itself, $\dfrac{38.61 \times 95}{100} = 36.68$ per cent.

On making these corrections we have:

	Original Analysis.	Corrected Analysis.
Saccharose	41.52	36.68
Sugars reducing	9.26	6.80
Other organic matter	11.66	18.96
Ash	11.50	11.50
Water	26.06	26.06
	100.00	100.00
Total sugar as reducing-sugar	52.94	45.41

If we call the possible yield of alcohol calculated from the total sugar in the original molasses 100, then the yield possible from the corrected analysis is only 85.8.

One of the most interesting but puzzling questions in connection with the investigation related to the manner in which the character of the unfermentable bodies, appearing as saccharose in the original analysis, changes during the course of the fermentation. If these bodies did not alter they could be estimated in the spent wash after fermentation, and there would be no difficulty in accounting for the low production of alcohol from the molasses. But the fact that only a small quantity of reducing-bodies is found in the spent wash, even on inversion of this with acids, makes it appear as if a loss of sugar actually took place.

When measured quantities of liquid were removed from a solution of molasses at different stages of the fermentation, and were treated with acid, and the reducing-bodies so produced estimated, it was found that they diminished rapidly during the earlier stages of the fermentation. Thus:

Attenuation.	Reducing-bodies (Expressed in Terms of Reducing-sugars). Grams per 100 c.c.
0.0	10.3
0.5	9.5
2.5	8.62
5.5	8.28
Fermentation complete	0.7

Hence when alcoholic fermentation had only just started (atten., 0.5), the quantity of reducing-bodies which could be produced by inversion with acids had already become very considerably diminished, and was very little in excess of the quantity (9.0 grms.) produced by treating the molasses with invertase.

A similar observation was made in the experiments with invertase. When inversion with invertase was complete, an estimation of the reducing-bodies produced by inversion with acids, including those already produced by invertase, showed that the quantity of these was not much in excess of these latter, whereas before the action of the invertase the quantity of reducing-bodies produced by the acid treatment was much greater. Thus if we call the quantity of reducing-bodies produced from a given weight of molasses by the action of acids 10.3, and the quantity by invertase 8.7 grms., then after inversion with invertase further treatment with acids produced a total quantity of only 9.0 grms., showing that a considerable change in the character of the bodies invertible by acids and not by invertase had taken place. This was quite apart from any loss of fermentable sugar during the inversion, which loss, as proved by subsequent fermentation, was very small. Besides, if it had been fermentable sugar which was disappearing owing to, say, bacterial action, the loss should have increased with the time, but it did not. Sufficient evidence has already done given that the loss of fermentable sugar due to bacterial action during the fermentation of the molasses could only have been very small, since even prolonged treatment with sulphuric acid failed to materially raise the yield, and further, if bacteria were present we should expect the wash to become acid. Under ordinary circumstances, however, the increase of acidity in the solutions during fermentation is slight.

It appears probable that the bodies, whatever they may be, which appear as saccharose in the analysis and which are inverted by acids but not by invertase, are decomposed by some enzyme in the yeast during the earlier stages of fermentation.

DISCUSSION.

Mr. J. A. Schofield asked if the ordinary methods of analysis, when applied to beet-molasses, also gave high results. It was rather strange that the sugar that seemed to disappear should not only have the rotary power of saccharose, but should also yield bodies with the same reducing power as invert-sugar.

Dr. R. Greig-Smith suggested that the apparent loss of sugars might arise from these particular bodies being readily decomposable, and thus supplying cell material for the growing yeast. During his researches on vegetable gums he had found some bodies that yielded, on hydrolysis, reducing substances that were not sugars capable of forming ordinary osazones, for the compounds melted at too low a temperature and yielded tarry bodies, with acetic acid. Possibly some similar substance might be present in molasses. With regard to sugar in molasses fermenting more quickly than pure sugar aided by Pasteur's nutrient, he thought this was due to the high proportion of salts present. He deprecated the assumption that some "enzyme" had been acting, when, as a matter of fact, the nature of the change was simply unknown.

Dr. Harker, in reply to Mr. Schofield, said that in beet-molasses reducing-sugars were absent, and raffinose was the only substance known to be present that made a correction necessary in the polariscopic reading. With regard to Dr. Greig-Smith's remarks, he thought the disappearance of the apparent saccharose was too rapid to be explained as due to its being used as food for yeast-cells. He was of opinion that the rapidity of fermentation in molasses was due to the large proportion of nitrogenous yeast foods rather than to the salts.

CHAPTER III.

THE DISTILLATION AND RECTIFICATION OF ALCOHOL.

Theory of Vapor Pressure and Boiling-point. Boiling-points of Mixtures of Ethyl and Methyl Alcohol. Boiling-points of Mixtures of Ethyl Alcohol and Water. Theory of Distillation. Simple Distillation. Constant Boiling Mixtures. Theory of Fractional Distillation. Theory of Compound Distillation. Dephlegmation. The Efficiency of Fractional Distillation. The Extraction of the Alcohol by Distillation. The Rectification of the Alcohol. History of the Distillation of Alcohol. Commercial Apparatus for the Distillation of Alcohol. American Alcohol-distilling Apparatus.

IF any liquid is introduced into an exhausted enclosure it evaporates until its vapor reaches a definite pressure, known as the vapor pressure of the liquid. This vapor pressure depends solely upon the temperature.

If the enclosure into which the liquid is introduced, instead of being exhausted, contains air or other gas, the liquid evaporates nevertheless to just the same extent as before. If, however, the liquid is placed in the open air the vapor is carried away by diffusion and the liquid continues to evaporate until it entirely disappears.

If the temperature is gradually raised the vapor pressure increases, and this surface evaporation becomes more rapid until suddenly a new phenomenon appears. This is at the point where the vapor pressure becomes equal to the pressure of the atmosphere.

The vapor, in order to escape, no longer needs to diffuse through the atmosphere, but is able to push it away bodily. Evaporation is now not confined to the surface. Bubbles of vapor rise from the interior and the liquid is said to boil. The boiling-point is therefore the temperature at which the vapor pressure becomes equal to the atmospheric pressure and the boiling-point is higher the greater this pressure is.

When the liquid is a mixture of two or more constituents, each is present in the vapor above the liquid, and each has a "partial" vapor pressure which depends on the composition of the liquid and the temperature. At a given temperature these partial vapor pressures are

64

never as great as the vapor pressures of the respective constituents in the pure state. The boiling-point of a mixture is the temperature at which the sum of the partial vapor pressures is equal to the atmospheric pressure. Usually the boiling-point of a mixture of two liquids lies between the boiling-points of the pure liquids, but this is not always the case. It is true of mixtures of common (ethyl) alcohol and wood alcohol (methyl alcohol), but it is not true of mixtures of ethyl acohol and water, as shown in the following tables. Table I gives the boiling-points, at the normal pressure of 760 mm., of mixtures of the first pair of liquids.

TABLE I.—METHYL ALCOHOL AND ETHYL ALCOHOL.

Per Cent Methyl Alcohol.	Boiling-point, Degrees Centigrade.	Per Cent Methyl Alcohol.	Boiling-point, Degrees Centigrade.
100.0	64.7	46.0	70.3
88.1	65.7	42.4	70.8
74.6	67.0	36.5	71.6
65.4	67.9	24.9	73.5
55.9	69.0	11.1	76.1
50.0	69.7	0.0	78.3
46.2	70.2		

Table II gives the boiling-points, at the normal pressure of 760 mm., of mixtures of the second pair.

TABLE II.—ETHYL ALCOHOL AND WATER.

Per Cent Ethyl Alcohol	Boiling-point, Degrees Centigrade.	Per Cent Ethyl Alcohol.	Boiling-point, Degrees Centigrade.	Per Cent Ethyl Alcohol.	Boiling-point, Degrees Centigrade.
100.0	78.300	88.0	78.445	55.0	81.77
99.5	78.270	87.0	78.530	48.0	82.43
99.0	78.243	86.0	78.575	37.0	83.76
98.5	78.222	85.0	78.645	35.0	83.87
98.0	78.205	84.0	78.723	29.0	84.86
97.5	78.191	83.0	78.806	26.0	85.41
97.0	78.181	82.0	78.879	22.0	86.11
96.5	78.179	81.0	78.968	20.0	87.32
96.0	78.174	80.0	79.050	18.0	87.92
95.5	78.176	79.0	79.133	13.0	90.02
95.0	78.177	78.0	79.214	10.0	91.80
94.5	78.186	77.0	79.354	8.0	93.10
94.0	78.195	76.0	79.404	7.0	93.73
93.5	78.211	75.0	79.505	5.5	94.84
93.0	78.227	73.0	79.683	4.5	95.63
92.5	78.241	71.0	79.862	3.0	97.11
92.0	78.259	69.0	80.042	2.0	98.05
91.0	78.270	67.0	80.237	1.5	98.55
90.0	78.323	65.0	80.438	1.0	98.95
89.0	78.385	63.0	80.642	0.5	99.65

Table I is calculated from the data of Haywood (Jour. Amer. Chem. Soc., 21, 996).

Table II is taken from the paper of Noyes and Warfel (Jour. Amer. Chem. Soc., 23, 467).

In order to show clearly the difference between the two cases the data given in the tables is plotted in Figs. I and II, and that part of the curve in Fig. II which is of special interest, namely, between 90 per cent and 100 per cent of alcohol, is plotted on a larger scale in Fig. III.

It is obvious from the diagrams that if we start with ethyl alcohol and add little by little the lower boiling methyl alcohol, the boiling-point of the mixture drops and steadily approaches the boiling-point of pure methyl alcohol. If, on the other hand, we add similarly to water suc-

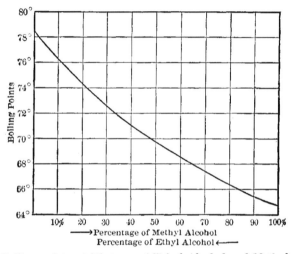

FIG. I.—Boiling-points of Mixtures of Ethyl Alcohol and Methyl Alcohol.

cessive portions of the lower boiling ethyl alcohol, the boiling-point drops as before, but when the alcohol in the mixture has reached about 90 per cent the boiling-point has already fallen to that of pure alcohol. As more alcohol is added the boiling-point continues to decrease until it is about 0.13° lower. With further additions of alcohol the boiling-point increases and approaches again that of pure alcohol.

According to the experiments of Young and Fortey (Trans. London Chem. Soc., 81, 717) the mixture of lowest boiling-point contains 95.57 per cent of alcohol by weight or 97.2 per cent by volume. It will be shown presently that the existence of this mixture of minimum boiling-point is of the very greatest importance in the technical distillation of alcohol. Such a unique mixture is known as a constant boiling mixture.

Theory of Distillation. Simple Distillation.—The process of distillation consists in leading the vapor from a boiling liquid into a cooler vessel, where it recondenses.

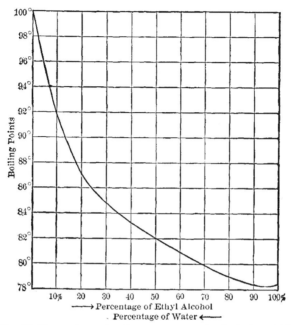

FIG. II.—Boiling-points of Mixtures of Ethyl Alcohol and Water.

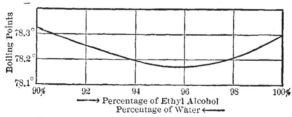

FIG. III.—Boiling-points of Mixtures of Ethyl Alcohol and Water from 90% to 100% on a Larger Scale.

The simplest apparatus for the purpose, which is shown in Fig. 18, consists of a glass flask (or a retort) in which the liquid or liquid mixture is boiled and the condenser into which the vapor thus formed is conducted and by which it is recondensed, the distillate being collected in the receiving-flask.

This form of condenser consists of two tubes between which a current of cold water flows in an upward direction or opposite to the flow of the distillate. The inner tube of this condenser as well as the outer is sometimes made of glass and in some instances of metal.

This form of condenser is called the "Liebig," from the illustrious chemist who invented it.

The flask in which the distillate collects is called the receiver. In using such an apparatus the process is called simple distillation. In practice the common still, a large boiler heated by fire or steam, supplies the place of the flask or retort of the laboratory apparatus, while the

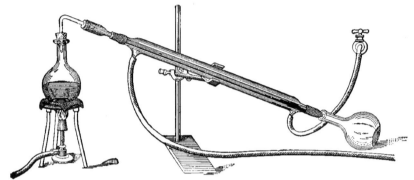

FIG. 18.—Laboratory Distilling Apparatus, with Liebig Condenser.

Liebig condenser is replaced by a spiral tube of copper (called a worm) which is immersed in a tank supplied with a current of cold water, the vapor thereby being exposed to a great degree of cold surface.

The tank or vessel containing the worm is called the condenser. Such an apparatus is called the common or simple still, and a representation of it is shown in Fig. 19, the distillate being collected in the receiver c at a. A represents the boiler and B the still-head of the still.

In the column still (compound still) this still-head of the simple still is replaced by a column or "dephlegmator," the theory of which and the principles governing its operation will be explained later on in this chapter.

Theory of Fractional Distillation.—When a pure liquid is distilled the boiling-point remains constant until the distillation is complete. When a mixture is distilled this is sometimes, but rarely, true. In all other cases the liquid which appears in the condenser has a lower boiling-point than the original mixture, while the residue in the still always has a higher.

This is a rule which was first devised by Konowalow (Annalen der Physik, 14, 341, 1881). It is unnecessary in a book of this sort to give the rigorous proof of this theorem. It will be sufficient to point out that any contradiction of this rule would incur a contradiction of the fundamental laws governing this phenomenon. Furthermore this rule has been repeatedly verified by a large number of practical experiments.

In general if the distillation of a mixture is stopped before it is completed, two mixtures are obtained, one in the receiver of the lower boiling-point and one left in the still of the higher boiling-point. If each of these portions is then partially distilled the distillate of the former has a still lower boiling-point, and the residue from the latter a still higher boiling-point.

This process of successive differentiation is known as fractional

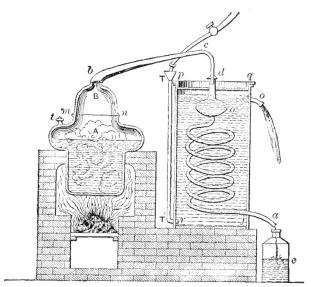

FIG. 19.—The Common or Simple Still.

distillation, and is one of the most common methods of separating the constituents of a liquid mixture.

An example of this process in its simplest form is given by Maercker.

A fermented mash liquor of 11.3 per cent of alcohol by weight was distilled in a simple still until the liquor remaining in the still was practically free from alcohol.

This residue was then discarded and the distillate redistilled until again a residue was left practically free from alcohol. This process was repeated five successive times and the results are recorded in the following table:

Alcoholic Mixture.	Per Cent Alcohol by Weight.
Original wash liquor....................	11.3
First distillate......................	32.3
Second distillate.....................	55.0
Third "	70.3
Fourth "	78.5
Fifth "	83.0

In Fig. 20 below are shown two kinds of flasks for fractional distillation in the laboratory, each flask being fitted with a thermometer,
the one on the right of cut having a T tube.

Ordinarily the process of fractionation is made somewhat more
complex than this by dividing each distillate into successive portions each
of which is then distilled in turn. The efficiency is thus increased,
but in any case such a fractional distillation carried on by means of a

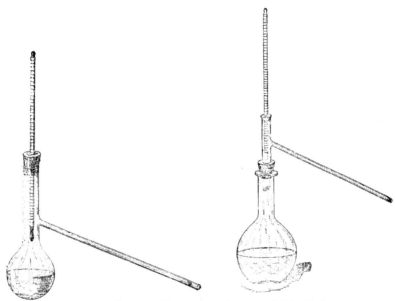

FIG. 20.—Flasks for Laboratory Fractional Distillation.

simple still is a tedious and laborious process, and this fact has led to
important modifications in stills used for fractionating.

Theory of Compound Distillation. Dephlegmation.—If the neck
of the distilling-flask, or the still-head, is constructed in such a way
that the liquid that condenses there does not return immediately to
the body of the still it remains in small pools. The composition of the
liquid in these pools varies and the boiling-point is lower the farther
the pool is from the body of the still. The vapor passing through
these pools on its way to the condenser changes in composition (becomes
richer in alcohol) as it progresses and finally when it enters the condenser it is leaving a liquid of much lower boiling-point than that in
the bottom of this still. As the mixture passes up the still-head it
is thus subjected to what is equivalent to a fractional distillation, while
the weaker alcoholic liquors run back gradually into the still. Such

an arrangement produces therefore a much more effective separation and much more highly concentrated alcohol than does a simple still. In Figs. 21 and 22 are shown two such arrangements for laboratory purposes known as the "rod-and-disc" still-heads, and the Linnemann dephlegmator, from Young's Fractional Distillation, page 163.

Other forms of laboratory dephlegmator apparatus are shown in Figs. 23 and 24, page 72.

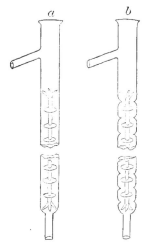

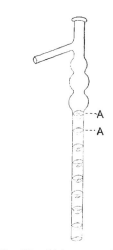

FIG. 21.—The "Rod-and-disc" Still-heads: (*a*) without, (*b*) with constrictions in the outer tube.

FIG. 22.—The "Linnemann" Dephleg mator.

In *a* this consists of a T tube and spherical bulbs and is the Wurtz dephlegmator. This is shown merely to include it among the different forms given. Linnemann's apparatus in another form of earlier date is shown by *b* in the same figure and has cups of platinum gauze in the vertical tube as shown.

Hempel's tube is shown by *c* in the same figure. It is filled with specially made glass beads, and shown provided with T tube and thermometer in this cut.

The Le Bel-Henninger tube shown by *d*, in Fig. 24, is usually provided with platinum cones to cause the obstruction which is effected by placing these cones on the constrictions between the bulbs blown on the vertical tube; each bulb is connected by a reflux tube with the one below it so that the liquid is carried back from bulb to bulb and not straight to the still.

The Glinsky dephlegmator, shown by *e* in Fig. 24, is provided with only one reflux tube, which carries the excess of liquid from

the large bulb to the tube below the lowest obstruction practically back
to the still. It is therefore faulty in construction, as no opportunity
is afforded the ascending alcoholic vapors to come in contact and be
washed by such drawn-off alcoholic liquid and thereby be enriched by it

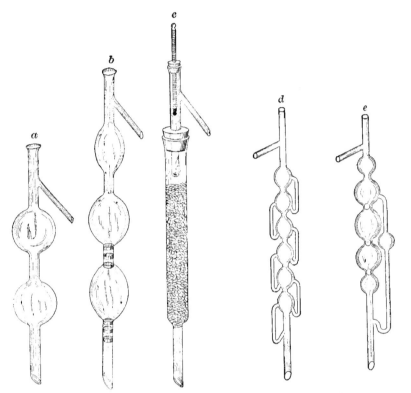

FIG. 23.—Laboratory Dephlegmator
Apparatus. a, Wurz; b, Linne-
man; c, Hempel.

FIG. 24.—d, Le Bel-Henninger's
Laboratory Dephlegmator; e,
Glinksky's Laboratory De-
phlegmator.

to the extent that they should. Another serious fault in construction
in these dephlegmators of Le Bel-Henninger and Glinsky consists in
the fact that the reflux tubes are external and unlike the Coffey still;
the returning liquid is thus exposed to the cooling action of the
air.

The laboratory dephlegmators of Brown and of Young and Thomas
follow the principle of the Coffey still more closely, the reflux tubes being
much shorter and being heated by the ascending vapor. In Fig. 25
the "Young and Thomas" dephlegmator is shown. In the wide
tube are sharp constrictions on which rest concave rings of platinum

gauze, *R*, and these support small glass reflux tubes, *T*, of the form shown in this cut. The narrow V-shaped part serves as a trap. The enlargement *A* prevents the reflux tube from slipping through the ring if the tube is inverted. One of the internal projections is shown at *B* in the tube *b*. A horizontal section of the tube at *B* is shown by *c*.

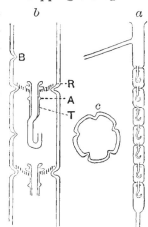

On comparing the efficiency of these different dephlegmators it was found by Young that for large quantities (400 grms.) of liquid Glinsky's apparatus was inferior to the Le Bel and also to that of Young and Thomas. With small quantities (50 grms.) of liquid he found that the Young and Thomas dephlegmator gave better results than either the Le Bel or the Glinsky dephlegmators. The first dephlegmator employed in the laboratory was devised by Linnemann, and has already been shown in its earlier form. In this dephlegmator, however, the liquid

Fig. 25.—The "Young and Thomas" Dephlegmator.

gradually accumulates until the quantity becomes unmanageable, when the distillation has to be discontinued until the liquid flows back to the still. This entailed waste of time and increased loss of alcohol by evaporation, and it was impossible to make an accurate record of the temperature. The Hempel dephlegmator, already shown in Fig. 23, is simple and efficient, but the amount of liquid (alcohol) which collects in this tube or still-head is excessive, and it is therefore unsuitable for the distillations of small quantities of liquid. The description just given of laboratory dephlegmators also serves as a history of their development. Commercial stills based on the principle of the "rod-and-disc" still-head and the dephlegmator just described will be discussed later.

The Efficiency of Fractional Distillation.—The efficiency of a fractional separation depends upon the character of the still and upon the number of fractions and redistillations. Moreover, the efficiency of each distillation is greater the slower it is and the more regular the heating. In practice it is necessary to some extent to sacrifice efficiency to speed.

It is frequently assumed that by perfecting our stills and our methods of fractionation it is possible to come as near as we please to effecting the complete separation of the constituents of a mixture. While this is true of some mixtures, it is not true of others, and the distinction between the two classes is of very great importance.

A mixture of ethyl and methyl alcohols after enough fractionations in an efficient still yields on the one side practically pure ethyl alcohol, on the other practically pure methyl alcohol, and we have every reason to believe that with an ideally perfect still the separation could be made complete. But with mixtures of ethyl alcohol and water this is far from being true. Young and Forty (Trans. London Chem. Soc., 81, 717) describe the results of a very efficient fractionation, starting with 92.6 per cent alcohol by weight. They used an eighteen-column dephlegmator and fractionally distilled seven times. By this means instead of absolute alcohol they obtained only 95.3 per cent alcohol. Even more significant is the experiment described by Le Bel (Comptes Rend., 88, 912), who showed that 98 per cent alcohol yielded a distillate *weaker* in alcohol (97.4 per cent) and a residue *stronger* in alcohol (99.5 per cent). The clue to this remarkable difference in behavior between a mixture of methyl and ethyl alcohol on the one hand and a mixture of ethyl alcohol and water on the other is obvious if we return to Figs. I, II, and III, pp. 66, 67. Let us consider first a mixture of ethyl alcohol and water containing 95.57 per cent by weight of alcohol. We have stated as a universal rule that a liquid never gives a distillate of higher boiling-point than its own. But in this particular case it is impossible for the mixture to yield a distillate of lower boiling-point than its own, for we see from the curve that it has the lowest boiling-point of any mixture of alcohol and water. When it distills, therefore, it must pass over at constant temperature and without change of composition. Such a unique mixture is known as a constant boiling mixture. All other mixtures distill invariably in such a way that the distillate is represented by a point lower down on the boiling-point curve, the residue by a point higher up on the curve. Whenever, therefore, in any pair of liquids there is one mixture of lowest boiling-point, then on (repeated) distillation the distillate will always tend toward the lowest boiling mixture. Thus upon repeated distillation of a mixture of methyl alcohol and ethyl alcohol the distillate will approach closer and closer to pure methyl alcohol, the residue to pure ethyl alcohol. But upon repeated distillation of a mixture of ethyl alcohol and water of less than 95.57 per cent the distillate will approach 95.57 per cent alcohol and the residue will approach pure water. If we started with a mixture stronger in alcohol than the constant boiling mixture described, then the distillate would again approach 95.57 per cent alcohol, while the residue would approach pure alcohol. No matter how perfect a still may be, therefore, it is hopeless to attempt to obtain absolute alcohol from dilute alcohol by mere distillation.

In order to obtain absolute alcohol some hygroscopic substances, such as quicklime or anhydrous copper sulphate, are employed as stated in Chapter II.   After digesting or allowing the strong alcohol to remain in contact with such substances in closed vessels for a sufficient length of time to separate the water from the alcohol, in such a constant boiling mixture as has been described, the absolute alcohol is recovered by careful distillation.   Metallic sodium is also used for such purposes.   It is thus seen that the assistance of chemistry is necessary in addition to that of physics and mechanics to solve the problems in the technical distillation of alcohol.

The curve showing the boiling-points of ethyl alcohol and water shows the slight minimum which we have commented upon.   In the

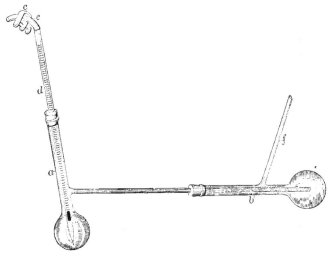

FIG. 26.—Laboratory Vacuum Distilling Apparatus.

case of mixtures of the higher liquid alcohols with water, this boiling-point minimum is more pronounced the higher the alcohol is in the series, and it is therefore impossible by mere distillation to come even as near a complete separation from water as in the case of ethyl alcohol.

Before discussing the technical distillation of alcohol two methods of distillation, known as distillation under reduced pressure and distillation with steam, may be mentioned.

These methods are chiefly used in cases where for fear of decomposition or for other reason it is undesirable to heat the substance to its normal boiling-point.   In Fig. 26 the air is exhausted from the distilling-flask in any convenient manner.

In Fig. 27 is shown Brühl's apparatus, whereby, in distilling under reduced pressure, the receiver can be changed in fractional distillations without breaking the vacuum.

Distillation with steam is chiefly used in the case of substances which are non-miscible with water. The steam passing through the liquid to be distilled becomes saturated with its vapor and the vapor condensed with the steam in the condenser is then readily separated from the condensed water in the receiver.

FIG. 27.—Brühl's Laboratory Vacuum Distilling Apparatus.

Such a laboratory steam distilling apparatus is shown in Fig. 28.

In case it is desired to superheat the steam used for such laboratory distillations as have been mentioned, it is done by passing the steam through a heated copper coil like the one shown in Fig. 29, page 77.

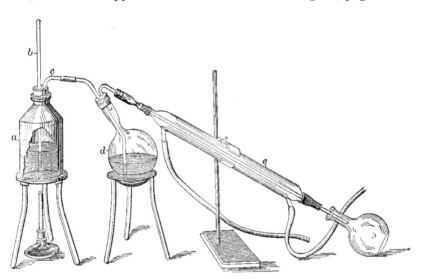

FIG. 28.—Laboratory Steam Distilling Apparatus.

The Extraction of the Alcohol by Distillation.—This is the fourth step in the processes involved in the manufacture of alcohol, as mentioned in Chapter II. We have shown by what has preceded that it is technically impossible to make use of the method of simple distillation for the production of high-proof alcohol.

This is because of the great number of repeated distillations required involving a consequent enormous loss of time and expense.

The fermented mash liquor or wash usually contains, as has been stated in Chapter II, from 10 to 12 per cent of alcohol.

It is the object of the alcohol distiller to extract and concentrate this alcohol from the wash and to obtain it at a high degree of proof.

The theory of compound distillation proceeds upon the idea of effecting this object in one operation in a compound apparatus, thus imitating the repeated vaporizations and condensations (repeated number of distillations) of the simple still necessary for this purpose, which we have

Fig. 29.—Laboratory Copper Coil for Superheating Steam.

described. A great saving of time is thus made and much less expense is involved. There is also much less loss of alcohol by evaporation. In the compound still many repeated vaporizations and condensations take place in a continuous manner, whereby both fractional distillation and fractional condensation occur as shown in the course of the vapors and the return flow of weaker alcohol through the chambers, the details of which are given, on an enlarged scale, in Fig. 30. The result is the constant increased concentration of the alcoholic vapors and the constant increased attenuation of the watery weak alcoholic liquor in its downward course through the chambers to the still, where it is finally discharged as spent wash.

In Fig. 30 the course of the vapor bubbling up through the pools of alcoholic liquid in the chambers is shown by the arrows. In the upper drawing the flow of returns, or weaker alcoholic liquid over heads, down through the chambers is indicated by the arrows. Finally the nearly pure alcohol vapor passes over to the final condenser to be recondensed and obtained as high-proof alcohol. In this country two distillation processes have been used. In the first the alcohol is obtained at 140 proof or 70 per cent; in the second the alcohol is rectified and obtained at the high proof desired.

The Rectification of the Alcohol.—In modern continuous stills, presently to be described, there is needed no filtration through charcoal (rectifi-

DETAIL OF COLUMN CHAMBERS

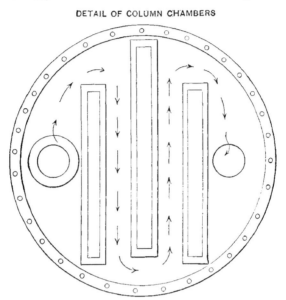

ARROWS INDICATE FLOW OF RETURNS OVER HEADS

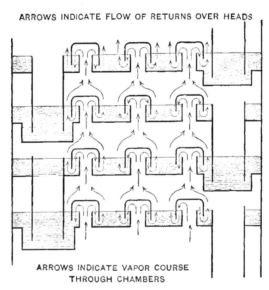

ARROWS INDICATE VAPOR COURSE
THROUGH CHAMBERS

FIG. 30.

cation) of the potable spirits produced. Formerly abroad, as in this country to-day, such filtration method was necessary to purify the spirit.

The name rectifying-still or rectifying-column still clings to the apparatus (dephlegmator) which accomplishes the purification in the cases of the modern stills.   In the case of denatured alcohol it is a matter of profit to remove the fusel-oil in making the alcohol, as it is a valuable product and consists largely of amyl alcohols, which are used as a base in the form of amyl acetate for the manufacture of water-proof lacquers, artificial leather, sanitary sheeting for hospitals, etc.

The strength of alcohol produced in distillation depends upon the efficiency of the still, its proper manipulation, and also upon the number of chambers or plate partitions in the rectifying-column, and whether one or more rectifying-columns are used.   It also depends upon the amount of cooling surface possessed by the dephlegmating apparatus, or fractional condenser, as it is now more properly called in the laboratory, or the "goose," as it is called in practice.

Formerly the rectification of the spirits marked a distinct (fifth) and last step in the processes involved in the manufacture of high-proof alcohol.

History of the Distillation of Alcohol.—Alcohol in a dilute form as an intoxicating beverage has been known among all races and conditions of people since very ancient times.   A common form of such alcohol is wine, the fermented juice of the grape.   All the juices of plants which contain sugar and all vegetable matters which contain starch will yield alcohol by fermentation.

The preparation of an alcoholic liquor by separating the more volatile portions of the fermented juices of fruits and infusions of grains by distillation does not appear to have been understood by the ancients according to Muspratt.   Ure says: "It seems to have been invented by the barbarians of the north of Europe as a solace to their cold and humid clime, and was first made known to the southern nations in the writings of Arnoldus de Villa Nova and his pupil, Raymond Lully of Majorca."

The first stills were naturally of the most primitive design and construction.   The contents were boiled by direct fire, and even to-day such a method of heating is used for special distillations.   The object of distillation is to obtain the alcohol in a more concentrated form from the fermented liquor.   The next step after the fermentation of the raw material in making alcohol, therefore, is the process whereby such fermented mash or wash liquor is subjected to distillation to extract the alcohol from it. By repeated distillations and rectifications, in one or more operations, the highly purified alcohol is obtained from such fermented liquor, or wash as it is often called, the high-proof alcohol obtained being known as commercial 95 per cent alcohol, Cologne spirits, and neutral spirit of high proof, as the case may be.

Before turning to the long and interesting development of the apparatus for the distillation of alcohol upon a commercial scale, whereby such great degree of perfection has finally been attained, it may be well to state that concerning the statement of Ure it has been ascertained that in the times of the Ptolemies the Greek-Egyptian chemists were acquainted with the art of simple distillation.*

COMMERCIAL APPARATUS FOR THE DISTILLATION OF ALCOHOL.

FOREIGN ALCOHOL-DISTILLING APPARATUS.

Édouard Adam's Still.—The origin of the first still which abolished to a great extent the use of the worm and substituted condensing vessels, which principle of fractional condensation, as well as the "heater" or dephlegmator (reflux condenser), has been retained with modifications in nearly all subsequent inventions of the kind, is due to a Frenchman named Édouard Adam, who is said to have been a distiller unacquainted with anything more than the routine of his trade. In 1801 he witnessed some experiments with a Woulfe apparatus at a chemical lecture in Montpellier, and was so impressed with its advantages that he soon after constructed a still upon the same principle. This succeeded so well that the whole process of distillation was soon completely changed. The use of Woulfe's apparatus is described in any technology or work on gas, and by referring to that it will be seen that Adam's still was one of the happiest adaptations of a laboratory appliance to a manufacturing purpose. The modification as made by M. Adam is represented in Fig. 31.

It will be noticed that the terminal egg-shaped copper vessels are connected on the one hand with the retort or boiler containing the fermented liquor or wine, and on the other with a worm which is immersed in a cooler, F. The neck of the retort passes into the first egg-shaped vessel, dipping below the surface of the liquor. It is perforated at its termination by minute holes through which the vapor passes. A pipe from the first egg leads to the second, also dipping below the surface of the liquor, and so on, from one to the next, whatever the number may be.

---

* Saridakes (from Lasche's Magazine, Vol. I, p. 189) gives the statement that "the origin of the art of distilling has been wrongly attributed to the Arabians, whose noticeable appearance in the world's history dates only since 622 A.D. The art is much anterior to the above date: it was originated by Greek-Egyptian chemists during the Hellenization of Egypt, under the reign of the Ptolemies, 330 to 323 B.C."

From the last egg a tube enters the globe B before passing into the worm, whose use will presently be explained.   From the next to the last egg, or from any one of the series, an extra tube, C, also passes into the globe B, by which arrangement one or more of the eggs may be dispensed with when the distillation does not need to be carried very high.   Another pipe, D, connects each egg and also the boiler with a small worm, V, which is used for testing the strength of the distillate in any one of the eggs, or from the boiler.   Another pipe, E, leads from the cooler F into the boiler, and another, H, into the cooler from the storehouse where the wines are kept.   The worm in the cooler F, moreover, leads into another worm in the cooler G.   This still is worked in the following manner: The

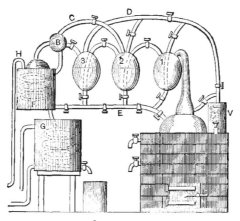

Fig. 31.—Édouard Adam's Still.

cocks connecting the upper tubes are closed, and those in the lower pipe, E, are opened.   The wine is pumped from the storehouse through the tube H into the cooler F, whence it flows into the boiler.   When this is about two thirds full the cock next it is closed and the wine is forced up into the first egg; when this is about half-filled the cock next it is closed, when the second egg is treated in the same manner; and so on through the series, except the last one, which serves as a condenser and is surrounded with cold water.   The lower cocks are now closed and the upper ones communicating between the eggs and with the worm are opened.   Heat is applied to the boiler and the mixture of alcoholic and watery vapor is carried into the first egg and there condensed by the wine quite rapidly in the beginning of the process, so that for a time no vapor passes over into the second egg.   The wine in the first egg, however, gradually comes to its boiling-point, which, by reason of its containing more alcohol than that in the boiler, is at a lower temperature.   In consequence the vapor which passes into the second egg has a greater percentage of alcohol than that which it received. This vapor, being condensed, will cause the liquor in the second egg to be stronger than in the first, and therefore to boil at a still lower temperature. The successive eggs as they recede from the boiler will thus contain stronger and stronger spirits, so that the last one may be made to receive alcoholic vapor of any desired strength. This is passed into the worm in F and condensed either in that or in the succeeding worm in the tub G below, which is filled with water, kept cool by a constant flow. The upper cooler, or wine-heater, containing the wine is kept closed, except that a pipe leads into the globe B. This arrangement is for the purpose of preventing loss of spirit by evaporation, which would be considerable at the temperature it attains by contact with the worm. The excise laws of Great Britain prevented the introduction of this still into that country until after their modification in 1815.

While, as is readily apparent from the above explanation, Adam's still was a very important contribution to the practice of the distillation of alcohol, nevertheless it was a periodic and not a continuous distilling apparatus.

The principle of continuous distillation of alcohol will next be described. While in Dorn's distilling apparatus by one operation spirit containing about 60 per cent of spirit is obtained, two important improvements in stills over his apparatus were made, one by Derosne in France and the other by Coffey in England. Both of these stills further perfected the process of continuous distillation.

Derosne's Still.—Édouard Adam's apparatus was in the meantime, from 1801 to 1815, much improved in France by Isaac Bérard, Cellier-Blumenthal, and Derosne. The modification of Cellier-Blumenthal, improved by Derosne and now called Derosne's still, is represented in Fig. 32, page 83. This still made possible the method of continuous distillation. It consists of two boilers (or tandem stills), A and A'; a first rectifier, C; a wine-heater, D, containing a dephlegmator; a condenser, F; a supply-regulator, E, for controlling the flow of wine from the reservoir G, which is accomplished by means of a float-valve.

The still is worked in the following manner: The boilers are about two thirds filled with wine, or the liquor to be subjected to distillation, through the cocks c, c'. The proper quantity is indicated by the glass gauges d, d'. Wine from the reservoir G is then let into the funnel J, by which the condenser F and the wine-heater D are filled. In the distillation the low-wine vapors pass from the lower into the upper

boiler through the pipe Z, the extremity of which is enlarged and perforated with small holes.   Here the vapors are condensed, increasing
the strength of the wine in the upper boiler and consequently lower-

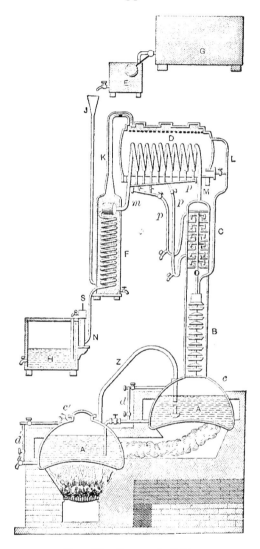

FIG. 32.—Derosne's Still.

ing its boiling-point.   The vapors ascend into the rectifiers B and C.
The lower rectifier B contains a number of shallow pans perforated
with holes, and a number of spherical discs, also perforated with holes,
placed above them in pairs, the convexity of each disc being upward,

and receiving the drip of the shallow pan next above it. This drip
is produced by warmed wine which flows from the wine-heater through
the pipe L. By these means the vapors ascending from the upper boiler
have their more watery portions condensed, while the alcoholic vapor
continues to ascend.

The dripping wine also has a portion of its alcohol expelled in the
form of vapor, which ascends with the vapor coming from below into
the upper rectifier through the orifice O in its base. This upper rectifier communicates through the tube M with a worm (which is the
dephlegmator) in the wine-heater D, the worm ending in the tube
m, which again terminates in the worm contained in the condenser F
through a cylindrical connection in its upper part. The worm in F
terminates in a small vessel, N, which is furnished with an alcoholometer. The alcohol in N flows from its upper part into the cistern H.
The upper rectifier C is divided into a number of compartments by
as many horizontal partitions, each disc having an orifice in its centre,
like the orifice at O. To each of these orifices on the upper side of the
partition is adjusted a short open vertical tube. A short distance
above each tube is placed an inverted pan, having its edges descending
about three fourths of an inch below the level of the upper orifice of
the tube. As the vapors ascend from the lower rectifier into the upper
one, a portion of them condense and collect upon the bottom of the
compartments until they rise slightly above the edges of the inverted
pans and nearly to the upper orifices of the tubes. When this takes
place the vapor can only pass upward by forcing its way under the
edges of the pans, by which means the more watery portion is still
further condensed, the (stronger) alcoholic vapor, having a higher
tension, retaining its gaseous form, and passing on through the tube M
into the dephlegmatory worm in the wine-heater, there to be partially
condensed; which process heats the wine surrounding the worm. A
phlegma collects in the lower convolutions, which may be drawn off
by means of the pipes p, p, p, and transferred at pleasure either into
the tube m or into the upper rectifier. The purer alcoholic vapors
which arise pass through the dephlegmator into the condensing worm
in the condenser F, whence they flow in liquid form into the vessel N
and thence into the reservoir or receiver H, while the spent wash liquor,
free from alcohol, is run off by the outlet-pipe from A'. The strength
of the alcohol produced by this still depends upon the number of windings of the dephlegmator and the number of partitions in the upper
rectifier. Derosne's still requires but little fuel, distills rapidly, and
yields a good spirit, which may be varied in strength at pleasure.

Pistorius' Still.—The distilling apparatus shown in Fig. 33 was invented by Pistorius, in Berlin, in the year 1817. This cut shows the still according to his original drawing in the works of Lüdersdorff-Pistorius on the manufacture of alcohol.

In operating this still the wash liquor is boiled by a direct fire in the lower boiler or still A. The weak alcoholic vapors evolved are conducted by the tube D into the second still C. In order to prevent the scorching or burning of the contents of these stills, they are provided with mechanical stirrers or agitators, by means of which the contents can be kept in motion.

The wash liquor in the second boiler or still C is brought to boiling by the alcoholic vapors entering it from the still A and also by the hot fluc-gases from the furnace fire under the still A. The alcoholic vapors from the still C escape into the rectificator E through the tube a, surmounted by the cap b, and must force their way through a pool or layer of alcoholic liquor in the bottom of E, becoming greatly enriched in alcohol thereby, after which they pass on through G to the rectifying-column H, H_2, H_3, which is cooled by water from the pipe h, and these still stronger alcoholic vapors are finally condensed as about 80 per cent alcohol in K and collected in practice from L in the receiver. Meantime the cold wash liquor is being heated in F, a saving in fuel being thus effected, and as this wash liquor is heated a partial or fractional condensation of the alcoholic vapors is thus accomplished, and the weaker alcoholic liquor so obtained furnishes the layer for the bottom of E, as mentioned above. The low wines also return from the rectifying-column into E through G, G, and also contribute to this layer or pool of weak alcohol in E. In practice the tubes L, G, G, and D are properly connected up, although in this drawing of Pistorius they are left open. It will thus be seen that E is really a "heater" or dephlegmator apparatus. The surplus low wines from E are returned to C. At the point c in the tube to B is a cock for condensing the vapors from A through the condenser m and collecting the distillate at f. When such a tested sample proves to be alcohol-free the contents of A are spent and this is run off. It is called the slop and is the residue from the distillation of the wash or fermented weak liquor. After A is emptied the contents of C are then run into A, and the hot wash liquor from the "heater" F is run into C; then F is refilled with cold wash liquor and the distillation again proceeds. Such a still is periodic and not continuous. This still possesses the advantages of the wash "heater" and of the rectifying-column. It has since been improved over this original design.

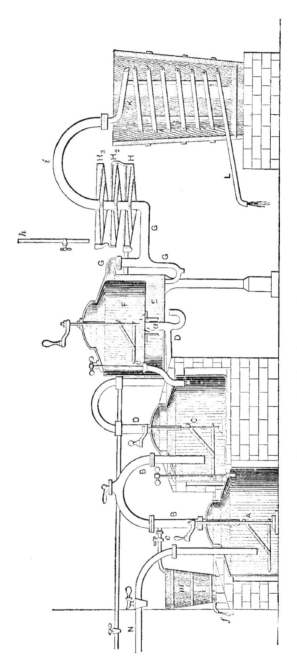

Fig. 33.—The Pistorius Distilling Apparatus.

Saint-Marc's Still.—In Fig. 34 is shown the distilling apparatus of Saint-Marc. In this still the number of plates was increased over that of the Pistorius still, which assisted in developing the process of continuous distillation. The discharge-pipe for the spent wash or residue from the distillation is shown at the bottom of the still in this cut. In this form this apparatus found employment in the English colonies for the distillation of rum. Saint-Marc was a veterinary surgeon on the staff of Napoleon I. and after the battle of Waterloo he went, in 1823, to England and became interested in the distillation of spirits, with the result that he there perfected this still and about the year 1827 took out a patent therefor.

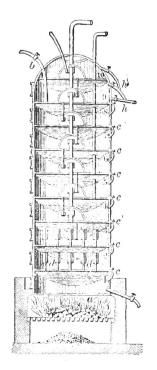

FIG. 34.—Saint-Marc's Distilling Apparatus.

The Coffey Still.—In 1832 an Englishman named Coffey patented the continuous form of distilling apparatus shown in Fig. 35. This still has proved to be of great value to the distiller. Its objects are two-fold:

1. To economize the heat as much as possible by exposing the liquid to a very extended heating surface;

2. To cause the evaporation of the alcohol from the wash by passing a current of steam through it.

In operating this still the wash is pumped from the reservoir M through L into the zigzag pipe m, which passes from top to bottom of the rectifier K. In circulating through this tube m the wash liquor is heated to quite an extent. Arrived at the last convolution of this tube in the rectifier, the heated wash passes by the tube m in at the top of the still. It falls and collects upon the top shelf or plate until this overflows, whence it falls on to the second shelf and so on to the bottom of the still. All the while steam, supplied by the tube b, passes upward through the tubes and perforations in these shelves. As the wash gradually descends in the still it becomes rapidly weaker, partly from condensation of the steam which is passed into it and partly from loss of alcohol, either evaporated or expelled by the steam, until when it arrives at the bottom it has parted with the last trace of alcohol. This spent wash is drawn off by the trapped pipe N.

At the same time the vapor as it rises through each shelf of the

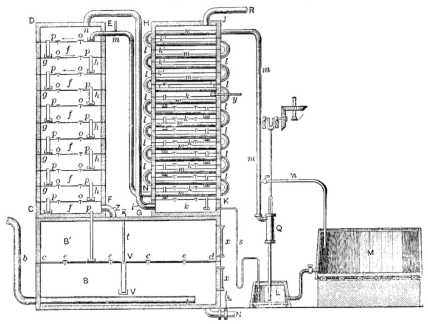

FIG. 35.—The Coffey Still.

still bubbles through the liquid on them and becomes continuously richer in alcohol, and thus contains less and less water in consequence of its condensation; it then passes from the top of the still in at the bottom of the lower compartment of the rectifier K. Here it ascends

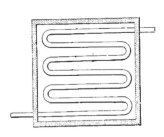

FIG. 36.—The Coffey Dephlegmator.

through perforated plates similar to those in the column of the still and bubbling through the liquid, between the windings of the descending wash-pipe, on the shelves until it is conducted through R into the finished spirit-condenser, to be finally recondensed as high-proof alcohol of about 91 per cent by weight.

The low wines run from the bottom of the rectifier K, where they collect, to L and are pumped into the top of the still with the wash, to be again distilled and thereby concentrated into high-proof alcohol. In order to still further economize heat, the water for supplying the steam-boiler is made to pass through a long coil of pipe immersed in the boiling but spent wash, by which means its temperature is raised before it enters the boiler.

This still in the larger sizes works off upward of 3000 gallons of wash per hour.

In Fig. 36 is shown the construction and design of the Coffey dephlegmator.

As pointed out earlier in this chapter it is enclosed, and the returning condensed alcoholic liquid is not thus exposed to the cooling action of the air, the wash flowing through the tubes of this dephlegmator being thus heated by the ascending alcoholic vapors.

The Ilges Automatic Continuous Distilling Apparatus.*—According to the investigations of Hayduck (Zeitschr. f. Spir.-Ind., 1890, No. 49), this apparatus furnishes pure spirit of a superior degree of strength and in the same process separates the fusel-oil. This apparatus is shown in Fig. 37, p. 90. The claims made for it are that it is simple to work, that it is economical in its use of steam and water, that the process is continuous and that by one operation pure 96 per cent spirit is made.

Referring to the cut shown in Fig. 37, the method of operating the still becomes readily apparent. The wash is supplied from the reservoir or tank to the still A by the action of the wash-regulator G. The steam-regulator F supplies the steam to the still. The discharge of the spent wash or slop is controlled by the slop-regulator C, and such slop is tested at Q. The alcoholic vapors, together with those of the fusel-oil, enter the dephlegmator D by the pipe a. The dephlegmator consists of eight or nine partitions or chambers filled with porcelain balls and cooling-tubes. The pure-spirit vapors are conveyed to the condenser E by the tube b. The low wines, together with the fusel-oil, run down through the dephlegmator chambers mentioned, becoming more and more enriched with fusel-oil until, at a strength of about 15 per cent alcohol by volume, they pass out of the dephlegmator through the tube c into the low-wine condenser M and give up their content of fusel-oil, which is drawn off.

The separated low wines are conveyed by the tube h to the fore-heater R over into the low-wine column O in order to be again distilled, and finally the spent low wines are discharged from the pipe i, k, free from alcohol and fusel-oil. The testing apparatus for the spent low-wine liquor is at P.

It is noticed that no use is made of any rectifying process (by filtration) involving charcoal batteries in connection with this still.

---

* Maercker's Handbuch der Spiritusfabrikation, 1898.

German Continuous Distilling Apparatus and Rectifying-still.—
In Figs. 38, 39, and 40 there is shown the Braunschweigische apparatus,
as follows: Fig. 38 shows a portion of the mash-column, which is equiva-

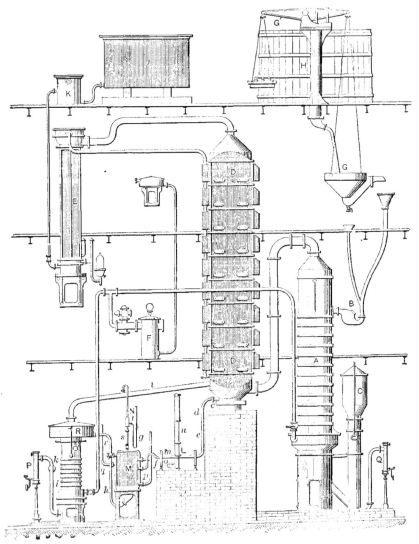

FIG. 37.—The Ilges Automatic Continuous Still.

lent to our American continuous beer-still. This German apparatus is
fitted with dephlegmator or mash fore-heater and sieve-column.

While the German apparatus shown in Figs. 39 and 40 distill continuously, the makers recommend that the separation of the fusel-oil and other impurities take place in a second rectifying apparatus for

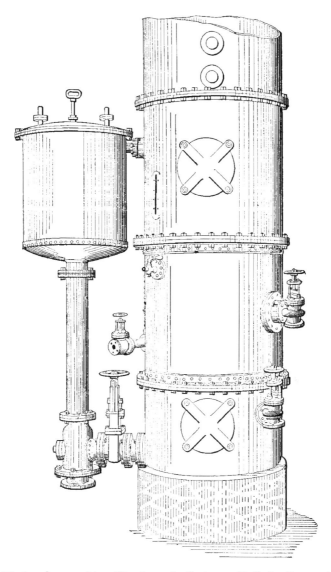

FIG. 38.—Mash-column with a Heating-tube System. Built by Braunschweigische Maschinenbau-Anstalt, Braunschweig, Germany.

periodical charging, which apparatus is shown in Fig. 40, page 93. It is claimed that in this manner great simplicity of service and security in working is obtained when contrasted with the complex automatic continuous alcohol-distilling apparatus which simultaneously separates the fusel-oil. In the United States such separate and periodic rectifying methods are also followed, as the descriptions to follow will show.

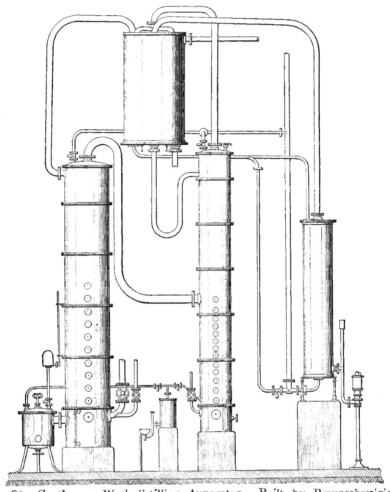

FIG. 39.—Continuous Wash-distilling Apparatus. Built by Braunschweigische Maschinenbau-Anstalt, Braunschweig, Germany.

The Periodic Wash-distilling Apparatus for Agricultural Spirit Distilleries.—In Fig. 41, page 94, is shown a periodic spirit-still quite similar in principle to the American three-chambered charging-still. This foreign still is claimed to possess considerable merit, and the advantages claimed for it are simplicity of construction, ease of working, small amounts of water and steam needed, quick extraction of the alcohol from the wash, and the high grade of the spirits produced.

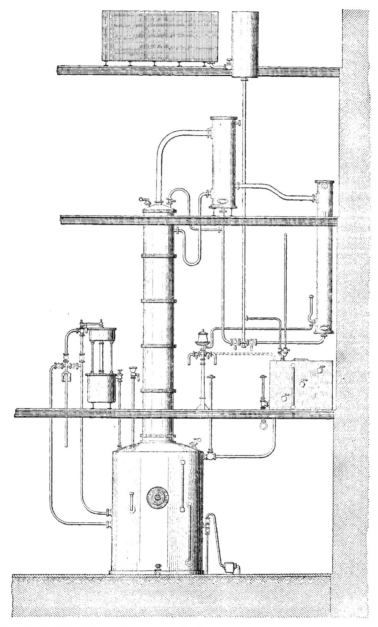

FIG. 40.—Alcohol Rectifying Apparatus. Built by Braunschweigische Maschinenbau-
Anstalt, Braunschweig, Germany.

The direct continuous rectifying apparatus shown in Fig. 42, page 95, is built by E. Barbet, Paris, France. The maker claims the following advantages for this still: The alcohol produced by it is of the best quality. It is especially adapted for the rectification of wines, but the reagent vessels, here shown, are necessary on account of the special impurities of wines. This type of rectifying-still, which has been tried in France

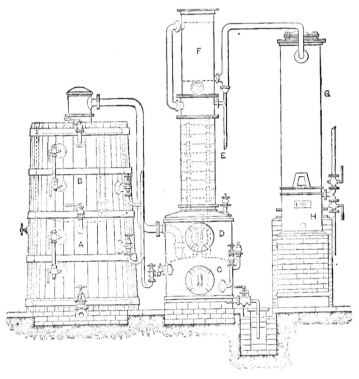

Fig. 41.—Distilling Apparatus, or Periodic Still. Built by Novák & Jahn, Prague, Austria.

and foreign countries, is claimed to be the most perfect of its kind. *EE'* is a necessary refiner, to which are adjusted the reagent vessels designed to purify the alcoholic vapors. The pasteurization acts, in the third place, as a complementary refining process, practically final. The wine takes the following course: It enters in the first place at the bottom of the wine-heater *M*, and from there it goes to the refining-plates at *E'*. Once arrived in the sub-chamber *E''* it is relieved of its most volatile impurities, gas and aldehydes. It then descends to the plates at *C*, where it is submitted to a more active boiling, which effects the entire exhaustion of the alcohol. The vapors, which are separated at the plates *C*, pass by the pipe ST to the rectificator proper, called G.   The wine-heater M and the refrigerator N, or condenser, furnish the retrogressions (returns) necessary to concentrate the alcohol to 96.5%. N shows the apparatus

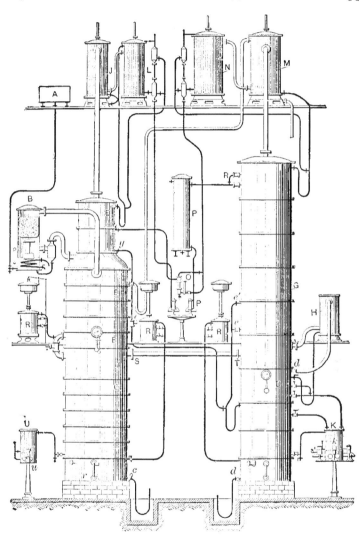

Fig. 42.—Direct Continuous Rectifying Apparatus. Built by E. Barbet, Paris, France.

which extracts the pasteurized alcohol, P the condensing apparatus, and P the testing apparatus.   As for those impurities which may remain, separated by the condenser N, they return to the testing apparatus E. At the base of the rectifying-column G the last refluxes are purified and extracted apart in the fusel-oil columns at D. H is the special condenser of the fusel-oil. These impurities pass out in a highly concentrated form and are recondensed in the refrigerator K. This apparatus produces a pure neutral spirit in one continuous operation. Barbet mentions that among the reagents used in these stills are fragments of marble and saline solutions.

In connection with Barbet's continuous rectifying apparatus, shown in Fig. 42, it will be of interest from the French standpoint to know that among the problems to be solved by rectification Sorel mentions " the difficulties caused by the principal bodies concurrently existing or present in the phlegms (or raw spirits), which are ethers formed by the reaction of the acids upon the alcohols; acids formed by the oxidation of the alcohols; glycerine, and sometimes acrolein as an accompanying product; acetaldehyde and the aldehydes which correspond to the divers homologues of ethyl alcohol; furfurol; ammonia, and a number of organic bases apparently existing in the phlegms as products formed because of the non-assimilation of the yeast, etc.

" All, or nearly all, of these substances are able to react one upon the other to produce new compounds, and are able to divide themselves and to transform themselves under the prolonged action of the water and the heat; one must therefore contend against a veritable Proteus. If these substances were anhydrous there would still be extreme difficulty experienced in separating them; the presence of water acts for some of them in the presence of the others to still further complicate the problem.

"The numerous chemical methods of treatment (for the separation of these substances) have been successively proposed and rejected; finally they have been wholly abandoned. It is, then, to the purely physical processes that the constructor of rectifying apparatus must address himself, and these methods demand a profound knowledge concerning the laws of physics of the most delicate character: the solubility of the different component parts one in the other, the vapor pressure of the different mixed liquids, specific heats, the latent heats of vaporization, density of the vapors, radiation, etc. Upon this profound knowledge and the rigorous choice of the proportions of the divers organic parts of the apparatus depend the success or failure of the apparatus itself."

The Stade Continuous Automatic Still.—An exceedingly effective type of continuous still for the extraction of alcohol direct from the wash is shown in Fig. 43, p. 98.

This is the automatic and continuous working still built by Geo. Stade, Berlin, Germany. This type as shown is called construction B, for cologne spirits and rum, separating in one operation the fusel-oil and impurities.   The strength of the refined spirit should be 96 per cent Tralles.

For making ordinary rum 90 to 92 per cent Tralles are sufficient as a rule.

The advantages claimed for this still are that no charcoal filters or rectifying apparatus are necessary for cleansing the raw spirit as distilled from the wash as has heretofore been customary in other and less modern makes of apparatus.

The product therefore suffers no deterioration, as no decomposition of the fusel-oil occurs, for by this new process of distillation the fusel-oil vapors are separately condensed and collected in an uninterrupted stream.

In sound wash experience the products of fermentation are found in a purer form in the wash than in the spirit as usually distilled from it; for although the wash contains fusel-oil perhaps averaging $\frac{4}{10}$ of 1 per cent for different washes as the quantity is different in different washes, the wash contains no volatile aldehydes or ethers.

In less modern types of stills aldehydes are formed by contact of the alcoholic vapors with the atmosphere in the cooler.

The final results of the older methods of rectifying show a further deterioration; for if the better products of the common rectifying process, i.e., the different high wines and the rectified spirits, after having been laboriously separated were combined afresh with the ordinary alcohol and the first and second runnings the mixture would be considerably more impure than the original raw spirit.

For the above reasons the makers of this type of still claim that their automatic still for refined spirit encounters none of these disadvantages inasmuch as it extracts directly from the wash the volatile substances therein contained, namely, the ethyl alcohol and raw fusel-oil, *separately* and *without* decomposition.

As to the size of this still it may be said that *its height* is 10 meters (a meter = 39.3 inches), *the floor-space* it occupies is 6 meters × 1.50 meters, and *its capacity* is 2500 gallons of wash liquor per hour.

The Wash-regulator. — The wash-regulator consists of a vat with overflow-pipe and the capacity of the wash-pump is so calculated that a continuous overflow takes place at full opening of the outlet-valve, in order to keep a constant level in this vat.

The wash outlet-pipe is connected with a graduated cock handled from the working platform below.   The outlet-opening of the vat has to be brushed out and cleaned after using so as to be sure this opening is clear of dead ferments.

The Still Water-regulator.—This works in the same way as the wash-regulator with constant level. The regulating outlet-cock is fixed on the spirit-condenser, but is handled from below, where a gradient is put up.

The overflow of this tank returns to the cool tanks as refresherator or to the suction-well. It is a most important requisite to have this water free from incrustation-forming salts, as otherwise the tubes in

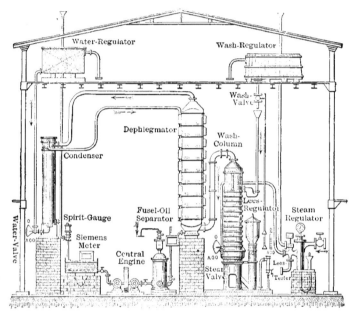

Fig. 43.—Patent Automatic and Continuous Working Still, Construction B. Built by Geo. Stade, Berlin, Germany.

the condenser and the dephlegmator get coated and cause great irregularities in the long run.

The Steam-regulator.—This is the most important of all. The change in pressure is effected by means of lead weights on the regulating piston; as a rule 0.5 atmosphere is the working pressure. However 0.3 to 0.7 atm. may be used if required. The apparatus is put up exactly level and care must be taken that all steam pumps and pipes are quite clean. A few days before starting the still, this steam-regulator must be tested and fully lubricated with gasoline and kerosene. No oil is allowed. The safety-valve of the steam-receiver is charged $\frac{1}{10}$ of an atmosphere higher than the working pressure of the regulator. Exhaust-steam from the central pumping-engine as well as exhaust from the sugar-works are led into this receiver.

All engines are to be lubricated by mineral-oil.

The direct steam enters the regulator after passing a reducing-valve at 3 to 4 atm. This secures even working of the pumping-engine and even quality of exhaust-steam for the receiver. This receiver is acting as steam accumulator for the still. The steam-receiver as well as all steam-pipes are covered with heat-insulating composition.

The condensed-water valve on the bottom of the receiver is always kept a little open.

In order to operate this still the proceeding is as follows: First see that all joints are tight, and in case of a new still the apparatus is completely filled with water for this purpose. The water is then discharged through the lees regulating-pipe and steam is turned on. The wash-regulator is now filled up. For starting, the wash-column steam-cock is put at 10%, rising to 40%. As soon as the dephlegmator becomes heated to the third or fourth body, the wash-cock is opened say 20 to 30%, and when the spirit appears in the spirit-gauge the water is put on gradually. All cocks and valves are fixed in such a manner that a maximum of wash is worked off. This maximum is reached as soon as wash appears in the wash gauge-glass. The wash-cock is then shut a little so that no wash or only very little appears in the glass. At the same time in the lees and singlings tester the small spirit hydrometers are visible.

The regulator analysis of lees and singlings will soon show at what position the small alcohol hydrometers or alcoholometers have to stand to avoid any possible loss.

Now the temperature of the singlings running from the dephlegmator is regulated by the water-cock on the condenser. If pure spirit is desired, the temperature for separation of the fusel-oil appears to be 87°–88° C., the best temperature being 87.8° C. As soon as the fusel-oil appears in the sight-glass of the separator it is drawn off either continuously or temporarily, while the singlings are returned to the wash-reservoir.

For manufacturing rum no separation of fusel-oil is looked for and the temperature may be kept from 89° to 92° C., according to the quality of the rum required. The strength of the refined spirit should be 96%; for making ordinary rum 90 per cent to 92 per cent Tralles are sufficient as a rule.

The spirit made is measured by the Siemens meter, shown at the left in Fig. 43. This still causes *no loss of alcohol*, while in filtering and rectifying fully 2½ per cent of alcohol is lost. The only by-product of this automatic still for refined spirit (when using molasses wash) is fusel-oil, which has a good market value.

All the exhaust-steam of the engines can be used in the distillation.

Only 250 kilograms (1 kilo = 2.20 lbs.) of steam are required for 1000 liters (a liter = 1 quart) of wash, which is equivalent to one ton of coal (of good quality) for 1000 imperial gallons = 1120 American gallons of molasses.

The construction of this still is such that very little expense for repairs is necessary.

The Ilges Automatic Rectifying-still,* used in Germany for producing pure 96 per cent alcohol (192° U. S. proof) continuously from the wash or from raw spirits, separating in one operation the fusel-oil and impurities, is illustrated in Fig. 44.

In this cut the details of the construction are plainly indicated by the vertical sectional drawings. This still is elaborated and still further improved over the earlier type of the similar Ilges still shown in Fig. 37, page 90.

It will be noticed that this improvement consisted principally in the addition of a second or additional rectifying-column. This still has three very important advantages or features:

1. It recovers or extracts 90 per cent of all the alcohol contained in the wash and produces it as an absolutely pure spirit of from 96 to 96.5 per cent strength by volume, or from 192 to 193 per cent U. S. proof.

2. It recovers all the fusel-oil of a strength of 80 per cent.

3. It recovers all the low wines at a strength of 97 per cent by volume or 194 per cent U. S. proof.

This still gives satisfaction no matter what the nature of the raw materials used for the mashes; whether the mashes are thick and turbid, whether the wash or raw spirits contain dregs or settlings, the product is equally good and is obtained free from all low wines, fusel-oil, or furfurol.

As an example of the ability and capacity of this still to also purify raw spirits the following example is given: A distiller owning one of these stills had been in the habit of distilling his mash; working six hours a day to do so, using a still heated directly by fire, he found that, by running night and day continuously with this still for an equal period of six months, in purifying the raw spirits from a distillery company he increased the quantity of alcohol so obtained by more than fourfold without any change in his methods.

---

* From Maercker-Delbrück's Handbuch der Spiritusfabrikation, 1903.

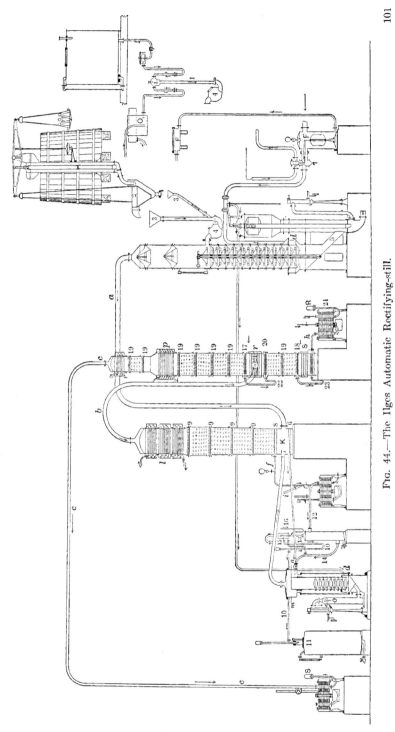

FIG. 44.—The Ilges Automatic Rectifying-still.

To return to the still shown in Fig. 44, it is seen that the wash is supplied automatically, through the pipe H, from the elevated wash reservoir or tank, to the still by the pipes 3 and 4.

In the case of distilling raw spirits, these are supplied to the still, from the elevated tank at the extreme right of the cut, mixed with warm water from the tank O, by connecting the pipe 4 to the still.

Steam is supplied to the still through the steam-regulator F at the lower right-hand side of this cut. The spent wash is discharged through the tube 5 in the slop or spent-wash regulator beside the still. This spent-wash or slop regulating apparatus is provided with a device for testing the slop by an alcohol hydrometer, to see if it is free from alcohol, before it is discharged.

The alcoholic vapors from the still are conveyed to the first rectifier K by the pipe a, entering the rectifier at its base by the tube 6. The object of this rectifier is to concentrate the alcohol to 96.5 per cent and to remove the fusel-oil.

At K there is an empty space in this first rectifier into which the vapors from the low-wine dephlegmator or cooler m enter by the tube 7, and where they are mixed with the vapors from the still. The space between K and l is completely filled with porcelain balls.

The high-proof alcohol vapors now pass from the first rectifier K by the tube b into the second rectifier at 21, through the dephlegmator r, being thus freed from practically all of the contained aldehydes, after which the condensed high-proof alcohol runs down through the porcelain balls in the chambers 19 and 18 through the tube 23, being conveyed in a zigzag manner, where the spirit is partially vaporized and deprived of the last traces of aldehydes in S, and the now absolutely pure alcohol vapors are now conveyed by the tube h to the final spirit-condenser and the pure 96.5 per cent alcohol is drawn off at R.

When the low-wine vapors mixed with the fusel-oil are separated and condensed by the dephlegmator l from the pure alcohol vapors, they run down through the chambers and are conducted by f into the low-wine condenser and thence into the fusel-oil separator by the pipe 12, and the fusel-oil is collected by the pipe 10 in the fusel-oil reservoir 11. The low wines pass on to the spent low-wine condenser, and their vapors (singlings) again pass into the first rectifier K by the tube 7 as stated. The spent low wines are tested at C before being discharged.

The tube c conveys the small amounts of the vapors of low wines (which get past the first to the second rectifying-column), containing the traces of aldehydes, to the condenser, where these bodies are recondensed and drawn off at S.

The Siemens Alcohol Meter.—In the description of the patent Stade continuous still, on pages 96–98, it was stated that such still was pro-

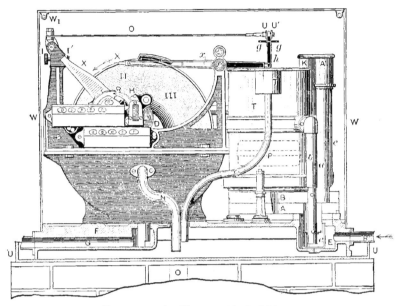

FIG. 45.—The Siemens Alcohol Meter.

vided with the Siemens alcohol meter. These meters can, of course, be used with any make of similar still of large capacities.   In Fig. 45 is

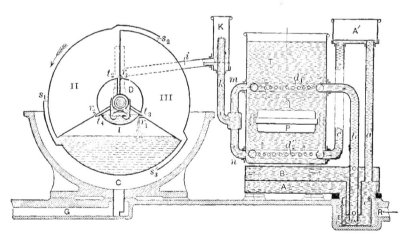

FIG. 46. —Sectional Drawing of the Siemens Alcohol Meter.

shown an illustration of this meter.   In Germany the wort is left to ferment for thirty hours, and is then conveyed to a patent still.   On issuing

from the condenser the spirit passes through a domed glass case in which
is a gauging-cup. In this cup, into which the spirit flows and from which
it overflows, there float a thermometer and a hydrometer, to indicate the
strength of the spirit passing. From this apparatus (similar in purpose
to the American separating-boxes) the spirit flows into a Siemens meter,
fitted with an indicator which records the quantity, reduced to the standard of absolute alcohol, of spirit transmitted, and from the meter the
spirit passes on to the receiver. A sectional drawing of this ingenious
metering apparatus is shown in Fig. 46.

AMERICAN ALCOHOL-DISTILLING APPARATUS.

The Continuous Beer-still.—Turning now to American apparatus,
in Fig. 47, p. 105, there is shown a patent continuous beer-still, with
tubular heater and condenser combined, and cooler for high- and low-
proof spirits. This still is made in capacities of from 300 gallons of
wash per hour to 13,000 gallons of wash per hour. It is also used for the
production of high wines, which are charged into the copper kettles as
shown in Fig. 48, page 106.

In using this continuous still for the production of high-proof
spirits the return-pipe M is used to carry back to the still the low wines,
or singlings, condensed by the cold beer passing through the tubes, which
are surrounded by the vapor from the still. For low-proof spirit the pipe
M is dispensed with, the vapor passing direct to the worm, or cooler.

Returning to Fig. 48, page 106, the *Alcohol and Cologne Spirit Apparatus*, it may be said that the kettles or stills are made, in capacities of
from 50 to 600 barrels, with a rectifying-column, goose condenser, and
final condenser, producing the highest grades of cologne spirits and
alcohol of a proof of 192 per cent or 96 per cent alcohol.

The cut shown in Fig. 49 on page 107 is the continuous "beer" still
shown in Fig. 47, with the addition of a goose condenser or tubular condenser, whichever is preferred, with return to top chamber of still, the
three or four top chambers being regular column chambers. The vapor
passes from the goose to a final condenser, then through the tail-box to
a small copper receiving-tank, from where it is drawn into the cistern, or
if below the required proof, is returned to the still by means of the steam-
syphon. By this method alcohol of 180 per cent proof, or 90 per cent
alcohol, can be produced by continuous distillation.

A Continuous-distilling and Redistilling Apparatus is shown in Fig.
50 on page 108. This cut represents an apparatus designed to fill the
needs of a distilling and redistilling process continuously. It consists of

the continuous beer-still fitted with brass boiling-caps and tubular condenser, the vapor outlet from which is discharged into the rectifying-kettle, which is supplied with a steam-boiling scroll, rectifier-column, goose, and

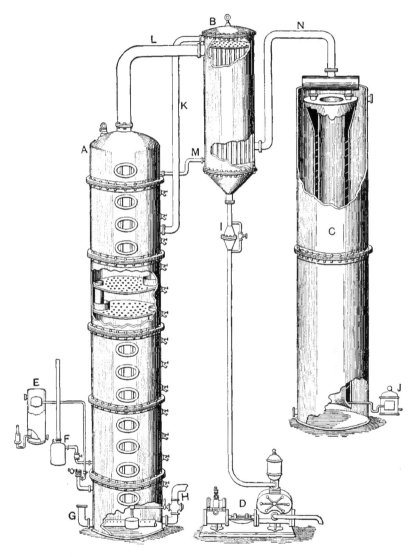

Fig. 47.—Continuous Beer-still. Built by Hoffman-Ahlers Co., Cincinnati, Ohio.

final condenser. It will produce a high-proof product, or it can be changed by means of gate-valves in the vapor-pipe into separate distilling and redistilling apparatus. The final condenser can be either a tubular or

worm condenser, whichever is preferred.   By this apparatus alcohol of
188 per cent proof or 94 per cent strength can be made.

From what has preceded in this chapter it is believed that no detailed
description of the four types of stills just described is necessary.   By
inspection of Figs. 47–50 the details of their construction are plainly evi-

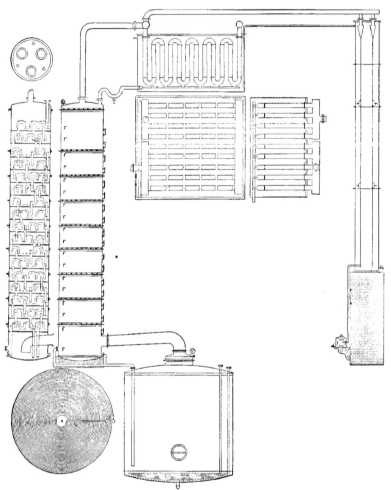

Fig. 48.—Alcohol and Cologne Spirit Apparatus.   Built by Hoffman-Ahlers Co.

dent, and we see that they are designed on the basis of the theories of
distillation which we have already discussed.

The Continuous Beer-still Apparatus.—This apparatus of the "continuous" type, shown in Fig. 51, p. 109, is simple in its construction and
operation and most effective in results, producing a clear, sweet, high

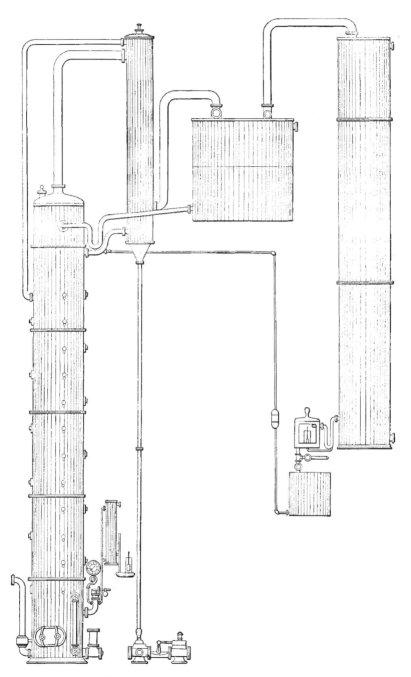

FIG. 49.—Continuous Beer-still with Goose Attached. Built by Hoffman-Ahlers Co.

wine of 150 per cent U. S. standard proof or 75 per cent alcohol by
volume.

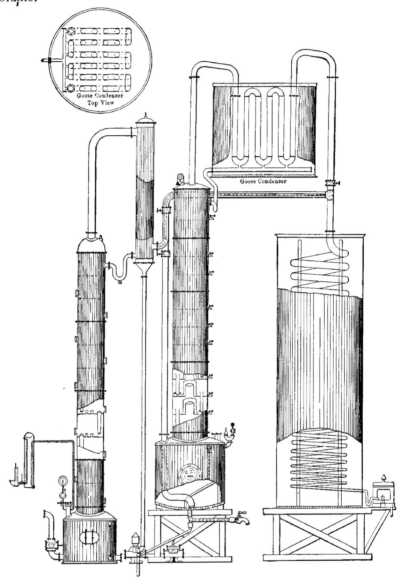

FIG. 50.—Continuous Distilling and Redistilling Apparatus.
Built by Hoffman-Ahlers Co.

In the operation of this apparatus the beer is delivered to the still
by means of the pump through the tubes of the heater. After entering
the still it flows over plate A, which is perforated with copper-capped

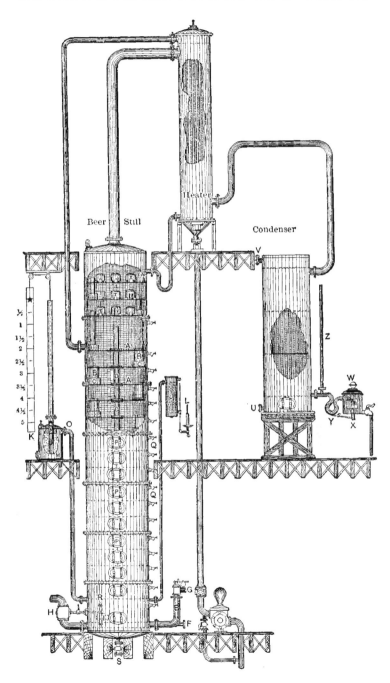

FIG. 5 1.—Continuous Beer-still, showing Heater and Condenser. Built by
The Vulcan Copper Works Co.

holes, to down pipe *B*, by which means it enters seal *C* and again over-flows plate *A* in the chamber below. This process is continued until the bottom chamber is reached, from which the spent beer is automatically discharged through the automatic waste-valve *H*. The level of the beer in the lower chamber is regulated by the float *1*, connected by means of a rod to automatic valve *H*.

Steam enters a perforated pipe in the bottom of the still through manifold *E*. Connections are made for both live steam *F* and exhaust-steam *G*. The steam entering the still at the bottom chamber passes upward through the tongued holes in the plates, thoroughly boiling out the beer flowing over the plate and carrying with it the alcoholic vapors to the next chamber above. After reaching the top chamber the vapors are conducted to the heater, passing downward and around the tubes (through which the beer is being pumped) to the final condenser.

This type of heater embodies several important improvements over the old style and performs a double function, namely, heating the beer and condensing the low-proof vapors, the latter being returned to the still. The high-proof vapors pass through to the final condenser to the tail-box *W*, where they are recondensed and conducted through pipes to the receiving-tanks.

A small portion of the vapors in the lower chamber are conducted to the slop-tester *J*. This consists of a small condenser, and by means of a hydrometer-stem any loss of alcohol is immediately detected.

The vessel *M* is also connected to the lower chamber, and the pressure carried in the still is registered on the tally-board *K* by means of the float *N* in the tube. The float rises or lowers according to the amount of pressure brought to bear on the surface of the water in the vessel *M*. The pressure will vary according to the number of chambers and ranges from one and a half to three pounds.

D are braces to support the centre of the plates in the stills of larger diameter; *P* are manheads; *R*, gauge-glasses; *S*, washout; *Q*, try-cocks; *U*, water inlet; *V*, water overflow; and *Z*, air-pipe. *Y* is a small pipe conducting the alcohol to hydrometer-cup *X*, so that the quality of the product can be readily seen during the entire operation of the appara-tus. This type of still is built as large as nine feet in diameter.

Following is a table of sizes of still and the number of gallons of wash they will handle per hour:

20″ diameter still.....................	400 gallons per hour.
24″ " "	500 " " "
30″ " "	1000 " " "
36″ " "	1500 " " "
40″ " "	2000 " " "
48″ " "	3000 " " "

Spirit Apparatus.—The apparatus shown in Fig. 52, page 112, is designed to raise to a higher proof the product of the continuous beer-still apparatus previously described, and is built in sizes to charge from 3 to 500 barrels.

The still proper on the lower floor is built either in a horizontal or upright form. The horizontal stills are smaller in diameter and greater in length, while the upright stills are greater in diameter and less in height.

These stills have steam-coils, running horizontally with the still, by means of which its contents are brought to the boiling-point. The coils have one or more steam inlets and outlets according to the size of still. The vapors pass upward from the still to the column by means of the dome and vapor-pipe on the top of the still.

The end of the vapor-pipe being submerged in the column, the vapors bubble through the liquid and ascend to the chamber above, the means of entrance being through the vapor-pipe and bonnet, necessitating the passing of the vapor through the liquid, or it returns twice in each chamber before it passes to the next chamber above.

Ample space is provided for the passage of the vapors between the top edge of the vapor-pipe and the bonnet, with a corresponding space between the lower edge of the bonnet and head or floor of the chamber. During this process the vapors grow stronger in proof as they ascend to the top of the column.

While the high-proof vapors are ascending, the returns are dropping back from chamber to chamber through the down pipes, and find their way back to the still by means of the trap in the bottom of the column as shown in the cut.

The liquid in each chamber is carried to the level of the down pipes as shown in the open section of the column. The vapor-pipes with their bonnet coverings are also plainly shown.

The vapors on emerging from the top of the column are conducted to a manifold connected to five sections of the "goose." They are here split up and pass upward and downward through the five sections until they reach the manifold or equalizing drum connecting the entire ten sections of the "goose" at the back end. The vapor after leaving the first five sections enters the next five sections and is forced upward and downward till it reaches the manifold on the front of the "goose" and passes on to the final condenser.

The "goose" is submerged in a tank of water and here the finer separations take place. Each of the bottom return bends is provided with a return pipe, and the returns, or low-proof alcohol, are conducted

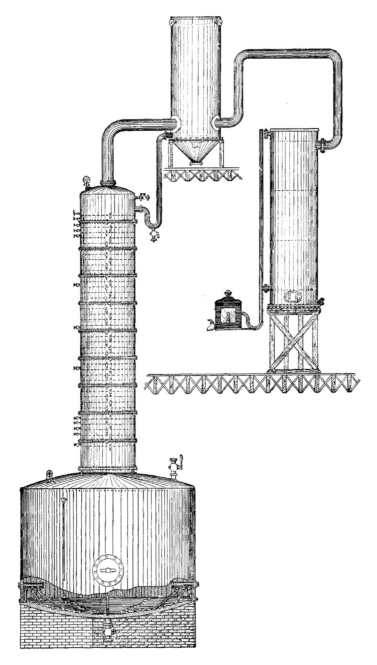

FIG. 52.—Spirit Apparatus.   Built by the Vulcan Copper Works Co.

back to the column by means of the trapped return pipe at the bottom of the "goose" tank.

The final condenser may be either of the Bevis or tubular form. The Bevis condenser consists of two cylinders, one within the other, leaving a space of about one half inch all around. A copper wire of one half inch or five eighths inch diameter is soldered spirally around, filling up the space between the two cylinders, thus forcing the vapors to travel between the spirals while being subjected to the cooling waters in which the condenser is submerged.

These condensers are built in sections and connected by means of brass bends, as shown in the open part of the cut. At the lower end of the Bevis condenser is the spirit outlet, to which is connected the tail-box, of the same pattern as described in connection with the continuous beer-still apparatus.

The return or wash-out cocks on the right of the column are for draining the chambers. The small cocks on the left of the column are test-cocks. The cock on the bottom of the trap in the return-pipe from "goose" to column is for running off the fusel-oil after the column has been in operation for some length of time. The smaller pipe entering the top of this trap and connected to the "goose" tank is used in washing out the column and charging the chambers of the column after they have been drained. The still is also provided with a gauge-glass, manhead, vacuum-valve, charge-cock, blow-out cock, and pressure-gauge.

Fig. 53 shows the "kettle" or upright still, which is provided with steam-coils, and with one or more steam inlets and outlets, according to the size of the still. The interior arrangement of the chambers in this type of column are of an entirely different construction from the one just described in Fig. 52.

This construction is plainly shown in the enlarged detail. The vapor-pipes with their bonnet coverings are rectilinear, splitting up the vapors more thoroughly and subjecting them to a more complete washing. The travel of the returns in their downward course over the heads or plates is also much longer than in the previously described column and the number of chambers more than twice as many.

The column being connected directly to the still, with the tubular separator in place of the "goose," and the tubular condenser make a compact apparatus, requiring much less space both in regard to floor-space and height as compared to the other type.

By referring to the cuts showing the detail construction of the heads or plates the upward course of the vapor and the downward course of the returns, or weaker alcoholic liquor, are plainly shown by the darts. (See Fig. 53, page 115, where the arrows indicate the flow of returns over heads and the vapor course through the chambers of the column of this still.)

The tubular separator has a diaphragm through its centre, with the sides and top riveted to the sides of the shell and upper-tube head, leaving it open on the lower end. The vapor enters the tubular condenser at the top, surrounds the tubes (through which the cooling-water is passing on its downward course), and passes through the bottom opening of the diaphragm on its upward course to the outlet and final condenser.

For the larger stills of this type, the separator furnished with this style of apparatus has several distinguishing features, making it a superior apparatus in every respect as compared with the old style of the same type. The features of this type are its simplicity, compactness, and efficiency. It produces a grade of alcohol eminently clean and satisfactory.

In Fig. 53 the arrows indicate flow of returns over heads and vapor course through chambers; the detail of column chambers is also shown.

In the field of distillery operation in the United States are to be found plants of the most tremendous size, the like of which can be seen in no other part of the world. These colossal establishments, in which from ten to fifteen thousand bushels of grain are handled daily, call for apparatus of the highest perfection in design and constructive detail to expeditiously and effectively accomplish the desired results. This applies in particular to the rectifying department of the distillery, where the success-determining factor of the entire operation is centred. The *spirit-rectifying apparatus* illustrated in Fig. 54 is in use in nearly all of the largest American distilleries. The Vulcan Copper Works Company, of Cincinnati, Ohio, are the builders.

The component parts of the apparatus as a whole are the still at the base, to which is connected the rectifying-column, from whence the vapors proceed into the goose separator and then into the final condenser. The still, which as here presented is horizontal in construction, is likewise built upright or kettle-shaped. The largest of these stills has a capacity of twenty-five thousand gallons. They are built of heavy copper-plate throughout, securely riveted and soldered. Heat is applied by means of longitudinal steam-coils firmly stayed in the bottom of the still. The foundation supports consist of brick or concrete saddle-piers spaced at requisite intervals and extending half-way up the sides in

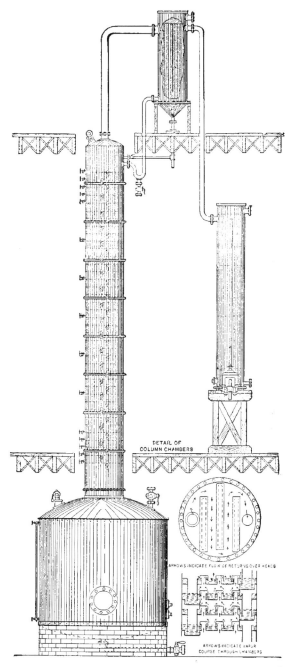

DETAIL OF
COLUMN CHAMBERS

ARROWS INDICATE FLOW OF RETURNS OVER HEADS

ARROWS INDICATE VAPOR
COURSE THROUGH CHAMBERS

FIG. 53.—The "Kettle" or Upright Still (Spirit Apparatus). Built by The Vulcan
Copper Works Co.

which the still rests. A glass gauge, manhead, charge-cock, and discharge-cock comprise the attachments. In the centre of the top is a dome in which the vapors are accumulated before passing over into the column.

A column of proportionate size to that of the still specified above is 6 feet in diameter and stands 40 feet high. It is composed of a series of individual chambers each containing an equipment of especially contrived boiling-pipes and caps so applied as to obtain a most thorough distribution and highly effective wash of the vapors as they ascend through the column chambers. Down-pipes for returning the products condensed out of the vapor also form a part of the equipment for each chamber. Out of the bottom chamber is a connection for carrying these accumulated returns back into the still. On this interior construction detail of the column is dependent the entire efficiency of the apparatus. Return-cocks are provided in all the chambers for draining the contents successively from one chamber to the next preparatory to cleansing the apparatus.

The goose separator consists of a series of copper-pipe sections, the individual pipes being connected one to the other by means of copper return-bends. There are six of these sections, each containing twenty pipes representing an aggregate of 1500 square feet of separating surface. The whole is contained in a steel water-tank 8 feet wide by 22 feet long by 8½ feet deep. The purpose of this separator is to effect a final minute and delicate separation of the vapors after leaving the column. The condensed products in this separator are returned into the upper-column chamber.

The condenser is of the internal tubular type, in which the vapors pass through the tubes and the cooling-water surrounds them. It is 60 inches in diameter and 24 feet high. The finished spirit discharges from the base of the condenser into a separating box with glass sides, through which the flow of the spirit can be observed.

The apparatus is particularly striking because of the simplicity of the operating detail and the entire absence of any intricate adjustments calling for attention from the operator. It produces an absolutely pure neutral spirit free from every contaminating impurity, 192 per cent U. S. proof, corresponding to 96 per cent by volume in strength.

A Distilling Apparatus, the invention of W. E. Lummus, Lynn, Mass., is shown in Fig. 55, page 118.

The combined effects of a baffle-plate and fractional condensation are effected by this construction. Cross-currents of the vapors are thus produced and the utmost degree of concentration of the vapor is aimed at by this device, while an extension of this one chamber shown can

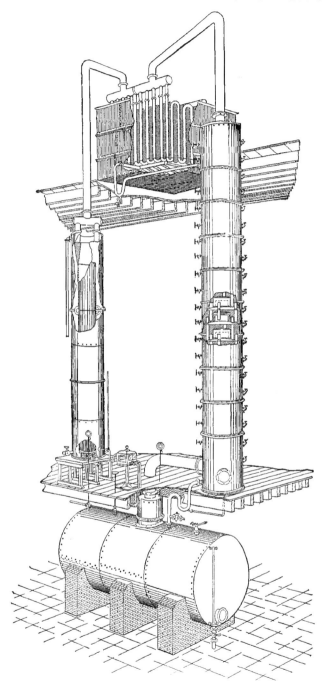

FIG. 54.—Spirit Apparatus. Built by The Vulcan Copper Works Co.,
Cincinnati, Ohio.

easily be made by bolting a number of other chambers together. The
rectangular form of the said chambers secures uniform action of the

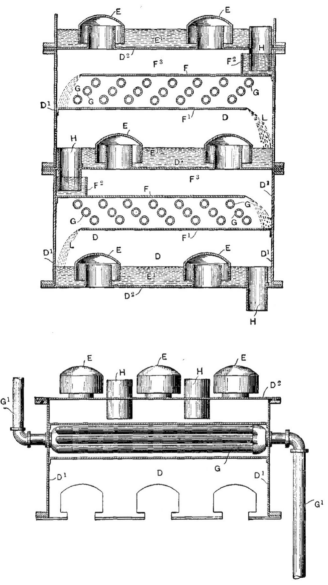

FIG. 55.—The Lummus Patent Distilling Apparatus.

liquids and vapors upon one another. The liquid descending the column
through the pipes *G* always moves in a general direction opposite to that

FIG. 56.—"Separating-boxes" for Spirit Distilleries.

of the ascending vapor, which bubbles through the pools of alcoholic liquid shown in the cut, and, as the temperature is highest in the bottom chamber, the liquid, which leaves each chamber at its hottest point, enters the next lower and warmer chamber at its coolest point and is therefore constantly encountering hotter vapor and absorbing more heat from the vapors in contact with the outside of the pipes G, which are the conductors for the condensing medium and are arranged in inclined rows, as shown, and act as deflectors to the ascending vapors.   This absorption of heat effects a fractional condensation of the least volatile vapors, which fall in a spray on the diaphragms FF' and joining the discard from the down pipes H (the returns) are swept down into the next lower chamber to be redistilled, this process continuing until the contents of the charge have all been distilled and thus separated into high-proof alcohol, which is finally condensed from the ascending vapors of pure alcohol, while the spent alcohol-free wash remains in the still, as this apparatus is intended not for continuous but periodic distillation.   Upon recharging the still the operation of distillation is again begun.

In Fig. 56., page 120, are shown two "separating-boxes."

The method of testing the strength of the spirit during the distillation by means of an alcohol hydrometer becomes readily apparent upon an inspection of Fig. 56.   The upper box shows a side pipe from which the spirit enters the hydrometer-jar inside this box on turning the cock. The lower box shows a different design for the same purpose.   The spirit as it is distilled and condensed flows through these boxes, which are locked and under the control of the U. S. inspector, to the receiving cistern.

Summary of Chapter III.

In summing up the different reasons for the very remarkable development in the intricate and delicate distilling apparatus shown and the perfection attained in these high-class types of practically perfect continuous and periodic fractionating stills no one advance in the long series was more notable than the application of steam to the purposes of distillation.

It rendered possible the extended application of the continuous-distilling method and practically revolutionized the art.

Some dilution occurs from the use of steam, but the quality of spirit produced is naturally much better.   The use of steam rendered possible the availing of the residue of the distillation, in case such was valuable, for an ingredient in the rations for feeding cattle, and in this country such residue or slop from distilling corn and grains is largely so employed. A still further marked advantage in the use of steam is the freedom from any obstructions due to accumulations of solid matter in the stills, and which is now prevented by the more active ebullition when the heat is supplied in this manner. This results in a much less cost for cleaning and repairing these intricate and expensive stills, a matter of great importance in the economics of the manufacture of alcohol.

In the choice of a still so many factors enter into the case that no arbitrary rule can be laid down. Local conditions, the nature of the mash, the cost of the water obtainable, the cost of the coal, etc., are, however, a few factors which may be mentioned.

An alcohol still is like any other piece of apparatus whatever be its nature, in that it should be chosen with the idea of its being as near perfectly adapted as possible to the conditions and the purposes in hand.

The production of alcohol and its extraction from the fermented mash liquor or wash has been explained in Chapters II and III.

After being distilled the alcohol in this country is received in cisterns or stored in tanks in accordance with the U. S. regulations for distilled spirits. From these tanks it is drawn off for the filling of packages by automatic barrel-fillers. The operation of these fillers is shown in the view given in Fig. 57 below.

FIG. 57.—Automatic Barrel-fillers.

CHAPTER IV.

ALCOHOLOMETRY.

The Determination of Alcohol by the Alcoholometer. The Determination of Alcohol by Distillation. The Alcohol Tables Adopted by the A. O. A. C. The U. S. Proof Gallon, Wine Gallon, and Taxable Gallon. The U. S. Alcohol Tables for the Control of Denatured Alcohol. The Detection and Determination of Ethyl and Methyl Alcohols in Mixtures by the Immersion Refractometer. The Determination of Methyl Alcohol in Denatured Alcohol by the Immersion Refractometer. Tests for the Detection of Acetone, Methyl Alcohol, and Ethyl Alcohol. The Denatured Alcohol Motor for Laboratory Power Purposes.

The Determination of Alcohol by the Alcoholometer.*—"The alcoholometer usually employed is known by the name of Gay-Lussac, from the chemist who first made practical use of it in the determination of alcohol. It is constructed in such a way as to read directly the volume of absolute alcohol contained in one hundred volumes of the liquid at a temperature of 15°.6. The instruments employed should be carefully calibrated and thoroughly cleaned by washing with absolute alcohol before use. The stem of the instrument must be kept free from any greasy substance, and this is secured by washing it with ether. After this last washing the analyst should be careful not to touch the stem of the instrument with his fingers. It is most convenient to make the determination exactly at 15°.6, but when made at other temperatures the reading of the instruments is corrected by tables which may be found in works especially devoted to the analysis of wines."

In this country the alcoholometer is used to some extent. A cut of the U. S. Customs hydrometer for alcohol and spirits is shown in Fig. 58.† This instrument has four scales; two scales in the stem. The one marked "Tralles" indicates the direct volume percentage of alcohol and water when floated in spirits. The second scale is the U. S.

---

* Wiley in "Principles and Practice of Agricultural Analysis," pp. 612–16. "The quantity of alcohol in a mixture may be determined by ascertaining the temperature of the vapors produced on boiling. This is the principle involved in the use of the ebullioscope. This method is not employed to any extent in this country."

† Furnished by Eimer & Amend, New York.

proof scale running from the mark P (being equal to proof or 53.71 per cent by volume of water and 50 per cent by volume of alcohol) up to 100 and down to 100, indicating in this way the number of degrees below the proof (below 50% alcohol), and above proof (indicating the degrees above 50% alcohol). The body of the hydrometer contains two sets of scales, one giving direct degrees of temperature in Fahrenheit, and the other three scales to the left and two to the right indicate the number of degrees to be added or deducted according to temperature. The same instrument is also made without the thermometer and without the temperature correction.

" In this country the official method is based upon the determination of the specific gravity by an instrument constructed in every respect like the alcoholometer, but giving the specific gravity of the liquor at 15°.6 instead of its percentage by volume in alcohol. The reading of the instrument having been determined at a temperature of 15°.6, the corresponding percentage of alcohol by volume or by weight is taken directly from the tables given further on." (A. O. A. C.)

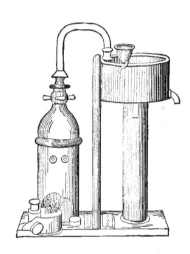

Fig 58.   Fig. 59.

Fig. 58.   The U. S. Customs Hydrometer for Alcohol and Spirits.
Fig. 59.   Metal Distilling Apparatus.

The Determination of Alcohol by Distillation.—" The metal apparatus employed in the laboratory of the Department of Agriculture for the distillation of fermented beverages in order to determine the percentages of alcohol by the method given above is shown in Fig. 59.

The apparatus consists of a retort of copper, carried on supports in such a way as to permit an alcohol or Bunsen lamp to be placed under it. It is connected with a block-tin condenser, and the distillation is received in a tall graduated cylinder, placed under the condenser, in such a way as to prevent the loss of any alcohol in the form of vapor.

"Exactly 300 cubic centimeters of the wine, or fermented beverage, are used for the distillation. Any acid which the wine contains is first saturated with calcium carbonate before placing in the retort. Exactly 100 cubic centimeters of distillate are collected and the volume of the distillate is completed to 300 cubic centimeters by the addition of recently distilled water. The cylinder containing the distillate is brought to a temperature of 15°.6, the alcoholometer inserted, and its reading taken with the usual precautions.

"*Official Method.* — The alcoholometers employed in the official methods are calibrated to agree with those used by the officers of the Bureau of Internal Revenue. They are most conveniently constructed, carrying the thermometer-scale in the same stem with that showing the specific gravity. It is highly important that the analyst assure himself of the exact calibration of the instrument before using it. Inasmuch as the volume of the distillate may not be suited in all cases to the use of a large alcoholometer, it is customary in this laboratory to determine the specific gravity by means of the hydrostatic balance. Attention is also called to the fact that in the official method directions are not given to neutralize the free acid of the fermented beverage before the distillation. Since the Internal Revenue Bureau is concerned chiefly with the determination of alcohol in distilled liquors, this omission is of little consequence. Even in ordinary fermented beverages the percentage of volatile acids (acetic, etc.) is so small as to make the error due to the failure to neutralize it of little consequence. In order, however, to avoid every possibility of error it is recommended that in all instances the free acids of the sample be neutralized before distillation. In this laboratory the distillations are conducted in a glass apparatus, shown in the accompanying figure. The manipulation is as follows:

"One hundred cubic centimeters of the liquor are placed in a flask of from 250 to 300 cubic centimeters capacity, fifty cubic centimeters of water added, the flask attached to a vertical condenser by means of a bent bulb tube, 100 cubic centimeters distilled, and the specific gravity of the distillate determined. The distillate is also weighed, or its weight calculated from the specific gravity. The corresponding percentage of alcohol, by weight, is obtained from the appended table and this figure multiplied by the weight of the distillate and the result divided by the weight of the sample gives the per cent of alcohol, by weight, contained therein. The percentage of alcohol by volume of the liquor is the same as that of the distillate and is obtained directly from the tables on pages 127–140.

"In distilled liquors about thirty grams are diluted to 150 cubic centimeters, 100 cubic centimeters distilled, and the per cent of alcohol, by weight, determined as above. The percentage of alcohol, by volume,

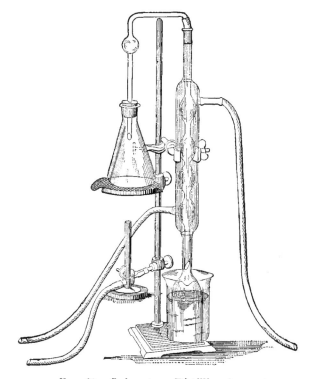

Fig. 60.—Laboratory Distilling Apparatus.

in the distillate is obtained from the tables mentioned. This figure, divided by the number expressing the volume in cubic centimeters of the liquor taken for the determination (calculated from the specific gravity) and the result multiplied by 100 gives the per cent of alcohol, by volume, in the original liquor.

"*Determining the Specific Gravity of the Distillate.*—The specific gravity of the distillate may be determined by the pyknometer, alcoholometer, hydrostatic balance, or in any accurate way. The volume of the distillate is not always large enough to be conveniently used with an alco-

holmeter, especially the large ones employed by the Bureau of Internal
Revenue. In the laboratory of the Agricultural Department it is customary to determine the density of the distillate by the hydrostatic
balance, consisting of an analytical balance and Westphal sinker. The
specific gravity is in each case determined at 15°.6, referred to water
of the same temperature, or if at a different temperature, calculated
thereto.

"*Calculating Results.*—The specific gravity of the alcoholic distillate
having been determined by any approved method, and corrected to a
temperature of 15°.6, the corresponding per cent of alcohol by volume
and by weight is found by consulting the following Tables I and II,
which are the official tables adopted by the Association of Official Agricultural Chemists, November 14–16, 1901. If the specific gravity found
fall between two numbers in these tables, the corresponding per cents
are determined by interpolation."

REFERENCE TABLES ADOPTED BY THE ASSOCIATION OF OFFICIAL AGRICULTURAL CHEMISTS.

(November 14–16, 1901.)

TABLE I.—SPECIFIC GRAVITY AND PERCENTAGE OF ALCOHOL.

(According to Squibb.)

Per Cent Alcohol by Volume.	Specific Gravity.		Per Cent Alcohol by Volume.	Specific Gravity.		Per Cent Alcohol by Volume.	Specific Gravity.	
	At $\frac{15.56°}{15.56}$ C.	At $\frac{25°}{15.56}$ C.		At $\frac{15.56°}{15.56}$ C.	At $\frac{25°}{15.56}$ C.		At $\frac{15.56°}{15.56}$ C.	At $\frac{25°}{15.56}$ C.
1	0.9985	0.9970	36	0.9578	0.9521	71	0.8875	0.8796
2	0.9970	0.9953	37	0.9565	0.9507	72	0.8850	0.8771
3	0.9956	0.9938	38	0.9550	0.9489	73	0.8825	0.8746
4	0.9942	0.9922	39	0.9535	0.9473	74	0.8799	0.8719
5	0.9930	0.9909	40	0.9519	0.9456	75	0.8769	0.8689
6	0.9914	0.9893	41	0.9503	0.9438	76	0.8745	0.8665
7	0.9898	0.9876	42	0.9490	0.9424	77	0.8721	0.8641
8	0.9890	0.9868	43	0.9470	0.9402	78	0.8696	0.8616
9	0.9878	0.9855	44	0.9452	0.9382	79	0.8664	0.8583
10	0.9869	0.9846	45	0.9434	0.9363	80	0.8639	0.8558
11	0.9855	0.9831	46	0.9416	0.9343	81	0.8611	0.8530
12	0.9841	0.9816	47	0.9396	0.9323	82	0.8581	0.8500
13	0.9828	0.9801	48	0.9381	0.9307	83	0.8557	0.8476
14	0.9821	0.9793	49	0.9362	0.9288	84	0.8526	0.8444
15	0.9815	0.9787	50	0.9343	0.9267	85	0.8496	0.8414
16	0.9802	0.9773	51	0.9323	0.9246	86	0.8466	0.8384
17	0.9789	0.9759	52	0.9303	0.9226	87	0.8434	0.8352
18	0.9778	0.9746	53	0.9283	0.9205	88	0.8408	0.8326
19	0.9766	0.9733	54	0.9262	0.9184	89	0.8373	0.8291
20	0.9760	0.9726	55	0.9242	0.9164	90	0.8340	0.8258
21	0.9753	0.9719	56	0.9221	0.9143	91	0.8305	0.8223
22	0.9741	0.9706	57	0.9200	0.9122	92	0.8272	0.8191
23	0.9728	0.9692	58	0.9178	0.9100	93	0.8237	0.8156
24	0.9716	0.9678	59	0.9160	0.9081	94	0.8199	0.8118
25	0.9709	0.9668	60	0.9135	0.9056	95	0.8164	0.8083
26	0.9698	0.9655	61	0.9113	0.9034	96	0.8125	0.8044
27	0.9691	0.9646	62	0.9090	0.9011	97	0.8084	0.8003
28	0.9678	0.9631	63	0.9069	0.8989	98	0.8041	0.7960
29	0.9665	0.9617	64	0.9047	0.8969	99	0.7995	0.7914
30	0.9652	0.9603	65	0.9025	0.8947	100	0.7946	0.7865
31	0.9643	0.9594	66	0.9001	0.8923			
32	0.9631	0.9582	67	0.8973	0.8895			
33	0.9618	0.9567	68	0.8949	0.8870			
34	0.9609	0.9556	69	0.8925	0.8846			
35	0.9593	0.9538	70	0.8900	0.8821			

REFERENCE TABLES, A. O. A. C.

TABLE II.—PERCENTAGE OF ALCOHOL.

(Recalculated from the determinations of Gilpin, Drinkwater, and Squibb.)

Specific Gravity at $\frac{60°}{60}$ F.	Alcohol. Per Cent by Volume.	Alcohol. Per Cent by Weight.	Alcohol. Grams per 100 c.c.	Specific Gravity at $\frac{60°}{60}$ F.	Alcohol. Per Cent by Volume.	Alcohol. Per Cent by Weight.	Alcohol. Grams per 100 c.c.
1.00000	0.00	0.00	0.00	0.99701	2.00	1.59	1.59
0.99992	0.05	0.04	0.04	0.99694	2.05	1.63	1.62
0.99984	0.10	0.08	0.08	0.99687	2.10	1.67	1.66
0.99976	0.15	0.12	0.12	0.99679	2.15	1.71	1.70
0.99968	0.20	0.16	0.16	0.99672	2.20	1.75	1.74
0.99961	0.25	0.20	0.20	0.99665	2.25	1.79	1.78
0.99953	0.30	0.24	0.24	0.99658	2.30	1.83	1.82
0.99945	0.35	0.28	0.28	0.99651	2.35	1.87	1.86
0.99937	0.40	0.32	0.32	0.99643	2.40	1.91	1.90
0.99930	0.45	0.36	0.36	0.99636	2.45	1.95	1.94
0.99923	0.50	0.40	0.40	0.99629	2.50	1.99	1.98
0.99915	0.55	0.44	0.44	0.99622	2.55	2.03	2.02
0.99907	0.60	0.48	0.48	0.99615	2.60	2.07	2.06
0.99900	0.65	0.52	0.52	0.99607	2.65	2.11	2.10
0.99892	0.70	0.56	0.56	0.99600	2.70	2.15	2.14
0.99884	0.75	0.60	0.60	0.99593	2.75	2.19	2.18
0.99877	0.80	0.64	0.64	0.99586	2.80	2.23	2.22
0.99869	0.85	0.67	0.67	0.99579	2.85	2.27	2.26
0.99861	0.90	0.71	0.71	0.99571	2.90	2.31	2.30
0.99854	0.95	0.75	0.75	0.99564	2.95	2.35	2.34
0.99849	1.00	0.79	0.79	0.99557	3.00	2.39	2.38
0.99842	1.05	0.83	0.83	0.99550	3.05	2.43	2.42
0.99834	1.10	0.87	0.87	0.99543	3.10	2.47	2.46
0.99827	1.15	0.91	0.91	0.99536	3.15	2.51	2.50
0.99819	1.20	0.95	0.95	0.99529	3.20	2.55	2.54
0.99812	1.25	0.99	0.99	0.99522	3.25	2.59	2.58
0.99805	1.30	1.03	1.03	0.99515	3.30	2.64	2.62
0.99797	1.35	1.07	1.07	0.99508	3.35	2.68	2.66
0.99790	1.40	1.11	1.11	0.99501	3.40	2.72	2.70
0.99782	1.45	1.15	1.15	0.99494	3.45	2.76	2.74
0.99775	1.50	1.19	1.19	0.99487	3.50	2.80	2.78
0.99768	1.55	1.23	1.23	0.99480	3.55	2.84	2.82
0.99760	1.60	1.27	1.27	0.99473	3.60	2.88	2.86
0.99753	1.65	1.31	1.31	0.99466	3.65	2.92	2.90
0.99745	1.70	1.35	1.35	0.99459	3.70	2.96	2.94
0.99738	1.75	1.39	1.39	0.99452	3.75	3.00	2.98
0.99731	1.80	1.43	1.43	0.99445	3.80	3.04	3.02
0.99723	1.85	1.47	1.47	0.99438	3.85	3.08	3.06
0.99716	1.90	1.51	1.51	0.99431	3.90	3.12	3.10
0.99708	1.95	1.55	1.55	0.99424	3.95	3.16	3.14

REFERENCE TABLES, A. O. A. C.

TABLE II.—PERCENTAGE OF ALCOHOL—(Continued).

Specific Gravity at $\frac{60°}{60}$ F.	Alcohol.			Specific Gravity at $\frac{60°}{60}$ F.	Alcohol.		
	Per Cent by Volume.	Per Cent by Weight.	Grams per 100 c.c.		Per Cent by Volume.	Per Cent by Weight.	Grams per 100 c.c.
0.99417	4.00	3.20	3.18	0.99149	6.00	4.80	4.76
0.99410	4.05	3.24	3.22	0.99143	6.05	4.84	4.80
0.99403	4.10	3.28	3.26	0.99136	6.10	4.88	4.84
0.99397	4.15	3.32	3.30	0.99130	6.15	4.92	4.88
0.99390	4.20	3.36	3.34	0.99123	6.20	4.96	4.92
0.99383	4.25	3.40	3.38	0.99117	6.25	5.00	4.96
0.99376	4.30	3.44	3.42	0.99111	6.30	5.05	5.00
0.99369	4.35	3.48	3.46	0.99104	6.35	5.09	5.04
0.99363	4.40	3.52	3.50	0.99098	6.40	5.13	5.08
0.99356	4.45	3.56	3.54	0.99091	6.45	5.17	5.12
0.99349	4.50	3.60	3.58	0.99085	6.50	5.21	5.16
0.99342	4.55	3.64	3.62	0.99079	6.55	5.25	5.20
0.99335	4.60	3.68	3.66	0.99072	6.60	5.29	5.24
0.99329	4.65	3.72	3.70	0.99066	6.65	5.33	5.28
0.99322	4.70	3.76	3.74	0.99059	6.70	5.37	5.32
0.99315	4.75	3.80	3.77	0.99053	6.75	5.41	5.36
0.99308	4.80	3.84	3.81	0.99047	6.80	5.45	5.40
0.99301	4.85	3.88	3.85	0.99040	6.85	5.49	5.44
0.99295	4.90	3.92	3.89	0.99034	6.90	5.53	5.48
0.99288	4.95	3.96	3.93	0.99027	6.95	5.57	5.52
0.99281	5.00	4.00	3.97	0.99021	7.00	5.61	5.56
0.99274	5.05	4.04	4.01	0.99015	7.05	5.65	5.60
0.99268	5.10	4.08	4.05	0.99009	7.10	5.69	5.64
0.99261	5.15	4.12	4.09	0.99002	7.15	5.73	5.68
0.99255	5.20	4.16	4.13	0.98996	7.20	5.77	5.72
0.99248	5.25	4.20	4.17	0.98990	7.25	5.81	5.76
0.99241	5.30	4.24	4.21	0.98984	7.30	5.86	5.80
0.99235	5.35	4.28	4.25	0.98978	7.35	5.90	5.84
0.99228	5.40	4.32	4.29	0.98971	7.40	5.94	5.88
0.99222	5.45	4.36	4.33	0.98965	7.45	5.98	5.92
0.99215	5.50	4.40	4.37	0.98959	7.50	6.02	5.96
0.99208	5.55	4.44	4.40	0.98953	7.55	6.06	6.00
0.99202	5.60	4.48	4.44	0.98947	7.60	6.10	6.04
0.99195	5.65	4.52	4.48	0.98940	7.65	6.14	6.07
0.99189	5.70	4.56	4.52	0.98934	7.70	6.18	6.11
0.99182	5.75	4.60	4.56	0.98928	7.75	6.22	6.15
0.99175	5.80	4.64	4.60	0.98922	7.80	6.26	6.19
0.99169	5.85	4.68	4.64	0.98916	7.85	6.30	6.23
0.99162	5.90	4.72	4.68	0.98909	7.90	6.34	6.27
0.99156	5.95	4.76	4.72	0.98903	7.95	6.38	6.31

REFERENCE TABLES, A. O. A. C.

TABLE II.—PERCENTAGE OF ALCOHOL—(*Continued*).

Specific Gravity at $\frac{60°}{60}$ F.	Alcohol.			Specific Gravity at $\frac{60°}{60}$ F.	Alcohol.		
	Per Cent by Volume.	Per Cent by Weight.	Grams per 100 c.c.		Per Cent by Volume.	Per Cent by Weight.	Grams per 100 c.c.
0.98897	8.00	6.42	6.35	0.98660	10.00	8.04	7.93
0.98891	8.05	6.46	6.39	0.98654	10.05	8.08	7.97
0.98885	8.10	6.50	6.43	0.98649	10.10	8.12	8.01
0.98879	8.15	6.54	6.47	0.98643	10.15	8.16	8.05
0.98873	8.20	6.58	6.51	0.98637	10.20	8.20	8.09
0.98867	8.25	6.62	6.55	0.98632	10.25	8.24	8.13
0.98861	8.30	6.67	6.59	0.98626	10.30	8.29	8.17
0.98855	8.35	6.71	6.63	0.98620	10.35	8.33	8.21
0.98849	8.40	6.75	6.67	0.98614	10.40	8.37	8.25
0.98843	8.45	6.79	6.71	0.98609	10.45	8.41	8.29
0.98837	8.50	6.83	6.75	0.98603	10.50	8.45	8.33
0.98831	8.55	6.87	6.79	0.98597	10.55	8.49	8.37
0.98825	8.60	6.91	6.83	0.98592	10.60	8.53	8.41
0.98819	8.65	6.95	6.87	0.98586	10.65	8.57	8.45
0.98813	8.70	6.99	6.91	0.98580	10.70	8.61	8.49
0.98807	8.75	7.03	6.95	0.98575	10.75	8.65	8.53
0.98801	8.80	7.07	6.99	0.98569	10.80	8.70	8.57
0.98795	8.85	7.11	7.03	0.98563	10.85	8.74	8.61
0.98789	8.90	7.15	7.07	0.98557	10.90	8.78	8.65
0.98783	8.95	7.19	7.11	0.98552	10.95	8.82	8.69
0.98777	9.00	7.23	7.14	0.98546	11.00	8.86	8.73
0.98771	9.05	7.27	7.18	0.98540	11.05	8.90	8.77
0.98765	9.10	7.31	7.22	0.98535	11.10	8.94	8.81
0.98759	9.15	7.35	7.26	0.98529	11.15	8.98	8.85
0.98754	9.20	7.39	7.30	0.98524	11.20	9.02	8.89
0.98748	9.25	7.43	7.34	0.98518	11.25	9.07	8.93
0.98742	9.30	7.48	7.38	0.98513	11.30	9.11	8.97
0.98736	9.35	7.52	7.42	0.98507	11.35	9.15	9.01
0.98730	9.40	7.56	7.46	0.98502	11.40	9.19	9.05
0.98724	9.45	7.60	7.50	0.98496	11.45	9.23	9.09
0.98719	9.50	7.64	7.54	0.98491	11.50	9.27	9.13
0.98713	9.55	7.68	7.58	0.98485	11.55	9.31	9.17
0.98707	9.60	7.72	7.62	0.98479	11.60	9.35	9.21
0.98701	9.65	7.76	7.66	0.98474	11.65	9.39	9.25
0.98695	9.70	7.80	7.70	0.98468	11.70	9.43	9.29
0.98689	9.75	7.84	7.74	0.98463	11.75	9.47	9.32
0.98683	9.80	7.88	7.78	0.98457	11.80	9.51	9.36
0.98678	9.85	7.92	7.82	0.99452	11.85	9.55	9.40
0.98672	9.90	7.96	7.85	0.98446	11.90	9.59	9.44
0.98666	9.95	8.00	7.89	0.98441	11.95	9.63	9.48

REFERENCE TABLES, A. O. A. C.

TABLE II.—PERCENATGE OF ALCOHOL—(Continued).

Specific Gravity at $\frac{60°}{60}$ F.	Alcohol.			Specific Gravity at $\frac{60°}{60}$ F.	Alcohol.		
	Per Cent by Volume.	Per Cent by Weight.	Grams per 100 c.c.		Per Cent by Volume.	Per Cent by Weight.	Grams per 100 c.c.
0.98435	12.00	9.67	9.52	0.98219	14.00	11.31	11.11
0.98430	12.05	9.71	9.56	0.98214	14.05	11.35	11.15
0.98424	12.10	9.75	9.60	0.98209	14.10	11.39	11.19
0.98419	12.15	9.79	9.64	0.98203	14.15	11.43	11.23
0.98413	12.20	9.83	9.68	0.98198	14.20	11.47	11.27
0.98408	12.25	9.87	9.72	0.98193	14.25	11.52	11.31
0.98402	12.30	9.92	9.76	0.98188	14.30	11.56	11.35
0.98397	12.35	9.96	9.80	0.98182	14.35	11.60	11.39
0.98391	12.40	10.00	9.84	0.98177	14.40	11.64	11.43
0.98386	12.45	10.04	9.88	0.98172	14.45	11.68	11.47
0.98381	12.50	10.08	9.92	0.98167	14.50	11.72	11.51
0.98375	12.55	10.12	9.96	0.98161	14.55	11.76	11.55
0.98370	12.60	10.16	10.00	0.98156	14.60	11.80	11.59
0.98364	12.65	10.20	10.03	0.98151	14.65	11.84	11.63
0.98359	12.70	10.24	10.07	0.98146	14.70	11.88	11.67
0.98353	12.75	10.28	10.11	0.98140	14.75	11.93	11.71
0.98348	12.80	10.33	10.15	0.98135	14.80	11.97	11.75
0.98342	12.85	10.37	10.19	0.98130	14.85	12.01	11.79
0.98337	12.90	10.41	10.23	0.98125	14.90	12.05	11.82
0.98331	12.95	10.45	10.27	0.98119	14.95	12.09	11.86
0.98326	13.00	10.49	10.31	0.98114	15.00	12.13	11.90
0.98321	13.05	10.53	10.35	0.98108	15.05	12.17	11.94
0.98315	13.10	10.57	10.39	0.98104	15.10	12.21	11.98
0.98310	13.15	10.61	10.43	0.98099	15.15	12.25	12.02
0.98305	13.20	10.65	10.47	0.98093	15.20	12.29	12.06
0.98299	13.25	10.69	10.51	0.98088	15.25	12.33	12.10
0.98294	13.30	10.74	10.55	0.98083	15.30	12.38	12.14
0.98289	13.35	10.78	10.59	0.98078	15.35	12.42	12.18
0.98283	13.40	10.82	10.63	0.98073	15.40	12.46	12.22
0.98278	13.45	10.86	10.67	0.98068	15.45	12.50	12.26
0.98273	13.50	10.90	10.71	0.98063	15.50	12.54	12.30
0.98267	13.55	10.94	10.75	0.98057	15.55	12.58	12.34
0.98262	13.60	10.98	10.79	0.98052	15.60	12.62	12.37
0.98256	13.65	11.02	10.83	0.98047	15.65	12.66	12.41
0.98251	13.70	11.06	10.87	0.98042	15.70	12.70	12.45
0.98246	13.75	11.11	10.91	0.98037	15.75	12.75	12.49
0.98240	13.80	11.15	10.95	0.98032	15.80	12.79	12.53
0.98235	13.85	11.19	10.99	0.98026	15.85	12.83	12.57
0.98230	13.90	11.23	11.03	0.98021	15.90	12.87	12.61
0.98224	13.95	11.27	11.07	0.98016	15.95	12.91	12.65

REFERENCE TABLES, A. O. A. C.

TABLE II.—PERCENTAGE OF ALCOHOL—(Continued).

Specific Gravity at $\frac{60°}{60}$ F.	Alcohol.			Specific Gravity at $\frac{60°}{60}$ F.	Alcohol.		
	Per Cent by Volume.	Per Cent by Weight.	Grams per 100 c.c.		Per Cent by Volume.	Per Cent by Weight.	Grams per 100 c.c.
0.98011	16.00	12.95	12.69	0.97808	18.00	14.60	14.28
0.98005	16.05	12.9J	12.73	0.97803	18.05	14.64	14.32
0.98001	16.10	13.03	12.77	0.97798	18.10	14.68	14.36
0.97996	16.15	13.08	12.81	0.97793	18.15	14.73	14.40
0.97991	16.20	13.12	12.85	0.97788	18.20	14.77	14.44
0.97986	16.25	13.16	12.89	0.97783	18.25	14.81	14.48
0.97980	16.30	13.20	12.93	0.97778	18.30	14.85	14.52
0.97975	16.35	13.24	12.97	0.97773	18.35	14.89	14.56
0.97970	16.40	13.29	13.01	0.97768	18.40	14.94	14.60
0.97965	16.45	13.33	13.05	0.97763	18.45	14.98	14.64
0.97960	16.50	13.37	13.09	0.97758	18.50	15.02	14.68
0.97955	16.55	13.41	13.13	0.97753	18.55	15.06	14.72
0.97950	16.60	13.45	13.17	0.97748	18.60	15.10	14.76
0.97945	16.65	13.49	13.21	0.97743	18.65	15.14	14.80
0.97940	16.70	13.53	13.25	0.97738	18.70	15.18	14.84
0.97935	16.75	13.57	13.29	0.97733	18.75	15.22	14.88
0.97929	16.80	13.62	13.33	0.97728	18.80	15.27	14.92
0.97924	16.85	13.66	13.37	0.97723	18.85	15.31	14.96
0.97919	16.90	13.70	13.41	0.97718	18.90	15.38	15.00
0.97914	16.95	13.74	13.45	0.97713	18.95	15.39	15.04
0.97909	17.00	13.78	13.49	0.97708	19.00	15.43	15.08
0.97904	17.05	13.82	13.53	0.97703	19.05	15.47	15.11
0.97899	17.10	13.86	13.57	0.97698	19.10	15.51	15.15
0.97894	17.15	13.90	13.61	0.97693	19.15	15.55	15.19
0.97889	17.20	13.94	13.65	0.97688	19.20	15.59	15.23
0.97884	17.25	13.98	13.69	0.97683	19.25	15.63	15.27
0.97879	17.30	14.03	13.73	0.97678	19.30	15.68	15.31
0.97874	17.35	14.07	13.77	0.97673	19.35	15.72	15.35
0.97869	17.40	14.11	13.81	0.97668	19.40	15.76	15.39
0.97864	17.45	14.15	13.85	0.97663	19.45	15.80	15.43
0.97859	17.50	14.19	13.89	0.97658	19.50	15.84	15.47
0.97853	17.55	14.23	13.92	0.97653	19.55	15.88	15.51
0.97848	17.60	14.27	13.96	0.97648	19.60	15.93	15.55
0.97843	17.65	14.31	14.00	0.97643	19.65	15.97	15.59
0.97838	17.70	14.35	14.04	0.97638	19.70	16.01	15.63
0.97833	17.75	14.40	14.08	0.97633	19.75	16.05	15.67
0.97828	17.80	14.44	14.12	0.97628	19.80	16.09	15.71
0.97823	17.85	14.48	14.16	0.97623	19.85	16.14	15.75
0.97818	17.90	14.52	14.20	0.97618	19.90	16.18	15.79
0.97813	17.95	14.56	14.24	0.97613	19.95	16.22	15.83

REFERENCE TABLES, A. O. A. C.

TABLE II.—PERCENTAGE OF ALCOHOL—(Continued).

Specific Gravity at $\frac{60°}{60}$ F.	Alcohol.			Specific Gravity at $\frac{60°}{60}$ F.	Alcohol.		
	Per Cent by Volume.	Per Cent by Weight.	Grams per 100 c.c.		Per Cent by Volume.	Per Cent by Weight.	Grams per 100 c.c.
0.97608	20.00	16.26	15.87	0.97406	22.00	17.92	17.46
0.97603	20.05	16.30	15.91	0.97401	22.05	17.96	17.50
0.97598	20.10	16.34	15.95	0.97396	22.10	18.00	17.54
0.97593	20.15	16.38	15.99	0.97391	22.15	18.05	17.58
0.97588	20.20	16.42	16.03	0.97386	22.20	18.09	17.62
0.97583	20.25	16.46	16.06	0.97381	22.25	18.13	17.66
0.97578	20.30	16.51	16.10	0.97375	22.30	18.17	17.70
0.97573	20.35	16.58	16.14	0.97370	22.35	18.21	17.74
0.97568	20.40	16.59	16.18	0.97365	22.40	18.26	17.78
0.97563	20.45	16.63	16.22	0.97360	22.45	18.30	17.82
0.97558	20.50	16.67	16.26	0.97355	22.50	18.34	17.86
0.97552	20.55	16.71	16.30	0.97350	22.55	18.38	17.90
0.97547	20.60	16.75	16.34	0.97345	22.60	18.42	17.94
0.97542	20.65	16.80	16.38	0.97340	22.65	18.47	17.98
0.97537	20.70	16.84	16.42	0.97335	22.70	18.51	18.02
0.97532	20.75	16.88	16.46	0.97330	22.75	18.55	18.06
0.97527	20.80	16.92	16.50	0.97324	22.80	18.59	18.10
0.97522	20.85	16.96	16.54	0.97319	22.85	18.63	18.14
0.97517	20.90	17.01	16.58	0.97314	22.90	18.68	18.18
0.97512	20.95	17.05	16.62	0.97309	22.95	18.72	18.22
0.97507	21.00	17.09	16.66	0.97304	23.00	18.76	18.26
0.97502	21.05	17.13	16.70	0.97299	23.05	18.80	18.29
0.97497	21.10	17.17	16.74	0.97294	23.10	18.84	18.33
0.97492	21.15	17.22	16.78	0.97289	23.15	18.88	18.37
0.97487	21.20	17.26	16.82	0.97283	23.20	18.92	18.41
0.97482	21.25	17.30	16.86	0.97278	23.25	18.96	18.45
0.97477	21.30	17.34	16.90	0.97273	23.30	19.01	18.49
0.97472	21.35	17.38	16.94	0.97268	23.35	19.05	18.53
0.97467	21.40	17.43	16.98	0.97263	23.40	19.09	18.57
0.97462	21.45	17.47	17.02	0.97258	23.45	19.13	18.61
0.97457	21.50	17.51	17.06	0.97253	23.50	19.17	18.65
0.97451	21.55	17.55	17.10	0.97247	23.55	19.21	18.69
0.97446	21.60	17.59	17.14	0.97242	23.60	19.25	18.73
0.97441	21.65	17.63	17.18	0.97237	23.65	19.30	18.77
0.97436	21.70	17.67	17.22	0.97232	23.70	19.34	18.81
0.97431	21.75	17.71	17.26	0.97227	23.75	19.38	18.84
0.97426	21.80	17.76	17.30	0.97222	23.80	19.42	18.88
0.97421	21.85	17.80	17.34	0.97216	23.85	19.46	18.92
0.97416	21.90	17.84	17.38	0.97211	23.90	19.51	18.96
0.97411	21.95	17.88	17.42	0.97206	23.95	19.55	19.00

REFERENCE TABLES, A. O. A. C.

TABLE II.—PERCENTAGE OF ALCOHOL—(Continued).

Specific Gravity at $\frac{60°}{60}$ F.	Alcohol.			Specific Gravity at $\frac{60°}{60}$ F.	Alcohol.		
	Per Cent by Volume.	Per Cent by Weight.	Grams per 100 c.c.		Per Cent by Volume.	Per Cent by Weight.	Grams per 100 c.c.
0.97201	24.00	19.59	19.04	0.96991	26.00	21.27	20.63
0.97196	24.05	19.63	19.08	0.96986	26.05	21.31	20.67
0.97191	24.10	19.67	19.12	0.96980	26.10	21.35	20.71
0.97185	24.15	19.72	19.16	0.96975	26.15	21.40	20.75
0.97180	24.20	19.76	19.20	0.96969	26.20	21.44	20.79
0.97175	24.25	19.80	19.24	0.96964	26.25	21.48	20.83
0.97170	24.30	19.84	19.28	0.96959	26.30	21.52	20.87
0.97165	24.35	19.88	19.32	0.96953	26.35	21.56	20.91
0.97159	24.40	19.93	19.36	0.96949	26.40	21.61	20.95
0.97154	24.45	19.97	19.40	0.96942	26.45	21.65	20.99
0.97149	24.50	20.01	19.44	0.96937	26.50	21.69	21.03
0.97144	24.55	20.05	19.48	0.96932	26.55	21.73	21.07
0.97139	24.60	20.09	19.52	0.96926	26.60	21.77	21.11
0.97133	24.65	20.14	19.56	0.96921	26.65	21.82	21.15
0.97128	24.70	20.18	19.60	0.96915	26.70	21.86	21.19
0.97123	24.75	20.22	19.64	0.96910	26.75	21.90	21.23
0.97118	24.80	20.26	19.68	0.96905	26.80	21.94	21.27
0.97113	24.85	20.30	19.72	0.96899	26.85	21.98	21.31
0.97107	24.90	20.35	19.76	0.96894	26.90	22.03	21.35
0.97102	24.95	20.39	19.80	0.96888	26.95	22.07	21.39
0.97097	25.00	20.43	19.84	0.96883	27.00	22.11	21.43
0.97092	25.05	20.47	19.88	0.96877	27.05	22.15	21.47
0.97086	25.10	20.51	19.92	0.96872	27.10	22.20	21.51
0.97081	25.15	20.56	19.96	0.96866	27.15	22.24	21.55
0.97076	25.20	20.60	20.00	0.96861	27.20	22.28	21.59
0.97071	25.25	20.64	20.04	0.96855	27.25	22.33	21.63
0.97065	25.30	20.68	20.08	0.96850	27.30	22.37	21.67
0.97060	25.35	20.72	20.12	0.96844	27.35	22.41	21.71
0.97055	25.40	20.77	20.16	0.96839	27.40	22.45	21.75
0.97049	25.45	20.81	20.20	0.96833	27.45	22.50	21.79
0.97044	25.50	20.85	20.24	0.96828	27.50	22.54	21.83
0.97039	25.55	20.89	20.28	0.96822	27.55	22.58	21.86
0.97033	25.60	20.93	20.32	0.96816	27.60	22.62	21.90
0.97028	25.65	20.98	20.36	0.96811	27.65	22.67	21.94
0.97023	25.70	21.02	20.40	0.96805	27.70	22.71	21.98
0.97018	25.75	21.06	20.44	0.96800	27.75	22.75	22.02
0.97012	25.80	21.10	20.47	0.96794	27.80	22.79	22.06
0.97007	25.85	21.14	20.51	0.96789	27.85	22.83	22.10
0.97001	25.90	21.19	20.55	0.96783	27.90	22.88	22.14
0.96996	25.95	21.23	20.59	0.96778	27.95	22.92	22.18

REFERENCE TABLES, A. O. A. C.

TABLE II.—PERCENTAGE OF ALCOHOL—(Continued).

Specific Gravity at $\frac{60°}{60}$ F.	Alcohol			Specific Gravity at $\frac{60°}{60}$ F.	Alcohol		
	Per Cent by Volume.	Per Cent by Weight.	Grams per 100 c.c.		Per Cent by Volume.	Per Cent by Weight.	Grams per 100 c.c.
0.96772	28.00	22.96	22.22	0.96541	30.00	24.66	23.81
0.96766	28.05	23.00	22.26	0.96535	30.05	24.70	23.85
0.96761	28.10	23.04	22.30	0.96529	30.10	24.74	23.89
0.96755	28.15	23.09	22.34	0.96523	30.15	24.79	23.93
0.96749	28.20	23.13	22.38	0.96517	30.20	24.83	23.97
0.96744	28.25	23.17	22.42	0.96511	30.25	24.87	24.01
0.96738	28.30	23.21	22.45	0.96505	30.30	24.91	24.04
0.96732	28.35	23.25	22.49	0.96499	30.35	24.95	24.08
0.96726	28.40	23.30	22.53	0.96493	30.40	25.00	24.12
0.96721	28.45	23.34	22.57	0.96487	30.45	25.04	24.16
0.96715	28.50	23.38	22.61	0.96481	30.50	25.08	24.20
0.96709	28.55	23.42	22.65	0.96475	30.55	25.12	24.24
0.96704	28.60	23.47	22.69	0.96469	30.60	25.17	24.28
0.96698	28.65	23.51	22.73	0.96463	30.65	25.21	24.32
0.96692	28.70	23.55	22.77	0.96457	30.70	25.25	24.36
0.96687	28.75	23.60	22.81	0.96451	30.75	25.30	24.40
0.96681	28.80	23.64	22.85	0.96445	30.80	25.34	24.44
0.96675	28.85	23.68	22.89	0.96439	30.85	25.38	24.48
0.96669	28.90	23.72	22.93	0.96433	30.90	25.42	24.52
0.96664	28.95	23.77	22.97	0.96427	30.95	25.47	24.56
0.96658	29.00	23.81	23.01	0.96421	31.00	25.51	24.60
0.96652	29.05	23.85	23.05	0.96415	31.05	25.55	24.64
0.96646	29.10	23.89	23.09	0.96409	31.10	25.60	24.68
0.96640	29.15	23.94	23.13	0.96403	31.15	25.64	24.72
0.96635	29.20	23.98	23.17	0.96396	31.20	25.68	24.76
0.96629	29.25	24.02	23.21	0.96390	31.25	25.73	24.80
0.96623	29.30	24.06	23.25	0.96384	31.30	25.77	24.84
0.96617	29.35	24.10	23.29	0.96378	31.35	25.81	24.88
0.96611	29.40	24.15	23.33	0.96372	31.40	25.85	24.92
0.96605	29.45	24.19	23.37	0.96366	31.45	25.90	24.96
0.96600	29.50	24.23	23.41	0.96360	31.50	25.94	25.00
0.96594	29.55	24.27	23.45	0.96353	31.55	25.98	25.04
0.96587	29.60	24.32	23.49	0.96347	31.60	26.03	25.08
0.96582	29.65	24.36	23.53	0.96341	31.65	26.07	25.12
0.96576	29.70	24.40	23.57	0.96335	31.70	26.11	25.16
0.96570	29.75	24.45	23.61	0.96329	31.75	26.16	25.20
0.96564	29.80	24.49	23.65	0.96323	31.80	26.20	25.24
0.96559	29.85	24.53	23.69	0.96316	31.85	26.24	25.28
0.96553	29.90	24.57	23.73	0.96310	31.90	26.28	25.32
0.96547	29.95	24.62	23.77	0.96304	31.95	26.33	25.36

REFERENCE TABLES, A. O. A. C.

TABLE II.—PERCENTAGE OF ALCOHOL—(*Continued*).

Specific Gravity at $\frac{60°}{60}$ F.	Alcohol.			Specific Gravity at $\frac{60°}{60}$ F.	Alcohol.		
	Per Cent by Volume.	Per Cent by Weight.	Grams per 100 c.c.		Per Cent by Volume.	Per Cent by Weight.	Grams per 100 c.c.
0.96298	32.00	26.37	25.40	0.96043	34.00	28.09	26.98
0.96292	32.05	26.41	25.44	0.96036	34.05	28.13	27.02
0.96285	32.10	26.46	25.48	0.96030	34.10	28.18	27.06
0.96279	32.15	26.50	25.52	0.96023	34.15	28.22	27.10
0.96273	32.20	26.54	25.56	0.96016	34.20	28.26	27.14
0.96267	32.25	26.59	25.60	9.96010	34.25	28.31	27.18
0.96260	32.30	26.63	25.64	0.96003	34.30	28.35	27.22
0.96254	32.35	26.67	25.68	0.95996	34.35	28.39	27.26
0.96248	32.40	26.71	25.71	0.95990	34.40	28.43	27.30
0.96241	32.45	26.76	25.75	0.95983	34.45	28.48	27.34
0.96235	32.50	26.80	25.79	0.95977	34.50	28.52	27.38
0.96229	32.55	26.84	25.83	0.95970	34.55	28.56	27.42
0.96222	32.60	26.89	25.87	0.95963	34.60	28.61	27.46
0.96216	32.65	26.93	25.91	0.95957	34.65	28.65	27.50
0.96210	32.70	26.97	25.95	0.95950	34.70	28.70	27.54
0.96204	32.75	27.02	25.99	0.95943	34.75	28.74	27.58
0.96197	32.80	27.06	26.03	0.95937	34.80	28.78	27.62
0.96191	32.85	27.10	26.07	0.95930	34.85	28.83	27.66
0.96185	32.90	27.14	26.11	0.95923	34.90	28.87	27.70
0.96178	32.95	27.19	26.15	0.95917	34.95	28.92	27.74
0.96172	33.00	27.23	26.19	0.95910	35.00	28.96	27.78
0.96166	33.05	27.27	26.23	0.95903	35.05	29.00	27.82
0.96159	33.10	27.32	26.27	0.95896	35.10	29.05	27.86
0.96153	33.15	27.36	26.31	0.95889	35.15	29.09	27.90
0.96146	33.20	27.40	26.35	0.95883	35.20	29.13	27.94
0.96140	33.25	27.45	26.39	0.95876	35.25	29.18	27.98
0.96133	33.30	27.49	26.43	0.95869	35.30	29.22	28.05
0.96127	33.35	27.53	26.47	0.95862	35.35	29.26	28.05
0.96120	33.40	27.57	26.51	0.95855	35.40	29.30	28.09
0.96114	33.45	27.62	26.55	0.95848	35.45	29.35	28.13
0.96108	33.50	27.66	26.59	0.95842	35.50	29.38	28.17
0.96101	33.55	27.70	26.63	0.95835	35.55	29.43	28.21
0.96095	33.60	27.75	26.67	0.95828	35.60	29.48	28.25
0.96088	33.65	27.79	26.71	0.95821	35.65	29.52	28.29
0.96082	33.70	27.83	26.75	0.95814	35.70	29.57	28.33
0.96075	33.75	27.88	26.79	0.95807	35.75	29.61	28.37
0.96069	33.80	27.92	26.82	0.95800	35.80	29.65	28.41
0.96062	33.85	27.96	26.86	0.95794	35.85	29.70	28.45
0.96056	33.90	28.00	26.90	0.95787	35.90	29.74	28.49
0.96049	33.95	28.05	26.94	0.95780	35.95	29.79	28.53

REFERENCE TABLES, A. O. A. C.

TABLE II.—PERCENTAGE OF ALCOHOL—(*Continued*).

Specific Gravity at $\frac{60°}{60}$ F.	Alcohol.			Specific Gravity at $\frac{60°}{60}$ F.	Alcohol.		
	Per Cent by Volume.	Per Cent by Weight.	Grams per 100 c.c.		Per Cent by Volume.	Per Cent by Weight.	Grams per 100 c.c.
0.95773	36.00	29.83	28.57	0.95487	38.00	31.58	30.16
0.95766	36.05	29.87	28.61	0.95480	38.05	31.63	30.20
0.95759	36.10	29.92	28.65	0.95472	38.10	31.67	30.24
0.95752	36.15	29.96	28.69	0.95465	38.15	31.72	30.28
0.95745	36.20	30.00	28.73	0.95457	38.20	31.76	30.32
0.95738	36.25	30.05	28.77	0.95450	38.25	31.81	30.36
0.95731	36.30	30.09	28.81	0.95442	38.30	31.85	30.40
0.95724	36.35	30.13	28.84	0.95435	38.35	31.90	30.44
0.95717	36.40	30.17	28.88	0.95427	38.40	31.94	30.48
0.95710	36.45	30.22	28.92	0.95420	38.45	31.99	30.52
0.95703	36.50	30.26	28.96	0.95413	38.50	32.03	30.56
0.95695	36.55	30.30	29.00	0.95405	38.55	32.07	30.60
0.95688	36.60	30.35	29.04	0.95398	38.60	32.12	30.64
0.95681	36.65	30.39	29.08	0.95390	38.65	32.16	30.68
0.95674	36.70	30.44	29.12	0.95383	38.70	32.20	30.72
0.95667	36.75	30.48	29.16	0.95375	38.75	32.25	30.76
0.95660	36.80	30.52	29.20	0.95368	38.80	32.29	30.79
0.95653	36.85	30.57	29.24	0.95360	38.85	32.33	30.83
0.95646	36.90	30.61	29.29	0.95353	38.90	32.37	30.87
0.95639	36.95	30.66	29.32	0.95345	38.95	32.42	30.91
0.95632	37.00	30.70	29.36	0.95338	39.00	32.46	30.95
0.95625	37.05	30.74	29.40	0.95330	39.05	32.50	30.99
0.95618	37.10	30.79	29.44	0.95323	39.10	32.55	31.03
0.95610	37.15	30.83	29.48	0.95315	39.15	32.59	31.07
0.95603	37.20	30.88	29.52	0.95307	39.20	32.64	31.11
0.95596	37.25	30.92	29.56	0.95300	39.25	32.68	31.14
0.95589	37.30	30.96	29.60	0.95292	39.30	32.72	31.18
0.95581	37.35	31.01	29.64	0.95284	39.35	32.77	31.22
0.95574	37.40	31.05	29.68	0.95277	39.40	32.81	31.26
0.95567	37.45	31.10	29.72	0.95269	39.45	32.86	31.30
0.95560	37.50	31.14	29.76	0.95262	39.50	32.90	31.34
0.95552	37.55	31.18	29.80	0.95254	39.55	32.95	31.38
0.95545	37.60	31.23	29.84	0.95246	39.60	32.99	31.42
0.95538	37.65	31.27	29.88	0.95239	39.65	33.04	31.46
0.95531	37.70	31.32	29.92	0.95231	39.70	33.08	31.50
0.95523	37.75	31.36	29.96	0.95223	39.75	33.13	31.54
0.95516	37.80	31.40	30.00	0.95216	39.80	33.17	31.58
0.95509	37.85	31.45	30.04	0.95208	39.85	33.22	31.62
0.95502	37.90	31.49	30.08	0.95200	39.90	33.27	31.66
0.95494	37.95	31.54	30.12	0.95193	39.95	33.31	31.70

REFERENCE TABLES, A. O. A. C.

TABLE II.—PERCENTAGE OF ALCOHOL—(Continued).

Specific Gravity at $\frac{60°}{60}$ F.	Alcohol.			Specific Gravity at $\frac{60°}{60}$ F.	Alcohol.		
	Per Cent by Volume.	Per Cent by Weight.	Grams per 100 c.c.		Per Cent by Volume.	Per Cent by Weight.	Grams per 100 c.c.
0.95185	40.00	33.35	31.74	0.94868	42.00	35.13	33.33
0.95177	40.05	33.39	31.78	0.94860	42.05	35.18	33.37
0.95169	40.10	33.44	31.82	0.94852	42.10	35.22	33.41
0.95161	40.15	33.48	31.86	0.94843	42.15	35.27	33.45
0.95154	40.20	33.53	31.90	0.94835	42.20	35.31	33.49
0.95146	40.25	33.57	31.94	0.94827	42.25	35.36	33.53
0.95138	40.30	33.61	31.98	0.94820	42.30	35.40	33.57
0.95130	40.35	33.66	32.02	0.94811	42.35	35.45	33.61
0.95122	40.40	33.70	32.06	0.94802	42.40	35.49	33.65
0.95114	40.45	33.75	32.10	0.94794	42.45	35.54	33.69
0.95107	40.50	33.79	32.14	0.94786	42.50	35.58	33.73
0.95099	40.55	33.84	32.18	0.94778	42.55	35.63	33.77
0.95091	40.60	33.88	32.22	0.94770	42.60	35.67	33.81
0.95083	40.65	33.93	32.26	0.94761	42.65	35.72	33.85
0.95075	40.70	33.97	32.30	0.94753	42.70	35.76	33.89
0.95067	40.75	34.02	32.34	0.94745	42.75	35.81	33.93
0.95059	40.80	34.06	32.38	0.94737	42.80	35.85	33.97
0.95052	40.85	34.11	32.42	0.94729	42.85	35.90	34.00
0.95044	40.90	34.15	32.46	0.94720	42.90	35.94	34.04
0.95036	40.95	34.20	32.50	0.94712	42.95	35.99	34.08
0.95028	41.00	34.24	32.54	0.94704	43.00	36.03	34.12
0.95020	41.05	34.28	32.58	0.94696	43.05	36.08	34.16
0.95012	41.10	34.33	32.62	0.94687	43.10	36.12	34.20
0.95004	41.15	34.37	32.66	0.94679	43.15	36.17	34.24
0.94996	41.20	34.42	32.70	0.94670	43.20	36.21	34.28
0.94988	41.25	34.46	32.74	0.94662	43.25	36.23	34.32
0.94980	41.30	34.50	32.78	0.94654	43.30	36.30	34.36
0.94972	41.35	34.55	32.82	0.94645	43.35	36.35	34.40
0.94964	41.40	34.59	32.86	0.94637	43.40	36.39	34.44
0.94956	41.45	34.64	32.90	0.94628	43.45	36.44	34.48
0.94948	41.50	34.68	32.93	0.94620	43.50	36.48	34.52
0.94940	41.55	34.73	32.97	0.94612	43.55	36.53	34.56
0.94932	41.60	34.77	33.01	0.94603	43.60	36.57	34.60
0.94924	41.65	34.82	33.05	0.94595	43.65	36.62	34.64
0.94916	41.70	34.86	33.09	0.94586	43.70	36.66	34.68
0.94908	41.75	34.91	33.13	0.94578	43.75	36.71	34.72
0.94900	41.80	34.95	33.17	0.94570	43.80	36.75	34.76
0.94892	41.85	35.00	33.21	0.94561	43.85	36.80	34.80
0.94884	41.90	35.04	33.25	0.94553	43.90	36.84	34.84
0.94876	41.95	35.09	33.29	0.94544	43.95	36.89	34.88

REFERENCE TABLES, A. O. A. C.

TABLE II.—PERCENTAGE OF ALCOHOL—(*Continued*).

Specific Gravity at $\frac{60°}{60}$ F.	Alcohol. Per Cent by Volume.	Alcohol. Per Cent by Weight.	Alcohol. Grams per 100 c.c.	Specific Gravity at $\frac{60°}{60}$ F.	Alcohol. Per Cent by Volume.	Alcohol. Per Cent by Weight.	Alcohol. Grams per 100 c.c.
0.94536	44.00	36.93	34.91	0.94188	46.00	38.75	36.50
0.94527	44.05	36.98	34.95	0.94179	46.05	38.80	36.54
0.94519	44.10	37.02	34.99	0.94170	46.10	38.84	36.58
0.94510	44.15	37.07	35.03	0.94161	46.15	38.89	36.62
0.94502	44.20	37.11	35.07	0.94152	46.20	38.93	36.66
0.94493	44.25	37.16	35.11	0.94143	46.25	38.98	36.70
0.94484	44.30	37.21	35.15	0.94134	46.30	39.03	36.74
0.94476	44.35	37.25	35.19	0.94125	46.35	39.07	36.78
0.94467	44.40	37.30	35.23	0.94116	46.40	39.12	36.82
0.94459	44.45	37.34	35.27	0.94107	46.45	39.16	36.86
0.94450	44.50	37.39	35.31	0.94098	46.50	39.21	36.90
0.94441	44.55	37.44	35.35	0.94089	46.55	39.26	36.94
0.94433	44.60	37.48	35.39	0.94080	46.60	39.30	36.98
0.94424	44.65	37.53	35.43	0.94071	46.65	39.35	37.02
0.94416	44.70	37.57	35.47	0.94062	46.70	39.39	37.06
0.94407	44.75	37.62	35.51	0.94053	46.75	39.44	37.09
0.94398	44.80	37.66	35.55	0.94044	46.80	39.49	37.13
0.94390	44.85	37.71	35.59	0.94035	46.85	39.53	37.17
0.94381	44.90	37.76	35.63	0.94026	46.90	39.58	37.21
0.94373	44.95	37.80	35.67	0.94017	46.95	39.62	37.25
0.94364	45.00	37.84	35.71	0.94008	47.00	39.67	37.29
0.94355	45.05	37.89	35.75	0.93999	47.05	39.72	37.33
0.94346	45.10	37.93	35.79	0.93990	47.10	39.76	37.37
0.94338	45.15	37.98	35.83	0.93980	47.15	39.81	37.41
0.94329	45.20	38.02	35.87	0.93971	47.20	39.85	37.45
0.94320	45.25	38.07	35.91	0.93962	47.25	39.90	37.49
0.94311	45.30	38.12	35.95	0.93953	47.30	39.95	37.53
0.94302	45.35	38.16	35.99	0.93944	47.35	39.99	37.57
0.94294	45.40	38.21	36.03	0.93934	47.40	40.04	37.61
0.94285	45.45	38.25	36.07	0.93925	47.45	40.08	37.65
0.94276	45.50	38.30	36.11	0.93916	47.50	40.13	37.69
0.94267	45.55	38.35	36.15	0.93906	47.55	40.18	37.73
0.94258	45.60	38.39	36.19	0.93898	47.60	40.22	37.77
0.94250	45.65	38.44	36.23	0.93888	47.65	40.27	37.81
0.94241	45.70	38.48	36.26	0.93879	47.70	40.32	37.85
0.94232	45.75	38.53	36.30	0.93870	47.75	40.37	37.89
0.94223	45.80	38.57	36.34	0.93861	47.80	40.41	37.93
0.94214	45.85	38.62	36.38	0.93852	47.85	40.46	37.97
0.94206	45.90	38.66	36.42	0.93842	47.90	40.51	38.01
0.94197	45.95	38.71	36.46	0.93833	47.95	40.55	38.05

REFERENCE TABLES, A. O. A. C.

TABLE II.—PERCENTAGE OF ALCOHOL—(Continued).

Specific Gravity at $\frac{60°}{60}$ F.	Alcohol.			Specific Gravity at $\frac{60°}{60}$ F.	Alcohol.		
	Per Cent by Volume.	Per Cent by Weight.	Grams per 100 c.c.		Per Cent by Volume.	Per Cent by Weight.	Grams per 100 c.c.
0.93824	48.00	40.60	38.09	0.93636	49.00	41.52	38.88
0.93815	48.05	40.65	38.13	0.93626	49.05	41.57	38.92
0.93805	48.10	40.69	38.17	0.93617	49.10	41.61	38.96
0.93796	48.15	40.74	38.21	0.93607	49.15	41.66	39.00
0.93786	48.20	40.78	38.25	0.93598	49.20	41.71	39.04
0.93777	48.25	40.83	38.29	0.93588	49.25	41.76	39.08
0.93768	48.30	40.88	38.33	0.93578	49.30	41.80	39.12
0.93758	48.35	40.92	38.37	0.93569	49.35	41.85	39.16
0.93749	48.40	40.97	38.41	0.93559	49.40	41.90	39.20
0.93739	48.45	41.01	38.45	0.93550	49.45	41.94	39.24
0.93730	48.50	41.06	38.49	0.93540	49.50	41.99	39.28
0.93721	48.55	41.11	38.53	0.93530	49.55	42.04	39.32
0.93711	48.60	41.15	38.57	0.93521	49.60	42.08	39.36
0.93702	48.65	41.20	38.61	0.93511	49.65	42.13	39.40
0.93692	48.70	41.24	38.65	0.93502	49.70	42.18	39.44
0.93683	48.75	41.29	38.68	0.93492	49.75	42.23	39.48
0.93679	48.80	41.34	38.72	0.93482	49.80	42.27	39.52
0.93664	48.85	41.38	38.76	0.93473	49.85	42.32	39.56
0.93655	48.90	41.43	38.80	0.93463	49.90	42.37	39.60
0.93645	48.95	41.47	38.84	0.93454	49.95	42.41	39.63

The United States Proof Gallon.—Considerable confusion exists in the public mind as to the precise meaning of the terms U. S. Proof Gallon, U. S. Wine Gallon, and U. S. Taxable Gallon.

In an endeavor to make the Government meaning clear, these terms will be explained in their above order.

U. S. Proof Gallon.—"Section 3249, Revised Statutes, provides that proof spirit shall be held to be that alcoholic liquor which contains one half its volume of alcohol of a specific gravity of seven thousand nine hundred and thirty-nine ten-thousandths (0.7939) at 60° Fahrenheit, referred to water at its maximum density as unity." It is thus seen that the U. S. proof gallon is one half alcohol *by volume or bulk* and therefore contains 50 per cent absolute alcohol, while 200 proof contains 100 per cent absolute alcohol *by volume.* The volume percentage of absolute alcohol multiplied by 2, therefore, gives the proof. The degree or per cent proof divided by 2 gives the percentage of absolute alcohol by volume.

U. S. Wine Gallon.—The U. S. wine gallon contains the same number of cubic inches as the U. S. standard gallon, viz., 231 cubic inches.

A wine gallon of high-proof alcohol is therefore a U. S. standard gallon.

The U. S. Taxable Gallon (in case of Distilled Spirits).—The present tax on distilled spirits is "$1.10 on each proof gallon or wine gallon when below proof, and a proportionate tax at a like rate on all fractional parts of such proof or wine gallon: *Provided*, that in computing the tax on any package of spirits all fractional parts of a gallon less than one tenth shall be excluded. . . . Under the above provisions, in computing the tax on any package of spirits, officers will exclude the hundredths of a gallon less than one tenth whenever they may arise. . . . When spirits are below proof the tax attaches to the wine gallons as heretofore. For example, in case of a package of spirits, when the loss is not excessive, if the contents are found to be 44.59 wine gallons and 44.15 proof gallons, the tax will be computed on 44.5 gallons." In this case the strength of the spirits was 99.2 degrees proof.

Other provisions for allowance for loss of spirits while in warehouse and further exact facts relating to the above can be found in the U. S. Internal Revenue Regulations and Instructions concerning the Tax on Distilled Spirits.

A barrel may hold, for instance, 50 wine gallons, 50 proof gallons, and 50 taxable gallons, and in this case the strength of the spirits is 50 per cent by volume or 100 U. S. proof or "proof," which means 50 per cent by volume, as described, and as there are 50 wine gallons, or bulk gallons, there results 50 taxable gallons on which $1.10 per gallon has to be paid.

Denatured alcohol is of course untaxed, but the above definitions with regard to distilled spirits have been given for the reasons stated.

In the control of denatured alcohol the tables published in the Gaugers' Manual, U. S. Internal Revenue, will be used.

The tables given on the following pages (pp. 143-145) were taken from the edition of 1900 of this manual. In testing spirits for their alcoholic strength in per cents of proof by these tables a gauger's cup, shown in Fig. 62, p. 142, and alcohol hydrometers, shown in Fig. 61, p. 142, are used. Proof or 100 will be indicated on the hydrometer when the temperature of the spirit is at 60° F. Tables for correction of temperature when it varies from 60° F. are supplied in this manual.

The gauger's cup is filled with the spirit to be tested according to the directions in this manual, and the hydrometer is carefully placed therein and the degree or per cent proof is read from the scale on the

stem at the surface of the spirits according to these published directions.
A complete set of five stems according to the Standard of the U. S.
Internal Revenue is shown in Fig. 61, ranging from water marked 0 to
absolute alcohol marked 200.

The British proof gallon is defined by law to be such spirit as at
the temperature of 51° F. shall weigh $\frac{1}{2}\frac{3}{3}$ of an equal measure of distilled water. Absolute alcohol contains 175¼ per cent by measure or

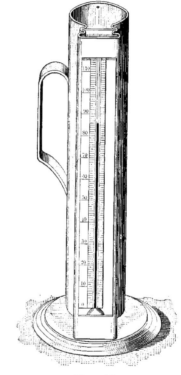

FIG. 61.   FIG. 62.

FIG. 61.—Spirit Hydrometer showing Set of 5 Stems According to the Standard
     Adopted by the U. S. Internal Revenue Dept. Furnished by Emil Grenier Co.,
     New York City.
FIG. 62.—Gaugers' Cup, with Thermometer. Furnished by Hoffman-Ahlers Co.,
     Cincinnati, Ohio.

volume of proof spirit in the English system. The percentage by *volume
of absolute alcohol* may be obtained by multiplying the percentage of
proof spirit by the factor 0.5706.

The percentage by *volume of proof spirit* may be obtained by dividing
the percentage of absolute alcohol by volume by 0.5706 or multiplying
it by 1.7525. The British proof gallon is further described in the
Appendix of this book.

TABLE

Giving the Respective Volumes of Absolute Alcohol and Water Contained in 100 Volumes of Spirits of Different Strength, and also the Specific Gravities of the Mixtures, Referred, for Convenience, to the Density of Water at 60° Fahr. as Unity.

(From Gaugers' Manual, p. 575, 1900, U. S. Internal Revenue.)

Per Cent Proof.	Alcohol.	Water.	Specific Gravity.	Per Cent Proof.	Alcohol.	Water.	Specific Gravity.
	Vols.	Vols.			Vols.	Vols.	
1	0.50	99.53	0.99929	41	20.50	81.26	0.97549
2	1.00	99.06	0.99858	42	21.00	80.81	0.97498
3	1.50	98.59	0.99787	43	21.50	80.36	0.97447
4	2.00	98.13	0.99716	44	22.00	79.91	0.97396
5	2.50	97.66	0.99645	45	22.50	79.47	0.97344
6	3.00	97.19	0.99574	46	23.00	79.02	0.97292
7	3.50	96.72	0.99503	47	23.50	78.57	0.97241
8	4.00	96.25	0.99431	48	24.00	78.12	0.97190
9	4.50	95.78	0.99360	49	24.50	77.67	0.97139
10	5.00	95.32	0.99289	50	25.00	77.22	0.97087
11	5.50	94.85	0.99224	51	25.50	76.77	0.97034
12	6.00	94.39	0.99160	52	26.00	76.32	0.96981
13	6.50	93.93	0.99098	53	26.50	75.87	0.96928
14	7.00	93.48	0.99036	54	27.00	75.42	0.96874
15	7.50	93.02	0.98974	55	27.50	74.97	0.96821
16	8.00	92.56	0.98911	56	28.00	74.52	0.96767
17	8.50	92.10	0.98849	57	28.50	74.06	0.96711
18	9.00	91.64	0.98787	58	29.00	73.61	0.96655
19	9.50	91.18	0.98725	59	29.50	73.16	0.96598
20	10.00	90.72	0.98663	60	30.00	72.70	0.96541
21	10.50	90.26	0.98608	61	30.50	72.25	0.96484
22	11.00	89.81	0.98552	62	31.00	71.79	0.96426
23	11.50	89.36	0.98497	63	31.50	71.33	0.96364
24	12.00	88.91	0.98441	64	32.00	70.87	0.96302
25	12.50	88.45	0.98386	65	32.50	70.42	0.96240
26	13.00	88.00	0.98330	66	33.00	69.96	0.96178
27	13.50	87.55	0.98275	67	33.50	69.49	0.96114
28	14.00	87.10	0.98220	68	34.00	69.03	0.96049
29	14.50	86.65	0.98167	69	34.50	68.57	0.95982
30	15.00	86.20	0.98114	70	35.00	68.10	0.95915
31	15.50	85.75	0.98063	71	35.50	67.64	0.95847
32	16.00	85.30	0.98011	72	36.00	67.17	0.95779
33	16.50	84.85	0.97959	73	36.50	66.70	0.95707
34	17.00	84.40	0.97907	74	37.00	66.23	0.95635
35	17.50	83.95	0.97856	75	37.50	65.77	0.95564
36	18.00	83.50	0.97804	76	38.00	65.30	0.95492
37	18.50	83.05	0.97753	77	38.50	64.82	0.95417
38	19.00	82.60	0.97702	78	39.50	64.35	0.95342
39	19.50	82.16	0.97651	79	39.50	63.88	0.95267
40	20.00	81.71	0.97600	80	40.00	63.41	0.95192

RESPECTIVE VOLUMES OF ALCOHOL AND WATER, AND SPECIFIC GRAVITY—

(*Continued*).

Per Cent Proof.	Alcohol.	Water.	Specific Gravity.	Per Cent Proof.	Alcohol.	Water.	Specific Gravity.
	Vols.	Vols.			Vols.	Vols.	
81	40.50	62.93	0.95112	121	60.50	43.16	0.91234
82	41.00	62.45	0.95031	122	61.00	42.65	0.91122
83	41.50	61.97	0.94950	123	61.50	42.14	0.91010
84	42.00	61.50	0.94869	124	62.00	41.63	0.90897
85	42.50	61.01	0.94785	125	62.50	41.12	0.90784
86	43.00	60.53	0.94701	126	63.00	40.61	0.90671
87	43.50	60.05	0.94617	127	63.50	40.10	0.90556
88	44.00	59.57	0.94532	128	64.00	39.59	0.90441
89	44.50	59.08	0.94446	129	64.50	39.07	0.90326
90	45.00	58.60	0.94359	130	65.00	38.56	0.90211
91	45.50	58.12	0.94271	131	65.50	38.05	0.90093
92	46.00	57.63	0.94183	132	66.00	37.53	0.89975
93	46.50	57.14	0.94093	133	66.50	37.01	0.89856
94	47.00	56.66	0.94003	134	67.00	36.50	0.89737
95	47.50	56.16	0.93909	135	67.50	35.98	0.89616
96	48.00	55.67	0.93815	136	68.00	35.46	0.89495
97	48.50	55.18	0.93721	137	68.50	34.94	0.89375
98	49.00	54.69	0.93627	138	69.00	34.42	0.89254
99	49.50	54.20	0.93532	139	69.50	33.90	0.89129
100*	50.00	53.71	0.93437	140	70.00	33.38	0.89003
101	50.50	53.21	0.93341	141	70.50	32.86	0.88878
102	51.00	52.72	0.93245	142	71.00	32.33	0.88753
103	51.50	52.22	0.93144	143	71.50	31.81	0.88627
104	52.00	51.72	0.93043	144	72.00	31.29	0.88500
105	52.50	51.22	0.92941	145	72.50	30.76	0.88374
106	53.00	50.73	0.92839	146	73.00	30.24	0.88247
107	53.50	50.23	0.92737	147	73.50	29.71	0.88119
108	54.00	49.73	0.92635	148	74.00	29.19	0.87990
109	54.50	49.22	0.92531	149	74.50	28.66	0.87860
110	55.00	48.72	0.92427	150	75.00	28.13	0.87730
111	55.50	48.22	0.92322	151	75.50	27.61	0.87599
112	56.00	47.72	0.92217	152	76.00	27.08	0.87467
113	56.50	47.22	0.92111	153	76.50	26.55	0.87334
114	57.00	46.71	0.92004	154	77.00	26.02	0.87200
115	57.50	46.21	0.91896	155	77.50	25.48	0.87067
116	58.00	45.70	0.91788	156	78.00	24.95	0.86933
117	58.50	45.19	0.91679	157	78.50	24.42	0.86796
118	59.00	44.69	0.91569	158	79.00	23.88	0.86659
119	59.50	44.18	0.91458	159	79.50	23.35	0.86522
120	60.00	43.67	0.91346	160	80.00	22.81	0.86384

* Proof: In mixing alcohol and water a contraction in volume ensues. There are required, therefore, to make 100 gallons of proof spirit, 50 gallons of absolute alcohol and 53.71 gallons of water.

RESPECTIVE VOLUMES OF ALCOHOL AND WATER, AND SPECIFIC GRAVITY—
(Continued).

Per Cent Proof.	Alcohol.	Water.	Specific Gravity.	Per Cent Proof.	Alcohol.	Water.	Specific Gravity.
	Vols.	Vols.			Vols.	Vols.	
161	80.50	22.28	0.86244	181	90.50	11.30	0.83216
162	81.00	21.74	0.86104	182	91.00	10.74	0.83046
163	81.50	21.20	0.85962	183	91.50	10.17	0.82876
164	82.00	20.66	0.85820	184	92.00	9.60	0.82706
165	82.50	20.12	0.85678	185	92.50	9.03	0.82527
166	83.00	19.58	0.85535	186	93.00	8.45	0.82348
167	83.50	19.04	0.85390	187	93.50	7.87	0.82165
168	84.00	18.50	0.85245	188	94.00	7.29	0.81981
169	84.50	17.95	0.85098	189	94.50	6.70	0.81790
170	85.00	17.41	0.84950	190	95.00	6.10	0.81598
171	85.50	16.86	0.84803	191	95.50	5.51	0.81394
172	86.00	16.32	0.84656	192	96.00	4.91	0.81190
173	86.50	15.77	0.84502	193	96.50	4.31	0.80983
174	87.00	15.22	0.84347	194	97.00	3.70	0.80776
175	87.50	14.66	0.84189	195	97.50	3.10	0.80566
176	88.00	14.11	0.84031	196	98.00	2.48	0.80356
177	88.50	13.55	0.83873	197	98.50	1.87	0.80137
178	89.00	12.99	0.83715	198	99.00	1.25	0.79918
179	89.50	12.43	0.83550	199	99.50	0.62	0.79690
180	90.00	11.87	0.83385	200	100.00 [1]	0.00	0.79461

[1] Absolute alcohol.

*The Detection and Determination of Ethyl and Methyl Alcohols in Mixtures by the Immersion Refractometer.—† The immersion refractometer used is the recently devised instrument made by Zeiss. The construction of the immersion refractometer is such that, as its name implies, it may be immersed directly in an almost endless variety of solutions, the strength of which within limits may be determined by the degree of refraction read upon an arbitrary scale. Thus, for example, the strengths of various acids and of a variety of salt solutions used as reagents in the laboratory, as well as of formaldehyde, of sugars in solution and of alcohol, are all capable of determination by the use of the immersion refractometer.

Fig. 63 shows the form used by the authors of this test. P is a glass prism fixed in the lower end of the tube of the instrument, while at the top of the tube is the ocular Oc, and just below this, on a level with the

---

* By Albert E. Leach and Hermann C. Lythgoe. Reprinted from the Journal of the American Chemical Society, Vol. XXVII, No. 8, August, 1905.
† From Leach's Food Inspection and Analysis.

vernier screw Z, is the scale on which is read the degree of refraction of the liquid in which the prism P is immersed. The tube may be held in the hand and directly dipped in the liquid to be tested, this liquid being contained in a vessel with a translucent bottom, through which the light is reflected.

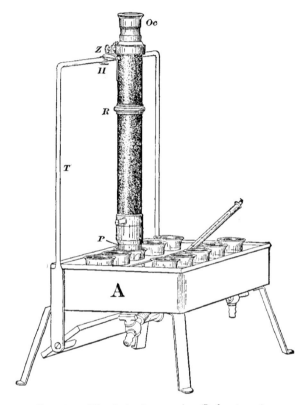

Fig. 63.—The Zeiss Immersion Refractometer.

But the preferable method of use is, however, that shown in Fig. 63, the Zeiss immersion refractometer. A is a metal bath with inlet and outlet tubes, arranged whereby water is kept at a constant level. The water is maintained at a constant temperature, which will be found of great convenience when the instrument is used constantly, especially with the solid fats. In the bath A are immersed a number of beakers containing the solutions to be tested. T is a frame on which is hung the refractometer by means of the hook H, at just the right height to permit of the immersion of the prism P in the liquid in any of the beakers in the row beneath. Under this row of beakers the bottom of the tank is composed of a strip of ground glass, through which light is reflected by an adjustable pivoted mirror. The temperature of the bath is noted by a delicate thermometer immersed therein, capable of reading to tenths of a degree.

Returning to the main refractometer-tube, R is a graduated ring or collar, which is connected with a sleeve within the tube with a compound prism near the bottom, the construction being such that by turning the collar R one way or the other, the chromatic aberration or dispersion of any liquid may be compensated for and a clear-cut shadow or critical line projected across the scale. By the graduation on the collar R the degree of dispersion may be read. Tenths of a degree on the main scale of the instrument may be read with great accuracy by means of the vernier screw Z, graduated along its circumference, the screw being turned in each case till the critical line on the scale coincides with the nearest whole number.

The scale of the instrument reads from -5 to 105, corresponding to indices of refraction of from 1.32539 to 1.36640. It should be noted that the index of refraction may be read with a greater degree of accuracy on the immersion refractometer than on the Abbé instrument. This instrumen is shown in Fig. 64 (the Abbé refractometer with temperature-controlled prisms).

A Zeiss heating apparatus for heating the metal bath A is shown in Fig. 65. A supply reservoir A is secured to the wall and is connected by means of a rubber inlet-tube G to the water-faucet C. The reservoir is provided with a waste overflow-pipe and with an outlet-tube D, the flow through the latter being regulated by the cock H. The tube D leads to the spiral heater HS, which is heated by a Bunsen burner.

From the heater the tube E conducts the warm water through the refractometer, from which it flows through the tube F, either directly into the sink or into the intermediate vessel B. The temperature of the water is regulated by adjusting the cock H and the height of the flame of the Bunsen burner. Such a heater is of great convenience when using this instrument with the solid fats. It can be obtained of the manufacturers.

For convenience of reference a table showing specific gravity and percentage of alcohol for use with this refractometer is given on pages 158–163 (according to Hehner).

The use of wood alcohol in various preparations which come within the domain of the public analyst for examination is apparently on the increase. It is especially to be looked for as an adulterant in medicinal preparations, liniments, tinctures, and in all varieties of flavoring and

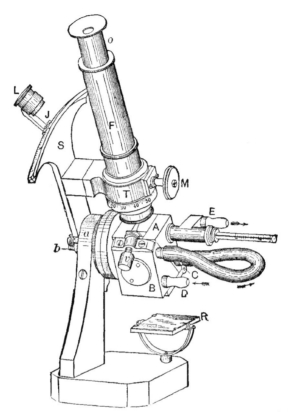

FIG. 64.—The Abbé Refractometer with Temperature-controlled Prisms.

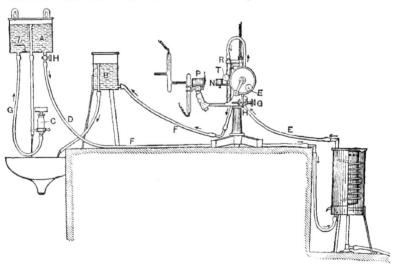

FIG. 65.—The Zeiss Heating Apparatus for all Forms of Refractometer.
Shown in Connection with the Pulfrich Refractometer.

other extracts high in alcohol. In Massachusetts we have found methyl alcohol in various pharmaceutical preparations, such as tincture of iodine, and in lemon and orange extracts.

Existing methods for the detection of wood alcohol, with one or two exceptions, are extremely unsatisfactory. Most of the older methods, such, for example, as the potassium permanganate test, depend upon the presence of acetone in the methyl alcohol. With the improved refining

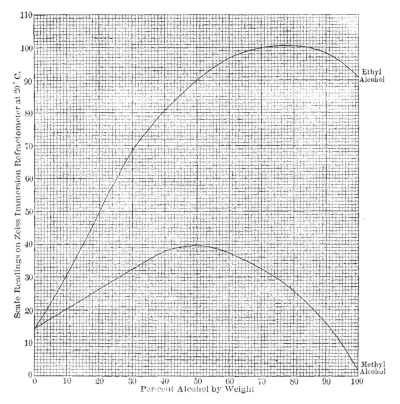

Diagram illustrating the Wide Difference in Refraction between Ethyl and Methyl Alcohol.

processes used at the present day wood alcohol is readily obtainable free from more than traces of acetone, so that it is impossible to distinguish it from ethyl alcohol by its odor. Crude wood alcohol with acetone present in marked degree is frequently capable of being indicated even in mixture with ethyl alcohol by the sense of smell. It is the refined or deodorized methyl alcohol sold under a variety of trade names, such as Columbian spirits, Hastings spirits, Colonial spirits, purified wood alcohol, etc., *that one finds as an adulterant of tinctures, extracts, and beverages.*

The most practical method hitherto used for the detection of methyl alcohol is that of Mulliken and Scudder,* which depends on the oxidation of the methyl alcohol in the sample to formaldehyde by the use of a red-hot spiral of copper wire, using, however, the hydrochloric acid and milk test for the detection of formaldehyde in the oxidized solution.†

Attention is further called to the German official process of Windisch,‡ a color reaction depending on the transformation of the methyl alcohol to methyl violet.

Methods for the quantitative determination of wood alcohol are even more rare. Duprey § has suggested a method of concentrating the alcohol by repeated distillation, after which part of the final distillate is oxidized to acetic acid, the latter being titrated with alkali, while the alcohol is determined in the other portion of the distillate from the specific gravity. Both methods with pure ethyl alcohol should give concordant results, whereas in presence of methyl alcohol a lower result is obtained by the oxidation process.

The specific gravity of absolute methyl and ethyl alcohol is practically identical, and it is also true that when mixed with varying proportions of water the specific gravity of both alcohols is so nearly the same (with the same proportions of water in each) that the same tables for computation of percentage of alcohol from the specific gravity may be used in one case as in the other.

A very important physical constant, however, which we have found to differ most widely in the two alcohols is the index of refraction, and it is on this property that we base our method for the detection and determination of methyl alcohol.

We use for this purpose the immersion refractometer of Zeiss. This instrument was fully described in a former paper by us.∥ To illustrate the wide difference in refraction between the two alcohols, the strongest commercial ethyl alcohol found on the market (the alcohol of the U. S. Pharmacopœia, which contains 91 per cent of absolute alcohol by weight) gives a reading with the immersion refractometer of 98.3° at 20° C., while the reading of methyl alcohol of 91 per cent strength by weight is 14.9°. Fifty per cent ethyl alcohol by weight has a refraction on the immersion refractometer of 90.3°, while the same strength (50 per cent) of methyl

---

* Am. Chem. Jour., 24, 444 (1900); *ibid*, 27, 892.

† Ann. Rept. Mass. State Board of Health, 1897, p. 558; Leach, Food Inspection and Analysis, p. 666.

‡ Vereinbar. z. Unters. v. Nahr. u. Genussm., Heft II, p. 130.

§ Analyst, 1, p. 4.

∥ Am. Chem. Jour., 26, 1196 (1904).

alcohol refracts on the instrument at 39.8°, all readings being made at 20° C. From this wide variation it is readily seen that there is no trouble in detecting even small amounts of methyl alcohol in mixtures. Table I

TABLE I.—PERCENTAGE BY WEIGHT OF ETHYL AND METHYL ALCOHOLS CORRESPONDING TO SCALE READINGS ON ZEISS IMMERSION REFRACTOMETER AT 20° C.

Scale Reading, 20° C.	Per Cent Alcohol by Weight.		Scale Reading, 20° C.	Per Cent Ethyl Alcohol by Weight.	Scale Reading, 20° C.	Per Cent Ethyl Alcohol by Weight.
	Methyl Alcohol.	Ethyl Alcohol.				
0			40	14.73	80	38.82
1			41	15.23	81	39.64
2	100.00		42	15.73	82	40.64
3	99.33		43	16.23	83	41.64
4	98.69		44	16.73	84	42.75
5	98.06		45	17.23	85	43.75
6	97.44		46	17.73	86	44.75
7	96.80		47	18.23	87	46.00
8	96.13		48	18.73	88	47.25
9	95.42		49	19.23	89	48.38
10	94.71		50	19.73	90	49.62
11		94.00	51	20.25		
12		93.28	52	20.77	91	50.87 100.00
13		92.55	53	21.29	92	52.66 99.00
14		91.75	54	21.81	93	54.00 98.00
15	1.34	90.92 0.33	55	22.33	94	55.80 97.00
16	3.00	90.08 1.00	56	22.85	95	57.60 96.00
17	4.67	89.25 1.62	57	23.38	96	59.60 95.00
18	6.34	88.45 2.25	58	23.90	97	61.75 94.00
19	8.00	87.64 2.93	59	24.43	98	64.00 91.60
					99	66.75 88.50
20	9.67	86.73 3.56	60	24.94	100	70.00 85.50
21	11.34	85.80 4.19	61	25.50		
22	13.00	84.80 4.82	62	26.06	101	75.00
23	14.67	83.60 5.39	63	26.60		
24	16.17	82.40 5.94	64	27.15		
25	17.72	81.20 6.50	65	27.71		
26	19.33	80.00 7.06	66	28.29		
27	20.93	78.75 7.58	67	28.88		
28	22.47	77.43 8.09	68	29.44		
29	23.96	76.00 8.64	69	30.00		
30	25.50	74.57 9.20	70	30.71		
31	27.18	73.14 9.76	71	31.47		
32	28.67	71.50 10.32	72	32.21		
33	30.33	70.00 10.87	73	32.93		
34	32.00	68.00 11.43	74	33.69		
35	33.50	66.00 11.99	75	34.43		
36	35.16	64.00 12.54	76	35.09		
37	37.00	62.00 13.10	77	35.99		
38	40.00	59.75 13.64	78	37.00		
39	43.93	14.19	79	37.90		

shows the percentage by weight at 20° C. of the two alcohols corresponding to each degree of scale reading on the refractometer.

The difference in refraction between the two alcohols varies considerably for different strengths. In the case of methyl alcohol, starting at zero (or water containing no alcohol), at which the reading on the immersion at 20° is 14.5, the refraction gradually increases with increasing strength of methyl alcohol up to about 50 per cent of the latter by weight, where the refraction reaches its maximum, after which for higher strengths of methyl alcohol it drops quite rapidly until at 100 per cent the refraction is but 2.0.

In the case of ethyl alcohol, starting, as before, with pure water and increasing the strength of the solution in alcohol, the refraction increases quite rapidly up to solutions of about 75 per cent strength, where it then drops slightly, but by no means to such an extent as in the case of methyl alcohol. It will thus be seen that by far the widest variations in refraction between the two alcohols take place above 50 per cent in strength.

From the peculiar shape of both alcohol curves, rising gradually to a maximum and then falling, no confusion should be caused by the fact that in some cases one scale reading may correspond to two different percentages of strength of the same alcohol.

The detection of wood alcohol by this method is comparatively simple and consists in submitting to refraction with the immersion refractometer the distillate which one makes for the determination of ethyl alcohol in the regular manner in alcoholic beverages, essences, tinctures, extracts, or whatever may be the nature of the substances to be examined. If the refraction of the liquid shows the percentage of alcohol agreeing with that obtained from the specific gravity in the regular manner, it may safely be assumed that no methyl alcohol is present. If, however, there is an appreciable amount of methyl alcohol the low refractometer reading will at once indicate the fact. If the absence in the solution of other refractive substances than water and the alcohols is assured this qualitative test by difference in refraction is conclusive, but if there is doubt a confirmatory test by the Mulliken and Scudder method * should be made.

Not only can methyl alcohol be thus readily detected, but the amount may be approximately and in some cases very accurately determined. Addition of methyl to ethyl alcohol decreases the refraction in direct proportion to the amount present. Hence the quantitative calculation may be readily made by interpolation in Table II, which follows, using

---

* Loc. cit. supra.

the figures for pure ethyl and methyl alcohol of the same alcoholic strength as the sample. The degree of accuracy of this calculation varies with the strength of alcohol. For instance, with an alcoholic strength of 10 per cent there is less exactness than at 50 per cent strength, where 1 per cent or even less can be readily determined. From this point on the delicacy of the process naturally increases, until at 90 per cent strength 0.1 per cent of methyl alcohol may be determined with accuracy.

TABLE II.—SCALE READINGS ON ZEISS IMMERSION REFRACTOMETER AT 20° C. CORRESPONDING TO EACH PER CENT BY WEIGHT OF ETHYL AND METHYL ALCOHOL.

Per Cent Alcohol by Weight.	Scale Readings.		Per Cent Alcohol by Weight.	Scale Readings.		Per Cent Alcohol by Weight.	Scale Readings.	
	Methyl Alcohol.	Ethyl Alcohol.		Methyl Alcohol.	Ethyl Alcohol.		Methyl Alcohol.	Ethyl Alcohol.
0	14.5	14.5	34	35.2	74.4	68	34.0	99.4
1	14.8	16.0	35	35.8	75.8	69	33.5	99.7
2	15.4	17.6	36	36.3	76.9			
3	16.0	19.1	37	36.8	78.0	70	33.0	100.0
4	16.6	20.7	38	37.3	79.1	71	32.3	100.2
5	17.2	22.3	39	37.7	80.2	72	31.7	100.4
6	17.8	24.1				73	31.1	100.6
7	18.4	25.9	40	38.1	81.3	74	30.4	100.8
8	19.0	27.8	41	38.4	82.3	75	29.7	101.0
9	19.6	29.6	42	38.8	83.3	76	29.0	101.0
			43	39.2	84.2	77	28.3	100.9
10	20.2	31.4	44	39.3	85.2	78	27.6	100.9
11	20.8	33.2	45	39.4	86.2	79	26.8	100.8
12	21.4	35.0	46	39.5	87.0			
13	22.0	36.9	47	39.6	87.8	80	26.0	100.7
14	22.6	38.7	48	39.7	88.7	81	25.1	100.6
15	23.2	40.5	49	39.8	89.5	82	24.3	100.5
16	23.9	42.5				83	23.6	100.4
17	24.5	44.5	50	39.8	90.3	84	22.8	100.3
18	25.2	46.5	51	39.7	91.1	85	21.8	100.1
19	25.8	48.5	52	39.6	91.8	86	20.8	99.8
			53	39.6	92.4	87	19.7	99.5
20	26.5	50.5	54	39.5	93.0	88	18.6	99.2
21	27.1	52.4	55	39.4	93.6	89	17.3	98.9
22	27.8	54.3	56	39.2	94.1			
23	28.4	56.3	57	39.0	94.7	90	16.1	98.6
24	29.1	58.2	58	38.6	95.2	91	14.9	98.3
25	29.7	60.1	59	38.3	95.7	92	13.7	97.8
26	30.3	61.9				93	12.4	97.2
27	30.9	63.7	60	37.9	96.2	94	11.0	96.4
28	31.6	65.5	61	37.5	96.7	95	9.6	95.7
29	32.2	67.2	62	37.0	97.1	96	8.2	94.9
			63	36.5	97.5	97	6.7	94.0
30	32.8	69.0	64	36.0	98.0	98	5.1	93.0
31	33.5	70.4	65	35.5	98.3	99	3.5	92.0
32	34.1	71.7	66	35.0	98.7			
33	34.7	73.1	67	34.5	99.1	100	2.0	91.0

Table II shows the refraction on the immersion refractometer corresponding to each percentage of alcohol, both ethyl and methyl, by weight, all readings being taken at exactly 20° C. This table will show at a glance whether a solution of given strength of alcohol as determined from the specific gravity contains ethyl or methyl alcohol or is a mixture of the two.

The fact should be borne in mind that in the examination of flavoring extracts it is difficult to so completely separate out the volatile oils as to prevent minute traces from appearing in the distillate. These, and indeed any volatile substances present in marked degree, appreciably affect the accuracy of the quantitative results, though mere traces do not cause serious error. The presence of notable amounts of acetone exercises also a marked effect, but the purified wood alcohol commonly used as an adulterant contains so little acetone that it may ordinarily be neglected in expressing approximate results. Pure acetone refracts considerably lower than ethyl alcohol.

Two or three examples of actual cases as found in the routine inspection of foods and drugs in Massachusetts will best illustrate the method of calculation. For determination of total alcohol from the specific gravity Hehner's alcohol tables were used (as given on pages 158–163).

(1) A lemon extract found by the polariscope to contain 4.9 per cent of lemon-oil by volume and 90.20 per cent of alcohol by volume at 15° was freed from lemon-oil by diluting four times with water, treating with magnesia in the regular manner and filtering. A measured portion of the filtrate was then distilled and the distillate made up to the measured portion taken. This distillate was found to have a specific gravity of 0.9736, corresponding to 18.38 per cent alcohol by weight,* and to have a refraction of 35.8 on the Zeiss immersion refractometer.

By interpolation in Table II the readings of ethyl and methyl alcohol corresponding to 18.38 per cent alcohol are 47.2 and 25.4 respectively, the difference being 21.8. 47.2 − 35.8 = 11.4. (11.4 ÷ 21.8)100 = 52.3. In this case 52.3 per cent of the alcohol present was methyl.

(2) An orange extract was found with 1.5 per cent of orange-oil and 83.2 per cent of alcohol by volume at 15° C. The specific gravity of

---

* Our methyl-ethyl alcohol tables being most conveniently worked out on the weight-per cent basis, the per cent by weight rather than by volume of the dilute distillate is here taken. Percentage of total alcohol in the extract as well as of lemon-oil we commonly express by volume. In this case the specific gravity 0.9736 corresponds to 22.55 per cent alcohol by volume. The per cent by volume of total alcohol in the extract, 90.20 at 15° C., is found by multiplying 22.55 by 4 to correct for the dilution. The alcohol tables used are given on pp. 158–163.

the one-fourth strength distillate, freed from oil as in the case of the lemon extract, was 0.9754, corresponding to 16.92 per cent alcohol by weight. Refraction of the distillate at 20° C. was 42.0. Readings of ethyl and methyl alcohol of 16.9 strength are, according to Table II, 44.3 and 24.5 respectively. Difference 19.8. $44.3 - 42 = 2.3$. $(2.3 \div 19.8)$ $100 = 1.2$. Thus, 1.2 per cent of the alcohol present was methyl.

(3) 6.3 c.c. of tincture of iodine, after titration with N/10 sodium thiosulphate (in the regular manner for determining its strength according to the U. S. Pharmacopœia), were neutralized with N/10 sodium hydroxide and distilled, collecting 25.2 c.c. of the distillate, corresponding to a dilution of 1:4 of the sample. The distillate contained 20.92 per cent alcohol by weight, refraction 27.5 at 20° C., indicating 99 per cent of the alcohol to be methyl. There is no doubt that the alcohol in this case was entirely methyl, the slightly high refraction of the distillate being due to the presence of a slight amount of volatile substance formed by decomposition of the tincture of iodine.

The accuracy of the method is shown in a general way by a series of experiments, the results of which are tabulated as follows:

TABLE III.—READINGS OF EXPERIMENTAL MIXTURES OF METHYL AND ETHYL ALCOHOLS.

Specific Gravity 15° C.	Per Cent Alcohol by Weight.	Scale Reading, 20° C.	Methyl Alcohol.		Ethyl Alcohol.	
			As Prepared, Per Cent.	As Found, Per Cent.	As Prepared, Per Cent.	As Found, Per Cent.
0.8190	91.36	33.9	68.52	69.88	22.84	21.48
0.8190	91.36	54.9	45.68	47.41	45.68	44.95
0.9239	47.41	51.9	35.56	35.42	11.85	11.99
0.8190	91.36	76.3	22.84	23.75	68.52	67.61
0.9326	43.43	62.4	21.71	21.38	22.71	22.05
0.9643	25.64	37.2	19.23	19.76	6.41	5.88
0.9207	48.86	77.5	12.21	11.77	36.65	37.09
0.9753	17.00	34.0	8.50	8.92	8.50	8.08
0.9666	23.92	50.2	5.98	6.48	17.94	17.44

* **The Determination of Methyl Alcohol in Denatured Alcohol by the Zeiss Immersion Refractometer.**—This method of Leach and Lythgoe just described is applied more particularly to the pure wood alcohol (which is practically free from odor and impurities, and would therefore be less desirable for denaturing purposes), but in the case of

---

* This procedure does *not* separate the two alcohols, but merely removes these other substances in order that the calculation may be made.

denatured alcohol which contains acetone and petroleum benzine a slightly different procedure is necessary. They recommend a test as follows: Take 25 c.c. of the sample of denatured alcohol and dilute to 100 c.c. with water; add about 5 grms. powdered magnesium carbonate, shake well, and filter.

The filtrate is free from petroleum benzine, but contains the acetone and the alcohols.

A measured portion of this filtrate 55 c.c. is washed into a distilling-flask and treated with 10 grms. of powdered potassium bisulphite and, after standing an hour, is distilled, taking 55 c.c. of distillate.

This distillate is free from acetone, but contains some sulphurous acid, and in order to remove this it is distilled with sodium hydroxide, the final distillate being made up to 55 c.c.

The specific gravity and refraction of this final distillate is taken, and the percentage of methyl and ethyl alcohols is calculated from the tables. The percentage of the alcohols in this last distillate must be multiplied by 4 to express the results in terms of the original sample. The alcohol tables used are given on pp. 158–163.

The Abbé refractometer may be used for approximate work, but does not give the accuracy which is obtained by the immersion refractometer.

A table which may be used in connection with the Abbé instrument is given as follows:

TABLE FOR USE WITH THE ABBÉ REFRACTOMETER.

Per Cent Alcohol by Weight.	Index of Refraction, nD. Methyl Alcohol.	Ethyl Alcohol.	Per Cent Alcohol by Weight.	Index of Refraction, nD. Methyl Alcohol.	Ethyl Alcohol.	Per Cent Alcohol by Weight.	Index of Refraction, nD. Methyl Alcohol.	Ethyl Alcohol.
0	1.3330	1.3330	10	1.3352	1.3395	20	1.3376	1.3467
1	1.3331	1.3336	11	1.3354	1.3402	21	1.3378	1.3474
2	1.3334	1.3342	12	1.3357	1.3400	22	1.3381	1.3481
3	1.3336	1.3348	13	1.3359	1.3416	23	1.3384	1.3488
4	1.3338	1.3354	14	1.3361	1.3423	24	1.3386	1.3495
5	1.3340	1.3360	15	1.3364	1.3429	25	1.3388	1.3502
6	1.3343	1.3367	16	1.3366	1.3437			
7	1.3345	1.3374	17	1.3369	1.3444			
8	1.3347	1.3381	18	1.3371	1.3452			
9	1.3350	1.3388	19	1.3374	1.3459			

Example of the Determination of Methyl Alcohol in Denatured Alcohol by the Zeiss Immersion Refractometer.

The sample of denatured alcohol was made by mixing

> 100 c.c. of commercial 95% alcohol;
> 10 c.c. of commercial wood alcohol;
> 0.5 c.c. of petroleum benzine.

This sample was then analyzed by the above method with the following result:

Specific gravity of final distillate 0.9707.
Refraction of final distillate 47.5.

> Alcohol corresponding to sp. gr. 19.08% by weight,
> $= 23.38\%$ by volume,
> Refraction of 19.08% ethyl $= 48.7$
> Refraction of methyl alcohol $= 25.9$
>
> _____
>
> 22.8

$$\left(\frac{48.7-47.5}{22.8}\right)100 = 5.26.$$

Hence 5.26% of the total alcohol is methyl alcohol;
$23.38 \times 4 \quad = 93.52\%$ total alcohol by volume;
$93.52 \times 0.526 = 4.92\%$ methyl alcohol by volume in sample;

_____

88.60% ethyl alcohol by volume in sample.

A second analysis gave results so close to this one that it was considered unnecessary to include it here.

The small amounts of pyroligneous impurities always present in commercial wood alcohol will have a slight effect upon the refraction of the distillate, making the percentage of methyl alcohol slightly less than it should be.

TABLES SHOWING THE SPECIFIC GRAVITY AND PERCENTAGE OF ALCOHOL

(According to Hehner.)

Specific Gravity at 15.6° C.	Absolute Alcohol.			Specific Gravity at 15.6° C.	Absolute Alcohol.		
	Per Cent by Weight.	Per Cent by Volume.	Grams per 100 c.c.		Per Cent by Weight.	Per Cent by Volume.	Grams per 100 c.c.
1.0000	0.00	0.00	0.00				
0.9999	0.05	0.07	0.05	0.9959	2.33	2.93	2.32
8	0.11	0.13	0.11	8	2.39	3.00	2.38
7	0.16	0.20	0.16	7	2.44	3.07	2.43
6	0.21	0.26	0.21	6	2.50	3.14	2.49
5	0.26	0.33	0.26	5	2.56	3.21	2.55
4	0.32	0.40	0.32	4	2.61	3.28	2.60
3	0.37	0.46	0.37	3	2.67	3.35	2.65
2	0.42	0.53	0.42	2	2.72	3.42	2.70
1	0.47	0.60	0.47	1	2.78	3.49	2.76
0	0.53	0.66	0.53	0	2.83	3.55	2.81
0.9989	0.58	0.73	0.58	0.9949	2.89	3.62	2.87
8	0.63	0.79	0.63	8	2.94	3.69	2.92
7	0.68	0.86	0.68	7	3.00	3.76	2.98
6	0.74	0.93	0.74	6	3.06	3.83	3.04
5	0.79	0.99	0.79	5	3.12	3.90	3.10
4	0.84	1.06	0.84	4	3.18	3.98	3.16
3	0.89	1.13	0.89	3	3.24	4.05	3.22
2	0.95	1.19	0.95	2	3.29	4.12	3.27
1	1.00	1.26	1.00	1	3.35	4.20	3.33
0	1.06	1.34	1.06	0	3.41	4.27	3.39
0.9979	1.12	1.42	1.12	0.9939	3.47	4.34	3.45
8	1.19	1.49	1.19	8	3.53	4.42	3.51
7	1.25	1.57	1.25	7	3.59	4.49	3.57
6	1.31	1.65	1.31	6	3.65	4.56	3.63
5	1.37	1.73	1.37	5	3.71	4.63	3.69
4	1.44	1.81	1.44	4	3.76	4.71	3.74
3	1.50	1.88	1.50	3	3.82	4.78	3.80
2	1.56	1.96	1.56	2	3.88	4.85	3.85
1	1.62	2.04	1.61	1	3.94	4.93	3.91
0	1.69	2.12	1.68	0	4.00	5.00	3.97
0.9969	1.75	2.20	1.74	0.9929	4.06	5.08	4.03
8	1.81	2.27	1.80	8	4.12	5.16	4.09
7	1.87	2.35	1.86	7	4.19	5.24	4.16
6	1.94	2.43	1.93	6	4.25	5.32	4.22
5	2.00	2.51	1.99	5	4.31	5.39	4.28
4	2.06	2.58	2.05	4	4.37	5.47	4.34
3	2.11	2.62	2.10	3	4.44	5.55	4.40
2	2.17	2.72	2.16	2	4.50	5.63	4.46
1	2.22	2.79	2.21	1	4.56	5.71	4.52
0	2.28	2.86	2.27	0	4.62	5.78	4.58

SPECIFIC GRAVITY AND PERCENTAGE OF ALCOHOL—*(Continued)*.

Specific Gravity at 15.6° C.	Absolute Alcohol.			Specific Gravity at 15.6° C.	Absolute Alcohol.		
	Per Cent by Weight.	Per Cent by Volume.	Grams per 100 c.c.		Per Cent by Weight.	Per Cent by Volume.	Grams per 100 c.c.
0.9919	4.69	5.86	4.65	0.9879	7.33	9.13	7.24
8	4.75	5.94	4.71	8	7.40	9.21	7.31
7	4.81	6.02	4.77	7	7.47	9.29	7.37
6	4.87	6.10	4.83	6	7.53	9.37	7.43
5	4.94	6.17	4.90	5	7.60	9.45	7.50
4	5.00	6.24	4.95	4	7.67	9.54	7.57
3	5.06	6.32	5.01	3	7.73	9.62	7.63
2	5.12	6.40	5.07	2	7.80	9.70	7.70
1	5.19	6.48	5.14	1	7.87	9.78	7.77
0	5.25	6.55	5.20	0	7.93	9.86	7.83
0.9909	5.31	6.63	5.26	0.9869	8.00	9.95	7.89
8	5.37	6.71	5.32	8	8.07	10.03	7.96
7	5.44	6.78	5.39	7	8.14	10.12	8.04
6	5.50	6.86	5.45	6	8.21	10.21	8.10
5	5.56	6.94	5.51	5	8.29	10.30	8.17
4	5.62	7.01	5.57	4	8.36	10.38	8.24
3	5.69	7.09	5.64	3	8.43	10.47	8.31
2	5.75	7.17	5.70	2	8.50	10.56	8.38
1	5.81	7.25	5.76	1	8.57	10.65	8.45
0	5.87	7.32	5.81	0	8.64	10.73	8.52
0.9899	5.94	7.40	5.88	0.9859	8.71	10.82	8.58
8	6.00	7.48	5.94	8	8.79	10.91	8.66
7	6.07	7.57	6.01	7	8.86	11.00	8.73
6	6.14	7.66	6.07	6	8.93	11.08	8.80
5	6.21	7.74	6.14	5	9.00	11.17	8.87
4	6.28	7.83	6.21	4	9.07	11.26	8.93
3	6.36	7.92	6.29	3	9.14	11.35	9.00
2	6.43	8.01	6.36	2	9.21	11.44	9.07
1	6.50	8.10	6.43	1	9.29	11.52	9.14
0	6.57	8.18	6.50	0	9.36	11.61	9.22
0.9889	6.64	8.27	6.57	0.9849	9.43	11.70	9.29
8	6.71	8.36	6.63	8	9.50	11.79	9.35
7	6.78	8.45	6.70	7	9.57	11.87	9.42
6	6.86	8.54	6.78	6	9.64	11.96	9.49
5	6.93	8.63	6.85	5	9.71	12.05	9.56
4	7.00	8.72	6.92	4	9.79	12.13	9.64
3	7.07	8.80	6.99	3	9.86	12.22	9.71
2	7.13	8.88	7.05	2	9.93	12.31	9.77
1	7.20	8.96	7.12	1	10.00	12.40	9.84
0	7.27	9.04	7.19	0	10.03	12.49	9.92

SPECIFIC GRAVITY AND PERCENTAGE OF ALCOHOL—(*Continued*).

Specific Gravity at 15.6° C.	Absolute Alcohol.			Specific Gravity at 15.6° C.	Absolute Alcohol.		
	Per Cent by Weight.	Per Cent by Volume.	Grams per 100 c.c.		Per Cent by Weight.	Per Cent by Volume.	Grams per 100 c.c.
0.9839	10.15	12.58	9.99	0.9799	13.23	16.33	12.96
8	10.23	12.68	10.06	8	13.21	16.43	13.03
7	10.31	12.77	10.13	7	13.38	16.52	13.10
6	10.38	12.87	10.20	6	13.46	16.61	13.18
5	10.46	12.96	10.28	5	13.54	16.70	13.26
4	10.54	13.05	10.36	4	13.62	16.80	13.33
3	10.62	13.15	10.44	3	13.69	16.89	13.40
2	10.69	13.24	10.51	2	13.77	16.98	13.48
1	10.77	13.34	10.59	1	13.85	17.08	13.56
0	10.85	13.43	10.67	0	13.92	17.17	13.63
0.9829	10.92	13.52	10.73	0.9789	14.00	17.26	13.71
8	11.00	13.62	10.81	8	14.09	17.37	13.79
7	11.08	13.71	10.89	7	14.18	17.48	13.88
6	11.15	13.81	10.95	6	14.27	17.59	13.96
5	11.23	13.90	11.03	5	14.36	17.70	14.04
4	11.31	13.99	11.11	4	14.45	17.81	14.13
3	11.38	14.09	11.18	3	14.55	17.92	14.23
2	11.46	14.18	11.26	2	14.64	18.03	14.32
1	11.54	14.27	11.33	1	14.73	18.14	14.39
0	11.62	14.37	11.41	0	14.82	18.25	14.48
0.9819	11.69	14.46	11.48	0.9779	14.91	18.36	14.58
8	11.77	14.56	11.56	8	15.00	18.48	14.66
7	11.85	14.65	11.64	7	15.08	18.58	14.74
6	11.92	14.74	11.70	6	15.17	18.68	14.83
5	12.00	14.84	11.78	5	15.25	18.78	14.90
4	12.08	14.93	11.85	4 ·	15.33	18.88	14.98
3	12.15	15.02	11.92	3	15.42	18.98	15.07
2	12.23	15.12	12.00	2	15.50	19.08	15.14
1	12.31	15.21	12.08	1	15.58	19.18	15.21
0	12.38	15.30	12.14	0	15.67	19.28	15.30
0.9809	12.46	15.40	12.22	0.9769	15.75	19.39	15.38
8	12.54	15.49	12.30	8	15.83	19.49	15.46
7	12.62	15.58	12.37	7	15.92	19.59	15.54
6	12.69	15.68	12.44	6	16.00	19.68	15.62
5	12.77	15.77	12.51	5	16.08	19.78	15.70
4	12.85	15.86	12.59	4	16.15	19.87	15.76
3	12.92	15.96	12.66	3	16.23	19.96	15.84
2	13.00	16.05	12.74	2	16.31	20.06	15.90
1	13.08	16.15	12.81	1	16.38	20.15	15.99
0	13.15	16.24	12.89	0	16.46	20.24	16.06

SPECIFIC GRAVITY AND PERCENTAGE OF ALCOHOL—(*Continued*).

Specific Gravity at 15.6° C.	Absolute Alcohol.			Specific Gravity at 15.6° C.	Absolute Alcohol.		
	Per Cent by Weight.	Per Cent by Volume.	Grams per 100 c.c.		Per Cent by Weight.	Per Cent by Volume.	Grams per 100 c.c.
0.9759	16.54	20.33	16.13	0.9719	19.75	24.18	19.19
8	16.62	20.43	16.21	8	19.83	24.28	19.27
7	16.69	20.52	16.28	7	19.92	24.38	19.36
6	16.77	20.61	16.35	6	20.00	24.48	19.44
5	16.85	20.71	16.43	5	20.08	24.58	19.51
4	16.92	20.80	16.50	4	20.17	24.68	19.59
3	17.00	20.89	16.57	3	20.25	24.78	19.66
2	17.08	20.99	16.65	2	20.33	24.88	19.74
1	17.17	21.09	16.74	1	20.42	24.98	19.83
0	17.25	21.19	16.81	0	20.50	25.07	19.90
0.9749	17.33	21.29	16.89	0.9709	20.58	25.17	19.98
8	17.42	21.39	16.97	8	20.67	25.27	20.07
7	17.50	21.49	17.05	7	20.75	25.37	20.14
6	17.58	21.59	17.13	6	20.83	25.47	20.22
5	17.67	21.69	17.20	5	20.92	25.57	20.30
4	17.75	21.79	17.29	4	21.00	25.67	20.33
3	17.83	21.89	17.37	3	21.08	25.76	20.46
2	17.92	21.99	17.46	2	21.15	25.86	20.52
1	18.00	22.09	17.54	1	21.23	25.95	20.59
0	18.08	22.18	17.61	0	21.31	26.04	20.67
0.9739	18.15	22.27	17.68	0.9699	21.38	26.13	20.73
8	18.23	22.36	17.76	8	21.46	26.22	20.81
7	18.31	22.46	17.82	7	21.54	26.31	20.89
6	18.38	22.55	17.90	6	21.62	26.40	20.96
5	18.46	22.64	17.97	5	21.69	26.49	21.03
4	18.54	22.73	18.05	4	21.77	26.58	21.11
3	18.62	22.82	18.13	3	21.85	26.67	21.18
2	18.69	22.92	18.19	2	21.92	26.77	21.25
1	18.77	23.01	18.27	1	22.00	26.86	21.33
0	18.85	23.10	18.34	0	22.08	26.95	21.40
0.9729	18.92	23.19	18.41	0.9689	22.15	27.04	21.47
8	19.00	23.18	18.48	8	22.23	27.13	21.54
7	19.08	23.38	18.56	7	22.31	27.22	21.61
6	19.17	23.48	18.65	6	22.38	27.31	21.68
5	19.25	23.58	18.73	5	22.46	27.40	21.76
4	19.33	23.68	18.80	4	22.54	27.49	21.83
3	19.42	23.78	18.88	3	22.62	27.59	21.90
2	19.50	23.88	18.95	2	22.69	27.68	21.96
1	19.58	23.98	19.03	1	22.77	27.77	22.01
0	19.67	24.08	19.12	0	22.85	27.86	22.12

SPECIFIC GRAVITY AND PERCENTAGE OF ALCOHOL—(*Continued*).

Specific Gravity at 15.6° C.	Absolute Alcohol.			Specific Gravity at 15.6° C.	Absolute Alcohol.		
	Per Cent by Weight.	Per Cent by Volume.	Grams per 100 c.c.		Per Cent by Weight.	Per Cent by Volume.	Grams per 100 c.c.
0.9679	22.92	27.95	22.18	0.9470	36.00	42.95	34.09
8	23.00	28.04	22.26	0.9452	37.00	44.06	34.96
7	23.08	28.13	22.33	0.9434	38.00	45.16	35.85
6	23.15	28.22	22.40	0.9416	39.00	46.26	36.72
5	23.23	28.31	22.47	0.9396	40.00	47.35	37.58
4	23.31	28.41	22.54	0.9376	41.00	48.43	38.44
3	23.38	28.50	22.61	0.9356	42.00	49.50	39.30
2	23.46	28.59	22.69	0.9335	43.00	50.57	40.14
1	23.54	28.68	22.76	0.9314	44.00	51.63	40.97
0	23.62	28.77	22.83	0.9292	45.00	52.68	41.81
0.9669	23.69	28.86	22.90	0.9270	46.00	53.72	42.64
8	23.77	28.95	22.97	0.9248	47.00	54.76	43.47
7	23.85	29.04	23.05	0.9226	48.00	55.79	44.28
6	23.92	29.13	23.11	0.9204	49.00	56.82	45.09
5	24.00	29.22	23.19	0.9182	50.00	57.84	45.91
4	24.08	29.31	23.27	0.9159	51.00	58.85	46.71
3	24.15	29.40	23.33	0.9135	52.00	59.84	47.50
2	24.23	29.49	23.40	0.9113	53.00	60.85	48.29
1	24.31	29.58	23.48	0.9090	54.00	61.84	49.08
0	24.38	29.67	23.55	0.9069	55.00	62.84	49.88
0.9659	24.46	29.76	23.62	0.9047	56.00	63.82	50.66
8	24.54	29.86	23.70	0.9025	57.00	64.80	51.44
7	24.62	29.95	23.77	0.9001	58.00	65.77	52.21
6	24.69	30.04	23.84	0.8979	59.00	66.74	52.98
5	24.77	30.13	23.91	0.8956	60.00	67.69	53.74
4	24.85	30.22	23.99	0.8932	61.00	68.64	54.49
3	24.92	30.31	24.05	0.8908	62.00	69.58	55.23
2	25.00	30.40	24.12	0.8886	63.00	70.52	55.98
1	25.07	30.48	24.19	0.8863	64.00	71.46	56.72
0	25.14	30.57	24.26	0.8840	65.00	72.38	57.46
0.9638	26.00	31.57	25.06	0.8816	66.00	73.30	58.19
0.9623	27.00	32.73	25.98	0.8793	67.00	74.22	58.91
0.9609	28.00	33.89	26.90	0.8769	68.00	75.12	59.63
0.9593	29.00	35.05	27.82	0.8745	69.00	76.01	60.34
0.9578	30.00	36.20	28.73	0.8721	70.00	76.91	61.05
0.9560	31.00	37.34	29.63	0.8696	71.00	77.78	61.74
0.9544	32.00	38.47	30.53	0.8672	72.00	78.66	62.44
0.9528	33.00	39.61	31.43	0.8649	73.00	79.54	63.14
0.9511	34.00	40.74	32.32	0.8625	74.00	80.40	63.83
0.9490	35.00	41.84	33.21	0.8603	75.00	81.28	64.52

The British proof gallon at 15.6° C. has a specific gravity of 0.9198 and contains 49.24 per cent of absolute alcohol by weight and 57.06 per cent of absolute alcohol by volume.

SPECIFIC GRAVITY AND PERCENTAGE OF ALCOHOL—(*Continued*).

Specific Gravity at 15.6° C.	Absolute Alcohol.			Specific Gravity at 15.6° C.	Absolute Alcohol.		
	Per Cent by Weight.	Per Cent by Volume.	Grams per 100 c.c.		Per Cent by Weight.	Per Cent by Volume.	Grams per 100 c.c.
0.8581	76.00	82.16	65.22	0.8254	89.00	92.54	73.46
0.8557	77.00	83.00	65.89	0.8228	90.00	93.29	74.05
0.8533	78.00	83.85	66.56	0.8200	91.00	94.00	74.62
0.8508	79.00	84.67	67.21	0.8172	92.00	94.71	75.18
0.8483	80.00	85.49	67.86	0.8145	93.00	95.42	75.75
0.8459	81.00	86.32	68.52	0.8118	94.00	96.13	76.31
0.8434	82.00	87.12	69.16	0.8089	95.00	96.80	76.85
0.8408	83.00	87.91	69.79	0.8061	96.00	97.49	77.39
0.8382	84.00	88.70	70.41	0.8031	97.00	98.14	77.90
0.8357	85.00	89.49	71.03	0.8001	98.00	98.78	78.41
0.8331	86.00	90.26	71.65	0.7969	99.00	99.37	78.89
0.8305	87.00	91.02	72.25	0.7939	99.97	99.98	79.37
0.8279	88.00	91.78	72.86		Abs.	Alc.	
				0.7938	100.00	100.00	79.38

Tests for the Detection of Acetone, Methyl Alcohol, and Ethyl Alcohol.

For the detection of acetone, methyl alcohol, and ethyl alcohol the following tests will be found of value. They are taken from Vol. I of Mulliken's "Identification of Pure Organic Compounds," 1903.

Tests for the Detection of Acetone.

Mulliken gives the following properties and tests in his Vol. I, "Compounds of Order I," "Identification of Pure Organic Compounds," 1903:

" p. 141, Acetone.

GENUS VII, KETONES.

Division B, Liquid Ketones.

Boiling-point (C. °). Specific Gravity. Ketones Colorless and Liquid.

56.5   0.819$^{0}_{4}$ † Acetone, Me.CO.Me.

            * Miscible with aq. alcohol or ether. Odor alcoholic-ethereal

            ** Identify by test 711, p. 148."

** "Test 711 (p. 148). *Acetone.* (Properties tabulated on p. 141.)

"1. Apply the color reactions with sodium nitroprusside, described in Test 701, p. 146, bearing in mind that since nearly all soluble ketones and aldehydes give colorations of some kind when thus treated, the result will be significant only when

* aq. = water, or aqueous.

† Placed before the name of a compound indicates that the position of the latter in the analytical system has been experimentally determined in the author's laboratory.

the colors obtained correspond closely to the specified hues of the color standard " (as published with Mulliken's book).

"This procedure is to be especially recommended for the preliminary examination of aqueous solutions and distillates supposed to contain at least several per cent of acetone. In examining such a solution, simply substitute 2 c.c. of it for the same volume of the solution of definite concentration prescribed in the general directions. Very dilute solutions should first be somewhat concentrated by a rectification with the assistance of a small distilling-tower. If a solution contains only 1% of acetone, the color of 'portion a' will at first be yellow-orange (YO) instead of orange; while 'portion b,' with acetic acid, will give a very pale tint of red, RT3, instead of R RT1, which, after standing for twenty minutes, will fade to a tone of the same hue, but so pale as to be barely distinguishable.

"2. Place in a dry 6-inch test-tube two drops of the ketone and 0.4 c.c. of cold water. Add 0.4 c.c. of benzaldehyde, 2.0 c.c. of strong alcohol, and 0.5 c.c. of a 10 per cent aqueous sodium-hydroxide solution. Mix by shaking. Boil very gently over a small flame for one minute, counting the time from the moment when the mixture first actually boils. If no precipitate appears, cool and shake vigorously. Filter off the crystals * and wash with 2 c.c. of cold strong alcohol. Recrystallize from 2 c.c. of boiling alcohol. Cool, and if necessary shake until crystals appear. Filter. Wash with 1 c.c. of cold alcohol. Press on filter-paper or porous tile. Then transfer to a watch-glass and dry half an hour or longer at 100°. In taking the melting-point raise the temperature at the rate of about one degree in twenty seconds.

"The product formed in this test is dibenzylideneacetone $(C_6H_5 \cdot CH:CH)_2 \cdot CO$. It crystallizes in pale yellow lustrous plates which melt at 111°-112° (uncor.).

"*Observations on the Application of Procedure 2 to Aqueous Solutions of Acetone.* —If a solution contains less than 75% of acetone, take 1 c.c. instead of two drops as above directed, and add no water. The quantities of the other reagents and the method of procedure may be allowed to remain unchanged. The test has been used for solutions containing as little as 2% of acetone. But with solutions between 5% and 2%, cooling and shaking after heating frequently gives only an emulsion. The addition of 1 c.c. of strong cold alcohol and shaking will, in such cases, produce a crystalline precipitate, which can then be treated in the usual manner.

"If the quantity of crystals obtained from an acetone solution after the first filtration is small, wash with 1 c.c. of alcohol (instead of 2.0 c.c.), and recrystallize from 1 c.c. of boiling alcohol (instead of 2 c.c.). If no crystals then appear on cooling and shaking, add cold water (0.5 c.c.–1.0 c.c. is usually enough) until the solution becomes turbid. Shaking will then produce crystals. Wash these with 0.5 c.c. of cold alcohol (instead of 1 c.c.). Crystals thus obtained from dilute alcohol will be found to melt at 0.5°–1.5° lower than those from strong alcohol. It is, on the whole, advisable to concentrate very dilute acetone solutions by distillation rather than to test them by this method at very low concentrations.

"For the detection of traces of acetone by this method, see Vorländer, Hobohm B. 29, 1840."

---

* If the precipitate, instead of consisting of crystals, is an oil or pasty mass, the procedure given requires no modification. Such products usually become crystalline, either during the washing with alcohol, or upon the cooling of the solution prepared from the washed oil.

Tests for the Detection of Methyl Alcohol.

"Genus VIII, Alcohols.

Methyl Alcohol (p. 160).

Boiling-point (C. °).	Specific Gravity.	Alcohols Colorless and Liquid, with Specific Gravity less than 0.90 at 20°/4°.
66	$0.798^{15}/_{15}$	† Methyl Alcohol, Me.OH
		Miscible with aq. Odor alcoholic
		* Identify by Test 819, p. 171."

"* Test 819 (p. 171). *Methyl Alcohol.* (Properties tabulated on p. 160.)

"1. (Color reaction). Dissolve one drop of the alcohol in 3 c.c. of water in a 6-inch test-tube. Wind a piece of rather light copper wire around a lead-pencil, so that the closely coiled spiral shall form a cylinder 2 cm. in length, while 20 cm. of the wire is left unbent to serve as a handle. Oxidize the spiral superficially by holding it in the upper part of the flame of a Bunsen burner; and then, while still at a red heat, plunge it into the alcoholic solution. (This treatment oxidizes a portion of the methyl alcohol to formic aldehyde.) Withdraw the spiral immediately and cool the test-tube with running water. Repeat the oxidation of the solution twice by the method given. Add one or two drops of 0.5 per cent aqueous solution of resorcin. Pour the mixture slowly into a second inclined test-tube containing 3–5 c.c. of pure concentrated sulphuric acid. The procedure and the phenomena in the test from this point on are the same as described in the latter part of Test 114–1 for formic aldehyde.

"Many methyl ethers and methyl esters that are sufficiently soluble in water to be tested by this method, and tertiary butyl alcohol, show the same behavior as methyl alcohol. Remember that the actual separation of bright-red solid flocks from the aqueous layer above the sulphuric acid after standing is essential to the proof that methyl alcohol is present.

"Many compounds besides those mentioned give traces of formic aldehyde when oxidized by a hot copper wire, but not enough to give a separation of the characteristic flocks. Test 114–2 for formic aldehyde will often show the presence of these traces, and therefore must not be substituted for Test 114–1. Ethyl, propyl, isopropyl, butyl, isobutyl, hexyl, and allyl alcohols, ethyl ether, and acetone give strong yellow, amber, ocherous, or dirty-greenish colorations; and, if present in relatively large quantities in mixtures containing methyl alcohol, will interfere with its detection by destroying the purity of color required in the flocks.

"Weak aqueous solutions suspected to contain methyl alcohol may be oxidized directly with the copper wire and then tested with resorcin in the usual manner, solutions much weaker than the one recommended in the procedure giving entirely satisfactory results.

"*In examining organic mixtures for methyl alcohol* the precautions mentioned in the following paragraphs should be observed:

"(a) Use for the test only that part of any mixture that can be completely distilled between 50° and 100°, and which, after distillation, gives a clear colorless solution when diluted with several volumes of water.

"(b) Make a blank experiment before oxidation with the copper spiral, by pouring 2 c.c. of a clear aqueous distillate of the proper boiling-point, to which one drop of 0.5 per cent resorcin solution has been added, so as to form a layer upon concentrated sulphuric acid in a test-tube. If a precipitate or strongly colored ring makes its appearance, the solution is not suitable for testing without preliminary treatment.

"(c) Do not test by this method any solution that is suspected to contain phenols or organic bases.

"* 2. Convert four drops of the alcohol into its 3, 5-dinitrobenzoate by the procedure detailed in the first paragraph of Test 814-1 for ethyl alcohol.

"Boil the reaction product with 12 c.c. of dilute ethyl alcohol (3:1). Cool, shake, allow to stand for a minute or two, and filter. Wash with 2 c.c. strong cold alcohol. Recrystallize from 12 c.c. of boiling dilute alcohol (3:1). Cool, shake, and allow to stand for a minute or two, and filter. Wash the crystals with 2 c.c. of cold strong alcohol. Dry at a temperature not above 100° and determine the melting-point.

"The crystalline methyl dinitrobenzoate obtained in this test melts at 107.5° (uncor.).

"(J) (p. 114). *Methyl Alcohol and other Lower Fatty Alcohols and Ketones.*—If the distillate (obtained as directed) is a clear solution without layers, and is odorless or has a mild alcoholic odor, remove 2 c.c., oxidize with a hot copper spiral, and examine for methyl alcohol by Specific Test 819. If no colored ring whatever appears in this test, the distillate does not contain any volatile alcohol provided for in this method or acetone; and unless some non-volatile alcohol can be separated from the salts remaining in the distilling-flask, the compound under examination must next be sought among the species of Genus VI, Acid Anhydrides and Lactones."

* The crystalline methyl 3, 5-dinitrobenzoate described suggests a hint worthy of a trial to see if such compound can furnish a quantitative method for estimating methyl alcohol, first purifying it by a preliminary treatment.

Tests for the Detection of Ethyl Alcohol.

"GENUS VIII, ALCOHOLS.

Ethyl Alcohol (p. 161).

Boiling-point (C. °).	Specific Gravity.	Alcohols, Colorless and Liquid, with Specific Gravity less than 0.90 at 20°/4°.
78.4	0.794$^{15.5}/_{15.5}$	† Ethyl Alcohol, Et.OH. Odor alcoholic Miscible with aq. ** Identify with Test 814, p. 168.

** "Test 814 (p. 168). *Ethyl Alcohol.* (Properties tabulated on p. 161.)

"The ready formation of iodoform at 50°-60°—but not in the cold—in Test 801 is the most convenient preliminary test for ethyl alcohol. The following very satisfactory confirmatory test is, of course, applicable only to a nearly pure alcohol containing not more than about 10 per cent of water. The same general procedure

† Placed before the name of a compound indicates that the position of the latter in the analytical system has been experimentally determined in the author's laboratory. The "specific descriptions" for such compounds are also based, for the most part, on experimentally verified data.

with slight modifications, may be used in the identification of many of the homologues of ethyl alcohol.

"1. Heat together gently in a 3-inch test-tube held over a small flame 0.15 grm. of 3, 5-dinitrobenzoic acid (see foot-note) and 0.20 grm. of phosphorus pentachloride.

NOTE.—This new reagent is listed by C. A F. Kahlbaum of Berlin at 8 marks per 100 grms., and may be obtained in New York from Eimer & Amend. It may also be readily prepared in the laboratory from benzoic acid.

When signs of chemical action are seen, remove the heat for a few seconds. Then heat again, boiling the liquefied mixture *very gently* for one minute. Pour out on a very small watch-glass and allow to solidify. As soon as solidification occurs remove the liquid phosphorus oxychloride with which the crystalline mass is impregnated by rubbing the latter between two small pieces of porous tile. Place the powder in a dry 5- or 6-inch test-tube. Allow four drops of the alcohol to fall upon it, and then stopper the tube tightly without delay." When employing this procedure for the propyl and butyl alcohols use six drops of the alcohol instead of four; for the alcohol must always be present in moderate excess. "Immerse the lower part of the test-tube in water having a temperature of 75°–85°. Shake gently and continue the heating for ten minutes.

"To purify the ester produced in the reaction crush any hard lumps that may form when the mixture cools with a stirring-rod, and boil gently with 15 c.c. of methyl alcohol (2.1) until all is dissolved, or for a minute or two." In testing for other alcohols than ethyl, all directions for the use of the solvent in this paragraph must be modified as elsewhere specified. *Cf.* tests for methyl, propyl, butyl, and isobutyl alcohols. "Filter boiling hot if the solution is not clear. Cool. Shake and filter. Wash with 3 c.c. cold methyl alcohol (2:1). Recrystallize from 9 c.c. of boiling methyl alcohol (2:1). Wash with 2 c.c. of the same solvent. Spread out the product on a piece of tile. Allow to become air-dry, and determine the melting-point.

"* Ethyl 3, 5-dinitrobenzoate, the product in this test crystallizes in white needles melting at 92°–93° (uncor.)."

The Denatured Alcohol Motor for Laboratory Purposes.—In connection with very small power capacities for laboratory purposes it is of interest to know that an alcohol motor for such work can be supplied. In Fig. 66 is shown such a motor.

These motors are operated by the expansive force of hot air. They are made in a number of sizes (six in all) using respectively from 3 to 10 pints of denatured alcohol per hour, and are used for very light work, like running a fan, stirrer, etc., in the laboratory. These motors can also be operated with gas. They oocupy a space of about $9\frac{1}{2} \times 18$ inches and run at 400 to 500 revolutions per minute. The fly-

---

* The crystalline ethyl 3, 5-dinitrobenzoate described suggests a hint worthy of a trial to see if such compound can furnish a quantitative method for estimating ethyl alcohol, first purifying it by a preliminary treatment.

wheel is 6 inches in diameter; belt pulleys 1¼, 2, and 3 inches in diameter. Where gas is not obtainable for these little motors, denatured alcohol

Fig. 66.—Hot-air Motor driven by Denatured Alcohol.
(Furnished by Eimer & Amend, New York.)

offers quite a satisfactory fuel solution for them, and may be preferred to gas for such intermittent uses of small power.

CHAPTER V.

THE COST OF ALCOHOL AND OF ALCOHOL-DISTILLING PLANTS.

Cost of Alcohol from Different Raw Materials. By-products in the Distillation of Alcohol. Fusel-oil. The Composition of Fusel-oil. The Value of the Slop or Spent Wash. The Manufacture of (Ethyl) Alcohol from Sawdust. Ethyl Chloride as a Refrigerant. Plan of Distillery for Distilling Alcohol from Corn. Cost of Buildings for Alcohol-distilling Plants. Cost of Alcohol-distilling Plants. Cost of Commercial Wood Alcohol (Methyl Alcohol)

Cost of Alcohol from Different Raw Materials.—*Cost of Alcohol from Corn.*—In calculating the cost of alcohol from corn in the United States the table on p. 170,* giving the corn crop for 1905, will be of interest.

Taking the cost of corn in the West at 40 cents per bushel and the yield of alcohol from one bushel of corn at five gallons of proof spirits, we have 8 cents as the cost of one gallon of proof spirits.

For commercial 95 per cent alcohol, or 190° proof, this cost would be $1.9 \times 8 = 15.2$ cents per gallon for the material alone at the distillery. To this cost must be added the manufacturing cost, the cost of the package or barrel, the freight charges, and the cost of the denaturing, which added charges would probably bring such cost to about 30 cents per gallon. With the further addition of the costs of distribution and the profits to be considered it would appear that completely denatured alcohol of 95 per cent strength, or 190° proof, would retail in the vicinity of about 40 cents per gallon.

Cost of Alcohol from Molasses.—As shown in Chapter II, the yield of alcohol from one gallon of the base molasses, from the manufacture of cane-sugar, is about 0.85 gallon of proof spirit in the most modern distilleries. At 7 cents per gallon for such molasses, one gallon of proof spirit costs $0.0823, and one gallon of 190° proof alcohol therefore costs $0.0823 \times 1.9 = 15.64$ cents, which is about the same cost for material alone as in the case of corn at 40 cents per bushel for material alone.

---

* Furnished by U. S. Dept. of Agriculture.

TABLE SHOWING THE CORN CROP OF 1905 IN THE UNITED STATES.

States and Territories.	Corn.				
	Acreage.	Yield per Acre.	Production.	Price per Bushel.	Total Farm Value.
	Acres.	Bush.	Bushels.	Cents.	Dollars.
Maine..............	13,000	34.3	445,900	69	307,671
New Hampshire......	27,045	37.0	1,000,665	69	690,459
Vermont............	58,238	34.7	2,020,859	68	1,374,184
Massachusetts........	44,799	37.5	1,679,962	70	1,175,973
Rhode Island........	10,011	32.5	325,358	71	231,004
Connecticut..........	55,595	42.7	2,373,906	71	1,685,473
New York...........	613,103	31.5	19,312,744	61	11,780,774
New Jersey..........	277,749	35.8	9,943,414	55	5,468,878
Pennsylvania........	1,441,797	38.9	56,085,903	54	30,286,388
Delaware...........	196,472	30.4	5,972,749	47	2,807,192
Maryland...........	628,795	36.9	23,202,536	48	11,137,217
Virginia............	1,859,610	23.4	43,514,874	53	23,062,883
North Carolina.......	2,704,772	13.9	37,596,331	64	24,061,652
South Carolina.......	1,878,978	10.9	20,480,860	74	15,155,836
Georgia.............	4,295,924	11.0	47,255,164	70	33,078,615
Florida.............	645,416	10.1	6,518,702	66	4,302,343
Alabama............	2,903,483	14.8	42,971,548	64	27,501,791
Mississippi..........	2,099,830	14.3	30,027,569	65	19,517,920
Louisiana...........	1,424,562	13.7	19,516,499	61	11,905,064
Texas..............	6,532,695	21.3	139,146,404	49	68,181,738
Arkansas...........	2,215,245	17.3	38,323,738	55	21,078,056
Tennessee...........	3,138,533	24.6	77,207,912	50	38,603,956
West Virginia........	765,541	29.8	22,813,122	53	12,090,955
Kentucky...........	3,195,072	29.7	94,893,638	43	40,804,264
Ohio...............	2,973,529	37.8	112,399,396	43	48,331,740
Michigan............	1,228,704	34.0	41,775,936	46	19,216,931
Indiana.............	4,597,804	40.7	187,130,623	38	71,109,637
Illinois.............	9,616,886	39.8	382,752,063	38	145,445,784
Wisconsin...........	1,473,613	37.6	55,407,849	42	23,271,297
Minnesota...........	1,507,614	32.5	48,997,455	33	16,169,160
Iowa...............	8,767,597	34.8	305,112,376	34	103,738,208
Missouri............	6,014,639	33.8	203,294,798	37	75,219,075
Kansas.............	6,977,467	27.7	193,275,836	33	63,781,026
Nebraska...........	8,035,115	32.8	263,551,772	32	84,336,567
South Dakota........	1,623,105	31.8	51,614,739	31	16,000,569
North Dakota........	89,405	27.5	2,458,638	36	885,110
Montana............	3,941	19.4	76,455	68	51,989
Wyoming............	2,107	26.9	56,678	75	42,508
Colorado............	116,659	23.8	2,776,484	47	1,304,947
New Mexico.........	39,423	25.3	997,402	69	688,207
Arizona.............	7,614	27.0	205,578	97	199,411
Utah...............	11,353	36.2	410,979	70	287,685
Nevada.............	....	......	....	......	....
Idaho..............	5,506	27.2	149,763	66	98,844
Washington..........	10,796	24.2	261,263	60	156,758
Oregon.............	17,556	23.0	403,788	59	238,235
California...........	56,592	32.0	1,810,944	76	1,376,317
Oklahoma.	1,902,948	25.3	48,144,584	32	15,406,267
Indian Territory......	1,905,131	32.7	62,297,784	37	23,050 180
United States......	94,011,369	28.8	2,707,993,540	41.2	1116,696,738

Cost of Alcohol from Potatoes.—Before considering this cost we call attention to the view shown in Fig. 67 of a scene representing harvesting potatoes near Greeley, Colorado. To return we may say that in Germany, where alcohol for industrial purposes is very largely made from potatoes, the yield of absolute alcohol (or 200° U. S. proof) is one gallon from 1.26 bushels of potatoes. In calculating at what price potatoes can be used for the making of industrial alcohol in the United States, it would appear that if the price is based on the cost, for materials alone, of alcohol from corn at 40 cents per bushel it would necessitate a price

Fig. 67.—Harvesting Potatoes on the Ranch of F. H. Badger, near Greeley, Colorado. (See Frontispiece.)

of from 12 to 14 cents per bushel for such potatoes. This is arrived at as follows: 1 bushel corn yields 5 gallons of proof spirits, 1.26 bushels of potatoes yield 2 gallons proof spirits, and a yield of 5 gallons of proof spirits requires 3.15 bushels of potatoes. In the case of corn at 40 cents per bushel, the price paid for such potatoes per bushel for making denatured alcohol could only be $\frac{40}{3.15}$, or about 13 cents per bushel. As to the availability of such cheap potatoes (the usual price in car-load lots at Chicago is fully 25 cents per bushel) the following data are given: In determining the price of potatoes the cost to the farmer for raising them is important. In Fig. 67 is shown a view entitled "Harvesting Potatoes on the Ranch of F. H. Badger, near Greeley, Colorado."

Concerning the cost per bushel for raising potatoes to the farmer

Mr. F. H. Badger writes the author as follows: "It costs the farmer 20 to 30 cents per bushel to raise potatoes, perhaps 25 cents per bushel will be about the average cost. The farmer will sell as first-class, marketable potatoes from 65 per cent to 90 per cent, the best fields running as high as 95 per cent. A very small amount is fed to cattle and pigs, as the well-shaped little potatoes are planted, and the culls are sold to the starch factories for 12 cents a bushel. Greeley, Colorado, is the centre of a potato district that raises about 8,000,000 bushels per annum, and if we take as an average 10 per cent of culls we will have some 800,000 bushels of cheap potatoes. The bulk of our potatoes are sorted up in the dug-out and the culls taken from the dug-out to the starch factory."

Messrs. Albert Miller & Co., Chicago, Illinois, one of the largest wholesale dealers in potatoes in this country, inform the author that "in the West the farmers figure that it costs, in an average season, about 10 to 12 cents per bushel to grow and load potatoes.

"We can contract them here at about 25 cents per bushel in almost any season. In fact we could contract almost any amount at this price, or might do it a little less if we took them field run. . . . There is no average price that strach factories pay. It depends of course upon conditions. When potatoes are scrace and high they use the culls. When they are cheap they buy them field run. As a rule they cannot afford to pay over 20 cents per bushel.

"The proportion of the potato crop that the farmer uses is a question that is impossible to answer. It would depend of course upon how much he raised. Some farmers will grow four or five acres and some one hundred acres."

Regarding the raising of potatoes in Maine the author is informed that the crop for 1905 in Aroostook County was approximately 13,000,000 bushels. The amount sold to the starch factories and used on the farm constitutes about 15 per cent of the crop.

The starch factories pay from 25 cents to 50 cents per barrel of 165 lbs. net for potatoes run of field. A bushel of potatoes weighs 60 lbs., making this average price 13.6 cents per bushel run of field. The average cost to the farmer for raising potatoes is about 25 cents per bushel. It is thus seen that the cost of potatoes at present is too high for their economical use in the manufacture of denatured or industrial alcohol.

It is of great interest to consider the conditions in Germany relative to this subject, and from the report of the U. S. Consul-General, Alexander M. Thackara, Berlin, Germany, Sept. 10, 1906, we learn that "in the campaign year 1904–5 the average price of potatoes was 42.58

mark ($10.13) per 1000 kilograms (2204.6 pounds) or 27.6 cents per bushel.

"The crop for 1905 was 1,775,579,073 bushels of 60 pounds each, an average of 217 bushels to the acre. With the exception of 1901 this crop exceeds all previous years. The value of this crop of 1905 was $490,059,948.

"In 1904 the potato crop of the United States was placed at 332,830,300 bushels, of a farm value of $150,673,392, or 45.2 cents per bushel.

"According to Dr. W. Behrens, one of Germany's experts, in 1901, out of the 26,250,000 hectares (65,000,000 acres) of arable land, 3,300,000 hectares (8,100,000 acres), or 12½ per cent, were planted in potatoes.

"The doctor now claims that Germany plants more potatoes in proportion to its area and number of inhabitants than any other civilized country.

"About 50 per cent of the potato crop in Germany may be safely estimated is used for human food purposes. The most important ingredient in potatoes—starch—is used for manufacturing alcohol and also pure starch and its products.

"The following table shows the production of alcohol in Germany for the past five campaign years and the materials from which the spirit was distilled.

"The figures show very clearly the great extent to which potatoes are used in the German alcohol distilleries.

"The figures represent hectolitres (1 hectolitre = 26.417 gallons)."

TABLE SHOWING PRODUCTION OF ALCOHOL IN GERMANY FOR THE PAST FIVE CAMPAIGN YEARS AND MATERIALS FROM WHICH THE SPIRIT WAS DISTILLED.

Materials.	1900–1901.	1901–2.	1902–3.	1903–4.	1904–5.
Potatoes.	3,302,780	3,519,171	2,649,952	3,045,605	2,877,344
Grain.	613,749	594,177	625,785	692,483	765,727
Molasses.	83,797	88,728	88,124	92,838	107,950
Others.	51,534	36,832	19,073	33,373	36,431
Total.	4,051,860	4,238,908	3,382,934	3,854,299	3,787,452
Gallons.	107,038,175	111,979,432	89,367,127	101,819,197	100,053,300

"In all the statistics in this report the gallon, unless specially mentioned otherwise, refers to the United States gallon of 231 cubic inches of pure alcohol."

As above shown, potatoes are very largely used for the production of alcohol in Germany. It would be of much importance to determine just exactly what is the cost of such production. Regarding this interesting phase of the subject, this report of Mr. Thackara states that "I have been unable to obtain satisfactory data regarding the cost of production of alcohol from the different materials. It depends upon many different conditions: the size of the distillery, the efficiency of the apparatus, and the methods used, upon whether or not the owners of the plants have other industries connected with them, upon the disposition which is made of the by-products, etc."

Cost of Alcohol from Sweet Potatoes.—*In the Azores the actual yield of absolute alcohol from 100 kilograms (220 pounds) of sweet potatoes is 10 to 12 liters (an average of 11.62 quarts as a liter=1.056 quarts). A bushel of sweet potatoes weighs 54 pounds and costs approximately 25 cents to 35 cents at the farm, run of field, i.e. small and large. On the above figures a bushel would yield about 1.5 gallons of U. S. proof spirits and would cost about 20 cents per gallon for the material alone. As this is an increase of about one third in cost as compared with corn at 40 cents per bushel for materials alone, it is seen that sweet potatoes are not an economical source for industrial alcohol. As a result of the methods used by the distillery here quoted, there was finally obtained from 90 to 95 per cent of pure alcohol, and 5 to 10 per cent of the impure quality for industrial uses, although about 600 per cent of pure alcohol and 40 per cent of the somewhat impure could be made if desired. The two distilleries formerly managed by M. Durot have been closed, as he writes, for three years. The closing down of this industry is a real disaster for the agricultural interests of this island according to M. Durot, as the culture of the sweet potato had been a source of revenue to the island for twenty years.

The author has been told that the cultivation of sugar-beets has now been introduced as a source of sugar and will largely replace the cultivation of the sweet potatoes.

Cost of Alcohol from Sugar-beets.—Taking the yield of 180° proof alcohol from sugar-beets in France from the example given in Chapter II we have a yield of 1 hectolitre (26.41 gallons) of 180° proof alcohol from 4400 lbs. or 2.2 tons of sugar-beets. At $5.00 per ton in the United States this is $11.00 cost, for materials alone, for this yield from sugar-beets, or a cost of about 42 cents per gallon for the 180° proof alcohol.

As the average yield of sugar per short ton of beets in the United

---

* Statement furnished the author by M. S. Durot, manager of a sweet-potato distillery at Isle de Terceira, Azores.

States is about 250 pounds, the yield of sugar is therefore about 12½ per cent, or about one fifth more than in case of the above French figures. This however would only lower the above cost of the alcohol to about 35 cents per gallon, based on the costs of the beets alone. Sugar-beets are therefore not an economical source of alcohol in the United States and cannot hope to compete with corn and with cane-molasses. About 50 pounds of beet-molasses are usually obtained in sugar-houses per ton of sugar. The greater part of such molasses is used as a cattle food, being mixed and dried with beet pulp, millers' refuse, chopped hay or straw, and other absorbent materials and marketed under the trade names of "sucrene," "blomo," etc. The feeding value of beet pulp, from making sugar, as compared with grain, has been placed at $4.00 per ton. In the manufacture of beet-sugar the abolition of the molasses is a very important point and continual experiments are made in this direction. Hence for the above reasons and because the beet-sugar industry is now successfully established in this country, the sugar-beet will not be utilized for the manufacture of alcohol in the United States.

By-products in the Distillation of Alcohol.—*Fusel-oil.*—In the fermented mash or wash liquor there are formed, as a result of the fermentation, a number of substances, all of which possess different boiling-points. In addition to the alcohol and water present, such a liquor contains fusel-oil. This is not a definite substance, but is a complex mixture, and varies somewhat in composition, according to the nature of the raw material from which the alcohol is fermented and the manner of fermentation used. To give an approximate idea of its composition, we may mention that it usually contains a large percentage of amyl alcohol and isoamyl alcohol, together with small amounts of compound ethers, higher alcohols, and small percentages of free fatty acids and esters.

* Karl Windisch gives the composition of 1 kilogram of fusel-oil, freed from water and ethyl alcohol, from potatoes as—

Normal propyl alcohol	68.54 gm.
Isobutyl alcohol	243.50 "
Amyl alcohols	687.60 "
Free fatty acids	0.11 "
Fatty acid ester	0.20 "
Furfurol and bases	0.05 "

* Arbeiten aus dem Kaiserlichen Gesundheitsamt, 1892, Bd. 8.

In 100 parts of free acids and acid esters from potato fusel-oil are contained—

Capric acid.	36	parts
Pelargonic acid	12	"
Caprylic acid.	32	"
Caproic acid.	14	"
Butyric acid	0.5	"
Acetic acid.	3.5	"

1 kilogram of fusel-oil from corn contains—

Normal propyl alcohol.	36.90	gm.
Isobutyl alcohol.	157.60	"
Amyl alcohols.	758.50	"
Hexyl alcohol.	1.33	"
Free fatty acids.	1.60	"
Fatty acid esters.	3.05	"
Terpenes.	0.33	"
Terpene hydrate.	0.48	"
Furfurol, bases, and heptyl alcohol.	0.21	"

In 100 parts by weight of the free acids and acid esters from corn fusel-oil are contained—

	Free Fatty Acids.	Fatty Acid Esters.
Capric acid.	44.1	40.7
Pelargonic acid.	12.9	14.2
Caprylic acid.	26.7	34.8
Caproic acid.	13.2	9.6
Butyric acid.	0.4	0.4
Acetic acid.	2.7	0.3

The terpene $C_{10}H_{16}$, as well as the terpene hydrate $C_{10}H_{18}O$, possesses even in extremely diluted condition the characteristic corn-brandy odor and contributes very essentially to the aroma of corn brandy. An identification of this particular terpene with any of the other known terpenes has not yet been effected, but this terpene appears to resemble phillandrene. The fusel-oil from potatoes, according to Kruis and Raymann, contains in one kilogram—

Ethyl alcohol.	48.88%
Normal propyl alcohol.	0.85%
Isobutyl alcohol.	4.19%
Amyl alcohol.	942.42%
Hexyl alcohol.	0.19%
Caprylic acid—ethyl ester.	0.26%
" " —amyl ester.	1.00%
Caprinic acid— " "	0.66%
Residue not determined.	1.45%

It may further be said that the researches of Pasteur, Le Bel, and Ley have proved that the amyl alcohol of fusel-oil really consists of a mixture of two primary amyl alcohols of nearly identical boiling-points and specific gravities. One of these (isobutyl carbinol) is optically inactive, but the other secondary butyl carbinol has the property of rotating the plane of a polarized ray of light to the left. For further study of fusel-oil the reader is referred to the authorities mentioned, as well as to Sorel's Rectification de L'Alcohol and to E. Houriers' Manual de la Distillation. Also to Bull. No. 65, U. S. Department of Agriculture, A. O. A. C., to Leach's Food Inspection and Analysis, and Maercker-Delbruck's Handbuch der Spiritusfabrikation, 1903, for methods and tests for the determination of fusel-oil.

Rabuteau's frequently cited statement that fusel-oil contains isopropyl alcohol has been refuted by later investigators.

The Value of the Slop or Spent Wash.—Any by-products of value which can be obtained in the distillation of alcohol will, of course, lower the initial cost of the alcohol, and hence could tend to lower the selling price of denatured alcohol.

The usual production of the valuable by-product, fusel-oil, has already been mentioned, and at the present time there are also the values of the residues from the distillation of corn and molasses to consider, as these will be the principal raw materials for the manufacture of alcohol at least for some time to come.

In Europe potash residues from the molasses used for distilling purposes are used extensively as manure. There is not enough potash in the residue from sugar-cane molasses to make it very valuable for this purpose. Inquiry reveals the fact that the residue from distilling cane-sugar molasses in the United States has very little value. It is difficult to arrive at an estimate of the value of the residue from the distillation in the case of corn for the purposes of a cattle food. All the refuse of the glucose factories and distilleries is used for feeding stuff, either directly or after drying, but figures are not readily available as to its worth for such purposes.

* An average of several analyses from distillers' grains shows:

Ash................................... 2.13 per cent.
Crude fibre........................... 15.50 " "
    " protein........................ 34.29 " "
    " fat............................ 10.51 " "
Pentosans............................. 23.91 " "
Cellulose, starch, and undetermined... 13.60 " "

* From Bureau of Chemistry, U. S. Department of Agriculture.

When properly dried and cured this is a very valuable concentrated food, containing a large amount of protein and fat, the two most expensive components of a ration from the feeder's standpoint.

In the Water Supply and Irrigation Paper, No. 179, Series L, Quality of Water, 14, of the Department of the Interior, United States Geological Survey, Charles T. Walcott, Director, are given, under the title "Prevention of Stream Pollution by Distillery Refuse," some very interesting and important facts as to the value of distillers' grains for a feeding-stuff, based on the investigations of Herman Stabler at Lynchburg, Ohio, an outline of which is here given. A plant for the evaporation of slop was installed at the Lynchburg distillery late in the autumn of 1905.

After twice screening the slop by brass screens, it was pumped to be filtered in two 40-plate presses. Each press is 20 feet in length and 3 feet in diameter and has a net filtering area of 230 square feet. The thin slop from both screens is received in large wooden tanks from which it is pumped to the evaporator.

The evaporating apparatus is of chief importance and will therefore be described in some detail. The machine used is the Hoffman-Ahlers triple-effect vacuum evaporator, a view of which is shown in Fig. 68. Each effect consists essentially of two chambers connected by four large pipes, and also by a great number of tubes, placed within the steam-chamber.

A sectional view of the arrangement of these tubes in the steam-chambers is shown, in the middle effect, in Fig. 68. This apparatus is capable of treating more than 40,000 gallons of the thin slop in twenty hours (guaranteed capacity 2700 gallons per hour) and reducing it 88 to 90 per cent in volume. It is now operated with 40 pounds of steam pressure in the first effect, a 3- or 4-inch vacuum in the second effect, and a 26-inch vacuum in the third effect. This apparatus costs, in place, $16,000.

The magma from the evaporator is added to the feed from the filter-presses, and the two are thoroughly mixed by passing through a screw-conveyer 1 foot in diameter and 40 feet in length. It is then dried by passing through a direct-heat rotary drier 40 feet in length and 6 feet in diameter and a steam rotary drier 20 feet in length and 6 feet in diameter.

The product of these machines is placed in sacks for shipment. The installation at Lynchburg proves that the cost figures can be reduced in the main by about 25 per cent, so that even under pioneer and imperfect conditions a substantial profit upon the investment is being made. The new feed is sweeter and has a more attractive odor. It has a higher specific gravity. Although chemical analysis shows that the protein and

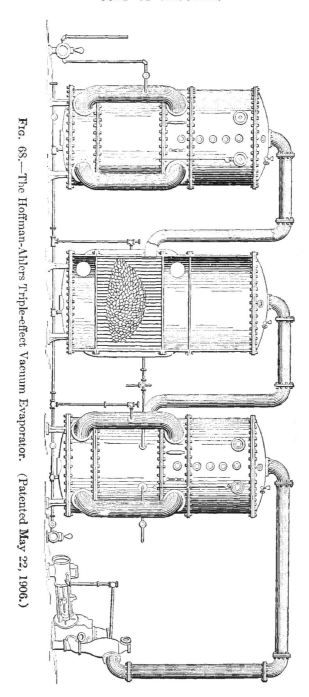

FIG. 68.—The Hoffman-Ahlers Triple-effect Vacuum Evaporator. (Patented May 22, 1906.)

fat content for corn and the fat content for rye are slightly decreased, this decrease is more than made up by the increased digestibility of the other constituents.

The paper quoted also contains the results of a series of chemical analyses made of these cattle-feed grains and of concentrated corn and rye slop by A. Lasché, Milwaukee, Wis.

In the summary of these results the paper states that about 45 gallons of waste slop liquor are discharged for each bushel of grain mashed, and that this liquor contains approximately 5 per cent (by weight) of solid matter, nearly half of which is held in solution. Also that stream pollution may be wholly avoided by means of evaporation recovery of cattle-feed grains from the slops. As applied to a distillery using daily 1750 bushels of corn for a season of 150 days and 1392 bushels of rye for a season of 50 days the following data regarding the process may be accepted as approximate:

(a) Cost of complete recovery plant........................ $52,000
(b) Annual profit over operating expenses on investment in complete plant for evaporation recovery, per cent. 73
(c) Cost of additional plant to add evaporation to recovery by screening...................................... $40,000
(d) Annual profit over operating expenses afforded by increased product, based on investment in additional plant to add evaporation to recovery by screening, per cent. 34

Ordinarily from 10 to 40 per cent of the slop cannot be profitably used and is run to waste. The trial at Lynchburg, Ohio, substantiates all the claims made for it and indicates that it will prove to be a rather greater source of profit than had been expected.

In connection with the drying of distillery slop or spent grains the Biles rotary steam drier and press may be mentioned. A view of these machines is shown in Fig. 69, p. 181, as installed in a one-story house. This press, with gradual low pressure, is claimed to deliver the feed at from 55 to 60 per cent moisture, the drying being done by either the Biles steam or direct-heat drier.

While there has been a considerable use of such slop in the past for cattle-feeding purposes, it would appear that this improved method, which has been described by Herman Stabler, offers greatly increased advantages and possibilities along these lines.

A short description of the composition of fusel-oil is here given. It is hoped to treat this important subject in a more extended manner in a later edition.

*The Manufacture of Ethyl Alcohol from Sawdust.—The conversion of the cellulose of sawdust or similar material into glucose and the alcoholic fermentation of this sugar have been frequently attempted on a large scale but accomplished only recently through the operation of methods devised largely by Claassen.

In ordinary soft woods we have a mixture of true cellulose and oxycelluloses, the latter of which may be rather easily hydrolyzed and converted into sugar. By the Claassen process this is accomplished by heating sawdust with sulphurous acid under pressure in large lead-lined

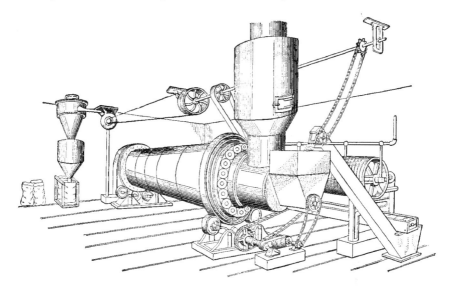

FIG. 69.—The Biles Rotary Steam Drier and Press.

drums. At the end of the operation on opening a valve the main portion of the sulphurous acid escapes and may be absorbed in water to be used in a second operation. This is perhaps the most important feature of the process, since in all the older processes the removal of the hydrochloric or sulphuric acid employed as a converting agent was found to be very difficult in practice and too expensive to admit of actual working. The Claassen process was first worked in America by the Lignin Inversion Company in an experimental plant at Chicago. In this plant it was found that a ton of dry pine sawdust would yield about 20 per cent of sugar, or about 400 pounds, three fourths of which was readily fermentible with yeast. Twenty-five gallons of 188°

---

* The author is indebted for this article to Prof. J. H. Long of the Northwestern University, Chicago, Ill.

alcohol (94 per cent by volume) was found to be a good working yield.

Following the demonstrations in this experimental plant the Claassen Lignin Company was organized to work the process on the commercial scale. A plant was built at Hattiesburg, Mississippi, in an important lumber region, and after much delay on account of defective machinery was brought finally to the condition of working efficiency.

A considerable quantity of high-grade ethyl alcohol has been produced and put on the market. The operating company seems to be convinced that the process can be worked at a profit. From latest reports it appears that the plant is being enlarged and that a new one is to be built on the Pacific Coast.

The alcohol secured in this process is of high grade and practically free from by-products occurring when certain other materials are worked up. The sawdust which is not converted into sugar is left in a condition for easy compression into briquettes, for direct use or conversion into charcoal.

The practical difficulties in the working of this Claassen process are largely physical, as the chemical conversion and fermentation seems to be simple enough. The most trouble has been encountered in the extraction of the treated sawdust so as to secure the sugar for fermentation. Several types of extraction batteries were tried before success was reached; experience in the beet-sugar extraction seemed to be of little value here, but at last accounts the difficulties had been overcome, and nothing seems to stand in the way of ultimate success in this new industry.

The available supply of raw material is enormous, and saving this may have some effect on the lumber industries.

Ethyl Chloride as a Refrigerant.—One of the many uses of alcohol that have been proposed is the manufacture of ethyl chloride to be used as a refrigerant.

On this subject Prof. John H. Long of the Northwestern University, Chicago, Ill., writes the author under date of August 9, 1906, as follows: "Some years ago I was very much interested in a plant used to cool a warehouse in Chicago in which ethyl chloride was the expanding agent. The warehouse was in the wholesale market district and was used for eggs, butter, poultry, etc.

" The refrigerator was successful, but the first cost of material was then high, as a relatively large amount had to be used: the chief advantage in the process was in the ease of recovery by compression. My connection with the matter was merely as consulting chemist.

"It was hoped by the people interested in this project to perfect a plant to be used in meat and fruit cars, the idea being to use a storage-cylinder and compression-pump in each individual car. The motion of the car-axle worked the pump. This worked all right as long as the car was moving, but if side-tracked some hours the temperature ran up. I have always thought the ethyl-chloride process worthy of more experimentation."

Plan of 200-bushel Daily Capacity Distillery.—It was intended to have published the plans for a 5000-bushel distillery, that is, a plant having a daily capacity of 5000 bushels of corn, for the manufacture of alcohol. It has been found necessary to postpone the preparation of these plans until a later edition of this book. Such a model plant is shown in Fig. 73, p. 187, and a careful inspection of the view shown in this cut will give a very good idea of the size, construction, and arrangement of an alcohol plant of the most modern type. In default of the plans mentioned above we present the plan of a 200-bushel daily capacity distillery, which will also serve to give quite a good idea, as the principle is the same, of the plan and arrangements in such a plant, the equipment, etc., for the production of high-proof alcohol. These plans were furnished by the Hoffman-Ahlers Co., Cincinnati, Ohio.

On the three following pages are shown the plans, as mentioned above, for a small distillery of a daily capacity of 200 bushels, or, approximately, 520 gallons of commercial 95 per cent alcohol. The scale to which these plans are drawn is 3/32 inch = 1 foot. From these plans we see the location of boiler, engine, and gearing, with grain elevator and mills, yeast- and mash-tubs, fermenters, beer-still, doubler, and condensers, by which those contemplating the erection of a distillery may obtain an idea of its practical construction. Regarding the details of the equipment of such a distillery it may be stated that it consists of a cold-water tank, grain-hopper, meal-hopper, Bevis condenser, beer-still, beer-heater, mash-tub, mash-tub stack, yeast-tubs, roller-mill, pipe-cooler, fermenter, beer-sink, boiler, engine, beer-pump. In the case of a molasses distillery, as no grinding-mills or mashing machinery are required, the cost will be less than for a distillery of this character. The approximate cost of this plant here shown is $20,000.

The continuous distillation for 190° proof is not recommended by these builders, as by so doing the fusel-oil is lost. This is a valuable product and can only be produced by fractional distillation, it being drawn from the rectifying-column. The fusel-oil is worth about $1.25 per gallon in barrel lots, and about two gallons are obtained to each 100 bushels of grain, which would mean an income of about $5 a day for a

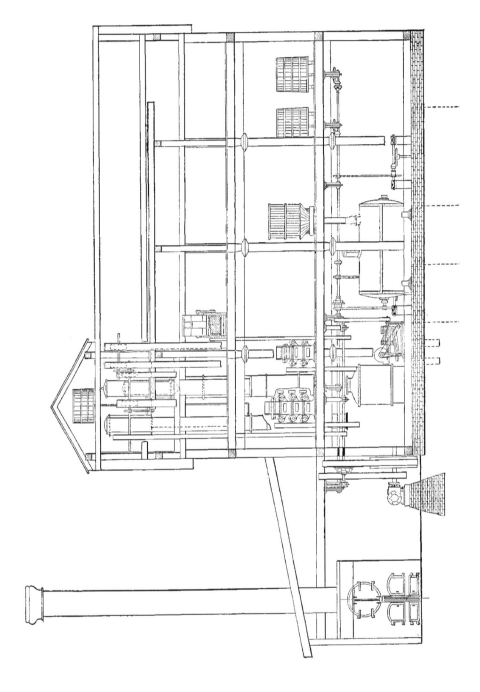

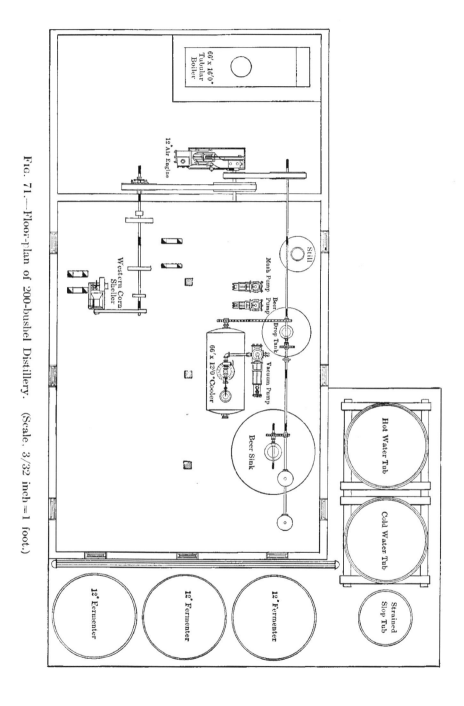

FIG. 71.—Floor-plan of 200-bushel Distillery. (Scale, 3/32 inch = 1 foot.)

200-bushel house. The apparatus as shown is complete for double distillation to produce alcohol of 190 per cent proof. The cost of such a distillery of 200 bushels' capacity, complete, without the land is about $20,000, including the requisite redistilling apparatus.

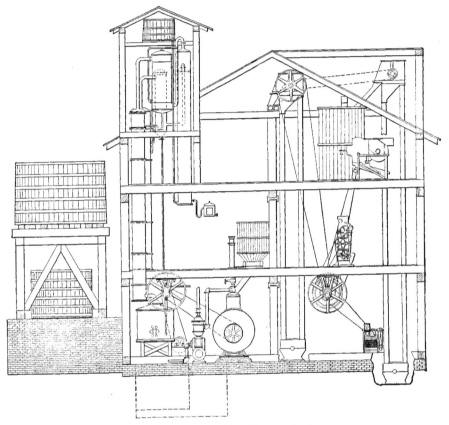

Fig. 72.—End Elevation of 200-bushel Distillery.   (Scale 3/32 inch = 1 foot.)

Cost of Buildings for Alcohol-distilling Plants.*—The most modern requirements call for as nearly fire-proof construction in these buildings as can be attained. The still-room or house is usually about five stories in height for the size or capacity of the plants we have described, i.e., of about 5000 bushels daily capacity, or 12,000 gallons daily capacity of molasses. For the above reasons this still-house should be built of con-

---

* These figures and diagrams were furnished through the kindness of Mr. Charles T. Main, Mill Engineer, Boston, Mass.

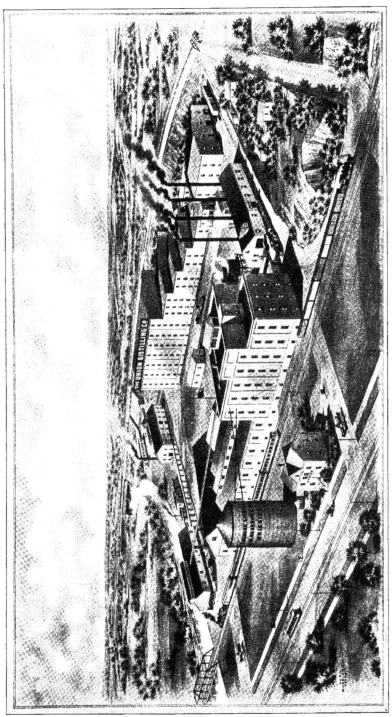

FIG. 73.—A Model Distillery (capacity 5400 bushels per day). Owned by The Union Distilling Company, Cincinnati, Ohio, Manufacturers of Denatured Alcohol, Grain Spirits, and Grain Alcohol.

187

crete and steel. The tanks for the storage of alcohol should be in part of this house.

The other buildings can be built of brick and hard pine. This is what is known as mill construction for textile manufacturing. This type is also known as the "slow-burning" type of buildings. Of course all the buildings of the plant can be built of concrete and steel, which is the best and most fire-proof construction yet devised. If this is done the cost for buildings will be about 15 per cent more than where brick and hard pine are used. Frame construction is undesirable in every way. The saving by the use of frame construction for walls instead of brick is not as great as many persons think. The only saving is in somewhat lighter foundations and in the outside surfaces of the building. The floor, columns, and roof must be the same strength and construction in any case. It will be of some assistance in approximating the cost of brick and hard-pine construction for buildings for alcohol manufacturing plants if a unit of cost in terms of square feet of floor-space can be ascertained. This is because there is a much wider range of cost than is commonly supposed, it being not an uncommon thing to hear the cost of such buildings (mill buildings) placed from only 60 to 80 cents per square foot of floor-space. The cost per square foot of floor-space depends upon the width, length, height of stories, and number of stories.

As the construction used in mill buildings for textile manufacturing purposes has become a standard type for many other kinds of manufacturing purposes as well as for the construction used in the most modern alcohol manufacturing plants the estimates and diagrams here presented apply equally as well to the cost of buildings for the latter purpose in terms of square feet of floor-space. The cost of labor in these estimates will be about one third of the total cost. These figures cover the cost of buildings designed to carry a floor load of about 100 pounds to the square foot. If greater floor loads than this are to be carried the cost of the buildings *will be increased.*

In the basis of estimates here given the *present* costs of the different materials, as well as the *present* average cost of labor, should be substituted for the values here given, as these costs vary of necessity from time to time. With these exceptions the principle here laid down applies fully to present-day costs of such buildings. The costs given include plumbing, but no heating or sprinklers.

Use of Diagrams.—1. The diagrams can be used to determine the probable approximate cost of proposed brick buildings to be used for manufacturing purposes, and these can be taken from the diagrams readily. For example, if it is desired to know the probable cost of a mill 400 feet long by 100 feet wide by 3 stories high, refer to the sheet showing the cost of three-story buildings. On the curve for buildings 100 feet wide, find the point where the vertical line of 400 feet in length cuts the curve, then move horizontally along this line to the left-hand vertical line, on which will be found the cost of 66 cents. For present prices of materials and labor add about 5 per cent, making the total about 70 cents per square foot.

The cost given is for brick manufacturing buildings under average conditions, and can be modified if necessary for the following conditions:

a. If the soil is poor or the conditions of the site are such as to require more than the ordinary amount of foundations the cost will be increased.

b. If the end or a side of the building is formed by another building the cost of one or the other will be reduced.

c. If the building is to be used for ordinary storage purposes with low stories and no top floors, the cost will be decreased about 10 per cent for large low buildings to 25 per cent for small high ones, about 20 per cent usually being fair.

d. If the buildings are to be used for manufacturing purposes and are to be substantially built of wood, the cost will be decreased about 6 per cent for large one-story buildings to 33 per cent for high small buildings, and 15 per cent would usually be fair.

e. If the buildings are to be used for storage with low stories and built substantially of wood, the cost will be decreased from 13 per cent for large one-story buildings to 50 per cent for small high buildings, and 30 per cent would usually be fair.

f. For office buildings the cost must be increased according to the finish.

The cost of very light wooden structures is much less than the above figures would give.

The table which follows the curves shows the approximate ratio of the costs of different kinds of buildings to the cost of those shown by the curves.

2. The diagrams can be used as a basis of valuation of different buildings.

A building, no matter how built or how expensive it was to build, cannot be of any more value for the purpose to which it is put than a modern building properly designed for that particular purpose. The cost of such a modern building is then the limit of value of existing buildings.

Existing buildings are usually of less value than new modern buildings for the reason that there has been some depreciation due to age, and that the buildings are not as well suited to the business as a modern building would be.

Starting with the diagrams as a base, the value can be approximately determined by making the proper deductions.

3. The diagrams can be used as a basis for insurance valuations after deducting about 5 per cent for large buildings to 15 per cent for small ones for the cost of foundations, as it is not customary to include the foundations in the insurable value.

Basis of Estimates.—The following table shows the costs which form the basis of the estimates, and these unit prices can be used to compute the cost of any building not covered by the diagrams.

The cost of brick walls is based on 22 bricks per cubic foot, costing $15.00 per thousand laid. Openings are estimated at 33 cents per square foot, including windows, doors, and sills.

Ordinary mill floors, including timbers, planking, and top floor, with Southern pine timber at $30.00 per thousand feet, board measure, and spruce planking at $20.00 per thousand, cost about 25 cents per square foot, which has been used as a unit price.

Ordinary mill roofs covered with tar and gravel, with lumber at the above prices, cost about 20 cents per square foot, and this has been used in the estimates.

Add to above for stairways, elevator-wells, plumbing, partitions and special work.

The present prices for materials and labor would increase the cost as shown on the diagrams about 5 per cent.

Deductions from Diagrams.—1. An examination of the diagrams shows immediately the decrease in cost as the width is increased. This is due to the fact that the cost of the walls and outside foundations, which is an important item of cost, relative to the total cost, is decreased as the width increases.

For example, supposing a three-story building is desired with 30,000 square feet on each floor.

If the building were 600 feet by 50 feet its cost would be about 80 cents a square foot.

If the building were 400 feet by 75 feet its cost would be about 71 cents a square foot.

If the building were 300 feet by 100 feet its cost would be about 68 cents a square foot.

If the building were 240 feet by 125 feet its cost would be about 66 cents a square foot.

2. The diagrams show that the minimum cost per square foot is

TABLE SHOWING RATIO OF COST OF BUILDINGS DESIGNATED, COMPARED WITH BRICK MILLS OF STANDARD CONSTRUCTION.

Superficial Feet of Floor in One Story.	FRAME MILLS.					
	One Story.	Two Stories.	Three Stories.	Four Stories.	Five Stories.	Six Stories.
1,250	0.859	0.675				
2,500	0.862	0.727				
5,000	0.888	0.779	0.751	0.726	0.703	0.674
7,500	0.895	0.791	0.765	0.738	0.716	0.690
10,000	0.904	0.801	0.775	0.749	0.727	0.703
15,000	0.913	0.816	0.792	0.769	0.747	0.724
20,000	0.919	0.833	0.810	0.787	0.765	0.743
25,000	0.923	0.847	0.824	0.802	0.781	0.758
30,000	0.927	0.858	0.835	0.814	0.795	0.770
35,000	0.930	0.865	0.844	0.821	0.804	0.778
40,000	0.933	0.870	0.848	0.828	0.810	0.786
45,000	0.936	0.873	0.852	0.832	0.815	0.792
50,000	0.939	0.875	0.855	0.836	0.818	0.797

Superficial Feet of Floor in One Story.	BRICK STOREHOUSES.					
	One Story.	Two Stories.	Three Stories.	Four Stories.	Five Stories.	Six Stories.
1,250	0.798	0.728				
2,500	0.845	0.725				
5,000	0.833	0.800	0.777	0.764	0.755	0.748
7,500	0.852	0.807	0.783	0.772	0.763	0.755
10,000	0.866	0.813	0.790	0.778	0.770	0.762
15,000	0.887	0.825	0.805	0.792	0.783	0.775
20,000	0.896	0.836	0.817	0.804	0.795	0.786
25,000	0.905	0.847	0.828	0.815	0.805	0.796
30,000	0.910	0.856	0.836	0.823	0.814	0.805
35,000	0.915	0.864	0.842	0.830	0.821	0.812
40,000	0.919	0.869	0.848	0.835	0.826	0.817
45,000	0.922	0.872	0.852	0.839	0.831	0.822
50,000	0.924	0.875	0.856	0.843	0.834	0.826

Superficial Feet of Floor in One Story.	FRAME STOREHOUSES.					
	One Story.	Two Stories.	Three Stories.	Four Stories.	Five Stories.	Six Stories.
1,250	0.696	0.505				
2,500	0.747	0.578				
5,000	0.744	0.602	0.561	0.531	0.508	0.483
7,500	0.765	0.625	0.581	0.551	0.530	0.506
10,000	0.784	0.645	0.602	0.574	0.552	0.527
15,000	0.810	0.678	0.638	0.610	0.588	0.563
20,000	0.824	0.703	0.667	0.637	0.614	0.590
25,000	0.834	0.720	0.685	0.655	0.632	0.608
30,000	0.841	0.733	0.697	0.667	0.645	0.621
35,000	0.848	0.741	0.706	0.677	0.655	0.632
40,000	0.855	0.749	0.715	0.687	0.665	0.643
45,000	0.861	0.758	0.723	0.697	0.676	0.653
50,000	0.869	0.767	0.732	0.707	0.686	0.664

reached with a four-story building. A three-story building costs a trifle more than a four-story. A one-story building is the most expensive. This is due to a combination of several features.

a. The cost of ordinary foundations does not increase in proportion to the number of stories, and therefore their cost is less per square foot as the number of stories is increased, at least up to the limit of the diagrams.

b. The roof is the same for a one-story building as for one of any other number of stories, and therefore its cost relative to the total cost grows less as the number of stories increases.

c. The cost of columns, including the supporting piers and castings, does not vary much per story as the stories are added.

d. As the number of stories increases, the cost of the walls, owing to increased thickness, increases in a greater ratio than the number of stories, and this item is the one which in the four-story building offsets the saving in foundations and roof.

3. The saving by the use of frame construction for walls instead of brick is not as great as many persons think. The only saving is in somewhat lighter foundations and in the outside surfaces of the building. The floor, columns, and roof must be the same strength and construction in any case.

PRICES AND OTHER DATA USED FOR ESTIMATING THE COST OF BRICK BUILDINGS FOR TEXTILE MANUFACTURING.

	FOUNDATIONS, including Excavations. Cost per Linear Foot.		BRICK WALLS. Cost per Square Foot of Surface.		Columns, including Piers and Castings.
	For Outside Walls.	For Inside Walls.	Outside Walls.	Inside Walls.	Cost of One.
One-story building....	$1.75	$1.50	$0.33	$0.40	$12.00
Two-story building...	2.50	2.00	0.37	0.40	12.00
Three-story building..	3.25	2.50	0.40	0.40	12.00
Four-story building ..	4.00	3.00	0.43	0.40	12.00
Five story building...	4.80	3.50	0.46	0.40	12.00
Six-story building....	5.80	4.00	0.50	0.40	12.00

ASSUMED HEIGHT OF STORIES.

From ground to first floor 3'
Buildings 25' wide, stories 13' high   Buildings 75' wide, stories 15' high
      "   50' "   "   14' "   "   100' "   "   16' "
                                            "   125' "   "   16' "

Floors, 25 cents per square foot of gross floor-space.
Roof, 20 cents per square foot. Roof to project 18" all around buildings.
Stairways, including partitions, $100 each flight.
Allow 1 stairway and one elevator tower for buildings up to 150' long.
    "   2 stairways "   "   "   "   "   "   " " 300' "
    "   3   "   "   "   "   "   "   " over 300' "
Plumbing, $75 for each fixture, including piping and partitions.
Allow 2 fixtures on each floor up to 5,000 square feet of floor-space and add 1 fixture for each additional 5,000 square feet of floor or fraction thereof.

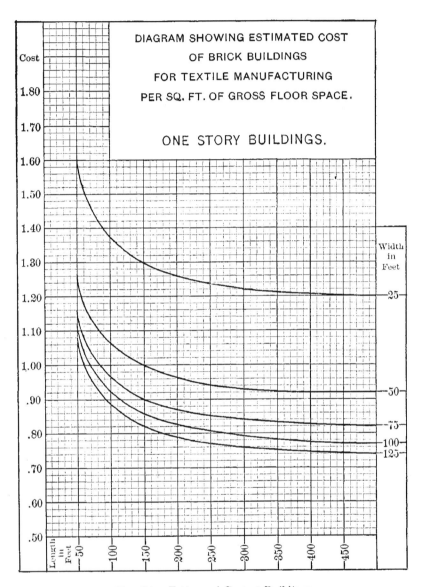

Fig. 74.—Estimated Cost of Buildings.

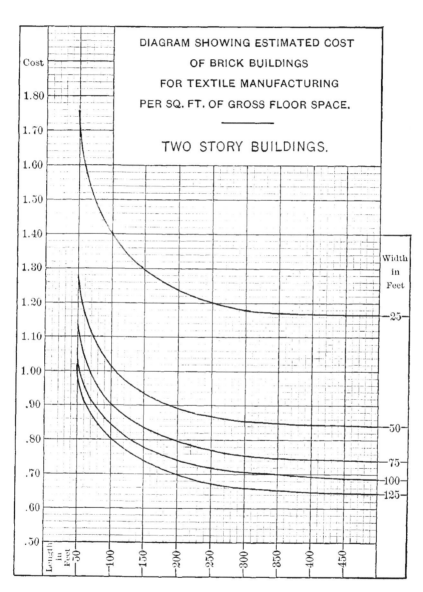

Fig. 75.—Estimated Cost of Buildings.

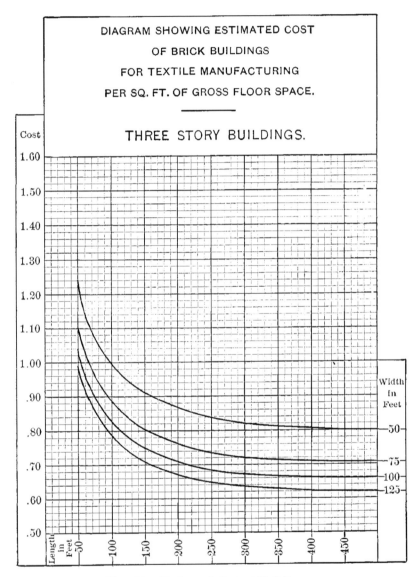

FIG. 76.—Estimated Cost of Buildings.

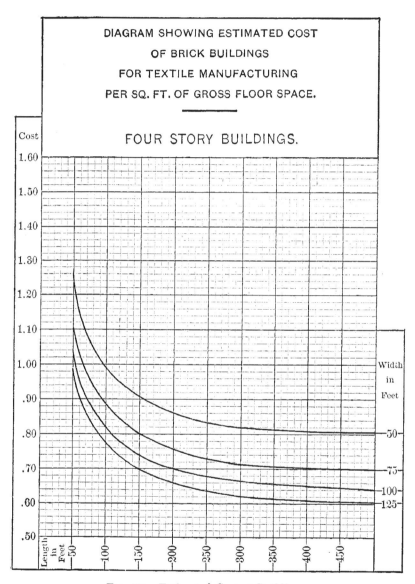

FIG. 77.—Estimated Cost of Buildings.

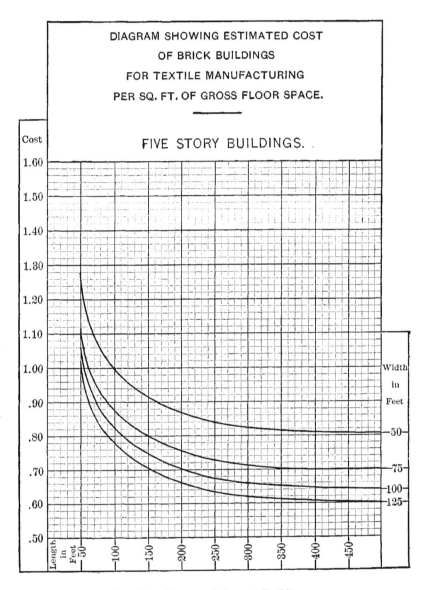

FIG. 78.—Estimated Cost of Buildings.

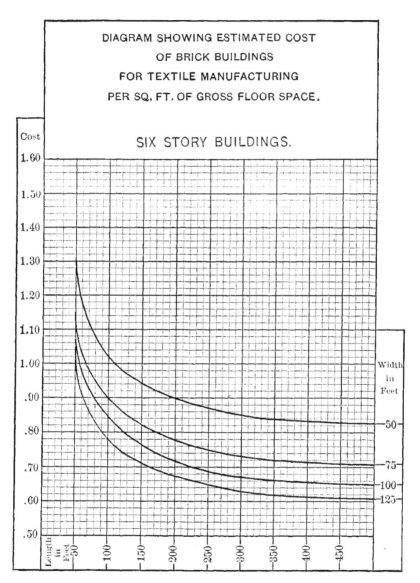

FIG. 79.—Estimated Cost of Buildings.

Cost of Alcohol-distilling Plants.—In continuation of the costs of alcohol-distilling plants it may be said that the larger the production the cheaper in proportion is the operating cost. The same rule holds as in the economics of any other manufacturing business. It costs almost as much, therefore, to operate a 2500-bushel corn plant as one of 5000 bushels daily capacity, and to operate a 6000-gallon molasses plant as one of 12,000 gallons daily capacity. In addition the larger part of the increase in cost from the smaller to the larger of these capacities is for increased apparatus. This being the case, it is merely a question of what is the minimum reasonable operating expense for such plants in terms of daily capacity of production. Experience has shown that such capacity, in case of corn, is 5000 bushels, and of molasses, 12,000 gallons. Each plant, in such a case, has the advantage at the start of the lowest operating expenses commensurate with sound business experience and successful operation.

The daily production of 95% alcohol in the case of the 5000-bushel corn plant is, in round numbers, about 13,000 gallons, while from the 12,000-gallon molasses plant it is about 5400 gallons per day. Several requirements may be broadly stated as also influencing the cost of alcohol-distilling plants. The warmer the water for use in the condensers, the more condensers are required for cooling purposes. The condensers of the Southern plants are of a different type from those in the North, and hence the construction varies. One of the principal items is to have good cool fresh water, and lots of it. As a rule, it is estimated in all the houses that it takes 500 gallons of water to make about $4\frac{1}{2}$ of whiskey or proof spirits, counting water for boilers, for mashing, and for the fermentation. Some plants without modern improvements take more water than others, but this is an average in figuring pumping capacity for a modern plant. In the grain-house grinding and mashing machinery and apparatus are required, as has been fully described in Chapter II. In a molasses-house no such machinery is required, and hence the cost of the latter is lessened by the proportional amount of money which such an equipment represents. The number of men required is, therefore, less than in the case of a grain-house. In redistilling and rectifying there is a shrinkage of alcohol according to the equipments of the house. In a house equipped with all the latest improvements the loss is not so great as in one not up to the standard. The shrinkage varies from 8 to 16 points, that is, from 0.08 to 0.16 of a gallon of proof spirits.

The consideration of a continuous still which will prevent such loss from double distillation by extracting the high-proof alcohol in one operation direct from the mash, while at the same time all the valuable fusel-oil is saved, is therefore of prime importance in the manufacture of alcohol for denatured alcohol. This has been fully explained in Chapter III. Such a type of still is necessarily very expensive. The construction of alcohol-distilling plants of the kind we are considering includes a five-story still-house of steel and concrete of fire-proof construction, a brick storehouse for the filled packages (barrels), and a corrugated-iron building for empty packages. The cost of a 5000-bushel corn distillery, with complete equipment of boilers, machinery, and apparatus, exclusive of land, is approximately $300,000. The cost of a molasses distillery of 12,000 gallons daily capacity, on the same basis of calculation, is approximately $180,000. No attempts have been made to itemize these estimates. They were given the author by contractors and builders of experience. Copper enters very largely into the question, and a price to-day would not, perhaps, represent the conditions a year hence. The same is also true of building materials and the proportion of the cost of labor to the total cost of these plants. For preparing denatured alcohol an additional building and appliances are required, also a denatured alcohol warehouse, and the sum of $20,000 must be added to the above estimates, in such case, for this additional equipment.

Cost of Commercial Wood Alcohol (Methyl Alcohol).—Methyl alcohol is obtained in the United States chiefly by the destructive distillation of wood. In Europe it is sometimes manufactured by the destructive distillation of peat and also from vinasse (the residue remaining after the distillation of fermented beet-root molasses), and Allen (Commercial Organic Analysis, Vol. I) points out that "methyl alcohol may be prepared by a variety of synthetical reactions."

The products from peat and vinasse are, however, inconsiderable, and are more or less incidental or by-products. The preparation of methyl alcohol by synthesis is not practiced on a commercial scale, as it is too expensive a process to admit of this being done at a profit.

The commercial demand for methyl alcohol for all purposes throughout the world is met by submitting wood to dry distillation, the methyl alcohol, together with many other products, being obtained from the liquor condensed from the vapors evolved. The residue from the distillation is charcoal, which finds wide employment as a domestic fuel and in the smelting of various ores, chiefly iron ores, for the production of charcoal or Swedish pig-iron.

The operation mentioned above is called destructive distillation because, in the process of vaporizing, the temperatures attained are so high that the original character of the wood is thereby destroyed and the product recovered by condensation represents a more or less accidental rearrangement of the elementary substances that were present in the wood. This destructive distillation as now carried on in the large modern works takes place in huge iron retorts or ovens called "by-product ovens," and is analogous to the operations involved and the appliances employed in the destructive distillation of coal.

These retorts or ovens are heated by fires maintained in furnaces below. The hot gases (products of combustion) circulate through flues in the side walls, so arranged as to cause an even distribution of heat throughout the charge of wood, with a maximum economy of fuel. Some uncondensable gases are given off during the process, and these, together with the "broken" charcoal (also called "breeze" and "brase") and residual tar, are employed as fuel in these furnaces.

The by-product oven or retort consists of massive masonry construction, open at each end, with heavy iron doors, and has a capacity of from three to four steel cars, into which the wood is packed. The wood is cut to a uniform length and of a maximum diameter of 4 to 5 inches. These cars are now run into the carbonizing-chamber of this oven or retort, after which the doors are closed and sealed air-tight by water-cooled rubber gaskets. (In the older types of these retorts they are built in pairs, and the covers are sealed air-tight by means of clay.)

In this modern "by-product oven" the wood is retorted or destructively distilled as has been described, the operation usually requiring twenty-four hours. When the distillation is finished, the cars containing the hot charcoal are drawn out of the oven, and cars newly charged with wood are run in, the furnace fires meanwhile being kept up.

To prevent spontaneous combustion of the hot charcoal, the cars containing it are at once run into steel chambers, which are then closed to exclude the air. Here this charcoal is left for about forty-eight hours, in order to allow it to cool to a point where it can be drawn out and remain exposed to the air without danger of its taking fire.

The tar produced in such a modern plant furnishes with the combustible waste gases, mentioned above, sufficient fuel for the heating needs of the entire retorting or destructive distillation of the wood. In some localities natural gas is used for fuel purposes. Coal is only necessary in the older retorting systems.

The character of the product obtained from this destructive distillation of wood depends to a considerable extent upon the temperature at which this distillation takes place, which is usually from 400° to 600° F. where iron retorts are employed, and the distillate consists of a weak complex liquid mixture of water, tarry substances, acetic acid (pyroligneous acid or wood vinegar), creosote, and wood naphtha, with small amounts of other organic substances, and it possesses an extremely repugnant odor and disagreeable taste.

Since the valuable portions of this distillate had their origin in the solid fibres of the wood and not in the sap or moisture, a greater economy of fuel is obtained by drying or seasoning the wood to the utmost degree practicable before it is "retorted" or distilled. For this reason wood is cut a year before being used. And further, since the resinous or tarry portions of the distillate are the least valuable and preponderate in fir or balsamic trees, only leaf or foliage woods are employed. In the United States, now the chief seat of this industry, maple, beech, and birch are the woods usually employed as giving the richest distillate capable of the most economical "after treatment." The liquid or distillate obtained as above described is now usually worked on an improved system known as the "gray acetate system," a name derived from one of its products, the so-called gray acetate of lime, and which has superseded the less profitable and less cleanly "brown acetate" process, which gave brown acetate of lime (an acetate containing a large percentage of undesirable and valueless tarry impurities).

Brown acetate of lime is sold on a basis of 60 per cent of real acetate of lime, while gray acetate of lime is sold on basis of 80 per cent. Both kinds usually run from 2 to 7 per cent over these figures.

Fig. 80 shows a graphic representation of the steps in the destructive distillation of wood and the products obtained by the "gray acetate system" in the manufacture of crude wood alcohol of 82 per cent in strength by Tralles' alcoholometer.

In explaining the improved process ("gray acetate" process) it may be said that the entire distillate from the destructive distillation of the wood is at once submitted to a second plain distillation, i.e., the liquor is evaporated at a temperature below the critical point at which the molecules break up to form new products. This distillation takes place in a copper still or in closed kettles connected by a vapor-pipe from the top to a suitable condenser and receiving-tank. As the distillation commences, the wood naphtha, which constitutes the most volatile portion of the liquor and is present to the extent of about $\frac{1}{2}$ of 1 per cent by weight of the original wood, begins to distill over and is collected until the boiling-point has reached about 110° C.

As the wood naphtha becomes exhausted, the crude acetic acid comes over very dilute and the distillation is continued until no more acetic acid can be obtained. About all the water comes off with the naphtha and acetic acid, so that the residue in the still consists of tar

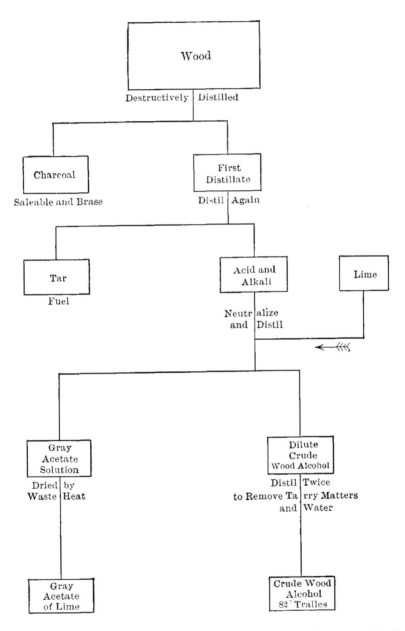

FIG. 80.—Graphic Representation of the Destructive Distillation of Wood in making Crude Wood Alcohol 82 per cent Tralles.

creosote, and other oils of low value. These are usually employed as liquid fuel in connection with a jet of steam, and thus contribute to the economy of this first distillation of the wood.

The second distillate thus obtained is now neutralized with lime and is again distilled. The distillate thus obtained consists of wood naphtha of about 32%. The residue of gray acetate of lime is a product which has a large variety of uses such as the manufacture of acetone, from which chloroform is now principally made; the manufacture of acetic acid, both commercial and pure, and for the making of acetates of various kinds for different manufacturing purposes. The wood naphtha 32%, or dilute crude wood alcohol, is now twice distilled to further remove tarry bodies and water and the product thus optained is the crude wood alcohol 82 per cent by Tralles' alcoholometer, and this is termed the strength in alcohol. As a matter of fact it is nothing of the sort, and such a figure, owing to the acetone and other substances present lighter than water, does not represent the real alcoholic strength in terms of absolute methyl alcohol. A content of acetone as high as 30 per cent is sometimes met with in such crude (82 per cent) wood alcohol.

Commercial Wood Alcohol (95 *per cent strength*).—This crude wood alcohol, 82 per cent, is now shipped to a refinery usually so located as to be central to many crude wood-alcohol plants in order to be assured delivery of the large quantities of such crude wood alcohol needed for the production of commercial wood alcohol (95 per cent strength), as well as for the saving in freights and for economical operation.

The refining process necessary to convert this unmerchantable crude wood alcohol into a condition or quality necessary for commercial purposes is analogous to those used in the refining of crude petroleum or mineral oils.

Several alkaline distillations involving the use of alkaline substances such as lime are necessary to remove the phenols, which are very persistent impurities.

A distillation with acid is sometimes employed to fix the ammonia and volatile basic substances. These chemical processes are combined with a series of fractional distillations in order to remove impurities for which chemical treatment alone will not suffice. The distillation apparatus employed is very expensive and of highly complicated construction. The final product thus obtained is commercial wood alcohol, which is usually sold at 95 per cent strength by Tralles' alcoholometer, and contains from 10 per cent to 20 per cent acetone and varying proportions of other organic impurities.

Usually there are required five gallons of crude 82 per cent wood alcohol to produce four gallons of commercial 95 per cent wood alcohol. As the cost at the plant for making the crude is about 39 cents a gallon, the cost of one gallon of the commercial is about 55 cents, 5 cents, being added for the manufacturing cost. In shipping this commercial wood alcohol 95 per cent, the price should include, in addition to the above, a cost of about 11 cents a gallon for freight and distribution charges, making the price about $67\frac{1}{2}$ cents a gallon when sold in large amounts.

Since the wood-alcohol industry was started the yield per cord of wood in gallons of crude wood alcohol 82 per cent has increased from $3\frac{1}{2}$ gallons to as high as 12 gallons. This result has been accomplished by the introduction of modern iron retorts and ovens to replace the charcoal kilns formerly employed, and by modern continuous steam distilling apparatus and special methods of rectification.

Commercial wood alcohol is a favorite denaturing agent abroad and possesses valuable properties for such purposes. It is an admirable denaturing agent, and any method tending to reduce its cost is of the highest importance. In view of the great progress and increased yields mentioned in the history of this industry, it may confidently be expected that the selling price of commercial wood alcohol may be reduced.[1] Sometimes commercial wood alcohol is still more highly rectified and refined up to strengths of from 97 to 98 per cent by volume of real methyl alcohol. Some of these products are so pure that only an expert is enabled to detect the difference between them and a sample of good-grade commercial 95 per cent (ethyl) alcohol. Such products are sold under the names of Manhattan Spirits, Columbian Spirits, Hastings' Spirits, Alcolene, Eagle Spirits, Colonial Spirits, and Lion d'Or. Concerning these purified products, which are methyl alcohol, it may be said that the laws of Massachusetts require that all methyl alcohol, whether crude or refined, be labeled "Wood Alcohol—Poison " in black letters of large gothic type.

---

[1] Since this prediction was made the selling price has dropped to 40 cents per gallon.

CHAPTER VI.

ALCOHOL AS AN ILLUMINANT.

The Incandescent Mantle for the Alcohol Lamp.   The Incandescent Alcohol
Lamp.   The Alcohol Illuminated-sign Lamp.   The German Incandescent Alcohol
Street Lights.   Cost of Lighting by Kerosene.   The Incandescent Welsbach Gas
Light.   Acetylene as a Source of Illumination.   The Electric Incandescent and
Arc Light.   Alcohol Compared to other Sources of Illumination.

THE use of alcohol for illuminating purposes dates back to the year
1833 in the United States.   In that year Augustus Van Horn Webb
introduced a substitute for the then existing portable lights, viz., candles
and whale-oil, calling it "spirit gas," being a mixture of alcohol and
spirits of turpentine.   His chief difficulty consisted in the weakness of
the alcohol, druggists' alcohol or spirits of wine about 80 per cent proof
being the only obtainable commercial alcohol, which in itself was not of
sufficient strength to incorporate and hold in solution under all temperatures the turpentine required to carbonize and impart body to the light
derived from alcohol.

Subsequent experiments resulted in the addition of other ingredients
such as gum-camphor, etc., whereupon he changed the name of the mixture to "camphorated gas."   The increasing demand for the "gas " or
fluid resulted in the invention of the alcohol column by John Wright,
whereby, by a process of exhaustive distillation, what was thereafter
known as 95 per cent alcohol was produced, this being of sufficient
strength to receive and retain in perfect solution the requisite quantity
of spirits of turpentine to impart light and maintain perfect combustion.

In 1838 Mr. Webb invented and introduced his "Webb's camphene
burner."   Ordinary spirits of turpentine containing too much rosin for
his purpose, he set about purifying it, and succeeded in relieving it of its
resinous properties.   This he submitted to the eminent chemist, Dr.
James R. Chilton, for analysis, who gave it the name of "camphene,"
which term Mr. Webb adopted in his patents, and from this period the
names "spirit gas " and "camphorated gas " were changed to "burning
fluid," a mixture of one part of Webb's camphene and four and a half
parts of 95 per cent alcohol.

207

The decade from 1830 to 1840 witnessed the introduction of high-proof alcohol and its use as a solvent for illuminating purposes, and the almost entire substitution of camphene and burning fluid for candles and whale-oil for artificial light. Indeed from 1840 to 1860 camphene and burning fluid were emphatically the "lights of the world," the former for fixed lamps, the latter for portable lamps.

The distillation of alcohol from high wines or common whiskey was then conducted exclusively by the rectifiers in the East, and so continued until the 'fifties, when distillers in Cincinnati and Illinois produced some 95 per cent alcohol which found its way to the Eastern market.

From 1850 to the outbreak of the Civil War the business of distilling alcohol and camphene, and the manufacture and sale of burning fluid, became a distinct and very extensive business in the city of New York.

From the adoption of alcohol for illuminating purposes in the manufacture of burning fluid until the outbreak of the war four fifths of the entire production of alcohol for home consumption was used in the manufacture of burning fluid. The remainder was used by druggists and in arts and manufactures.

Late in the 'fifties experiments were made in the production of coal-oil for illuminating purposes by the decomposition (destructive distillation) of coal, chiefly the Albert coal. Shortly thereafter came the discovery of petroleum, which led to the introduction of kerosene oil, or refined petroleum, for burning purposes, Samuel Downer of Boston being mainly instrumental in bringing it before the public. Many may recall the article known as "Downer's kerosene."

At this period, say 1860 to 1864, attention was called to refining petroleum for illuminating purposes, thus furnishing a substitute for the camphene and burning-fluid lights. The price of camphene rose from 35 cents per gallon prior to the war to $3.80 per gallon in 1864-5; and the imposition of the tax on distilled spirits (which included alcohol from necessity, it being so intimately and indissolubly connected with the spirit used by rectifiers, and almost identical with high-proof or cologne spirit) increased its cost beyond the possibility of using it for burning fluid in competition with kerosene oil.

The progress made in refining petroleum and the invention of lamps for burning it during the interval of the disuse of burning fluid and camphene rendered it an acceptable substitute for burning fluid and camphene, and owing to its marvelous cheapness it became, and in all probability may continue to be, "the people's light." The abolition of burning fluid caused a reduction of four fifths, or 80 per cent, in the consumption of alcohol. The remaining small percentage of the product met the requirements of druggists and that used in the arts and manufactures.

It is interesting here to notice that, on the authority of the Hon. David A. Wells, Commissioner of Internal Revenue from 1866 to 1870, written October 11, 1887, the use of proof spirits for the "burning fluid " above referred to, "in 1860, in places where coal-gas was not available, was all but universal, and necessitated a production and consumption of at least 25,000,000 gallons of proof spirits per annum, which in turn would have required the production and use of some 10,000,000 to 12,000,000 bushels of corn. In Cincinnati alone the amount of alcohol required every twenty-four hours by this industry was equivalent to the distillate of 12,000 bushels of corn. Each gallon of alcohol used in this 'burning fluid ' requiring 1.88 gallons of proof spirits for its manufacture." Therefore the 25,000,000 gallons of proof spirits used per annum referred to were equal to about 13,157,894 gallons of commercial alcohol of 95 per cent strength.

The almost complete disuse of alcohol in an industrial way in the United States on account of the tax, as described, naturally prohibited any development of apparatus for using alcohol, and our inventive faculties and abilities were turned in other directions.

On this account the apparatus shown in this book is necessarily largely of foreign make. As time passes we may speedily hope for a change in this respect, and that American inventive genius will improve on these problems already solved and solve those as yet partially developed

The Incandescent Mantle for Alcohol Lamps.—The adaptation of the mantle for use with the alcohol lamps for illuminating purposes marked a notable improvement in the efficiency of this lamp and made it a success.

There is therefore no longer any need of mixing purified spirits of turpentine or camphene with alcohol, as was necessary heretofore to produce a luminous flame. The importance of this invention renders of much interest a brief description of the discovery and manufacture of the modern mantle.

* About the year 1880 a young German, Dr. Karl Auer, while working in Professor Bunsen's laboratory, finding that for his chemical experiments on the rare earths he needed a very light thin filament, conceived the idea of saturating a cotton fibre with a solution of the rare earth, and then burned out the cotton, leaving behind the skeleton of the earth desired.

---

* Mr. H. S. Miner, chemist for the Welsbach Company, has kindly furnished these facts for the author.

The invention by Professor Bunsen of the gas-burner which bears his name gave a greater stimulus to the development of incandescent gas-lighting than any one thing up to the work of Dr. Auer, and in fact without this invention even his work would have been of little practical value.

The experiment of Dr. Auer was successful, and he eventually conceived the idea of working out a new system of illumination.

After very exhaustive experiments he settled upon the composition of the present mantle, which consists practically of 99 per cent thoria and 1 per cent ceria, and this composition gives practically the best lighting efficiency.

The present process by which a mantle is made is to knit or weave a cotton fabric, saturate it with a solution of the rare earths above mentioned, after which the fabric is dried and the asbestos loop or ring is attached to the top. The fabric is then incinerated, during which process the thread is entirely removed and the earthy matter only remains. After being subjected to a hardening process over an intense gas-flame, the mantle is dipped in a collodion solution, which strengthens it so it will resist the shocks incidental to handling and transportation. A thousand hours is considered the reasonable burning life of a mantle.

The Incandescent Alcohol Lamp.—Before taking up the kinds and details of these lamps it will be of interest to compare alcohol with kerosene for lighting purposes. In order to ascertain the cost of lighting by alcohol as compared to that of kerosene, the most widely used illuminant, careful duplicate photometric tests were made by the Electrical Testing Laboratories of New York and the reports of such tests were submitted by the author at the Congressional "free-alcohol" hearings held in Washington, D. C., February–March, 1906.

The lamps shown in Fig. 81, p. 212, are those referred to in the photometric tests of alcohol versus kerosene as illuminants, the tests being as follows:

The first test, made February 2, 1906, gave the following data (Report No. 1870, Orders Nos. 1783 and 1784).

Lamp.	One Gallon will Last		Candle-power.	Candle-power Hours.
	Hrs.	Min.		
Alcohol....................	58	52	25	1471
Oil.......................	87	0	9	783

The specific gravity of the denatured alcohol used in the above test was 0.8180, or about 94.5 per cent by Tralles' scale. The specific gravity of the kerosene used was 0.7930, and it was purchased from a local dealer.

This test included the French "Boivin" incandescent-mantle alcohol lamp and a flat-wick kerosene lamp such as is in common use in this country, using a good quality of alcohol and kerosene. The deduction to be made from this report is that if we had two lamps of equal candle-power and equal capacity, one burning alcohol and the other kerosene, the alcohol lamp would burn nearly twice as long as the kerosene lamp.

This is shown by the figures, because had the kerosene lamp been 25 candle-power it would have burned about thirty-one hours as against about fifty-nine hours for the 25 candle-power alcohol lamp.

In order to determine just exactly what burners of identical shape would burn of alcohol and kerosene in a given time, a second test was made March 3, 1906, by the same authorities, as follows (Report No. 1917, Order No. 1859):

Lamp.	One Gallon will Last		Candle-power.	Candle-power Hours.
	Hrs.	Min.		
Alcohol.	57	5	30.35	1732
Oil.	28	40	30.8	883

The kerosene used in the above test was purchased from a dealer in the vicinity. The specific gravity of this kerosene was 0.7950. The specific gravity of the denatured alcohol used in this test was 0.8240, or about 92.6 per cent by Tralles' scale.

It is also a matter of interest to know that extended photometric tests were made in 1900 by Professor E. Rousseau, of the University of Brussels, Belgium, to determine the comparative value of alcohol and kerosene as illuminants. In the first series of such tests he used alcohol of 96.4 per cent in strength, and in the second series alcohol of 94.2 per cent in strength by the centésimal alcoholometer. These tests demonstrated a difference in favor of alcohol of fully two to one, and are confirmed by the American tests just given. The author quoted from this report of Professor E. Rousseau at the Congressional "Free Alcohol" hearings held at Washington, D. C., February–March, 1906.

This American test, mentioned above, in which a round-wick, central-draft kerosene-burning lamp was used, in comparison with the "Boivin" incandescent-mantle alcohol lamp using a Welsbach mantle, shows conclusively that with two lamps of equal candle-power and equal capacity a gallon of alcohol possesses about twice the illuminating value of a gallon of kerosene. These lamps are shown in Fig. 81. The "Boivin" alcohol burner in the lamp tested is easily regulated by means of a vapor screw valve so that the amount of light furnished can be diminished or increased at pleasure. The consumption of alcohol is also correspondingly diminished or increased. Under all circumstances these photometric tests show alcohol to possess about twice as much value as kerosene for lighting purposes. Denatured alcohol therefore can easily compete successfully with kerosene at twice the cost per gallon. Moreover kerosene can only be increased to one half the selling price of denatured

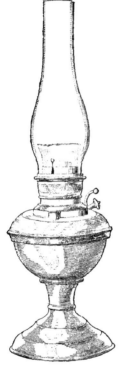

Fig. 81.

Kerosene Lamp.   French Alcohol Lamp.

alcohol for illuminating purposes at any given time, as these figures show. In discussing the comparative costs of alcohol and kerosene for illuminating purposes there are a number of features to consider besides the simple economics of the matter. These may be considered as follows:

1. *Safety of the Alcohol Lamp.*—The alcohol lamp is much safer than the kerosene lamp, as a fire started from alcohol is readily extinguished by water, which mixes with alcohol in all proportions. Such is not the

case with kerosene, as the throwing on of water only serves to spread the fire.

2. *Quality of the Light Furnished.*—The white light furnished by the alcohol lamp is akin to daylight in its quality, and being also extremely steady and uniform, it is preferable to the yellow light of the kerosene lamp.

3. *The Heat Given Off by Radiation.*—This is much less in the case of the alcohol lamp than from a kerosene lamp of equal candle-power, because the flame of the kerosene lamp owes its luminosity to the particles of carbon present, which, not being perfectly burnt, become incandescent in the flame and radiate of necessity a considerable degree of heat, as any one who has read beside the usual large round-wick kerosene lamp, such as was used in these photometric tests referred to, can testify. These conditions do not occur in the alcohol lamp, as the *mantle* becomes incandescent and not the flame. The flame of alcohol when burned in the wick lamp is, as is well known, of a pale bluish color and practically non-luminous. Hence the adaptation of the incandescent mantle to the alcohol lamp made it a commercial success, as has been shown.

4. *Maintenance of the Alcohol Lamp.*—As the alcohol lamp burns no wick, it is free from this troublesome feature invariably connected with the use of kerosene. The alcohol lamp does not smoke and is practically odorless. The fitting on of the mantle is easy and simple. The occasional replacing of the suction-wick used in the reservoir (body) of the lamp is quickly accomplished. The lighting of the alcohol lamp is more easily done than with kerosene, as the removal of the chimney or raising it is unnecessary. There is also much less vitiation of the atmosphere from burning denatured alcohol than in the case of kerosene, as we shall show later.

Turning now to the details of the construction of the alcohol lamp, we will discuss them under the following heads:

The Burner.—Fig. 82 shows the incandescent-mantle alcohol "Boivin" burner. This consists of the little alcohol reservoir-pump, the suction-wick, the alcohol vaporizing-tube, V shape in form, and the mantle. Just below the mantle is a small circular-shaped asbestos-lined copper channel, in which a little alcohol is ignited by a match in lighting this lamp.

The suction-wick merely brings the alcohol, by capillary attraction, to the V-shaped vaporizing-tube. The tiny pump in the reservoir (body) of the lamp furnishes the alcohol necessary in order to light this lamp. This is done as follows: The vapor screw valve V is opened by

unscrewing it, and the spring lever *O* is pushed down to operate the
pump. The alcohol so brought up to the igniting channel is lighted with
a match through the small opening above *O*. In about thirty seconds
the heat so produced vaporizes the alcohol furnished by the suction-wick.
This vapor burns as a gas, making the mantle white-hot, after which
the lamp burns automatically.

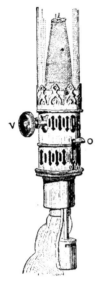

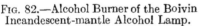

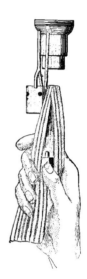

FIG. 82.—Alcohol Burner of the Boivin   FIG. 83.—Method of Changing the Suc-
   Incandescent-mantle Alcohol Lamp.   tion-wick in the Boivin Alcohol Burner.

This burner is as easily regulated as gas, the amount of light furnished, and hence of alcohol used, being reduced at will. It is claimed
that this burner consumes a liter (about one quart) of alcohol in fourteen
burning-hours, giving a light of 40 candle-power.*

A smaller alcohol burner is also made by E. Boivin, claimed to be of
20 candle-power and to consume one liter (about one quart) of alcohol
in twenty-eight burning-hours. These burners are intended for the
French denatured (not carbureted) alcohol of 90 per cent strength, but
will also burn U. S. completely denatured alcohol.

In Fig. 83 the suction-wick for this alcohol burner is shown, and
also the method of changing this wick. The wick is made of cotton,
very loosely twisted, and half an hour after being put in place it readily
becomes saturated with alcohol and the burner is then ready for use. ·

* French Standard Carcel.

This suction-wick lasts for months and is therefore very infrequently renewed, although this is readily done. The cuts showing the kerosene and alcohol lamps used in the tests referred to are shown in Fig. 81, p. 212. As with kerosene lamps, the form, design, and materials of the alcohol lamp may be varied at pleasure, depending upon the cost. Some of these lamps are of beautiful design and finish.

The "Boivin" French incandescent street light "La Parisienne" is shown by Fig. 84. This light is also used in France for interiors.

Fig. 84.   Fig. 85.

Fig. 84. Boivin Incandescent Alcohol Light for Interiors and also Out-of-door Use: "La Parisienne."
Fig. 85. Students' Alcohol Lamp.

Some of the uses claimed for it are for halls, stores, studios, railway stations, wharves, etc. This light has an illuminating power, it is claimed, of from 40 to 200 candle-power, according to the number of burners supplied, each burner giving 40 candle-power.

In the other cuts we are shown, as in Fig. 85, the students' or

reading alcohol lamp.   In Fig. 86 is shown the bracket reflector alcohol
lamp.   The alcohol lamp for projecting screen-pictures or views is shown
in Fig. 87.

The alcohol lamp, as shown in Fig. 85, gives a very satisfactory light
for the purposes of study.   As the lamp needs practically no attention
while burning, it contributes greatly to the comfort of the user.   It is
readily moved and convenient in shape.

The alcohol lamp shown in Fig. 86 is used as a source of illumination
where the reflector is of great service.   The focusing and concentration
of the rays of light by the reflector greatly enhances the lighting efficiency of this lamp.   It is very practical in construction and possesses
great durability.

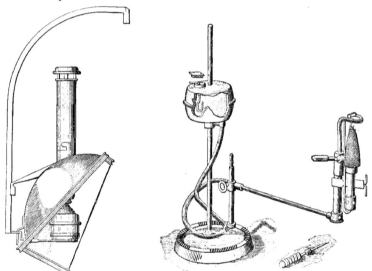

FIG. 86.—Bracket Reflector Alcohol   FIG. 87.—Alcohol Lamp for Projecting
               Lamp.   Screen Pictures or Views.

In the alcohol lamp shown in the Fig. 87 we possess a superior
source of illumination for the purposes intended.   The views shown by
this lamp are very distinct and strongly mark the contrasting light and
shade.   This light may also prove of value in commercial photography.

The copy of the U. S. patent, No. 781,490, granted January 31,
1905, to Emile Boivin, of Paris, France, for the radiation-burner for spirit-
lamps, is herewith appended.   The details are shown in Fig. 88, p. 218,
and Fig. 89, p. 219.

No. 781,490.   Patented January 31, 1905.

UNITED STATES PATENT OFFICE.

EMILE BOIVIN, OF PARIS, FRANCE

RADIATION-BURNER FOR SPIRIT-LAMPS.

SPECIFICATION forming part of Letters Patent No. 781,490, dated January 31, 1905.

Application filed December 7, 1903.   Serial No. 184,135.

To all whom it may concern:

Be it known that I, EMILE BOIVIN, a citizen of the Republic of France, and a resident of Paris, France, have invented certain new and useful Improvements in Radiator-burners for Spirit-lamps, of which the following is a specification.

The spirit-lamp burner which forms the object of the present application is distinguished from other burners of the kind by the novel arrangement in the chamber for the mixture of gases of a heating-radiator, the object and advantage of which is to insure dry vapors and a suitable form for the flame—that is to say, the form of a candle-flame—which renders the mantle incandescent, and when the radiator and the parts dependent thereon are thoroughly heated the mantle furnishes and maintains its maximum illuminating power, while a great saving of spirit is effected.

The object and advantages of the radiator, which is the essential feature of the invention, are as follows:

First.   After the lamp has been alight for some time this radiator becomes heated throughout and transmits this heat by contact to the interior of the tubes c, in which vaporization is effected.   This transmission of heat is intended to dry the vapors thus produced and to render them suitable for partial and complete combustion.

Second.   Independently of the form of the flame produced by the radiator as mentioned above the radiator proper, c, in consequence of its special form and the vertical slots formed in it promotes the movement of the dry vapors which come from the mixing-chamber d.

In order to make the invention quite clear, it is illustrated in the accompanying drawings.

Figure 1 is an elevation of the burner surmounted by the heating-radiator and the rod for supporting the mantle; Fig. 2, a vertical section through A B in Fig. 4; Fig. 3, a plan of the heating-radiator; Fig. 4, a horizontal section through C D in Fig. 2; Fig. 5, a plan of the ejector shown in Figs. 1, 2, and 6; Fig. 6, a vertical section of the burner, taken at right angles to Fig. 2; and Fig. 7, a plan of the burner.

As shown in Figs. 1 and 2, the burner consists of a central tube a, which dips into the reservoir or body of the lamp.   This tube is furnished with a suitable internal wick b.   At a certain height the tube a is surmounted by two flat tubes c, placed sufficiently apart for receiving between them a mixing tube or chamber d, Figs. 1, 2, and 4. The mixing-

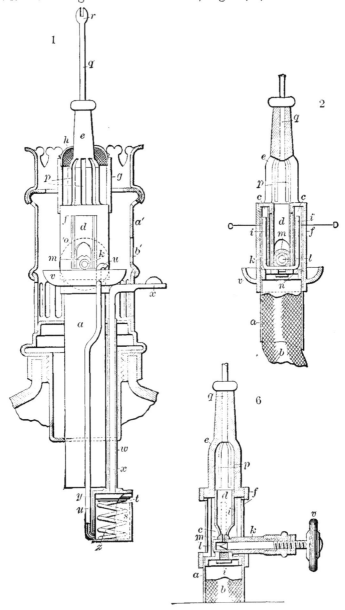

FIG. 88.—Sectional Drawings showing the Construction and Details of the Radiation-burner for the Boivin Patent Alcohol Lamp.

chamber d is brazed to the tube c and to the bottom of the radiator e, through which it runs. To the circumference of the base of the radiator

e the heater f is likewise brazed, which is formed by a tube open at the two ends and having two diametrically opposite openings. On the top of the heater f is a head-piece formed by a ring g, closed at one end by wire gauze h, through which the upper part of the radiator extends. The two side tubes c are closed at the top by their abutments and by being held in a circular recess formed in the base of the radiator e. In the interior of each of these tubes is one arm of a U-shaped tube i, the junctional horizontal part of which tube i is drilled with a hole communicating with the holes in a pipe k, with an internal regulating-valve l, which passes across an ejector m, arranged on and brazed to the top of the tube a. The base of the ejector m is drilled with two holes n registering with the two flat tubes c and permitting the passage of the spirit-vapors from the wick up into said flat tubes. The regulating-valve l, by means of which the vaporizing operation can be started or the action of the burner be stopped, is operated from the outside by a milled nut o, Figs. 1, 6, and 7. The radiator e is slightly conical and hollowed out inside. In the sides thereof are a number of vertical slots p. The top of the radiator,

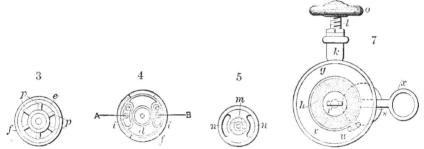

FIG. 89. — Sectional Drawings showing Details of the Radiation-burner for the Boivin Patent Alcohol Lamp.

which runs through the gauze wire h, receives the rod q and mantle-holder r. The radiator is placed over the mixing-chamber, and is intended to diffuse the vapors issuing from the ejector m in order to give them a desired form and heat them more and more until a complete diffusion thereof is effected. This heating is effected by conduction— that is to say, through the conductive power of the radiator to the heater and from the heater to the tubes c without any external action.

The igniting of the burner may be effected in any manner, but preferably by the device described in relation to Figs. 1 and 7 of the accompanying drawings. This device consists of a cylinder s, drilled near the top with an opening t, through which the spirit enters from the body of the lamp. To the bottom of this device an elevating-tube u is fitted, the top of which enters the igniting-pan v and is then bent toward the bottom of the vessel. The upper part of the cylinder s carries a tube w, which acts as a guide for the rod x of a piston y, arranged in the cylinder and the top of which is under the permanent action of a spring z. The upper part of the piston-rod is bent outside the gallery a' in order that it may be lowered when the ignition is effected. An orifice b' is formed in the gallery a' to allow of the introduction of a match and the igniting of the spirit which has been forced out of the cylinder s into the vessel v by means of the piston y. This arrangement is suitable where simple refined spirit is employed for lighting purposes; but when for any reason whatever carbureted spirit is employed, this spirit would not be suitable for the ignition, and therefore I reserve the right of isolating the above-described pump device in a reservoir-tube which is immersed in the body of a lamp and into which spirit is poured suitable for several ignitions.

The burner thus described acts as follows: The lighting or priming is effected as stated. The spirit is drawn up by capillary action near to the ejector m. The vaporization begins in the central tube a and the vapors ascend to the side tube c, which they enter, thence escaping through the ejector and reaching the mixing-tube d become mixed, are diffused and heated by the radiator e, and finally pass through the wire gauze h, taking the form desired for the mantle.

What I claim, and desire to secure by Letters Patent, is—

1. In an incandescent-lamp burner, the combination with a mixing-chamber, of two upright vaporizing-tubes adjacent thereto, and a U-shaped pipe having a leg in each tube and provided with an aperture in its horizontal part in line with said mixing-chamber.

2. In an incandescent-lamp burner, the combination with a wick-tube, of two flat vaporizing-tubes extending up therefrom and closed at their upper ends, a mixing-chamber between said vaporizing-tubes, a U-shaped pipe having a leg in each flat tube and provided with an aperture in line with said mixing-chamber, and a radiator above said mixing-chamber.

3. The combination with a wick-tube, of an ejector having a base closing the top of said tube and provided with two holes, vaporizing-tubes registering with said holes, a heater having open sides and inclosing and supporting said tubes, a mixing-chamber between the vaporizing-tubes, a U-shaped pipe in said tubes having its horizontal portion extending across said ejector and provided with an aperture communicating with the ejector, a valve controlling said ejector, and a slotted radiator surmounting said heater above the mixing-chamber.

In testimony that I claim the foregoing, I have hereunto set my hand this 23d day of November, 1903.

EMILE BOIVIN.

Witnesses:
EDMOND LECAUTWEIER,
H. C. COXE.

In describing the Phœbus Incandescent Alcohol Lamp, of which a cut is shown in Fig. 90, it may be said that the manipulation of this lamp is practically the same as those heretofore described in this chapter. The lamp is lighted at A by a match. It is extinguished by closing the screw vapor-valve B. In filling the lamp the alcohol is put in at the orifice C. D is the regulator. For a table lamp for reading purposes a shade is placed upon the support E. The small rubber bulb shown, when com-

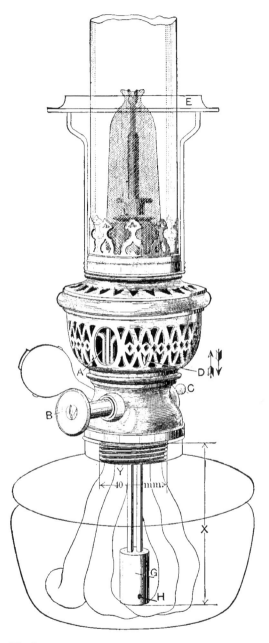

FIG. 90.—The Phœbus Incandescent Alcohol Lamp. Made by Beese & Co., Dresden, Germany.

pressed, forces a little alcohol into the lighting chamber A. This bulb is readily detachable, being provided with a metallic connection. The lamp is here shown without the base in order to show the details. Any design and material is supplied for the base by the manufacturers.

The accompanying cut shows the Phœbus Hanging Billiard Incandescent Alcohol Lamp. This lamp is of a beautiful design and furnishes a very agreeable light for its purpose. The style shown is the large model, and is finished in rich reddish brown or sea-green.

FIG. 91.—Phœbus Alcohol Billiard Lamp.

The ornate hanging Phœbus lamp (Fig. 92) is finished in an exquisite variety of designs. As the manipulation of this lamp is readily suggested by the cut, no description is necessary. The lamp is appropriately used for hall-lighting purposes.

The Phœbus (small model) Indoor Alcohol Lamp, as shown in Fig. 93. is supplied with a clear-glass globe and is very effective in its power of illumination.

In Fig. 94, p. 224, is shown the beautifully decorated Phœbus Indoor Alcohol Lamp. This lamp is furnished with a rich bead shade, which can be had in any colors desired. The globe supplied with this lamp admits of an abundant illumination and a pleasing quality of light.

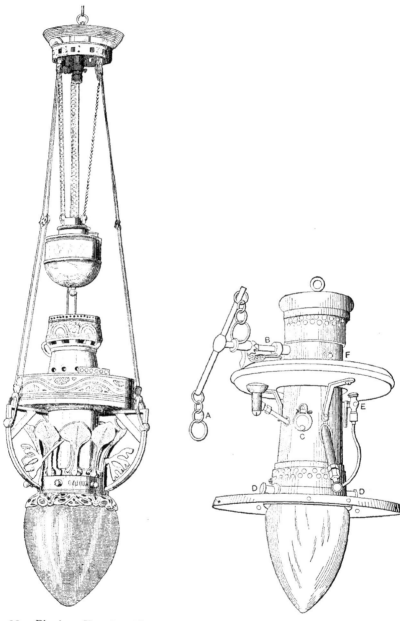

FIG. 92.—Phœbus Hanging Alcohol
Lamp for Indoor Use.

FIG. 93.—Phœbus Small Model Indoor
Alcohol Lamp.

From the cut here given an idea is obtained of the appearance and finish of the Phœbus Indoor Alcohol Light with ground-glass globe, shown in Fig. 95.

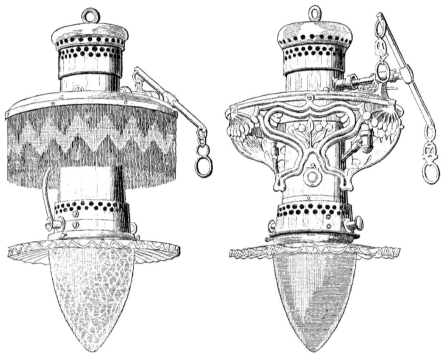

FIG. 94.—Phœbus Indoor Alcohol Light with Bead Shade.

FIG. 95.—Phœbus Indoor Alcohol Light with Bronze Design.

For the purposes of **Illuminating Sign Lamps** or **Art Lamps** the Phœbus lamp shown in Fig. 96 is an extremely satisfactory light. Any character of illuminated sign can be availed of with the transparent shade. The lamp is largely used for drug-stores, restaurants, hotels, etc.

The German Incandescent Alcohol Street Lights.—The German Incandescent Alcohol Street Light "Alba" is shown in Fig. 97, p. 226. This light is guaranteed storm and rain proof. Each lamp is fully guaranteed. The consumption of alcohol per burning-hour is ¼ liter (¼ quart), and the light thus furnished is claimed to be 220 candlepower.* "This light is also recommended for interior as well as for out-of-door uses, as it is claimed to be smokeless and odorless." Alcohol below 90 per cent in strength cannot be used in this light.

* Kerzen Standard.

The details of the construction of this "Alba" light are shown by Fig. 98, p. 227. They are as follows:

A is the little reservoir for holding the quantity of alcohol necessary to light the lamp. *B* is the principal or large alcohol reservoir of the lamp. *C* is the lever-valve by which the alcohol needed for lighting is drawn into *A* from *B*. *D* is the lighting-funnel. *E* is the heating-cup.

FIG. 96.—The Phœbus Alcohol Illuminating Sign Lamp.

F is the main-cock. The balance of the parts are described by Fig. 98 itself.

In order to light this alcohol light the proceeding is as follows, assuming that it has been all prepared, all ready to light: First close the main-cock *F*, then open the lever-valve *C* by pulling it down for twenty seconds in order to allow the amount of alcohol needed for priming to flow into *A*. The lever-valve *C* is then closed. The alcohol meanwhile flows into *E*, where it is lighted by a match through *D*.

The alcohol is permitted to burn for about a minute in order to facilitate the formation of the alcohol vapor, and after waiting for a minute, as mentioned, which is the very earliest that the lighting should be attempted,

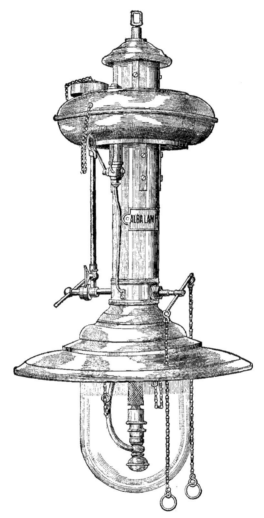

Fig. 97.—The "Alba" Alcohol Light.   Made by Schwintzer and Gräff, Berlin, Germany.

the alcohol that was in E now having *all* been burned, the lamp is ready for lighting. This is accomplished by opening the main-cock F by drawing or pulling down the ring and chain shown attached to F, when after the lighting is effected the lamp burns automatically.

If the main-cock is opened too soon or the above vaporizing for a minute is disregarded, then the alcohol itself runs down, in place of the alcohol-vapor, into the burner and the mantle is broken down from its

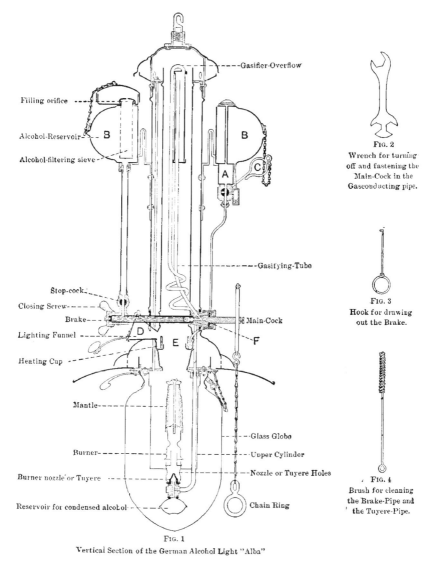

FIG. 1
Vertical Section of the German Alcohol Light "Alba"

FIG. 98.—Vertical Section of the "Alba" Alcohol Light.

strap by the pressure. However this is not material, as by removing the glass globe the broken mantle can be replaced by a new one.

The light is extinguished by closing the main-cock *F* by drawing down the chain attached as shown.   The alcohol-brake or regulating device for controlling the flow of alcohol is very ingenious and effective. It consists either of brass-wire cloth, wound about a central wire, or of a perforated brass tube packed with asbestos.   The alcohol flows by gravity slowly through this regulator controlled in addition by a thumb-screw, and is "gasified " and burned in the mantle.   The alcohol-brake is also used in many alcohol stoves and prevents any danger of "back-firing."   The details of construction are shown in the vertical section of the "Alba " light in Fig. 98.

The German Standard Alcohol Street Lamp.—Another form of alcohol street light for circumstances where other forms of illumination are not obtainable, as well as from the point of safety and absence of smoke or odor, is the Standard light, which has given satisfaction.   This lamp is shown in Fig. 99, p. 230.   With regard to the details of the lamp they may be described as follows: The alcohol is kept in the closed spirit-basin.   From this a small tube leads down to the asbestos wick or gas-generator.   This gas-generator is enclosed in brass netting and receives the spirit in its lower part.   The pressure of the spirit in the basin continuously pushes a small quantity of spirit through the generator-tube, which in its upper part is exposed to the heat developed by the burning spirit lamp.   No back-firing is possible, as it is prevented by the asbestos.   In the upper part of the wick the spirit is now transformed into vapor.   This vapor, or spirit-gas, enters the gas-tube leading down to the burner, keeping the Auer mantle at full heat, and in this manner the light is produced continuously.   To start the lamp a basin is fixed underneath the gas-generator, and in opening the main-cock (in order to light the lamp) a small quantity of spirit, just enough to start the lamp, runs into this small basin.   Here it is now lighted.   It heats up the wick and generates and ignites the gas, which shortly afterwards enters the burner.   The lighting can be done by an ordinary match, but where a number of lamps are used a special lighting instrument is preferable. To put out the light nothing more is required than to pull down the arm marked Z, and the light is extinguished at once.   From this description it will be seen that simplicity of construction is one of the vital points of these lamps, and this is the reason that they burn for months without requiring any other attention than filling and lighting.   The manipulations otherwise necessary in connection with this light are very simple also.   There is only the exchange of the generators or wicks and the renewing of the Auer mantle once after burning, say about 500 hours, and this can be done by any one without special knowledge.   It may be stated that the consumption of alcohol in this light is about 1 liter (= 1.056

quarts) in ten burning-hours, and it develops about 70 candle-power of light. The cost per burning-hour of this light varies with the price of the alcohol. As a rule the spirit used is about 172° American proof, as claimed by the maker.

The cost of 95% strength denatured alcohol in Germany is 29.69 cents per U. S. gallon.

Cost of Lighting by Kerosene.—From the tests mentioned on pages 210 and 211 we find that a gallon of good kerosene burned in a 9-candle-power lamp lasted 87 hours. At a cost of 15 cents per gallon at retail for kerosene this lamp would cost, for this amount of light on these figures, about 17/100 of a cent per burning-hour. The kerosene burned in the 30.8-candle-power lamp lasted 28 hours and 40 minutes. At a cost of 15 cents per gallon at retail for kerosene the 30.8-candle-power lamp would cost, for this amount of light about 0.52 cent per burning-hour.

Kerosene is burned as a vapor by means of a reservoir using 20 pounds pressure and having a piped system to the incandescent-mantle lights. Each light has a vaporizing-chamber below it, and once this has been heated, to start it, the lighting is automatic. As there is, however, a very tiny hole for the kerosene to be admitted to the heaters, any dirt occurring in the kerosene will stop these small holes and hence shut off the lights. Very high efficiencies in candle-power of light are claimed for this system.

Portable incandescent-mantle kerosene lamps are made abroad and are being experimented with in this country. The shape of the mantle is rather conical and the mesh rather open. The great delicacy of adjustment needed and the almost constant attention required to prevent the deposition of soot (carbon) on the mantle in these lamps, however, renders their general use somewhat difficult.

* **The Incandescent Welsbach Gaslight.** — In the development of the Welsbach light the results of experiments conducted by Thomas Drummond in the year 1826 constituted practically the first step in incandescent lighting. He used a stick of lime in an oxyhydrogen flame, producing the "lime-light" which with various modifications has been in continuous use practically ever since. With the introduction of uncarbureted water-gas a number of devices in the forms of baskets, combs perforated cylinders, etc., were invented to produce a luminous flame from this "blue gas." Typical among these are the lamps of Clammond and Fohnehjelm.

---

* The author is indebted to Mr. H. S. Miner, chemist of the Welsbach Company, for these facts.

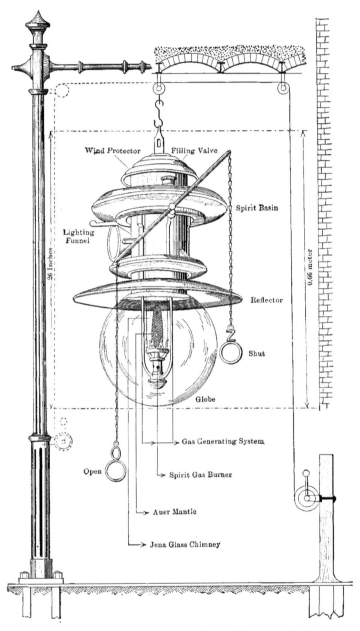

Fig. 99.—The Standard Incandescent Alcohol Street Lamp, made by George Stade, Berlin, Germany.

The invention and the perfecting of the incandescent mantle by Dr. Karl Auer about the year 1880, as already described on page 209, brought the development of the incandescent gaslight to a successful commercial basis.

In Fig. 100 is presented a cut of the standard Welsbach lamp, and in Fig. 101 is shown one of their inverted or "reflex" types of lamp. In explanation of Fig. 100 it may be said that the Standard Welsbach light using an 8-inch clear-glass chimney gives practically 100 candle-power horizontal illumination with a consumption of 4.5 cubic feet per hour on 21 candle-power water-gas containing about 650 B.T.U., when burned at 20/10 inches pressure. This produces an efficiency of 22.2 candle-power per cubic foot. This efficiency will vary on different

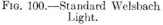

FIG. 100.—Standard Welsbach
Light.

FIG. 101.—The Inverted or "Reflex"
Welsbach Lamp.

gases and under different conditions of consumption. The standard used in these Welsbach-light tests is a 10-candle-power Harcourt pentane lamp.

The Welsbach reflex inverted light shown in Fig. 101 consumes 3.5 cubic feet of gas per hour, and while the horizontal candle-power is not so great as in the case of the upright burner, the light below the horizontal is considerably greater, reaching in one photometric test, using "Reflex" burner, "Reflex" mantle, and 8-inch-deep cone mirror reflector, as high as 277 candle-power directly beneath the light and from 95 to 230 candle-power at lesser angles compared to the horizontal candle-power.

With regard to the directions and care needed in using the Welsbach light it may be said that the instructions are as follows: The

Bunsen tube should be securely screwed to the fixture-nipple after the threads of the same have been coated with white lead or soap, and then the gallery should be slipped over the Bunsen tube. The mantle should be carefully removed from the box and mounted on the burner. Then burn off the protecting coating, igniting at the top, and place the glassware in position. The gas should then be turned on and lighted, and the gas-adjusting device at the base of the burner should be manipulated until the best light is obtained. The glassware should be removed occasionally and thoroughly washed and dried, at which time the gallery-carrying mantle should be taken off the Bunsen tube and any dust removed by blowing upward through the burner. The gallery with the glassware should then be replaced on the fixture.

As to care in handling the mantle it can be said that on account of the extreme fragility of the mantle it is necessary at all times to use the greatest care. The presence of dust in the burner-tube will cause the mantle to carbonize. Many persons suppose that the mantle is then worthless. After the dust has been blown out of the burner, this carbon deposit may be burned off by turning down the gas with the adjusting device at the base of the burner. Mantles giving a mellow-white light are most preferable, as they are stronger and maintain their light-giving qualities for a longer time. It may be stated that the reasonable burning life of a mantle is 1000 hours.

Acetylene as a Source of Illumination.—Acetylene gas is growing in importance as a source of illumination for special purposes, such as for lamps used with automobiles, steam and naphtha launches, and lighting-plants for hotels and houses. For this reason it has seemed desirable to compare its uses as an illuminant with alcohol. Acetylene is also used in the Government lighthouses in our Southern rivers and bays for range-lights in marking dangerous shoals.

The generation of acetylene gas from calcium carbide is explained in Chapter VII, and the properties of acetylene compared with other substances used for fuel and lighting purposes. At the present time the cost of acetylene is prohibitive for its use for general purposes of light, heat, and power. There are difficulties not yet wholly overcome which also prevent such general uses.

In Fig. 102 is shown the Acetylene Hanging Arc Lamp made by Klemm & Co. It is arranged for four acetylene burners and is furnished with a clear ground globe or alabaster globe as desired. This lamp is used, according to the manufacturers, as an indoor lamp for lighting stores and offices. It is provided with an 18-inch opal reflector and is finished nickel-plated.

* The cost of lighting depends entirely upon the price paid for the carbide, which at the present time can be had at retail for $3.50 per hundred pounds. The makers claim 5 cubic feet of gas per pound, but

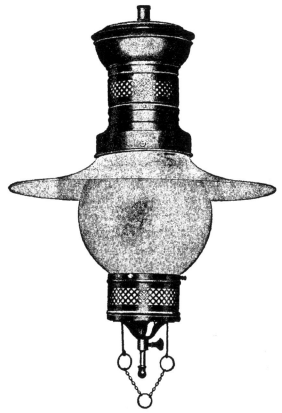

FIG. 102.—Acetylene Hanging Arc Lamp. Made by Klemm & Co., Philadelphia, Pa.

in practice it is found that $4\frac{1}{2}$ cubic feet is the average yield per pound at the burner. On this latter basis the gas costs 0.777 cents per cubic foot.

The efficiency of different makes and different sizes of burners vary. The best burners of large size yield 48 candle-power per cubic foot consumed. The standard burner generally used for acetylene consumes $\frac{1}{2}$ cubic foot per hour and gives 24 candle-power approximately. If a

---

* From data supplied by Mr. N. Goodyear, manager engineering department of J. B. Colt Company, New York.

16-candle-power burner were made, it would cost 0.259 cents per burning hour to maintain it.

Regarding the qualities of acetylene the reader is referred to Bulletin 57, Department of Agriculture, State of Pennsylvania, containing a report "On the Application of Acetylene Illumination to Country Homes," by George Gilbert Pond, Ph.D. Writing from Harrisburg, Pa., regard-

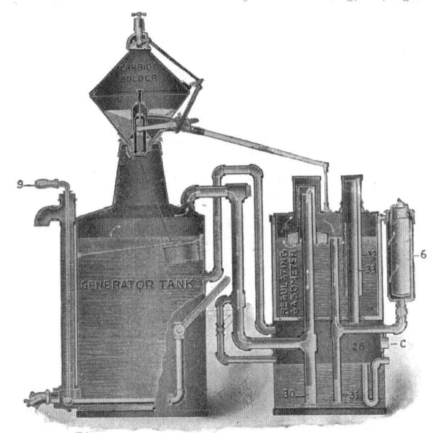

FIG. 103.—Acetylene-gas Generator. Made by J. B. Colt Co., New York City.

ing this report, Mr. John Hamilton, Secretary of Agriculture, says, under date of December 30, 1899: "The new illuminant, acetylene, which has now been tested to a considerable extent, has attracted the attention of residents in rural districts, and if found to be safe and easily controlled will supply a brilliant and cheap illuminant very much needed. . . . This department makes no recommendations in the use of acetylene gas, and only presents the subject for the information of the public, leaving each individual to judge for himself as to its desirability for his use."

In Fig. 103 is shown a sectional view of the Colt Acetylene Generator which is of the carbide feed type, the carbide being only fed as the gas is required. An inspection of this cut shows the method of feeding the carbide. The feed mechanism is positive and the valve, which is double, is provided with a rubber seat surrounded with a metal cylinder. The inner valve descends when working on a clean seat, and makes a tight joint, which is a distinctive and unique feature of this generator.

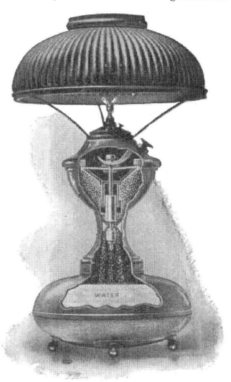

Fig. 104.—The Beck-Iden Acetylene Lamp.

Fig. 105.—Sectional View of the Beck-Iden Acetylene Lamp.

The safety devices on the cold-generators are carefully planned and constructed. Simplicity of operation and efficiency are marked features of this generator.

The Beck-Iden Household Acetylene Lamp.—* The Beck-Iden Acetylene Lamp is shown in Fig. 104, which gives an illustration of it, while the sectional view of the same lamp, given in Fig. 105, shows the construction and details of the manner in which the carbide is fed to the

---

* The makers of this lamp furnish this statement.

water. Heretofore numerous attempts have been made to construct acetylene lamps in which the water was fed to the carbide, but until the above-mentioned lamp was produced acetylene lamps for household use were in disfavor. The Beck-Iden lamp, owing to the fact that it feeds carbide to the water, precludes any after-generation of acetylene gas when the feed is stopped. The success with which it has met is due to this fact. By this process of feeding the lamp can be started or stopped at will. The carbide used is in a finely granulated condition, being contained in the urn of the lamp, while the water is in the lower part or water-fount.

In starting the lamp the screw on the side marked E is turned on. This permits the carbide to flow downward into the water. There is a

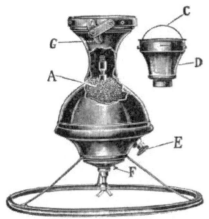

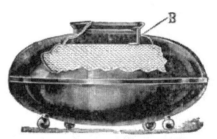

Fig. 106.—Sectional View of Beck-Iden Aectylene Lamp, Separated for Filling.

Fig. 107.—Sectional View of Water-fount of Beck-Iden Acetylene Lamp.

plug connected to a small gas-holder or diaphragm located in the top of the lamp, and as the gas generated by the dropping of the carbide into the water fills the gas-holder, this plug is raised and closes the feed-opening, and holds it closed so that no more carbide can fall until the gas in the holder is nearly used up by passing through the burner. When this occurs the plug again opens automatically to drop in a small quantity of carbide for the further generation of the gas. In this manner the operation above outlined is repeated automatically until the shut-off screw E is turned off, when the remaining gas in the lamp will pass out at the burner, be consumed in about half a minute, and the light then goes out. The charge of carbide for this lamp is about 1½ pounds, lasting from 9 to 10 hours, and furnishes about 40 candle-power of light at an expense of 1 cent an hour. On a 16-candle-power basis the cost of lighting is said to be approximately $\frac{1}{3}$ cent per hour. When the carbide is exhausted it is about like whitewash and pours out readily from the water-fount. The refilling of the water-fount with fresh water each time the lamp is filled is as necessary as the placing of more carbide in the lamp. It is claimed that there is not enough gas in a whole charge of the lamp to asphyxiate. Different sizes of burners are furnished. The burning duration of the charge is less the larger the burner used. In filling the lamp with carbide the top is separated, as shown in Fig. 106, from the water-fount. Fig. 107 shows the water-fount. This lamp was accepted by the National Board of Fire Underwriters, having passed the necessary tests of safety. The lamp is portable and the quality of light given is like daylight; the lamp when burning is odorless and free from any soot, smoke, or dirt.

The Electric Incandescent and Arc Lights.—This source of illumination is so well known that a brief description of it will suffice for the purposes of our comparison with alcohol. Improvements which are being made in the filaments will it is claimed increase the burning life for the incandescent lamp to double the present figure, or from about 480 hours to nearly 1000. Where cheap power for the generating of electricity prevails as we have indicated, or where conditions warrant, as in our large cities, this form of illumination has met with a very general and deserved use. The cost of electric-lighting on a 16-candle-power basis in very large cities is not over $\frac{3}{4}$ cent per hour, as the price of electricity is arranged on what is, in effect, a sliding scale of prices, so that the larger the use the less is the price paid for it.

This results in a reduction in many cases of from $\frac{3}{4}$ cent per lamp hour for a 16-candle-power-lamp basis to as low as $\frac{1}{4}$ cent and to an even lower price in some instances on this basis.

Summary of Chapter VI.

We shall make no attempt to give a precise comparison of the illuminating value of alcohol compared to the other sources that have been considered. So many factors enter into such a statement that it can only be made after very careful photometric tests conducted at one time and under identical conditions. In addition we have neither the cost of nor the standardized denatured alcohol as yet for such a precise test.

As it will be shown in the next chapter that denatured alcohol vitiates the atmosphere least of all the open-flame illuminants, besides possessing the other advantages we have mentioned, it will be seen that the matter of the selling price of denatured alcohol, while of very great importance, will probably not prevent some use of it for illuminating purposes, no matter what it is.

In case of a reasonably low price, if it could sell for 25 cents per gallon for instance, denatured alcohol could actively compete with kerosene, the illuminant which it appears destined to replace, just as in this country, previous to 1860, alcohol, as has been shown, replaced the cheaper candle and the whale-oil lamp.

CHAPTER VII.

THE FUEL VALUE OF ALCOHOL COMPARED WITH THE OTHER USUAL LIQUID FUELS.

The Williams Bomb Calorimeter. The Thermal Efficiency of a Fuel. The Fuel Value of Denatured Alcohol. Calculations of the Volume of Air Necessary for Complete Combustion of Alcohol, Gasoline, Kerosene, and Crude Petroleum. Ratio of Prices of Various Fuels. Ratio of Vitiation of the Atmosphere by Combustion of these Fuels. Table of the Calorific Value of the Usual Liquid Fuels. Alcohol Heating and Cooking Apparatus and Stoves.

BEFORE considering the subject proper it may be of interest to indicate in what manner the fuel value of any combustible, be it a solid or a liquid fuel, may best be determined, as well as to briefly describe a form of bomb calorimeter recently perfected by Mr. Henry J. Williams, of Boston, that is to-day in all probability the most convenient and reliable instrument yet devised for obtaining such results with accuracy.[*]

The instrument is shown in Fig. 108, which is a vertical section of the apparatus with all parts in position for making a combustion of coal. Fig. 2 shows a plan of the bomb. Fig. 3 shows the upper portion of the casing of the electric stirrer. Fig. 4 shows a plan of the calorimeter and water-jacket with attachments for firing. Fig. 5 shows the bomb in position in the calorimeter-can and its connection to the automatic electric contact for firing. Fig. 6 shows the calorimeter-can and cover. Figs. 7, 8, and 9 show the platinum crucible and details of the platinum crucible-stand.

The Williams **Bomb Calorimeter** represents the *closed* type of calorimeters in which the combustion takes place in an atmosphere of

---

[*] The perfecting of this instrument was originally started in 1895 with the late Prof. Silas W. Holman, of Boston, to whom full credit is due for suggesting many valuable features of the apparatus. Due acknowledgment is also made to Prof. Peter Schwamb, of the Mass. Institute of Technology, who, in 1897, designed the form of bomb that, with but slight modifications, has been adopted.

239

oxygen gas. The bomb is made of aluminum bronze, which transmits heat much more rapidly than steel. It is spherical in form, with the exception of a short neck through which it is charged and by means of which it can be sealed. The spherical form secures the maximum strength and capacity attainable, with the minimum weight and bulk of metal,

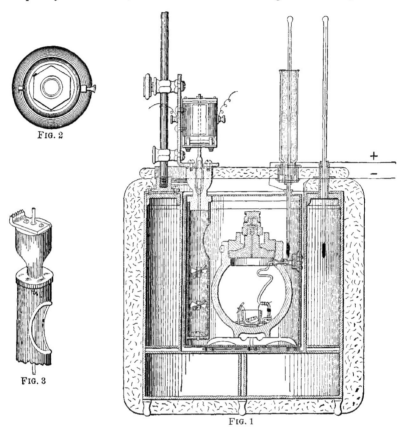

Fig. 2

Fig. 3

Fig. 1

Fig. 108.—The Williams Bomb Calorimeter.

so that the bomb requires less water to cover it, owing to its compact form, than if it had any other shape.

The bomb is closed by a lid, which is pressed directly downward by means of a nut which screws into the neck of the bomb and which bears upon a restricted area of the convex upper surface of the lid quite near its centre. The outer edge of this lid, underneath, where the area is greater, is brought into crushing contact with a light ring washer of tin resting upon a flat shoulder within the neck of the bomb. All twisting of the lid is thus avoided and all binding due to the crushing of the washer is prevented, while a tight joint is invariably secured with but little effort. A light check-valve, which the interior pressure within the bomb forces upward when the oxygen is shut off, serves to automatically confine the gas. The check-valve and closing-nuts replace the long projecting stem or pin-valve of the Mahler bomb, and they are so

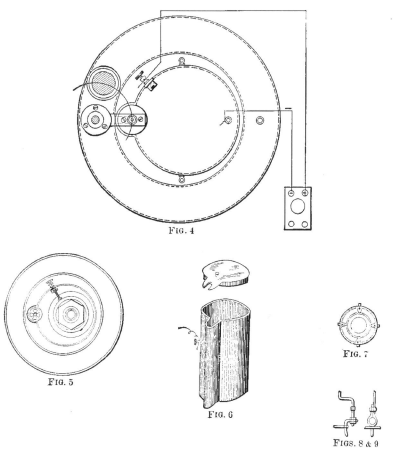

FIG. 4

FIG. 5

FIG. 6

FIG. 7

FIGS. 8 & 9

FIG. 109.—Details of the Williams Bomb Calorimeter.

disposed as to make it possible to completely submerge the bomb, so that no heat developed within it can escape measurement.

The calorimeter-can has a side-chamber adapted to exactly fit the casing of the electric stirrer, and a cover which effectually prevents escape of heat due to evaporation of liquid from the surface.

The shape of the bomb and calorimeter-can are such that 1500 grams of water suffice to completely cover the bomb, an amount which is from 32 to 37 per cent less than is required to only partially cover the Mahler bomb. In consequence the range of temperature obtained by the combustion of a given weight of coal is much greater than Mahler obtains, being 4 degrees where he would obtain only from 2.52 to 2.72 degrees, and the small but unavoidable errors incidental to the reading of thermometers are thereby greatly reduced.

The outside of the bomb is nickel-plated, while its interior walls are very heavily coated with pure gold, which protects them perfectly against corrosion and furnishes a sound and durable lining which transmits heat far more quickly and perfectly than enamel. In making a calorimeter test of coal the finely pulverized coal is compressed in the form of a little disc in which a deep slot can be cut to facilitate its adjustment to the fuse-wire. The platinum crucible-stand has a deep crucible, across the top of which the loop of platinum fuse-wire hangs, upon which the slotted lump of coal, weighing exactly 1 gram, can be slipped. From this it cannot get disconnected, for it is supported by the sides of the crucible. When all adjustments, which are readily made, are completed, the crucible-stand is lowered bodily into the bomb, which is firmly held in a screw-clamp, and the upper extremity of the crucible-stand is adjusted to its side in electrical contact with an insulated knob, outside of the bomb, through which an electric current may be conveyed to the fuse-wire.

The arrangements are such that nothing can disturb the integrity of the adjustments when they are once made, so that miss-fires are of very rare occurrence. Moreover the coal being in one piece, the crucible of deep form, and the crucible-stand entirely in the bottom of the bomb, losses of fuel by scattering when oxygen is admitted, or by spilling, cannot occur.

The stirring-apparatus consists of an electric motor, held in position on a rod above the calorimeter, whose shaft, provided with propeller-blades, is sufficiently prolonged to reach to the bottom of the calorimeter-can. The shaft revolves within a light metal casing, open above and below, in such manner that a rapid stream of water is drawn up from under the bomb and is thrown out above and around it. The stirring is rapid and perfect and requires no attention whatever, while the speed of the propellers is sufficiently constant to have made it possible to determine with the greatest accuracy the exact frictional effect of the stirrer and to apply to the determinations the proper correction therefor.

Finally the water-jacket which surrounds the calorimeter not only has the usual outside covering of felt and enamel cloth, but its top has also been provided with a heavy flat cover of non-conductive material, so that the space within which the operations and measurements are conducted is *absolutely protected* against the influence of the surroundings, and is only exposed to such influences as can definitely and accurately be known. To make doubly sure of this the water-jacket is provided with an electric stirrer of its own, so that its true temperature at all times is no longer open to doubt.

The bomb having been charged, placed within the calorimeter-can, covered with a known weight of water, both covers put on and the thermometers adjusted, the two electric stirrers are set in motion and the stirring takes place automatically. The influence of the water-jacket upon the calorimeter is carefully observed and when it is found to be uniform the charge is fired. The rise of temperature during combustion is noted through a series of readings until the maximum is reached and the readings are continued after the maximum, to determine the after-influence of the water-jacket upon the calorimeter. Proper correction is made for the amount of heat introduced through the fuse-wire, the melting of which is timed with an accurate stop-watch, from the dropping of the needle of an ammeter placed in circuit.

After the combustion the bomb is removed from the calorimeter, placed in the screw-clamp, the products of combustion drawn out and analyzed, if desired, to prove that the combustion was complete, the acids formed by the combustion washed down and carefully drawn out, and the nitric and sulphuric acids formed determined by appropriate methods. A somewhat elaborate calculation is now required to correct the determination for the influence of the surroundings, acids formed, fuse and stirrer, but these corrections can all be made with the utmost precision by calculation from the very accurate and reliable data which have been obtained. In short a result is obtained which accurately and positively indicates the true calorific value of the fuel, without appreciable loss of any kind, provided that the accuracy of all the instruments used has been carefully verified.

The above instrument therefore furnishes the means of determining with very great accuracy the true calorific power of combustibles, it being assumed, of course, that all the precautions which it is necessary to take in securing reliable samples have been observed.

This same bomb calorimeter is equally well adapted to determine with accuracy the calorific value or heating-power of liquid fuels, such as alcohol, gasoline, kerosene, fuel-oil, or other combustible liquids, but the manipulation of the instrument has to be slightly modified to suit the particular fuel operated upon.

A few of the more noteworthy features in the construction of the bomb calorimeter above described are: That the bomb is nearly spherical in form, that it is completely submerged and incorrodible, that, owing to its shape, a minimum amount of water is required to cover it, and that the calorimeter chamber is completely protected from outside influences. Moreover, all operations being either automatic or under full control, the readings of the thermometers are *thoroughly reliable*, because they are not altered by influences about which little or nothing can be accurately known, as is too often the case in the use of other calorimeters. It is not too much to say for this instrument, therefore, that it is justly entitled, *on its merits*, to be considered far superior to any other bomb calorimeter yet devised, both in convenience of handling and in accuracy, and it is equally well adapted for determining the calorific value of *any* combustible substance of whatsoever nature, be it a solid, a liquid, a gas, or a food.

The usually accepted unit of heat, the French calorie, is used in the calculations, this being the amount of heat required to raise the temperature of one kilogram of water one degree Centigrade. French calories can be reduced to British thermal units by simple multiplication by the factor 1.8.

The values obtained in an accurate bomb calorimeter, which is the *closed* form of calorimeter, indicate the total or actual heating power of the fuel per pound or per kilogram, but we must bear in mind that the figures so obtained cannot, for a number of reasons, ever be realized in practice. We must discriminate, therefore, between the *actual* calorific power as determined by the bomb and the *realizable* calorific power which we should expect to reach in practice. With liquids this difference is most important.

In the bomb, on the one hand, practically the whole of the water produced during the combustion, as well as any water of dilution present in the combustible (such as in denatured alcohol), is changed into steam or vaporized and then recondenses, and while doing so gives out its latent heat, which is included in the measurement. In practice, on the other hand, when the liquid is burned, this vapor seldom if ever escapes at a lower temperature than 212° F., and the latent heat of vaporization is necessarily lost. As with liquids the heat of vaporization of the water is generally a very large quantity, it is preferable to calculate the amount of latent heat lost during this vaporization into the corresponding number of calories, which are then deducted from the total calories found by calorimeter test. The remaining calories or their equivalent British thermal units then represent the *available* heat-power or calorific value of the fuel as it is used in practice.

The Thermal Efficiency of a Fuel.—The thermal efficiency obtained from a fuel is the ratio of the heat-units expended in useful work to the original heat-units available in such fuel. If the greatest thermal efficiency is to be secured two essential conditions must be complied with:

First. In the internal-combustion engine or motor the denatured alcohol or other fuel *must be completely consumed.*

Second. The temperature of the exhaust-gases *must be as low as possible.*

This subject will be more fully discussed in Chapter VIII, where the use of denatured alcohol for power will be taken up.

The Fuel Value of Denatured Alcohol.—A comparison of the respective calorific values of commercial (ethyl) alcohol of 95 per cent strength by volume and of denatured alcohol of a specified composition is given in the following table.

Fuel Values of Alcohols, Theoretical and as Obtained by Calorimeter Tests. (Henry J. Williams.)

Fuel.	Available B.T.U. per Pound. All Water Vaporized from and at 212° Fahr.	
	Theory.	By Calorimeter.
Commercial 95% alcohol (ethyl)............	10,769	10,504
Denatured* alcohol.....................	10,551	10,355

Commercial alcohol bought for 95 per cent ethyl alcohol by volume proved to be only 94.5 per cent alcohol by volume, which, by Smithsonian tables, for a specific gravity of 0.8180 at 15°.5 C., corresponds to only 91.5 per cent absolute alcohol by weight. The theoretical calorific value of this commercial alcohol was calculated as follows.

---

* As the U. S. regulations for denatured alcohol had not been issued at the date of this writing, the composition of the denatured alcohol here mentioned had to be arbitrarily decided upon. It was made up as follows:

100 liters commercial ethyl alcohol............ 95% (Druggists')
10 " commercial wood alcohol............ 95%
½ liter pure pyridine (E. Merck & Co.'s)

Corresponding to a percentage composition by weight of—

90.40% commercial ethyl alcohol.................. 95%
9.04% commercial wood alcohol.................. 95%
0.56% pure pyridine [1] (E. Merck & Co.'s)

The specific gravity of this denatured alcohol was 0.8192 at 60° F.

[1] Pure pyridine was used because the commercial pyridine, such as is used abroad, was not vailable.

Composition on the Basis
of 1 Gram.

Carbon.................	0.4776
Hydrogen..............	0.0796, which by combustion forms water, 0.7164 gm.
Water.................	0.3578
	0.9150
Water of dilution.........	0.0850
	1.0000

We therefore have:

Carbon.................	0.4776 gm. $\times$ 8080° = 3859°.0
Hydrogen..............	0.0796 gm. $\times$ 34500° = 2746°.2

$\qquad$ 6605°.2 calories obtained by
$\qquad$ combustion.

From which we must deduct the calories required
to vaporize all the water present in the form of
steam.

Total water = 1.1592 gms. $\times$ 537° $\qquad$ = 622.5

$\qquad$ 5982°.7 $\times$ 1.8 = 10,769 B.T.U.
$\qquad$ per pound.

The theoretical calorific values of denatured alcohol of the composition given above are obtained by an entirely similar though more complex calculation.

Commercial wood alcohol is of very variable as well as uncertain composition. It invariably contains large quantities of acetone as well as other impurities which greatly affect its heating value. Unless the quantity of all of these is known the theoretical calculation can only be of casual interest.

Analysis showed that the commercial wood alcohol used had practically the following composition:

Methyl alcohol................	77 per cent by weight
Acetone.....................	15 " " " "
Water.......................	8 " " " "
	100

and that the theoretical calorific power of absolute methyl alcohol is, by calculation, found to be 8248 B.T.U. per lb., while that of acetone is 12,407. We therefore have:

$$0.77 \times 8248 \quad = 6351 \text{ B.T.U.}$$
$$0.15 \times 12407 \quad = 1861 \text{ ``}$$

$$\overline{8212} \text{ ``}$$
Less $0.08 \times \quad 537 \times 1.8 = \quad 77 \text{ ``}$

8135 B.T.U. per lb. =theoretical calorific power of commercial wood alcohol.

The theoretical calorific power of pure pyridine being 14,424 B.T.U. per lb., we should have for denatured alcohol of the above composition:

Ethyl alcohol, 90.40% × 10769 = 9735 B.T.U.
Wood alcohol, 9.04% × 8135 = 735 "
Pyridine, 0.56% × 14424 = 81 "

= 10551 B.T.U. per lb. =theoretical calorific power of the denatured alcohol specified.

From what has preceded and from theoretical calculations it would appear that the low fuel value of denatured alcohol, as compared with gasoline, kerosene, and fuel oil, were unfavorable to alcohol. On this phase of the subject attention is called to a table of M. Henri Dupays, in the *Engineering Magazine* of February, 1904, where the following values for different combustibles, obtained in a Mahler calorimeter, are given:

Substance.	Calorific Power.		
* Denatured alcohol..............	5,906 calories per kilo	(10,631 ‡ B.T.U. per lb.)	
† 50% carbureted alcohol........	7,878 " " "	(14,180 " " ")	
Light petroleum essence (mean)....	10,500 " " "	(18,900 " " ")	
American crude oil..............	10,913 " " "	(19,643 " " ")	
American refined petroleum.	11,047 " " "	(19,884 " " ")	

And M. Dupays remarks: "These figures certainly do not appear favorable for alcohol. On the other hand, we must remember that, owing to the lower heat generated by the combustion of alcohol, a motor using

---

* This denatured alcohol was made up as follows:
    100 liters pure ethyl alcohol (probably commercial 95% alcohol)
    10 liters methyl alcohol containing $\begin{cases} 20\% \text{ acetone} \\ 0.5 \text{ gram heavy benzol} \end{cases}$

† Carbureted alcohol is denatured alcohol to which a hydrocarbon has been added in varying proportions.

‡ It should be noted in the above table that no mention is made of what becomes of the water-vapor resulting from the combustion, whether it is condensed or remains in the form of vapor. As shown (p. 248), this might affect the results over 1100 B.T.U. or even more, and it should be stated, as these results seem to be much higher than we should expect.

that fuel will run more smoothly than if one of the other substances has been employed. Further, a kilogram of alcohol requires less air for complete combustion than does a kilogram of mineral oil (petroleum): according to Ringelmann, 1894, 1.4, and according to Sorel, 1.3 to 1.5, the theoretical amount. This decreases the heat losses in the exhaust-gases (of motors, engines, etc.) and gives a higher thermal efficiency."

In the theoretical calculation for denatured alcohol it may be of interest to note that the quantity of heat required to drive out, in the form of steam, all the water formed during the combustion of the various components is a very large quantity.

The summarized loss of latent heat not available for doing work is shown by the following calculation to be for the denatured alcohol (pp. 245-247):

$$
\begin{aligned}
90.40\% \text{ of } 622^{c}.5 \text{ for ethyl alcohol} &= 562^{c}.7 \\
9.04\% \text{ of } 583^{c}.2 \text{ for commercial wood alcohol} &= 52^{c}.7 \\
0.56\% \text{ of } 305^{c}.9 \text{ for pure pyridine} &= 1^{c}.7 \\
\hline
&617^{c}.1
\end{aligned}
$$

$617.1 \times 1.8 = 1111$ B.T.U. to vaporize all the water formed.

Calculations of the Volume of Air Necessary for Complete Combustion of Alcohol, Gasoline, Kerosene, and Crude Petroleum.—

We may assume for the purposes of this discussion that these bodies have the chemical composition indicated by the formulæ given below:

Ethyl alcohol.	C_2H_5OH
Methyl alcohol.	CH_3OH
Gasoline (hexane).	C_6H_{14}
Kerosene (decane).	$C_{10}H_{22}$
Crude petroleum.	$C_{11}H_{24}$

This latter is variable in composition. In general it contains about 85 per cent carbon and 15 per cent of hydrogen by weight, but its elementary composition gives no idea of the variety of hydrocarbons contained in it.

If we show the complete combustion of these different fuels by means of chemical equations the results will be indicated as follows:

Ethyl Alcohol		Oxygen		Carbon Dioxide		Water
C_2H_5OH	$+$	$3O_2$	$=$	$2CO_2$	$+$	$3H_2O.$
46		96		88		54

By this equation we see that 96 parts of oxygen by weight are necessary for the complete combustion of 46 parts, by weight, of ethyl alcohol, and by this combustion there are produced 88 parts, by weight, of carbon dioxide and 54 parts, by weight, of water.

As the atmosphere consists of 20.9 per cent by volume and 23.1 per cent by weight of oxygen, it is seen that from $\dfrac{96 \times 100}{23.1}$ we find 415 parts, by weight, of air are necessary for the complete combustion of 46 parts, by weight, of absolute ethyl alcohol.

Hence we find that one (1) part of absolute ethyl alcohol by weight requires $\dfrac{415}{46}$, or about nine (9) parts of air by weight, for its complete or perfect combustion.

Methyl Alcohol		Oyxgen		Carbon Dioxide		Water
$2CH_3OH$	$+$	$3O_2$	$=$	$2CO_2$	$+$	$4H_2O.$
64		96		88		72

From this equation we find that 64 parts, by weight, of absolute methyl alcohol require 96 parts, by weight, of oxygen for its perfect combustion, or one (1) part of absolute methyl alcohol, by weight, requires six and one half (6.5) parts of air by weight.

Gasoline		Oxygen		Carbon Dioxide		Water
$2C_6H_{14}$	$+$	$19O_2$	$=$	$12CO_2$	$+$	$14H_2O.$
172		608		528		252

In this case 172 parts, by weight, of gasoline need 608 parts, by weight, of oxygen for perfect combustion, or 172 parts, by weight, of gasoline require $\dfrac{608 \times 100,}{23.1}$ or 2632 parts, by weight, of air and 1 part, by weight, of gasoline requires $\dfrac{2632}{172}$ or 15.3 parts, by weight, of air.

Kerosene		Oxygen		Carbon Dioxide		Water
$2C_{10}H_{22}$	$+$	$31O_2$	$=$	$20CO_2$	$+$	$22H_2O.$
284		992		880		396

Hence in the case of kerosene we find that one (1) part by weight requires about fifteen and one tenth (15.1) parts of air by weight for perfect combustion.

Crude Petroleum		Oxygen		Carbon Dioxide		Water
$C_{11}H_{24}$	$+$	$17O_2$	$=$	$11CO_2$	$+$	$12H_2O.$
156		544		484		216

By theory also we see that one (1) part of crude petroleum by weight needs about fifteen and one tenth (15.1) parts of air by weight for complete combustion.

To find the number of cubic feet of vapor from a given weight of any of these liquid fuels.

Find first the vapor density, that is, the specific gravity of the substance in the state of vapor referred to hydrogen as a unit.

It is a well-known chemical fact that the vapor density is one half the molecular weight.

Multiplying the vapor density by the weight of an equal volume of hydrogen, as for example a liter or a cubic foot, we find the weight of a liter or a cubic foot of the vapor. In the case of ethyl alcohol, C_2H_5OH, the molecular weight is $2 \times 12 + 5 + 16 + 1 = 46$, the vapor density consequently is 23. The weight of a cubic foot of hydrogen is 2.54 gms., that of alcohol vapor $2.54 \times 23 = 58.36$ gms. considered as a vapor under standard conditions; that is, at zero degrees of the Centigrade scale and 760 mm. barometric pressure.

Hence in the case of 1 cubic foot of absolute liquid ethyl alcohol we find the number of cubic feet of vapor it will produce, by theory, as follows:

One (1) cubic foot absolute ethyl alcohol will weigh 49.61 lbs. One (1) pound avoirdupois = 453.6 gms. Therefore 49.61 lbs. $\times$ 453.6 = 22,503 gms., which is the weight of 1 cubic foot of absolute ethyl alcohol.

22,503 divided by 58.36 = 388 cubic feet of absolute ethyl alcohol vapor (considered as a vapor at 0° C. and 760 mm. barometric pressure) from 1 cubic foot of absolute liquid ethyl alcohol.

As the above calculation is made for alcohol vapor at a temperature of 0° C. and 760 mm. barometric pressure, it is necessary to correct it to the boiling temperature of absolute ethyl alcohol, 78.4° C. (for the purposes of this discussion, as the alcohol will be vaporized in the internal-combustion engine), which correction is effected by the well-known formula

$$V:V'::273:273+78.4 \quad \text{or} \quad 388:V'::273:351.4=499.$$

Hence one cubic foot of liquid absolute ethyl alcohol will furnish 499 cubic feet of vapor at the boiling-point of absolute ethyl alcohol, 78°.4 C. As from the preceding equation one part of absolute ethyl alcohol by weight requires nine (9) parts of air by weight for complete combustion, we find that one cubic foot or 49.61 lbs. of absolute ethyl alcohol require 49.61×9 or 446 lbs. of air for complete combustion; hence 499 cubic feet of vapor of absolute ethyl alcohol require 7113 cubic feet of air (from

$446 \div 0.0627$, the weight in pounds avoirdupois of one cubic foot of air at 78.4° C.) for complete combustion, or $7113 \div 499 =$ about 14.25 cubic feet of air to 1 cubic foot of absolute alcohol vapor, for complete combustion, at the temperature of boiling alcohol, or 78.4° C. A graphic representation of the volume of oxygen needed to secure perfect combustion of a given volume of either of these fuels is shown by the following equations:

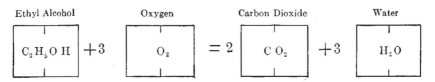

$$\text{Ethyl Alcohol} \quad \boxed{C_2H_5OH} \; +3 \; \boxed{O_2}^{\text{Oxygen}} \; = 2 \; \boxed{CO_2}^{\text{Carbon Dioxide}} \; +3 \; \boxed{H_2O}^{\text{Water}}$$

This equation shows in the case of ethyl alcohol that one volume of alcohol vapor requires three volumes of oxygen, or about fourteen and three tenth volumes of air for perfect combustion, while there are produced two volumes of carbon dioxide and three volumes of water in the form of steam.

In the same way we may represent the volumes of oxygen required in the case of these other fuels, and from this figure multiplied by 4.78 we obtain the volume of air requisite for perfect combustion in each case. These different cases are shown as follows:

$$\text{Methyl Alcohol} \quad 2\,\boxed{CH_3OH} \; + 3 \; \boxed{O_2}^{\text{Oxygen}} \; = 2 \; \boxed{CO_2}^{\text{Carbon Dioxide}} \; +4 \; \boxed{H_2O}^{\text{Water}}$$

Showing that one volume of methyl alcohol-vapor requires one and one half (1.5) volumes of oxygen, or about seven and two tenth (7.2) volumes of air, for complete combustion.

$$\text{Gasoline} \quad 2\,\boxed{C_6H_{14}} \; +19 \; \boxed{O_2}^{\text{Oxygen}} \; = 12 \; \boxed{CO_2}^{\text{Carbon Dioxide}} \; +14 \; \boxed{H_2O}^{\text{Water}}$$

From which graphic representation we find that one (1) volume of gasoline-vapor requires nine and one half (9.5) volumes of oxygen, or forty-five and four tenths (45.4) volumes of air, for its complete combustion.

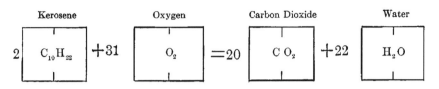

By which equation it is seen that one (1) volume of kerosene vapor requires fifteen and one half (15.5) volumes of oxygen, or seventy-four (74) volumes of air, for its perfect combustion.

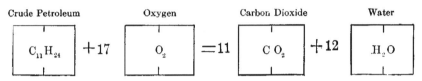

Using this graphic representation we find from this equation that one volume of crude petroleum-vapor requires seventeen volumes of oxygen, or about eighty-one and three tenth (81.3) volumes of air, for its perfect combustion.

The U. S. regulations prescribe the following formula for completely denatured alcohol (see Appendix, this book, p. 385):

100   parts, by volume, of ethyl alcohol (not less than 180° proof).
10   "   "   "   approved methyl alcohol.
½ part "   "   "   petroleum, or coal-tar benzine.

(For copy U. S. Specifications, see Circular No. 680, Chapter IX, pp. 352–354, this book.)

* For example, using gallons in the above formula we have a mixture containing in 100 gallons approximately 90½ of ethyl alcohol, 9 of methyl alcohol, and ½ of benzine. This corresponds to 81.45 gallons absolute ethyl alcohol×6.61 lbs.=538.38 lbs. alcohol. The 9 gallons approved methyl alcohol×6.916 lbs.=62.24 lbs.

As 100 c.c. such approved methyl alcohol must contain an average of 20 grams of acetone and other substances estimated as acetone, the per cent of these substances estimated as acetone will be $\dfrac{20 \times 100}{83} = 24.08$ per cent by weight. Therefore the 9 gallons of approved methyl alcohol consist, approximately, of 62.24−14.98=47.26 lbs. of approved methyl

---

* While this calculation is based on a theoretical assumption of the precise quantities of the various substances composing completely denatured alcohol of 180° proof, or 90 per cent by volume in strength, it is believed that it will be substantially true in practice.

alcohol of 85.66 per cent by weight = 40.48 lbs. absolute methyl alcohol and 14.98 lbs. of acetone. The half-gallon of petroleum benzine will weigh $\dfrac{0.800 \times 8.33 \text{ lbs.}}{2} = 3.33$ lbs. The complete combustion of acetone is shown by theory from the equation

Acetone		Oxygen		Carbon Dioxide		Water
C_3H_6O	+	$4O_2$	=	$3CO_2$	+	$3H_2O.$
58		128		132		54

From this equation it is seen that one part of acetone by weight requires 2.2 parts of oxygen, and therefore $\dfrac{2.2 \times 100}{23.1} = 9.52$ parts of air by weight for its complete combustion. This equation also shows that the complete combustion of one part of acetone by weight produces 2.27 parts, by weight, of carbon dioxide. Hence in 100 gallons of this completely denatured alcohol we have $538.38 + 40.48 + 14.98 + 3.33 = 597.17$, or 597 lbs. in round numbers of combustible matter or fuel, requiring from the preceding equations 5302 lbs. of air for complete combustion, as follows:

Absolute ethyl alcohol. $538.38 \times 9 = 4845.42$ lbs. of air
Absolute methyl alcohol. . . . . $40.48 \times 6.5 = 263.12$ " " "
Acetone. . . . . $14.98 \times 9.52 = 142.61$ " " "
Petroleum benzine (taken as gasoline) . . . . . . $3.33 \times 15.3 = 50.95$ " " "

100 gallons, or 694 lbs.. of completely denatured alcohol require $\quad 5302.10$ lbs. of air
Or 1 lb. requires 7.64 lbs. of air, or 1.764 lbs. of oxygen.

The carbon dioxide produced from the complete combustion, by theory, of the 100 gallons of completely denatured alcohol mentioned is found from the preceding chemical equations, as follows:

Absolute ethyl alcohol. . . . . 538.38 lbs. $\times 1.91 = 1028.31$ lbs. carbon dioxide
Absolute methyl alcohol. . . . . 40.48 " $\times 1.37 = 55.46$ " " "
Acetone. . . . . 14.98 " $\times 2.27 = 34.00$ " " "
Petroleum benzine (taken as gasoline). . . . . 3.33 " $\times 3.06 = 10.19$ " " "

100 gals., or 694 lbs., of completely denatured alcohol $= 1127.96$ " " "
Hence 1 lb. of such completely denatured alcohol produces 1.625 lbs. carbon dioxide when complete combustion occurs.

In case the coal-tar benzine, which can also be used, is employed as one of the denaturants by the U. S. regulations as an alternative to the petroleum benzine, the quantity of air required for the complete combustion by theory of half a gallon of it in the above example is very close to that required for the petroleum benzine. This is because the former, boiling between 150° C. and 200° C. consists largely of commercial toulene and xylene, with possibly some naphthalene dissolved and some slight sulphur impurity. Calculations based on the assumption that such benzine consisted largely of toluene and xylene give the following results by theory for complete combustion expressed in the form of chemical equations:

$$
\underset{92}{\underset{\text{Toluene}}{C_7H_8}} \quad + \quad \underset{288}{\underset{\text{Oxygen}}{9O_2}} \quad = \quad \underset{308}{\underset{\text{Carbon Dioxide}}{7CO_2}} \quad + \quad \underset{72}{\underset{\text{Water}}{4H_2O}},
$$

$$
\underset{212}{\underset{\text{Xylene}}{2C_8H_{10}}} \quad + \quad \underset{672}{\underset{\text{Oxygen}}{21O_2}} \quad = \quad \underset{704}{\underset{\text{Carbon Dioxide}}{16CO_2}} \quad + \quad \underset{180}{\underset{\text{Water}}{10H_2O}},
$$

from which it is seen that one part by weight of toluene requires 3.13 parts of oxygen, or 13.54 parts of air by weight, and one part by weight of xylene requires 3.17 parts of oxygen, or 13.72 parts of air by weight, by theory, for complete combustion. Hence in the calculation for the complete combustion of the completely denatured alcohol above, the coaltar benzine is quite close to the petroleum benzine and is practically the same.

Note.—On December 10, 1906, since the above was written, an amendment to the U. S. regulations by Circular No. 686 was issued, permitting the use of methyl alcohol and pyridine bases, as denaturants, by the following formula:

"To every 100 parts by volume of ethyl alcohol of the desired proof (not less than 180°) there shall be added two parts by volume of approved methyl alcohol and one half of one part by volume of approved pyridine bases—for example, to every 100 gallons of ethyl alcohol (of not less than 180° proof) there shall be added two gallons of approved methyl alcohol and one half gallon of approved pyridin bases."

Circular No. 686 is given in full in Chapter IX and also in the U. S. regulations in the Appendix of this book.

The theoretical B.T.U. in one pound of such completely denatured alcohol of 180° proof, mentioned in Circular No. 686, calculated from the preceding equations, is about 10,000.

For purposes of illumination, the ratio of the vitiation of the atmosphere by this completely denatured alcohol of Circular No. 686 corresponds substantially to that given for the U. S. formula just described.

*Neither coal-tar benzol nor ergin, the latter also a coal-tar product, have been used in the United States for internal-combustion engines, their cost being prohibitive for such purpose.

In Germany ergin, which is much preferred to benzol, is considered safer, and is cheaper than benzol.

---

* Statement furnished by The Otto Gas Engine Works of Philadelphia, Pa.

Ergin has a specific gravity of 0.90, flashes at 95° F., and its boiling-point is above 212° F. In internal-combustion engines it can be used very much like alcohol, in that it will stand a very high compression, up to 190 lbs. per square inch.

Ratio of Prices of these Various Fuels.—In comparing the ratio of the prices of these various fuels, it may be stated that the following table probably represents the average price, the highest-priced being given first:

1. Benzol,	5. Kerosene,
2. Ergin,	6. Fuel oil,*
3. Denatured alcohol,	7. Crude petroleum.
4. Gasoline,	

The choice of a fuel is not wholly dependent upon the price, as in case of denatured alcohol it will be shown that it is safe, hygienic, and that any one can use it; while in the case of these other fuels mentioned the exhaust-gases from the engine or motor are apt to be detrimental to health, and in case of fire at sea or on the land water will not help to put it out. As gasoline, kerosene, and crude petroleum do not mix with water, a fire will merely spread, as these fuels will float and burn on water. In the case of denatured alcohol, however, as it will easily mix with water, any fire which might accidentally occur is therfeore readily extinguished.

Denatured alcohol when burned fouls the atmosphere much less than any of these other liquid fuels we have mentioned.

The exhaust-gases from an alcohol-engine or motor are cooler and not detrimental to health, as is very apt to be the case with gasoline and other hydrocarbon fuels.

The ratio of air necessary for the complete combustion of all the above fuels should be somewhat exceeded in practice over the above theoretical calculations, in order to be sure the fuel is burned as completely as the conditions will admit.

The more imperfect the combustion the more wasteful is the performance of the engine or motor, and the liability of deposits of soot (blackening) in the cylinder is greatly increased if the amount of air introduced is not enough in the case of fuels other than alcohol. With denatured alcohol an insufficient amount of air entails a great loss of mechanical efficiency in the engine or motor, and liability to formation

---

* Fuel oil, while oftentimes crude petroleum, is usually a residue from which the lighter portions have been separated.

of products, through incomplete combustion, which may corrode (rust) the cylinder and exhaust-valves.

In Germany this latter condition has not been seriously encountered. In France, where the law requires wood alcohol to be present in much larger amount in the denatured alcohol, some complaints have arisen from this source.

In order to deduce some practical results from the preceding equations a table is here given showing the volume of air by theory required for complete combustion of given amounts of various fuels, with exception of benzol and ergin, whose high cost compared to the other fuels precludes their use.

TABLE SHOWING VOLUME OF AIR, BY THEORY, REQUIRED FOR COMPLETE COMBUSTION OF GIVEN AMOUNTS OF FUELS.

Kind of Fuel.	Ratio of Air to Fuel by Weight.	Air Required per Pound of Fuel. Cu. Ft.	Air Required per U. S. Gallon of Fuel. Cu. Ft.	Air Required per Cubic Foot of Fuel. Cu. Ft.
* U. S. completely denatured alcohol, 180° proof....................	7.64	99.87	694	5,193
72° gasoline........................	15.3	200.0	1,156	8,572
135° F., fire-test kerosene	15.1	197.4	1,293	9,684
† Fuel oil...........................	15.4	201.3	1,389	10,409
Crude petroleum, average Penna.......	15.4	201.3	1,389	10,409

* See page 253.

† Fuel oil is taken as of the same elementary composition as crude petroleum or 85 per cent of carbon and 15 per cent of hydrogen by weight.

For specific gravities and weights used in calculating above table see table, p. 258.

From the above table the markedly less amount of air required for the complete combustion of the denatured alcohol, compared to other usual liquid fuels, is readily apparent. Even absolute ethyl alcohol only requires about 117.6 cubic feet per pound for complete or perfect combustion. This feature is a decided advantage in case of denatured alcohol.

It will also be of interest to compare acetylene gas with these other fuel substances, and for this purpose it is thus mentioned in the next section of this chapter.

Ratio of Vitiation of the Atmosphere by Combustion of these Fuels.—As the use of acetylene gas generated for small capacities for lighting purposes from calcium carbide is attaining quite a degree of importance for some special uses, it is interesting to ascertain the ratio of air by weight necessary for the complete combustion of acetylene gas. This is found from the equation

Acetylene Gas		Oxygen		Carbon Dioxide		Water
$2C_2H_2$	$+$	$5O_2$	$=$	$4CO_2$	$+$	$2H_2O,$
52		160		176		36

from which we find that 3 parts, by weight, of oxygen, or about 13 parts, by weight, of air are required for the perfect combustion of one part, by weight, of acetylene gas. In such combustion there are produced from one part, by weight, of acetylene gas about 3.38 parts, by weight, of carbon dioxide.

In order to show the weight of oxygen required, and the weight of carbon dioxide formed, for the combustion of the same weight of each of these fuels the following table is given.

In this table the ratio of vitiation of the atmosphere given is deduced from the weight of carbon dioxide produced, in each case, from the same weight of each fuel.

TABLE SHOWING WEIGHT OF OXYGEN REQUIRED AND WEIGHT OF CARBON DIOXIDE PRODUCED BY THE PERFECT COMBUSTION OF EACH OF THE FUELS NAMED AND THE RATIO OF VITIATION OF THE ATMOSPHERE.

Kinds of Fuel.	Pounds of Oxygen for One Pound of Fuel.	Pounds of Carbon Dioxide Produced per Pound of Fuel.	Ratio of Vitiation of the Atmosphere.
Denatured alcohol 180° proof *........	1.764	1.625	100
72° gasoline.........................	3.53	3.070	188
135° F., fire-test kerosene	3.49	3.098	190
Fuel oil †............................	3.487	3.102	191
Crude petroleum.....................	3.487	3.102	191
Acetylene gas.......................	3.076	3.38	208
Coal gas.	2.793	2.18	134

Note.—One pound of acetylene gas = 13.74 cubic feet.

Specific gravity = 0.90 (referred to air).

One pound of coal gas = 31.0 cubic feet.

Specific gravity = 0.40 (referred to air).

* See page 253.

† Fuel oil is taken as of the same elementary composition as crude petroleum or $C_{11}H_{24}$.

In the above table the weight of carbon dioxide produced from one pound of denatured alcohol 180° U. S. proof is taken as unity, or 100, and it is the lowest of these fuels in ratio of vitiation of the atmosphere.

The denatured alcohol therefore fouls the atmosphere much less than these other fuels when burned in lamps, stoves, or used in explosive types of engines. This fact is of marked advantage in the case of alcohol.

The following table of comparison of these fuels is given as being of convenience in matters of reference.

TABLE SHOWING THE SPECIFIC GRAVITY, DEGREES BEAUMÉ, FLASHING-POINT, AND WEIGHT PER U. S. GALLON AND CUBIC FOOT OF CERTAIN FUELS.

Kind of Fuel.	Specific Gravity.	Degrees Beaumé.	Flashing-point, Degrees F.	Pounds in One Gallon, U. S. Stand.	Pounds in One Cubic Foot.
Ethyl alcohol 90 per cent, or 180° U. S. proof	0.8339	38	58.1	6.95	52
Ethyl alcohol 94 per cent, or 188° U. S. proof	0.8200	41	about 61	6.84	51.20
Ethyl alcohol 95 per cent, or 190° U. S. proof	0.8161	42	61.7	6.80	50.95
Ethyl alcohol, absolute or 200° U. S. proof	0.7938	46	81	6.61	49.61
* Gasoline 76° Beaumé	0.678	76	below 32	5.65	42.32
* Gasoline 72° Beaumé	0.6930	72	" 32	5.78	42.86
* Kerosene 135° F., fire test	0.786	48	125	6.55	49.06
* Kerosene 150° F., fire test	0.788	48	134	6.57	49.19
Fuel oil	0.8284	39	140	6.90	51.71
Crude petroleum, average Penna	0.8100	43	70	6.75	50.56
Ergin	0.900	25.5	95	7.50	56.18

* From Gill's Oil Analysis, and Gill and Healey, Tech. Quar., Vol. XV, p. 74.

For practical fuel purposes the specific gravity and strength of methyl alcohol may be taken as the same as the (ethyl) alcohol in the above table.

For convenience of reference the following table shows the calorific value of the usual liquid fuels.

TABLE SHOWING THE CALORIFIC VALUE OF THE USUAL LIQUID FUELS.

Kind of Fuel.	B.T.U. per Pound.	B.T.U. per Gallon.	B.T.U. per Cu. Foot.
* Denatured alcohol, specific gravity 0.8192	10,355	70,621	529,451
† 72° gasoline	18,900	109,242	810,054
135° kerosene	18,520	121,306	908,591
Fuel oil	19,000	131,100	982,490
‡ Crude American petroleum	19,630	132,502	992,492
‡ Refined American petroleum	19,880		
Coal gas	19,375		625
Pure benzol (by theory)	18,031		
‡ Carbureted alcohol from— 50% petrol 50% French methylated spirits }	14,200		

* See page 245.
† Gill and Healey, Tech. Quar., Vol. XV, p. 74, 1902.
‡ Bull. Assoc. Chem. Soc.; Journ. S. I. C., Vol. XXIV, p. 1218.

The Beaumé Hydrometer referred to is shown in the subjoined Fig. 110. In this cut is also shown the Hydrometer-jar (Fig. 111), which is filled with the liquid to be tested, and the hydrometer immersed therein.

The proper precautions as to temperature having been taken, the degree in strength, in terms of the Beaumé scale, are at once read from the scale of the hydrometer. This hydrometer-jar happens to be shown in a reduced size as compared with the hydrometer proper. The actual jar is, of course, of sufficient height to allow the hydrometer to sink its length in the liquid so as to fully include the use of the whole scale.

The table given on p. 260 is of convenience for converting scale of Beaumé degrees lighter than water into specific gravity and vice versa for experiments and work in practice.

Alcohol Heating and Cooking Apparatus and Stoves.— The alcohol self-heating flat-iron is shown in Fig. 112. This is heated by converting the alcohol into a gas and burning the vapor thus formed. It makes a very convenient heat-avoiding implement for use in summer-time.

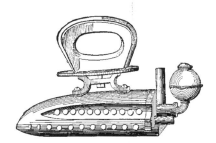

Fig. 110.—Beaumé Hydrometer. Fig. 111.—Hydrometer-jar, Lip Form. Fig. 112.—Foreign Alcohol Self-heating Flat-iron.

In Fig. 113, p. 260, is shown a foreign type of alcohol cooking-stove, the advantages of which are common to all alcohol stoves. These advantages can be stated to be freedom from smoke, soot, ashes, and dirt.

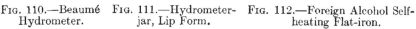

* Table Showing Relation of Beaumé Degrees to Specific Gravity and the Weight of One United States Gallon at 60° F.

Beaumé.	Specific Gravity.	Pounds in U. S. Gallons.	Beaumé.	Specific Gravity.	Pounds in U. S. Gallons.	Beaumé.	Specific Gravity.	Pounds in U. S. Gallons.	Beaumé.	Specific Gravity.	Pounds in U. S. Gallons.
10	1.0000	8.33	31	0.8695	7.24	52	0.7692	6.41	73	0.6896	5.75
11	0.9929	8.27	32	0.8641	7.20	53	0.7650	6.37	74	0.6863	5.72
12	0.9859	8.21	33	0.8588	7.15	54	0.7608	6.34	75	0.6829	5.69
13	0.9790	8.16	34	0.8536	7.11	55	0.7567	6.30	76	0.6796	5.66
14	0.9722	8.10	35	0.8484	7.07	56	0.7526	6.27	77	0.6763	5.63
15	0.9655	8.04	36	0.8433	7.03	57	0.7486	6.24	78	0.6730	5.60
16	0.9589	7.99	37	0.8383	6.98	58	0.7446	6.20	79	0.6698	5.58
17	0.9523	7.93	38	0.8333	6.94	59	0.7407	6.17	80	0.6666	5.55
18	0.9459	7.88	39	0.8284	6.90	60	0.7368	6.14	81	0.6635	5.52
19	0.9395	7.83	40	0.8235	6.86	61	0.7329	6.11	82	0.6604	5.50
20	0.9333	7.78	41	0.8187	6.82	62	0.7290	6.07	83	0.6573	5.48
21	0.9271	7.72	42	0.8139	6.78	63	0.7253	6.04	84	0.6542	5.45
22	0.9210	7.67	43	0.8092	6.74	64	0.7216	6.01	85	0.6511	5.42
23	0.9150	7.62	44	0.8045	6.70	65	0.7179	5.98	86	0.6481	5.40
24	0.9090	7.57	45	0.8000	6.66	66	0.7142	5.95	87	0.6451	5.38
25	0.9032	7.53	46	0.7954	6.63	67	0.7106	5.92	88	0.6422	5.36
26	0.8974	7.48	47	0.7909	6.59	68	0.7070	5.89	89	0.6392	5.33
27	0.8917	7.43	48	0.7865	6.55	69	0.7035	5.86	90	0.6363	5.30
28	0.8860	7.38	49	0.7821	6.52	70	0.7000	5.83	95	0.6222	5.18
29	0.8805	7.34	50	0.7777	6.48	71	0.6965	5.80			
30	0.8750	7.29	51	0.7734	6.44	72	0.6930	5.78			

* From Gill's Oil Analysis.

The examples of French alcohol heating apparatus shown in the cuts below are used in a similar manner to those already described.

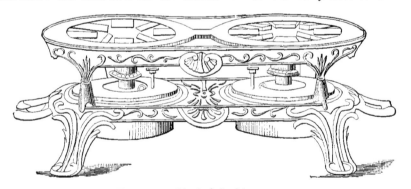

Fig. 113.—Alcohol Cooking-stove.

An exceedingly useful burner is provided for laboratory purposes by the Bunsen alcohol burner shown in Fig. 116.

The alcohol heating-stove shown in Fig. 117, p. 262, is a very satisfactory source of heat for laboratory and other purposes. It will be noticed that it is supplied with an adjustable notched ring, by which the heating support can be placed close to, or at a distance from, the flame, which

FIG. 114.—Boivin Alcohol Heating-stove and Extinguishing-cap.

FIG. 115.—French Curling-tongs and Alcohol Heater.

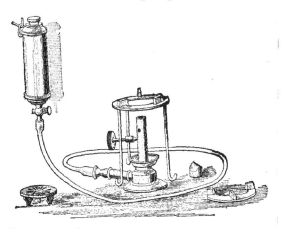

FIG. 116.—Alcohol Bunsen Burner for Laboratory.

is a very clever contrivance. Its principles of construction and method of burning the alcohol are similar to other stoves of this character.

Another form of foreign alcohol cooking-stove is shown in Fig. 118,

FIG. 117.—Alcohol Heating-stove, Adjustable.   Whitall, Tatum & Co.,
New York City.

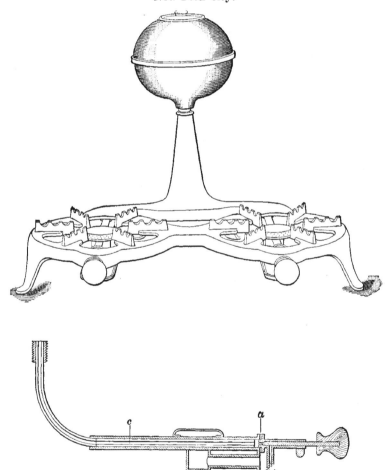

FIG. 118.—The upper cut shows the Barthel Alcohol Cooking- or Heating-stove
with two burners. The lower cut shows section of the burner. Made by
G. Barthel.

p. 262. This stove has two burners, the alcohol-reservoir being shown at the top.

The details of the burner are shown in the longitudinal vertical section of the drawing at the lower part of Fig. 118. It is claimed this stove does very satisfactory work with spirit of 90 per cent strength or 180° U. S. proof, although 95 per cent strength or 190° U. S. proof is also recommended. To light the stove a little alcohol is flowed into the igniting-channel just beneath the burner. The alcohol-valve is then closed and the spirit ignited with a match. Before the flame dies out the alcohol-valve is opened again and the spirit-gas flame is developed. The alcohol-valve is only opened two complete revolutions for this purpose, as a complete supply is thus obtained.

The height of the flame is adjusted by means of the alcohol supply-valve. When this valve is closed the flame is extinguished. The burner can be used for several hundred hours, after which it should be cleaned, or a new burner can be inserted as desired.

In the accompanying figure, 119, an alcohol laboratory burner is shown which burns half a pint of alcohol in 90 minutes with full flame. The flame-tube is 18 mm. in diameter (about 0.7 inch), and is claimed to melt a 3-mm. copper wire in 1½ minutes. The flame is 7 inches in height, and a heat equal to from two to three ordinary Bunsen burners is claimed to be produced by this burner.

The supply of air and height of flame may be regulated by the movable valve in the burner-tube. If the opening in the burner-tube becomes clogged, clean it with the needles furnished with the lamp; never use a pin. It is most important not to enlarge this opening. In using this burner the basin must first be filled with spirit. The suction-wick in this lamp merely brings the alcohol by capillary attraction to the vaporizing-chamber or

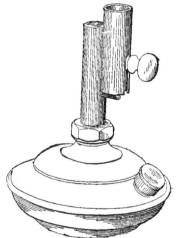

Fig. 119.—Barthel's Alcohol Laboratory Burner.

tube, where it is burned as a gas. The flame is perfectly blue and smokeless, and when the burner is not in use there is no loss of spirit by evaporation.

A soldering and paint-removing lamp or torch is shown in the illustration, Fig. 120, p. 264. It will be noticed that this lamp has no pump, as is the case with gasoline. It is therefore much simpler to operate and equally satisfactory in its results. To start this torch, al! that is necessary is to light a little alcohol in the igniting-dish, shown at the left of the cut, when the alcohol very quickly begins to vaporize and the gas is ignited at the mouth of the torch. The suction-wick shown in Fig. 121, supplies the alcohol to this vaporizing-tube. The vapors then issue from the nozzle inside the blowpipe and are ignited. The nozzle is shown in

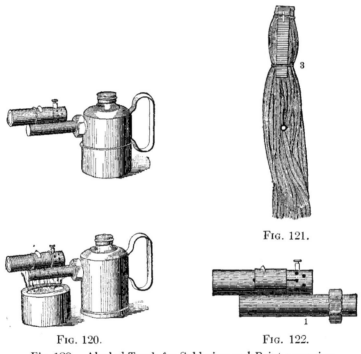

Fig. 121.

Fig. 120.   Fig. 122.

Fig. 120. Alcohol Torch for Soldering and Paint-removing.
Fig. 121. Suction-wick for Torch. Fig. 122. Lamp-nozzle for Torch.

Fig. 122. In renewing the wick the brass plate of the wick must be placed above, toward the blowpipe, the wick being pushed right up to the end of the wick-tube. The brass cup, which fits on the container, holds the correct charge for the lamp. After emptying this into the container of the lamp, the cap is screwed down tightly. The measuring-cup when inverted serves to ignite the lamp, as shown above.

In the Alcohol Bunsen Burner shown in Figs. 123 and 124 the flame is regulated by the controlling screw, but the flame should never be smaller than $1\frac{1}{2}$ inches. After continued use the wire gauze, which should always rest on the four spikes inside the tube, must be renewed. For a stronger flame a wider-mesh gauze should be taken. The passages in

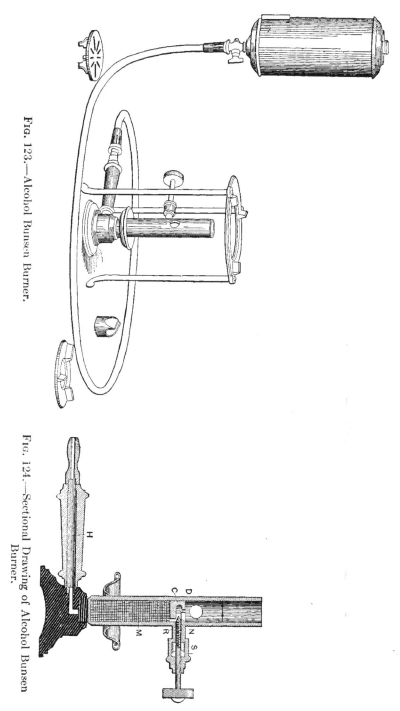

Fig. 123.—Alcohol Bunsen Burner.

Fig. 124.—Sectional Drawing of Alcohol Bunsen Burner.

the handle *H* and the body *M*, and occasionally the nozzle of the burner *D* and valve *C*, will become clogged in the course of from 500 to 1000 hours' use. The pricker is then used to restore the size of the flame. Only iron-wire gauze is recommended when heating vessels, as, on account of the heat of this burner, brass will fuse. In Fig. 123 the alcohol-reservoir, the flexible tube for supplying alcohol to the burner, and also the sectional drawing of this burner are shown.

American Alcohol Cooking-stoves.—The Quick Work Stove Company, of Cleveland, Ohio, furnish the following statement concerning the cuts

Fig. 125.—No. 32, Cabinet Alcohol Cooking-stove. Made by the Quick Work Stove Co., Cleveland, Ohio.

of their alcohol cooking-stoves, which are shown in the following pages: "We have been experimenting for the past three years to produce a good alcohol stove for use in foreign countries where tax-free denatured alcohol is used, and for this purpose we print our circular in both English and Spanish. We mention a number of points of interest concerning

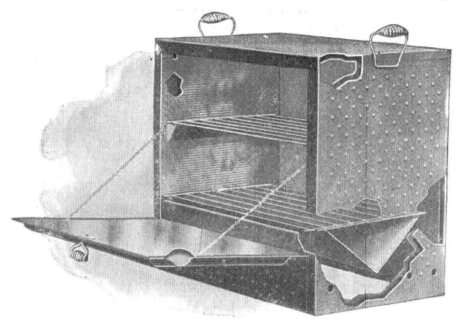

Fig. 126.—Oven of the Quick Work Stove.

perfected alcohol stoves which we shall incorporate in our next circular. Our stove, using a single burner with the fire turned on full, lasts about

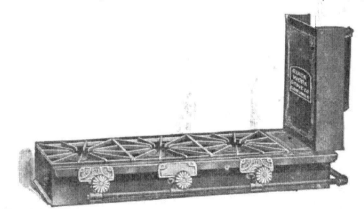

Fig. 127.—Three-burner Hot-plate, No. 44, of the Quick Work Stove.

$2\frac{3}{4}$ hours. In another test we kept water on our cooking-stove at the boiling-point for six hours using one quart of alcohol as fuel. This shows what saving can be made by an economical operator. We find the results of burning gasoline and alcohol are about the same, but submit that, taking everything into consideration, alcohol is far ahead of any other liquid fuel. Our stoves require no more care or attention than any ordinary

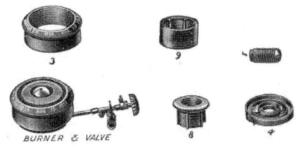

FIG. 128.—This cut shows Burner and Valve complete and the various Parts of the Burner for the Quick Work Alcohol Stove.

cooking-stove to maintain them in good working order. In the case of jelly, for instance, being boiled over and the vaporizer becoming filled, all that is necessary to do is to remove the burner parts and scrape the dirt out of the vaporizer. The burners are made of annealed cast iron,—not cheap metal or tin,—and are the most effective, durable, and expensive burner made. The construction of our hot-plate or platform stoves is very compact, and if well crated they will stand long and severe trips by rail or water. Any part of our stoves can be replaced without having to purchase a whole new stove. Our system of generating fuel into gas enables more air to be mixed with the gas than any other stove on the market. This results in complete combustion of the fuel, which is a

FIG. 129.—Sectional view of complete Burner for Quick Work Alcohol Stove.

very desirable feature. As soon as a meal is prepared, the fuel-valve is shut and no further fuel is consumed. All surplus heat is also avoided, which is not the case with wood, coal, or charcoal. The oven with our stove becomes thoroughly heated in about ten to fifteen minutes. These

Ready for use, 6¼ inches high.

Closed, 3¾ inches high.

FIG. 130.—Traveling Companion, capacity 1 pint. Nickel-plate, complete with Egg-holder and Tea or Coffee-maker. Made by S. Sternau & Co., Brooklyn, N. Y.

The stand, lamp, extinguisher, egg-holder, handle, and silver-plated tea- or coffee-maker fit inside the cup. The handle is non-heating ebonized wood and is removable.

This traveling companion is exceedingly convenient for heating milk or soups, cooking cereals, boiling eggs, etc. For travelers, tourists, picnickers, sportsmen, etc., it is of great utility. For use in the nursery or in the sick-room it is invaluable. The lamp holds one half gill, which will burn about twenty-three minutes. All of the alcohol lamps shown here are the very best that have been produced after an experience of twenty-three years.

stoves are portable, very convenient, and reliable in case of sickness where hot water is quickly wanted. If, as time passes, the use of alcohol as a fuel becomes general, the consumption for cooking purposes should certainly be very large. In Fig. 125, p. 266, is shown the No. 32 Cabinet Cooking-stove. This stove comprises four burners, and the illustration shows it to be of an efficient character and fine, durable construction."

American Alcohol Cooking Apparatus.—The following illustrations show some of the utensils for cooking purposes used in conjunction

FIG. 131.—Coffee-machine Set. Consists of coffee-machine with Sterno-Inferno burner, alcohol flagon, cream-pitcher, sugar-bowl, wind-shield, and oblong tray, size 12×18 inches. Capacity of coffee-machine 2½ pints or 14 after-dinner cups.

The Sterno-Inferno burner is the latest modern alcohol lamp; holds one gill, and will burn about one hour. This coffee-machine distills the coffee and thus extracts only the wholesome properties of the coffee. Coffee should never be boiled, because boiling extracts the unwholesome properties, dissipates the aroma, and spoils the flavor. With the foregoing coffee-machine coffee of a quality that never varies can always be made on the table. These unusual and convenient features one cannot fail to appreciate. When any of the parts of the coffee-machine are worn out they can be replaced without getting a new machine complete.

with alcohol lamps. Each article has been designed so as to be durable and practical in every respect, as well as appealing to the eye, and is made in the most skillful way of solid copper. Besides being furnished in polished copper, each article is also supplied in either nickel or silver-

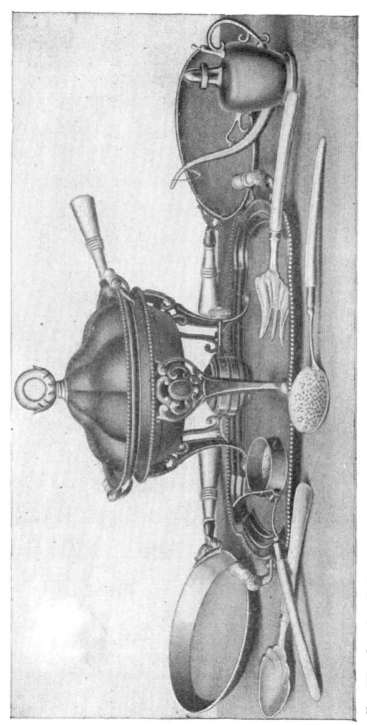

FIG. 132.—Complete Chafing-dish Outfit Trimmed with Genuine Ivory. Consists of three-pint chafing-dish with alcohol lamp, toaster, spoon, fork, omelet-pan, skimmer, egg-poacher, half-pint alcohol flagon, and oblong tray, size 12 × 18 inches; all trimmed with genuine ivory, excepting the flagon. The lamp holds one-half gill and will burn about twenty-four minutes.

This outfit is rich in appearance and a delight to those who appreciate the convenience of the chafing-dish for preparing hot luncheons in many ways.

271

plate, excepting the spoon, fork-skimmer, egg-poacher, and toaster, which are made of nickel-silver, and also furnished in silver-plate highly

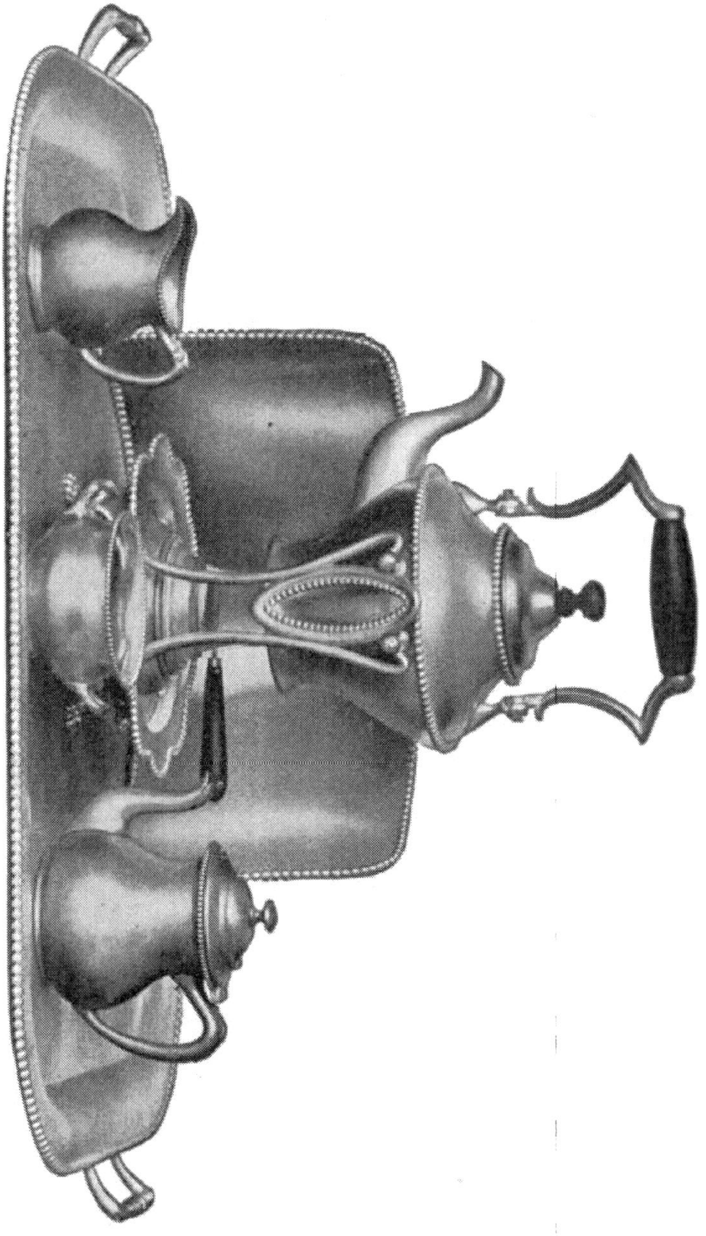

FIG. 133.—Teakettle Set, trimmed with solid beaded edge. Consists of teakettle and stand, fitted with ventilated asbestos lamp, sugar-bowl, cream-pitcher, wind-shield, teapot, and oblong tray, size 14×22 inches. Capacity of kettle, 2½ pints; capacity of pot, 1 pint; extreme height of kettle and stand, 12 inches. The alcohol lamp fitted to teakettle holds one half gill and will burn about eighteen minutes. The foregoing set is very satisfactory for an afternoon tea-service.

burnished. The apparatus shown in Figs. 130–133 is made by S. Sternau and Co., Brooklyn, N. Y.

The alcohol-gas stove shown in Fig. 134 is manufactured by Glogau & Co., Chicago, Ill. It is of durable construction and a very convenient

form of heating apparatus for small capacities. This stove is about five inches in width and height, weighs about eight ounces, and the reservoir holds nearly half a pint of alcohol. The materials are brass and the finish is nickel-plate. Wherever gas is not available or desirable, and for emergency heating necessities, light housekeeping, etc., it is extremely useful.

FIG. 134.—Glogau's Alcohol-gas Stove.

The principle of its operation consists in the fact that it vaporizes the alcohol and then burns it in the form of a gas, making an exceedingly steady flame and reliable source of heat. A quart of water is boiled in about eight minutes. The best results demand that the best spirits procurable be used for fuel. As an illustration of the universal use which the merit of this stove has obtained, it can be mentiond that it is used in the camps and hospitals of the United States, German, British, and French armies.

The Kerosene Burner for Steamer Automobiles.—This burner is manufactured by the National Oil-heating Company of Melrose, Mass.

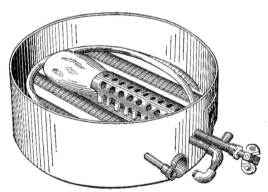

FIG. 135.—Kerosene Burner for Steamer Automobiles. Easily adaptable for use with alcohol.

It is started by a small alcohol burner or hand lamp specially designed for the purpose, which in a few moments heats the kerosene to the vaporizing temperature and ignites it. The alcohol vaporizing lamp is then withdrawn and the kerosene is soon ignited in the burner, where it automatically maintains its own combustion. A pipe from the kerosene pressure-tank to the main burner and one from the small pilot-light tank to the pilot light is all the piping necessary. The general appearance of this burner is similar to all steamer automobile burners in that the main vaporizing-coil lies across the burner forcing the gas into the mixing-tube, the kerosene being fed to the burner under pressure. The burner is closed at the bottom and there is no opportunity for back-firing. The flame and gases can only pass out through the boiler and stack. Should alcohol be obtainable at a reasonable price the above burner can be easily adapted for its use.

Foreign Alcohol Heating-stoves.—In the accompanying cut is shown the French alcohol heating-stove made by E. Boivin et Cie.,

FIG. 136.—Alcohol Heating-stove.

Paris, France. This stove is beautifully finished, as are all articles of French manufacture. The highly planished or polished fluted copper reflector in the front of the stove concentrates the rays of heat and throws them forward into the apartment, greatly conserving the amount of alcohol consumed. The advantages claimed for this stove are the absence of any objectionable flue products, a heating effect not obtained by any other (alcohol) system and no danger of explosion. It is also stated that the stove is regulated with a cock in the same manner as the ordinary gas-stove, and that the consumption of alcohol is reduced to a minimum, the heating effect equaling that of the gas-stove. In this stove the alcohol is first vaporized and then burns as a gas. The details of the manipulation of this stove are as follows:

R, alcohol-reservoir, which is filled with denatured alcohol of 90 per cent strength; *B*, alcohol-lighting cock; *C*, alcohol-igniting channel; *D*, alcohol-feeding cock; *E*, handle for opening or closing shutter to view the operation of the burner.

Note.—It is recommended for the best results in heating that the reservoir be kept well filled.

Important Notice.—Do not open the cock *D* while the alcohol is burning in the igniting-channel *C*, and be careful that the cock *D* is *always closed* when the stove is not in use.

This stove is merely an example of one type of alcohol stove used for heating purposes.

CHAPTER VIII.

ALCOHOL AS A SOURCE OF POWER.

The Deutz Alcohol-engine. The Deutz Alcohol-motor or Portable Engine American Alcohol-engines. The Alcohol-motor for the Automobile. The Diesel Engine. The Kerosene-oil Engine. The Gasoline-engine and its Adaptation to Alcohol. Comparison of the Economy of the Steam-engine with Other Types of Engines. The Gas-engine Compared with Other Types of Engines. Outline of the Methods Used in Testing Internal-combustion Engines.

The Deutz Alcohol-engine.—As the experience with alcohol engines has been extremely limited in the United States, it will be of advantage

Fɪɢ. 137.—Deutz Engine for Use with Alcohol, Gasoline, Kerosene, or Ergin.

to conisder the progress made by Germany in this respect. This nation has been a leading exponent in the development and uses of denatured

277

or industrial alcohol for the past twenty years. For this reason we will begin with a description of the design and construction of the engines built by the Deutz Gas-engine Works of Cologne-Deutz, Germany, which company have furnished the author with the data here given through the kindness of their American branch house, the Otto Gas-engine Works, of Philadelphia, Pa. We show in Fig. 137, p. 275, an illustration of the Deutz alcohol engine, type E–12, of 20 horse-power.

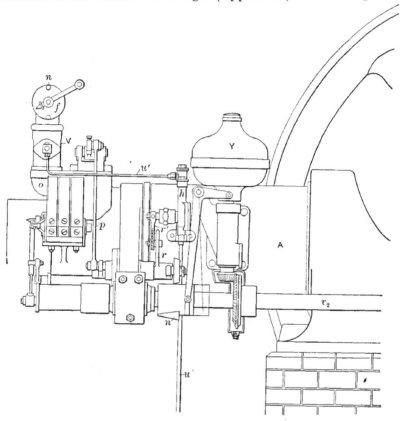

FIG. 138.—Side Elevation of Type E–12, Deutz Alcohol Engine.

The original Otto or Deutz engines have been built in Germany for a period of about forty years, the type of the Otto gas-engine being the pioneer in single-acting explosive engines.

"The original Otto engines types E–10, M–10, and E–12 are single-acting explosive engines. The cylinder being closed at one end, a mixture of air and gasoline, kerosene or alcohol vapor is exploded in the cylinder, the resulting pressure moving a piston which transmits power throughthe connecting-rod and crank to the fly-wheel shaft.

"The engine operates on the 4-stroke cycle principle, that is at every fourth piston-stroke, or every two full revolutions of the crank-shaft, a

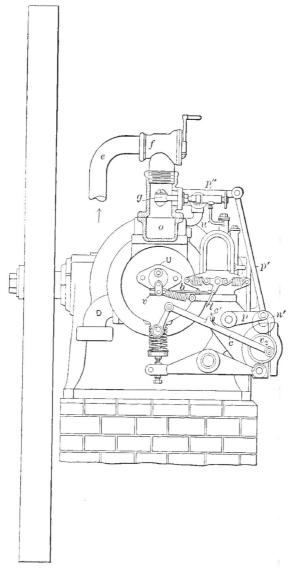

Fig. 139.—Cross-section of Type E–12, Deutz Alcohol Engine.

power impulse is generated.   When the piston is at the end of its inner stroke there remains between the piston-head and the inside end of the cylinder a certain clearance space—the compression space, filled with

air or the products of previous combustion, and beginning with this
position of the piston the following cycle of operations takes place:

"First (forward) stroke of the piston. During the outstroke of the
piston an explosive mixture of gaosline, kerosene, or alcohol-vapor and
air is drawn into the cylinder (charging period).

"Second (backward) stroke of the piston. The explosive mixture
is compressed in the clearance space (compression period).

"Third (forward) stroke of the piston. At the inner dead-center the
compressed charge is ignited, and the resulting high increase in pressure
drives the piston forward (working or power period).

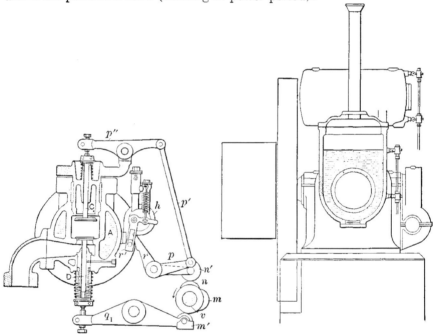

FIG. 140.—Vertical Section of Cylinder- FIG. 141.—Cross-section of Cooling-
head. water Jacket, by Evaporation.

"The strong impulse thus given to the fly-wheel suffices to keep
it in motion during the three following successive piston-strokes.

"Fourth (backward) stroke of the piston. The products of combustion are expelled into the atmosphere through the open exhaust-valve.

"Close uniformity and regulation of speed of the engine is secured by
the use of a proportionally heavy fly-wheel.

"The engines of types E–10, M–10, and E–12 can be operated with
gasoline, kerosene, alcohol, or ergin. If built for gasoline or kerosene
and changed for operating on alcohol or ergin, the compression must be

increased. Generally the engines are tested at the shops for one particular fuel only.

"The types enumerated differ somewhat, as follows:

"Type E–10 is a slow-speed engine and can be furnished equipped with either cooling by water circulation or cooling by evaporation (see paragraph describing methods of cooling). The charge is formed by means of a spraying device, the fuel being admitted to this device either through the pump or a float-valve.

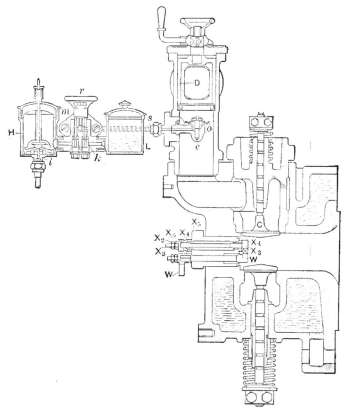

Fig. 142.—Longitudinal Section of Cylinder-head.

"Type M–10 has a higher speed and is built only for the method of cooling by evaporation. This method of cooling is recommended in places where water is scarce. The charge is admitted in the same manner as in type E–10.

"Type E–12 is also a high-speed engine, but is being built for either circulation or evaporation method of cooling. This type is equipped with the latest designed vaporizer.

"The types M-10 and E-12, as provided with cooling method by evaporation, are especially designed for portable engines.

"The accompanying illustrations show the working parts of type E-12 and the details of construction and design.   Fig. 138 (p. 278)
shows a side elevation of this engine and the most important parts of the valve-motion. Fig. 139 (p 279) illustrates a cross-section of the engine on the lines I–II of Fig. 138.   Fig. 140 (p. 280) illustrates a vertical section through the cylinder-head in which the fuel for the charge is supplied by a pump. Fig. 141 (p. 280) represents a cross-section through the cooling-water jacket, with cooling method by evaporation; Fig. 142 shows a longitudinal section through the cylinder-head in which the charge is formed

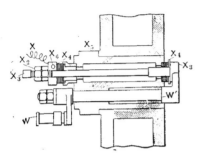

Fig. 143.—Current-interrupter for the Electric Igniting Apparatus.

by means of the new vaporizer; and Fig. 143 shows the current-interrupter for the electric igniting apparatus on a larger scale, being a vertical longitudinal section through the end of the cylinder-head.

"*Formation of Charge.*—a. When using fuel-pump and spraying device. The fuel (gasoline, kerosene, alcohol, or ergin) is contained in a tank placed beside the engine and connected to the pump h through the pipe u.   During each charging period the pump forces a fixed quantity of fuel through the connection u' and the sprayer g into the mixing-chamber O, which it enters as a finely divided spray. At the same time the air drawn in through the action of the piston enters the mixing-chamber through the air-cock f and the air-pipe e. While passing the sprayer the air is intimately mingled with the atomized fuel and is forced together with the fuel through the open inlet-valve C into the cylinder space A.   The fuel is here evaporated, both by heat radiating from the cylinder-walls as well as through direct contact with these hot walls.

"For the purpose of being able to start a kerosene-, alcohol-, or ergin-engine while the cylinder-walls are still cold, a gasoline starting-device has been provided from the cylinder-head, consisting of a small gasoline-reservoir which is connected with the mixing-chamber O by means of a small pipe fitted with a spray-nozzle. Before starting this reservoir is filled with gasoline. While the engine is being turned a small quantity of gasoline is drawn during the charging period into the mixing-chamber, entering the air-current through the spray-nozzle, being immediately vaporized on account of its high volatility and forming with the air an explosive mixture. After the engine has been running for a short time on the mixture generated in this manner as a gasoline-engine, and after the cylinder-walls have been sufficiently heated, the fuel-pump can be put in action and the engine be operated on kerosene, alcohol, or ergin.

"*Fuel-pump* (Fig. 140).—The fuel-pump h is a single-acting plunger-pump and fitted with a vertical plunger operated from below and with automatic suction- and delivery-valves. The plunger is actuated by means of a lever located in the pump-casing and connected to the outer lever r'. The roller n' while mounting the inlet-cam actuates the plunger from the lever r during its suction-stroke, and while the roller descends from the cam (towards the end of the suction period of the engine) the plunger actuated by a spring completes its discharge-stroke.

"The fuel is therefore injected only during the second half of the charging period, thus securing a favorable formation of the charge and reliable ignition.

"In order to change the stroke of the pump, and consequently the quantity of fuel injected, the roller of the pump-lever r' acting upon the lever-arm r is slideable and adjusted in a slot of the lever r'.

"The fuel-pump is equipped with a hand-lever (not shown in illustration), by means of which the connections u' are filled with fuel before the engine is started. In order to determine whether the fuel has reached the sprayer g, a test-valve v has been provided immediately before the sprayer. As soon as the liquid reaches this level, if this valve is open the fuel will be expelled in a fine stream. Furthermore, this test-valve enables one to control the proper working of the pump at any time during the operation of the engine.

"*b. When using Vaporizer.*—The fuel is admitted to the float-casing H, Fig. 142, flowing from a tank placed beside the engine through the connections u, while a float in the casing H acts upon the needle-valve i, so that the level of the liquid in the casing H is maintained at a constant height. For instance, if the level of the liquid rises, the float will be lifted and will close the needle-valve so that a lesser amount or no fuel can enter the casing H. The constant level of the fuel must always be below the openings o of the sprayer e connected with the casing H by means of the connections s. During each charging-stroke of the engine a partial vacuum is formed in the mixing-chamber E in accordance with the amount of opening of the inlet-valve (see paragraph 'Regulation '). This depression causes the fuel to be drawn out of the float-casing H and be atomized into fine streams through the sprayer o. The air entering through the cock d and passing the sprayer e with great velocity, atomizes the streams of fuel, intimately mingles with the fuel, and with this fuel enters the cylinder, where evaporation takes place, the same as when using the pump and sprayer described above. In order to effect evaporation the engine must be started with gasoline.

" The shut-off device of the evaporator consists of a small hand-wheel r, fitted with a projection which causes the valve k to be opened when turning the hand-wheel and thus connecting the starting-reservoir with the sprayer e. As the valve m remains closed the engine draws fuel from the starting-reservoir. After the engine has been running for a while the hand-wheel r is turned so that the projection opens the valve m; the valve k closes automatically, and fuel can therefore only be admitted from the float-casing. The hand-wheel can also be turned so that neither of the valves is open, causing the engine to stop. The vaporizer operates entirely automatically.

"*Ignition.*—The ignition of the charge in the cylinder is effected by the electric spark. A current is generated in a magneto-electric apparatus through induction by imparting an oscillating motion to the finely wound armature moving between the poles of a horseshoe magnet. While the current is most intense the circuit inside of the cylinder is interrupted by means of a contact-lever and a spark is generated which ignites the charge.

"The ignition device consists of a number of horseshoe magnets between the poles of which a finely wound armature is rotatably held in two bearings. Upon one end of the armature-shaft is located a lever t, which operates the armature, and which is actuated from the gear-shaft by means of a connecting-rod c with tongue c' (see Fig. 139). The connecting-rod is pivoted to an eccentric guide-pin, so that by turning the eccentric the point of ignition can be varied.

"Two springs attached to the lever of the armature-shaft and the stationary casing are so arranged that a line drawn through the four points at which the springs are fastened will go directly through the centre of the armature-shaft when the apparatus is at rest. At every other revolution of the engine these springs are put in tension by means of the tongue c', which moves the lever to one side. After the lever has been released the tension of the springs cause it to snap back into its original position. This causes the armature to move rapidly, and during that time a current is generated. A rod b connected with the lever acts upon the lever w of the igniter W whenever the armature lever is released.

"*The circuit-breaker* consists of the igniter-flange x^5 (Fig. 143), the firing-pin x^3, and the two-arm igniter-lever w-w'. The firing-pin is insulated at both ends by means of the mica washers x^4. When the inner arm w' of the igniter-lever rests against the firing-pin x^3, the electric current from the armature of the ignition device passes into the frame of the engine, and through this back into the armature by way of the wire x, the firing-pin x^3, and the igniter-lever w'. Ordinarily a spring acting upon the lever-arm w of the igniter-lever causes the igniter-lever to rest against the firing-pin, and the current generated can then pass as described above. As soon, however, as the rod b' connected with the lever t imparts a shock to the lever w, the lever w' is separated from the firing-pin, the circuit is interrupted, and the electric spark is generated.

"*Valve-motion.*—All movable parts of the valve-motion are actuated by means of a gear-shaft w^2 running alongside of the engine and rotating at half the number of revolutions of the crank-shaft. This gear-shaft is noiselessly operated from the crank-shaft by means of a pair of worm-gears. Cam-sleeves located upon the gear-shaft act upon the levers of the various valves. The exhaust-valve D is actuated by means of the cam m, the roller m', and the lever q, while the inlet-valve C is operated by the cam n, the roller n', and the lever connection p, p', and p''. While the exhaust cam-sleeve, which carries the exhaust-cam m is keyed tightly to the gear-shaft, the inlet cam-sleeve can be shifted upon the shaft through the action of the governor. The fuel-pump h is operated simultaneously with the inlet-valve, in that the arm r mounted upon the hub of the lever p actuates the pump-lever r'.

"*Regulation.*—The speed is regulated by varying the volume of the charge while maintaining a constant proportion of the components of the charge. As soon as the speed exceeds the normal to the least extent, the governor Y shifts the inlet cam-sleeve fitted with a conical cam n, so that a lower portion of the cam acts upon the inlet-valve roller. In this way the inlet-valve C is opened to a lesser extent and the stroke of the fuel-pump h is diminished; the total volume of the charge is therefore decreased and consequently the explosion and impulse becomes weaker, resulting in a proportional decrease of the speed. The governor therefore always regulates the fuel consumption in accordance with the power developed by the engine while maintaining a constant speed.

"*Cooling.*—The burning of the charge in the cylinder generates a high temperature, making it necessary to cool the cylinder and cylinder-head. This cooling is accomplished through circulation by passing water either from a main under pressure or through circulation from a cooling-water tank through the water-jacket (Fig. 140), or through cooling by evaporation (Fig. 141), in which method the water-jacket of the cylinder is extended upward in the shape of a box closed by a cover fitted with a funnel for filling cooling-water. The steam generated by the heating of the cooling-water escapes through a pipe attached to the cover.

"*Facilitating Starting.*—In order to facilitate starting, a second cam not shown in the illustration is mounted upon the exhaust cam-sleeve, known as the starting-cam. This cam is not in action while the engine is running; while starting, however, the exhaust roller is shifted so that it is operated by both cams. A portion of the charge in the cylinder is thus expelled through the open exhaust-valve during the compresssion period, thereby diminishing the resistance which would otherwise make turning by hand difficult."

The Alcohol-motor.—The following statement is also furnished the author by the Deutz Gas-engine Works of Cologne-Deutz, Germany:

"The great desire to secure a native fuel, such as alcohol, which could be easily produced from raw agricultural materials in Germany, as well as the importance therefore of the need of also obtaining the highest perfected type of alcohol-using motors for portable uses in Germany, gave rise, in the year 1902, through the efforts of the German Agricultural Association, to a competitive exposition in Mannheim, open to all visiting motors, the features of the alcohol-using motor to be that it should be portable, and also able to be successfully used for technical and agricultural purposes as against the common kerosen and gasoline motors, which latter had in turn replaced and succeeded steam-power for such uses.

"Their low running cost and maintenance, and not the least their merit in the less danger from their causing fires, has all tended to universally introduce these motors for industrial agricultural operations.

"The unbearable odor of kerosene acts as a restraint in the extension of its universal use as well as its great tendency to sootiness, while with gasoline the development of its use is offset by having to import it from foreign countries, as the supply, in case of a foreign war, would be cut off.

"In addition to this the control by the excise officers of the premiums granted by the government on engine gasoline affords a great deal of annoyance to the users of gasoline-engines.

"The efforts of the motor manufacturers had been long ago directed to producing from agricultural sources a native combustible or fuel which could be economically used in motors, and this was successfully accomplished, as demonstrated by the tests made at Mannheim by Prof. E. Mayer.

"*The Deutz Alcohol-motor, or Portable Engine.*—Considering the fluctuations in load met in practice, a 16-H.P. Otto Deutz alcohol portable engine gave the most favorable results, viz., 389 grams (about 13.7 ozs. avoirdupois) with normal and 507 grams (about 17.8 ozs. avoirdupois) per effective horse-power hour with half-load. For maximum brake-load effect the consumption is reduced to only 365 grams (about 12.8 ozs. avoirdupois) per effective horse-power hour.

"The accompanying illustration (Fig. 144) shows such a Deutz alcohol portable engine, which is not only used in summer for threshing and other agricultural purposes, but particularly as well also in the winter,

Fig. 144.—Threshing in Germany. The Deutz Alcohol Portable Engine

on account of its uniform speed, in the generation of electricity for lighting purposes.

"A further employment of the alcohol-motor is that of the perfected Deutz locomotive for mining-railway and field-railway uses, for which purposes the more expensive use of horses, on account of their cost to feed as well as the unsanitary conditions resulting therefrom, have gradually been superseded. This locomotive is shown in Fig. 145.

"The illustration shown in Fig. 146 is a locomotive for forest-railway use by the Grand Ducal Hessian Chief-Forestry in Kelsterbach.

"At the present time, of all the Deutz locomotives now being used, more than one third are run with alcohol. An extremely desirable feature in enabling these new alcohol-motors to attempt to compete with steam-locomotives is their much greater freedom from risks of causing fire by the sparks thrown out by the steam-locomotive, as with alcohol this is effectually precluded. This feature renders them especially desirable for agricultural uses. In Fig. 147 is shown the passenger railway at Exposition Park, Lima, Peru, equipped with a Deutz alcohol-locomotive.

"The stationary Deutz alcohol-engines are also wholly preferred to steam, and there has been an uninterrupted installation of such alcohol-engines since 1901.

"The fuel consumption of these alcohol-engines for the average sizes (from 8 to 25 H.P.) is from 370 to 380 grams (about 13 ozs. to 13.4 ozs.

Fig. 145.—Mining Railway of the Krupp Collieries "Hannover" and "Hannibal," Westphalia. Equipped with the Deutz Alcohol-locomotive.

avoirdupois) per effective horse-power hour, and when using alcohol of a calorific value of 6000 calories, or 10,800 B.T.U., there is obtained a thermal efficiency of some 22 per cent. The sizes shown in these cuts are nominally 8 H.P., but can easily develop 10 H.P.

"These most favorable figures of the fuel consumption are for the greater part due to the high compression (10 to 14 atmospheres) generated, which is made possible by the water always present in considerable amount in the alcohol consumed.

"In no other country has such progress been made in the employment of alcohol for industrial and technical uses as in Germany.

"The development of the industrial uses of alcohol merits most attention, therefore, in the case of Germany, as that country enjoys a leading position among other nations in this respect.

"This condition of affairs has been largely attained by the efforts of the great agricultural and industrial distilleries, as well as by the intelligent attitude and legislation on the part of the governments, because from their correct understanding of the great importance of this matter they have constantly striven to grant such legislation as will furnish earnest incentives for the production of alcohol and the creation of new

Fig. 146.—Forest Railway of the Grand Ducal Hessian Chief Forestry in Kelsterbach Equipped with the Deutz Alcohol-locomotive.

methods for its industrial use. And such legislation has endeavored in every way to facilitate and to expedite such ends.

"The great extent of such use is shown by the fact that there was used in Germany, in the years 1887 and 1888, some 38,000,000 liters (about 10,000,000 U. S. gallons) of alcohol for technical purposes, and in the years 1900 and 1901 this great quantity had increased to 112,000,000 liters (about 29,500,000 U. S. gallons), and especially has the consumption of alcohol denatured with the standard denaturing agent increased to the extent of some 79,000,000 liters (about 20,740,000 U. S. gallons) in the years 1902 and 1903."

"The association formed in 1899 for the purpose of utilizing alcohol, and which represents the majority of the German alcohol manufacturers, also considers it their chief aim to stimulate in every way the increase of the use of all kinds of spirits."

The Mietz and Weiss Alcohol-engine.—In the building of alcohol-engines by this firm the only change necessary was simply to increase the

Fig. 147.—Passenger Railway at Exposition Park, Lima, Peru. Equipped with the Deutz Alcohol-locomotive.

compression over the kerosene-oil engine which they have so long supplied and the merits of which are so well recognized.

A peculiarity of the use of alcohol is the necessity of a higher degree of compression than in the case of the petroleum products in order to secure the greatest efficiency.

A general view of the Mietz & Weiss double-cylinder marine oil- or alcohol-engine is shown in Fig. 148. These engines are made in a variety of sizes up to 50 horse-power.

As the ignition takes place from the rise in temperature by the compression of the gases in the combustion spaces of the cylinders, no electrical sparking devices or batteries are required. This feature contributes very largely to the reliability of these alcohol-engines, as there are no such devices to get out of order.

FIG. 148.—General View of the 7, 10, 15, 30, and 50 Horse-power Double-cylinder Mietz & Weiss Marine Oil or Alcohol Engine. Front View.

291

Fitted into the cylinder-head is a pear-shaped hollow cast-iron ball opening into the combustion-chamber of the cylinder. The end of this ball is directly in line with the injection-nozzle of the alcohol feed-pipe

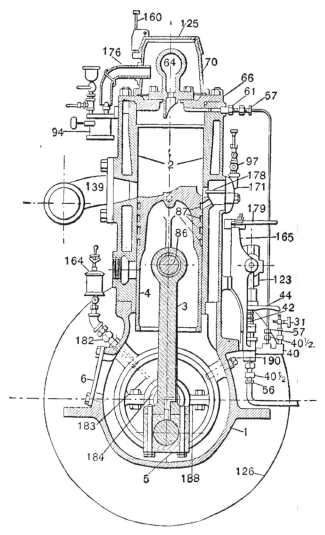

FIG. 149.—Sectional View of the Mietz & Weiss Marine and Vertical Oil- or Alcohol-engine, showing the cylinder and crank-case, piston, connecting-rod, and crank-shaft; also the igniter-ball and the ports showing the method of taking in the air and exhausting the gases.

entering the side of the cylinder. In starting the engine the igniter-ball is heated to a dull red by means of the hydrocarbon lamp attached to the engine and operated by compressed air from a small tank. When the igniter-ball is heated, which operation takes a few minutes, the engine is ready for starting, maintaining the ignition temperature automatically so long as it is in operation.

The simplicity of construction, there being no valves, no cams, no gears, and no vaporizer or electrical sparking device to get out of order, enable good results to be obtained from these engines without any special mechanical knowledge or skill. The governor is of the centrifugal balanced type. In the case of these engines for marine uses it is unaffected by the rolling of the boat or vessel. The speed of the engine can also be regulated by means of a throttle or hand-regulator, which limits the stroke of the pump or throws it away from the governor eccentric, entirely thereby stopping the flow of alcohol and stopping the engine.

A sectional view of this engine is shown in Fig. 149. In this sectional view the parts are explained as follows:

64 is thei gnitor-ball; 2 is the cylinder; 3 is the connecting-rod; 4 is the piston; 164 is the lubricating-oil well; 179 is the regulator-handle; 61 is the injection-nozzle.

A general view of the triple-cylinder Mietz & Weiss marine oil- or alcohol-engine is shown in Fig. 150, p. 295. These engines are furnished in sizes from 22 to 75 horse-power. The number of cylinders in these engines can be easily increased owing to the principle involved in the admission of the liquid fuel for the explosive charge, and the method of governing, whereby the charge is admitted practically in an automatic manner to the cylinders in rotation after the piston has closed the exhaust-port and begins its compression period.

In comparing alcohol and kerosene at the present time as fuel for these engines in constant operation, the point of advantage in economy will lie heavily in favor of kerosene. There is the advantage in case of alcohol over kerosene of absence of disagreeable odors. The same advantage holds in case of alcohol compared to gasoline. Another advantage in favor of alcohol over gasoline is its safety, as it will mix with water in case of fire, and as it is not so readily volatilized it is also much safer on this account than gasoline. In the case of kerosene, on account of its absence of volatility at ordinary temperatures, alcohol has not the same advantage. In case of accident by fire, as kerosene will not mix with water, alcohol has the advantage over kerosene.

As before stated, the complete reliability of these engines is not affected by any question of vaporization of the alcohol, because they are so constructed that the handling of alcohol is a normal operation for this engine.

The Weber Alcohol-engine.—In Fig. 151, p. 297, is shown a cut of the Weber alcohol-engine which is very similar in mechanical detail to

FIG. 150.—General View of the 22, 45, and 75 Horse-power Triple-cylinder Mietz & Weiss Marine Oil or Alcohol Engine. Front View.
305

the gasoline-engine built by the same firm, the Weber Gas-engine Company. This alcohol-engine is provided with a high-speed centrifugal governor, and the governing is accomplished by holding the air-valve

FIG. 151.—Alcohol-engine, 26 H.P. Built by Weber Gas- and Gasoline-engine Co.

and mixture-valve closed with exhaust-valve held open. This type of engine and method of governing is particularly well adapted for alcohol use.

The vaporizer is so arranged that at different altitudes, also during different atmospheric conditions, the vaporizer will admit the proper amount of alcohol and air for perfect combustion. The amount of fuel consumed would be in proportion to the load on the engine, and the governor itself will take of this very nicely.

The compression with this engine is quite a little higher than the compression carried in the gasoline-engine, and owing to less heat having to be absorbed by the water-jackets than in the case with the gasoline-engine the economy is quite high.

This company has found under actual conditions that the fuel consumption per horse-power per hour is about the same pound for pound whether using alcohol or gasoline. This alcohol-engine requires no external heating arrangements, as the engine will start on the first turn on the alcohol alone.

Some engines require the use of gasoline for the first few revolutions in order to warm up different portions of the engine before alcohol is turned on. With this engine as this company build it, however, there is not required anything other than the drawing of the charge of alcohol-vapor into the engine-cylinder and compressing same, when the engine will immediately start in operation. The engine is provided with a pump for keeping the supply of alcohol at a certain height in the vaporizer, and it can also be fitted with a gravity tank if so desired.

When using alcohol in one of these engines it is especially noticeable that the engine is not vitiated to the extent that it is when gasoline is used for fuel. This company mentions that their gas-engines, however, will work with perfect success on alcohol with but very slight changes. They have taken their regular gasoline-engine and have used alcohol in it directly after the gasoline has been exhausted. They have also taken the same engine and operated it with alcohol without first starting it on gasoline. The percentage of clearance in the cylinder of the Weber gas-engine is 5 per cent. The percentage of clearance in the Weber alcohol-engine is $3\frac{3}{4}$ per cent.

Gasoline Traction-engine as a Plowing-engine, and the Adaptation of Alcohol in Place of Gasoline.—During recent years there has been a rapid and remarkable advancement in the development of implements and machinery devoted to farm uses. But comparatively few years ago threshing-machines were operated by horse-power, while now a machine operated by horses is a rarity. The universal success of the traction-engine for threshing has caused it to be used for other power purposes, such as feed-grinding, freighting, plowing, etc. We show in Fig. 152 the Hart-Parr Company's 20-horse-power, nominal, traction-engine. This company are large builders of the types of internal-combustion engines, especially adapted for such purposes. They also manufacture portable and stationary engines of the same kind. With respect to the use of alcohol in these engines they make the following statement: "We have watched with a great deal of interest, and added our efforts to help bring about the free use of alcohol for power purposes. We have made a considerable study of the methods of utilizing this fuel, and expect soon to conduct extended experiments and arrive at definite results. Our engine is so constructed that alcohol can be used as fuel with very little change. By reducing the clearance space in the cylinder we will add the proper degree of compression and thus furnish the efficient use of alcohol as fuel.

"We have developed the feeding or carbureting devices with a view to utilizing such fuel, and believe that they are as well adapted for

FIG. 152.—Gasoline Traction- or Plowing-engine. Built by the Hart-Parr Co., Charles City, Iowa. This engine can be easily adapted for use with alcohol.

it as any that can be constructed. In enclosed situations within doors, where the odors from kerosene fuel are considerable, it is quite likely that alcohol will take the place even if it does not sell as low as petroleum fuel. We have several hundred of our traction-engines in very successful operation through the Western States and Canada, and recently made a shipment to the Hawaiian Islands.

"In the greater portion of the United States, where kerosene is very cheap or where the distillates of the Western country are produced, it will be a long time before alcohol will be low enough in price to compete with these fuels for traction-engine use.   In Fig. 153 is shown a

FIG. 153.—Plowing Scene, using the Hart-Parr Company's Traction engine

plowing scene, using the Hart-Parr Company's 20-horse-power, nominal, traction-engine.   Formerly our traction-engine was used entirely with gasoline as fuel.   The use of kerosene has greatly reduced the expense of operation of these engines. Kerosene can be purchased in our section at about 8 cents per gallon and yields a little more power per gallon than does gasoline. In the sugar-growing regions, and probably in territories lying so far distant that the freight on petroleum fuel makes it too expensive, the use of alcohol will commence even in traction-engines of the character which we are building. Accordingly this subject is of deep interest to us. We candidly admit that the great majority of the gasoline traction-engines previously offered have been failures. Experience, however, shows that the first crude machines in all kinds of labor-saving machinery are but the stepping-stones to the later and more efficient product.

"After years of patient efforts and work, repeated attempts and failures, we have succeeded in producing the first really successful gasoline traction-engine put on the market. We claim that our traction-engine is superior in economy to the steam-engine for the above-named purposes.

"In addition we claim there is no danger of setting fires by sparks as with the steam traction-engine. Our traction-engine is more convenient to operate than the best of steamers and is not troubled with leaky flues."

Power Uses of Alcohol.—The traction sawing-machine, for sawing cord-wood, which is shown in Fig. 154, is built by the Olds Gas Power

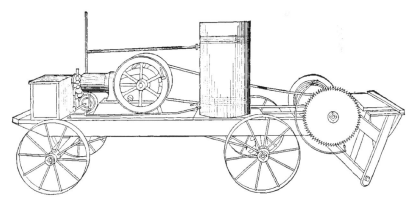

Fig. 154.—Traction Sawing-machine. Built by the Olds Gas Power Company.

Company and illustrates one of the many uses to which gasoline- and alcohol-engines can be put. This company claim to be the largest manufacturers of gas- and gasoline-engines in the United States. They will be ready to furnish a simple (mixer) attachment to their engine as soon as denatured alcohol is available, so that their engine can be used with the same ease, reliability, and economy with this fuel as is now the case with the use of the present fuels.

The consideration of freedom from fire, combined with compactness, comparatively light weight, ease of operation, and lack of danger, make these engines particularly adaptable for general use by people with comparatively little mechanical experience. The lack of danger from fire makes them more desirable for farm use than any other power. Farmers in general now realize that it is almost as essential to have one of these engines as it is to have a plow.

The money and time saved by using them for pumping water, electric lighting, cutting fodder, churning, separating cream, sawing wood, loading and unloading hay, grain, etc., amounts to the saving of the labor of from one to three men, which is something in these times of scarcity of help that must be considered by every farmer.

They are also indispensable where power is necessarily portable, on account of their light weight and compactness. A few of the uses to which they are put in this direction are for running portable sawmills, hoisters for unloading vessels, for building-contractors, sewer and viaduct work, filling coal-pockets, hoisting and hauling ice, etc. They are also valuable as a source of power for the spraying of the foliage of trees, shrubbery, etc., for the extermination of the gypsy and brown-tail moths and other insect pests.

In addition these engines furnish power for the blacksmiths, wheelwrights, grain-elevators, and all manufacturing where power is needed; also for municipal and private water-pumping and electric-light stations. In fact there are so many uses for this form of power that to enumerate them all would take more space than is available in this work.

While the demand for Olds engines has been constantly increasing, this company expect a very much larger demand for them at the time denatured alcohol is made available in all rural districts, as it undoubtedly will be within a very few years after the law authorizing this product goes into effect.

The Alcohol-motor for the Automobile.—If denatured alcohol can be furnished at a price that will admit of its use for power purposes, the consumption of it will be greatly increased. It would appear that the field open for such use of alcohol at the present time consists in engines of a capacity of 50 horse-power or less, and that its use as an alternative fuel to gasoline offers a strong incentive for its development on these lines. Taking up the question of the alcohol-motor for trackless vehicles, such as automobiles, truck-wagons, etc., it is of interest to review the results of foreign experience in this respect.* At the International Competitive Exposition held in Paris, France, in 1902, of motors and apparatus using denatured alcohol, the best results obtained were with a mixed fuel, consisting of 50 per cent methylated spirits and 50 per cent of a hydrocarbon fuel. In a number of trials of several good motors, operated successively with denatured alcohol alone and then with the same fuel 50 per cent carbureted, the superiority of the latter was as about seven parts consumed to ten parts of the former. In the report of M. Sorel to the Minister of Agriculture he stated, among other conclusions, that from the review of the motors by the jury, of which he was a member, the best motors required at least one and a half times the quantity of air theoretically necessary for completely utilizing the whole of the carbon of the denatured alcohol alone, or of the 50 per cent carbureted denatured alcohol in practice.

M. Sorel further stated that the results with certain motors were satisfactory, while those with others were not; also that the combustion appeared never to be complete, as was shown by the presence of appreciable quantities of acetic acid in the exhaust-gases. If the proper amount of air for the complete consumption of either alcohol was not supplied, incomplete combustion ensued, attended with a considerable degree of loss in efficiency of the motor.

It may be further stated that from the results of the tests there appeared to be an economy in 1902 over similar tests in 1901 of about 15 per cent. These results are the more interesting because they show an improvement in the operation of the automobiles which was evidently related *to the consumption of the fuel.* This is shown from the fact that the types of these vehicles have varied but little; the construction of the motors was practically the same, as well as the mechanical devices for the transmission of power and the variation of the speeds between 1901 and 1902. The manufacturers appear to have directed their efforts principally in the utilization of alcohol by elevating the temperature of the carbureter or of the explosive mixture at its entrance into the cylinder, and by the increasing of the compression. The jury also state that for automobiles weighing more than 500 kilos (1100 lbs.) the lowest consumption per kilometric ton was 87.10 c.c., or 73 grams of carbureted alcohol (50 per cent of hydrocarbon fuel and 50 per cent of the methylated or denatured alcohol).

---

* From the Ministère de l'Agriculture. Concours International de Moteurs et Appareils, utilisant L'Alcool Dénaturé, ayant en lieu à Paris en Mai 1902.—Rapports des Jurys, 1902.

In considering the facts brought out by the trials referred to there are two factors which throw some light upon the somewhat unsatisfactory results. One is that perhaps the 10 per cent content of methyl alcohol in the denatured alcohol was too high, and the other is that it may be possible to still further improve the alcohol-motor for such uses in America. No serious complaints are experienced in Germany from the corrosion of explosive-engine cylinders or exhaust-valves from formation of acetic acid. In Germany only about $1\frac{1}{4}$ per cent of methyl alcohol and $\frac{1}{4}$ liter of methyl violet dye, together with from 2 to 20 liters of benzol, are used to denature 100 liters of alcohol. Possibly the much smaller quantity of methyl alcohol in the German denatured alcohol for motor use may partly account for their freedom from this difficulty in their portable alcohol-motors and stationary engines. It may also be partly due to their superior construction and efficiency. As to improvements in the present American types of explosive motors, looking to their being adapted for use with alcohol, it may be said that competent engineering authorities believe that a successful alcohol-motor for automobiles can be made and will shortly come into use.

Some changes in design are needed from the explosive motors now in use, and it would appear that as mixed fuels are unreliable, apparently combining the disadvantages of each and thus overcoming their good points, it is more probable that with a small and separate gasoline-tank connected with the vaporizer or mixer by a small pipe fitted with a spray-nozzle the motor could be easily started with gasoline, on account of its high volatility, in a few moments, after which the alcohol fuel could be turned on and used at pleasure and with certainty of results. Or an auxiliary alcohol heating device, consisting of a special alcohol torch-lamp arranged to heat up the alcohol vaporizer for starting the alcohol motor might be used.

In any event, if alcohol can successfully run explosive stationary and portable agricultural motors—and practical experience has so demonstrated on the authority of competent engineers, as already explained—it is able also to successfully operate the automobile explosive motor. If motors for using alcohol are so adapted, the question of its cost in view of its many advantages will with some automobile owners not bar its use.

In considering the second method, as above stated for using alcohol in the automobile motor, the author is pleased to show in Fig. 155 a French alcohol carbureter designed for such adaptation. This cut and the following description were sent to the author by M. Henri Dupays, of Paris, France:

"The carbureter proper and the distributor consist of two distinct parts united by the tube *t*. The distributor is operated periodically, at the moment of the aspiration (suction) of the air by a vertical movement induced by the mechanism of the motor through the rod *T*.

"This distributor is, in effect, a sort of force-pump, consisting of a tube *D*, resting in the combustible (fuel) contained in the secondary reservoir *A*, which is provided with a float *C* operating the valve *H*, thus maintaining the fuel at a constant level in the reservoir *A*. A rod *K*, fastened to *T*, maintains a larger or smaller space in the bottom of the tube *D* by means of the small piston *p*. This rod *K* passes through the piston *p* and is of sufficient length to pass through the small hole

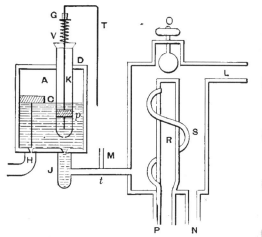

Fig. 155.—The Mechanical Distributing Carbureter used on the Bruhot Alcohol-Motors.

in the lower end of the tube *D*. This rod *K* is fastened to the tube *D* by the spring *V* held by the nut *G*, solid on *K*, on the upper part of the tube *D*.

"When the rod *T* is lowered it operates the rod *K* of the tube *D* by the intermediate nut *G* and the spring *V*, the space in the bottom of *D* being already filled with fuel. The tube *D* when it is lowered fits tightly on the seat of the valve of the vessel *J* under the reservoir *A*.

"When the tube *D* is forced down on the seat of this valve in *J* by the movement of the rod *T*, the combustible held in the lower part of *D* is completely separated from the liquid outside of this tube in the reservoir *A*, while the rod *T* continues its movement and overcomes the tension of the spring *V*, the lever *T* is lowered more and more and the rod *K* being also simultaneously lowered its end opens the escape-valve of J, while the fuel contained in the tube D is forced by the piston p into J and escapes through the tube t into the vaporizer.

"When T is again raised all the parts resume their original positions and the tube D is recharged with the liquid fuel.

"The fuel is thus periodically pumped in definite measured quantities into the carbureter, where it falls upon the coils of the heated spiral tube S and upon the walls of the vaporizer, which is heated by the exhaust-gases from the motor.

" The vaporization is facilitated by the small quantity of air drawn in through the pipe M, as well as by the air which enters by N and is heated by contact with S and R and finally with that of the cold air arriving by O.

"The explosive mixture or charge is conveyed by the pipe L to the cylinder of the motor. The exhaust-gases from the motor enter the vaporizer at P in the spiral tube S and are expelled through the cylinder R."

In the description, of which the above is a translation, it is not stated how vaporization is effected in order to start the alcohol-engine or motor when cold. It is evident that heat in some form must be used to first heat up this vaporizer. Whether this is done by an auxiliary alcohol blast-lamp or torch is not stated.

Neither is any mention made as to whether the cold-alcohol motor is first started with gasoline from a small tank, after which the alcohol fuel is turned on and used, the heat of the exhaust-gases neutralizing the cooling due to evaporation.

M. Dupays further writes the author on the whole question of denatured alcohol in France as follows: "My opinion has not changed from that definitely given by me at the end of my article, published in *The Engineering Magazine*, New York, U. S. A., in February, 1904." This article of M. Dupays was entitled "Mechanical and Commercial Aspects of the Alcohol-motor." The editors in a note published with this article state that "alcohol has, further, qualities which recommend it strongly for use in internal-combustion motors applied to the driving of automobiles, and it is in this relation that M. Dupays discusses it most fully. His intimate connection with the most notable experimental researches which have been made in this direction give him especial standing as an authority." In this article M. Dupays mentioned that "the best carbureter from a mechanical point of view will be the one which introduces automatically into each cylinder that quantity of alcohol which may be constant or variable, depending on the system of governing employed, which is strictly necessary to do the work, and in which the temperature is such as to insure rapid and complete evaporation of this charge in the least volume of air required to produce complete combustion. Carbureters fulfilling these conditions for alcohol exist." "Constructed originally to be used in connection with shale-oil, they have acted perfectly when alcohol, either pure or carbureted, was substituted. It might be difficult to show that the vaporizers now used with light mineral oils give equal satisfaction."

In this article, however, M. Dupays gave no view or sectional drawing to show the appearance and construction of such a vaporizer. In order to ascertain just what was the construction and what were the principles governing such alcohol vaporizer, the author, after reading this article of M. Dupays, entered into correspondence with him, resulting in the securing of a cut and special description of such an alcohol carbureter from M. Dupays. It is this special alcohol vaporizer which forms the subject of this description, and a sectional view of which has been shown in Fig. 155. on page 305. In this same magazine article, already mentioned, M. Dupays concludes as follows:

"In spite of the liberal encouragement given by the (French) government, and in spite of the rapid strides made in perfecting the mechanical appliances, the industrial development of alcohol as a fuel is at present nearly at a standstill." "And this rather distressing condition of affairs is due entirely to those whose own interests should prompt them to foster the growth of the industry; for at the present price of the commodity alcohol cannot compete successfully with its rivals." After enumerating several reasons to account for Germany's successful experience with denatured alcohol, M. Dupays concludes his article, mentioned above, as follows: "But the most important cause is found in the application (in Germany) of the principle of co-operation. The syndicate of agricultural distillers, which controls 80 per cent of the output, sells its entire product through a single agency—the Centrale für Spiritus Verwerthung (office for the sale of alcohol)—established in 1899. The commercial organization of this company is in many ways remarkable; it has succeeded in assuring to the manufacturer a satisfactory profit, and to the public a condition which in France is still a thing to be hoped for in the future, namely, a low price for alcohol."

The American Diesel Engine.—In this comparison of alcohol for power purposes with the usual liquid fuels, the use of which has been perfected after a long period of experiments, it is also of interest to consider the Diesel engine, which uses crude petroleum or fuel oil. This engine is a practical heat-engine, in which no system of igniting or mixing device is used, and it has met with deserved success. In Fig. 156 is shown a 225-horse-power triple-cylinder Diesel engine. The action of this engine is on the four-stroke or Otto cycle, which has been already explained in detail under the title of "Otto Alcohol-engine," at the beginning of this chapter.

The Diesel engine differs from all previous internal-combustion engines in compressing a full charge of air to a point above the igniting-point of the fuel, whether liquid or gaseous, then injecting this fuel for a certain period (variable according to load) into this red-hot air, where it burns with limits of pressure and temperature under perfect control. There are no explosions as in all other gas- or oil-engines, but steady combustion at predetermined, much lower temperature and without essential increase in pressure, the combustion line being practically an isothermal.

A small petroleum pump lifts the fuel into the chamber. A special compressor serves to compress air to inject the fuel and to store a surplus in an air-tank for starting the engine when cold. The fuel used is the common fuel oil or crude oil of Pennsylvania, Texas, or California. In speed regulation for sudden changes of load the Diesel engine will show a control equal to the best types of automatic engines. An extremely sensitive governor controlling the quantity of fuel injected for each stroke regulates the heat and therefore the expansive power of the air which is its medium.

The first experiments in 1893 by Rudolph Diesel, an eminent engineer of Munich, Germany, had in view mainly small machines, and these were more properly called by the appropriate name of motors. As more extended and complete experiments were made, the sizes have increased up to 450 horse-power, and 750-horse-power units are about to be placed in construction.

The compression of the air for the fuel mixture in the cylinder of this engine reaches 800 pounds per square inch, and is cooled before introduction to the fuel-valve, which opens and a charge of liquid fuel mixed with this compressed air is blown into the already red-hot air in the cylinder.

After the fuel needle-valve closes, the hot gases expand until the piston has traveled 90 per cent of its stroke, when the exhaust-valve opens to relieve the pressure before commencement of the next upward or exhaust stroke. The pressure at opening of the exhaust-valve for normal load is generally 35 pounds per square inch and the temperature about 700° Fahrenheit.

The absolute efficiency claimed for this engine is about 28 per cent, and in their larger units an absolute efficiency of 30 per cent is the standard performance and is frequently excelled in practice. In calculating the

Fig. 156.—225-horse-power Triple-cylinder Diesel Engine as installed in the Light and Power Plant of the German Tyrolean Alps. Exhibited at the World's Fair, St. Louis, 1904.

efficiency of the Diesel engine the losses as actually found in tests made on a 20-horse-power Diesel motor in New York were taken. This is a very high efficiency. With these engines in large sizes the heat losses through the exhaust-gases can in many cases be largely reduced by utilizing this heat for heating water or for producing steam for the heating of workrooms or for various mechanical purposes. In case of the loss of heat to the cooling-water, it may be said such heated water can be used for these same purposes, it being a question of temperature and quantities whether these two sources of such heated water are to be separately utilized or first combined. With these engines no difficulty has been experienced in operating alternating-current generators in parallel. By the use of such a cheap and universally obtainable fuel as crude petroleum or fuel oil, and in the case of such large horse-power units, this Diesel engine possesses special and unique advantages in the field where conditions call for such a type of engine. The larger the size horse-power used in these engines the more heat is generated from the two causes above mentioned. The conditions should therefore be such that this heat can be profitably utilized on a large scale, as has been pointed out above, so as to reduce the heat losses to the lowest possible point in the use of these engines. As the engines are of the stationary type, and are tending more and more to larger sizes, they do not conflict with portable alcohol-motors and alcohol marine engines in sizes up to 50 horse-power. The same may be said of engines for agricultural purposes or for individual uses in cities, where the odor of the exhaust-gases from crude petroleum or fuel oil may be objectionable, and where other factors may determine, in case alcohol can be obtained at a low enough price, that the latter type of engine should be used.

The Mietz & Weiss Kerosene-oil Engine.—It is of interest to also consider kerosene oil as a fuel for power purposes in this chapter in comparison with alcohol. For this purpose the following interesting test from the *Engineering News* of September 15, 1904, Vol. LII, No. 11, is taken:

TESTS OF AN OIL-ENGINE WITH STEAM INJECTION.

A test of a 15-H.P. engine of this type was conducted in the testing department of Mietz & Weiss, of New York, by Messrs. Charles Wineburgh and S. J. Goldwater. An abstract of these results is given below.

Fuel.—The fuel used was ordinary American kerosene oil. Analysis showed the composition to be

Carbon, 84.98 parts;
Hydrogen, 15.02 parts by weight.

The available B.T.U. per pound found by means of the calorimeter, calculated to represent the heat available in the engine, was 18,520.

Abstract from Table I.   Summary of data and results:

Number of run.	6
Approximate load	Full load
Duration of run, hours.	2
Oil pints, total.	32.01
Jacket-water, total, pints.	79.48
Revolutions per minute.	283.5
Explosions per minute.	283.5
Brake-load, pounds, net.	230.3
Ratio air to oil by weight.	32.4
Specific heat of exhaust-gases.	0.244
Maximum pressure, pounds per sq. in. abs	185
Compression pressure, pounds per sq. in. abs.	114
B.T.U. per D.H.P. per hour.	16,000
Thermal efficiency from I.H.P., power end.	0.209
" " " " net	0.193
" " " D.H.P.	0.159
Maximum thermal efficiency.	0.445

Fig. 157, p. 312, shows a general view of the Mietz & Weiss kerosene-oil engine with evaporating-jacket.   Fig. 158, p. 312, gives a longitudinal vertical section of the same engine.   The starting of this engine is effected as follows: The engine being in good working order in every respect, the kerosene-tank is filled.   The water is then turned on to the water-jacket of the cylinder.   By means of the kerosene blue burner furnished with each engine the combustion-chamber is heated externally for a few minutes to the temperature necessary for combustion.   The combustion-chamber is indicated at I in the cut.   The air needed for the explosion charge is now admitted to the cylinder and compressed by a throw of the engine fly-wheel by hand.   The charge of oil is now introduced into the combustion-chamber by the hand-lever of the oil-pump.   An explosion occurs, the engine starts up, and after this runs automatically.

The kerosene blue burner, furnished with each engine for the external heating of the combustion chamber, is shown in Fig. 158, p. 312.   The use of alcohol in this make of engine compared to kerosene has already been discussed under the preceding section entitled The Mietz & Weiss Alcohol-engine.

Endurance Test of the Kerosene-oil Engine.—The kerosene-oil engine gives a satisfactory record for continuous work with but little cost for

repairs.   In a case coming under the personal notice of the author, such
an engine used for pumping water ran $4\frac{1}{2}$ hours on an average per day
for a year.   One revolution of the pump $=8.8$ U. S. gallons.   The average

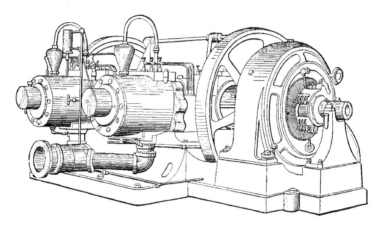

FIG. 157.—The Mietz & Weiss Direct-coupled Kerosene-oil Engine and Generator.

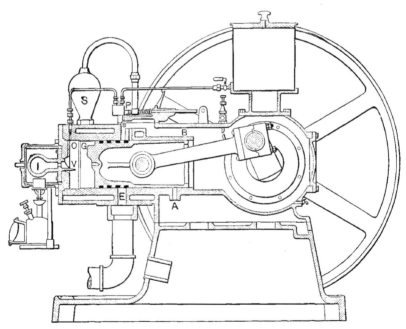

FIG. 158.—Section of engine shown in Fig. 157, with Evaporating-jacket.

number of gallons of water pumped per day was 91,048.   The average
number of gallons of oil used for pumping per day was $8\frac{3}{4}$.

FIG. 159.—The Foos Gasoline-engine.

This engine has run for seven years without repairs except a new cap for the combustion-chamber. This was originally made of cast iron, but this cracked and one made from cast steel was substituted with very satisfactory results, it being free from this defect. The combustion-chamber showed some deposit of soot, but required cleaning only at infrequent intervals. Altogether this engine proved to be a satisfactory and economical source of power for this purpose.

The Gasoline-engine and its Adaptation to Alcohol.—In Fig. 159, p. 313, is shown the regular 50-horse-power gasoline-engine as made by The Foos Gas-engine Company. In starting their small-size types of engines, all that is necessary is to throw the switch in contact, open the fuel-valve to the proper starting-point, and revolve the fly-wheel so as to complete the four-stroke cycle, after which an explosion is obtained and the engine takes its charge automatically until the rated speed is attained, at which the governor takes hold and either throttles or cuts the charge out entirely, according to which type of governor is used.

To start their larger-size engines the switch is thrown in contact, the fuel-valve and crank properly set, and by means of compressed air the first four-stroke cycle is completed, after which the operation of the engine is the same as just described for the smaller sizes. These engines also start easily in using alcohol and run right along on alcohol. When making tests of engines to be recorded at their works, this company usually give an endurance test of about ten hours.

They have made more elaborate efficiency tests in connection with gas, but have also made a number of minor tests with gasoline. They find that the *brake* thermal efficiency ranges on their engines from 18 per cent to 28 per cent, the maximum having been obtained from a 50-horse-power engine operating on gas. Their experience has been that, owing to gasoline being drawn into an engine in a liquid state, the thermal efficiency obtained is not as high as when the same engine is using gas.

The indicated efficiency ranges from 23 per cent to 33 per cent. The average mechanical efficiency is 87 per cent. The 50-horse-power gasoline-engine shown in the cut is fitted with a combination fuel-valve.

The Foos Co., can furnish these engines so equipped that they can be used with either gas or gasoline, changing from one fuel to the other without stopping the engine, but do not furnish this type as a regular equipment.

On the smaller sizes of these engines a horizontal pump is furnished and with this exception all sizes are built in the same way as in the case of the regular 50-horse-power engine shown in the cut. This engine operates on gasoline, naphtha, distillate, etc. As nearly all the principal working parts are assembled on one side, the engine can be installed to

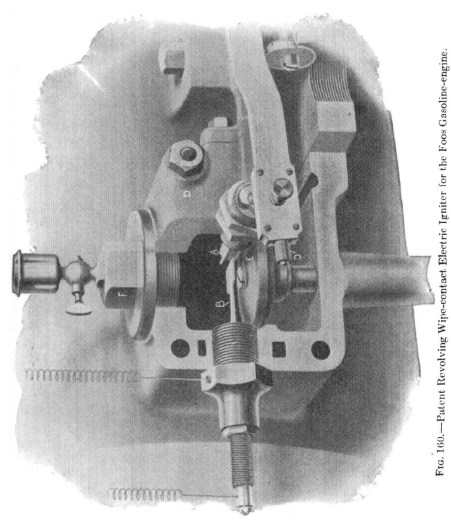

FIG. 160.—Patent Revolving Wipe-contact Electric Igniter for the Foos Gasoline-engine.

the best advantage and free access be had to the devices for regulating speed, fuel, and air-supply, time of ignition, and for starting the engine. Such advantageous features are, however, usually furnished by all the leading engine manufacturers. From letters from users of these engines, covering a long period of years, it is seen that the endurance and length of life of these engines is extremely satisfactory.

The ignition system of the Foos engine is shown in Fig. 160. It consists essentially of a patent revolving wipe-contact electric igniter with two independent electrodes, the stationary and revolving, each carrying a steel point, the two coming in contact each time a spark is necessary. The electric spark is the only mode of firing which can be used with all kinds of fuel, accurately timed, and which can always be relied upon to enable starting the engine upon a moment's notice.

In the cut shown, the revolving blade A, coming in contact with the spring B at each rotation, emits a large electric spark of high temperature, while at the same time the wiping contact of the two parts removes any burnt carbon or scale, preventing the incrustation of their edges, which in ordinary constructions is the cause of so much trouble. This rubbing action keeps the points of contact brightly polished, and thus insures continuous and even ignition. A large contact surface is thus ensured, a point of much importance, and any needed adjustment for wear is easily made, while the blades can be quickly renewed at trifling cost.

On the larger Foos engines the time of ignition can be adjusted while the engine is in motion by turning the thumb-screw C on the end of the igniter-rod, and this is used also to retard the impulses in starting up, which avoids any possibility of the engine starting backward. The igniter is situated in the inlet-valve E, as shown in Fig. 161. Its location thus exposes it least to the heat of the cylinder, and the igniters blades being in the direct course of the incoming charge are cooled by every fresh intake of gas and air entering the cylinder. The spark is thus produced where the mixture is the purest and most easily ignited. Either part of the igniter can be removed independently and the action and spark inspected by simply removing the cap F.

The inlet- and exhaust-valves of the Foos engine are shown in Fig. 161. These valves belong to the vertical poppet type, and are stated by this company to be far superior to the horizontal poppet-valves which so often leak by reason of their not seating properly on account of the wear on their stems and guides.

The inlet-valve E and exhaust-valve D are in separate castings, which are thoroughly water-jacketed, attached to opposite sides of the cylinder, and communicate by large ports with the combustion-chamber C. It is not necessary to detach the castings to remove the valves. The inlet-valve can be taken out by simply unscrewing the plug F and the exhaust-valve by unscrewing the plug H.

Suction in the cylinder is not relied upon in these engines, as in case of most engines, to open the inlet-valve.   It is lifted positively by a lever A and closed by its own weight and by a strong spring B.   This company state that suction-valves are usually enclosed in a casing in the cylinder or head, where they soon become distorted and destroyed by the heat.

The inlet-valve being opened by the cam, there is practically no vacuum to prevent the cylinder being filled with the charge at atmospheric pressure, and it not being closed until the proper point in the stroke assists in preventing the vacuum suggested.

Fig. 161.—The Inlet- and Exhaust-valves for the Foos Gasoline-engine.

The fuel-valve regulates the supply of fuel and is positive in its action, like all the other valves in this make of engine.

In these engines the piston passes over no ports and is free from the destructive friction occasioned by the improper lubrication and loss of efficiency caused by such construction.

The valve-gear is operated by steel cams driven by machine-cut gears of a form indicating the highest efficiency.   By adjusting with a common wrench the screws carried by the lift-levers A, any wear or looseness in the valve mechanism may be quickly and wholly taken up.

With regard to the percentage of clearance space in these Foos gasoline-engines in which the cylinder-bore ranges from $4\frac{1}{2}$ to 16 inches, the ratio of the combustion-chamber to piston displacement varies from 34 to 40 per cent for gasoline, while for gas this percentage runs from 22 to 28. In this engine there are no working parts in the cylinder-head. Consequently the clearance is decreased behind the piston by simply casting a cylinder-head in which there is a projection that extends into the counterbore of the cylinder; the only eliminating point is a place in which a greater compression would be a detriment.

In reference to the use of the Foos engine with alcohol, this company state that they are still experimenting on this line. They have, however, reached results which warrant them in saying that their engines, when used with this fuel, will start easily and run right along on alcohol just the same as on gasoline.

Comparison of the Economy of the Steam-engine with Other Types of Engines.—Before making this comparison we will discuss the economy of steam as a source of power by itself. The use of steam as a source of power and the construction of the steam-engine are so well known that a brief description of its uses is all that is needed in this respect. By passing steam under pressure through the cylinder of a steam-engine the energy represented by the expansive force of the steam is availed of for useful work.

In order to do this the back or exhaust valve of the cylinder is set at the least number of pounds pressure above that of the atmosphere as is possible for economical use of the steam. Such back pressure is varied according to conditions and circumstances. A simple engine is one in which the steam is expanded but once. The steam is usually admitted into the cylinder at from 80 to 100 lbs. pressure per square inch and exhausts or leaves the cylinder at about 2 to 3 lbs. pressure unless the exhaust-steam is used for heating or manufacturing purposes. After the steam has expanded in the cylinder as described, it has lost the greater part of its pressure and is allowed to escape by the exhaust-valve as mentioned. This valve is usually set so that about 2 to 3 lbs. pressure is left in the exhaust-steam.

In order to economize or use the heat left in this exhaust-steam various methods are used according to circumstances. In some manufacturing establishments where a considerable amount of hot water is required this exhaust-steam can be used to heat such water. By a device called a feed-water heater, such exhaut-steam can be used to previously heat the water used for the steam-boilers. The water obtained by this condensation of such exhaust-steam is incapable of being used except for purposes where the presence of traces of oil from the cylinder of the engine will make no difference.   There is, however, so much waste in using the simple type of steam-engine that in order to more fully economize the heat left in the exhaust-steam mentioned much more effective types of steam-engines have been invented.   One of these types is the simple condensing-engine.   The economy derived from the use of this type is effected for the reason that a greater number of expansions is obtained than in the non-condensing engine, and the temperature of the escaping steam is very much lower.

In one of these types of engines the steam is expanded twice—once in the high-pressure cylinder and again in the low-pressure cylinder—after which the exhaust-steam is condensed.   Such an engine is called a compound condensing steam-engine.   They are built both in vertical and horizontal design.   By condensing the exhaust-steam from the low-pressure cylinder a vacuum is obtained of some 27 inches, thus rendering very effective the exhaust-steam from the high-pressure cylinder after it passes into the low-pressure cylinder, there to be again expanded. The water heated by condensing the exhaust-steam from the low-pressure cylinder, if it can be used, represents a still further gain in economy. Another type of such engines is the triple-expansion steam-engine, in which the steam is expanded three times, after which the steam is condensed as described.   In a compound-condensing engine the steam is admitted at a pressure of 125 to 150 lbs., and exhausts into the low-pressure side or cylinder at a pressure of 5 to 10 lbs.   In the triple-expansion type of engine the steam is admitted to the first high-pressure cylinder at 165 to 200 lbs. per square inch of pressure, to the second cylinder at 50 lbs. pressure, and to the third at 5 to 10 lbs. pressure.

The economy of using steam in engines is still further enhanced by several other methods, which are as follows: The flue-gases from the boilers are made to give up some of their heat by passing them through a so-called "economizer."   This apparatus, or economizer, consists of a series of iron pipes filled with circulating water which absorbs heat from the escaping gases from the boiler-furnace on their way to the chimney and thus raises the temperature of the feed-water.   This hot water so produced can be at once used in the steam-boilers.   The water heated by condensing the exhaust-steam from the engine can be used for various purposes about the manufacturing plant where hot water is required. The heat in the exhaust-steam from the feed-pumps and the steam-cylinders of the condenser is made use of to heat the feed-water for the steam-boilers.

A few figures showing the comparative total coal consumption in pounds, the fixed charges on plant at 11 per cent, cost of attendance, cost of plant per horse-power on these various types of engines will demonstrate very clearly the advances along the lines of economy in operation and maintenance which have been made. These comparative figures are shown in the table submitted herewith. It is a promising attempt to secure a unit of cost in the comparative expense of steam as a source of power.

* TABLE OF YEARLY COST OF STEAM-POWER WITH FAIRLY STEADY LOAD, 308 DAYS, 10 HOURS PER DAY.

Type of Engine.	Horse-power of Engine.	Cost of Plant per H.P., including Buildings.	Total Coal Consumption in Pounds per H.P. per Hour.	Fixed Charges on Plant at 11 Per Cent.	Cost of Attend-ance.
Engine and boiler combined	10	$76.00	7.00	$83.60	$157.00
Simple non-condensing....	10	190.00	7.00	209.00	157.00
" "	20	139.00	5.25	305.80	209.00
" "	30	114.00	4.50	376.20	261.00
" "	75	72.00	3.50	594.00	470.00
Simple condensing........	10	193.00	6.00	212.30	157.00
" "	20	143.00	4.68	314.60	209.00
" "	30	118.00	3.91	389.40	261.00
" "	75	80.00	3.03	660.00	470.00
" "	100	71.00	2.75	781.00	587.00
Compound condensing....	100	93.00	2.25	1023.00	770.00
" "	500	63.00	1.75	3465.00	1694.00
" "	1000	53.50	1.75	5885.00	3080.00
" "	2000	50.00	1.75	11000.00	4620.00

* This table was compiled by Mr. Charles T. Main in January, 1898, and with due allowances for the rise in prices of engines and building materials since that date it is substantially correct at the present time. Mr. Main is a mill engineer of Boston, Mass. The table has been very kindly contributed by him. The complete table, of which the above is a part, is not given, as it is unnecessary to do so for the scope of comparisons made by the author below.

On the simple engines above one man attends engine, fires boiler, and is supposed to do other work besides.

On the 10-horse-power plant one fourth of his time is charged to attendance and three fourths on the 100-horse-power plant.

On the compound condensing-engine one man at $15 per week is charged up to the 100-horse-power engine; one man at $15 per week, one man at $12 per week, and one man at $6 per week are charged up to the 500-horse-power engine; one man at $18, two men $24, and two men $18 per week are charged up to the 1000-horse-power engine; one man at $24 per week, four men $48 per week, and two men $18 per week are charged up to the 2000-horse-power engine.

The wastefulness of the small type of steam-engine of the simple non-condensing type is strikingly illustrated by the above table, as well as the great economy resulting from the use of the large-size condensing types of engines already mentioned.   Roughly speaking, the waste entailed by using the small sizes of non-condensing steam-engines is fully 25 per cent over that of the larger sizes of condensing-engines.

From what has been said concerning the usual type of small-sized non-condensing steam-engines, and also from the probability that sizes of from 10 horse-power to 50 horse-power of alcohol-engines will be used at first in the United States, and also for the reason that the steam-engine possesses only about one half the thermal efficiency of the internal-combustion type of engine, it can be seen that there exists a wide field for the stationary type of alcohol-engine.   The extent of its use will largely depend upon the selling price of the denatured alcohol.   No steam-boiler is required for the alcohol-engine.   The cost for attendance is small compared to that required in the case of steam-engines of equal size horse-power.   The portability of the above sizes of alcohol-engines enables them to be easily set up and used, for instance, about the farm.   The above reasons all point to the probability of these engines being largely used in the United States for agricultural power purposes.

The fact that the fire under the steam-boiler must be constantly maintained so as to be ready for power demands at a moment's notice makes the fuel cost under conditions where intermittent power is wanted quite excessive.   This is not the case with the alcohol-engine.   When the engine stops the use and the cost of the fuel also stops.

In comparing the economy of the steam-engine with these other types of engines (internal-combustion engines) for the purposes of electric lighting and large development of power for manufacturing purposes, etc., it is still recognized that the great uniformity and reliability in the performance and endurance of the steam-engine, as well as its economy in the large sizes of the condensing types of engines mentioned, entitle it to very favorable consideration as a prime source of power.   Whether the rotary or turbine type of steam-engine will supplant the older reciprocating types in large-sized steam-engines is a feature that necessarily does not call for discussion in this book.

It may, however, be remarked that even the present types of internal-combustion engines are still built upon the design of the reciprocating type of engine, and it would seem, as has been pointed out by Warren in his article, "A Combination of Pressure Generator and Rotary Engine," published in the *Engineering Magazine*, February, 1904, that "in the present state of development of the internal-combustion engine it is undoubtedly true that the gain in thermal efficiency shown by the internal-combustion type of engine over the steam-engine is practically offset by the mechanical limitations and disadvantages which it presents."

It has long ago been recognized that we are far from obtaining with the steam-engine the full mechanical equivalent of heat, even when working under the most favorable circumstances.   Even with the most economical types of steam-engines only some 15 per cent of the power of which the fuel is capable is obtained.   To find a more economical means than this of converting heat into mechanical effect is one of the great problems of the present age.

The Gas-engine Compared with Other Types of Engines.—In comparing other types of engines with the simple gas explosive type of engine it may be mentioned at the start that the gas-engine was the pioneer in this type of power producers, the Otto gas-engine, or four-cycle engine, the principles of which are described in this chapter, as used for alcohol, gasoline, and kerosene fuels, being one of the earliest and the leading engine of this kind.

Where natural gas or blast-furnace gas can be availed of the gas-engine is very economical to use.   It is also used largely in cities where cheap illuminating-gas can be procured, and such engines are also now furnished and run with their own small gas-producer plant for the simple and economical production of coal-gas for such purpose.

* At the recent meeting of the Iron and Steel Institute in London, July 24–26, 1906, attended by American and Continental electrical engineers, it was stated that there were ordered by German iron-works and collieries, from March 1 to July 1, 1906, 31 gas-engines of about 36,150 horse-power, and that of forty-nine German smelting-works thirty-two had already gas-engines at work and nine had ordered such engines.   There were at work 203 engines of about 184,000 horse-power, and in course of erection and cn order 146 engines of about 201,-000 horse-power, making a total of 380,000 horse-power.

The recent gas-engine development since 1902 described above, includes large-sized engines, of from 500 horse-power to 2500 horse-power, and their use is largely local for the reason that shipyards, steel-works, and plants requiring large powers make use of such engines.   In some of the shipyards in Glasgow steam-power has been largely supplanted by gas,

---

* From the Iron and Coal Trades Review, Friday, July 27, 1906, sent the author by the Secretary of the Iron and Steel Institute of London, England.

which is generated by a special "producer" plant whose waste products are said to be recovered and sold.

In steel-works where the iron blast-furnaces, rolling-mills, etc., can be assembled this source of power promises to be of great importance and effect considerable economy. In the case of waste gases from iron-furaces and gases from coke-ovens there will be rendered available sources of power for the cheap generation of electricity where local conditions seem to warrant.

It will thus be recognized that the gas-engine is to become of vast importance in a special field, and in such large sizes under such unique conditions that alcohol cannot become a competitor for producing power along these lines. As such development will be largely local in its character and in large sizes of engines, it will not conflict with the smaller sizes of explosive engines used throughout this country, in which class alcohol will probably find its first large employment if the price is sufficiently low. A further reason for calling attention to the gas-engine is because its principles of working have been largely followed by the internal-combustion or explosive engines, using these other fuels which we have discussed.

It is entirely beyond the scope of this book to attempt any extended explanation of how the different tests showing the efficiency of gas-engines are made, as the mathematics involved and the complex and intricate procedure adopted preclude any such treatment of this phase of the subject.

Outline of the Methods Used in Testing Internal-combustion Engines.—It will, however, be of interest to sketch in outline the theory of the methods used in the testing of engines of this type. We will say, therefore, that the object of the test is to find that fractional part of heat supplied in the fuel which is realized in useful work *whatever fuel is used.* In order to do this we have to determine the input and output.

In the case of input the measurement is *the cubic feet or weight of fuel used for a given time and its heating capacity.*

In the case of output the measurement is (*a*) *power developed in the cylinder.* This is obtained from indicator-cards which represent the history of the pressure at each point of revolution, and from the average pressure thus obtained, together with the dimensions of the engine and the number of the revolutions, the power may be computed and is the indicated horse-power. (*b*) *Power delivered at pulley measured by brake or electrically,* and is the brake horse-power. The ratio of these different quantities, representing the fractional part of the heat in terms of power utilized, are termed *efficiencies.*

The indicated efficiency $= \dfrac{\text{Indicated horse-power}}{\text{Input}}$.

The brake efficiency $= \dfrac{\text{Brake horse-power}}{\text{Input}}$.

The mechanical efficiency $= \dfrac{\text{Indicated horse-power}}{\text{Brake horse-power}}$.

As a standard of reference we use the efficiency which would be obtained in a "perfect" or ideal gas-engine, i.e., an engine undergoing no loss of heat and no loss of power through friction.

Without going into the mathematics necessary to prove the problem, it may be stated that the ideal thermal or heat efficiency depends solely upon the proportions of the engine and not at all upon the nature of the fuel used.

Thus let $PD =$ the volume of piston displacement

and $\qquad C =$ the volume of clearance space,

that is, all the space left between the piston and cylinder-head and gas-ports up to the valve, then the efficiency is given by the formula

$$\text{Efficiency} = 1 - \left(\frac{C}{C + PD}\right)^{.4}.$$

To find how nearly the actual engine approaches the ideal conditions we have only to divide the actual efficiency by the ideal efficiency, which is explained as follows:

Actual efficiency $= \dfrac{\text{Output}}{\text{Input}}$.

Output $=$ I.H.P.

Input $=$ the total heat of combustion of the burning fuel (alcohol or any fuel).

Both output and input must be expressed in the same terms or units. To change British thermal units to foot-pounds multiply by 778.

As an example of the calculation of the best possible efficiency of an engine using alcohol compared to the ideal or theoretical efficiency, we give an alcohol-engine (the Otto or Deutz engine) possessing 18 per cent clearance. Then the piston displacement being 100 per cent, by logarithms, we find

Log $C = \log 18$ $= 1.2553$
Log $(PD+C) = \log (100+18) = 2.0719$
Subtract

$$9.1834 - 10$$
$$.4$$

$$\text{Log} \left(\frac{C}{PD+C}\right)^{.4} = 3.67336 - 4$$

$$= 9.6734 - 10.$$
Number corresponding $= 0.4714,$

$E = 1 - 0.4714$ (number corresponding) $= 52.9\%$ efficiency.

In the case of a similar size horse-power (Otto or Deutz) gas- or gasoline-engine the clearance is 28 per cent. In this case the best possible efficiency calculates to 45.6%.

The American Diesel engine has 7 per cent clearance including valve-chambers, and the best possible efficiency calculates to 66.4%, but is not realized in practice. The Diesel cycle is supposed to depart somewhat from the Otto cycle so that its theoretical efficiency would be higher. To find the theoretical temperature after compression we calculate it from the equation

$$T = T_0 \left(\frac{PD+C}{C}\right)^{.4}.$$

$$T = 1273° \text{ F.}$$

We assume, for the purposes of calculation, that the initial temperature $T_0 = 600°$ Fahr. absolute, as was found in one case, although this value should be first determined in the case of any actual experiment and test. By calculation, as follows, we obtain the value of T, assuming adiabatic compression (no heat being given out or taken in) of a perfect gas; the relation between temperature and volume is shown by

$$T v^{.4} = T_0 v_0^{.4}.$$

Applied to the Deutz or Otto alcohol-engine under consideration, with 18 per cent clearance, we have

$$PD+C = v_0 = 118$$
$$C = v = 18$$
$$T_0 = 600 \text{ (by assumption as explained above)}.$$

$$T = T_0 \left(\frac{v_0}{v}\right)^{.4}$$

$\log v_0 = \log 118 = 2.0719$
$\log v = \log 18 = 1.2553$

$\overline{0.8166}$
$.4$

$\overline{0.3266}$
$\log T_0 = \log 600 = 2.7782$

$\overline{3.1048}$
$T = 1273°$ F. absolute temperature,
$461°$ absolute zero.

$\overline{}$
$t = 812°$ F.

The temperature of the charge has thus been increased from 139° F. at admission to 812° F. at the end of compression, or 673° F.

When ignition occurs there will be a further increase in temperature due to heat of combustion. The theoretical value of this assuming no heat loss and instantaneous combustion would be |

$$\frac{\text{B.T.U. evolved by combustion}}{\text{Specific heat at constant volume of gaseous mixture}} = \begin{cases} \text{Degrees increase} \\ \text{in temperature.} \end{cases}$$

This is never realized because of heat losses and because the combustion is not instantaneous. What this theoretical increase would be for alcohol can be computed by assuming weight of fuel per revolution, heat of combustion, and percentage mixture. The actual or initial temperature mentioned above at admission of the fuel charge must be determined by experiment, as has been said, and will vary with quantity of charge, size and speed of engine, mass of metal, etc. To guard against preignition the actual temperature must not exceed that at which the substance will burn, and such temperatures have to be determined by actual experiment.

SUMMARY OF CHAPTER VIII.

In a general way it can be stated that the clearance in the cylinder depends upon the nature of the fuel and also on the size and speed of the engine.

Thus for each engine there is a definite clearance which gives the maximum economy for any given fuel and speed. For power installations this must be taken into account, but for smaller engines, such as are used in automobiles, where economy is a secondary consideration, some deviation from the best clearance is permissible. Thus without much loss of economy it might be possible to burn alcohol in a motor designed for some other fuel.

In the Otto gas-engine the average consumption per horse-power per hour when using illuminating-gas of approximately 650 B.T.U. is 18 cubic feet, with natural gas about 12 to 15 cubic feet, according to the quality of the gas, and with producer-gas about 100 cubic feet. The field for each of these types of engines we have described has been pointed out and such comparisons as can be made in a book of this scope have been given.

The question of the standardization of denatured alcohol in the United States for the purposes of power has still to be solved, although the presence of about 15 per cent, by weight, of water would appear to be the lowest usable quality for such use. This strength of alcohol is about 180° U. S. proof.

CHAPTER IX.

LAWS AND REGULATIONS FOR DENATURED ALCOHOL.

In Foreign Countries. Law for Denatured Alcohol in the United States. Cost of Denaturing Alcohol in Foreign Countries. Cost of Denaturing Alcohol in the United States. Properties of Denaturing Materials. Special Denaturing Methods in Foreign Countries. Tests Prescribed by Foreign Countries for the Denaturing Materials Used. Tests Prescribed by the United States for the Denaturing Materials Used. Completely Denatured Alcohol and Specially Denatured Alcohol in the United States. Recovery of Denatured Alcohol is permitted by the United States Regulations. Spirit Varnishes.

Laws and Regulations for Denatured Alcohol in Foreign Countries.

Laws and Regulations for Methylated Spirits in the United Kingdom. (Abstract of the English Regulations.)

Duty-free Spirit.

I. Methylated Spirit. There are two kinds of methylated spirit:

A. *"Ordinary" Methylated Spirit for use in manufacturing operations* —This consists of a mixture of 90 parts of ordinary ethylic alcohol of a strength of 60 to 66, o. p. (i.e., containing from 91 to 95 per cent of real alcohol) and ten parts of wood naphtha of an approved type.

Methylated spirit can only be made by

1. Distillers;
2. Rectifiers, i.e., persons who redistill duty-paid spirit;
3. Licensed methylators.

B. *"Mineralized" Methylated Spirit.*—This is the methylated spirit which is sold by retail to the general public for use for burning in spirit lamps, for cleansing and domestic purposes generally, and also to some extent for mixing with paints, stains, varnishes, etc., and for polishing purposes by cabinet-makers, etc.

In making "mineralized" methylated spirit, the alcohol is first mixed with the wood naphtha, as in making the "ordinary" methylated spirit.

329

After mixing with the wood naphtha, the whole contents of the vat of "ordinary " methylated spirit, or a portion of the spirit not less than 100 gallons, removed to another vat, is further mixed with three eighths of one per cent (0.375 per cent) of an approved "mineral naphtha." This mineral naphtha is an ordinary light mineral oil, having a specific gravity of from 0.800 to 0.830. The addition of this mineral oil does not interfere with the purposes for which this spirit is mainly used, viz., burning in spirit lamps, etc.

With regard to the denaturing of alcohol in England, it may be said that a new law went into effect October 1, 1906, a copy of which is reprinted, in part, in the Journal of the Society of Chemical Industry, No. 16, Vol. XXV, August 31, 1906. The purpose of the new law from which this abstract is made is to reduce the amount of methyl alcohol in the methylated spirits for industrial purposes from 10 to 5 per cent. This allows a cheaper denatured alcohol in addition to the former mineralized methylated spirit. In the mineralized methylated spirits for lighting and general use, the 10 per cent of approved wood alcohol is still retained and the three eighths of 1 per cent of approved mineral naphtha. The form of denatured alcohol above permitted by these new regulations is termed industrial methylated spirits. This new law will thus effect a larger use for industrial purposes of the new kind of denatured alcohol. Certain products which could not be made with the ordinary denatured alcohol under the old law are now permitted to be manufactured with industrial methylated spirits. These products are sulphuric ether, ethyl chloride, methyl chloride, and ethyl bromide, chloroform, and hydrate of chloral for use as a medicine or in any art or manufacture; and no objection is made to the substitution of methylated spirits in the preparation of soap, compound camphor, aconite, and belladonna liniments of the British pharmacopœia. No methylated spirits nor any derivative thereof, except sulphuric ether, ethyl chloride, methyl chloride, ethyl bromide, chloroform, and hydrate of chloral, can lawfully be present in any article whatever capable of being used either wholly or partially as a beverage or internally as a medicine.

It is also of importance to note that these new British regulations permit the exportation of methylated spirits (denatured alcohol).

The New British Excise Regulations for Industrial Alcohol and Methylated Spirits.*—The Commissioners of Inland Revenue, in pur-

---

* The author is indebted to Mr. Charles G. Cresswell, General Secretary of the Society of Chemical Industry, London, England, for copy of the Statutory Rules and Orders, 1906, No. 622, containing these regulations.

suance of the powers vested in them, hereby prescribe the following regulations which are to be observed from and after the 1st day of October, 1906:

Part I.—As to spirits other than methylated spirits.

1. In taking account of the quantity of spirits in the spirit store of a distiller the officer must carry to the debit side of the account the quantity of spirits computed at proof, which shall be from time to time duly conveyed into the store from the spirit receiver in the distillery, and must carry to the credit side of the account the quantity so computed, which shall have been sent out under permit.

2. There must be legibly cut, branded, or painted with oil-colour upon the head of every cask in warehouse containing racked or blended spirits, in addition to the other marks required to be thereon, the word "Racked" or the letter "R" in the case of racked spirits, and the word "Blended" in the case of blended spirits.

3. The manner in which a permit or certficate is to be cancelled is to be by writing in large letters in ink across the same the word "Received," and the day and the hour of the receipt, or by drawing lines in ink across the permit or certificate, so as to prevent it from being again used for the removal of spirits.

Part II.—As to spirits received for use in the arts and manufactures under section 8 of the Finance Act, 1902.

* 4. The allowance payable under section 1, subsection 1, of the Revenue Act, 1906, in respect of spirits received for use under section 8 of the Finance Act, 1902, shall be paid to the person authorized to receive the spirits on production by him to the Collector of Inland Revenue for the collection within which the spirits are authorized to be received for use, of a certificate signed by the officer who shall have taken account of the spirits on receipt, and countersigned by the supervisor of the district, setting forth the quantity of spirits at proof which shall have been so received.

Part III.—As to methylated spirits.

5. All spirits to be used for methylation must be conveyed under bond to the premises where the methylation is to take place, and must

---

* A copy of this British Revenue Act, 1906, is given in the Appendix of this book. The author has been furnished with this copy through the courtesy of Sir William Crookes, member of the Departmental Committee on Industrial Alcohol, which reported to both houses of Parliament in 1905.

there remain without alteration or change in the cask or package in which the same are delivered until an account of the spirits has been taken by the proper officer of Inland Revenue.

6. An authorised methylator must at the time of methylation mix with and dissolve in all spirits then methylated other than industrial methylated spirits as defined by the Revenue Act, 1906, in addition to the matter prescribed by section 123 of the Spirits Act, 1880, a quantity not less than three eighths of 1 per cent by volume of mineral naphtha of a specific gravity of not less than 0.800, and the mineral naphtha shall before the mixing thereof be examined and approved by the Principal of the Government Laboratory or other officer appointed in that behalf.

7. The account to be kept by an authorised methylator of any industrial methylated spirits, and any mineralised methylated spirits prepared or received by him, and of the sale or delivery thereof, shall be in the forms prescribed in the first and second parts, respectively, of the first schedule hereto annexed. The methylator shall enter in the appropriate account daily, and at any time when required by an officer, the quantity of methylated spirits made or received, and the separate quantities sent out, both in bulk and at proof, and he must keep the accounts at all times open for inspection by any officer of Inland Revenue.

8. Essential oil or other flavouring matter must not without the express sanction of the Commissioners of Inland Revenue be added to or mixed with methylated spirits.

9. Methylated spirits may be removed by a maker of methylated spirits from the place of methylation for exporttion under the following regulations, viz.:

(a) The methylator must give the proper officer 12 hours' written notice of his intention to export, and state in the notice the number of gallons to be exported and the time at which the officer's attendance will be required, which must be between the hours of 8 A.M and 2 P.M.

(b) The quantity exported at any one time must not be less than 10 gallons.

(c) The spirits may be exported in casks or other vessels, each containing not less than 10 bulk gallons, or they may be exported in smaller vessels containing any number of complete gallons, provided the vessels are packed in cases or packages containing not less than 10 bulk gallons each.

(d) The casks or vessels must be marked and numbered in the prescribed manner, and be accompanied on removal by a permit written by the methylator and endorsed by the officer.

10. A retailer of methylated spirits must not sell or have in his possession for sale any methylated spirits other than mineralized methylated spirits, nor any methylated spirits containing any essential oil or other flavouring matter; but this regulation shall not prevent a retailer of methylated spirits, if duly authorized by the Commissioners, receiving or having in his possession industrial methylated spirits for use in an art or manufacture carried on by him.

11. *A retailer of methylated spirits—*

(*a*) Must not receive or have in his possession at any one time a greater quantity of methylated spirits for sale than 200 gallons;

(*b*) Must not receive methylated spirits from a retailer of methylated spirits in a quantity exceeding four gallons at a time; and

(*c*) Must not sell to or for the use of any one person more than four gallons of methylated spirits at a time.

12. The account to be kept by a retailer of methylated spirits shall be in the form given in the second schedule hereto annexed.   The account is to be at all times open to inspection by any officer of Inland Revenue.

13. A retailer of methylated spirits must not use methylated spirits in any art or manufacture carried on by him unless he has been authorised by the Commissioners of Inland Revenue to do so.

14. A person who has been authorised to receive methylated spirits for use in any art or manufacture carried on by him, whether he holds or does not hold a licence as a retailer of methylated spirits, must obtain all methylated spirits received by him from an authorised methylator, and in the manner directed by subsection 4 of section 124 of the Spirits Act, 1880.

15. A retailer of methylated spirits, and a person authorised to receive methylated spirits, must on receiving any methylated spirits accompanied by a permit, or a document in the nature of a permit, keep the permit or document and deliver it to the officer of Inland Revenue who first inspects his premises after the receipt thereof.

16. The allowance payable under section 1, subsection 1, of the Revenue Act, 1906, shall, as regards spirits used in making industrial methylated spirits, be paid to the authorised methylator, on production by him to the Collector of Inland Revenue of the collection in which the methylating premises are situate, of a certificate signed by the supervisor and the officer who shall have witnessed the methylation, setting forth the quantity of spirits at proof which have been used for that purpose.

17. The regulations of June 15th, 1891, relating to the manufacture

First Schedule.

First Part.

FORM OF STOCK ACCOUNT OF INDUSTRIAL METHYLATED SPIRITS TO BE KEPT BY AN AUTHORISED METHYLATOR.

M......................., *Authorised Methylator.*

Industrial Methylated Spirits Made or Received into Stock.				Industrial Methylated Spirits Sent Out of Stock Accompanied by a Permit.						
Date of Receipt or Mixing.	Bulk Gals.	Strength O.P.	Gals. at Proof.	Date of Sending Out or Delivery.	No. of Permit	Name of Person to Whom Sent or Delivered.	Of What Place.	Bulk Gals.	Strength O.P.	Gallons at Proof.

Second Part.

FORM OF STOCK ACCOUNT OF MINERALISED METHYLATED SPIRITS TO BE KEPT BY AN AUTHORISED METHYLATOR.

M................................, *Authorised Methylator.*

Mineralised Methylated Spirits Made or Received into Stock.				Mineralised Methylated Spirits Sent Out of Stock Accompanied by a Permit.						
Date of Receipt or Mixing.	Bulk Gals.	Strength O.P.	Gals. at Proof.	Date of Sending Out or Delivery.	No. of Permit	Name of Person to Whom Sent or Delivered.	Of What Place.	Bulk Gals.	Strength O.P.	Gallons at Proof.

Second Schedule.

FORM OF STOCK ACCOUNT TO BE KEPT BY A RETAILER OF METHYLATED SPIRITS.

Requisition.			Permit.				Account of Sales.				
Date.	No. of.	Gallons Requisitioned.	Date.	From What Methylator Received.	Of What Place.	Gals.	Date.	Full Name of Person to Whom Sold.	Of What Place and Address.	Trade or Occupation.	Gallons and Parts of a Gallon Sold.

and sale of spirits, and that of November 17th, 1900, relating to permits are hereby annulled as from September 30th, 1906.

Dated this 11th day of August, 1906.

Signed by order of the Commissioners of Inland Revenue.

J. B. MEERS, Secretary.

ALCOHOL FOR INDUSTRIAL PURPOSES.—The Revenue Bill, which includes facilities for the use, without payment of duty, of spirits in arts and manufactures (J. S. C. I., 1905, 397–426; ib. 706) has received the Royal assent. After having been considered in Committee, the report stage passed the House of Commons without discussion on July 27, and the bill was read a first time in the House of Lords on the same date. The second reading was carried without dissent on July 31, and the third reading took place on the same afternoon. Rules and regulations for the use of duty-free spirit will be issued on October 1st next.

Laws and Regulations of Denatured Alcohol in Germany. (Abstract of Regulations.)*—Spirit for employment in industrial operations, vinegar-making, cleaning, heating, cooking, lighting, as well as for educational or scientific purposes, may, after having been denatured according to the regulations, or, in special cases, *without denaturing* on proof of the spirit having been so used, be granted freedom from the spirit taxes on the following conditions:

The freedom from duty includes—

(a) The release from the *"consumption"* tax and its *additions.*

(b) The refunding of the *"fermenting-vat"* tax, at the rate of 0.16 mark per liter of pure alcohol, so far as the spirit has been subjected to it.

(c) The return of the *"distilling"* tax at the rate of 0.06 mark per liter of pure alcohol.

Duty-paid spirit and spirit containing more than 1 per cent of fusel-oil are not admitted for denaturing. The denaturing is either *complete*, i.e., such as is deemed sufficient to make the spirit undrinkable or *incomplete*, i.e., such as requires the employment of other means for the prevention of the improper employment of such spirit.

General denaturing agents for complete denaturing:

4 parts wood naphtha
and 1 part pyridine bases,

---

* From Report of the Departmental Committee on Industrial Alcohol to the British Parliament, 1905.

to each liter of which may be added 50 grams of lavender-oil or rosemary-oil. Of this mixture 2½ liters are added to each hectolitre of alcohol.

German methylated spirit therefore contains 2 per cent of wood naphtha and 0.5 per cent pyridine bases with, optionally, 0.125 per cent of a lavender- or rosemary-oil.

For *incomplete* denaturing the following substances (special denaturing agents) may be used. They are to be added for denaturing purposes in the undernoted quantities per hundred liters of the spirit

(*a*) For industrial uses of all kinds:

> 5 liters of wood spirit
> or 0.5 liter of pyridine bases.

[For other examples of incomplete denaturing, see Appendix.]

Pure Duty-free Alcohol.

Pure alcohol, without denaturing, may be delivered duty free—

(*a*) To *certain hospitals, lying-in hospitals,* and lunatic asylums, as well as to public scientific institutions.

For use in motor-cars, etc., alcohol is completely denatured by the use of 1.25 liters (1.32 quarts) of the general denaturing agent, 0.25 liter (0.26 quart) of a solution of methyl violet dye, and 2 to 20 liters (2.11 to 21.13 quarts) of benzol to every hectolitre (26.4 gallons) of alcohol. For manufacturing there are many formulæ allowed for incompletely denatured alcohol for special purposes. Among these may be mentioned: For varnishes and polishes of all kinds, 2 liters (2.11 quarts) of wood alcohol and 2 liters of petroleum benzine, or 0.5 liter of turpentine (0.53 quart); for transparent soap, various chemical preparations; see Appendix at the back of this book. For general use on a large scale for industrial and manufacturing processes of all kinds, what is classed as "wood-spirit denatured" alcohol is allowed to be made and sold under special conditions. This consists of a mixture of 100 liters of alcohol of not less than 90 per cent (or 180° U.S. proof) with 5 liters of wood naphtha. There is also allowed for industrial uses 1/2 liter pyridine bases to 100 liters of spirit.

Laws and Regulations in France for Denatured Alcohol.

Duty-free Spirit.

(Abstract of French Regulations.)

Spirits may be denatured by the "general process" or by "special processes." Denaturing by the "special processes" is usually carried out at the factories where the spirit is to be used.

General Denaturing Process.—Ten liters of wood spirit of at least 90° (58 o. p.) and containing 25 per cent acetone, and 2.5 per cent of "impurities pyrogenées" for 100 liters of spirit. Spirit denatured by this reagent is divided into two classes:

(1) For lighting, heating, and for making "finish."

(2) For manufacturing purposes.

For lighting, heating, etc., this spirit must contain, in addition to the general denaturing agent, 0.5 per cent of heavy benzine distilling between 150° and 200° C. when used for heating and lighting and 4 per cent gum-resin for "finish."

For manufacturing purposes, such as making varnishes, solid extracts, solidified spirits, plastic substances, alkaloids, fulminate of mercury, transparent soap, insecticides, etc., the spirit is denatured by this general denaturing agent.

Certain industries cannot use methylated spirit, and the use of specially denatured alcohol, adapted to the particular necessities of each manufacturer, is permitted. As examples of this class can be mentioned ethers, simple and compound, for which the alcohol is mixed with 10 per cent of ether-making residues and 10 per cent sulphuric acid, to denature it.

For the manufacture of chloroform, some chloride of lime in solution is mixed with the alcohol in order to denature it. For chloral and chloral hydrate the alcohol is denatured by a current of chlorine-gas. For making collodion the alcohol is denatured by the addition of an equal volume of ether, and to this mixture 6 grams guncotton for each liter of alcohol are added.

Laws and Regulations of Denatured Alcohol in Austria-Hungary.

Duty-free Spirit.

Ordinary methylated spirit is made by mixing with alcohol of at least 90° (58 o. p.) 2 per cent wood naphtha, $\frac{1}{2}$ per cent pyridine bases, and a trace of phenolphthalein.

A tax equivalent to about one third of a penny a gallon is charged for denaturing.

For varnishes, fulminate of mercury, hat-making, etc., $\frac{1}{2}$ per cent of turpentine is the denaturing agent.

For vinegar the spirit is mixed with "anhydride."

Very small quantities of pure alcohol are used for scientific purposes under certain conditions free of duty.

Laws and Regulations of Denatured Alcohol in Russia.

Duty-free Spirit.

(Abstract of Russian Regulations.)

Persons wishing to use spirit duty free must apply to the Minister of Finance. Permission is generally limited *to one year.* Security for the duty (bond) must be given.

The quantity of spirit allowed is determined each year and "depends on the productive power of the manufactory, conditions for disposal of manufactured article, scale of annual consumption of spirit," etc. The spirit is issued from distilleries, rectifying-works, etc., on production of the order of the Finance Minister. It is received and examined at the factories by excise officers and, *after having been denatured,* is placed under revenue seal in a special store, and is only issued as required by an excise officer. Accounts of receipt and issue are strictly kept and sent to auditing authorities at the end of each year.

As a general rule a special Excise Controller is attached to each works for constant supervision of the proper use of the duty-free spirit, and the proprietor of the works is bound to provide him with proper dwelling accommodation and with furniture and fuel.

Foreign spirits cannot be imported duty free.

Law for Denatured Alcohol in the United States.

COPY OF UNITED STATES LAW, APPROVED JUNE 7, 1906, PERMITTING UNTAXED DOMESTIC DENATURED ALCOHOL FOR INDUSTRIAL USES.

[PUBLIC—No. 201.]

An Act For the withdrawal from bond, tax free, of domestic alcohol when rendered unfit for beverage or liquid medicinal uses by mixture with suitable denaturing materials.

Be it enacted by the Senate and House of Representatives of the United States of America in Congress assembled, That from and after January first, nineteen hundred and seven, domestic alcohol of such degree of proof as may be prescribed by the Commissioner of Internal Revenue, and approved by the Secretary of the Treasury, may be withdrawn from bond without the payment of internal-revenue tax, for use in the arts and industries, and for fuel, light, and power, provided said alcohol shall have been mixed in the presence and under the direction of an authorized Government officer, after withdrawal from the distillery warehouse, with methyl alcohol or other denaturing material or materials, or admixture of the same, suitable to the use for which the alcohol is withdrawn, but which destroys its character as a beverage and renders it unfit for liquid medicinal purposes; such denaturing to be done upon the application of any registered distillery in denaturing bonded warehouses specially designated or set apart for denaturing purposes only, and under conditions prescribed by the Commissioner of Internal Revenue with the approval of the Secretary of the Treasury.

The character and quantity of the said denaturing material and the conditions upon which said alcohol may be withdrawn free of tax shall be prescribed by the Commissioner of Internal Revenue, who shall, with the approval of the Secretary of the Treasury, make all necessary regulations for carrying into effect the provisions of this Act.

Distillers, manufacturers, dealers and all other persons furnishing, handling, or using alcohol withdrawn from bond under the provisions of this Act shall keep such books and records, execute such bonds and render such returns as the Commissioner of Internal Revenue, with the approval of the Secretary of the Treasury, may by regulation require. Such books and records shall be open at all times to the inspection of any internal-revenue officer or agent.

SEC. 2. That any person who withdraws alcohol free of tax under the provisions of this Act and regulations made in pursuance thereof, and who removes or conceals same, or is concerned in removing, depositing, or concealing same for the purpose of preventing the same from being denatured under governmental supervision, and any person who uses alcohol withdrawn from bond under the provisions of section one of this Act for manufacturing any beverage or liquid medicinal preparation, or knowingly sells any beverage or liquid medicinal preparation made in whole or in part from such alcohol, or knowingly violates any of the provisions of this Act, or who shall recover or attempt to recover by redistillation or by any other process or means, any alcohol rendered unfit for beverage or liquid medicinal purposes under the provisions of this Act, or who knowingly uses, sells, conceals, or otherwise disposes of alcohol so recovered or redistilled, shall on conviction of each offense be fined not more than five thousand dollars, or be imprisoned not more than five years, or both, and shall, in addition, forfeit to the United States all personal property used in connection with his business, together with the buildings and lots or parcels of ground constituting the premises on which said unlawful acts are performed or permitted to be performed: *Provided*, That manufacturers employing processes in which alcohol, used free of tax under the provisions of this Act, is expressed or evaporated from the articles manufactured, shall be permitted to recover such alcohol and to have such alcohol restored to a condition suitable solely for reuse in manfacturing processes under such regulations as the Commissioner of Internal Revenue, with the approval of the Secretary of the Treasury, shall prescribe.

SEC. 3. That for the employment of such additional force of chemists, internal-revenue agents, inspectors, deputy collectors, clerks, laborers, and other assistants as the Commissioner of Internal Revenue, with the approval of the Secretary of the Treasury, may deem proper and necessary to the prompt and efficient operation and enforcement of this law, and for the purchase of locks, seals, weighing beams, gauging instruments, and for all necessary expenses incident to the proper execution of this law, the sum of two hundred and fifty thousand dollars, or so much thereof as may be required, is hereby appropriated out of any money in the Treasury not otherwise appropriated, said appropriation to be immediately available.

For a period of two years from and after the passage of this Act the force authorized by this section of this Act shall be appointed by the Commissioner of Internal Revenue, with the approval of the Secretary of the Treasury, and without compliance with the conditions prescribed by the act entitled "An Act to regulate and improve the civil service," approved January sixteenth, eighteen hundred and eighty-three, and amendments thereof, and with such compensation as the Commissioner of Internal Revenue may fix, with the approval of the Secretary of the Treasury.

SEC. 4. That the Secretary of the Treasury shall make full report to Congress at its next session of all appointments made under the provisions of this Act, and the compensation paid thereunder, and of all regulations prescribed under the provisions hereof, and shall further report what, if any, additional legislation is necessary, in his opinion, to fully safeguard the revenue and to secure a proper enforcement of this Act.

Approved, June 7, 1906.

Cost of Denaturing Alcohol in Foreign Countries.*—"*With respect to the cost of denaturing in the United Kingdom* it may be said that this cost touches a part only of the question of the price of the spirit used for industrial purposes. An influence on price even more important lies at an earlier stage of production of the spirit, viz., in the conditions

---

* From Report of the Departmental Committee on Industrial Alcohol to the British Parliament, April, 1905; see Appendix, this book.

under which spirit can alone be manufactured in this country.   The duty on spirit used as a beverage in the United Kingdom is very heavy, and in imposing this duty it is essential to the protection of the revenue to impose on the manufacture of spirit such restraints as may be necessary to prevent any spirit from escaping payment of duty; and a consequence of such restraints must be to cause an appreciable enhancement in the cost of manufacture.   Only an approximation can be reached as to what the measure of this enhancement may be, as it is not susceptible of precise determination.   For our purpose it is sufficient to take the figures that have been established by law and practice as representing an enhancement of the cost of producing plain British spirits by 3d. the proof gallon, or an increase of about 50 per cent on the cost that would otherwise prevail in the production of industrial alcohol.   It is patent that producers thus hampered could not hope to compete successfully either in the home or in foreign markets against rivals not similarly hampered, unless some counterpoise were provided to the burdens that fiscal restrictions impose upon them.   Accordingly the law does provide such a counterpoise in the case of the home market by making the duty on imported spirits exceed the duty on British spirits by an amount equivalent to the burdens on the home producer,—this is called the "Surtax"; and in the case of foreign markets by granting to the home producer allowances calculated on the same basis.   These export allowances are at the rates of 3d. per proof gallon on plain spirits, and 5d. per proof gallon on compounded spirits and it is the higher of these two allowances that is taken as determining the measure of the ' surtax ' on all imported spirits other than rum or brandy, on which the 'surtax' is 4d. the proof gallon. The final result, upon the price of industrial spirit, of all the measures taken to protect the revenue may be stated as follows: Spirit used in manufacture is commonly about 64 overproof (about 93 per cent on the continental standard of pure alcohol) and is plain spirit.   Therefore the price of a bulk gallon of the spirit is about 5d. (10 cents, or about 8½ cents per U. S. bulk gallon) more than it would have been but for excise restrictions.   The cost of methylating (or denaturing) may be put at between 3d. and 4d. per bulk gallon (7 cents, or about 6 cents per U. S. bulk gallon), so that of the price eventually paid by the manufacturer, which at present may be taken at from 20d. to 22d. per bulk gallon for large quantities at wholesale price, about 8½d. (17 cents) is attributable to precautions on behalf of the revenue (about 14 cents per U. S. bulk gallon).

" *Cost of Denaturing in Germany.*—In Germany the production of spirit is a state-aided enterprise, the primary purpose of which is not so much the production of spirit on economic lines as the encouragement of agriculture in the less fertile provinces of the Empire, which lie on its eastern frontiers, and in which the conditions of soil and climate are so unfavorable. Without some such encouragement the country would be in serious danger of depopulation. It may be said that the fundamental principle of the scheme is to make those interested in the production of alcohol sharers with the state in the revenue collected on spirit used for potable purposes. Thus in the year ended on 30th September, 1903, there was collected from the taxes on spirit a total sum of £10,000,000, out of which a sum of £3,100,000 was given back to persons interested in the trade. But of this sum of £3,100,000 apparently some £700,000 had been already levied as tax on the producers, so that their net subvention would be £2,400,000 (about $11,688,000). In the same year the total production of spirit in Germany was, in round figures, 132,000,000 proof gallons, and accordingly the state subvention in that year represented a bonus of nearly $4\frac{1}{2}d.$ per proof gallon on all the spirit produced. The figures must, of course, vary from year to year according to the circumstances of production and consumption; but probably not very widely. This bounty, be it $4\frac{1}{2}d.$ (9 cents) per gallon or more or less, is retained by the producers or distributors as a rule, and only under certain circumstances do the German users of spirit secure a share in it. The cost of complete denaturing is definitely known to be only a little more than $1d.$ the bulk gallon (about 1.7 cents per U. S. bulk gallon). In this case, however, there is all the economy that results from simplicity, regularity, and magnitude in the operations."

It may be said that it costs at present a little over 2 cents a gallon to completely denature alcohol in Germany. Alcohol of 90 and 95 per cent strength by volume is used in making denatured alcohol. The selling price at retail for denatured alcohol is, for 95 per cent strength by volume, 33 pfennigs per liter, or 29.69 cents per gallon; 90 per cent strength by volume, 30 pfennigs per liter, or 27 cents per gallon. The selling prices at wholesale range from 28 to 29 pfennigs per liter, or from 25.2 to 26.1 cents per gallon. The German data are taken from the report of U. S. Consul-General Alexander M. Thackara, Berlin, Germany, September 10, 1906.

Cost of Denaturing in France.—"In France, since January 1, 1902, a drawback of 9 francs per hectolitre of pure alcohol (about $2\frac{1}{2}d.$ per proof gallon) has been allowed on alcohol used for lighting and heating to compensate for cost of methylating (or denaturing) and to enable this spirit to compete with petrol (gasoline) in motor-cars, etc. Denatured alcohol pays a statistical tax of 0.25 franc per hectolitre of pure alcohol (about 7d. per 100 proof gallons) and also 0.80 franc per hectolitre (about 1s. 10d. per 100 proof gallons) to cover the expense of the examination of the samples and the supervision of the denaturing operations." (This makes a cost of 1.05 francs per hectolitre of pure alcohol, exclusive of the denaturing materials, or 21 cents per 26.41 U. S. gallons of pure alcohol.)

U. S. Consul-General Robert P. Skinner reports as follows: "Denatured alcohol is composed, according to French law at the present time (August 6, 1906), of one hundred parts of industrial ethyl alcohol grading 90° (90 per cent) at a temperature of 15° C., of ten parts of methyl alcohol industrially denominated methylene, and which itself is composed of 75 per cent of methyl alcohol, 25 per cent of acetone, a certain quantity of impurities, and finally a one-half part of heavy benzol, boiling between 150° and 200° C., and differing essentially from pure benzol, which indicates a density of 0.88 at 15° C. and boils at 80.4° C."

The price of alcohol at 90°, which serves as a basis, is very variable and depends upon the demand and supply in the Paris market, which is held daily. The price is actually about 43 francs ($8.30) per hectolitre (26.41 U. S. gallons) naked, base 90°, with a premium for quality over 90°, and the tax on manufacture, i.e., 1.63 francs (31 cents) per hectolitre (26.41 U. S. gallons) of pure alcohol taken at the distillery. The cost of transportation is to be added to this price. For your information let me say that we have seen the market reach 26 francs ($5.01) in 1901 and 57 francs ($11) in 1905. Thus you see how difficult it is to establish an average price for this article which is so much speculated upon. Methylene responding to the requirements of the law is worth from 80 to 100 francs ($15.44 to $19.30) per hectolitre (26.41 U. S. gallons), and benzine from 45 to 65 francs ($8.68 to $12.54)."

On the above formula the cost of denaturing a hectolitre of alcohol is, for an average of these prices for the denaturing materials, 9.50 francs ($1.90 for 26.41 U. S. gallons, or about 7.2 cents per gallon). The rebate of 9 francs per hectolitre of pure alcohol is, for a hectolitre of denatured alcohol which contains about 81.5 liters of pure alcohol, about 7.335 francs. The government tax of 1.05 francs per hectolitre of pure alcohol makes the tax on 81.5 liters of pure alcohol (contained in one hectolitre of the denatured alcohol) as 0.856 franc, which, added to 9.50 francs, = 10.356 francs; less the rebate of 7.335 francs gives 3.021 francs per hectolitre as the cost of denaturing in France. This is equal to about 60½ cents per 26.41 U. S. gallons, or about 2.2 cents per gallon. "Denatured alcohol cannot be sold at this time (August 6, 1906) at retail in France for less than 55 centimes (11 cents) per liter " (about 44 cents per U. S. gallon).

The cost of denaturing in *Russia, Switzerland, Holland, Austria-Hungary,* and *Belgium* are difficult to ascertain. Some data are given in the "Report on Industrial Alcohol," pp. 422-85, in the Appendix of this book.

Cost of Denaturing Alcohol in the United States.—With regard to the cost of denaturing alcohol in the United States, it may be said that such a figure or cost is difficult to estimate on account of the fact that it is not certain what the price of the approved methyl alcohol will be, and what proportion of costs the Government restrictions as to denaturing will add. This will be explained in Chapter X. Given the cost of the approved methyl alcohol, the additional cost mentioned above and the cost of the petroleum, benzine, or the alternative coal-tar "benzine," the calculation is easily made on the Government formulæ for completely denatured alcohol, one of which is as follows: 100 gallons of ethyl alcohol of not less than 180° proof, 10 gallons of approved methyl alcohol, and $\frac{1}{2}$ gallon of the petroleum or coal-tar "benzine." See also p. 355, this chapter.

It will be of interest to know that coal-tar benzine boiling between 150° and 200° C. costs about 25 cents per gallon in this country and that the cost of the pyridin bases here is about the same as in Germany, about $1.50 per gallon. Both these bodies have been prescribed as denaturants by the United States Government.

Properties of Denaturing Materials.—The materials which are used for denaturing alcohol for general industrial uses both in this country and abroad have characteristics and properties which render the alcohol to which they have been added extremely repugnant to the taste and entirely unfitted for human consumption.

Wood alcohol or methyl alcohol is usually the principal one of several ingredients chosen, and its fatally poisonous properties and injurious effects upon the optic nerve, as well as the entire nervous system generally, are so well known that further mention, here, is unnecessary.

Chemical research is active all the time, on account of economic reasons, to find cheaper sources of denaturing agents in order to cheapen the cost of denatured alcohol, as well as in some cases abroad to allow of pyridine, one of the denaturing agents in Germany, being used for other purposes, and thus prevent a rise in the price (see Appendix, p. 441). In cases where special denaturing materials are permitted and used, these substances are, as a rule, the same as those used in the manufacture in question. Manufacturers who are allowed to denature alcohol at the factory or works have to do so abroad under very strict supervision of excise officials.   After the special denaturing agent is mixed with the alcohol it is usually kept in sealed tanks in care of trusted employees until it is used.   In many such cases the alcohol is thereby rendered unfit for use other than as intended.

Special Denaturing Methods in Foreign Countries.—In the United Kingdom spirits denatured with other substances than wood alcohol can be used subject to the special permission of the Government.   The denaturing substance is, as a rule, one used in the manufacturing operations involved (as castor-oil in making transparent soap).   Traders using these specially denatured spirits have to pay the cost of the revenue supervision.

Undenatured alcohol is allowed to be used by universities, colleges, and other public institutions for research and teaching under certain conditions.   See Appendix, pp. 458, 467.

In Germany *special denaturing agents* are allowed for *incomplete* denaturing.   "The list includes a number of manufacturing purposes, for which a different denaturing agent is permitted in each case."   See Appendix, p. 465.

"*Pure alcohol without denaturing* is permitted duty-free under certain restrictions by the Government."   See Appendix, pp. 465–66.

"Special denaturing substances are permitted by the French Government."   See Appendix, pp. 472–73.

The Swiss Government permit specially denatured alcohol.   See Appendix, p. 476.

For the Russian regulations as to special denaturing agents permitted see Appendix, p. 481.

The Dutch regulations for special denaturing substances are given on p. 482 of the Appendix.

Specially denatured alcohol is fully discussed in Chapter X under Uses of Alcohol.

Tests Prescribed by Foreign Countries for the Denaturing Materials Used.—The present legal provisions or regulations in Germany relating to the nature of the components of the methylating substance are given on p. 468 of the Appendix.   A comparison between these and those here given from Mr. Dalley's Report, pp. 342–6, will show but little difference, the "acetone" in the wood spirit being at present estimated by a volumetric process in which the acetone, aldehydes, and higher ketones are estimated by the formation of iodoform according to Messinger's method.

The details of the Government tests for the denaturing agents imposed in the other foreign countries permitting denatured alcohol can be found by consulting the report of Henry Dalley, Jr., 1896–7, already mentioned.   The countries covered in the report mentioned are Great

Britain, France, Germany, Belgium, Switzerland, The Netherlands, Italy, Sweden, Norway, and Austria-Hungary.

The examination of the wood naphtha used at present for methylating in Great Britain is given in the Appendix, on pp. 452–3, under the head of The United Kingdom.

In France the present restrictions as to the quality of the wood spirit used in methylating are given on p. 472 of the Appendix.

On p. 475 of the Appendix are described the present regulations concerning the denaturing mixture used in Switzerland.

* The Volumetric Estimation of " Acetone " by the Formation of Iodoform according to Messinger's Original Method.

"For the analysis are used:
  I. One fifth normal iodine solution.
  II. One tenth normal thiosulphate of sodium.
 † III. Hydrochloric acid, sp. gr. 1.025.
  IV. Caustic potash (56 gm. KOH in 1 liter water).
  V. A glass flask of 250 c.c. capacity, with tightly-fitting stopper.
  VI. A 1-c.c. pipette graduated in hundredths or in tenths.
 VII. Starch solution."
    (The correction for any nitrite present.)

"Since the caustic potash nearly always contains nitrite, it is necessary, before commencing the analysis, to add to 20 c.c. of above solution of KOH from 1–2 dg. of iodide of potassium; after adding the above HCl acid in slight excess, the liberated iodine is, with starch solution, titrated with the 1/10 N. hypo. above. The cubic centimeters thus needed are deducted from the number of cubic centimeters 1/10 N. hypo. used in the analysis."

Making the Analysis.—"Use 20 c.c. of the above KOH solution, or if the methyl alcohol is of the highest acetone content, 30 c.c. of the KOH solution (always exactly measured) and 1–2 c.c. of the methyl alcohol ‡ to be tested, which are put into the stoppered flask and well shaken. A measured quantity of the 1/5 N. iodine solution, from 20 to 30 c.c., is run into the flask drop by drop, shaking from one to one half minute or until the solution settles clear, then the above HCL acid is

---

 *The Volumetric Estimation of Acetone in Methyl Alcohol. J. Messinger, Berichte der Deutschen Chemischen Gesellschaft, Vol. XXI, 2, July–December, 1888, pp. 3366–73.

 † The same number of cubic centimeters of the above HCl acid are used as of the above KOH solution.

 ‡ In testing pure commercial methyl alcohol from 10 to 15 c.c. are used.

added, an excess of 1/10 N. hypo. solution is run in, starch solution added and titrated back with the iodine solution.

"The calculation of the analysis is made in the following way:

"One mol acetone (58) uses three mols iodine (762) to make one mol iodoform:

$$762:58 = m:$$

$m =$ quantity of iodine found.

$y =$ corresponding quantity acetone.

$$y = m \cdot 7\frac{58}{762} = 0.7612\ m.$$

"In order to prove the accuracy of this process I have made up weighed quantities of c. p. acetone (from bisulphite) with c. p. methyl alcohol (from oxalate) reduced to 100 c.c., and in such a manner that this solution represented from 0.2–2% of acetone.

"I have further tested acetone in a water solution and also in some of the commercial methyl alcohols."

In several such estimations Messinger obtained the following results:

	Calculated.	Found.			
		1st Test.	2d Test.	3d Test.	4th Test
Acetone, per cent	2.05	2.04	2.03	2.04	2.03.

'The above estimations are merely a few of such tests taken from quite a number as furnished by Messinger in this article.

The following legal provisions relating to the nature of the components of the general methylation (denaturing) substance in Germany are taken from the First Report on Alcohol, Methylated, Unmethylated, and Untaxed, by Henry Dalley, Jr., 1896–7:

"Tests prescribed for the denaturing materials used in Germany.

1. Wood Spirits.

"The wood spirits should be colorless or faintly yellowish. On distilling 100 volumes of wood spirits under normal barometric condition of 760 millimeters pressure of mercury up to a temperature of 75° C., at least 90 volumes should pass over. The wood spirits should admit of being mixed with water in any proportion without notable turbidity. The content of the wood spirits in acetone should exceed 30 per cent. The wood spirits should contain at least 1 per cent, but not more than 1.5 per cent, of constituents which discolor bromine."

2. The Pyridine Bases.

"The mixture of pyridine bases should be colorless or faintly yellowish. Its water content should not exceed 10 per cent. On distilling 100 volumes of the mixture under normal barometric condition of 760 millimeters up to a temperature of 140° C. at least 90 volumes should pass over. The mixture should admit of being mixed with water in any proportion without notable turbidity, and should be free from ammonia."

"Instructions for Testing the Wood Spirits and the Pyridine Bases.

"I. Wood Spirits.

"1. *Color.*—The color of the wood spirits should not be darker than that of a solution of 2 cubic centimeters of one tenth normal solution of iodine in a liter of distilled water.

"2. *Boiling-point.*—One hundred cubic centimeters of wood spirits should be placed in a metallic retort having a distilling-tube which is furnished with a bulb connected with a Liebig condenser by a lateral tube. Through the upper opening an officially certified thermometer with centigrade scale is introduced, whose mercury bulb stands below the connecting-tube. The retort is so moderately heated that the distillate runs off in drops from the condenser. The distillate is caught in a graduated glass cylinder, and if the thermometer shows 75 degrees and the barometer is normal, at least 90 cubic centimeters should have passed over.

"When the reading of the barometer departs from the normal, there for every 30 milimeters 1 degree should be allowed; that is to say, for example, at 770 milimeters 90 cubic centimeters should pass over at 75.3 degrees; at 750 milimeters 90 cubic centimeters should pass over at 74.7 degrees.

"3. *The Capacity to Mix with Water.*—Twenty cubic centimeters of wood spirits should give with 40 cubic centimeters of water a clear or only a faintly opalescent mixture.

"4. *Separation with Sodium Lye.*—On shaking 20 cubic centimeters of wood spirits with 40 cubic centimeters of sodium lye of 1.3 specific gravity, after half an hour at least 5 cubic centimeters of the wood spirits should have separated.

"5. *Proportion of Content in Acetone.*—One cubic centimeter of a mixture of 10 cubic centimeters of wood spirits with 90 cubic centimeters of water are shaken in a narrow mixing cylinder with 10 cubic centimeters of double normal sodium lye (80 grams of sodium hydroxide in a liter). Thereupon 5 cubic centimeters of double normal solution of iodine (254 grams of iodine to the liter) are added while the mixture is again shaken. The separating iodoform is taken up in 10 cubic centimeters of ether of the specific gravity of 0.722 by vigorously shaking. From the layer of ether, which separates after a short rest, 5 cubic centimeters are brought by means of a pipette on a watch-crystal that has been weighed and on it slowly evaporated. Then the watch-crystal is placed for two hours over sulphuric acid and weighed; the increase in weight should not be less than 0.07 gram.

"6. *Capacity to Take Up Bromine.*—One hundred cubic centimeters of a solution of potassium bromate and potassium bromide, prepared according to the instructions below, are compounded with 20 cubic centimeters of sulphuric acid diluted as explained below. To this mixture, which represents a bromine solution of 0.703 gram of bromine, wood spirits are added from a burette graduated to 0.1 cubic centimeter in drops with constant stirring, piolonged until permanent discoloration takes place. The discoloration ought not to require more than 30 cubic centimeters and not less than 20 cubic centimeters of wood spirits.

"The test for the capacity to take up bromine must always be made in full daylight."

"Instructions for the Preparation of the Constituents of the Bromine Solution.

"(a) *Bromine Salts.*—After drying for at least two hours at 100 degrees and cooling in the dryer, 2.447 grams of potassium bromate and 8.719 grams of potassium bromide, which have previously been tested for purity, are weighed and dissolved in water and diluted to 1 liter.

"(b) *Diluted Sulphuric Acid.*—One volume of concentrated sulphuric acid is mixed with three volumes of water. The mixture is allowed to cool."

II. Pyridine Bases.

"1. Color same as in wood spirits.

"2. *Behavior toward Cadmium Chloride.*—Ten cubic centimeters of a solution of 1 cubic centimeter of pyridine bases in 100 cubic centimeters of water are mixed with 5 cubic centimeters of 5 per cent water solution of anhydrous melted cadmium chloride and are vigorously shaken; thereupon a distinct crystalline precipitate should at once ensue. With 5 cubic centimeters of Nessler's reagent, 10 cubic centimeters of the same solution of pyridine bases ought to give a white precipitate.

"3. *Boiling-point.*—Proceed as in wood spirits, but the distillate should amount to at least 90 cubic centimeters only when the thermometer has risen to 140 degrees.

"4. *Capacity to Mix with Water.*—As in wood spirits.

"5. *Water Content.*—On shaking 20 cubic centimeters of bases and 20 cubic centimeters of sodium lye of 1.4 specific gravity and allowing to stand for some time, at least 18.5 cubic centimeters of the bases ought to be separated.

"6. *Titration of the Bases.*—One cubic centimeter of pyridine bases dissolved in 10 cubic centimeters of water is mixed with normal sulphuric acid until a drop of the mixture on congo paper produces a distinct blue border, which immediately disappears again. Not less than 10 cubic centimeters of the acid solution ought to be used in producing this reaction.

"To prepare congo paper, filter-paper is passed through a solution of 1 gram of congo red in 1 liter of water and dried."

"*Instructions for Testing Animal Oil, Oil of Turpentine, and Ether.*

I. ANIMAL OIL.

"1. *Color.*—The color of the animal oil should be blackish brown.

"2. *Boiling-point.*—On distilling 100 cubic centimeters in the manner described for wood spirits, not more than 5 cubic centimeters should pass over below 90 degrees, but at least 50 cubic centimeters should have passed over when the temperature has risen to 180 degrees.

"3. *Pyrrol Reaction.*—Two and five tenth cubic centimeters of a 1 per cent alcoholic solution of animal oil are diluted with alcohol to 100 cubic centimeters. If a pine-wood shaving moistened with concentrated hydrochloric acid is introduced in 10 cubic centimeters of that solution containing 0.025 per cent of animal oil it should show a distinct red color after a few minutes.

"4. *Behavior toward Chloride of Mercury.*—Five cubic centimeters of the 1 per cent alcoholic solution of the animal oil, on being mixed with 5 cubic centimeters of a 2 per cent alcoholic solution of chloride of mercury, should give at once a voluminous flaky precipitate. Five cubic centimeters of the 0.025 per cent alcoholic solution of animal oil mixed with 5 cubic centimeters of the solution of the chloride of mercury should at once show a distinct turbidity."

II. TURPENTINE-OIL.

"1. *Specific Gravity.*—The specific gravity of the oil of turpentine ought to be between 0.855 and 0.865 at 15 degrees C.

"*2. Boiling-point.*—On distilling 100 cubic centimeters in the manner given for wood spirits not more than 5 cubic centimeters should pass over under 150 degrees, but at least 90 cubic centimeters should have passed over when the temperature has risen to 160 degrees.

"*3. Capacity to Mix with Water.*—Twenty cubic centimeters of oil of turpentine are vigorously shaken with 20 cubic centimeters of water. If, after standing for some time, the two layers have separated and have become clear, the upper layer should carry at least 19 cubic centimeters."

III. ETHER.

"*1. Specific Gravity.*—Specific gravity of the ether should not be more than 0.730.

"*2. Capacity to Mix with Water.*—Twenty cubic centimeters of ether are shaken with 20 cubic centimeters of water. After settling the layer of ether should carry at least 18 cubic centimeters."

IV. SHELLAC SOLUTION.

"Ten grams of the solution on evaporating on the water-bath and subsequent heating of the evaporated residue in the drying-chamber for half an hour up to a temperature of 100 to 105 degrees should have at least 3.3 grams of shellac."

Tests Prescribed by the United States for the Denaturing Materials Used. Completely Denatured Alcohol and Specially Denatured Alcohol in the United States.—"Sec. 58" of "Regulations No. 30, United States Internal Revenue," provides that "alcohol denatured by the use of methyl alcohol and benzine as provided in Section 26 of these Regulations is to be classed as *completely denatured alcohol.* Alcohol denatured in any other manner will be classed as *specially denatured alcohol.*"

"*Denaturing Agents.*"

Completely Denatured Alcohol.

"Sec. 26" provides: "Unless otherwise specially provided, the agents used for denaturing alcohol withdrawn from bond for denaturing purposes shall consist of methyl alcohol and benzine in the following proportions: To every one hundred parts by volume of ethyl alcohol of the desired proof (not less than 180°) there shall be added ten parts by volume of approved methyl alcohol and one half of one part by volume of approved benzine; for example, to every 100 gallons of ethyl alcohol (of not less than 180 degrees proof) there shall be added 10 gallons of approved methyl alcohol and one half gallon of approved benzine.

" Alcohol thus denatured shall be classed as completely denatured alcohol.

" Methyl alcohol and benzine intended for use as denaturants must be submitted for chemical test and must conform to the specifications which shall be hereafter duly prescribed." These specifications are as follows:

CIRCULAR No. 680.

SPECIFICATIONS FOR METHYL ALCOHOL AND BENZINE, SUBMITTED FOR APPROVAL AS DENATURING MATERIALS.

TREASURY DEPARTMENT.
OFFICE OF THE
COMMISSIONER OF INTERNAL REVENUE,
WASHINGTON, October 30, 1906.

The second paragraph of section 1 of the act approved June 7, 1906, for the withdrawal from bond, tax free, of domestic alcohol to be rendered unfit for beverage or liquid medicinal purposes by the admixture of denaturing materials provides as follows:

The character and quantity of the said denaturing material and the conditions upon which said alcohol may be withdrawn free of tax shall be prescribed by the Commissioner of Internal Revenue, who shall, with the approval of the Secretary of the Treasury, make all necessary regulations for carrying into effect the provisions of this Act.

Pursuant to this authority, and in conformity with the terms of section 26 of regulations No. 30, the following specifications are prescribed for methyl alcohol and benzine submitted for approval as denaturing materials.

METHYL ALCOHOL.

The methyl alcohol submitted must be partially purified wood alcohol obtained by the destructive distillation of wood. It must conform to the following analytical requirements:

Color.—This shall not be darker than that produced by a freshly prepared solution of 2 c.c. of N/10 iodine diluted to 1000 c.c. with distilled water.

Specific Gravity.—It must have a specific gravity of not more than 0.830 at 60° F. (15.56° C.), corresponding to 91° of Tralles' scale.

Boiling-point.—One hundred c.c. slowly heated in a flask under conditions as described below must give a distillate of not less than 90 c.c. at a temperature not exceeding 75° C. at the normal pressure of the barometer (760 m.m.).

One hundred c.c. of wood spirit are run into a short-necked copper flask of about 180–200 c.c. capacity, and the flask placed on an asbestos plate having a circular opening of 30 mm. diameter. In the neck of this flask is fitted a fractionating tube 12 mm. wide and 170 mm. long, with a bulb just 1 centimeter below the side tube, which is connected with a Liebig's condenser having a water-jacket not less than 400 mm. long. In the upper opening of the fractionating tube is placed a standardized thermometer, so adjusted that its mercury bulb comes in the centre of the bulb. The distillation is conducted in such a manner that 5 c.c. pass over in one minute. The distillate is run into a graduated cylinder, and when the temperature of 75° C. has been reached at the normal barometric pressure of 760 mm., at least 90 c.c. shall have been collected.

Should the barometer vary from 760 mm. during the distillation, 1° C. shall be allowed for every variation of 30 mm. For example, at 770 mm. 90 c.c. should have distilled at 75.3°, and at 750 mm. 90 c.c. should have distilled at 74.7° C.

Miscibility with Water.—It must give a clear or only slightly opalescent solution when mixed with twice its volume of water.

Acetone Content.—It must contain not more than 25 or less than 15 grams per 100 c.c. of acetone and other substances estimated as acetone when tested by the following method (Messinger):

Determination of Acetone.—1 c.c. of a mixture of 10 c.c. wood naphtha with 90 c.c. of water is treated with 10 c.c. of double normal soda solution. Then 50 c.c. of N/10 iodine solution are added while shaking, and the mixture made acid with dilute sulphuric acid three minutes after the addition of the iodine. The excess of iodine is titrated back with N/10 sodium thiosulphate solution, using a few drops of starch solution for an indicator. From 15.5 to 25.8 c.c. of N/10 iodine solution should be used by the spirit.

The solution should be kept at a temperature between 15° and 20° C.;

Calculation: X = grams of acetone in 100 c.c. of spirit;

$\qquad Y$ = number of c.c. of N/10 iodine solution required;

$\qquad N$ = volume of spirit taken for titration.

Then, $X = \dfrac{Y \times 0.096672}{N}$.

Esters.—It should contain not more than 5 grams of esters per 100 c.c. of spirit, calculated as methyl acetate and determined as follows:

Five c.c. of wood spirit are run into a flask, and 10 c.c. normal sodium hydroxide free from carbonates are added, and the flask connected with a return condenser and boiled for two hours. Instead of digesting at boiling temperature the flasks may be allowed to stand overnight at room temperature and then heated on a steam-bath for thirty minutes with an ordinary tube condenser. The liquid after digestion is cooled and titrated with normal sulphuric acid, using phenolphthalein as an indicator.

$$\text{Methyl acetate, grams per } \left. \begin{array}{l} 100 \\ \text{c.c. of spirit} \end{array} \right\} = \frac{.074 \times \text{c.c. of N/ soda required} \times 100.}{\text{c.c. spirit taken}}$$

Bromine Absorption.—It must contain a sufficient quantity of impurities derived from the wood, so that not more than 25 c.c. or less than 15 c.c. shall be required to decolorize a standard solution containing .5 gram of bromine, as follows:

The standard bromine solution is made by dissolving 12.406 grams of potassium bromide and 3.481 grams of potassium bromate (which is of tested purity and has been dried for two hours at 100° C.) in a liter of water. Fifty c.c. of the standard solution containing .5 gram of bromine are placed in a glass-stoppered flask having a capacity of about 200 c.c. This is acidified by the addition of 10 c.c. of diluted sulphuric acid (1 to 4) and the whole shaken and allowed to stand a few minutes. The wood alcohol is then allowed to flow slowly into the mixture, drop by drop, from a burette until the color is entirely discharged. The temperature of the mixture should be 20° C.

In addition to the above requirements the methyl alcohol must be of such a character as to render the ethyl alcohol with which it is mixed unfit for use as a beverage.

BENZINE.

The benzine submitted for approval must be a hydrocarbon product derived either from petroleum or coal-tar. If derived from petroleum, it must have a specific gravity of not less than .800. If derived from coal-tar it must have a boiling-point of not less than 150° or more than 200° C.

It must be of such character as to impart a decided odor to ethyl alcohol when mixed with it in the proportion of one half of one part by volume."

JOHN W. YERKES, *Commissioner.*

Approved:

C. H. KEEP, *Acting Secretary of the Treasury.*

An amendment to the United States Regulations permitting the use of methyl alcohol and pyridin bases for denaturing is as follows.

CIRCULAR No. 686.

AMENDMENT OF SECTION 26, REGULATIONS NO. 30, CONCERNING DENATURED ALCOHOL.

TREASURY DEPARTMENT,
OFFICE OF COMMISSIONER OF INTERNAL REVENUE,
WASHINGTON, December 10, 1906.

Section 26 of the regulations and instructions concerning denatured alcohol, issued September 29, 1906, is amended by inserting after the words "approved benzine," in the ninth line of said section, the following:

"Or methyl alcohol and approved pyridin bases, in the following proportions: To every 100 parts by volume of ethyl alcohol of the desired proof (not less than 180°) there shall be added two parts by volume of approved methyl alcohol and one-half of one part by volume of approved pyridin bases—for example, to every 100 gallons of ethyl alcohol (of not less than 180° proof) there shall be added 2 gallons of approved methyl alcohol and one-half gallon of approved pyridin bases."

NOTE.—Methyl alcohol intended for use as a denaturant must conform to the specifications prescribed in Circular No. 680.

Pyridin bases intended for use as a denaturant must conform to the following specifications:

Specifications for pyridin bases submitted for approval as a denaturing material.

PYRIDIN BASES.

1. *Color.*—The liquid must meet the same requirements as to color that are imposed upon wood alcohol. (See Circular No. 680.)

2. *Reaction with Cadmium Chloride.*—Ten c.c. of a solution of 1 c.c. of pyridin bases in 100 c.c. of water are treated with 5 c.c. of an aqueous solution of anhydrous fused cadmium chloride and the mixture vigorously shaken. Within ten minutes an abundant crystalline separation should take place.

3. *Behavior with Nessler's Reagent.*—With 5 c.c. of Nessler's reagent, 10 c.c. of the pyridin bases must give a white precipitate.

4. *Boiling-point.*—When 100 c.c. are subjected to the determination of the boiling point in the same manner as prescribed for wood alcohol, at least 50 c.c. must distil at 140° C. and at least 90 c.c. at 160° C.

5. *Miscibility with Water.*—The same requirements must be met as are imposed upon wood alcohol. (See Circular No. 680.)

6. *Content of Water.*—When 20 c.c. of pyridin bases are shaken with 20 c.c. of a solution of caustic soda, with a specific gravity of 1,400, and the mixture allowed to stand for some time, at least 18.5 c.c. of the pyridin bases must separate from the solution.

7. *Alkalinity.*—One c.c. of pyridin bases dissolved in 10 c.c. of water are titrated with normal sulphuric acid until a drop of the mixture placed upon Congo paper shows a distinct blue border which soon disappears. It must require not less than 9.5 c.c. of the acid solution to produce the reaction.

The Congo paper is prepared by treating filter-paper with a solution of 1 gram of Congo red in 1 liter of water, and drying it.

JOHN W. YERKES, *Commissioner.*

Approved:

LESLIE M. SHAW, *Secretary of the Treasury.*

The Recovery of Denatured Alcohol is Permitted by the United States Regulations.—For small capacities to recover denatured alcohol below the standard proof we show here, in Fig. 162, a still especially designed for this purpose. By its use the alcohol can be raised to 190° proof. This apparatus consists of a copper kettle, with steam-boiling scroll, rectifying-column with tubular condenser and return to top chamber of rectifying-column, and also a final tubular condenser with connection to receiving-box. These stills can be made with a kettle capacity of 250 to 1500 gallons. In Fig. 163 is shown a similar apparatus for this purpose. In the case of those manufacturers who use denatured alcohol in such a manner that its recovery is possible, these stills can be profitably used, and the recovered alcohol be redenatured on the manufacturers' premises in the denatured-alcohol store-room, which must be provided for such purpose, in accordance with the United States Regulations.

The apparatus shown in Fig. 163 is for recovering denatured alcohol which has been reduced in strength by reason of the use to which it has been put. No matter how great this reduction, it can be brought back to its original state of high concentration by treatment in this apparatus.

The product is charged into the still, which is the large cylindrical vessel at the base. The same is provided with a closed coil through which steam circulates, the heat from which vaporizes the contents. The vapors pass into the column, which consists of a series of chambers provided with means for condensing and separating the water mixed with the alcohol-vapors. Such a separation takes place in each of the individual chambers, and on leaving the column at the top the vapors are

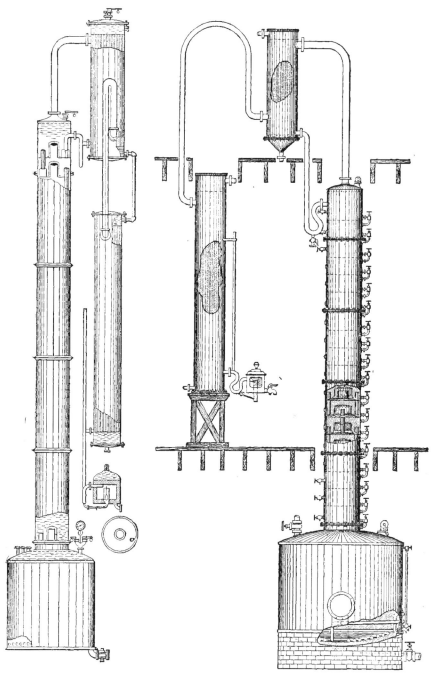

FIG. 162.—Apparatus for Recovering Denatured Alcohol.
Built by Hoffman-Ahlers Co.

FIG. 163.—Apparatus for Recovering Denatured Alcohol. Built by Vulcan Copper
Works.

further treated in the separator adjoining the column.   Here, by means of water circulating through tubes and the vapor surrounding them, a further minute and delicate condensation and separation takes place which completes the concentrating process.   The vapors then pass into a final condenser where they are cooled and from which the finished product is withdrawn.

The loss of alcohol by this recovering process is very slight, the apparatus being so designed that for all practical purposes it can be considered as nothing.   The amount of concentrated alcohol obtained from each running will be proportionate to the strength of the initial charge.

The apparatus is assembled complete and all parts are marked.   The operation of the apparatus is easy and simple, as there are no intricate or sensitive working parts to be looked after or to get out of order.   Users of denatured alcohol whose product can be recovered should investigate thoroughly the recovery of their alcohol.   This still is furnished in the following sizes: Capacity of still, 250, 500, 750, 1000, 1250, 1500, 2000 and 2500 gallons.

Spirit Varnishes.—One of the most important technical uses of alcohol is in the manufacture of varnishes and lacquers.   Among the gums which are so employed shellac may be mentioned as the chief. The use of tax-free denatured alcohol should greatly lower the cost of spirit varnishes.

Fry, in his book on Italian varnishes,* says: "M. Mailand did one great service to M. J. B. Vuillaume and his other followers in that he taught them to use oxygenated turpentine in forming their mixtures."

It may be said that such turpentine is soluble in alcohol, whereas the ordinary or unoxidized spirits of turpentine is not soluble, thus admitting of tempering the ordinary spirit varnish so it will be more flexible.

Sadtler † recommends "using bleached shellac dissolved in alcohol and copal varnish to produce the finest grade of spirit varnish.   In the preparation of this copal varnish the copal must be first fused or rather submitted to dry distillation (by direct heat) until about 15 per cent of its weight in oily distillation products has been distilled off."   It is the same with amber.   The residue is then perfectly soluble in alcohol

---

* The Varnishes of the Italian Violin-makers of the Sixteenth, Seventeenth, and Eighteenth Centuries and their Influence on Tone.   By George Fry, F.L.S., F.C.S.   London, 1904.

† A Handbook of Industrial Organic Chemistry, 1895.   By Samuel P. Sadtler, Ph.D., F.C.S.

It is then allowed to cool, after which this residue is powdered and mixed with sand and covered with 95 per cent alcohol, heated to boiling for some time, with a return condenser, and is then filtered. Sadtler says the addition of elemi resin imparts toughness to the copal varnish. The various resins used are shellac, gum-lac, sandarac, mastic, and dammar. Colored spirit varnishes are made by the addition of alcoholic extracts of dragon's-blood, cochineal, annatto, gamboge, turmeric, and even solutions of the aniline colors.

An ingenious method for fusing amber, copal, etc., is to prepare two brass tubes about $1\frac{1}{2}$ inches in diameter, one 14 inches long, the other 3 inches, united by a screw-coupling nut, the top of this tube being closed with a loose brass cap provided with an air-vent.

This brass tube is held in an iron ring over a gas-lamp, the nut mentioned providing the support for the tube. The tube dips into water. About 3 inches from the bottom of this brass tube a perforated brass plate $\frac{1}{4}$ inch thick sets in between the longer or upper tube and the lower or shorter tube. The water in the dish which receives the fused gum is kept boiling hot by an additional gas-lamp. Heat is now applied to the tube, the gum is put into it, and the latter soon fuses and drops into the hot water, while the more volatile oily portions escape as tarry gases and smoke from the top of the tube.

The fused gum is removed from the hot water as it runs down from the heated tube, after which it is dried and powdered, and when really dry is used in making spirit varnish.

Several methods are in use for the varnishing of violins.

One is to partly color the wood and when dry the surface is prepared and varnished with a partly colored varnish.

The other method is to properly prepare the surface of the wood and varnish with a colored varnish. It is claimed by some that the tone of the instrument is not injured by this latter method. Another theory is that the two-color effect (dichroic) of the Venetian violin varnishes was caused by the property of the varnish itself, for the reason that this valuable color effect was given it by the peculiar preparation the varnish underwent.

Some specially prepared powdered English colors in red, brown, and yellow are used in violin varnishes. The different violin-makers maintain a great degree of secrecy about the ingredients, the proportions, and the colors they use in their varnishes which, as a rule, they prepare themselves, the varnishes made being oil or oil and turpentine varnishes. In the finishing of factory-made violins, made abroad, spirit varnishes are largely used.

The price of shellac has increased very largely during recent years. Any promising substitute for it is therefore of interest.* "Dr. Thomas B. Osborne, New Haven, Conn., took out patents for the extraction of zein some years ago." Mr. Williams further states that "the zein was extracted with 95% grain alcohol from dry gluten meal, the product resulting after the commercial removal of starch from Indian corn, and about 30% approximately of this gluten meal was soluble. An 18% solution of zein and alcohol, with an equal percentage of resin, dissolved, made a very fine transparent varnish, superior to shellac." From this statement it does not appear whether ordinary resin or the better variety —the white winter resin—was used. It would seem that with the tax-free denatured alcohol for use as a solvent and the substitute for shellac above mentioned as though this matter were worthy of experiment. In the testimony given at the Free Alcohol hearings before the Committee of Ways and Means of the House of Representatives, February–March, 1906, it appeared that grain alcohol was markedly superior to wood alcohol for the making of spirit varnishes, lacquers, etc., and in the finishing of wood in the manufacture of furniture, cars, pianos, etc. There is therefore opened up a large field for the use of tax-free denatured alcohol, for manufacturing purposes along these lines in place of the large amounts of wood alcohol previously used.

* Statement furnished by Mr. Henry J. Williams, Boston, Mass.

CHAPTER X.

DENATURED ALCOHOL IN THE UNITED STATES.

The Impracticability of Purifying Denatured Alcohol.   The Possibilities of Industrial Alcohol in the United States.

The Impracticability of Purifying Denatured Alcohol.—The foundation of the idea of an industrial alcohol rests upon the fact that the methods at present adopted to completely denature alcohol are effective. The experience of England and Germany in the administration of their laws relating to the manufacture and uses of denatured alcohol shows that such laws are administered without any considerable degree of fraud, such frauds as have resulted being so inconsiderable as to practically render official action unnecessary.

Some frauds were formerly experienced in France, but have since 1894 been rendered more difficult by the legal addition of a quantity of benzol and aniline (malachite) green to the usual denatured alcohol. At present the use of this green has even been discontinued. It may also be stated that no nation having once enacted legislation permitting denatured alcohol has ever repealed such laws, no matter how great their exigencies in way of revenue may have been. On the contrary the tendency is always to liberalize such legislation and to extend the use of such alcohol in every way possible.

The testimony at the Congressional hearings held at Washington, D. C., February–March, 1906, relative to the repeal of the internal revenue tax on domestic denatured (industrial) alcohol shows that the experience in the future of the United States under the law recently enacted permitting industrial alcohol under these conditions will be the same as that of the other countries mentioned in respect to frauds upon the Government.

The points made at these hearings were that the illicit fermentation and distillation of whiskey, or "moonshining," as it is called, would be more profitable than the attempt to rectify denatured alcohol for drinking purposes; that it would be practically impossible to obtain an efficient rectifying-still for fraudulent use, and that existing laws and regulations,

361

fully as liberal as the proposed bill, are now in force without loss to the United States Government through fraud.

The further fact was brought out that from the letters and petitions, in favor of such legislation for industrial alcohol, received from chemical societies, leading universities, technical schools, agricultural colleges, scientists, and chemists in general, that they all consider alcohol as a chemical and not as a beverage, that is, something to be used industrially. There is no distinction, therefore, in the minds of these people and of these authorities to be drawn between industrial alcohol and other chemicals simply because degenerates and those criminally inclined sometimes drink this alcohol. Letters from such above chemists who had resided in England and Germany proved the impracticability of purifying denatured alcohol.

The author had the honor of representing the American Chemical Society and the Society of Chemical Industry through their New England Sections at these "free-alcohol" hearings already mentioned. On the topic under discussion he gave, as the result of his experiments, testimony to the effect that the denaturing agents in the samples of industrial alcohol which he exhibited could only be removed by distillation and with the most extreme difficulty and consequent great cost, and it is therefore far easier and cheaper to make whiskey illicitly in the first place.

Along the same lines as this discussion at these same hearings, Dr. H. W. Wiley, Chief of the Bureau of Chemistry of the U. S. Department of Agriculture, testified, stating that he appeared by authority of the Secretary of Agriculture and as a member of the Committee on the Use of Alcohol in the Industries Free of Tax, appointed by the American Chemical Society, which embraces a membership of 3000 of the more prominent chemists of this country. Dr. Wiley said: "It is not a question whether a chemist working for days and sometimes for weeks may be able to separate the pure product from the mixture, because that is the function of the chemist. The question, it seems to me, is whether such a separation could be made in such a way as to make it a commercial success in the face of the penitentiary, which would confront the effort on all occasions. I want to say further that I do not believe you can denature alcohol in such a way as to make it so impotable that somebody will not drink it without purification, because there are some men so depraved that they would not hesitate to drink anything that even looked like alcohol. You cannot be certain that some manufacturer will not attempt to evade the law. Let us admit all of these points without question.

"I have prepared a large number of denatured samples of alcohol, starting with pure ethyl alcohol and adding common reagents which you have heard about—methylated spirits, pyridine, etc. I have made up denatured alcohol and then diluted it to proof, that is, 50 per cent by volume of ethyl alcohol. Then I have distilled both of these bodies in a (simple) still such as a moonshiner would use, and then I have distilled that again to show you that the distillate is still absolutely unfit for use. Now if these are impracticable, as we have proved them to be, I do not think this committee need fear that anybody is going to the trouble and expense and run the risk incident to accomplishing this purpose. I think these samples will demonstrate to you the impossibility and impracticability of attempting to rectify denatured alcohol. I think the cost of restoring denatured alcohol to pure alcohol would be greater than to manufacture and pay the tax on a fresh portion of properly made alcohol."

Other and equally as strong arguments were presented at the above-mentioned hearings as to existing laws and regulations, fully as liberal as the legislation proposed, which are enforced without loss to this Government, through fraud, as follows:

"Under section 3282 of the Revised Statutes, acts of March 1, 1879, and June 14, 1879, the manufacturers of vinegar are allowed to distill alcohol from grain free of tax, and to convert such alcohol into vinegar under a nominal supervision by internal-revenue officials. . . .

"Alcohol is granted free of tax to producers of sweet wines under sections 42 to 49, inclusive, of the tariff act of October 1, 1890, as amended by the tariff act of August 28, 1894. . . . Under this law 3,430,829 proof gallons of alcohol in the form of grape brandy were used free of tax in fortifying (bringing up the alcoholic strength) of sweet wines during the fiscal year ending June 30, 1905 (see page 5 of the last annual report of the Commissioner of Internal Revenue)." The total quantity of alcohol delivered free of tax to the sweet-wine producers was shown "to be about *seven* times the estimated quantity (presented) of taxed grain alcohol now used in the industries of the United States." Also that "careful inquiry shows that not once since the enactment of this law has the Commissioner of Internal Revenue reported to Congress that the revenue from distilled spirits is endangered by the illicit recovery of such alcohol and its sale in competition with taxed whiskey." *

It was further explained that "sweet wine of domestic production

---

* A charge of three cents a gallon is now laid upon each taxable gallon of brandy used in the fortification of wines. See Annual Report of the Commissioner of Internal Revenue, 1906.

may be freely purchased in large quantities at a comparatively low price per gallon and the alcohol recovered therefrom by a simple process of distillation." Quoting further, we find from testimony at these hearings that "the fact that the law is not violated to an extent demanding official action is probably the best proof which can be obtained that untaxed domestic denatured alcohol requiring a complicated process of fractional distillation to render it potable (drinkable) would not endanger the present revenue derived from distilled spirits." Another point brought out was: "It is quite important to note that the materials from which whiskey may be illicitly distilled are always at hand in every household in the country, while denatured, industrial alcohol would have to be purchased in considerable quantities and removed to the place where the illicit recovery of the alcohol is intended to be carried on." From the mass of testimony presented at the hearings mentioned on this phase of the subject under discussion, as well as from that quoted immediately above, we can anticipate that if pure alcohol in the form of brandy can be administered by this Government free of tax without appreciable frauds being committed, then the same experience should be realized in the administration of the law recently enacted and approved, which permits tax-free domestic *denatured* alcohol for industrial uses. We can also believe that our experience in this respect will parallel that of England, Germany, France, and the other nations here mentioned and be equally satisfactory.

The Possibilities of Industrial Alcohol in the United States.—In discussing this phase of the subject there are three vital features to be considered which may be stated as follows:

1. The selling price of denatured alcohol.

2. The variety of its uses.

3. To what extent improvements can be made to increase the efficiency of alcohol motors, engines, lamps, etc., in order thus to contribute largely to the use of such alcohol.

1. *The Selling Price of Denatured Alcohol.*—The probable cost of making commercial alcohol of 95 per cent strength from either corn or molasses at the distillery we have shown to be about 15 cents a gallon for the materials alone. To this cost must be added the manufacturing cost, the cost of the package or barrel, the freight charges, and the cost of denaturing, which added charges would probably bring such cost to about 30 cents a gallon. To this cost must be added the cost of distribution and the profits, so that it would appear that completely denatured alcohol would retail for about 40 cents a gallon. Corn and cane-molasses are the only two raw materials at the present time worthy of

serious consideration as a source of industrial alcohol. These two products are the most economical from which to make alcohol in the United States, as past experience has shown; they can be readily obtained in ample quantities for such purposes. There is no risk, therefore, of any shortage in their supply or of irregularity in deliveries. The corn crop of the United States for 1905 was shown to have been 2,707,993,540 bushels. A bushel of corn will make on an average about 2.63 gallons of 95 per cent alcohol. To supply a demand of 10,000,000 gallons per year of alcohol about 3,802,281 bushels of corn are required. When we consider the amount of such commercial alcohol which can be made from even one per cent of this enormous corn crop, the number of gallons being approximately 70,000,000, some idea is had of the practically limitless supply of alcohol which this raw material can furnish. With regard to molasses as a raw material for alcohol, it is probable that some 50,000,000 gallons of the low grade which can be used for this purpose are yearly available for this country. From figures previously given this amount would furnish approximately 22,000,000 gallons of such alcohol. In the West corn will be largely used to make alcohol. This is because of its abundance and for the reason that it is the cheapest raw material in that part of the country for such purpose. For a similar reason molasses will be used in the cities of the Atlantic seaboard for making alcohol. The question of how largely the corn alcohol and the molasses alcohol can compete against each other throughout the country is a difficult one to answer. Several factors enter into such a problem, among which are the value of the residue from distilling corn as a cattle food; how much damaged or "heated" corn can be obtained at a lower price which will still answer for making alcohol, and the question of freight charges and transportation. The residue from the distillation of the molasses used for alcohol has been investigated to some extent abroad. In this country inquiry seems to develop the fact that so far it has but little, if any, real value. The question of transportation charges applies equally to molasses alcohol in this matter of competition. Whether molasses alcohol will be made in the Hawaiian Islands, denatured, and shipped to San Francisco to compete with the corn alcohol of the West is a question of the future.

In connection with the manufacture of alcohol from cane-molasses, just mentioned, it will prove of interest to know that ten of the beet-sugar factories of Michigan sent their molasses to a distillery in that State, and, as appeared in the Philippine hearings before the Committee of Ways and Means, produced therefrom about a million gallons of proof alcohol. This statement is taken from "Report No. 2888, Fifty-ninth Congress,

First Session, Tax-free Denatured Alcohol, April 4, 1906, submitted by Mr. Payne from the Committee on Ways and Means " [to accompany H. R. 17453].

At the present time it would seem that the selling price of denatured alcohol would not be dependent upon any scarcity of the supply of the raw materials for its manufacture. It has been pointed out that the largest possible yields of alcohol can be aimed at when making it for denatured alcohol. This fact, together with possible future improvements in the methods of manufacture to help lower the cost, will help to offset any rise in the price of raw materials, but to how complete an extent is problematical. Efforts are being made and will continue to be made to find a cheaper and as effective a denaturant as the wood alcohol. Attention in this respect is called to the yearly report of the Society for the Manufacture of Alcohol in Germany for 1906. This report also contains many other facts of interest concerning the manufacture of alcohol in Germany.

Molasses has already advanced to about 7 cents per gallon and we may therefore look for some increase in the price of corn. Any increase in price of molasses over 7 cents per gallon may be said to increasingly interfere with its ability to furnish alcohol at a cost to compete with corn at 40 cents per bushel, as shown by the calculation given.

The sugar-planters will endeavor in the future as in the past to increase their yields of sugar. This will tend to decrease the amounts of molasses made, as molasses is merely a by-product in the making of sugar. The increasing use of molasses as an ingredient in cattle feed is assuming a considerable degree of importance, and large amounts of it are so used. These two facts will both tend to decrease the supply of molasses available for alcohol in the future, but to what extent cannot, of course, be stated.

A higher price for molasses will stimulate importations of it to this country and make it profitable for planters to transport it from the interior sugar plantations to the coast for shipment. This may offset to some extent he prospect of a decreasing supply from the causes mentioned above.

As to low-priced and damaged corn it may be taken for granted that the farmer, whose present prosperity in this country is a matter of satisfaction to all, will on this account in the future be able to hold and to properly cure his corn to a much greater degree than in the past. He will be just as anxious to obtain a higher price by so doing as we should under similar circumstances. The future supply of such low-grade corn may therefore be diminished. The selling of denatured alcohol at nearly cost will enable the distiller to run his plant practically all the time, and the fixed charges of his plant will be partly, perhaps largely, borne by such alcohol. His profits he can therefore make in large measure from the tax-paid spirits or alcohol which he makes. He thus has a strong incentive to so sell all the denatured alcohol possible. From what has been stated it will be apparent that, under the present Government restrictions in this country as well as from the other reasons given, the farmer will be unable to practically engage in the distilling of alcohol.*

He can, however, sell or barter his farm products which are suitable for the economical production of alcohol to the distiller and have his margin of farm profits, based on his unit of cost for the raising of such products, to enable him to buy such alcohol in a way more cheaply than by a strictly cash transaction. In the West the farmer will be within reasonable transportation distance of the distillers, and if our Government should later on permit the transportation of denatured alcohol in tank-cars it would lessen the freight charges and reduce the cost of such alcohol to him as well as to users in other parts of our country. The further granting, later on, by our Government of permission to the distillers to convey the alcohol from the distillery to their denaturing-house by a properly secured, locked, and sealed pipe under strict Government supervision, will help materially to lessen the cost of denaturing, as it will avoid all costs for packages, teaming, labor, and the extra supervision and attendance on the part of the distiller. For this and other reasons the cost for denaturing alcohol in this country is difficult to determine. It can be said that considerable quantities of wood alcohol will be available January 1, 1907, when the new law permitting denatured alcohol goes into effect. Competition may therefore force down the selling price of this approved methyl alcohol prescribed by this Government. Probably still further improved methods of manufacture will be sought in making wood alcohol in order to lessen its cost and by so doing the cost of the denaturing of alcohol. If we take the cost of the approved methyl alcohol as that of the alcohol which it is to denature, we have the ideal condition, as there is then no increased cost due to denaturing the alcohol. It is probably too much to expect that such conditions will obtain, but it is hoped that such may be the case. Another factor in determining the selling price of denatured alcohol for the general purposes of light, heat, and power is that of the proper standardization of it for illuminating, heating, and power purposes.

It will be noted that the Government regulations merely state the

---

* Since this was written supplementary legislation has been enacted in this country which will probably result in the removal of the hindrances and restrictions mentioned. This legislation is given on p. 489.

lowest strength of denatured alcohol permitted, viz., 180° proof, or 90 per cent by volume. For the purposes of distribution and the convenience of the user it is important to have as few strengths or grades come into use as is possible. It is, however, of equal, if not of more, importance for the user and the public to know that they are receiving the grade which standardization has determined as the best for their particular use.

* Let us also consider the selling price of denatured alcohol in Germany, which may afford some comparison of what the maximum price in this country should be. Denatured alcohol sells at a much lower cost in Germany than in any of the other countries which permit its use.

It is for this reason, as well as because of the special efforts constantly put forth by Germany to develop and increase to the utmost every possible industrial use of alcohol, that that nation enjoys a position so far in the lead with respect to this subject. It may be said that it costs a little over 2 cents a gallon to completely denature alcohol in Germany. Alcohol of 90 and 95 per cent strength by volume is used in making denatured alcohol.

The selling price at retail for denatured alcohol is, for 95 per cent strength by volume, 33 pfennigs per liter, or 29.69 cents per gallon; 90 per cent strength by volume, 30 pfennigs per liter, or 27 cents per gallon. At wholesale the prices range from 28 to 29 pfennigs per liter, or from 25.2 to 26.1 cents per gallon. These figures were also given in Chapter IX, but are repeated here on account of their great importance. The distribution of spirit is practically controlled in Germany by a society known as the "Centrale für Spiritus Verwerthung," with its head offices in Berlin. At the end of the campaign the society adjusts with the distillers the losses or profits, based on the fixed price, resulting from the operations of the society in disposing of the spirit. In 1906 this price was 42 marks ($10.50) per hectolitre (26.41 gallons), or 40 cents a gallon, as against 56 marks ($14) per hectolitre (26.41 gallons), or 53 cents a gallon last year.

As a bonus on denatured alcohol, on the alcohol exported, and the alcohol used in the manufacture of exported goods, a portion of the mash-tub tax and the distillation tax is rebated. This rebate during the last campaign year in Germany amounted to $6,140,657, so that the cost of alcohol for drinking purposes was increased a little over $6,000,000 for the benefit of the industrial use of the spirit.

2. *The Variety of its Uses.*—In considering the variety of the uses for completely denatured alcohol, or industrial alcohol, in this country, we can first take the demand for wood alcohol for manufacturing pur-

* From Report U. S. Consul.

poses, which figure was shown to be about 8,000,000 gallons for the year 1905, from the testimony given at the "Free Alcohol" Congressional hearings held at Washington, D. C., February–March, 1906. This amount can be replaced by completely denatured alcohol. In addition, if the price of the latter practically cuts that of the former in two, there should be a largely increased demand for it over even the above figures. Depending upon the selling price, it would appear from the above facts, as well as from the natural increase in manufacturing, that a demand for some 12,000,000 gallons during the first year of the new law would be a fair estimate for manufacturing uses throughout this country. When we consider the further possible uses, such as lighting, heating, cleaning, and cooking these figures will easily reach 16,000,000 gallons if the selling price be sufficiently low. As alcohol burns twice as long as kerosene, giving the same amount of light, it can easily compete with kerosene at 15 cents a gallon for portable household illumination, and by some will be used in preference to kerosene even at a greater disparity in cost.

Under certain conditions, as where gas or electricity is not available, the alcohol street lights we have shown should be largely used. They are storm and rain proof. The testimony at the hearings referred to above showed also, according to German shop tests, that in round numbers alcohol compares equally well with gasoline as regards consumption for fuel purposes in internal-combustion engines and motors, in spite of the fact that gasoline possesses about 1.6 times the heating value of alcohol. This was because of the much increased compression that could be used with safety in such tests in the case of alcohol. The much greater safety of alcohol over gasoline is another potent factor in favor of the former, as well as the fact that it will mix with water, and a fire once started may be readily extinguished, while with gasoline such is not the case, as the addition of water for such a purpose merely spreads the fire. What this means on power-boats and fishing-craft only those who have had such an experience can understand. Already the price of gasoline has dropped in the East from about 23 cents per gallon for 76° (July 1, 1906, soon after the denatured alcohol act was approved and became a law) to about 17 cents per gallon for 70° at the present time, and no more 76° gasoline is now said to be obtainable.

It is thus seen that, whether industrial alcohol wholly substitutes gasoline for lighting and small power purposes or not, it will prevent future increases of price in this fuel. It will thus protect and benefit the owners of automobiles and power-boats who still prefer to use gasoline, because by replacing gasoline for agricultural power purposes alcohol can liberate large amounts of gasoline for automobile and power-boat use.

With regard to the competition of denatured alcohol with kerosene or crude petroleum or fuel oil for power purposes it cannot hope to compete with these fuels, on account of their low cost. In addition any disparity in price is made even more emphatic, because the consumption of the fuel increases, of course, with the size of the engine. As has been shown in the case of the automobile, the possibilities of the consumption of industrial alcohol for fuel for other types of internal-combustion engines, such as stationary and portable for agricultural and individual power purposes, are very great. Such use could easily be put at a very large figure under proper conditions, and could easily equal, if not exceed, that for all these other uses combined.

Turning now to the possibilities of specially denatured alcohol in this country, it may be stated that as large uses are found for such alcohol abroad they should also be possible here with us.

Some of the important manufacturing purposes for which completely denatured alcohol cannot be used are in the making of sulphuric ether, chloroform, acetic ether, smokeless powder, fulminates, photographic films, dry plates and papers, and aniline colors and dyes made from coal-tar. In making sulphuric ether in France undenatured alcohol is partially or specially denatured with residue from making ether and with oil of vitriol (sulphuric acid). The large use of ether as an anæsthetic in surgery and technically as a solvent for fats is well known. In France undenatured alcohol specially denatured with chloride of lime is permitted for making chloroform. The importance of the uses of chloroform in this country as an anæsthetic and for technical purposes is well known. In the United States the Government has undenatured alcohol, tax free, for the making of smokeless powder. Such alcohol can be specially denatured for this purpose with an equal volume of ether, and 6 grams of guncotton for each liter of alcohol added, under government supervision and restrictions. On account of the use of ether in smokeless powder, and because such ether is first made from alcohol, the importance of permitting specially denatured alcohol in this country for these purposes can be readily understood.

It has been calculated that tax-free alcohol would cut the price of smokeless powder more than one half. The manufacture of fulminates would be of importance to this country, and the testimony at the hearings mentioned showed that the industry had been obliged to leave the country because tax-free alcohol was not obtainable. In Germany tax-free alcohol is permitted for making smokeless powders, fuses, and fulminates, as well as for making the varnishes used in finishing these substances. Permission has to be obtained and the same regulations as are applicable to the buying, storage, and use of "wood naphtha denatured " spirit (see Appendix, this book), and the keeping of "control books " and other accounts are enforced.   In this connection it may be stated that tank-cars are also permitted abroad for the transportation of pure or undenatured alcohol, greatly reducing the charge for freight and handling.   Special denaturing agents are permitted in Germany only at the factory where the alcohol is to be used for the manufacture of photographic paper, dry films, and emulsions therefor, of chloride, bromide iodide of silver and gelatine, and similar preparations.   Permission must also be obtained from the chief office of the province to use such specially denatured alcohol.

For the manufacture of aniline colors and dyes (coal-tar colors) Germany also permits, tax free, specially denatured alcohol.   Some of the substances used in obtaining such colors and also intermediate products are used to denature such alcohol.   About ten per cent of the total dyes made by Germany require the use of alcohol in their manufacture, while the research work necessitated by their coal-tar color industries also calls for the use of considerable pure alcohol.   It is interesting to note that carboys of absolute alcohol are now shipped to the United States for the use of scientific and technological schools from Germany. These facts show not only the business enterprise of the Germans, but their increasing technical efforts, and their great supremacy in all matters pertaining to the chemical and allied industries.   Although this is not wholly due to tax-free alcohol for the past twenty years, still we may safely assume it to have been one of the great contributing causes for such success.   In the United States it would appear that tax-free alcohol should also be permitted under Government regulations for all these purposes, and is necessary to put our country on at least an equal basis with Germany in these respects.   Concerning the use of incompletely or partially denatured alcohol in Germany during 1904–5, we quote from the report of U. S. Consul-General Alexander M. Thackara, Berlin, Germany, September 10, 1906, as follows:

USE OF INCOMPLETELY DENATURED ALCOHOL IN GERMANY DURING 1904–5.

For soap-making..	5,250 gallons
" making lanolin......................................	25,780 "
" photographic paper, dry plates, emulsions, etc............	14,160 "
" manufacture of celluloid...............................	684,000 "
" " " varnishes and polishes...................	1,270,000 "
" " " chemical preparations and other purposes...	1,520,000 "
" " " sulphuric or common ether...............	2,131,000 "
" " " chloroform.............................	7,053 "
" " " iodoform..............................	10,567 "
" surgical dressings....................................	11,800 "
	5,679,610 gallons

With regard to the total quantity of alcohol used in the industries
in Germany during the past campaign year, 1904-5, the highest ever
known, these amounts are as follows:

Completely denatured alcohol. . . . . 26,000,000 gallons
Alcohol for the manufacture of vinegar. 4,000,000   "
Incompletely or partially denatured alcohol. 7,000,000   "

      Total quantity used. . . . . 37,000,000 gallons

In 1887–8 there were used only some 10,250,000 gallons for industrial purposes. The completely denatured alcohol used for power, light,
and heat in 1904-5 was 26,000,000 gallons, while in 1887–8 only some
3,600,000 gallons were so used, showing the consumption of alcohol for
power, light, and heat has increased over seven times in the past seventeen years.

In France in 1903 (latest available statistics) the following amounts
of pure alcohol were used for similar purposes, viz.:

Ether and explosives. . . . . 1,405,338 gallons
Drugs and chemical preparations.   613,162   "
                                       ‾‾‾‾‾‾‾‾‾‾‾‾‾
                                    2,018,500 gallons

The above figures show that a substantial amount of pure alcohol under
the conditions mentioned was used in these two countries in the year
1903. Imitation silk as made abroad also calls for the use of a large
quantity of alcohol for solvent purposes.

In the United States there was withdrawn, free of tax, during the
fiscal year ending June 30, 1905, an aggregate of 2,112,830 taxable
gallons of alcohol merely for scientific purposes and for the use of the
United States Government.

From the report of U. S. Consul-General A. M. Thackara, already
quoted, we find the latest complete statistics regarding the alcohol situation in France to be as follows:

The last year for which complete statistics are available, covering
the manufacture, denaturation, importation, and various uses of alcohol
in France, presents the interesting record tabulated on page 373, giving
materials from which alcohol was manufactured.

Tax was paid on the quantity used for beverages and other purposes.

The present wholesale price of grain alcohol, in France, ranges from 50
to 55 francs ($9.65 to $10.61) per hectolitre of 26.42 gallons, according to
quality. This would be equivalent to 36 to 40 cents per gallon. Methyl
or wood alcohol is imported into France mainly from Great Britain and

Materials.	Hectolitres.
Grain and potatoes.	352,928
Molasses.	670,969
Beets.	926,159
Wine.	26,810
Apples and pears.	2,274
Lees of wine.	54,903
All other material.	104,997
Imported, mainly from Germany and Holland.	92,000
Total supply.	2,139,040
Equal to (gallons).	56,513,436

METHODS OF CONSUMPTION.

The methods of consumption are shown in the following table:

	Hectolitres.
Drinking and other purposes.	1,308,903
Denatured.	374,598
Converted to vinegar.	87,285
Consumed free at distilleries.	98,070
Leakage.	4,704
Losses through accident.	4,503
Exported.	284,207
Total.	2,162,270
Equal to (gallons)	57,127,173

Germany. Its present wholesale price in Paris is about 77 francs ($14.86) per hectolitre, or approximately 56 cents per gallon.

From the above statistics it is seen that 374,598 hectolitres, or about 9,893,133 gallons, of denatured alcohol were used in that year. There was also used 87,285 hectolitres of alcohol, or about 2,305,196 gallons, which was converted into vinegar.

From what has preceded it appears that there is considerable opportunity in the United States for the technical use of pure alcohol, *to be specially denatured under Government control and regulations, and that in no case does any one of these manufactured products mentioned, on page 370, contain any alcohol in the finished article.*

At present the law does not provide for the use, free of tax, of alcohol which is wholly undenatured, when used for domestic purposes, except as stated. It can also be stated that exportation of methylated spirits (denatured alcohol) is permitted under the new excise regulations in the United Kingdom by the British Government, quoted in Chapter IX. It would therefore seem as though our Government could, under proper restrictions, permit alcohol either completely denatured by the U. S. regulations or denatured according to foreign formulæ acceptable to our Government, under the new law, to be exported.

3. *To what extent improvements can be made to increase the efficiency of alcohol motors, engines, lamps, cooking-stoves, etc., in order thus to contribute largely to the uses of such alcohol.*—In Chapter VIII the possibilities of the uses of alcohol for the automobile motor have already been indicated and the probable line upon which its development will proceed. Broadly stated, it may be said that a great amount of experimenting remains to be done in this country with regard to the development and perfecting of all the above alcohol-using apparatus in order to adapt it to our conditions. We are in a pioneer state with regard to this whole problem. Many of our manufacturers of such apparatus are therefore at work at the present time investigating these problems, and any close judgment as to the possibilities of industrial alcohol is thus seen to be impracticable. The best we can do is to consider, as we have done, the experience of foreign countries in this respect and the amounts of industrial alcohol used by them for these various purposes, and base our estimates upon such data.

The employment of alcohol for stationary and marine engines has also been shown in Chapter VIII and quite fully described and summarized. Improvements can and will be made in alcohol engines and motors by manufacturers in this country. The rate of progress in this respect will depend directly upon the demand for such engines, and this demand in turn rests largely upon the price of the denatured alcohol. The same can be said of alcohol lamps and cooking- and heating-stoves. Like the profitable manufacture of the alcohol itself, the profitable manufacture of apparatus to use it successfully depends upon the tenets of, and hard-headed adherence to, strict business principles and economics.

That American genius will fully meet all the demands along these lines from our fellow-countrymen and successfully solve the problem of industrial alcohol is the hope and belief of the author.

APPENDIX.

UNITED STATES REGULATIONS AND INSTRUCTIONS CONCERNING THE DENATURATION OF ALCOHOL AND THE HANDLING AND USE OF SAME UNDER THE ACT OF CONGRESS OF JUNE 7, 1906.

REGULATIONS No. 30, U. S. INTERNAL REVENUE.

SEC. 1. The following regulations are issued pursuant to an act of the Congress providing for the withdrawal from bond, tax free, of domestic alcohol to be rendered unfit for beverage or liquid medicinal uses by the admixture of denaturing materials.

The act in question is as follows:

"*Be it enacted by the Senate and House of Representatives of the United States of America in Congress assembled,* That from and after January first, nineteen hundred and seven, domestic alcohol of such degree of proof as may be prescribed by the Commissioner of Internal Revenue and approved by the Secretary of the Treasury, may be withdrawn from bond without the payment of internal-revenue tax, for use in the arts and industries, and for fuel, light, and power, provided said alcohol shall have been mixed in the presence and under the direction of an authorized Government officer, after withdrawal from the distillery warehouse, with methyl alcohol or other denaturing material or materials, or admixture of the same, suitable to the use for which the alcohol is withdrawn, but which destroys its character as a beverage and renders it unfit for liquid medicinal purposes; such denaturing to be done upon the application of any registered distillery in denaturing bonded warehouses specially designated or set apart for denaturing purposes only, and under conditions prescribed by the Commissioner of Internal Revenue with the approval of the Secretary of the Treasury.

" The character and quantity of the said denaturing material and the conditions upon which said alcohol may be withdrawn free of tax shall be prescribed by the Commissioner of Internal Revenue, who shall, with the approval of the Secretary of the Treasury, make all necessary regulations for carrying into effect the provisions of this Act.

" Distillers, manufacturers, dealers, and all other persons furnishing, handling, or using alcohol withdrawn from bond under the provisions of this Act shall keep such books and records, execute such bonds, and render such returns as the Commissioner of Internal Revenue, with the approval of the Secretary of the Treasury, may by regulation require. Such books and records shall be open at all times to the inspection of any internal-revenue officer or agent.

" SEC. 2. That any person who withdraws alcohol free of tax under the provisions of this Act and regulations made in pursuance thereof, and who removes or conceals same, or is concerned in removing, depositing, or concealing same

375

for the purpose of preventing the same from being denatured under governmental supervision, and any person who uses alcohol withdrawn from bond under the provisions of section one of this Act for manufacturing any beverage or liquid medicinal preparation, or knowingly sells any beverage or liquid medicinal preparation made in whole or in part from such alcohol, or knowingly violates any of the provisions of this Act, or who shall recover or attempt to recover by redistillation or by any other process or means, any alcohol rendered unfit for beverage or liquid medicinal purposes under the provisions of this Act, or who knowingly uses, sells, conceals, or otherwise disposes of alcohol so recovered or redistilled, shall on conviction of each offense be fined not more than five thousand dollars, or be imprisoned not more than five years, or both, and shall, in addition, forfeit to the United States all personal property used in connection with his business, together with the buildings and lots or parcels of ground constituting the premises on which said unlawful acts are performed or permitted to be performed: *Provided*, That manufacturers employing processes in which alcohol, used free of tax under the provisions of this act, is expressed or evaporated from the articles manufactured, shall be permitted to recover such alcohol and to have such alcohol restored to a condition suitable solely for reuse in manufacturing processes under such regulations as the Commissioner of Internal Revenue, with the approval of the Secretary of the Treasury, shall prescribe.

" Sec. 3. That for the employment of such additional force of chemists, internal revenue agents, inspectors, deputy collectors, clerks, laborers, and other assistants as the Commissioner of Internal Revenue, with the approval of the Secretary of the Treasury, may deem proper and necessary to the prompt and efficient operation and enforcement of this law, and for the purchase of locks, seals, weighing-beams, gauging instruments, and for all necessary expenses incident to the proper execution of this law, the sum of two hundred and fifty thousand dollars, or so much thereof as may be required, is hereby appropriated out of any money in the Treasury not otherwise appropriated said appropriation to be immediately available.

" For a period of two years from and after the passage of this act the force authorized by this section of this act shall be appointed by the Commissioner of Internal Revenue, with the approval of the Secretary of the Treasury, and without compliance with the conditions prescribed by the act entitled "An act to regulate and improve the civil service," approved January sixteenth, eighteen hundred and eighty-three, and amendments thereof, and with such compensation as the Commissioner of Internal Revenue may fix, with the approval of the Secretary of the Treasury.

" Sec. 4. That the Secretary of the Treasury shall make full report to Congress at its next session of all appointments made under the provisions of this act, and the compensation paid thereunder, and of all regulations prescribed under the provisions hereof, and shall further report what, if any, additional legislation is necessary, in his opinion, to fully safeguard the revenue and to secure a proper enforcement of this act."

Approved, June 7, 1906.

Part I.*

DENATURING BONDED WAREHOUSES.

Sec. 2. The proprietor of any registered distillery may withdraw from his distillery warehouse, free of tax, alcohol of not less than 180 degrees proof or strength, to be denatured in the manner hereinafter prescribed.

A distiller desiring to withdraw alcohol from bond for denaturing purposes under the provisions of this act shall, at his own expense, provide a denaturing bonded warehouse, to be situated on and constituting a part of the distillery premises. It shall be separated from the distillery and the distillery bonded warehouse and all other buildings, and no windows or doors or other openings shall be permitted

---

* Persons desiring information as to distilleries will be supplied on request with the proper regulations.

in the walls of the denaturing bonded warehouse leading into the distillery, the distillery bonded warehouse or other room or building, except as hereinafter provided. It must be constructed in the same manner as distillery bonded warehouses are now constructed, with a view to the safe and secure storage of the alcohol removed thereto for denaturing purposes and the denaturing agents to be stored therein. It must be approved by the Commissioner of Internal Revenue. It shall be provided with closed mixing tanks of sufficient capacity. The capacity in wine gallons of each tank must be ascertained and marked thereon in legible letters, and each tank must be supplied with a graduated glass guage whereon the contents will be at all times correctly indicated. All openings must be so arranged that they can be securely locked. Suitable office accommodation for the officer on duty must be provided.

SEC. 3. The denaturing bonded warehouse shall be used for denaturing alcohol, and for no other purpose, and nothing shall be stored or kept therein except the alcohol to be denatured, the materials used as denaturents, the denatured product, and the weighing and gauging instruments and other appliances necessary in the work of denaturing, measuring, and gauging the alcohol and denaturing materials.

These bonded warehouses must be numbered serially in each collection district, and the words "Denaturing bonded warehouse No. ——, district of ——," must be in plain letters in a conspicuous place on the outside of the building.

In case the distiller's bond has been executed before the erection of such warehouse the consent of the sureties to the establishment of the denaturing warehouse must be secured and entry duly signed made on the bond.

DENATURING MATERIAL ROOM.

SEC. 4. There shall be provided within the denaturing bonded warehouse a room to be designated as the denaturing material room. This room is to be used alone for the storage of denaturing materials prior to the denaturing process. It must be perfectly secure, and must be so constructed as to render it impossible for any one to enter during the absence of the officer in charge without the same being detected.

The ceiling, inside walls, and floor of said room must be constructed of brick, stone, or tongue-and-groove planks. If there are windows in the room the same must be secured by gratings or iron bars, and to each window must be affixed solid shutters of wood or iron, constructed in such manner that they may be securely barred and fastened on the inside. The door must be substantial, and must be so constructed that it can be securely locked and fastened.

SEC. 5. At least two sets of tanks or receptacles for storing denaturing material must be provided, and each set of tanks must be of sufficient capacity in the aggregate to hold the denaturing material which it is estimated the distiller will use for thirty days. A set of tanks shall consist of one or more tanks for storing methyl alcohol, and one or more tanks of smaller capacity for storing other denaturing materials. The capacity of each tank must be ascertained and marked in legible figures on the outside.

The tanks must not be connected with each other, and must be so constructed as to leave at least 18 inches of open space between the top of the tank and ceiling, the bottom of the tank and the floor, and the sides of the tank and walls of the denaturing material room. Each tank shall be given a number, and this number must be marked upon it. There shall be no opening at the top except such as may be necessary for dumping the denaturing material into the tank and thoroughly plunging or mixing the same. Said opening must be covered so that it may be locked. Likewise the faucet through which the denaturing material is drawn must be so arranged that it can be locked. Each tank must be supplied with a graduated glass gauge whereby the contents of the tank will always be shown.

CUSTODY OF DENATURING BONDED WAREHOUSE.

SEC. 6. The denaturing bonded warehouse shall be under the control of the collector of the district and shall be in the joint custody of a storekeeper, storekeeper-gauger, or other designated official and the distiller.

No one shall be permitted to enter the warehouse except in the presence of said officer, and the warehouse and room shall be kept closed and the doors, exterior and interior, securely locked except when some work incidental to the process of denaturing or storing material is being carried on. Standard Sleight locks shall be used for locking the denaturing bonded warehouse and the denaturing material room, and they shall be sealed in the same manner and with the same kind of seals as distillery bonded warehouses and cistern rooms are now sealed. Miller locks shall be used in securing the faucets and openings of the mixing tanks and the denaturing material tanks.

The officer in charge of the denaturing bonded warehouse, material room, and tanks shall carry the keys to same, and under no circumstances are said keys to be intrusted to any one except another officer who is duly authorized to receive them.

Application for Approval of Denaturing Bonded Warehouse.

Sec. 7. Whenever a distiller wishes to commence the business of denaturing alcohol he must make written application to the collector of the district in which the distillery is located for the approval of a denaturing bonded warehouse.

Such application must give the name or names of the person, firm, or corporation operating the distillery, the number of the distillery, the location of the same, the material of which the warehouse is constructed, the size of same, width, length, and height, the size of the denaturing material room therein, and the manner of its construction, the capacity in gallons of each tank to be used for denaturing alcohol or for holding the denaturing agents, and the material of which said tanks are constructed.

Such application must be accompanied by a diagram correctly representing the warehouse, the mixing tanks, denaturing material room, and denaturing material tanks, with all openings and surroundings. It must show the distillery and all the distillery bonded warehouses on the premises, with dimensions of each.

The application may be in the following form:

To collector of ——— district of ———.

Sir: The undersigned ——— ——— doing business under the name or style of ——— hereby makes application for the approval of a denaturing bonded warehouse which he has provided as required by law, situated upon and constituting a part of the premises known as Distillery No. ——— at ———, in the county of ———, and State of ———.

Said denaturing warehouse is constructed of

———————————————————————————————————

———————————————————————————————————

———————————————————————————————————

(Here describe accurately the denaturing warehouse, giving the height, width, and depth; the mixing tank or tanks and the capacity of each in gallons; also the size in height, width, and depth of the denaturing material room; the denaturing material tanks, and the capacity in gallons of each; also the openings of the denaturing warehouse and denaturing material room.)

——— ———,
Distiller.

Examining Officer to Inspect Warehouse.

Sec. 8. Upon receipt of the application and accompanying diagram the collector shall detail one of his deputies or some other officer who shall visit the distillery and make a careful examination of the proposed denaturing bonded warehouse.

Such officer shall ascertain whether or not said warehouse and mixing tanks and denaturing material room and tanks are constructed in conformity with the regulations, the statements made in the application, and the representations on the diagram.

Sec. 9. If the deputy collector finds that the statements in the application are true and that the denaturing warehouse and material room are constructed in conformity with the law and regulations, he shall make report and recommendation in the following form:

I hereby certify that I have visited the distillery premises described in the foregoing application for the approval of a warehouse in which to denature alcohol by ——— proprietor of distil ery No. —— in the district of ——— and have carefully examined the proposed warehouse and mixing tanks, and the denaturing material room and tanks; that I have measured said warehouse, room, and tanks; that I have examined said distillery premises, and the distillery and distillery bonded warehouses located thereon, and have found the statements and representations made in the application and diagram hereto attached to be in every respect true and correct.

I find that said proposed denaturing warehouse, mixing tanks, denaturing material room, and denaturing material tanks, and everything connected with the same are constructed in strict conformity with all requirements of the law and regulations.

I recommend that said denaturing warehouse be approved.

——— ———,
Deputy Collector ——— *District of* ——— —.
This report shall be affixed to the application.

APPROVAL OF WAREHOUSE.

Sec. 10. The collector shall examine the deputy's report and if, after such examination, he is satisfied that the warehouse and all its parts are constructed in conformity with the law and regulations, he shall indorse his approval on the application and shall transmit the original, together with the diagram, to this office.

If the Commissioner of Internal Revenue is satisfied, after examining the application and reports, that the denaturing warehouse is situated and constructed in compliance with the law and regulations, he shall approve same and notify the collector of said approval.

DENATURING WAREHOUSE BOND TO BE GIVEN.

Sec. 11. After receipt of notice of the approval of said warehouse the distiller may withdraw from his distillery warehouse, free of tax, alcohol of not less than 180 degrees proof or strength, and may denature same in said denaturing warehouse in the manner hereinafter indicated, provided he shall first execute a bond in the form prescribed by the Commissioner of Internal Revenue, with at least two sureties, unless, under the authority contained in an act approved August 13, 1894, a corporation, duly authorized by the Attorney-General of the United States to become a surety on such bond, shall be offered as a sole surety thereon. The bond shall be for a penal sum of not less than double the tax on the alcohol it is estimated the distiller will denature during a period of thirty days, and in no case is the distiller to withdraw from bond for denaturing purposes and have in his denaturing warehouse in process of denaturation a quantity of alcohol the tax upon which is in excess of the penal sum of the bond.

Sec. 12. If, at any time, it should develop that the denaturing warehouse bond is insufficient the distiller must give additional bond.

Sec. 13. The bond herein provided for must be executed before the distiller can withdraw from distillery bonded warehouse, free of tax, alcohol to be denatured, and if he desires to continue in the business of denaturing alcohol, said bond must be renewed on the first day of May of each year or before any alcohol is withdrawn from bond for denaturing purposes. It must be executed in duplicate in accordance with instructions printed thereon. One copy is to be retained by the collector and one copy is to be transmitted to the Commissioner of Internal Revenue.

It shall be in the following form:

DENATURING WAREHOUSE BOND.

KNOW ALL MEN BY THESE PRESENTS: That we, ——— ——— of ———, as principal, and ——— ——— of ———, as sureties, are held and firmly bound to the UNITED STATES OF AMERICA in the full and just sum of ——— dollars, lawful money of the United States; to which payment, well and truly to be made, we bind ourselves jointly and severally, our several heirs, executors, and administrators, firmly by these presents.

Sealed with our seals and dated the ——— day of ———, 190—.

The condition of the foregoing obligation is such that whereas the above bounden principal, under the provisions of the act of June 7, 1906, has constructed a warehouse for denaturing alcohol on the premises of distillery No. ———, situated at ———, in the county of ———, State of ———, and said warehouse has been duly approved; and whereas said principal intends to withdraw from the distillery bonded warehouse belonging to said distillery situated on the distillery premises, alcohol free of tax for the purpose of denaturing same in the denaturing warehouse;

Now, therefore, if the aforesaid principal shall *immediately* upon the withdrawal from the distillery bonded warehouse aforesaid of all alcohol intended for denaturing purposes transfer same to the denaturing warehouse aforesaid, and in said denaturing warehouse, denature said alcohol in accordance with the terms of the entry for withdrawal of same and in conformity with the law and all rules and regulations duly prescribed in relation to the denaturing of alcohol; and if said principal shall in the transferring from distillery warehouse to denaturing warehouse, and in the handling and disposing of said alcohol, comply with all the law and regulations aforesaid; if he shall pay the tax of one dollar and ten cents per proof gallon on all alcohol withdrawn by him from distillery bonded warehouse free of tax for denaturing purposes and disposed of in any manner, either in transit from the distillery bonded warehouse to the denaturing warehouse or after it has been deposited in the denaturing warehouse, without first having denatured said alcohol in such manner as may have been prescribed by the Commissioner of Internal Revenue, with the approval of the Secretary of the Treasury, and if he shall pay all penalties incurred by him and all fines imposed on him for violation of any of the provisions of the law relating to the withdrawal of, transferring of, denaturing of, and disposing after denaturation of alcohol, withdrawn free of tax, then this obligation is to be void, otherwise, to remain in full force and effect.

——— ——— [SEAL.]
——— ——— [SEAL.]
——— ——— [SEAL.]

SEC. 14. The collector, upon receipt of the bond, shall examine same and investigate as to the sureties thereon.

If he finds the bond properly executed and the sureties sufficient, he shall approve the bond, and thereafter, during the life of the bond, the distiller may withdraw from his distillery warehouse, free of tax, alcohol to be denatured under such regulations as may hereinafter be prescribed.

CONDITIONS UNDER WHICH ALCOHOL IS WITHDRAWN.

SEC. 15. Not less than three hundred (300) wine gallons of alcohol can be withdrawn at one time for denaturing purposes.

When a distiller who is a producer of alcohol of not less than 180 degrees proof and who has given the denaturing warehouse bond as aforesaid desires to remove alcohol from the distillery bonded warehouse for the purpose of denaturing, he will himself, or by his duly authorized agent, file with the collector of internal revenue of the district in which the distillery is located the following notice in triplicate:

NOTICE OF INTENTION TO WITHDRAW FOR TRANSFER TO DENATURING BONDED WAREHOUSE.

———, ———, 190—.

———— ————,
Collector ——— *District of* ———.

SIR: The undersigned distiller and owner of ——— packages of alcohol, the serial numbers of which are ———, produced at distillery No. ———, in the ———

district of ———, and now stored in the distillery bonded warehouse No. —— at said distillery, desires to withdraw same under section 1 of the act of June 7, 1906, for denaturing purposes, and requests that said spirits be regaged.*

Respectfully,

——— ———, *Distiller.*

Sworn to before me this —— day of ———, 190—

——— ——— [SEAL.]

Upon the receipt of such notice the collector will at once append to each copy the following:

COLLECTOR'S ORDER TO GAUGER.

OFFICE OF COLLECTOR OF INTERNAL REVENUE,

—— DISTRICT, ———.

SIR: You will proceed to distillery warehouse No. ——, of ———, at ———, and there inspect and gauge, according to law and regulations, the alcohol which ——— desires to withdraw and transfer to denaturing bonded warehouse, and you will mark upon each package so regauged the number of wine gallons and proof gallons therein contained, and you will make report of your gauging on the certificate hereunto appended, and sign and deliver same to applicant.

——— ———,

Collector.

SEC. 16. Upon the receipt of the foregoing the officer designated will at once proceed carefully and thoroughly to inspect each package, ascertaining the actual wantage, proof, and contents without reference to the marks on the casks. In case the spirits are withdrawn on day of entry, regauge is not necessary, and the entry gauge shall be accepted. He will make return on each copy of the order for inspection in the following form:

GAUGER'S REPORT OF SPIRITS GAUGED.

I hereby certify that pursuant to the above order the following-described spirits deposited in distillery bonded warehouse No. —— by ——— ——— on the —— day of ——— 190— have been inspected and gauged by me this —— day of ——— 190— and found to be as follows:

			Contents when deposited in warehouse.					Contents when application for withdrawal is made.				
No. of Packages.	Marks and Serial Nos. of Packages.	Nos. of Warehouse Stamps.	Wine Gallons.	Degree of Proof.	Proof Gallons.	Taxable Gallons.	Amount of Tax.	Wine Gallons.	Degree of Proof.	Proof Gallons.	Taxable Gallons.	Amount of Tax.

And I further certify that the difference between the quantity, as shown by the marks and stamps on the cask, and the quantity as shown by my inspection, made in pursuance of the above order, is ——— wine, ——— proof, and ——— taxable gallons.

——— ———,

U. S. Gauger.

* If spirits are withdrawn same day as entered omit regage.

Upon receipt of the gauger's report the distiller will indorse thereon an entry for withdrawal for transfer to denaturing bonded warehouse, which shall be in the following form:

ENTRY FOR WITHDRAWAL FOR TRANSFER TO DENATURING BONDED WAREHOUSE.

—— DISTRICT, STATE OF ——.

—— ——, 190—.

The undersigned requests that the spirits described in the foregoing certificate and report of gauger, now in distillery bonded warehouse No. ——, owned by —— and situated in ——, county of ——, State of ——, in the —— district of said State, may be transferred therefrom and delivered into the denaturing bonded warehouse situated at my said distillery, to be denatured under the provisions of the act of June 7, 1906.

Number of Packages.	Marks and Serial Numbers of Packages.	Number of Warehouse Stamps.	Wine Gallons.	Degree of Proof.	Proof Gallons.	Taxable Gallons.	Amount of Tax.

—— ——. *Distiller.*

TAX COLLECTED ON DEFICIENCY.

SEC. 17. Upon receipt of the foregoing entry for withdrawal, the collector shall examine same, and, if it shall appear from the report of regauge, as made by the gauger, that there is an excessive loss in any package, under the provision of the act of August 28, 1894, as amended by act of March 3, 1899, then the collector shall collect the tax on such deficiency and shall indorse upon each copy of the order for inspection permit for the delivery of the spirits to be transferred to denaturing bonded warehouse in the following form:

PERMIT FOR TRANSFER TO DENATURING BONDED WAREHOUSE.

OFFICE OF COLLECTOR OF INTERNAL REVENUE,

—— DISTRICT OF THE STATE OF——,

——, ——, 190—.

SIR: The tax on —— gallons of the deficiency of —— gallons ascertained under section 50 of the act August 28, 1894, as amended, as shown by the accompanying report of —— gauger, having been paid to me and good and sufficient denaturing bond, dated ——, 190—, having been executed as required by law and filed in this office, said bond covering all distilled spirits to be transferred from distillery bonded warehouse to denaturing bonded warehouse for denaturing purposes, you are hereby directed to deliver said spirits to —— to be transfererd by him in your presence and under your supervision to the denaturing bonded warehouse of said —— on his distillery premises.

The gauger will affix the proper marks and brands in your presence.

—— ——, *Collector.*

To —— ——, *Storekeeper.*

SPIRITS TRANSFERRED TO BE MARKED.

Upon receipt of the permit by the storekeeper the packages of distilled spirits described in notice of intention to withdraw may be withdrawn from distillery bonded warehouse without the payment of the tax, and may be transferred to the denaturing bonded warehouse on the distillery premises; but before the removal of said spirits from the distillery bonded warehouse, the gauger, in addition to marking, cutting, and branding the marks usually required on withdrawal of spirits from warehouse, will legibly and durably mark on the head of each package, in letters and figures not less than one-half an inch in length, the number of *proof* gallons then ascertained, the date of the collector's permit, the object for which the spirits were withdrawn, and his name, title, and district.

Such additional marks may be as follows:

Withdrawn under permit issued Jan'y 10, 1907
For Denaturing Purposes
Proof gallons, 84
William Williams, U. S. Gauger,
5th Dist. Ky.

Entries in Record 18 and Reports 86 and 87.

SEC. 18. In his record 18 the storekeeper will enter said packages of spirits in *red ink* and will show that they were withdrawn free of tax for denaturing purposes. The storekeeper's reports on Forms 86 and 87 shall also show that the spirits were withdrawn for denaturing purposes and without the payment of the tax under the provisions of the act of June 7, 1906.

Immediately upon the withdrawal of the spirits, as above indicated, the storekeeper will transmit the duplicate permit to the collector, who will note upon the original permit in his possession the withdrawal of the spirits therein mentioned.

Collector's 94a.

SEC. 19. The collector will take credit for all spirits so withdrawn, on the appropriate line of his bonded account (Form 94a), for the month during which such withdrawals were made.

He will also make proper entry on the inside page of that account as to the quantity covered by each permit, and will forward each of such duplicate permits (with the distiller's entry for withdrawal) with his bonded account as a voucher for such entry.

Spirits Transferred to Denaturing Bonded Warehouse.

SEC. 20. When the packages of spirits are marked and branded in the manner above indicated they shall at once, in the presence and under the supervision of the storekeeper, be transferred to the denaturing bonded warehouse.

Record of Spirits Received in Denaturing Bonded Warehouse.

SEC. 21. The officer in charge of the denaturing bonded warehouse shall keep a record of the spirits received in said denaturing bonded warehouse from the distillery bonded warehouse and the spirits delivered to the distiller for denaturing purposes.

Upon the *debit* side of said record, in columns prepared for the purpose, there shall be entered the date when any distilled spirits were received in denaturing bonded warehouse, the date of the collector's permit, the date of withdrawal from distillery bonded warehouse, the number of packages received, the serial numbers of the packages, the serial numbers of the distillery warehouse stamps, and the wine and proof gallons.

Upon the *credit* side of said record shall be entered the date when any spirits were delivered to the distiller for denaturing purposes, the date of the collector's permit for withdrawal, the date of withdrawal from distillery bonded warehouse, the number of packages so delivered, the serial numbers of the packages, the serial numbers of the distillery warehouse stamps, and the wine and proof gallons.

Immediately upon the receipt of any distilled spirits in the denaturing bonded warehouse, and on the same day upon which they are received, the officer must enter said spirits in said record.

Likewise, on the same date upon which any spirits are delivered to the distiller for denaturing purposes, said spirits must be entered on said record.

SEC. 22. A balance must be struck in the record described in above section at the end of the month showing the number of packages and quantity in wine and proof gallons of spirits on hand in packages on the first day of the month, the number of packages and quantity in wine and proof gallons received during the month. the number of packages and quantity in wine and proof gallons delivered to the distiller during the month, and the balance on hand in packages and wine and proof gallons at the close of the month.

RETURN ON FORM 86b.

SEC. 23. On all days on which any spirits are entered into the denaturing bonded warehouse, or on which any spirits are delivered to the distiller for denaturing purposes, the officer must make in duplicate a return on Form 86b as follows:

SPIRITS ENTERED IN DENATURING BONDED WAREHOUSE AND DELIVERED TO DISTILLER FOR DENATURATION.

RETURN for the —— day of ——— 190— of distilled spirits entered into and withdrawn from denaturing bonded warehouse belonging to distillery No. ——, carried on by —— ——, in the —— collection district of the State of ———.

Entries.

Number Packages.	Serial Number Packages.	Serial Number D. W. S.	Date of Permit.	Date of Withdrawal.	W. G.	P. G.

Deliveries to Distiller for Denaturing Purpose.

Number Packages.	Serial Number Packages.	Serial Number D. W. S.	Date of Permit.	Date of Withdrawal.	W. G.	P. G.

I hereby certify that the distilled spirits above reported were deposited into said denaturing bonded warehouse or were delivered to the distiller for denaturing purposes (as the case may be) in my presence, and that the information given concerning the serial numbers and contents of the packages, and the serial numbers of the stamps, was obtained by me on actual examination of the marks, brands, and stamps on said packages and not from any return made by the gauger.

—— ——, *U. S. Officer.*

Dated at —— this —— day of ———, 190—.

MONTHLY RETURN OF SPIRITS ENTERED IN WAREHOUSE AND DELIVERED TO DISTILLER.

SEC. 24. The officer in charge of the denaturing bonded warehouse must also make in duplicate at the end of each month and forward to the Collector of Internal Revenue a monthly return to be a transcript of and to be made up from the officer's record 18b.

Said return must show in detail the spirits deposited in the denaturing bonded warehouse, also the spirits delivered to the distiller for denaturing purposes and the spirits remaining in the denaturing bonded warehouse at the end of the month. Separate entries must be made of each day's work and the spirits must be described in the same manner as they are in the return 86b and the book, Form 18b.

OFFICE FORM 15b.

SEC. 25. Collectors in whose districts alcohol is being withdrawn from bond for denaturing purposes shall provide themselves with a record (Office Form 15b) in which shall be kept the individual account of each distiller in the district who has qualified for the purpose of denaturing alcohol. This record is to be made up from reports on Form 87b. It must show the date upon which any spirits were deposited in denaturing warehouse, the serial numbers of the packages deposited, the number of packages and the proof gallons. Said record must likewise show in detail the deliveries to the distillers for denaturing purposes.

DENATURING AGENTS.

COMPLETELY DENATURED ALCOHOL.

SEC. 26. Unless otherwise specially provided, the agents used for denaturing alcohol withdrawn from bond for denaturing purposes shall consist of methyl alcohol and benzine in the following proportions: To every one hundred parts by volume of ethyl alcohol of the desired proof (not less than 180°) there shall be added ten parts by volume of approved methyl alcohol and one-half of one part by volume of approved benzine; for example, to every 100 gallons of ethyl alcohol (of not less than 180 degrees proof) there shall be added 10 gallons of approved methyl alcohol and ½ gallon of approved benzine.* Alcohol thus denatured shall be classed as completely denatured alcohol.

---

* An amendment to the U. S. Regulations permitting the use of methyl alcohol and pyridin bases for denaturing is as follows:

"Section 26 of the regulations and instructions conerning denatured alcohol, issued September 29, 1906, is amended by inserting after the words 'approved benzine,' in the ninth line of said section, the following:

"'Or methyl alcohol and approved pyridin bases, in the following proportions: To every 100 parts by volume of ethyl alcohol of the desired proof (not less than 180°) there shall be added two parts by volume of approved methyl alcohol and one-half of one part by volume of approved pyridin bases—for example, to every 100 gallons of ethyl alcohol (of not less than 180° proof) there shall be added 2 gallons of approved methyl alcohol and one-half gallon of approved pyridin bases.'

"NOTE.—Methyl alcohol intended for use as a denaturant must conform to the specifications prescribed in Circular No. 680 (see Chapter IX, this book).

"Pyridin bases intended for use as a denaturant must conform to the following specifications:

"*Specifications for pyridin bases submitted for approval as a denaturing material.*

"PYRIDIN BASES.

"1. *Color.*—The liquid must meet the same requirements as to color that are imposed upon wood alcohol. (See Circular No. 680.)

"2. *Reac ion with cadmium chloride.*—Ten c.c. of a solution of 1 c.c. of pyridin bases in 100 c.c. of water are treated with 5 c.c. of an aqueous solution of anhydrous fused cadmium chloride and the mixture vigorously shaken. Within ten minutes an abundant crystalline separation should take place.

"3. *Behavior with Nessler's reagent.*—With 5 c.c. of Nessler's reagent, 10 c.c. of the pyridin bases must give a white precipitate.

"4. *Boiling-point.*—When 100 c.c are subjected to the determination of the boiling-point in

Methyl alcohol and benzine intended for use as denaturants must be submitted for chemical test and must conform to the specifications which shall be hereafter duly prescribed.

DENATURANTS DEPOSITED IN WAREHOUSE.

SEC. 27. As the distiller's business demands, he may bring into the denaturing bonded warehouse, in such receptacles as he may wish, any authorized denaturant. Such denaturants shall at once be deposited in the material room; thereafter they shall be in the custody and under the control of the officer in charge of the warehouse. Before any denaturant is used it must be dumped into the appropriate tank and after the contents have been thoroughly mixed, a sample of one pint taken therefrom. This sample must be forwarded to the proper officer for analysis. The officer will then securely close and seal the tank.

No part of the contents of the tank can be used until the sample has been officially tested and approved, and report of such test made to the officer in charge of the warehouse.

If the sample is approved the contents of the tank shall, upon the receipt of the report, become an approved denaturant and the officer shall at once remove the seals and place the tank under Government locks.

If the sample does not meet the requirements of the specifications, the officer shall, upon the receipt of the report of nonapproval, permit the distiller, provided he desires, to treat or manipulate the proposed denaturant so as to render it a competent denaturant. In such case another sample must be submitted for approval. If the distiller does not desire to further treat the denaturant, the officer shall require him immediately to remove the contents of the tank from the premises.

RECORD OF DENATURANTS RECEIVED.

SEC. 28. The officer shall keep a denaturing material room record. This record shall show all material entered into and removed from the denaturing material room.

There shall be proper columns on the *debit* side in which are to be entered the date when any material is received, the name and residence of the person from whom received, the kind of material, the quantity in wine gallons, and, if methyl alcohol, in proof gallons, the date upon which the material was dumped into the tank, the number of the tank, the date upon which sample was forwarded, and the number of the sample, and the result of the official test.

On the *credit* side of said record shall be entered, in proper columns, the date upon which any material was removed from the denaturing material room for denaturing purposes, the kind of material, the number of the tank from which taken, the number of the sample representing the tank and sent for official test, the number of wine gallons, and, if methyl alcohol, the number of proof gallons.

NOTE.—For regulations regarding specially denatured alcohol, see page 394.

MONTHLY RETURNS OF DENATURANTS RECEIVED.

SEC. 29. A balance shall be struck in this record at the end of each month whereby shall be shown the quantity of material of each kind on hand in the de-

---

the same manner as prescribed for wood alcohol, at least 50 c.c. must distil at 140° C. and at least 90 c.c. at 160° C.

"5. *Miscibility with water.*—The same requirements must be met as are imposed upon wood alcohol. (See Circular No. 680.)

"6. *Content of water.*—When 20 c.c. of pyridin bases are shaken with 20 c.c. of a solution of caustic soda, with a specific gravity of 1,400, and the mixture allowed to stand for some time, at least 18.5 c.c. of the pyridin bases must separate from the solution.

"7. *Alkalinity.*—One c.c. of pyridin bases dissolved in 10 c.c. of water are titrated with normal sulphuric acid until a drop of the mixture placed upon Congo paper shows a distinct blue border which soon disappears. It must require not less than 9.5 c.c. of the acid solution to produce the reaction.

"The Congo paper is prepared by treating filter paper with a solution of 1 gram of Congo red in 1 liter of water and drying it."

naturing material room on the first day of the month, the quantity received during the month, the quantity rejected and removed from the premises during the month, and the quantity delivered to the distiller for denaturing purposes during the month, and the quantity on hand at the end of the month.

The officer shall, at the end of each month, prepare in duplicate, sign, and forward to the collector of internal revenue a report which shall be a transcript of said record.

DISTILLER TO KEEP RECORD OF DENATURANTS.

SEC. 30. The distiller shall also keep a record, in which he shall enter the date upon which he deposits any material in the tanks of the denaturing material room, the name and address of the person from whom said material was received, and the kind and quantity of the material so deposited; also he shall enter in said record the date upon which he receives any material from the denaturing material room, the kind and quantity of such material so received, and the disposition made of same.

NOTICE OF INTENTION TO DENATURE SPIRITS.

SEC. 31. The distiller shall, before dumping any spirits or denaturants into the mixing tank, give notice to the officer in charge of the denaturing warehouse in proper form in duplicate, and enter in the proper place thereon (in the case of distilled spirits) and in the proper column the number of the packages, the serial numbers of same, the serial number of the warehouse stamps, the contents in wine and proof gallons and the proof as shown by the marks, the date of the withdrawal gauge, and by whom gauged.

In case of denaturing agents he shall enter in the proper place and in the proper columns the number of gallons, the kind of material, and the number of the denaturing material tank from which same is to be drawn.

The contents of the several packages of alcohol, as shown by the withdrawal gauge, shall be accepted as the contents of said packages when dumped for denaturing purposes unless it should appear from a special showing made by the distiller that there has been an accidental loss since withdrawal from distillery bonded warehouse.

Upon receipt of this notice the officer in charge of the denaturing warehouse shall, in case of the packages of alcohol, inspect same carefully to ascertain whether or not they are the packages described in the distiller's notice. He will then cut out that portion of the warehouse stamp upon which is shown the serial number of the stamp, the name of the distiller, the proof gallons, and the serial number of the package. These slips must be securely fastened to the form whereon the gauging is reported and sent by the officer with his return to the collector.

TRANSFER OF DENATURANTS TO MIXING TANKS.

SEC. 32. The distiller, unless pipes are used, as herein provided, shall provide suitable gauged receptacles, metal drums being preferred, with which to transfer the denaturing agents from the material tanks to the mixing tanks. These receptacles must be numbered serially and the number, the capacity in gallons and fractions of a gallon, the name of the distiller, and the number of the denaturing bonded warehouse marked thereon in durable letters and figures. They shall be used for transferring denaturing material from the material tanks to the mixing tanks and for no other purpose. The distiller must also provide suitable approved sealed measures of smaller capacity. The gauged receptacles are to be used where the quantity to be transferred amounts to as much as the capacity of the smallest gauged receptacle in the warehouse. The measures are to be used only when the quantity of material to be transferred is less than the capacity of the smallest gauged receptacle.

SEC. 33. The distiller may provide metal pipes connecting the material tanks and the mixing tanks and the denaturant may be transferred to the mixing tanks through these pipes. Such pipes must be supplied with valves, cocks, faucets, or other proper means of controlling the flow of the liquid, and such valves, cocks, or faucets must be so arranged that they can be securely locked, and the locks attached thereto must be kept fastened; the keys to be retained by the officer in charge, except when the denaturing material is being transferred to the mixing tanks.

In the event pipes are used as above provided, the glass gauges affixed to the material tanks must be so graduated that tenths of a gallon will be indicated.

Before any material is transferred from a material tank to a mixing tank the officer must note the contents of the material tank as indicated by the glass gauge. He will then permit the denaturant to flow into the mixing tank until the exact quantity necessary to denature the alcohol, as provided by the regulations, has been transferred. This he will ascertain by reading the gauge on the material tank before the liquid has begun to flow and after the flow has been stopped. He should verify the quantity transferred by reading the gauge on the mixing tank before and after the transfer.

SEC. 34. The officer in charge of the denaturing warehouse will be held strictly accountable for any errors in the quantities of denaturants added. It is important that his measurements should be absolutely correct. He must know that the measures and the gauged receptacles provided by the distiller and the graduated gauges affixed to the tanks are correct. He must from time to time apply such tests to these measures, gauged receptacles, or graduated gauges, as the case may be, as will satisfy him that they are correct. If he finds the measures, gauged receptacles, or graduated gauges to be incorrect, he shall refuse to permit the distiller to transfer any denaturant to the mixing tanks until appliances have been provided whereby the exact quantity of denaturants used may be ascertained.

The distiller must provide all scales, weighing beams, and other appliances necessary for transferring the denaturing materials, gauging or handling the alcohol, or testing any of the measures, receptacles, or gauges used in the warehouse, and also a sufficient number of competent employees for the work.

CONTENTS OF MIXING TANK TO BE PLUNGED.

SEC. 35. The exact quantity of distilled spirits contained in the packages covered by the distiller's notice having been ascertained by the officer and the spirits having been dumped into the mixing tank, and the quantities of the several denaturants prescribed by the regulations having been ascertained by calculation and added as above provided to the alcohol in the mixing tank, the officer must cause the contents of the tank to be thoroughly and completely plunged and mixed by the distiller or his employees.

OFFICER TO MAKE RETURNS OF DUMPED MATERIAL.

SEC. 36. The officer will make return on the proper form, wherein he will show the number of packages of distilled spirits inspected by him and dumped in his presence by the distiller, the serial numbers of said packages, the serial numbers of the warehouse stamps affixed to said packages, the proof gallon contents of said packages, and the name of the gauger who made the withdrawal gauge.

He shall also report on said form the number of drums of the several kinds of denaturants gauged by him and dumped in his presence, the serial numbers of said drums, the quantity in wine gallons, and, in the case of wood alcohol, the quantity in proof gallons of each kind of denaturant gauged and dumped, the serial numbers of the tanks from which the denaturants were drawn, and the tank sample number of said denaturant.

DRAWING OFF AND GAUGING DENATURED PRODUCT.

SEC. 37. The distiller may from time to time, as he wishes, in the presence of the officer, draw off from the tank or tanks the denatured product in quantities of not less than 50 gallons at one time, and the same must at once be gauged, stamped, and branded by the officer and removed from the premises by the distiller.

Kind and Capacity of Packages Used.

Sec. 38. He may use packages of a capacity of not less than five gallons or not more than one hundred and thirty-five (135) gallons, and each package must be filled to its full capacity, such wantage being allowed as may be necessary for expansion.

All packages used to contain completely denatured alcohol must be painted a *light green*, and in no case is a package of any other color to be used.

Alcohol to be Immediately Denatured.

Sec. 39. No alcohol withdrawn from distillery warehouse for denaturing purposes shall be permitted to remain in the denaturing bonded warehouse until after the close of business on the second day after the said alcohol is withdrawn, but all alcohol so withdrawn must be transferred, dumped, and denatured before the close of business on said second day.

Application for Gauge of Denatured Alcohol.

Sec. 40. When the process of denaturing has been completed and the distiller desires to have the denatured alcohol drawn off into packages and gauged, he shall prepare a request for such gauge on the proper form. The request shall state as accurately as practicable the number of packages to be drawn off and the number of wine and proof gallons contents thereof.

This notice shall be directed to the collector of internal revenue, but shall be handed to the officer on duty at the denaturing bonded warehouse.

Sec. 41. If the officer shall find upon examination of the proper record that there should be on hand the quantity of denatured alcohol covered by said notice, he shall proceed to gauge and stamp the several packages of denatured alcohol in the manner herein prescribed, and shall make report thereof on the proper form.

In no case will the officer gauge and stamp denatured alcohol the total quantity in wine gallons of which taken together with any remnant that may be left in the denaturing tank exceeds in wine gallons the sum of the quantity of distilled spirits and denaturants dumped on that day and any remnant brought over from previous day.

How Denatured Alcohol shall be Gauged.

Sec. 42. The gauging of denatured alcohol shall, where it is practicable, be by weight. The officer shall ascertain the tare by actually weighing each package when empty. Then, after each package has been filled in his presence, he shall ascertain the gross weight, and, by applying the tare, the net weight.

He shall then ascertain the proof in the usual manner, and by applying the proof to the wine gallons content the proof gallons shall be ascertained.

The regulations relating to the gauging of rectified spirits, so far as they apply to apparent proof and apparent proof gallons, shall apply to denatured spirits. Where it is for any reason not practicable to gauge denatured alcohol by weight, using the tables that apply in the case of the gauging of distilled spirits, the gauging shall be by rod.

Return on Form 237a.

Sec. 43. Having gauged each of said packages, the officer shall make return on Form 237a, whereon he shall first certify that he has carefully examined the distiller's denaturing account, and that the aggregate contents of the several packages embraced in said return, added to any balance that may be on hand after they are withdrawn, does not exceed in proof gallons the quantity shown to be in the mixing tank by the distiller's denaturing account. Usually there will be a slight loss in proof gallons in process of denaturation. If there is a material loss, however, the officer should ascertain the cause and should include the explanation in his report.

The return must also show in the proper columns in detail the capacity of each package, its gross weight, tare, net weight, if gauged by weight, indication, temperature, net wine gallons contents, proof, proof gallons contents, apparent proof, apparent proof gallons contents, the serial number of the denatured alcohol stamp affixed to the package, and the serial number of the package.

This return must be in duplicate, and must be forwarded to the collector of the district.

MANNER OF MARKING HEADS OF PACKAGES.

SEC. 44. *Upon each head* of the package shall be stenciled in *red* letters, of not less than 1½ inches in length by 1 inch in width, the words "DENATURED ALCOHOL."

Upon the stamp head of the package there shall be stenciled the serial number of the package, the name of the distiller denaturing the spirits, the number of the denaturing bonded warehouse at which the spirits were denatured, and the district and State in which it is located, the date upon which the contents of the pacakge were denatured, and the serial number of the denatured alcohol stamp.

PACKAGES TO BE NUMBERED SERIALLY.

SEC. 45. Packages of denatured alcohol must be numbered serially as they are withdrawn and gauged. The serial number for every denaturing bonded warehouse must begin with number 1 with the first cask denatured, and no two or more packages denatured at the same denaturing bonded warehouse shall be numbered with the same number. A change of person or persons operating a distillery and denaturing bonded warehouse will not be taken to require a new series of numbers for the packages of spirits thereafter denatured at such warehouse.

STAMPS FOR DENATURED ALCOHOL.

SEC. 46. The following form of stamp for denatured alcohol is hereby prescribed:

STAMP FOR DENATURED ALCOHOL, NO. ——.

Issued by —— ——, collector of the —— district, State of ——, to —— ——, denaturer of alcohol in said collection district, ——, ——, 19—, —— proof gallons, —— wine gallons.

—— ——, *U. S. Officer.*

These stamps are to be made of white paper, the lettering to be red. They are to be bound in book form, each book containing 150 stamps, only one denomination being contained in each book. The denominations are to be 5, 10, 20, 30, 40, 50, 60, 70, 80, 90, 100, 110, 120, and 130 gallons, respectively, with proper number coupons attached to each, and each coupon representing one gallon.

In using the coupons on said stamps the same rule will be followed in dealing with fractional parts of gallons as are observed in the case of rectifier's stamps; that is to say, if the fraction is less than five-tenths of a gallon it must be dropped, and if it is more than five-tenths it is called the next unit above. Connected with each stamp is its corresponding stub, which the officer must fill out in accordance with the facts in the case.

The stamp must be signed by the officer, and he will enter upon it the date upon which he affixes it to the package, the number of wine and proof gallons, the number of the denaturing bonded warehouse, and the name of the denaturer.

SEC. 47. Stamps for denatured alcohol will be intrusted to the officer assigned to the denaturing bonded warehouse. He must keep these stamps continuously in his possession, and when not in actual use the book must be deposited in a safe and secure place in the denaturing bonded warehouse under lock and key, to which no one shall have access at any time except himself.

The officer must make a daily report to the collector of all denatured alcohol stamps used, and for whom used.

Disposition of Books, Stubs, etc.

Sec. 48. When all the stamps in any book have been used, the book with the stubs will be returned to the collector, who shall forward it to this office. The stubs and unused coupons must remain in the book.

Officers are advised that they will be held strictly responsible for all denatured alcohol stamps delivered to them, and they are cautioned against affixing such stamps to packages which do not correctly represent the character of the contents. They must know that all the statements on the heads of the packages are strictly true.

Duties of Officer in Regard to Mixing Tank.

Sec. 49. The mixing tank is absolutely under control of the officer in charge of the warehouse. If it becomes necessary for him to leave the denaturing bonded warehouse during the process of denaturing, he must close and lock all openings to said tank and must retain the key in his possession, and all other persons must leave the building.

When the work of the day is done the officer must ascertain the quantity in wine and proof gallons of any remnant of denatured alcohol that may be on hand, and on each day be ore any further denaturing is done he must, before anything is dumped into the denaturing tank, ascertain the quantity in wine and proof gallons of any remnant that may be in the tank.

Record of Operations to be Kept by Officer.

Sec. 50. The officer assigned to duty at the denaturing bonded warehouse shall, in a book prescribed for that purpose, keep a true and correct record of the operation at said denaturing bonded warehouse.

Said book shall show on the debit side, in the case of distilled spirits, the date upon which the spirits were dumped, the number of packages dumped, the serial numbers of said packages, the serial numbers of the warehouse stamps, the date of permit, the date of withdrawal from the distillery warehouse, the name of the officer who made the withdrawal gauge, the wine gallons and proof gallons. In the case of denaturing agents, said record must show on said *debit* side the date on which said denaturing agents were dumped, the kind of material, the number of the denaturing tank from which taken, the tank sample number of the denaturant, the date upon which the sample was inspected, the quantity in wine gallons, and, if methyl alcohol, the quantity in proof gallons dumped.

If there is more than one dump made during the day *separate* entries must be made for each dump, but the totals for the day must be carried forward and entered. in the proper columns in *red* ink.

On the *credit* side of said record must be entered the denatured product drawn from dump. The entries must be made in the proper columns and must show the number of packages of denatured alcohol drawn from dump, the serial numbers of the denatured stamps, the date upon which said packages were withdrawn from dump and gauged, the number of wine gallons and the number of proof gallons, and to whom delivered and the hour removed from the denaturing premises.

If there is more than one lot drawn off and gauged during the day, a separate entry must be made for each lot, but the total wine and proof gallons drawn off and gauged for the day must be carried forward and entered in *red* ink in a column prepared for that purpose.

There must also be columns in said book in which to enter the remnant brought over from the previous day, the total quantity of distilled spirits and denaturants dumped during the day, the quantity withdrawn from dump and gauged during the day, and the quantity left in the mixing tank at the close of business.

Denatured Alcohol to be Removed from Warehouse.

Sec. 51. Not later than the close of business on the day following that upon which the work of drawing off and gauging the denatured spirits is completed, the distiller must remove said denatured alcohol from the denaturing bonded warehouse. He may either remove the alcohol to a building off the distillery premises, where he can dispose of it as the demands of the trade require, or he may dispose of it in stamped packages direct to the trade from the denaturing bonded warehouse

Record Showing Alcohol Received and Disposed of to be Kept by Distiller.

Sec. 52. The distiller must keep a record (Form 52d and 52e) in which he shall show, respectively, all denatured alcohol received from the officer in charge of the warehouse and disposed of by him.

Upon the "Received" side he shall enter the date upon which he receives any denatured alcohol from the denaturing bonded warehouse, the number of packages received, the serial numbers of the packages, the date upon which the alcohol was denatured, the name of the officer, the kind and percentage of the denaturants used, the serial number of the denatured alcohol stamp, and the aggregate wine and proof gallons. These entries must be made on the same day the denatured alcohol is received.

On the "disposed of" side the distiller must show the date upon which he disposes of any denatured alcohol, the name and address of the person or firm to whom sold or delivered, if a manufacturer, the kind of a manufacturer, the kind and percentage of the denaturing agents used, the number of packages, the serial numbers of the packages, the serial numbers of the denatured alcohol stamps, and the aggregate wine and proof gallon contents.

These entries must be made before the goods are removed from the denaturing bonded warehouse, if sold direct from there, or from the salesroom of the distiller off the premises, if sold from there.

Sec. 53. Spaces and columns must be provided for at the bottom of said record wherein can be shown the quantity of denatured alcohol brought over in stock from the previous month, the quantity received during the month, the quantity disposed of during the month, and the quantity remaining on hand at the end of the month. In this statement must be shown the number of packages brought over, received, disposed of, and on hand, the serial numbers of said packages. the serial numbers of the denatured stamps, the wine gallons, and the proof gallons,

Monthly Transcript.

Sec. 54. Before the tenth day of each month the distiller must prepare a complete transcrpit of this record, must swear to same, and must forward it to the collector of the district.

Said affidavit shall be in the following form:

I, ——— ———, do state on oath that I am ——— of denaturing bonded warehouse No. ——— in the ——— district of ———, and the above is a true, correct, and complete statement of the denatured alcohol received by me from said denaturing bonded warehouse, of the denatured alcohol disposed of, to whom disposed of, and of the denatured alcohol on hand at the end of the month.

Collectors to Keep Accounts with Denaturers.

Sec. 55. Collectors must keep an exact account with each denaturer of alcohol on record (Form 39a) in such manner as to be constantly advised as to the state. of the denaturer's business, and they must exercise such supervision over the issue of stamps for denatured alcohol as will prevent fraud in their use.

The entries in said record 29a must be made daily. Said entries are to be made from the officer's returns on Form 122a and 237a. Under the heading "Material dumped for denaturation" must be entered in the case of distilled spirits the date of the dumping, the number of packages, the serial numbers of the packages, the serial numbers of the warehouse stamps, the date of the collector's permit for withdrawal, the date of withdrawal from distillery bonded warehouse, the name of the withdrawal gauger, and the wine and proof gallons.

In the case of denaturants there must be entered in proper columns the serial numbers of the tanks from which the denaturants were drawn, the tank sample number of the denaturant, the dates upon which said samples were inspected, and the number of gallons of each of the several kinds of denaturant dumped.

Under the heading "Alcohol Denatured," in the proper columns, shall be entered the date of denaturation, the numbers of package denatured and gauged, the serial numbers of said packages, the serial numbers of the denatured stamps attached to them, the name of the officer, and the quantity of alcohol in wine and proof gallons denatured and gauged.

Proper columns and spaces shall be provided at the bottom of this record where shall be entered at the end of each month the quantity in wine and proof gallons of denatured alcohol remaining in denaturing tanks brought over from previous month, the quantity of material dumped for denaturation during the month, the quantity drawn from the denaturing tank. gauged, and removed from the premises during the month, and the quantity left in the mixing tank at the end of the month.

Distiller's Return to be Compared with Collector's Record.

Sec. 56. The distiller's return on Form 52d should be compared with this record at the end of each month. The number of packages, serial numbers of the packages, and number of gallons received by the distiller from denaturing bonded warehouse should agree with the 39a as made up from the officer's 2 37a.

Manner of Handling and Testing Samples of Denaturants.

Sec. 57. When the distiller at any denaturing bonded warehouse has dumped into any material tank a quantity of a proposed denaturant as hereinbefore provided, the officer shall draw a sample from said tank. A heavy glass bottle, which must be provided by the distiller, shall be used as a container for said sample. The bottle must be securely closed and sealed, and a label affixed thereto, showing the serial number of the denaturing material tank from which the sample was taken, the date it was drawn from the tank, and the name of the officer sending it.

The sample shall be securely packed and sent by express to the most convenient laboratory for test. All expenses in connection with the forwarding of samples must be borne by the distiller.

As soon as practicable the necessary tests of the sample shall be made in the laboratory and report made of its character.

One copy of the report should be sent to the collector of internal revenue of the district, and the other should be sent to the officer in charge of the denaturing bonded warehouse.

Part II.

DEALERS IN DENATURED ALCOHOL AND MANUFACTURERS USING DENATURED ALCOHOL.

Sec. 58. Alcohol denatured by use of methyl alcohol and benzine as provided in section 26 of these regulations is to be classed as *Completely denatured alcohol.* Alcohol denatured in any other manner will be classed as *Specially denatured alcohol.*

Denatured Alcohol Not to be Stored on Certain Premises, and Not to be Used for Certain Purposes.

Sec. 59. Neither completely nor specially denatured alcohol shall be kept or stored on the premises of the following classes of persons, to wit: dealers in wines, fermented liquors or distilled spirits, rectifiers of spirits, manufacturers of and dealers in beverages of any kind, manufacturers of liquid medicinal preparations, or distillers (except as to such denatured alcohol in stamped packages as is manufactured by themselves), manufacturers of vinegar by the vaporizing process and the use of a still and mash, wort, or wash, and persons who, in the course of business, have or keep distilled spirits, wines, or malt liquors, or other beverages stored on their premises. *Provided,* That druggists are exempt from the above provisions.

Cannot be Used in Manufacturing Beverages, etc.

Sec. 60. Any one using denatured alcohol for the manufacture of any beverage or liquid medicinal preparation, or who knowingly sells any beverage or liquid medicinal preparation made in whole or in part from such alcohol, becomes subject to the penalties prescribed in section 2 of the act of June 7, 1906.

Under the language of this law it is held that denatured alcohol cannot be used in the preparation of any article to be used as a component part in the preparation of any beverage or liquid medicinal preparation.

Permits Required.

Sec. 61. Persons who wish to deal in completely denatured alcohol must secure permits from the collector of internal revenue of the district in which the business is to be carried on.

Every person who sells or offers for sale denatured alcohol in the original stamped package shall be classed as a *wholesale dealer in denatured alcohol,* and denatured alcohol shall not be sold in quantities of 5 gallons or more except in the original stamped packages.

Every person who sells or offers for sale denatured alcohol in quantities of *less* than 5 gallons shall be classed as a *retail dealer in denatured alcohol.*

The same person may be both a wholesale and a retail dealer, but the retail and the wholesale business will be considered separate, and permits must be secured for each.

Collectors are authorized to issue permits on the forms herein prescribed upon application duly made.

Said permits are to be numbered serially in the same manner in which special-tax stamps are now numbered, and are to be on the forms herein prescribed.

Application for Permit to be Filed with Collector.

Sec. 62. A person, firm, or corporation desiring to secure a permit to sell denatured alcohol must make application on the following form:

[FORM 11a.]

The undersigned, ——— ———, states on oath that he is a member of the firm (corporation) of ———, doing business at ———, and said firm (corporation) consists of ——— ——— and is located at ———, in the county of ——— and State of ———. The premises of said concern are located on ——— street, and are described as follows: ——— and said premises constitute all of the premises used by ——— in ——— said business; that no part of said premises is used by any one in the business of a distiller, manufacturer of wines or malt liquors, a dealer in wines, malt liquors, or distilled spirits (except druggists), a rectifier of spirits, a manufacturer of or dealer in any kind of beverages, a manufacturer of any liquid medicinal preparation, or a manufacturer of vinegar produced by any vaporizing process from mash, wort, or wash, or by any person (except druggists) who in the course of his business keeps or stores distilled spirits, wines, or malt liquors thereon.

Applicant binds himself and his ——— to comply with the law and all the regulations relating to the handling and sale of denatured alcohol.

He desires to deal in denatured alcohol in the original stamped package (or in quantities of less than five gallons), and he therefore requests that a permit be issued to him to receive denatured alcohol in stamped packages upon his premises and to sell same in original stamped packages (or in quantities of less than five gallons).

(Signed) ———— ————.

Subscribed and sworn to before me this —— day of ————, 190—.

———— ————.

In the case of individuals the application must be signed and sworn to either by the inividual himself or by his duly authorized attorney in fact, and either a general power of attorney or a power specially authorizing the attorney in fact to act must accompany the application.

In the case of corporations the application must be signed and sworn to by the duly authorized officer or agent of the corporation, and a certified copy of the minutes of the board of directors authorizing the party, either generally or specially, to perform the act must accompany the application.

Permits Expire June 30 Each Year.

Sec. 63. Applications to deal in denatured alcohol must be made to the collector of internal revenue of the district in which it is proposed to do business on or before the first day of July of each year, or before any denatured alcohol is received on the premises, and said application will expire on the 30th of June ensuing.

In case a dealer in denatured alcohol moves his place of business before the expiration of the fiscal year for which the permit was issued he must make application for the transfer of his permit to the place to which he moves.

Permits to be Canceled under certain Conditions.

Sec. 64. If it should appear on proper showing made at any time that the party to whom a permit to deal in denatured alcohol has been issued has wilfully violated any of the provisions of the law or regulations relating to the using or handling of denatured alcohol, it shall be the duty of the collector of internal revenue to cancel the permit.

Appeal for rehearing may be made to the Commissioner of Internal Revenue in any case where a permit has been canceled, and the Commissioner may, if he thinks the facts justify it, reverse the action of the collector in canceling the permit.

Form of Permit.

Sec. 65. The collector's permit will be in the following form:

This is to certify that. application having been made to me in due form, permission to engage in the business of wholesale (retail) dealer in denatured alcohol is hereby given to ———— ————, at ————, on the following-described premises ————, said permit to expire on June 30, ————.

Right to cancel this permit is hereby reserved, should it at any time appear on proper showing made that the said party has wilfully violated any of the provisions of law or regulations regarding denatured alcohol.

———— ————,

Collector ———— *District.*

Collectors to Keep Record of Dealers, Denaturers, etc.

Sec. 66. Collectors shall keep a record (Book Form 10a), in which shall be entered the names of all distillers who have qualified as denaturers of alcohol in the district, and the names of all wholesale and retail dealers in denatured alcohol; also manufacturers using specially and those using completely denatured alcohol. Said record shall show the name of the party, his residence, and the date, number, and whether he is a dealer, distiller, or manufacturer. This record shall be open to public inspection.

Wholesale Dealers to Keep Record.

Sec. 67. Wholesale dealers in denatured alcohol shall keep a record, in which they shall enter all the denatured acohol received and disposed of by them.

On the received side they shall enter the date upon which the package of denatured alcohol was received, the name and address of the persons from whom received, the district and State in which the alcohol was denatured, the number of packages received, the serial numbers of the packages, the serial numbers of the stamps, and the wine and proof gallons.

These entries shall be made in said record upon the day on which the dealer receives the denatured alcohol and before it is removed from his premises or any of the packages are broken.

On the disposed-of side of said record the dealer shall enter the date upon which he disposes of any denatured alcohol, the name and address of the person to whom disposed of, whether the purchaser is manufacturer or dealer, the name of the denaturer and the district in which the alcohol was denatured, the number of packages, the serial numbers of the packages, the serial numbers of the denatured alcohol stamps, and the aggregate number of wine and proof gallons.

These entries must be made *before* the alcohol is removed from the premises.

In case the dealer is a retail dealer and the alcohol is charged off to himself as a retail dealer, the entries must be made in said record before the package is opened or any alcohol is drawn from it.

Columns and spaces must be arranged in said record in which at the end of the month the dealer must enter the number of packages, the serial numbers of the packages, and the quantity in gallons of denatured alcohol on hand on the first day of the month, received during the month, disposed of during the month, and on hand at the end of the month.

Wholesale Dealer to Make Monthly Transcript.

SEC. 68. The dealer must make a transcript of this record each month, must swear to it before some officer authorized to administer oaths, and must forward it to the collector of the district before the 10th day of the ensuing month.

Said affidavit may be in the following form:

I, ——— ———, do state on oath that I am ———, of the business of ———, wholesale dealer in denatured alcohol, and that the above is a true, correct, and complete transcript of the record showing the business done by ———, as such wholesale dealer in denatured alcohol, and that said record is in every respect a true and correct record of the business done by said dealer during the month of ———, 190—, and of the balance of alcohol on hand at the end of said month.

Subscribed and sworn to before me this —— day of ———.

——— ———.

Record always Open to Inspection of Officers.

SEC. 69. This record must be open at all times to the inspection of all internal revenue officers or agents. It must be preserved by the dealer for two years. Wholesale dealers in denatured alcohol must keep a sign in legible and durable letters posted in a conspicuous place on the outside of their building, as follows:

"Wholesale Dealer in Denatured Alcohol."

Bills of Lading, etc., to be Preserved by Dealers.

SEC. 70. All denaturers of alcohol and wholesale dealers in denatured alcohol must preserve for two years all bills of lading, express receipts, dray tickets, and other similar papers showing shipment of denatured alcohol, and such papers must be submitted to any internal-revenue officer or agent who makes request for same for inspection.

Assistance to be Furnished Officers.

SEC. 71. Dealers in denatured alcohol shall keep the permits issued to them posted in a conspicuous place. They must furnish internal-revenue officers or agents the help and all the facilities necessary to handle the packages of denatured alcohol when said officers are making inspections.

Retail Dealers to Keep Record.

Sec. 72. Retail dealers in denatured alcohol shall keep a record, in which they shall enter the date upon which they receive any package or packages of denatured alcohol, the person from whom received, the serial numbers of the packages, the serial numbers of the denatured alcohol stamps, the wine and proof gallons, and the date upon which packages are opened for retail.

The transcript of each month's business as shown by this record must be prepared, signed, and sworn to and forwarded to the collector of internal revenue of the district in which the dealer is located before the 10th of the following month. This transcript must be signed and sworn to by the dealer himself or by his duly authorized agent.

Labels to be Placed on Retail Packages.

Sec. 73. Retail dealers in denatured alcohol must provide themselves with labels upon which the words "Denatured Alcohol" have been printed in plain, legible letters. The printing shall be red on white. A label of this character must be affixed by the dealer to the container, whatever it may be, in the case of each sale of denatured alcohol made by him.

Stamps to be Destroyed when Package is Empty.

Sec. 74. As soon as the stamped packages of denatured alcohol are empty the dealer or manufacturer, as the case may be, must thoroughly obliterate and completely destroy all marks, stamps, and brands on the packages.

The stamps shall under no circumstances be reused, and the packages shall not be refilled until *all* the marks, stamps, and brands shall have been removed and destroyed.

Manufacturers Using Completely Denatured Alcohol to Secure Permit.

Sec. 75. Manufacturers desiring to use completely denatured alcohol, such as is put upon the market for sale generally, may use such alcohol in their business subject to the following restrictions:

A manufacturer using less than an average of 50 gallons of denatured alcohol per month will not be required to secure permit from the collector or to keep records or make returns showing the alcohol received and used.

Manufacturers who use as much as 50 gallons of completely denatured alcohol a month must procure such alcohol in stamped packages, and before beginning business the manufacturer must make application to the collector of the proper district for permit, in which application he will state the exact location of his place of business, describing the lot or tract of land upon which the plant is located, and must keep the alcohol in a locked room until used.

Sec. 76. The permit shall be in the following form:

PERMIT TO MANUFACTURER TO USE COMPLETELY DENATURED ALCOHOL.

It appearing upon application duly made by ———— ———— that, under the act of June 7, 1906, ———— ———— should be permitted to use completely denatured alcohol, in quantities of more than 50 gallons per month, at ————, factory of ———— ————, in the county of ————, State of ————, in the manufacture of ————, permission is hereby given said ———— ———— to procure completely denatured alcohol in stamped packages and use same in such manufacture at said place. This permit expires ———— ————, 190—.

———— ————,
Collector ———— District ————.

Every Facility for Examination to be Afforded Officers.

Sec. 77. Denaturers of alcohol, dealers in denatured alcohol, and persons who use it must afford every facility to revenue officers and employees whose duty it is to make investigation as regards such alcohol. The premises upon which the alcohol is denatured or sold or in any manner handled must be open at all hours of the day or night (if the same should be necessary) to revenue agents, inspectors, and deputy collectors; and all books, papers, or records of every kind, character, or description relating to the alcohol handled by such persons must be submitted to any revenue officer for inspection and the officer must be permitted to make transcripts or copies of such books or papers, provided in the discharge of his duty he finds it necessary.

Officer to Take Samples.

Sec. 78. Should any revenue officer for any reason suspect that any beverage or liquid medicinal preparation contains denatured alcohol, he must secure samples of the suspected goods and forward them to his superior officer, who will forward them to the proper chemist for analysis. Such samples should be so marked as to identify them. Any internal-revenue officer is authorized to take samples of denatured alcohol, wherever found, and at such times as it may be deemed necessary, said samples to be submitted to the proper official for examination. These samples will, under no circumstances, be more than will be needed for analysis or examination.

Part III.

SPECIAL DENATURANTS.

Sec. 79. As the agents adapted to and adopted for use in complete denatural tion render the alcohol denatured unfit for use in many industries in which ethyl-alcohol, withdrawn free of tax, can be profitably employed, therefore, in order to give full scope to the operation of the law, special denaturants will be authorized when absolutely necessary. Yet the strictest surveillance must be exercised in the handling of alcohol incompletely or specially denatured.

Formula for Special Denaturants to be Submitted to the Commissioner.

Sec. 80. The Commissioner of Internal Revenue will consider any formula for special denaturation that may be submitted by any manufacturer in any art or industry and will determine (1) whether or not the manufacture in which it is proposed to use the alcohol belongs to a class in which tax-free alcohol withdrawn under the provisions of this act can be used, (2) whether or not it is practicable to permit the use of the proposed denaturant and at the same time properly safeguard the revenue. But one special denaturant will be authorized for the same class of industries, unless it shall be shown that there is good reason for additional special denaturants.

The Commissioner will announce from time to time the formulas of denaturants that will be permitted in the several classes of industries in which tax-free alcohol can be used.

Application for Permits to Use Special Denaturants.

Sec. 81. Manufacturers desiring to use specially or incompletely denatured alcohol in their business must make application to the collector of internal revenue of the district in which the business is located. In this application the following information must be given: The location of the plant; the name and address of each partner or the corporate name, if a corporation; a complete description of each building on the manufacturing premises as to dimensions, partitions, apartments, or openings; a complete description of the room or place in which it is proposed to keep the denatured alcohol stored as to dimensions, openings, and kind of materials of which constructed; the kind of business carried on and in which it is proposed to use the denatured alcohol; the special denaturants desired to be used and the reasons for desiring to use such special denaturants; the quantity of denatured alcohol it is estimated will be used until the 1st of the next July following; and if alcohol is recovered in the process of manufacture, the manner in which it is recovered, its condition when recovered, and the percentage so recovered.

STOREROOM TO BE SET ASIDE—HOW CONSTRUCTED.

SEC. 82. A room or building must be prepared and set aside in which to store the denatured alcohol after it is brought upon the premises, and such room or building shall be numbered serially in each collection district.

Said room must be on the manufacturing premises, and it must be used for storage of denatured alcohol, alcohol recovered in the process of manufacture, for the work of restoring and redenaturing such recovered alcohol, and for no other purpose.

It must be securely constructed in such a manner as to render entrance impossible during the absence of the person in whose charge it is placed.

The doors and windows must be so constructed that they may be securely fastened. All necessary openings must be under a prescribed lock, the key to be kept by the person designated to have charge of the storeroom.

A sign, "Denatured Alcohol Storeroom No. —," must be placed over the main door of the room.

FORM OF APPLICATION, AND TO WHOM MADE.

SEC. 83. The application made to the collector by the manufacturer must be in duplicate and in the form prescribed below; and a diagram showing the buildings on the manufacturing premises and their relation to each other must accompany the notice:

NOTICE BY MANUFACTURERS.

Notice is hereby given that ——— ——— of the ——— of ——-—, county of ——— and State of ——— intend—, under the name or style of ——— ———, to carry on, after the —— day of ——— 190—, on the premises owned by ——— ———, situate No. —— street, in the ——— of ———, county of ——— and ——— of ———.

(Name of all partners interested in the business, if a firm, or name of corporation if a corporation, with residence.)

(Particular description of the lot or tract of land on which the buildings used in the business are located.)

(Size and description of all buildings on the manufacturing premises and material of which constructed. Purpose for which used.)

(Statement of the title under which the premises on which the manufacturing business is situated is held and the name or names of the owners thereof.)

Said ——— ———- desires to use specially denatured alcohol, at ——— proof, in manufacture of the said ———, the alcohol to be denatured by the use of the following agents as denaturants, ——— ———, and ha—— provided and set aside a storeroom on said premises in which to store said denatured alcohol, said storeroom being described as follows: ——— ———

It is estimated that ——— proof gallons of denatured alcohol will be used in the manner indicated between the —— day of ——— and the —— day of July, 190—.

Subscribed and sworn to before me this —— day of ———, 190—.

SEC. 84. This notice will be given in all cases before beginning business or before using specially denatured alcohol in said business, and on the first day of July of each succeeding year in cases where the business is continued.

The name of every person interested in the business as a partner must be stated in the proper space, except in the case of notices given by incorporated companies, when the names and addresses of the officers of the corporation should be given.

The signature to the notice when given by an individual must in all cases be made by the manufacturer in person, or in his name by his authorized agent or attorney in fact.

In case of a firm, the signature must be made in the firm name by a member of the firm or by some person duly authorized as above.

In case of a corporation, the signature must be made in the name and under the seal of the corporation by the proper officer thereof.

Collector to Cause Plant to be Inspected.

Sec. 85. Upon receipt of the foregoing notice the collector will, either by himself or one of his deputies, proceed to the manufacturing plant described in the application and notice and inspect same. He will ascertain whether or not the statements in the notice and representations on the accompanying diagram are true and correct, and if he finds they are, he will indorse on the notice the following:

I hereby certify that I have examined the premises of ———— ————, described in the within application and accompanying diagram, and I find the statements and representations therein made to be true and correct.

———— ————,
———— Collector, ———— District ————.

Collector to Examine Appplication.

Sec. 86. One copy of the application will be retained by the collector and the other will be forwarded to the Commissioner of Internal Revenue. The collector will examine the application and will determine—

First. Whether alcohol withdrawn from bond free of tax under the provisions of this act can be used in the manufacture of the article or articles it is proposed to manufacture at said place.

Second. Whether the denaturants proposed have been authorized by the Commissioner of Internal Revenue for the class of industry in question.

Third. Whether the premises can, under these regulations, be used for the storage of denatured alcohol—that is to say, whether or not they come within one of the classes of premises upon which denatured alcohol cannot be stored.

Fourth. Whether the room in which it is proposed to store the denatured alcohol to be brought upon the premises and used for manufacturing purposes, as indicated, is safe and secure and meets the requirements of the regulations.

If the collector finds favorably on all the above propositions he will approve the application.

Sec. 87. If the industry in which it is proposed to use the denatured alcohol has not been held by the Commissioner of Internal Revenue to be an industry in which alcohol withdrawn under the provisions of this act can be used, or if the proposed formula of denaturants has not been duly authorized, the collector will take no action upon the application until the Commissioner has passed upon it and has duly advised him.

Manufacturers to Give Bond.

Sec. 88. If the application is approved the manufacturer shall at once be notified, but before the use of specially denatured alcohol is permitted on the premises, or at the place designated in the application, the manufacturer shall file with the collector a bond in the prescribed form, said bond to be renewed annually on the first day of July and to run until the first day of the following July.

FORM OF MANUFACTURER'S BOND.

Know all men by these presents, that ———— ————, of ————, as principal, and ———— ————, of ———— and ———— ———— of ————, as sureties, are held and firmly bound unto the United States of America in the sum of ——— dollars, to be paid to the said United States; for the payment whereof we bind ourselves, our heirs, executors, and administrators, jointly and severally, firmly by these presents.

Witness our hands and seals this —— day ———, nineteen hundred and——.

The condition of this obligation is such that whereas the above-bounden principal is engaged in the business of manufacturing ——— ——— at ———, in the county of ———, State of ———, and intends to use in said manufacture alcohol withdrawn from bond free of tax and denatured in the following manner: ——— said alcohol so denatured to be secured from any distiller with whom the said principal can make satisfactory arrangements and transported from denaturing bonded warehouse to said principal's manufacturing premises above described.

Now, therefore, if the entire quantity of alcohol so secured at denaturing bonded warehouse or warehouses is transported to the place of business of the said ——— ———, and is securely stored in the denatured alcohol storeroom designated and set aside as such at said place and is there safely kept until it is needed for use in the manufacture of ——— by said ——— ——— and is used by said ——— ——— for the purposes specified and for no other purposes, and if the said ——— ———, or their agents or employees, shall faithfully comply with all the requirements and regulations prescribed by the Commissioner of Internal Revenue and approved by the Secretary of the Treasury in relation to the transporting of denatured alcohol from denaturing bonded warehouses to manufacturing establishments, the storing of said alcohol on manufacturing premises, and the keeping of records and the making of returns and reports, then this obligation to be void, otherwise to remain in full force and effect.

And the obligors for themselves, their heirs, executors, administrators and assigns, do further covenant and agree with the United States, in case said denatured alcohol, or any part thereof, is diverted from the purpose for which it is intended, either in transit from the denaturing bonded warehouse to the manufacturing establishment, or after it has been stored in said manufacturing establishment, or shall be used for any purposes other than those specified above, well and truly to pay, or cause to be paid, to the collector aforesaid double the legal tax on the whole amount of alcohol so wrongfully diverted and used.

The true intent of this obligation is that it will operate both as a transporting and a warehousing bond. Liability under it is to attach as soon as *any* alcohol specially denatured at *any* denaturing bonded warehouse shall leave said warehouse to be transported to the manufacturing premises of the principal herein. It is to cover said alcohol while in transit to said manufacturing establishment and after it is stored in the designated storeroom at said establishment. It is intended to save the United States harmless because of any neglect or wrongful act on the part of the principal or any of ——— agents or employees done in connection with or in relation to said denatured alcohol, no matter whether said act or acts be the independent act of the principal or his agents, or in act or acts done pursuant to a conspiracy or an agreement with some officer or agent of the United States.

———— ————.
———— ————.
———— ————.

Signed, sealed, and delivered in the presence of—

———— ————.

The penal sum of this bond shall be the amount of the tax on the estimated quantity of denatured alcohol that the manufacturer will use during the year the bond is intended to cover, and at no time shall the manufacturer have on his premises a quantity of denatured alcohol the tax upon which is more than one-half of the penal sum of the bond. The manufacturer may, at any time it may appear that the bond for any year is insufficient, give an additional bond.

There must be at least two sureties to the bond and they must make the usual affidavit on Form No. 33, unless under authority contained in the act of August 13, 1894, a corporation duly authorized in writing by the Attorney-General of the United States to do business under said act shall be offered as sole surety.

The Christian names of the signers must be written in the body of the bond and so signed to the bond. The residence of each signer must be stated in the boy of the bond.

Each signature must be in the presence of two witnesses, who must sign their names as such, and a seal of wax or wafer must be attached to each signature.

COLLECTOR TO APPROVE BOND.

SEC. 89. The bond, after being duly executed, will be deposited with the collector of internal revenue, who will examine it carefully. He will also investigate as to the solvency of the sureties. If he finds the bond to be sufficient, he will approve it and forward it to the Commissioner of Internal Revenue, together with his certificate to the effect that he has examined the bond and finds it made in accordance with the regulations, and that the sureties are sufficient.

If upon receipt and examination of the bond the Commissioner approves it, he will notify the collector, and thereafter, during the life of the bond, it will be lawful for the manufacturer to receive and transport to his manufacturing premises from any distiller who is a denaturer of alcohol, alcohol denatured in the manner prescribed in the application and bond.

COLLECTOR TO ISSUE PERMIT.

SEC. 90. Upon the approval of the bond, the collector shall issue a permit to the manufacturer, which shall be numbered serially and shall be in the following form:

MANUFACTURER'S PERMIT.

This is to certify, whereas ——— ———, manufacturers of ———, in the county of ———, State of ———, on the —— day of ———, 190—, made application for permit to use alcohol denatured in special manner, to wit, by the use of ———, and the said application having been approved, said manufacturers gave bond as required by law, and the same has been approved.

Therefore the said manufacturers are hereby authorized and permission is hereby given them to receive and have transported to their premises and stored in their designated storeroom for denatured alcohol, alcohol denatured in the manner above indicated.

This permit expires July 1, 190—.

——— ———,
Collector District ———.

MANUFACTURER TO GIVE NOTICE OF DENATURER FROM WHOM ALCOHOL IS SECURED.

SEC. 91. Manufacturers who have given bond and received the permit and are thereafter authorized under the restrictions herein prescribed to use alcohol denatured with special denaturants may secure from any distiller who is a denaturer of alcohol the alcohol to be used in said business.

The manufacturer shall give notice to the collector of the district in which his establishment is located in the following form in duplicate if the manufacturing establishment and the denaturing bonded warehouse at which the alcohol is denatured are in the same collection district, and in triplicate if they are in different districts.

———
Collector, District of ———:

You are hereby notified that I have arranged with ——— ———, proprietor of distillery No. ———, located at ———, in the district of ———, to supply ——— ——— from denaturing bonded warehouse No. ———, located at ———, in the —— district of ———, with alcohol denatured in accordance with the terms of —— application approved on the —— day of ———, 190—, in the following manner, to wit: ——— Said alcohol to be used in the manufacture of ———

in ——— establishment located at ———, in the district of ———. The alcohol is to be transported to ——— premises by ——— and ———.

(Signed) ——— ———.

Upon receipt of this notice the collector shall retain one copy in his office. The other copy he shall forward to the Commissioner of Internal Revenue, and, if the manufacturing establishment and the warehouse at which the alcohol is to be denatured are in different districts, the third copy shall be forwarded to the collector of the district in which the denaturing bonded warehouse is located.

Notice to Officer at Denaturing Bonded Warehouse.

Sec. 92. The collector of the district in which the denaturing bonded warehouse is located shall forward to the officer in charge of said warehouse a notice in the following form:

You are hereby notified that ——— ———, manufacturer of ———, located at ———, in the district of ———, ha— been duly authorized to use in the manufacture of said ——— at said establishment alcohol specially denatured in the following manner, ——— and the said ——— ha— given notice that —— he —— ha—— arranged with ——— ———, proprietor of distillery No. ——, to supply alcohol so denatured from denaturing bonded warehouse No. ——, in the ——— District of ———.

You are hereby authorized to permit said distiller to withdraw from bond, free of tax, alcohol to be denatured in the manner indicated, the quantity to be withdrawn during the current fiscal year not to exceed ——— gallons.

——— ———,
Collector, District ——.

Regulations Prescribed in Case of Completely Denatured Alcohol to Apply.

Sec. 93. The regulations prescribing the manner in which alcohol is to be withdrawn from warehouse, transferred to denaturing bonded warehouse and dumped, the manner in which the denaturants are to be brought upon the premises, stored and tested, in the case of completely denatured alcohol, apply in case of specially denatured alcohol; likewise the regulations prescribing the manner in which completely denatured alcohol is to be drawn off, after being denatured, gauged, marked, etc., apply in case of specially denatured alcohol. In the case of specially denatured alcohol the following marks, in addition to those prescribed for completely denatured alcohol, must be put upno the stamp-head.

Denatured for ———, proprietor of storeroom for specially denatured alcohol, No. —— in the district of ———.

Special and Complete Denaturants Not to be Mixed.

Sec. 94. In no case is completely denatured alcohol to be mixed with specially denatured alcohol and special denaturants are to be kept completely separate from denaturants used in complete denaturation. The officer in charge of the warehouse must be careful to see that denaturing material tanks are empty before any special or complete denaturing agents are dumped. Likewise he must be careful to see that the mixing tanks are empty before any dumps, either for special or complete denaturation, are made.

Specially Denatured Alcohol to be at Once Put in Transit.

Sec. 95. As soon as specially denatured alcohol is gauged and the packages are properly marked and stamped, it must be removed from the denaturing bonded warehouse and put in transit to the manufacturer for whom it was denatured, and under no circumstances must any other disposition be made of any part of it.

Reports at Warehouse, etc.

SEC. 96. Reports, records, etc., relating to the alcohol after it has been denatured, and to be made and kept by the officer and the distiller, must, in the case of specially denaturated alcohol, contain columns and spaces for showing and must show the name and address and number of the manufacturer to whom the alcohol was sold, and the following additional reports must be made by the officer and the distiller:

———— ————

Collector ———— *District of* ————.

You are hereby notified that I have this day delivered to ———— ————, proprietor of distillery No. ————, district of ————, the following packages of specially denatured alcohol:

Number of Packages.	Serial Number, Packages.	Serial Number, Stamps.	Wine Gallons.	Proof Gallons.

Said alcohol was denatured at ———— denaturing bonded warehouse No. ————, located at ————, in the ———— district of ————, and it was disposed of to ———— ————, proprietor of manufacturer's storeroom No. ————, located at ————, in the district of ————, in accordance with specifications as stated in the notice of ———— ————, 190—, and it has this day been forwarded to ———— ————, at ————, by ———— ————, there to be delivered to said manufacturer.

———— ————,
United States Officer.

This report shall be made in triplicate, one copy to be sent to the collector of the district in which the denaturing bonded warehouse is located, one to the collector of the district in which the manufacturing establishment is located, and one to the Commissioner of Internal Revenue.

Notice of Shipment of Specially Denatured Alcohol.

SEC. 97. The distiller shall prepare and forward a report in the following form:

———— ————,

Collector;

You are hereby notified that I have this day received from ———— ———— denaturing bonded warehouse No. ————, located at ————, in the ———— district of ————, the packages of specially denatured alcohol described below and have forwarded them to ———— ————, manufacturer of ————, and proprietor of manufacturer's storeroom for specially denatured alcohol No. ————, located at ————, in the district of ————.

Number of Packages.	Serial Number, Packages.	Serial Number, Stamps.	Wine Gallons.	Proof Gallons.

———— ————,
Proprietor of Distillery No. ————.

Alcohol to be Promptly Forwarded and Notice of Receipt Given.

SEC. 98. It shall be the duty of the officer in charge and the distiller to see that the denatured alcohol is promptly delivered from the denaturing bonded warehouse to the common carrier.

The manufacturer must immediately upon the receipt of the alcohol store it in his designated storeroom for denatured alcohol, and must at once prepare report in the following form:

NOTICE OF RECEIPT OF ALCOHOL.

OFFICE OF ——— ———,
——— ———.

——— ———,
Collector ——— *District* ———:

You are hereby notified that I have this day received from ——— ———, carrier, the packages of denatured alcohol hereinafter described, received at ——— on the ——— day of ———, 190—, by ——— ———, from ——— ———, proprietor of distillery No. ———, in the ——— district of ———, and denatured at ——— in denaturing bonded warehouse No. ———, in the ——— district of ——— in accordance with the formula authorized on the ——— day of ———, 190—. Said alcohol has been stored in designated storeroom for specially denatured alcohol on ——— premises and will not be removed from there except as it is needed for use in the manufacture of ———. Said storeroom is in the custody and control of ——— ———.

Respectfully,

——— ———, *Manufacturer.*

This report shall be made in duplicate, one copy to be forwarded to the collector of the district in which the alcohol was denatured and the other to the collector of the district in which the manufacturing plant is located.

MANUFACTURER'S ALCOHOL RECORD.

SEC. 99. The manufacturer must keep a record in which he shall enter on the "Received" side the date upon which he receives any denatured alcohol on his premises, the number of packages received and the name and address of the distiller, the district in which denatured, the name of the officer who gauged the alcohol, the serial numbers of the packages, the serial numbers of the denatured alcohol stamps, the number of wine gallons, and the number of proof gallons.

These entries must be made at the time the denatured alcohol is received in the storeroom and before any of it is withdrawn from the packages or is used in manufacture.

On the "Disposed-of" side of the record must be entered the denatured alcohol used in manufacture. The entries must show the date upon which any packages of denatured alcohol are broken for use in manufacture, the number of packages, the name and address of the distiller who denatured the alcohol, the name of the officer who affixed the denatured alcohol stamp, the serial numbers of the packages, the serial numbers of the denatured alcohol stamps, the wine gallons, and the proof-gallons contents of the packages.

This record must have spaces and columns in which can be entered the number of packages and the quantity in wine and proof gallons of unbroken packages brought over in stock from previous month, of broken packages brought over from previous month, total of such packages brought over, of packages received during the month, of packages used during the month, of unbroken packages on hand at the end of the month, of broken packages on hand at the close of the month, and the total on hand at the end of the month.

TRANSCRIPT TO BE MADE OF RECORD.

SEC. 100. A transcript of this record must be prepared, sworn to, and forwarded to the collector of internal revenue of the district for each month before the tenth day of the following month.

The affidavit above referred to must be in the following form:

STATE OF ———,
COUNTY OF ———.

On this day personally appeared before me ——— ———, duly designated custodian of the storeroom for specially denatured alcohol No. ——— of the ——— district of ———, of denatured alcohol received and to be used at the manufacturing establishment of ——— ———, manufacturer of ———, at ———, in the county of ———, State of ———, and on oath states that the above is a true and correct statement on the debit side of the specially denatured alcohol received in said storeroom, and on the credit side, of the specially denatured alcohol charged off for use in manufacturing ——— at said manufacturing establishment, and that all of the alcohol delivered from said storeroom was delivered in exactly the same condition as when received at said storeroom and was delivered for use in manufacturing ——— and was so used.

——— ———, *Custodian* ———.

Subscribed and sworn to before me this —— day of ———, 190—.

This affidavit must be made by the person who has the custody of the storeroom, whether it be the manufacturer himself or one of his employees.

Manufacturer's Record of Alcohol Used and Articles Produced.

Sec. 101. The manufacturer must also keep a book in which shall be entered the quantity of goods produced and finished each month and in which specially denatured alcohol was used, and at the close of business each month and before the 10th of the following month the manufacturer must make and forward to the collector of internal revenue a transcript of this record and must affix an affidavit in the following form:

State of———,
County of ———.

On this day personally appeared before me ——— ———, who on oath states that the above is a true, correct, and complete statement of the goods manufactured during the month last past and in the manufacture of which denatured alcohol was used at the place of business of ———, located at ———, in the county of ———, State of ———.

Subscribed and sworn to before me this —— day of ———, 190—.

This affidavit must be made by the manufacturer himself, the manager of the business, superintendent, bookkeeper, or other person who has knowledge of the facts.

Care should be taken to see that both of the above-prescribed records and the reports made therefrom are in every respect true and correct. Failure to keep these records correctly and to make correct reports from them promptly as prescribed by these regulations is a breach of the bond required of the manufacturer and he incurs the liabilities growing out of such breach.

The affidavits may be made before any revenue officer authorized under the law to administer oaths. Such officer is not permitted to make any charge for such service. In the event it is not practicable to have these returns sworn to before a revenue officer they may be sworn to before any officer authorized by State or Federal law to administer oaths.

Custodian of Storeroom to be Designated.

Sec. 102. The manufacturer must either be the custodian in person of the storeroom for specially denatured alcohol or he must designate some one of his employees to be the custodian. The manufacturer must notify the collector of the district of the person who has been designated as the custodian of the storeroom, and if for any reason a change is made the collector must be promptly notified.

No one must be permitted to go into the storeroom in the absence of the custodian. The door of the storeroom must be provided with suitable lock for securely fastening it, and the custodian must carry the key to the lock. It will be his duty, together with the manufacturer (provided he is an employee and not the manufacturer), to see that none of the denatured alcohol brought upon the premises is diverted from the use for which it was denatured. He must keep the denatured-alcohol storeroom record herein provided for and must prepare, sign, and swear to the returns.

If the manufacturer is a corporation the custodian of the storeroom for specially denatured alcohol and the person who is to keep the record of denatured alcohol used and articles manufactured and make the returns herein prescribed must be named by the board of directors or other governing power and a certified copy of the minutes of the meeting at which said persons were so designated must be forwarded to the collector of the district.

Manager to Make Affidavit.

Sec. 103. The manufacturer or the manager of the business, provided the manufacturer is a corporation, must, in the event some one other than himself keeps one or both of the records and makes one or both of the returns herein prescribed, make the following affidavit to such of the returns as he does not personally prepare and swear to.

State of ———,
County of ———.

I, ——— ———, state on oath that I am ——— ——— of the business of ——— and that from my knowledge of said business gained as such ———, I verily believe the above stated accounts are correct and that the above affidavit of ——— ——— is in every particular true.

———————,
—————— ———.

Subscribed and sworn to before me this ——— day of ——, 190—.

Collector to Keep Record of Manufacturer's Operations.

Sec. 104. The collectors of internal revenue of the several districts shall keep in a record specially prepared for the purpose an account of each manufacturer in the district using specially denatured alcohol.

Said record shall be made up from the reports of officer showing the shipment of denatured alcohol to the manufacturer, and the reports of the manufacturer on the proper forms.

Said record must show the date upon which any alcohol was shipped from the denaturing bonded warehouse, the date it was received by the manufacturer, the name of the distiller, the location and number of the denaturing bonded warehouse at which it was denatured, the number of packages in the lot, the serial numbers of such packages, the serial numbers of the denatured alcohol stamps, the wine gallons, and the proof gallons.

Said record must also show the number of packages, serial numbers of such packages, serial numbers of the stamps and quantity of alcohol charged off for use in the manufacturing business, and the quantity used in such business. It must also show the quantity of the manufactured article in proper denominations produced each month. There must also be columns and spaces in which to enter the quantity of alcohol on hand in unbroken packages at the beginning of the month, the quantity in broken packages, the quantity received during the month, the quantity used in the business during the month, the quantity on hand in broken packages at the close of the month, the quantity on hand in unbroken packages, and the total quantity on hand.

Alcohol to be Used as Received.

Sec. 105. Specially denatured acohol must be used in the manufacture of the products exactly as stated in the manufacturer's application and in the collector's permit, and it cannot be used in any other manner, and manufacturers using such alcohol must complete the work of manufacture of the products specified in their notice and bond on the premises upon which they are authorized by their permit to use alcohol.

Manufacturer Quitting Business May Dispose of Alcohol to Other Manufacturer.

Sec. 106. In the event any manufacturer using specially denatured alcohol for any reason quits the business of manufacturing the commodities authorized by his permit and there remains on hand in his storeroom a quantity of specially denatured alcohol, he may dispose of such alcohol to another manufacturer in the same class of business provided he gives notice to the collector of internal revenue. When such notice is given, a deputy collector or other officer will visit the manufacturer's place of business and check the alcohol on hand against the manufacturer's record. If the quantity on hand is found to agree with the manufacturer's record and the alcohol is in the same condition as it was when denatured, the officer will report to the collector, who will issue a permit authorizing the transfer of the denatured alcohol to the premises of the manufacturer to whom the alcohol has been disposed of. The purchaser must be a regularly qualified manufacturer and must be authorized to use alcohol specially denatured in the manner and under the formula under which the alcohol transferred was denatured.

Provisions Applicable to Manufacturers Using Either Specially or Generally Denatured Alcohol.

Sec. 107. Under no circumstances will denaturers, manufacturers, or dealers, or any other persons, in any manner treat either specially or completely denatured alcohol by adding anything to it or taking anything from it until it is ready for the use for which it is to be employed. It must go into manufacture or consumption in exactly the same condition that it was when it left the denaturer. Diluting completely denatured alcohol will be held to be such manipulation as is forbidden by law.

Sec. 108. Manufacturers using either specially or completely denatured alcohol must store it in the storeroom set apart for that purpose, the place for deposit named in the bond and application, and nowhere else. Likewise they must deposit recovered alcohol in said storeroom as fast as it is recovered. It will be held to be a breach of the bond and a violation of the law if any alcohol of any kind, character, or description should be found stored at any other place on the premises.

Collector to be Notified of Change in Plant.

Sec. 109. If there are any material changes in the manufacturing establishments at which either specially or completely denatured alcohol (where permit is required) is used, either in the plant or in the methods of manufacture, or if there is any change in the ownership of the establishment, new application must at once be filed, new bond given (if bond is necessary), and new permit granted by the collector.

Sec. 110. Persons who use alcohol denatured in any manner except as is expressly authorized by the law will be held to be liable for double the amount of the tax on all the alcohol so used, in addition to the penalties, civil and criminal, expressly provided by the act of June 7, 1906.

Part IV.

ALCOHOL RECOVERED, RESTORED, AND REDENATURED.

Sec. 111. Section 2 of the denatured alcohol law provides:

That manufacturers employing processes in which alcohol used free of tax under the provisions of this act is expressed or evaporated from the articles manufactured shall be permitted to recover such alcohol and to have such alcohol restored to a condition suitable solely for reuse in manufacturing processes under such regulations as the Commissioner of Internal Revenue, with the approval of the Secretary of the Treasury, shall prescribe.

Alcohol to be Restored on Premises Where Used or in a Restoring Plant.

Sec. 112. The work of recovering alcohol and restoring it to conditions suitable for reuse in manufacturing processes must be done on the premises on which said alcohol was originally used or at a duly authorized restoring plant, and it must be reused in the same manufacturing establishment in which it was originally used (except as provided in Part V of these Regulations).

Still May be Used.

Sec. 113. If in restoring alcohol to a condition suitable for reuse a still is necessary, the manufacturer may set up on his premises such still and any other apparatus that may be necessary for use in connection with or independent of the still in the work of recovering such alcohol. The still must be registered in the same manner in which the law and regulations require that all stills set up be registered. It cannot be used for any other purpose than to recover by redistilling alcohol that has been withdrawn from bond free of tax for denaturing purposes, denatured, and then used by the manufacturer.

Application to be Used.

Sec. 114. A manufacturer desiring to recover and reuse such alcohol must in his application for permit to use denatured alcohol in his business, in addition to the statements required to be made in said application, state fully the manner in which he intends to recover alcohol, the condition as to proof, purity, etc., of the alcohol when it is recovered, the percentage of alcohol used in said business which he proposes to recover, and the estimated quantity in proof gallons of alcohol he expects to recover during the year. If it is necessary before redenaturing said alcohol to redistil or otherwise treat it in order to restore it to a condition suitable as to proof and purity for use in the particular manufacture for which it is intended, the process must be explained, and if a still is used the capacity of the still must be set out in full and the other apparatus used in connection with the still must be described.

The application for permit must, in addition to the form heretofore prescribed (see Sec. 83), contain the following:

Said ———— ———— desires to recover alcohol used in said business in the following manner, ————: The condition of said alcohol when recovered as to purity and proof will be ————; the percentage of alcohol used in said business which said ———— ———— expects to recover is ————, and the total quantity —he— expect— to recover during the year beginning with July 1, 190—, is ———— proof gallons. In the process of restoring alcohol to a condition suitable for use, the following apparatus will be used, ———— and the said ———— ———— desires to re-denature the alcohol so recovered or restored, provided redenaturation is necessary, in the storeroom for denatured alcohol on said premises in the following manner ————:

The bond prescribed in the case of manufacturers using specially denatured alcohol (see Sec. 88) must, in addition to the provisions in the form set out, contain the following additional provisions:

And whereas the said ———— ———— proposes to recover alcohol used in said manufacture in the following manner ————, said alcohol when so recovered to be in the following condition as to proof, etc., ————, and proposes to restore said alcohol to a condition suitable for reuse in the following manner ————, and proposes to redenature said alcohol so recovered and restored, provided redenaturation is necessary, before reusing same in the storeroom for denatured alcohol on said premises.

Now therefore if the said ———— ———— shall remove all of said alcohol so recovered and restored to a condition suitable for reuse to ———— storeroom for denatured alcohol on said premises as soon as it is so recovered and restored, shall safely keep said alcohol in said storeroom until it shall have been redenatured, provided redenaturation is necessary, shall pay double the tax of one dollar and ten cents on each proof gallon of all alcohol recovered and reused in any manner without having first been redenatured, and shall fully, promptly, and faithfully comply with all the law and regulations relating to the recovering and restoring to a condition fit for reuse and the redenaturing of alcohol that has been withdrawn from bond without the payment of the tax.

Bond to be Executed by Manufacturer Using Completely Denatured Alcohol.

SEC. 115. No manufacturer's transportation and storage bond being required of a manufacturer using in his business completely denatured alcohol, in case such manufacturer desires to recover and redenature such alcohol so that it may be reused he must execute a bond containing the provisions of the two above prescribed paragraphs. The penal sum of said bond shall be double the tax on the alcohol it is estimated the manufacturer will recover and redenature in thirty days. Said bond must be executed in duplicate and must be approved by the collector of the district in the same manner as manufacturer's bonds heretofore prescribed. He must also provide storeroom for the denatured alcohol used by him and must designate some one to act as custodian thereof, and he must keep such records and make such returns as are required in case of manufacturers using specially denatured alcohol.

The permit issued to the manufacturer by the collector must contain, in addition to what is contained in the form heretofore prescribed, the following:

And the said ———— ———— is hereby further authorized and permission is given ———— to recover and restore to a condition suitable for use in said manufacture alcohol in the following manner ———— ————. Said alcohol must be stored in the denatured-alcohol storeroom on said manufacturer's premises and must be redenatured in said storeroom before it is reused, provided redenaturation is necessary.

Alcohol to be Stored in Storeroom as Recovered.

SEC. 116. The manufacturer must draw off the alcohol as it is recovered into packages and must immediately store it in exactly the same condition as it is when recovered in the storeroom for denatured alcohol, and it shall thereafter be in charge of the custodian of said warehouse. Alcohol recovered at such establishment and placed in the warehouse for denatured alcohol will not be redistilled or otherwise treated except in the presence of the proper officer.

Still Used for Recovering Alcohol Only, etc.

SEC. 117. The still employed in redistillation will not be used for any purpose except to redistil alcohol for redenaturation, and it will not be used except in the presence of the proper officer. When the still is not being used the furnace door or cocks controlling the steam connections will be securely locked and the collector will keep the keys to said locks in his possession.

Application to have Alcohol Restored and Redenatured.

SEC. 118. At such intervals as the necessities of the business may demand, and when the manufacturer has a sufficient quantity of recovered alcohol on hand to justify the sending of an officer to his place of business, he may make application to the collector of the district for an officer to be detailed to supervise the work of redistilling or otherwise treating the recovered alcohol and the redenaturing of it. Such application will be in the following form:

———— ————,
Collector ———— *District of* ————:
You are hereby notified that there is stored in the storeroom for denatured alcohol on the manufacturing premises of ———— gallons of alcohol, ———— proof, which was

withdrawn from bond, free of tax, and denatured, and which was used in the process of manufacturing ——— and recovered at said place. Request is hereby made that an officer be sent to said place of business to supervise the work of restoring and redenaturing said alcohol.

——— ———,
Manufacturer.

COLLECTOR TO DETAIL OFFICER TO VISIT MANUFACTUREING PLANT.

SEC. 119. Upon receipt of the manufacturer's notice the collector will detail an officer to proceed to the manufacturing premises in question and supervise the work of restoring to suitable condition and redenaturing the alcohol mentioned in the notice. The instructions of the collector shall be in the following form:

——— ———,
‘——— ———.

——— ———, manufacturer of ———, and proprietor of storeroom for the denatured alcohol No. —, in this district, located at ———, has notified me that ——— ——— ha— stored in ——— storeroom ——— gallons of alcohol of ——— proof, recovered in process of manufacture, and ——— desire ——— to have said alcohol restored to a condition suitable for use in the manufacture of ——— and redenatured (if necessary) in the following manner ——— at said storeroom.

You are hereby instructed to proceed at once to said manufacturing establishment and supervise the work of restoring and redenaturing said alcohol in the manner indicated. You will gauge, mark, stamp, and brand the packages of redenatured alcohol and will make due return of same.

——— ———,
Collector ——— *District of* ———.

OFFICER TO VISIT MANUFACTURING ESTABLISHMENT.

SEC. 120. Upon receipt of these instructions the officer will proceed at once to the manufacturing establishment, and will supervise the work of restoring and redenaturing the alcohol in accordance with the regulations.

The agents to be used in redenaturing must be brought into the storeroom and must be inspected by the officer immediately upon his arrival there. He must take samples of each denaturant and forward them, properly marked and labeled, to the nearest laboratory. If the denaturants are in two or more packages he must secure an equal part from each package so that the sample will be a respresentative one.

The packages or tanks containing the denaturants must be sealed and must remain sealed until the officer receives the report upon the samples sent.

SEC. 121. If the report is favorable to the samples, the officer in charge of the storeroom may, after the receipt of the report, permit the denaturing agents to be used in accordance with the general or special specifications, as the case may be, in redenaturing alcohol at said storeroom.

If the report is unfavorable the proposed denaturants shall at once be removed from the storeroom by the manufacturer.

While the officer is at the manufacturing establishment supervising the work of restoring and redenaturing the alcohol, the storeroom will be in his custody and he must carry the key to it.

RESTORING, REDENATURING, AND GAUGING THE ALCOHOL.

SEC. 122. The process of restoring the alcohol to a condition suitable for use will be carried on in the presence and under the supervision of the officer. If in the process of restoring the alcohol to a condition suitable for reuse it is necessary to remove it from the storeroom, it will be returned to said storeroom as rapidly as it is restored and drawn off into suitable packages. The officer will, in having the packages filled with the restored alcohol, leave a wantage equal in volume to the denaturants to be added. He will ascertain by weight the wine and proof gallons in each package before any denaturant has been added. He will then cause the denaturants to be added to the package and will gauge, mark, stamp, and brand the package of redenatured alcohol.

The same kind of packages and stamps prescribed by these regulations for alcohol denatured at denaturing bonded warehouses will be used for alcohol redenatured at storerooms for denatured alcohol. Packages of redenatured alcohol shall be numbered serially, beginning with number one, at each storeroom.

PACKAGES TO BE MARKED, STAMPED, AND BRANDED.

Sec. 123. The officer shall put the following marks, stamps, etc., on the package when he gauges it:

On the stamp head he shall stencil the following:

The serial number of the package, the date of redenaturation and gauge, the wine gallons, proof and proof gallons, the name of the manufacturer and the number of the storeroom, the State and the district, the name and title of the officer, and the number of the denatured alcohol stamp affixed to the package. The words "Redenatured alcohol" must be placed upon each head of the package.

The stamp must be affixed and signed by the officer. The stamps will be furnished by the collector as they are needed, and the officer must take the books of unused stamps with him when he has finished the work of restoring and redenaturing alcohol and return them to the collector.

OFFICER TO MAKE RETURN AND KEEP RECORD.

Sec. 124. Having gauged and marked the several packages of redenatured alcohol the officer will make return of such gauge, wherein he will show in proper columns in detail the capacity of each package, its gross weight, tare, net weight, indication, temperature, net wine gallons contents, proof and proof gallons contents before the denaturants were added, the net wine, proof and proof gallons contents after the denaturants were added, apparent proof, apparent proof gallons contents, the serial number of the package, and the serial number of the denatured alcohol stamp affixed to it.

Sec. 125. The officer shall keep a record in which he shall enter in proper columns and spaces in detail on the debit side the quantity of recovered alcohol in wine and proof gallons found in the storeroom when he arrived at the establishment, the quantity in wine and proof gallons of alcohol restored each day, the manner in which said alcohol was restored, the quantity in wine and (if possible) proof gallons of the several denaturants used each day, the kind of denaturants used, and the numbers of denaturant samples sent to the laboratory.

On the credit side shall be entered in the proper columns, the date upon which any alcohol is redenatured, the number of packages, the serial numbers of the packages, the serial numbers of the denatured alcohol stamps on said packages, and the wine and proof gallons.

OFFICER TO MAKE REPORT OF OPERATIONS AT STOREROOM.

Sec. 126. At the end of each month, or as soon as the work of restoring the alcohol to suitable condition and the redenaturing of it is completed, the officer must make a transcript in duplicate from this record and forward it to the collector.

MANUFACTURER TO KEEP RECORD.

Sec. 127. The manufacturer must keep a record in which he shall enter daily in proper spaces and columns the quantity in wine and proof gallons of alcohol recovered by him and placed in storeroom, the quantity of denaturants placed in said storeroom for redenaturing purposes, and the quantity of alcohol, in wine and proof gallons, restored to a condition suitable for use, and the quantity of each denaturant used.

He shall also enter in said record daily the quantity of alcohol redenatured in his storeroom, the serial numbers of the packages, the serial numbers of the denatured alcohol stamps, and the wine and proof gallons of the redenatured alcohol.

Manufacturer to Make Transcript and Report.

Sec. 128. He must prepare a transcript of this record at the end of the month, and before the 10th day of the following month he must swear to same and forward it to the collector of internal revenue. The affidavits to this report must be made by the custodian of the storeroom and the manager of the business and must be in the following form:

State of ———,

County of ———:

I, ——————, state on oath that I am custodian of the storeroom for denatured alcohol, No. ——, at the manufacturing establishment of ——— ———, manufacturers of ——— at ———, in the county of ———, State of ———, and that the above is a true, correct, and complete statement of the alcohol withdrawn from bond, free of tax, and denatured at denaturing bonded warehouse, recovered in said manufacturing establishment, restored to condition suitable for reuse at said place and redenatured in said storeroom for denatured alcohol (or that such redenaturation was not found necessary), and that no alcohol which was recovered and restored at said place was used in any manner until after it had been redenatured, nor was any redenatured alcohol used in any manner except in the manufacture of ——— at said place.

——— ———,
Custodian Storeroom No. ——.

I, ——— ———, state on oath that I am ——— ———, of the above-described business, and from my knowledge of the business I believe the above report of business done to be true, correct, and complete, and the statements contained in the above affidavit of ——— ———, custodian at said storeroom, to be in every respect true and correct.

——— ———,
——— ———.

The above two affidavits were subscribed and sworn to before me this —— day of ———, 190—.

——— ———.

Manufacturer to Make Entry in Record of Alcohol Received and Disposed of, etc.

Sec. 129. The manufacturer must also enter on his record of denatured alcohol received and disposed of the packages of alcohol redenatured at said storeroom. On the "Received" side of said record must be shown the date upon which the alcohol was received from redenaturation. The alcohol must be treated in the same manner on said record as it was when received originally.

In the summary on said record the quantity of alcohol received from redenaturation and reused must be shown in items separate from the denatured acohol coming into the stock originally from dealers and denaturers.

Collector to Keep Account with Manufacturer of Alcohol Restored.

Sec. 130. The collector must keep an account with each manufacturer who recovers, restores, and redenatures alcohol. This record must be made from the reports of the chemist, officer in charge of the storeroom, and manufacturer. It must show the quantity of alcohol recovered and deposited in storeroom each day, the quantity restored to a condition suitable for reuse, the quantity and kind of denaturants used in denaturing said alcohol, the name of the officer supervising the restoring of and redenaturing of said alcohol, the number of packages and the serial number of same, and the quantity in wine and proof gallons of alcohol redenatured, gauged, and delivered to the manufacturer for reuse.

Alcohol not to be Redenatured unless Necessary.

Sec. 131. Manufacturers who recover alcohol will not be required to have said alcohol redenatured if it retains a sufficient quantity of the original denaturants to prevent its use as a beverage. If necessary, this may be determined by the chemical examination of samples taken for this purpose and forwarded to the nearest laboratory. In the event it is not necessary to redenature the alcohol the manufacturer must deposit it in his storeroom in suitable packages and make application to the collector of internal revenue to have it regauged and restamped. The collector will detail an officer to visit the storeroom and regauge and restamp the alcohol. When it has been regauged and restamped the alcohol will be taken up on proper records by the officer and the manufacturer, and will appear on the monthly reports in the same manner as though it had been redenatured. The officer making the regauge will make a report in the same manner as is required when alcohol is redenatured on the manufacturer's premises, except that the report will not show that the goods are redenatured.

Part V.

RESTORING AND REDENATURING PLANTS.

Sec. 132. Centrally located plants may be established for the purpose of restoring to a condition suitable for reuse and for redenaturing, if necessary, alcohol recovered by manufacturers; these plants to be located at such places as the Commissioner of Internal Revenue may deem necessary.

Warehouse: How Constructed.

Sec. 133. A warehouse constructed in the manner in which distillery warehouses are constructed must be provided. This warehouse to be used for the purpose of storing recovered denatured alcohol received from manufacturing establishments. Either an apartment in this warehouse or a separate warehouse may be provided in which to redenature and store the restored alcohol. This apartment or separate warehouse, as the case may be, must be constructed in the same manner as denaturing bonded warehouses heretofore described. It must be supplied with mixing tanks, and a room to be used as a denaturing material room must be provided. The apartment used as a denaturing bonded warehouse must be separated from the apartment used as a storage room for the recovered alcohol received from manufacturers, and there must be no openings or doors between the two apartments. The denaturing material room must be constructed in the same manner as similar rooms are constructed at denaturing bonded warehouses, and all of the appliances required at denaturing bonded warehouses must be supplied.

Cistern Room to be Provided.

Sec. 134. A cistern room constructed in the same manner as are cistern rooms at registered distilleries must be provided. In the process of restoring the recovered alcohol by redistillation, it must be received into the cisterns direct from the worm or condenser in the same manner as distilled spirits are received into the cisterns at registered distilleries.

The cisterns and cistern room must be supplied with the same kind of locks as are required for similar rooms at registered distilleries.

Sec. 135. When the restoring and redenaturing plant is in operation it must be under the supervision and control of a storekeeper-gauger or other officer designated by the collector of internal revenue.

This officer shall carry the key to the warehouse or warehouses used in connection with the plant and the cistern and cistern rooms. When operations at the plant are suspended for the day he shall lock the steam valves controlling the supply of steam to the several parts of the plant, and such other appliances as will prevent the plant from being operated during his absence. Under no circumstances is he to permit any work to go on during his absence, and he shall exercise the same kind of surveillance over the plant as is exercised at registered distilleries.

APPLICATION TO BE MADE TO COLLECTOR.

SEC. 136. Any person desiring to establish a plant at which denatured alcohol recovered at a manufacturing establishment may be restored and redenatured shall make application to the collector of internal revenue in the district in which such plant is to be located.

In this application he shall state the exact location of said plant. He shall describe all of the buildings located on the premises. In this description he shall give the size of each building, the materials of which it is constructed, and their location with reference to each other. He shall describe all of the apparatus intended to be used in the work of restoring alcohol.

If one or more stills are used he shall describe each still accurately, giving the capacity of each, together with all of the connections and other apparatus used therewith. He shall describe the cisterns, cistern rooms, warehouses, or tanks constituting a part of the plant, giving the capacity of each cistern or tank in gallons.

The application may be in the following form:

To Collector of Internal Revenue,
    —— *District of* ——.

SIR: Notice is hereby given that I have erected for the purpose of restoring denatured alcohol and redenaturing it a plant located at ——, State of ——, described as follows: ——

[Here given description of the plant, together with the cistern, cistern room, still or stills, warehouse, etc., as required above.]

and you are hereby requested to cause such proposed restoring and redenaturing plant to be inspected with a view of determining whether or not it is constructed in compliance with the law and regulations.

    —— ——,
               Proprietor.

A diagram upon which is shown the entire plant with all the buildings located on the premises must be submitted with this application.

Upon receipt of the application the collector will, either himself, or by one of his deputies, visit and inspect the premises. He will determine whether or not the plant is constructed in accordance with the regulations, and whether or not the statements made in the application and the representations made on the diagram are true.

If he finds that the statements are correct and that the plant is constructed in accordance with the regulations, he will so indorse upon the application, and the collector will forward same to the Commissioner of Internal Revenue.

If the Commissioner is of the opinion that the establishment of the plant is necessary, and that it is constructed in accordance with the law and regulations, he will approve it and will so advise the collector.

BOND FOR RESTORING AND REDENATURING PLANT.

SEC. 137. Upon receipt of notice from the Commissioner of Internal Revenue that the restoring and redenaturing plant has been approved, the collector shall notify the proprietor of the plant of such approval, and thereafter he may receive upon his premises, restore, and redenature alcohol, provided he shall first make a bond in the following form:

Know all men by these presents, That —— ——, of ——, as principal, and —— ——, of ——, as sureties, are held and firmly bound unto the United States of America, in the sum of —— dollars, for the payment whereof to the

United States we bind ourselves, our heirs, executors, and administrators, jointly and severally, firmly by these presents.

The condition of this obligation is such that whereas the above bounden principal has established a plant for restoring and redenaturing alcohol, located at ———, and whereas said plant has been approved by the Commissioner of Internal Revenue and the said principal has been authorized to receive upon his premises and store in his warehouse alcohol withdrawn from bond, free of tax, denatured, used at manufacturing establishments and recovered in the process of manufacture, and has been authorized to restore such alcohol so received to a condition suitable for reuse in manufacturing processes, and has been authorized to redenature such alcohol at his redenaturing warehouse located at said plant, Now, if the said ——— ——— shall, in the operation of his restoring and redenaturing plant, bring into the warehouse specially set aside for that purpose, all of the recovered alcohol consigned to him by manufacturers wherever located, shall safely store in said warehouse all of said alcohol so received, shall restore all of said alcohol to a condition suitable for reuse in manufacturing processes and redenature it in his redenaturing apartment or warehouse, in the manner prescribed by regulations; and if he shall pay the tax of one dollar and ten cents per proof gallon upon all the alcohol that may be consigned to him by any manufacturer and not properly stored in said warehouse, or stored in said warehouse and not duly restored, or duly stored and restored and not duly redenatured by him, and if he shall in all respects comply with all of the requirements and provisions of the law and regulations in relation to storing, restoring, redenaturing, and disposing of said alcohol, then this obligation is to be null and void, otherwise to remain in full force and effect.

It is the intent and purpose of this obligation that it shall operate as a transportation, warehousing, restoring, and redenaturing bond, and that liability under it shall attach the moment any recovered alcohol is put in transit by a manufacturer to the principal herein; while it is in transit to him; after it has been deposited in the warehouse located on his restoring and redenaturing plant; while it is in process of being restored; after it has been deposited in his redenaturing apartment or warehouse; while it is in process of redenaturation, after it has been redenatured, and while it is in transit to any manufacturer to whom it may be consigned.

——— ———. [SEAL.]
——— ———. [SEAL.]
——— ———. [SEAL.]

Signed and sealed in the presence of—

——— ———.

PENAL SUM OF BOND.

SEC. 138. The bond required of the proprietor of a restoring and redenaturing plant shall be in the penal sum of not less than the tax on the alcohol it is estimated will be restored and redenatured thereat in thirty days, and in no event shall it be less than five thousand dollars or more than one hundred thousand dollars. The sureties may be either personal sureties or a corporate surety duly authorized to make bonds under the existing laws.

QUANTITY OF ALCOHOL TO BE RETURNED TO MANUFACTURER.

SEC. 139. Alcohol restored and redenatured at a plant established for that purpose may be restored to a condition suitable for reuse in manufacturing processes only. Alcohol recovered by any manufacturer using either specially or completely denatured alcohol may be restored and redenatured in accordance with the regulations herein prescribed, but in each case the manufacturer sending alcohol to such plant to be restored and redenatured must receive back from such plant a quantity of alcohol equal to that sent to the plant to be restored and redenatured, less any reduction in quantity attending the necessary process of restoration. In no event shall a manufacturer receive any greater quantity of alcohol from a restoring and redenaturing plant than is sent to such plant by him, allowance being made, of course, for the denaturants added; and in no event shall alcohol redenatured at a restoring and redenaturing plant be delivered or disposed of for reuse to anyone except a manufacturer who had delivered recovered alcohol to such plant.

No Other Business to be Carried on.

Sec. 140. No business can be carried on on the premises of a restoring and redenaturing plant except such business as is incident to the work of receiving, depositing, restoring, and redenaturing alcohol received there, and no tax-paid alcohol can be received on these premises.

Sec. 141. The premises of all restoring and redenaturing plants shall at all times be open to the inspection of duly authorized internal-revenue officers, and they shall have the right to observe the process and methods employed, and take such samples of the product of the plant as in their judgment may be necessary.

Plant to be Secured on Suspension.

Sec. 142. When the plant is suspended the officer in charge must securely lock all valves and cocks controlling the supply of steam, and the furnace doors; likewise he must securely lock the cistern rooms and warehouses connected with the plant and deliver the keys to the collector of the district; and when the plant suspends operations it must be placed in such condition by the officer that it can not be operated during his absence, or until notice has been given to the collector by the proprietor of his intention to resume work.

When the proprietor of the restoring and redenaturing plant desires to suspend operations, he shall give the collector of internal revenue notice of such intention; and when he desires to resume operations he shall likewise give notice, and the collector will thereupon assign an officer to the establishment who shall have custody and control of it during the period of operations.

Proprietor of Restoring Plant to Own Real Estate.

Sec. 143. In his application for permit to operate a restoring and redenaturing plant the proprietor must state the name of the person or persons holding the fee-simple title to the real estate upon which the plant is located. In the event the title is not in the proprietor of the plant, he must secure the consent of the owners of such fee-simple title in the same manner as is required in the case of registered distilleries.

Manufacturer to Keep Record and Send Notice of Shipment.

Sec. 144. A manufacturer using denatured alcohol and recovering it in process of manufacture, and desiring to have such alcohol restored to a condition suitable for reuse in manufacture at a restoring and redenaturing plant, must deposit such alcohol as it is recovered in the designated storeroom on his manufacturing premises, in the same manner as required of manufacturers who restore alcohol on their own premises.

He must keep a record, in which he shall enter the quantity of alcohol in wine and proof gallons recovered each day and stored in his storeroom. At such times as he may desire, he may ship such recovered alcohol to a restoring and redenaturing plant, but before it leaves his storeroom he must put it into suitable packages, and upon the head of each package he must place the following marks:

Denatured alcohol recovered at the manufacturing establishment of ——— ———, storeroom No. ——, located at ———, in the district of ———, ——— wine gallons, ——— proof gallons, serial No. ——.

He must number these packages serially, beginning with No. 1.

Upon the credit side of his record he shall enter the date upon which he sends any recovered alcohol to the restoring and redenaturing plant, the name of the proprietor of the plant to which it is sent, the number of packages, the serial numbers of the packages, and the wine and proof gallons.

Sec. 145. Upon the date upon which he places in transit any recovered alcohol he must prepare a notice, in which he shall state the number of packages, the serial numbers of the packages, the wine and proof gallons, and the name of the restoring and redenaturing plant to which the recovered alcohol is sent.

This notice must be in triplicate, provided the restoring and redenaturing plant is located in one district and the manufacturing establishment is located in another. If they are both in the same collection district, then it may be prepared in duplicate. One copy of the notice is to be sent to the collector of the district in which the manufacturing plant is located, another copy to the collector of the district in which the restoring and redenaturing plant is located (provided it is in another district), and the remaining copy to the officer in charge of the restoring and redenaturing plant.

As soon as the recovered alcohol reaches the restoring and redenaturing plant the proprietor of the establishment must deposit it in the warehouse located on the premises, and it must remain in this warehouse until it is ready to be redistilled and restored.

Record to be Kept by Proprietor of Restoring Plant.

Sec. 146. The proprietor of the restoring and redenaturing plant must keep a record in which he shall enter the date upon which he receives any recovered alcohol. In this record he must give the name and address of the manufacturer from whom the alcohol was received, the number of packages, the serial numbers of the packages, the wine and proof gallons.

Upon the credit side he shall enter the date upon which he sends any redenatured alcohol to the manufacturer, the name of the manufacturer, the number of packages, the serial numbers of the packages, the name of the officer inspecting the packages, the serial numbers of the stamps, and the wine and proof gallons.

At the end of the month and before the 10th day of the ensuing month he must prepare and forward to the collector of internal revenue a transcript of this record. Said transcript will constitute his return for the month and must be duly sworn to.

Officer to Keep Records and Make Returns.

Sec. 147. The officer in charge of the restoring and redenaturing plant must keep a record in which he shall enter the date upon which any recovered alcohol is deposited in the warehouse, the name and address of the persons from whom received, the number of packages, the serial numbers of the packages, and the wine and proof gallons.

Upon the credit side of this record he shall enter the date upon which he delivers any alcohol to the proprietor of the plant for restoring purposes, the name and address of the persons from whom the alcohol was received, the number of packages, the serial numbers of the packages, and the wine and proof gallons.

From this record he shall make a report each day to the collector, in which he shall show the number of packages of recovered alcohol entered into the warehouse on that date, the name and address of the persons from whom it was received, the serial numbers of the packages, and the wine and proof gallons.

This report shall also show the quantity of recovered alcohol delivered from the warehouse to the proprietor of the plant for restoring purposes; the name and address of the persons from whom received, the serial numbers of the packages, and the wine and proof gallons.

The above record and report shall be designated as a warehouse record and report. The report shall be made at the close of business on each day. At the end of the month the officer in charge of the plant shall make a monthly report, which shall be a transcript of this record.

Restored Alcohol to be Removed from Cistern Room to Denaturing Room.

Sec. 148. As fast as the alcohol is restored it shall be drawn off into packages from the cisterns in the cistern room and shall be gauged and transferred to the denaturing warehouse and at once redenatured. These packages shall be numbered serially, beginning with No. 1 for each restoring plant.

Redenaturing Warehouse Record.

Sec. 149. The officer in charge of the plant shall keep a record to be known as the denaturing warehouse record, in which he shall enter each day the number of wine and proof gallons of restored alcohol received from the cistern room and deposited in the denaturing warehouse, the number of packages, and the serial numbers of the packages.

Upon the debit side of this record he shall enter the number of wine and proof gallons of alcohol delivered to the proprietor of the plant each day for redenaturation, the number of packages, and the serial number of each package.

From this record he shall make daily returns showing the quantity of alcohol restored, gauged, and deposited in the denaturing bonded warehouse and delivered to the proprietor of the plant for redenaturation.

He shall likewise keep a record of the denaturants brought upon the premises and deposited in the material room. This record shall be similar to the record kept for the same purpose at denaturing bonded warehouses operated in connection with distilleries.

Officer to Keep Redenaturation Record.

Sec. 150. The officer shall keep a record of alcohol redenatured, gauged, marked, stamped, branded, and delivered to the proprietor of the restoring and redenaturing plant. This record shall be similar to the record kept in denaturing warehouses operated in connection with distilleries.

The packages of alcohol redenatured at a restoring and redenaturing plant must be numbered serially, beginning with No. 1, and no two packages must have the same number. The packages of alcohol redenatured at restoring and redenaturing plants must be gauged, marked, stamped, and branded in the same manner as such packages are gauged, marked, stamped, and branded at denaturing bonded warehouses operated in connection with distilleries.

Upon the head of the package must be stenciled the name of the proprietor of the restoring and redenaturing plant, the district and State in which it is located, the serial number of the package, the serial number of the stamp, and the wine and proof gallons, and the words "Redenatured alcohol" must be placed thereon in legible letters.

Alcohol Sent Out from Redenaturing Plants.

Sec. 151. If the alcohol is redenatured by the use of special denaturants, then the same kind of notices as are given to the several collectors in the case of especially denatured alcohol sent out from denaturing bonded warehouses operated in connection with distilleries must be prepared and forwarded to the collector. Likewise, the manufacturer receiving the alcohol must give a notice to the collector of his district similar to that required in a case of specially denatured alcohol received direct from denaturing bonded warehouse. The manufacturer must charge himself on his record with the alcohol received in the same manner as is required in the case of alcohol received direct from denaturing bonded warehouse.

Collectors to Keep Records.

Sec. 152. Collectors in whose districts restoring and redenaturing plants are operated shall be provided with records in which shall be kept the account of each plant. In this record shall be entered the quantity in wine and proof gallons of recovered alcohol daily received and deposited in the warehouse at said plant, the number of packages, the serial numbers of the package, and the names of the manufacturers from whom received.

Said record shall also show the quantity of alcohol in wine and proof gallons delivered to the proprietor of the plant each day to be restored, the names and addresses of the persons from whom received, the number of the packages, and the serial numbers of the packages.

Collectors shall also keep records similar to those kept in case of denaturing bonded warehouses, showing the quantity of alcohol deposited in said redenaturing warehouse, the quantity of denaturants deposited in the material room, the quantity of alcohol and denaturants dumped each day, and the quantity of redenatured alcohol withdrawn from dump, gauged, and delivered to the denaturer.

Persons desiring information as to the operation of distilleries for the production of alcohol will be furnished with all the laws and regulations controlling upon application made to collectors of internal revenue or to this Office. The several forms herein prescribed will be furnished collectors on requisition; and the Catalogue numbers given such forms will be furnished at an early date.

JOHN W. YERKES,
Commissioner of Internal Revenue.

This September 29, 1906.
Approved:

    C. H. KEEP,
        Acting Secretary of the Treasury.

REPORT OF THE BRITISH DEPARTMENTAL COMMITTEE ON INDUSTRIAL ALCOHOL, PRESENTED TO BOTH HOUSES OF PARLIAMENT BY COMMAND OF HIS MAJESTY.

TERMS OF REFERENCE.—To inquire into the existing facilities for the use, without payment of duty, of spirits in arts and manufactures, and in particular into the operation of Section 8 of the Finance Act, 1902, and to report whether the powers conferred upon the Commissioners of Inland Revenue by this section permit of adequate facilities being given for the use of spirits in manufactures and in the production of motive power, or whether further facilities are required; and if it should appear to the Committee that the present facilities are inadequate, to advise the further measures to be adopted, without prejudice to the safety of the revenue derived from spirits, and with due regard to the interests of the producers of spirits in the United Kingdom.

To The Right Honourable J. AUSTEN CHAMBERLAIN, M.P., chancellor of the Exchequer.

SIR,

1. We have the honour to submit to you the following Report of our proceedings and conclusions in connection with the inquiry, which, in August last, you invited us to undertake into the question of facilities for the use of Spirit in Arts and Manufactures.

INTRODUCTORY REMARKS.

2. In interpreting the terms of reference, we have considered that the main objects of our inquiry were to ascertain the extent to which alcohol is, or might be, employed in arts and manufactures, or in the production of heat, light, or motive power; and to determine the conditions of greatest freedom that could be accorded to its use for those purposes, consistently with adequate safety to the revenue derived from spirit as an article of human consumption.

3. We have, therefore, confined our attention almost exclusively to these points; and have not attempted to deal fully with allied questions, such as possible changes in the methods of producing spirit, or in the materials from which it may be obtained, or such as the actual or possible sources of supply. These questions, important as they are in themselves, seemed to us somewhat remote from the purpose immediately in view; and their investigation would have unduly enlarged and prolonged our labours.

4. We did, however, for special reasons, take some evidence on the question of the production of spirit from potatoes; enough to satisfy us that in the present agricultural conditions of this country it would not be possible to found a profitable industry on the employment of potatoes as a material for distillation.

5. In order to obtain evidence, we addressed ourselves to the Association of Chambers of Commerce of the United Kingdom, and to the Chambers of Commerce of London, Liverpool, Manchester and Birmingham; and the majority of witnesses examined by us were gentlemen selected for us by those bodies, as representatives competent to speak on behalf of the several industries in which alcohol is, or might be, employed. Of the rest, some came at their own request, while others came on our direct invitation. In addition to oral evidence, much information was laid

before us in the form of memoranda prepared for us by the Board of Inland Revenue, in regard to the regulations in this and other countries governing the use of spirit for industrial purposes, as to the quantities of spirit so used, and as to the Rules and Regulations laid down by the Board of Inland Revenue under the Act of 1902. These memoranda are printed as appendices to the evidence. Lastly, as in the evidence of certain of the witnesses who came before us much stress was laid upon the system and regulations established in Germany in connection with the industrial use of alcohol, we felt it was very desirable to procure information at first hand upon that subject; and we accordingly obtained your authority to send a deputation to Germany for that purpose. The report of this sub-committee is annexed in immediate continuation of this Report.

Conditions Governing the Use of Spirits for Industrial Purposes.

6. The use of methylated (denatured) spirit duty free was first authorised in 1855 by the Act 18 & 19, Vict., c. 38. The present law on the subject is contained in the Spirits Act, 1880, as amended by the Customs and Inland Revenue Act, 1890, and Section 8 of the Finance Act, 1902.

7. The practice resulting from the law has been as follows:

Up to the year 1855, spirit could not be used duty free by the public under any circumstances. From 1855 to 1861 it could be used duty free for manufacturing purposes only, if methylated according to the prescribed process.

From 1861 to 1891 spirit could be used duty free for any purpose other than consumption directly or indirectly as a beverage, or internally as a medicine, provided it was mixed with wood-naphtha to the extent of one-ninth of its volume. But, if used in large quantities, as for manufacturing purposes, it could not be purchased from a retailer of methylated spirit, but only from a methylator, and the user was subject to Excise supervision.

From 1891 to 1902, the use of this kind of methylated spirit (which came to be described as "ordinary" methylated spirit) was confined to manufacturing purposes, subject to the same conditions as before; while for general purposes a spirit, consisting of the above spirit with an addition of .375 per cent. of mineral naphtha (petroleum), and known as "mineralised" methylated spirit, was brought into use. It is only in this spirit that retailers are permitted to deal.

Since 1902, the two kinds of methylated spirit have continued to be used as before. But an alternative to their use has been opened to manufacturers, under which spirits may be employed after being subjected to some special process of denaturing, appropriate to the particular industry, or possibly even in a pure state, should circumstances be held by the Board of Inland Revenue so to require.

8. Advantage has been taken of the Act of 1902 by a certain number of manufacturers. But, in examining the witnesses who have come before us, we have been surprised to find in some quarters a very inadequate acquaintance with its provisions, and much failure to appreciate its significance; and we are disposed to think that the beneficial effects of the Act have, on this account, been less widely diffused than they might have been. It may reasonably be expected that, as a result of this enquiry, enterprising traders will more largely avail themselves of the provisions of this Act.

Hindrances to the Use of Spirit for Industrial Purposes in the United Kingdom.

9. The "Ordinary" Methylated Spirit is open to certain objections as a material or instrument of manufacture. In a few cases it is unsuitable by reason either of the chemical properties or of the smell of the wood-naphtha it contains. But even where its character is not a serious objection, it is still always open to this disadvantage, that it is somewhat heavily enhanced in cost as compared with pure spirit. For not only does the wood-naphtha, which must be present to the extent of 10 per cent., cost more than double the price of the equivalent quantity of spirit, but now and again it tends to make the mixture less efficient for the purpose in view than it would be without this ingredient.

10. It was to meet these objections that legislation was undertaken in 1902; and, so far as they are concerned, we consider that Section 8 of the Finance Act of that year does all that is possible in respect of the character of spirit. For it has entirely removed all difficulty in the way of procuring a spirit suitable in character for any industrial purpose. It has also to some extent mitigated the objection on the score of cost, inasmuch as the special processes of denaturing authorised by the Board of Inland Revenue are commonly less expensive to the manufacturer than is the case with "Ordinary" Methylated Spirit. On the other hand, the cost of these processes is enhanced by the charges for Excise supervision.

11. But the cost of denaturing touches a part only of the question of the price of the spirit used for industrial purposes. An influence on price, even more important, lies at an earlier stage of production of the spirit, viz., in the conditions under which spirit can alone be manufactured in this country. The duty on spirit used as a beverage in the United Kingdom is very heavy, and in imposing this duty it is essential to the protection of the revenue to impose on the manufacture of spirit such restraints as may be necessary to prevent any spirit from escaping payment of duty; and a consequence of such restraints must be to cause an appreciable enhancement in the cost of manufacture. What the measure of this enhancement may be is not susceptible of precise determination; and even an approximation to it can only be reached by persons with a minute and practical knowledge of all the details of manufacture and of trade on the one hand, and of what is required for the protection of the revenue on the other. We have, therefore, not attempted to investigate all the elements that enter into the calculation, but have accepted the figures that have been established by law and practice as applicable to the present situation. These figures will be found in Appendix No. I., together with a full explanation of the manner in which they have been reached. For our purpose it is sufficient to say that they may be taken as representing an enhancement of the cost of producing plain British spirits by 3d. the proof gallon, or an increase of about 50 per cent. on the cost that would otherwise prevail in the production of industrial alcohol. It is patent that producers thus hampered could not hope to compete successfully, either in the home or in foreign markets, against rivals not similarly hampered, unless some counterpoise were provided to the burdens that fiscal restrictions impose upon them. Accordingly, the law does provide such a counterpoise—in the case of the home market, by making the duty on imported spirits exceed the duty on British spirits by an amount equivalent to the burdens on the home producer—this is called the "Surtax"—and in the case of foreign markets, by granting to the home producer allowances calculated on the same basis. These export allowances are at the rates of 3d. per proof gallon on plain spirits, and 5d. per proof gallon on compounded spirits, and it is the higher of these two allowances that is taken as determining the measure of the "Surtax" on all imported spirits other than Rum or Brandy, on which the "Surtax" is 4d. the proof gallon. The final result upon the price of industrial spirit of all the measures taken to protect the revenue may be stated as follows. Spirit used in manufacture is commonly about 64 overproof (about 93 per cent. on the continental standard of pure alcohol), and is plain spirit. Therefore, the price of a bulk gallon of the spirit is about 5d. more than it would have been but for excise restrictions. The cost of methylating may be put at between 3d. and 4d. per bulk gallon, so that of the price eventually paid by the manufacturer, which at present may be taken at from 20d. to 22d. per bulk gallon for large quantities at wholesale price, about 8½d. is attributable to precautions on behalf of the revenue.

12. The two considerations (a) of the conditions in which spirit must be used, and (b) of the price at which it can be procured, affect different industries in very varying degrees. Either consideration may be of vital importance to a particular industry. But, speaking generally, we have no hesitation in saying, on the evidence before us, that, taking the whole range of industrial enterprises employing alcohol, the question of price is infinitely the more important of the two. The number of cases in which it has been conclusively shown that ordinary methylated spirit is seriously detrimental by reason of its character, are remarkably few, whereas the cases are numerous in which a difference of, say, 6d. per bulk gallon in the price of alcohol might make all the difference between profit or loss in the carrying on of an enterprise.

13. To illustrate this, we will briefly review the evidence laid before us in respect of some of the more important industries employing alcohol, and in doing so will include such general observations as occur to us.

COAL TAR COLOUR INDUSTRY.

14. We take this first because it has figured very prominently in the discussions which have led up to the present inquiry. In the course of those discussions, it has frequently been asserted that the Coal Tar Colour Industry, which originated in this country, and at one time flourished in this country, has been lost to us very largely, if not mainly, by reason of the obstacles in the way of a cheap and untrammelled supply of alcohol. In view of the prominence given to this asertion, we thought it desirable, even at the risk of travelling somewhat beyond the immediate purpose of our inquiry, to procure authentic evidence upon the subject. With that object we invited to appear before us Dr. W. H. Perkin, the discoverer in 1856 of the first Coal Tar Colour, Mr. R. J. Friswell, who was engaged in the manufacture of aniline dyes from 1874 to 1899, and Professor Meldola, who was similarly engaged from 1870 to 1885, and to whose memorandum appended to his evidence we desired to call special attention. We had also before us, as a witness nominated by the London Chamber of Commerce, Professor A. G. Green, whose name is associated with a well-known work on Organic Colouring Matters. Further, our Sub-Committee that visited Germany had an opportunity of learning the views of many persons connected with the colour industry in that country.

15. On a review of all the evidence, pro and con, we are satisfied that, regarded as a statement of historical fact, the assertion that the Coal Tar Colour Industry has been lost to this country on account of obstacles to the use of alcohol is destitute of substantial foundation.

16. In the earlier days of the industry alcohol was used almost wholly as a solvent, and for that purpose methylated spirit is suitable. Moreover, when alcohol first began to be used as a constituent of dyes, and until some time after the decadence of the industry in this country had become marked, the margin of profit on the manufacture was so great that the difference in price even between duty-free and duty-paid alcohol was a matter that could practically be left out of consideration.

17. It would take us too far afield to examine at length into the causes that did, in fact, contribute to the decadence of the industry in this country and to its rapid development in Germany. But much infomation on the subject will be found in the evidence, and here we will confine ourselves to saying that, in our opinion, the cause which predominated over all others was the failure of those responsible for the management and for the finance of the industry here, during the years 1860–1880, to realise the vital importance of its scientific side, and their consequent omission to provide adequately for its development on that side.

18. But while we say this in the interest of historical accuracy, it by no means follows that either we, or the authorities we have quoted, think that what was true of the period 1860–1880 is true of the present time. On the contrary, it is unquestionable that, in some branches of the colour industry, with alcohol playing a considerable part as a constituent of certain dyes, and with profits cut down by competition to a narrow margin, the circumstances under which, in respect of condition and of price, alcohol can be used have become of importance. But here, too, it is necessary to guard against exaggeration. Large classes of the Coal Tar Colours—alizarine, indigo, and by far the greater number of the azo dyes—require no alcohol for their manufacture either directly or indirectly, and these represent by far the larger proportion of all the colours produced. We have had varying estimates given to us of the proportion of the whole output that demands alcohol, and they range from the 10 per cent. of the German authorities to the 20 per cent. to 25 per cent. of Professor Green. Therefore, for at least 75 per cent. of the whole industry, alcohol does not enter into account even now, and these branches could be prosecuted in this country, as indeed they now are, whatever the conditions in regard to the use of alcohol might be.

19. Nevertheless, even where alcohol is not immediately required for the manufacture of a dyestuff, the utilisation of waste products and the development of new methods may be hampered by a want of alcohol; while, for those dyestuffs for

which alcohol is essential, its price and the conditions of its use are matters of great moment. We are of opinion, therefore, that, if the hope is to be entertained of recovering any considerable portion of this trade, more favourable conditions must be established in respect of the use of alcohol.

20. We may observe that in the manufacture of dyestuffs, or of the intermediate products for their manufacture, the part played by methylic alcohol is far more important than is that of ethylic alcohol. Methylic alcohol is not produced by fermentation and it was not until the process of its manufacutre was so far perfected as to bring it into possible competition with ethyl alcohol that it was thought necessary to subject it to the charge of the spirit duties. This was done by an Act of 1865; and in 1898 its use was prohibited in the preparation of beverages or of medicines for internal use. Its chemical character differs so much from that of ethyl alcohol that its presence in any product can readily be detected by analysis. In view of these facts, we think that exceptional treatment may be accorded to methylic alcohol, in the manner described later.

SMOKELESS POWDERS.

21. On the question whether in this industry ordinary methylated spirit is unsuitable or detrimental in character, the evidence laid before the Committee appears to us conflicting and inconclusive. We are inclined to think that the true position is that the question has never been thoroughly sifted. As Sir W. Crookes put it to us, it is known that very slight chemical variations in the materials employed may produce very marked variations in the quality of the powder produced, more especially as regards its stability; to determine whether the chemical composition of ordinary methylated spirit (or of methylated ether) would or would not affect the stability or other properties of a powder, would demand costly experiments extending over many years; and there has not been any sufficient inducement to undertake such experiments. The act of 1902 still further diminishes the inducement, and all the more so because there is probably no single industry in which exceptional advantages as regards the use of spirit could be accorded with less risk to the revenue. The workmen employed are of necessity men of steady and trustworthy character; they are subject to the strictest supervision; and the manner in which spirit enters into the process of manufacture give but little opening for peculation.

22. But the question of the price of spirit and ether is one of vital importance to the manufacturer of smokeless powder of which nitro-cellulose is a constituent.* The quantity of alcohol used, either directly in the form of spirit or indirectly in the form of ether, for the production of one pound of this powder is very large. What the exact amount may be it is difficult to determine, because so much depends upon the amount of spirit that may be recovered from any operation, and this varies as between one operation and another, and as between one factory and another. But one witness gave us to understand that a difference of 6d. per gallon in the price of spirit would make a difference of 7d. per pound in the cost of the powder produced; and it is manifest that even a much smaller difference than that would turn the scale between profit and loss.

PHARMACEUTICAL PRODUCTS—FINE CHEMICALS.

23. In this branch of industry alcohol plays a very important part. In Section 4 of our Sub-Committee's report, the subject is very fully treated, and we will not here repeat what is there stated. We will merely observe that for a large, and probably increasing, number of substances, such as the synthetic perfumes, antipyrine, phenacetin, sulphonal, and so on, alcohol at a price not in excess of that at which it stands in competing countries, and usable under conditions not inimical to the quality and character of the compounds produced, is essential to the existence of the industry. The industry presents certain features of difficulty because, in the first place, there are large numbers of pharmaceutical preparations in which the

---

* It is an open question amongst the authorities whether the powder of the future will be one requiring alcohol for its preparation.

alcohol remains as free spirit, and which must continue to be made from duty-paid spirit; and because, in the second place, the preparations are so numerous and so various in character that there are difficulties in making a single process of denaturing applicable to them all. But these difficulties have been satisfactorily overcome in Germany, and we see no reason why they should not be overcome here. We are, however, of opinion that the manufacture of synthetical chemical products with duty-free alcohol would have to be completely and effectually separated from the manufacture of preparations (as, for example, tinctures) in which the alcohol remains as such, and which, therefore, must be made with duty-paid spirit.

Ether.

24. The production of ether has become a most important industry, large quantities being required for manufacturing purposes (*e.g.*, smokeless powder. artificial silk, etc.) and for refrigerating purposes. For most, if not for all, of these purposes, ether made from ordinary methylated spirit is quite suitable. But, inasmuch as it requires much more than a gallon of strong spirit to produce a gallon of ether, the price of spirit is manifestly a consideration of primary moment to this industry. Incidentally we may mention that, in the course of the evidence, the question was raised whether the present rates of import duty on ethers are the correct equivalents of the duty payable on the spirit necessary to produce them.

Artificial Silk.

25. This industry is not at present prosecuted in this country, although it employs many thousands of workpeople on the Continent. Some five or six years ago an attempt was made to introduce it, and a factory was established at Wolston, near Coventry. but after working for nearly two years (1899–1900) it was closed. At that time the excise authorities had no power to allow the use of spirit in any other form than that of ordinary methylated spirit, and in the opinion of Mr. Cash, who was Chairman of the company from its formation until some six months before it was wound up, and who attended as a witness before us, the obligation to use methylated spirit was one of the causes of the failure of the enterprise. The evidence on this point is far from conclusive. But it is unquestionable that the operations of manufacture in this industry are extremely delicate, and that the difficulties to be overcome in any case great and numerous. To add to the difficulties that are inevitable one that can be avoided would manifestly be most undesirable; and, therefore, if using methylated spirit creates a fresh difficulty, it should by all means be avoided. For the manufacture of artificial silk, the price of alcohol is a consideration of vital importance, as the combined ether and spirit required to produce one pound of the finished article represents nearly a gallon of strong spirit.

Lacquers, Varnishes, etc.

26. These are usually made with the ordinary methylated spirit, where spirit enters into the manufacture. (Spirit is not required for lacquers that are applied cold.) In a few rare cases pure duty-paid spirit is employed for the finest kinds of lacquer. On the question whether methylated spirit is detrimental to the character of the product, the evidence submitted to us was conflicting—some witnesses insisting that it is detrimental, another, representing a considerable section of the trade, maintaining that it is not. Specimens of goods treated with lacquer made with pure spirit, with ordinary methylated spirit, and with wood-naphtha, respectively, were submitted to us; and we are bound to say that any distinction between them was scarcely perceptible to the unprofessional eye.

27. However this may be, we consider that for this trade neither the character nor the price of spirit under existing conditions creates any serious hindrance, except, perhaps, for goods exported. For in the home market the trade enjoys a considerable measure of practical protection, owing to the fact that imported lacquers and varnishes containing spirit are charged full spirit duty on the quantity of spirit contained.

MOTOR VEHICLES.

28. Spirit is not used at present in this country as a fuel for motor vehicles. Nor is it so used to any great extent either in Germany or in France, in spite of the fact that both these countries are most desirous of encouraging the use of a material that is indigenous, in preference to a material like petrol that has to be imported. Where spirit is used for motor or other engines in those countries, it is almost entirely for agricultural engines. For motor cars, spirit presents certain special difficulties, which require to be overcome, the principal being the behaviour of alcohol in very cold weather, and the tendency of the acids generated by its combustion to cause corrosion of the metal surfaces with which they come in contact.

29. For the moment, therefore, the question of the use of spirit for motor cars is not ripe for consideration from the point of view of our inquiry. Should it hereafter become so, it is manifest that alcohol used for this purpose must be denatured in the most effectual and most permanent manner. Happily this will not present any difficulty, as there is no evidence to suggest that the mineralised methylated spirit in common use in this country is in any way unsuitable or detrimental for this purpose.

30. Any question, therefore, of the use of spirit for motor vehicles will be one of price, and as at present the price of petrol is about half the price of methylated spirit, we think that close investigation of the matter may be delayed until such time as there may be an approximation between the prices of petrol and spirit sufficient to create a practical alternative of choice between the two.

GENERAL CONCLUSIONS.

31. On all the facts before us we have arrived at the following general conclusions:

(i) That where spirit is used for general and universal purposes, such as heating or lighting, the present "mineralised" methylated spirit is perfectly satisfactory, both to the revenue and to the public, in respect of character, and that at present no better method of denaturing is available. In respect of price, the cost of mineralised methylated spirit is enhanced by some 40 per cent. by reason of measures necessary for the protection of the revenue. But to countervail such enhancement would be merely to relieve the whole community of a burden in one direction by putting upon it an equivalent burden in another, seeing that the cost of relief would necessarily have to be made up to the Exchequer from some other source of taxation. Thus there would be no real balance of gain to the community as a whole from arrangements that would of necessity be somewhat complex, and would entail a certain cost in their application. We think, however, that, having regard to the practical security that is provided for the revenue by the process of denaturing adopted in the case of this spirit, the regulations in regard to distribution might be appreciably relaxed in respect of the quantities that retailers may keep in stock, or may sell at any one time to a customer. We recommend that the regulations should be left to be prescribed from time to time by the Board of Inland Revenue, instead of being stereotyped in the Statutes.

(ii) That where spirit is used for industrial purposes, the Finance Act of 1902 provides adequate and entirely satisfactory machinery for securing that the spirit may be used in a condition that is suitable and appropriate to each particular purpose of manufacture. The machinery is elastic—much more so than is the corresponding machinery in Germany—and it permits of every reasonable process of denaturing, or even, in the last resort, of the use of spirit in a pure state. For more t..an this it would be impossible to ask.

(iii) That something more is required in order to place spirit used as an instrument or a material of manufacture on a footing satisfactory in the matter of cost. Anything in the nature of a bounty is undesirable. But seeing that on the price of spirit the very existence of cetain industries may depend, and that for all industries using alcohol the price of spirit is an important factor for that portion of trade that lies outside the home market, we are strongly of opinion that it is desirable to make such arrangements as will free the price of industrial spirit from the enhancement due to the indirect influence of the spirit duties. It would surely be disastrous if, to the mischief that the drinking of alcohol causes by diminution in the efficiency of labour, the taxation of alcohol should be allowed to add the further mischief of narrowing the openings for the employment of labour.

32. In our opinion, there is only one way in which the influence of the spirit duties can be satisfactorily counteracted in favour of industrial alcohol. To diminish the Excise restrictions on the manufacture of alcohol might mitigate the influence, but probably not to any great extent. For with a duty of over 1000 per cent. on the prime cost of an article, revenue control must of necessity be strict. Moreover, the gain to industry would be made at the risk of the revenue, and a duty that yields over £20,000,000 per annum to the Exchequer is a public interest that cannot be trifled with. To relieve imported spirit from the surtax which is needed to counterbalance the burden imposed on production in this country by the Excise regulations would be manifestly unfair; and its effect would be to give to the State-aided spirits from Germany or Russia a practical monopoly of the market in this country for industrial spirit. The only adequate course, it seems to us, is to neutralise, for industrial spirit, the enhanced cost of production due to Excise control, in the same way as the enhanced cost is neutralised for exports, viz: by granting an allowance on such spirit at such rate as may from time to time be taken as the equivalent of the increase in cost of production due to revenue restrictions. At the present time, the rate is taken at 3d. per proof gallon for plain spirits, and the allowance would accordingly be at this rate, and should be paid equally on all industrial spirit whether it be of British or of foreign origin.

33. We do not suggest that the cost of methylation should be borne by the State, although a strictly logical application of the principle of attempting to put industrial alcohol on the footing that it would occupy, if there were no duties on spirit, might seem to require this further concession. For we hold that the manufacturer using alcohol has so strong an interest in rendering it unpotable for his own protection that he may fairly be asked to accept denaturing as a necessary incident of use, the cost of which he should bear.

34. At the same time we think that the charge on the manufacturer might reasonably be limited to paying the cost of the denaturing agents and of the mixing of them with the spirits; and that he should not be required to pay the cost of regular attendance of the Excise officers which is given wholly in the interests of the revenue. Attendances at irregular times, at the special request and for the special convenience of the manufacturer, might, if necessary, continue to be charged against him.

35. We think that for ordinary methylated spirit (which will continue to be used for many industrial purposes for which it is not, in the words of the Act of 1902, "unsuitable or detrimental") the formula of methylation may safely be modified, and the proportion of wood-naphtha reduced, so that the mixture may consist of ninety-five volumes of spirit to five of wood-naphtha. This will at once somewhat cheapen the methylated spirit, and will also diminish any prejudicial effect that the chemical properties of wood-naphtha may have for certain manufactures; while it will continue to "earmark" the spirit sufficiently to allow of detection by analysis, should the methylated spirit be used for any improper purpose. It must be remembered that this kind of methylated spirit can only be used by persons holding an authority from, and under heavy bond to, the Commissioners of Inland Revenue (whereby its employment is subject to control and supervision, which can be graduated according to circumstances), and that consequently the risk of fraud is limited.

36. We have mentioned that we think that methylic alcohol used for industrial purposes might be accorded special treatment. We understand that the Board of Inland Revenue do not consider that it would be safe to revert to the position obtaining before 1865, when methylic alcohol was regarded as wholly outside the scope of the spirit duties: and their opinion receives support from the fact that in France the law has recently been altered so as to define more precisely the degree of purity which shall render methylic alcohol liable to duty. The object we have in view can, however, be sufficiently met without taking methylic alcohol out of the

charge for duty. It would meet all requirements in respect of methylic alcohol, if it were exempted from the condition of the proviso to Section 8 of the Act of 1902, which requires payment of the surtax on all imported spirit used for manufacture, and if the Board of Inland Revenue should exercise their discretion under the section in the matter of denaturing in such a way as to permit the use of methylic alcohol practically pure. This, we understand, they would be willing to do; and exemption from the surtax would be fully justified, inasmuch as the manufacture of methylic alcohol in the United Kingdom is not, in fact, subjected to any restrictions that enhance the cost of its production.

37. While making the concessions above described, we think it would be right, in the interests of the revenue, that special denaturing agents authorized for use in particular industries, should be subject to official test; and further that manufacturers who are authorised to employ specially denatured alcohol should be required to keep such books as may be prescribed, showing the receipts and issues of spirit, the manner in which it has been distributed to the several branches or departments of the factory, and the quantities produced of the articles manufactured with it.

38. We believe that the recommendations we have made, if adopted, will place the manufacturers of this country in respect of the use of alcohol in industry on a footing of equality, in some respects of advantage, as compared with their competitors abroad. Amongst the witnesses who appeared before us, we found a very general impression that, in Germany at any rate—and Germany is our most formidable competitor in this field—spirit could be used in manufacture duty-free and pure, with scarcely any restraint. This is very far from being the case, as the Report of our Sub-Committee shows. As regards price, the grant of the export allowance would, we believe, make the average price of industrial spirit in the United Kingdom even lower than the average price in Germany. The price, exclusive of the cost of any denaturing, would, under present conditions, be about 7d. the proof gallon, or about 11½d. the bulk gallon at 64 over proof—the strength common in industrial spirit. That is as low as the minimum price paid by users in Germany in the year 1902, when spirit was abnormally low, and is much below the figures of 1s. 3½d. per proof gallon, and of 2s. 1½d. per bulk gallon prevailing in Germany at the present time. Further, the price of spirit in this country, where all materials may be freely used, and where none of general use are subject to taxation, is a stable price. In Germany the conditions of production tend to wide and rapid fluctuations in price.

39. At the same time, it would be a mistake to suppose that any facilities given for the use of spirit in this country are likely to create such an increased demand for spirit as to produce any shortage of supply, and so to lead to a rise in price. This point is fully discussed in Section 9 of our Sub-Committee's Report, and we see no reason to dissent from the conclusion that any increase in the demand for industrial spirit must for a long time to come lie well within the limit of 3½ millions of proof gallons. This estimate serves also to assign a limit within which the charge to the Exchequer, resulting from the proposed allowance of 3d. per proof gallon on industrial spirit, will be confined. The present consumption of such spirit is about 3½ million proof gallons, on which the allowance would aggregate £40,000. The utmost expansion that can be regarded as attainable within a measurable distance of time would double that sum, and it may safely be assumed that any immediate expansion will be moderate and gradual.

40. For convenience of reference we summarise our several recommendations.

(i) That an allowance be granted to all industrial spirit, whether of British or foreign origin, at the rate from time to time prevailing for the allowance to British plain spirits on export:

(ii) That imported methylic alcohol be relieved from the obligation to pay the surtax imposed by the proviso to Section 8 of the Finance Act, 1902; and that methylic alcohol be accorded favourable treatment in the matter of denaturing:

(iii) That "ordinary" methylated spirit should contain only 5 per cent. wood-naphtha, instead of 10 per cent.

(iv) That no charge should be made on manufacturers for the regular attendance of Excise officers to supervise denaturing operations or the use of denatured spirit, in factories taking the benefit of Section 8 of the Finance Act, 1902.

(v) That where spirit is allowed to be denatured with special agents such agents should be subject to official test and approval; and that accounts should be kept by the user showing receipts of spirit into store, the issues thereof from store in detail, and the quantities of goods produced.

(vi) That in the manufacture of fine chemicals and pharmaceutical products, spirit specially denatured should be allowed only where the manufacture is kept entirely separate from the manufacture of tinctures and other preparations in which spirit remains as spirit in the finished product.

(vii) That the regulations governing the sale by retail of mineralised methylated spirit should be made less stringent and more elastic.

Any special cases, such as that of smokeless powder, not touched by the above recommendations, can always be met under the powers conferred by Section 8 of the Act of 1902.

41. In concluding our Report, we desire to express our indebtedness to our Secretary, Mr. E. C. Cunningham, whose service in that capacity has been of the greatest value to the Committee.

We have the honour to be, Sir,
Your obedient Servants.

H. W. PRIMROSE,
WILLIAM CROOKES,
W. H. HOLLAND,
JOHN SCOTT MONTAGU,
LOTHIAN D. NICHOLSON,
WM. SOMERVILLE,
T. E. THORPE,
THOMAS TYRER.

E. C. CUNNINGHAM (Secretary).
23rd March, 1905.

Dear Mr. Chancellor of the Exchequer,

After carefully re-perusing the above report in its final form, we shall esteem it a favour if you will kindly allow us to modify our assent to the somewhat emphatic opinion expressed in paragraph 15, and to say that whilst obstacles to the use of Alcohol have not been shown to be the sole, nor even the main, cause of the loss of the Coal Tar Colour Industry to this country, we are nevertheless of opinion that they have been shown to be one of the contributing causes of that unfortunate result.

Yours sincerely,
W. H. HOLLAND,
JOHN S. MONTAGU.

31st March, 1905.

REPORT OF SUB-COMMITTEE ON THEIR VISIT TO GERMANY.

We have the honour to report that we left London on the morning of January 14th, returning on the 26th.

We spent six days in Berlin, and while there we received the most cordial and unremitting attention from Privy Counsellors Koreuber and Dr. von Buchka, to whom, through our Ambassador, we had been referred by his Excellency the Secretary to the Imperial Treasury. We desire to record our sense of the very great obligation under which we feel to those gentlemen.

From Berlin we went on to Heidelberg and Darmstadt, returning through Cologne.

We give the result of our inquiries in full detail in separate sections relating to the several heads. The outcome of them may be briefly summarised as follows:

(1) That the German system, in regard to the use of spirit for industrial purposes, is correctly stated in Appendix No. III., as laid before the Committee:

(2) That this system, while designed on liberal and comprehensive lines, is rigidly enforced, and allows of no exceptions in practice to the rules as laid down. Consequently, with the exception of smokeless powder, no article can be manu-.

factured in Germany with duty-free spirit, *unless* it be subjected before use to *some* process of denaturing:

(4) That the price of spirit in Germany for industrial purposes fluctuates very widely; that at the present time it is considerably higher than the price of similar spirit of British manufacture in this country; and that even in normal years its price is not as much below the price in this country as the Committee have been led to suppose:

(5) That the consumption of spirit in Germany for domestic and industrial purposes affords no standard by which to measure the possible consumption for similar purposes in the United Kingdom.

Section 1.

Official Regulations.

The whole of our first day in Berlin we spent in going carefully through the published official regulations as to use of spirit duty-free for industrial and other purposes with Privy Counsellor Korcuber, of the Imperial Treasury, and Dr. von Buchka, the Head of the Chemical Branch of that Department.

As a result we are enabled to state that the abstract of the regulations as given in Appendix No. III. is perfectly accurate, and that practice conforms exactly to the regulations.

Accordingly the rules and practice of the German Empire may be briefly described as follows:

(1) Spirit may be used duty-free in a pure, undenatured state, only in a very limited number of cases, viz:

(a) In public, *i.e.*, State, or municipal, hospitals:

(b) In similar scientific institutions:

(c) For making smokeless powder, fuses and fulminates.

(2) For all other purposes, without exception, duty-paid spirit must be used, *unless* the spirit be subjected to some *authorised* process of denaturing prior to use.

(3) The authorised processes of denaturing fall into two main classes, according as they result in:

A. Complete Denaturing.

B. Incomplete Denaturing.

(4) The processes authorised for "Complete Denaturing" are two, viz:

(a) An admixture with every 100 litres of spirit of $2\frac{1}{2}$ litres of a mixture containing 4 parts of wood-naphtha and 1 part of pyridine bases. (To this mixture 50 grams of lavender or rosemary oil may be added optionally, to counteract the smell of the pyridine bases. But the addition is seldom made.) Spirit thus denatured is what is used for domestic purposes—heating, lighting and cooking. It is seldom used for industrial purposes. The only purpose of that kind for which its employment is considerable is the manufacture of cheap varnish.

(b) An admixture with the spirit of half the quantity (viz., $1\frac{1}{4}$ litres per 100 litres of spirit) of the above denaturing mixture, together with an addition of $\frac{1}{4}$ litre of a solution of methyl violet dye and of benzol in quantities that may range from 2 to 20 litres to every 100 litres of spirit.

Although spirit thus treated is classed as completely denatured, its use is limited to agricultural and motor engines, and the process would seem to fall more properly into Class B.

The spirit thus denatured is used in practice almost entirely for agricultural engines, as no satisfactory solution has yet been found of certain difficulties which beset the use of spirit for motor cars.

(5) The processes authorised for "Incomplete Denaturing" are numerous. They consist:

(a) Of two alternative processes of general application, viz.:

The addition to every 100 litres of spirit of either 5 litres of wood-naphtha,

or $\frac{1}{2}$ litre of pyridine bases.

(b) Of numerous processes of special application.

These are fully set out in Appendix No. III. But the processes applicable to the most numerous and most important industries, including coal tar colours and chemical preparations, are the four alternatives of

An addition to every 100 litres of spirit of 10 litres of sulphuric ether,
or 1 litre of benzol,
or ½ litre of turpentine,
or .025 litre of animal oil.

(6) We may observe that the above regulations are applicable only to ethyl alcohol. Methylic alcohol does not fall within the charge to spirit duty in Germany, and may be used freely for industrial purposes, without control by the Revenue authorities.

(7) The schedule of authorised denaturing agents cannot be varied by the Executive. Any amendment of it, or addition to it, must be sanctioned by the Bundesrath, or Federal Council of the Empire; and the procedure for obtaining such sanction occupies many months, probably never less than six.

We add from our notes a few general observations and others bearing upon points referred to by witnesses who have given evidence before the Committee.

(i) The rules are strictly enforced and no exceptions to them are allowed.

(ii) The Revenue authorities regard them as being as little stringent as is compatible with the safety of the spirit revenue, even with the present low duty on spirit. They considered that, if the duties were ever to be raised, it would be necessary to revise the regulations, and to make them less lenient in certain directions.

(iii) The revenue authorities regard as a valuable safeguard to the revenue the obligation on manufacturers to keep "stock accounts" and "control books." They do not consider that it causes to manufacturers any serious difficulty or inconvenience.

(iv) For lacquer-making a considerable quantity of wood-naphtha denatured spirit is used in Nüremberg, Baden and Bavaria. Elsewhere turpentine is almost universally employed as the denaturing agent. No lacquers, polishes or varnishes can be made in Germany with pure duty-free spirit, or with admixture only of shellac.

(v) *Photographic Collodion.*—It is the common opinion in Germany that the British-made collodion is better than the German.

(vi) *Edible Oils.*—No special process of denaturing is prescribed for these. Therefore the general incomplete denaturing agents must be used, *i.e.*, wood-naphtha or pyridine bases—see above 5 (a).

(vii) All alcohol-containing medicines must now be made with duty-paid spirit, even veterinary medicines. The privilege of using pure undenatured duty-free alcohol for such purpose was taken away in October, 1903.

(viii) Tinctures are not allowed drawback on exportation, unless manufactured under Excise supervision (in bond).

No drawback, or allowance in the nature of drawback, is given under any circumstances in respect of articles manufactured with denatured spirit.

SECTION 2.

It was our desire to see the working of the system in factories typical of as many of the principal industries using alcohol as it might be possible for us to visit without unduly extending the period or the circuit of our tour. We failed, however, to accomplish this object in respect to factories for the production of synthetic perfumes, of varnish, and of coal tar colours, for the following reasons:

Synthetic Perfumes.

Dr. von Buchka very kindly addressed, on our behalf, the firm of Messrs. Schimmel of Leipsic, the principal manufacturers in Germany of synthetic perfumes. But those gentlemen informed him that it was against the rule of their establishment to admit visitors, and that they regretted that to this rule they could make no exception.

Varnish.

This industry is not carried on to any great extent in Berlin. But Dr. Wittelshöfer, managing director of the Centrale für Spiritus Verwerthung, kindly made efforts, on our behalf, to obtain admission to the one important establishment of the kind in the city. Owing, however, to the absence of the principal partners, there was no one who possessed the requisite authority to give permission for our visit during the days we were in Berlin, and we did not think it worth while to prolong our stay for the purpose of obtaining an opportunity, as the facts and position in regard to lacquer and varnish are so clear as not to demand any further special elucidation.

Coal Tar Colours.

Before leaving England, Dr. Thorpe had addressed to Dr. Glaser—a personal friend of his, and a former director (now a member of the Advisory Committee) of the Badische Anilin und Soda Fabrik of Ludwigshafen—a request that we might be permitted to visit that establishment. The directors felt some difficulty in acceding to this request. They, however, deputed Dr. Ehrhardt, one of their chemists, to wait upon us at Heidelberg with Dr. Glaser, in order to explain their position, and to give us such information as he properly could in regard to the special subject of our inquiry. We, accordingly, had the advantage of a conversation of some two hours duration with him and Dr. Glaser together, and from our notes of it we abstract the following items.

Dr. Ehrhardt felt great difficulty in offering an opinion as to the proportion of coal tar dyes, whether by way of value or of quantity, which require the use of alcohol in their manufacture, but was inclined to accept as probably correct an estimate which had been given to us in Berlin by a very competent authority, and which placed the proportion at 10 per cent. of the whole. He observed that indigo and alizarine, neither of which requires the use of alcohol, would account for at least one half of the production of the Badische Fabrik. In addition there was a large class of azo colours which made up a large proportion of the rest of the colouring matters made by the company, and of which only a very few individuals require alcohol.

Asked whether, in these circumstances, it might not be possible to engage profitably in the manufacture of the 90 per cent. of dyestuffs that need no alcohol, while neglecting those that required alcohol, Dr. Ehrhardt remarked that such an enterprise would be at a disadvantage as regards the by-products for the profitable utilisation of which research, demanding alcohol, was necessary.

On the question of the proportion that the cost of alcohol bore to the total cost of production of coal tar colours, Dr. Ehrhardt felt unable to offer an opinion; but he regarded as quite possible an estimate of $\frac{1}{2}$ per cent. which had been given to us in Berlin by the authority previously mentioned.

Duty-free alcohol in a pure state is not allowed under any circumstances, not even in the laboratory.

The denaturants employed by the Badische Fabrik are animal oil, pyridine, and sometimes the colour to be manufactured.

The importation into Germany of English-made colours or intermediate products is small and is confined to a few specialities.

The total number of persons employed in the Fabrik is between 7,000 and 8,000, of whom a large number are boys; no women. Of these only a very few could ever have access to the spirit used, at a stage at which it might conceivably be drunk, and those few would always be under supervision.

There is no particular tendency at the Fabrik to avoid the use of alcohol, the restrictions not being found seriously burdensome.

On the general question of the causes which have led to the great development of the coal tar industry in Germany, and its decline, or at any rate, its stagnation in Great Britain, we had much interesting talk with Dr. Glaser and Dr. Ehrhardt, and also on the following day at Mannheim with Dr. Caro, who may be regarded as one of the principal founders of the industry in Germany. They all agreed that, as an historical fact, the question of alcohol had little or nothing to do with the matter. Dr. Caro pointed out that the movement had begun, and had reached a point of considerable advancement before the time at which the use of alcohol otherwise than as a solvent—a purpose for which methylated spirit is perfectly suitable—had been appreciably developed, and before the time at which reduction in the selling price of dyestuffs through competition had rendered economy in production of serious importance.

They were unanimously of opinion that the real cause of the failure of the dye industry to develop in the United Kingdom was the lack of appreciation by British manufacturers of the importance of the scientific side of the industry. Thirty and forty years ago the whole business was conducted by the manufacturer, without much thought of its scientific aspects, and without any adequate recognition of the place of the trained chemist in connection with it.

In Germany the case was different. There the rise of the industry coincided with an immense development of activity in the study of organic chemistry and in its application to industry, stimulated largely by the influence of Kekulé, his coadjutors and immediate followers. Dr. Glaser gave it as his opinion that Kekulé's conception of the chemical structure of benzol was the germ out of which has grown the modern colour industry. The output of chemists by the German Universities was relatively enormous, and has continued to be so for the past forty years, and the services of competent chemists became obtainable at salaries of no more than £100 per annum. Consequently, they are engaged by hundreds to act practically as foremen in the works, and the whole of the subordinate supervision was in the hands of scientifically trained men. This was of immense advantage to the business of manufacture, and at the same time it provided a large field from which to select the more competent men for the work of research and invention; and those thus advanced were given a leading part in the management and in the profits of the business.

Nothing of the kind was possible in England at that time. Perhaps it is not so, even now.

At the same time these gentlemen all recognised that as things are at the present day, when alcohol enters so largely into the composition of colouring matters, and when the profits on the manufacture of coal tar dyes and intermediate products have been cut down by competition to a narrow margin, the question of alcohol, of the price at which it can be procured, and of the facilities given for its employment, has become a matter of great, if not of cardinal, importance.

SECTION 3.

Operation of Complete Denaturing.

By the courtesy of the Brennspiritus Gesellschaft we were given an opportunity of visiting their methylating premises in Warschauer Strasse, in the eastern quarter of Berlin, and there witnessing the operation of preparing the "completely" denatured spirit which is used in Germany for household purposes—heating, lighting, cooking, etc., and which thus corresponds to the mineralised methylated spirit we are familiar with in this country.

On the occasion of our visit, the spirit for denaturing was contained in twenty-eight casks, holding some 600 litres (132 gallons) apiece. These had been conveyed to the methylating premises direct from a distillery, under Revenue seal, and accompanied by an official despatch giving particulars of the distinctive number, tare, seals, content, etc., of each cask. The operation of denaturing was superintended by two Revenue officials, whose attendance has, as usual, to be paid for by the methylator. The first duty of these officers is to see the casks weighed. The weighing machine was situated just outside the room provided for the officers, who, after testing the weights, watched the weighing operation from inside. As each cask was rolled on to the machine, an employé of the methylator called out its distinctive number, tare, and gross weight to the nearest half kilogram. The casks were not gauged on the methylating premises, the quantity of spirit being ascertained from its weight and strength alone.

The operation of weighing was performed in a remarkably expeditious manner, the whole of the twenty-eight casks being weighed in about twenty-five minutes.

For the subsequent operations, the casks are arranged in rows—bungs upwards. The Revenue officers first proceed to verify the seals, passing one on each side along the rows, and assuring themselves that the seals of each cask are intact and correspond in number and position with the entries on the despatch. An employé of the methylator follows them, and, as each set of seals is checked, knocks off the seal and Revenue fastening over the bung-hole and withdraws the bung in readiness for sampling.

The spirit in each cask is next roused by a wooden rod inserted through the bung-hole, to ensure that the spirit shall be of uniform strength throughout. A sample is then taken from each cask, and its temperature and apparent strength ascertained by the alcoholometer. The standard strength is then deduced by the help of tables. The alcoholometer is provided by the methylator at his own expense; and each instrument must be officially tested before it is brought into use.

The Revenue officers having completed their check, and determined the content of each cask in terms of 100 per cent. alcohol, the quantity of denaturing mixture requisite for each cask is calculated.

The denaturing mixture, consisting of four parts of wood-naphtha to one part of pyridine bases, is received in iron drums, ready mixed, from the factory where it is prepared, in this case the factory at Fürstenwalde, which we subsequently visited. The drums are kept under Revenue seal, and may only be opened in the presence of a Revenue officer. The quantity of denaturant required for each cask is drawn off in a graduated can and emptied into the cask through the bung-hole. The Revenue officers keep a running account of the quantity drawn off from the store drum, from time to time, on a label attached to the drum.

After the addition of the denaturant, the Revenue officers must satisfy themselves that a thorough mixture of the spirit and denaturant is effected by stirring with a wooden rod, or by rolling the cask about; and the denatured spirit is then free from further Revenue control.

As the time at our disposal was limited, we did not wait to see the whole of the twenty-eight casks denatured; but we were informed that the whole operation would probably be completed in some three to four hours from its commencement. We have already remarked on the expeditious manner in which the casks were weighed; and we were also struck by the methodical and systematic way in which the casks were arranged in rows, after weighing, for the subsequent operations. A considerable saving of time is, of course, effected by not gauging the contents of the casks; but in regard to the salient feature in which the operation we have described differs from a methylation in this country, viz., the fact that the spirit is denatured in the casks themselves, instead of being emptied into a vat and there mixed with the denaturant, we were given to understand that this is not regarded as saving an appreciable amount of time in the operation of denaturing. The method has obvious advantages when it is intended to send out the denatured spirit in cask; but we were not surprised to hear that, when the spirit is intended for bottling, and especially when very large quantities are denatured at one time, the methylator prefers to pump the spirit from the casks into a vat or tank and add the denaturing mixture there.

Before leaving the premises, we paid a short visit to the bottling-room, where a staff of some twenty or thirty men and women, assisted by the latest labour-saving machinery, were engaged in washing, filling, labelling, and stoppering the bottles in which the spirit is sent out for sale by retail. Each bottle contains one litre, and the price at which it is sold is indicated on the label. This price is fixed from time to time by the Centrale, and is at present forty pfennigs per litre. The present price is, however, abnormally high. In ordinary times, we gathered that it ranges from twenty to twenty-five pfennigs.

SECTION 4.

Pharmaceutical Products—Fine Chemicals.

As is well known, Germany has long enjoyed a pre-eminence in the manufacture of the products classed generically as "fine" chemicals, in contradistinction tor "heavy" chemicals such as the mineral acids, alkalis, bleaching powder, alum, etc., mainly inorganic substances, which hitherto have been the chief staple chemical products of this country. Germany too has made almost exclusively the now numerous pharmaceutical products, which are definite organic compounds, often of complicated chemical constitution, largely obtained by synthetic processes and which may be said to depend upon the industrial application of the laboratory processes and methods of modern organic research.

As it is frequently alleged in this country that this pre-eminence is largely, if not entirely, due to the facility and comparative cheapness with which ordinary alcohol, both pure and suitably denatured, is obtained by chemical manufactures in Germany, it was of great importance to our inquiry to obtain trustworthy first-hand information on the subject.

We accordingly solicited permission to visit the establishments of E. Mer k in Darmstadt, and of the Chemische Fabrik Auf Actien (Vorm. E. Schering) at Berlin. selecting these as among the most representative and most comprehensive manufactories of these particular classes of products, and to have the opportunity of conferring with those responsible for their direction and management. Both factories have a world-wide reputation and have branch houses or agencies in almost every country in both hemispheres.

Permission was readily granted in each case, and every facility was afforded to us to acquire information on the special subject of our inquiry and to see operations involving the use of alcohol, its custody and control, methods of denaturing, processes of recovery, Revenue checks, etc. We cannot too gratefully acknowledge the courtesy with which we were received, the readiness with which such information as we could reasonably ask for was given, and the freedom with which illustrative or typical processes, some of them unique, were exhibited and explained.

Whilst at Berlin we were invited by Dr. Böttinger of the well-known Bayer Company to visit the newly-erected factory at Leverkusen, but as we were at the same time informed that they do not use or denature any spirit in Leverkusen, we were reluctantly obliged, on account of the short time at our disposal, to decline the opportunity of seeing what Professor Witt described as the best appointed works of the kind in Germany.

At the Charlottenburg branch of the Chemische Fabrik Auf Actien (Vorm. E. Schering), which we visited first, we were received by Dr. O. Antrick. By arrangement with the company, we so timed our visit as to be able to witness a denaturing operation on the large scale, having learned from Dr. Antrick that such an operation had been arranged for prior to our application.

The denaturant mainly in use in this factory is animal oil, which is mixed under the direction of the Revenue officers, in the proportion required by the regulations. The sample of the bone-oil used must be of the character officially prescribed. It is received at the works under revenue seal, accompanied by a certificate of its validity from a sworn chemist, recognised by the revenue authorities. The only other denaturant employed in this works is ether, which is admixed under the direction of the Revenue officers to the extnet of 10 per cent. The ether employed must be certified to be of the official character before addition.

All expenses of methylation, not only the cost of the denaturants themselves but the fee for the chemists' analyses and certificates, as well as the charges for the attendance of the officer, the cost of handling, mixing, pumping, etc., are borne by the manufacturers, who are required to furnish the gauge glasses, standardised hydrometers, weighing machines, mixing machines, mixing rods, office furniture. in fact everything needed to carry out the process as prescribed, without charge to the State.

12,000 hectolitres of alcohol are employed in the course of a year. The proportion of ether alcohol to bone-oil alcohol used is roughly as 2 to 7. No duty-free pure alcohol is allowed.

The denaturing operation we actually witnessed was with ether. The alcohol as received was contained in sealed iron puncheons or drums, each of which, after inspection of the validity of the seal, was weighed, the weighing machine being so placed that the Revenue officers seated at a table, within the building in which the alcohol was to be subsequently stored, could readily check the weights and compare them with the particulars on the despatches. The strength of the alcohol was then ascertained by the alcoholometer, the temperature noted, and the necessary corrections made, as indicated in the official tables. After the officers had verified the particulars, the alcohol was pumped or forced by compressed air into the store-receivers, iron tanks of known capacity secured with locks and provided with gauges; the calculated quantity of ether was then added and the mixture thoroughly stirred by mechanical means. Formerly the admixture was made by a stream of compressed air, but this led to so large a loss of ether by volatilisation that mechanical stirring is now preferred. The room in which the various tanks of denatured alcohol are contained is a specially constructed and well-arranged building, and all precautions are taken to avoid any illicit use of the spirit. The users of the alcohol are required to keep an account of successive withdrawals, and each department and branch factory must also keep an account of receipt and expenditure on a prescribed form. These accounts are from time to time examined and verified by the Revenue officers, who record the dates of their visits and affix their signatures.

The amount of clerical work needed, and the system of verification and control in force, struck us as greater and more detailed than English users of alcohol under the 1902 regulations have hitherto been subjected to. Dr. Antrick considered, however, that in a works of the magnitude and character of Schering's, the system was not too irksome, and they had little difficulty in complying with the official requirements, although he admitted that in smaller works there were occasional complaints of the rigour of the system. We had further an opportunity of witnessing operations in which the denatured spirit was employed and partially recovered, and we saw the method of recovery and rectification of the alcohol in actual use. We were also shown how the recovered alcohol was stored, brought to account, and how the necessary re-denaturing was effected.

The factory of E. Merck, of Darmstadt, is now situated in new premises in the Frankfurter Strasse, some distance outside the town. It is an old-established business, and is under the direction of four grandsons of the original founder. It may be said to have developed out of the old pharmacy of the same name in Darmstadt, which has existed for nearly two centuries and which is still maintained by the firm.

The new works, which are still in process of being finished as regards approaches and certain internal arrangements, are among the most complete and best appointed of their kind in the world. They consist of a number of detached and specially planned factories, under individual control and with special staffs of chemists and workmen, together occupying a very large area of ground, with convenient railway access from Arheilgen on the Main-Neckar line. 1,200 workmen are employed and 290 clerks and chemists. The firm deals in upwards of 6,000 products, 3,000 of which are made upon these premises. There are branch manufacturing establishments in Moscow and in New York. In the latter no preparation involving the use of alcohol is made.

All the denaturants allowed by the regulations, including the special ones used in the manufacture of iodoform, chloroform and ethyl bromide, are employed. The official completely denatured alcohol, containing wood-naphtha and pyridine bases, is used, but not for many purposes and only in small quantities. In all about 100,-000 kilos of alcohol are denatured annually, in addition to which large quantities of duty-paid spirit are used, over which there is no official control. The use of pure alcohol without duty is not allowed. No precise estimate could be given, at the time, of the number of the 3,000 products which needed alcohol, but two of the partners, including the head of the actual factory management, agreed that it could not exceed 20 per cent. The value of the alcohol used, as compared with the value of the finished products, could not at once be ascertained; it, of course, varies largely with the different products, but was probably not more than from 15 to 20 per cent. Special methods are employed for removing the last traces of the denaturants from the finished products, some of which were described to us. Owing to the number of denaturants allowed no particular difficulty seems to occur in this respect, although in some cases duty-paid alcohol must be employed. It may here be stated that the principle of *ad hoc* denaturation is not regarded with favour by the German Revenue officials, and in many cases the privilege of employing it has been withdrawn.

We inspected the spirit stores and inquired into the methods of custody, control and distribution of the duty-free alcohol, and we had also the opportunity of witnessing a denaturing operation. The method, in principle, was precisely similar to that we had seen at Charlottenburg, although the arrangements for the convenience of the Revenue officials were slightly different. These officers are required to attend for denaturing about twice a week. The cost of attendance is about 6 marks per officer per day—say 24 marks a week. Sometimes, however, a third officer is required. The cost of this attendance is considered of less consequence than the trouble it involves. We were informed that the present price of Prima spirit is 67 marks per 100 kilos (= 2s. 2d. per bulk gallon), which does not include the vat tax, but includes the distillery tax, which amounts to 7.16 marks per 100 kilos. For purposes of rebate, a running account is kept and the payments are made about every three months. No export business involving drawbacks on exportation is done at Darmstadt.

We inspected some of the control books relating to alcohol in the separate factories. The superintending chemist in charge of each department is personally responsible for the accuracy of the control book, and for the proper use of the spirit served out to him.

As regards ether, we were informed that this article may not be retailed, except when made from duty-paid spirit. A pharmacist may only receive it under permit, and may not sell it for medicinal purposes, unless prescribed by a physician. This procedure is adopted with a view of stopping the practice of drinking ether as an intoxicant.

In hospitals, ether may, by special permission, be used duty free for anæsthetical purposes, and its use is also permitted, duty free, in the laboratories of those educational institutions which are allowed to use duty-free alcohol.

After having had the advantage of discussing this aspect of the general question with many persons well qualified to express an opinion, we have little doubt that the pre-eminence of Germany, in these particular branches of applied chemistry, is due to the same causes which have contributed to her success in the so-called coal tar colour industry. Alcohol in that industry has played at most a very subordinate part in its development, and although it is true that it plays a relatively much more important part in the manufacture of "fine" chemicals and of pharmaceutical products, the extraordinary development in Germany, which has occurred during the last fifteen or twenty years, in the discovery and utilisation in medicine of synthetic organic substances, is primarily due to the influence of the schools of chemistry, to the ardour and success with which organic chemistry in its highest developments is cultivated, and to the skill, energy and resourcefulness with which it is sought to turn the results of investigation to immediate practical account. The same conditions which have led to the synthesis and manufacture of alizarin and indigo—two of the most important vegetable dyestuffs, but which, like the great group of the azo colouring matters, require little or no alcohol for their production —have equally led to the discovery and commercial production of the long list of organic products of definite composition, but of complicated constitution, which under a variety of names, more or less fanciful, find an application, more or less permanent, in therapeutics. It is easy to trace how the growth of such a business as that of Merck is the direct outcome of the extraordinary development of chemistry, due to the genius and influence of Liebig, Wöhler, and Bunsen, and their contemporaries and immediate successors.

These men made Germany the nursery of chemists; their influence led to a great extension of laboratories and of laboratory training, not only among the German universities, but gradually in every academic centre throughout the world. The elder Merck was quick to take advantage of his opportunity. A pharmacist of the old school, who made the greater number of the products in which he dealt, and an experienced operative chemist, well versed in all the chemical methods of his time, he was ready to undertake the manufacture of the various reagents—the so-called fine chemicals and the materials for research—which the rapidly multiplying laboratories in Germany needed.

SECTION 5.

Agricultural Distilleries; Marienfelde.

Finding that there was in the neighbourhood of Berlin an example of an agricultural distillery, we took advantage of the opportunity and paid a visit to it.

It was situated at Marienfelde, some ten miles to the south of Berlin, on a large and apparently very flourishing farm. The distillery was at work, and we were enabled therefore to study the system in operation.

The procedure is as follows:

The potatoes (which must be produced on the land of the proprietor) are first washed by machinery. They are then steamed and pulped, and driven through a strainer into the mash-tun where they are mixed with a small percentage of malt. The wort is then passed into the fermenting vats. Each vat is gauged, and its content marked on the outside, together with the number of the vat. The wash is left to ferment for thirty hours, and is then conveyed to the still, which is of the patent-still type. On issuing from the condenser the spirit passes first through a domed glass case in which is a cup. In this cup, into which the spirit flows and from which it overflows, there float a thermometer and a hydrometer, to indicate the strength of the spirit passing. From this apparatus the spirit flows into a (Siemens) meter, fitted with an indicator which records the quantity, reduced to the standard of pure alcohol, of spirit transmitted, and from the meter the spirit passes on to the receiver.

The system of control does not require the continuous attendance of Excise officers, but is compounded of—

(1) Mechanical contrivances,
(2) Book entries,
(3) Liability to visitation at any time.

(1) *Mechanical Contrivances.*

Up to the point at which the wash passes into the still, these are limited to the gauging of the vats and to the plumbing under Revenue seal of all joints of the pipes leading from the vats to the still. From that point onwards to the receiver every vessel is locked and sealed, and no access to the spirit can be obtained by the distiller. As the manager expressed it to us, "Up to this point I am treated as an honest man. Afterwards I am no longer trusted."

In the smaller distilleries the meter, which no doubt is an expensive apparatus, is dispensed with, and the quantity of spirit distilled is ascertained by the Excise officer from the receiver. Whether there be a meter or not, the receiver is of course under lock, and is not accessible to the distiller.

(2) *Book Entries.*

The regulations require entry of the quantity of materials used. But we understood that this was regarded as of little practical value, and that little attention was paid to such records. It is manifest that they cannot be susceptible of any real check.

The important entries are those of the times of charging and discharging the several fermenting vats, and of the quantities of wash in each. These entries can of course be checked against the spirit found in the receiver, and on them is computed the vat-tax and the distillery tax, which have to be paid by the distiller.

(3) *Liability to Visitation.*

It will be seen that the control under (1) and (2) provides no security against abstraction of wash from the fermenting vats. Visitation at frequent and uncertain intervals would seem to be an essential feature of the system, and we gathered that at Marienfelde the visits of Excise officers were even unpleasantly frequent. Whether they are so in more remote distilleries may be open to doubt.

In any case we are of opinion that the system of control rests so heavily upon confidence that, while it may be satisfactory with a low duty on spirits and with a system of rebates of duty that makes the Excise a source of profit to the smaller distiller, it could not safely be adopted where the duty is as high as it is in the United Kingdom and invariable in its incidence.

The distillery at Marienfelde is one of the best and largest type of argicultural distilleries. Its "contingent" is 600 hectolitres per annum, or about 23,000 proof gallons of spirit. Out of the total number of agricultural distilleries in the German Empire there are not more than some 2,000 or 3,000 of similar size and character.

The vast majority of the agricultural distilleries are to be found in the eastern provinces of Prussia and Saxony, where the soil is poor, and the cost of conveying agricultural produce to a remunerative market is high; and it is not quite clear to us how it can be commercially profitable on a fertile farm close to Berlin to convert potatoes into spirit. The manager informed us that in the present year, even with the abnormally high price of spirit, he would realise on his potatoes used for distillation no more than from £2 to £2 5s. per ton, whereas if sold for consumption as potatoes, they would realise some £4 per ton. He was, however, compelled to use them in the distillery, in order to maintain his "contingent," which might be reduced if he should fail in any season to reach his prescribed production of 600 hectolitres. Moreover we doubt whether the above figure of return on the potatoes included the bonus of 20 marks (£1) per hectolitre on the amount of the contingent. This would be equal to more than another £1 per ton for the potatoes used.

We think the explanation of the maintenance of this distillery is that it is kept up to some extent as a convenient object lesson in the neighbourhood of Berlin, for the instruction of Excise officers, and to illustrate the teaching at the Institut für Gährungsgewerbe und Stärke-fabrikation in Berlin, an institution established by the trades, with assistance from the Government, for the purpose of giving instruction in brewing, distilling, and other processes in which fermentation is employed.

We were informed that in normal years the return from potatoes used in the agricultural distilleries does not exceed some 25s. per ton (exclusive presumably of bonuses), and in many cases is less. The average is about 20s. per ton.

The yield of alcohol from a ton of potatoes may be taken at about 25 gallons of pure alcohol, or about 44 proof gallons.

Section 6.

Vinegar Factory.

We visited a large establishment in Berlin for the manufacture of vinegar from alcohol, one of several worked by the same proprietors (Messrs. Kühne) in different parts of the Empire.

The process is exceedingly simple. The spirit, after the account has been taken in the usual way by the Excise officers, is poured, together with the prescribed quantities of vinegar and water, through a scupper in the pavement of the receiving floor into tanks in the basement. From these the mixture is pumped up to the topmost floor of a high building, whence it percolates down through a series of vats, floor by floor, filled with wood shavings and containing the food for the organisms which effect the conversion, and arranged so as to secure the maximum of exposure of the liquid to the air. The liquid finally returns to the basement in the form of the finished product (vinegar), the whole circuit occupying not more than three or four hours.

The quantity of vinegar produced of the strength of 7 per cent. of acetic acid is about 10 times the quantity of alcohol used.

There is a loss of some 30 per cent. of the alcohol by evaporation.

In this industry the control over the spirit employed is less exacting than in the case of any other industry in Germany. From the time when the spirit is denatured no further control is exercised over it. No books have to be kept to show how it has been disposed of, or what the yield of vinegar has been; nor is there any regular visitation of the manufacturing premises by the Excise officers. The one and only regulation imposed for the protection of the Revenue is a prohibition against keeping a still on the premises. It is true that the condition of the denatured spirit is such that there need be no apprehension of its being drunk on the premises or without purification. But even so, the system of control seems dangerously confiding, and the authorities of the Treasury frankly admitted that it could not be justified in principle.

The Government, however, have been reluctant to disturb it; partly because it is of long standing, and is not believed to lead to abuse in practice, but principally because this process of vinegar making can even now with difficulty hold its own against the process of manufacture from pyroligneous acid, and because it is feared that any curtailment of the present privileges of the industry would seriously endanger its very existence.

It is, however, felt that if at any time the duty on spirits should be raised in Germany it would be hardly possible to maintain the present system of control without modification.

In these circumstances it seems highly improbable that the process, which is at present not practised in the United Kingdom, could with advantage be introduced into this country.

The quantity of spirit used for the manufacture of vinegar in the German Empire was, for the year 1903, over 6,000,000 proof gallons.

The quantity used in the factory we visited is about 150,000 proof gallons.

Section 7.
A German Methylating Factory: Fürstenwalde.

Much, if not the greater portion, of the partially denatured spirit used by German manufacturers is denatured in the works in which it is actually employed, and this is invariably the case where the volume of spirit handled is large. Owing, however, to the fact that the freight-charges on pure alcohol are higher than on the denatured spirit—a difference which the German chemical manufacturers are struggling to remove—and to other circumstances, arrangements are made whereby manufacturers requiring only a relatively small quantity of denatured spirit, either complete or partial, may obtain it from professed methylators, working under Revenue supervision.

At the suggestion of Dr. Koreuber and Dr. von Buchka, who were kind enough to accompany us, we visited such an establishment at Fürstenwalde, a town on the Spree, about thirty miles south-east of Berlin, and within easy railway communication of the district of Posen where much of the agricultural spirit is made.

We were received by the proprietors of the establishment, Drs. B. Hecker and W. Zeidler, one of whom made up for us, in turn, every form of denatured alcohol which the regulations permitted the firm to prepare. The origin, character and sources of supply of each denaturant were described to us, and samples of the various articles, officially certified to be in conformity with the prescribed nature, were shown to us.

The wood-naphtha used for denaturing contains much less methyl alcohol than is customary in this country; as a rule, the quantity does not exceed 55 per cent. On the other hand, the regulations prescribed that it must contain at least 25 per cent. of acetone—a relatively expensive substance, probably not so useful as an indicative or "earmarking" material as methyl alcohol, and, as we are given to understand, somewhat prejudicial to the use of wood-naphtha and of methylated spirit in certain manufacturing operations.

The "pyridine bases" employed come largely from England, although other sources of supply are available. The price, owing to the increasing demand for these substances as the raw material for the manufacture of a number of special products, has risen considerably of late, and although used in only relatively small quantity, and for the most part in connection with the completely denatured spirit intended for heating, lighting and power, this increase in price is beginning to be felt. Considering the comparatively high prices of spirit in Germany at the present time, and the consequent restriction in the demand for general or household purposes, which is by far the largest outlet for industrial spirit in that country, any cheapening of the cost of denaturing becomes a matter for serious consideration.

The addition of lavender or rosemary oil, which is optional, and to the extent of 0.125 per cent., to the completely denatured spirit is seldom made, except for special purposes, as in soap-making. This addition was originally suggested to meet a possible popular prejudice against the use of denatured spirit in households, owing to the pungent smell of the pyridine bases. The prejudice, if it ever existed, apparently no longer obtains, although it must be stated that the German methylated spirit is far more disagreeable, as regards smell, than that in common use in England.

The Fürstenwalde Works mix considerable quantities of the general denaturant—that is the mixture of four parts of wood-naphtha and one part of pyridine bases—and which as already stated is added to the spirit in the proportion of $2\frac{1}{2}$ litres to every 100 litres of alcohol. The volume of the mixed denaturant made per annum is at present 800,000 litres—which is about one-third of the whole made in Germany.

We saw the operation of preparing the mixture. The wood-naphtha was received in iron drums, the tare of which is known. It is examined and certified as to character. The weight of the wood spirit having been ascertained, by the arrangements and in the manner already described, the requisite proportion of authenticated pyridine base contained in carboys is calculated, and that amount is weighed out. The wood-naphtha is then poured into a tank, and forced by air pressure into the receiver, after which the "pyridine base" is added.

The denaturing solution is distributed in drums, sealed by the Revenue authorities and bearing labels certifying that the mixture is in accordance with law. The drums when received by the consignee can only be unsealed by a Revenue Officer. A running account is then kept on an attached label on each drum of the successive quantities withdrawn for denaturing purposes.

Section 8.

Artificial Silk Factory.

By the courtesy of Dr. Bottler, whom we met in Berlin, and who is managing director of an artificial silk factory at Jülich, near Cologne, we were enabled to pay a visit to that establishment.

In the process followed in this case alcohol plays a very important part, seeing that something like a gallon and a half of proof spirit is required, either in the form of ether or of spirit, to produce 1 lb. of the finished product.

The process is as follows:

Nitro-cellulose is dissolved in a mixture of ether and alcohol, consisting of sixty parts of ether and forty of alcohol, and the solution thus obtained, which is in effect collodion, is after filtration driven under pressure, until it finally emerges, through a number of fine glass tubes. On contact with the air the solution solidifies and the threads thus formed are picked up on bobbins, sixteen of the primary threads being immediately twisted into a single thread which becomes the unit for further operations.

The ether used in the factory is purchased from outside, not manufactured on the spot.

The alcohol comes in under Excise seal in the usual way, and is denatured in accordance with the regulations by being mixed with 10 per cent. of ether. The denaturing is carried out in the presence of the Revenue officers and under their supervision. The denatured spirit is stored in a metal tank, under Revenue lock and fitted with an indicator outside showing the quantity present in it.

Copper-zinc vessels are used, in preference to iron, to avoid injury to the ethered alcohol from corrosion.

From the tank the denatured spirit, when required for use, passes through closed pipes to the vessel in which the nitro-cellulose is dissolved—the additional ether required being added at this point. While in the dissolving chamber the spirit is not accessible to the workmen employed in the factory; and speaking generally we should say that the conditions of this manufacture lend themselves to the establishment, without much cost or difficulty, of an effective control over the spirit employed.

We may mention that Dr. Bottler informed us that very great difficulties had been met with in perfecting the process of manufacture, and that although the factory had been in operation for over two years, it was only within the ten days preceding our visit that he was able to feel confident that all the difficulties had been overcome. Into those difficulties the obligations in respect of denaturing did not enter, and the experience of this factory is sufficient to show that the embarrassments which attended a similar experiment made some years ago at Coventry, and which were there attributed to the character of the methylated spirit that the promoters were compelled to use, may arise from more causes than one.

Production and Price of Spirit in Germany.

The production of spirit in Germany is a State-aided enterprise, of which the primary purpose is not so much the production of spirit on economic lines as the encouragement of agriculture in the less fertile provinces of the Empire, which lie on its Eastern frontiers, and in which the conditions of soil and climate are so unfavorable that without some such encouragement the country would be in serious danger of depopulation.

To enter into the history and details of the system, interesting though they be, would be to go beyond the province of our inquiry. We shall, therefore, confine our attention as closely as we can to the two points which are of interest to our Committee, viz.: the effect of the system on the price of spirit for industrial purposes and its effect upon the price of spirit for export.

The system is essentially communistic in character, and its effects can be better seen by studying its results broadly and as a whole, rather than by attempting to trace its influence upon the interests of individuals.

Looking at it from this point of view, it may be said that the fundamental principle of the scheme is to make those interested in the production of alcohol sharers with the State in the revenue collected on spirit used for potable purposes.

Thus in the year ended on 30th September, 1903, there was collected from the taxes on spirit a total sum of £10,000,000, out of which a sum of £3,100,000 was given back to persons interested in the trade. But of this sum of £3,100,000 apparently some £700,000 had been already levied as tax on the producers, so that their net subvention would be £2,400,000. In the same year the total production of spirit in Germany was in round figures £132,000,000 proof gallons, and accordingly the State subvention in that year represented a bonus of nearly 4½d. per proof gallon on all the spirit produced. The figures must, of course, vary from year to year, according to the circumstances of production and consumption; but probably not very widely.

The question for us is whether this bounty, be it 4½d. per gallon or more or less, is retained by the producers or distributors, or whether it goes, in whole or in part, to cheapen spirit to the consumers.

Our conclusion is that as a rule it is retained by the producers in respect of all spirit consumed in Germany, and that only under certain circumstances do the German users of spirit secure share in it.

We will endeavour shortly to give the grounds on which we form this conclusion.

The system of subvention, as established in Germany, stimulates production, but at the same time it provides within itself an arrest of the stimulus after a certain measure of production has been reached. For the *maximum* bounty that can be secured in respect of any spirit, and which may be put at about 11d. per proof gallon, is obtainable only in respect of a certain limited output, called the Contingent. The total of such output is the equivalent of the amount of spirit estimated to be required for consumption as drink;—and therefore of the amount of spirit on which alone tax will be ultimately levied; and the Contingent of each distiller is the share annually alloted to him of such amount. On that share it is possible, in favourable circumstances, for a distiller to obtain the maximum bounty of 11d. the proof gallon. But as soon as his production exceeds this allotted Contingent, one portion of the bounty, representing about 6d. per proof gallon, automatically ceases, and on the excess production the distiller can at most obtain 5d. per proof gallon. Only the smallest distilleries can obtain the maximum bounty of this kind; and as a distillery increases in size and output the bounty diminishes until with the larger distilleries it becomes non-existent. Thus the system of subvention gradually ceases to operate as a stimulant to production, and it may perhaps be said that the system gives no encouragement to produce more than such an amount of spirit as is sufficient to satisfy the demand for consumption for all purposes within the protected German market, and to provide a moderate margin for stock.

The distribution of spirit produced in the German Empire is practically a mon poly of an association called the Centrale für Spiritus Verwerthung, which is representative of the producers of spirit, and which acts as intermediary between them and the consumers for 90 per cent. of all the spirit produced. The policy of this Association coincides with the Governmental policy in tending to restriction of production within the limits above indicated, and in so far as this policy is successful it is clear that, with practically prohibitive duties on the importation of spirit, the user of spirit in Germany is not likely to be able to secure for himself any portion of the benefit of the State bounties. He may only do so to a limited extent, when the general policy of the State and of the Association is defeated by unforeseen variations either in the supply or in the demand of any period.

With the spirit exported the case is somewhat different. For this must frequently represent a surplus, of which the Association desires to relieve the home market; and it may be assumed with some confidence that, in order to get rid of such surplus, a price is in the circumstances usually accepted which represents a transfer to the purchaser of a part, or even of the whole, of the State bounty.

Another feature of the system in its bearing upon the price of spirit to German users is this, that it tends to great fluctuations of price. For the general principle of the system being to limit production relatively to home consumption, no safeguard is provided against the contingency that has arisen this year of a shortage in production due to a failure of that which provides four-fifths of the material used in distilling, viz.: the potato crop.

Thus our conclusion is that the German user of spirit is not generally benefitted by the State aid given to the production of spirit, and at times is injured by it.

The evidence of facts seems to support these theoretical deductions. At the present moment, as we were informed by a large user of spirit, the price charged for spirit of the first quality, such as is necessary for the finer purposes for which spirit is used, is, free of all duty, 50 marks per hectolitre—at the German standard of pure alcohol. At the British standard of proof spirit this is approximately equal to 50s. per 38 proof gallons, or a little over 1s. 3½d. per proof gallon. The price of similar spirit of British manufacture in the United Kingdom is about 10d. per proof gallon. Three years ago the minimum price for such spirit was in Germany 7d. per proof gallon, and the average price for the year 1902 was 8½d. In the United Kingdom the price of British spirit was the same as now. The year 1902 was, however, altogether an exceptional year in Germany, and manufacturers have little expectation of seeing similar prices recur, unless, as one gentleman put it to us, the Centrale Association should be dissolved and competition between producers introduced.

Moreover, in 1902 the Centrale was pursuing the policy of endeavouring to cheapen spirit for industrial purposes by charging higher prices for spirit used for consumption as drink, and lower for industrial spirit. This policy has, however, broken down, in consequence, we surmise, of a tendency noticeable in Germany, as it is in this country, to a decrease in consumption of spirituous liquors. In consequence of contracts made for long terms of years, the policy is still in operation in respect of spirit used for industrial locomotives and other engines. But as the contracts expire, it is anticipated that the policy will be modified, if not abandoned, even in this category of consumption.

It will be seen from the above figures that at the present time the price of industrial spirit in Germany is substantially higher than it is in the United Kingdom; that the price is subject to violent fluctuations; and that although at times it has been, and probably will again be, appreciably below the British price, it is doubtful whether its normal level in future will show any very material advantage to the German user.

As regards the cost of denaturing by special agents, it is hardly possible to name an average figure. In all cases the cost of manipulation, of attendance of Excise officers, of vessels and instruments, has to be borne by the manufacturer, and one manufacturer estimated these for us as at least 2 marks per hectolitre, or about 1d. per bulk gallon of strong spirit. In addition there is the cost of the denaturing agent, which varies very much according to the substance used. Our informant estimated that in his case the average of the whole cost of denaturing might be taken at 7 marks per hectolitre of strong spirit, or almost 4d. per bulk gallon. We are inclined to think this too high an estimate, seeing that the cost of "complete" denaturing is definitely known to be only a little more than 1d. the bulk gallon. In that case, however, there is all the economy that results from simplicity, regularity and magnitude in the operations.

A question that pressed itself strongly upon our attention, during our visit to Germany, was how far the consumption of spirit for domestic and industrial purposes in that country could be taken as a measure of the possible consumption for similar purposes in the United Kingdom, and we think it may be useful that we should offer to the Committee some observations upon it.

In the year to 30th September, 1903, the consumption in Germany was—

	Proof gallons.
For domestic use........................(about)	33,900,000
For motor and other engines........................	1,100,000
For industrial purposes........................	14,000,000
Total........................	49,000,000

In the year to 31st March, 1903, the consumption in the United Kingdom for similar purposes was—

	Proof gallons.
For domestic use........................(about)	2,200,000
For industrial use........................	3,300,000
Total........................	5,500,000

At first sight these figures suggest somewhat startling possibilities. But, if the facts be examined, it will be found that the possibilities of extended use of spirit in England shrink to very moderate dimensions.

In the first place the large consumption of spirit in Germany for domestic purposes, for heating, cooking and lighting, is due not to the absolute cheapness of spirit, or to any special advantage that it possesses as an agent for producing heat and light, but is due solely to its cheapness as compared with other agents, coal, gas or oil.

Of these oil is the agent that most directly competes with spirit, and in Germany oil, in the interests of alcohol, is subjected to a duty of 3 marks per cwt., or nearly 2½d. per gallon. In the United Kingdom its importation is free—consequently the comparison stands thus:

	Price of Methylated Spirit per bulk gallon.	Petroleum. per gallon.
In Germany........................	1s. 0d. (normal) 1s. 9½d. (present)	10½d.
In the United Kingdom........................	2s. to 2s. 6d.	5d. to 7d.

The price given above for petroleum in Germany is the price in Berlin, and there it is cheaper than spirit. Consequently in Berlin spirit, which has to compete with gas as well as with oil, is very little used for domestic purposes; probably not more so than in this country. In the rural districts oil is probably dearer than in Berlin, and more difficult to procure, whereas methylated spirit is of universal distribution —(it enjoys preferential railway rates)—and of uniform price, and it is therefore in these rural regions that the main consumption takes place. In the United Kingdom with cheap gas and cheap oil, no conceivable reduction in the price of methylated spirit would make spirit able to compete with them in price, and price must always be the determining motive of choice for the mass of the people. For though spirit has certain advantages in directions other than price, they are not of any marked significance in themselves, nor are they of a character to appeal very powerfully to the masses.

Accordingly we may dismiss almost entirely the use of spirit for domestic purposes as offering an opening for expansion in the demand for spirit in the United Kingdom.

With spirit for industrial purposes the case is different. But even here a large abatement must be made from the German figures before they can be taken as a possible measure of British consumption. Of the 14,000,000 proof gallons used in 1902-3, 6,350,000 gal'ons were employed for a purpose, vinegar-making, which, as we show elsewhere, is not present, or likely to be present in the United Kingdom. Another 2,650,000 gallons is used for polishes, varnishes, etc., an industry which in this country enjoys somewhat special advantages and which may be supposed to have reached a pretty full measure of development, under which it employs some 1,800,000 gallons of spirit.

This leaves some 5,000,000 proof gallons used in Germany for miscellaneous industrial purposes, for which in this country we use some 1,500,000 proof gallons.

On these figures one may say that the increased demand that might arise for spirit in this country, in consequence of an extension in its use for industrial purposes, may safely be placed at less than 3,500,000 proof gallons.

H. W. PRIMROSE,
T. E. THORPE.

E. C. CUNNINGHAM, Secretary.
27th February, 1905.

APPENDICES FROM MINUTES OF EVIDENCE TAKEN BEFORE THE BRITISH DEPARTMENTAL COMMITTEE ON INDUSTRIAL ALCOHOL, PRESENTED TO BOTH HOUSES OF PARLIAMENT BY COMMAND OF HIS MAJESTY.

APPENDIX No. I.

DUTIES AND ALLOWANCES ON BRITISH SPIRITS AND DUTIES ON FOREIGN SPIRITS.

The duty (Excise) on British spirits is at present 11s. per gallon at proof.

When British spirits are exported (or used for certain operations in bond), not only is the duty of 11s. remitted, but an allowance also is paid by the Inland Revenue at the rate of 3d. per proof gallon on plain spirits and of 5d. per proof gallon on compounded spirits.

These allowances are commonly spoken of as the "allowances on British spirits."

The duty (Customs) on Foreign Spirit is at present—

On Brandy and Rum 11s. 4d. per proof gallon,
On other sorts 11s. 5d. per proof gallon,
(with certain special rates for liqueurs and performed spirits and for spirits imported in bottle).

The difference (4d. or 5d. as the case may be) between the duty on British spirits and that on Foreign spirits is commonly spoken of as "the Surtax on Foreign spirits," or more briefly as "the Surtax."

Both the Allowances and the Surtax which date from 1860 (when the old protective duties were done away with) aim at the same purpose, which is, not to put the British producer of spirits in a position of advantage as compared with his foreign or colonial competitor, but to save him from being placed in a position of disadvantage.

In imposing a heavy duty on British spirits, it is necessary at the same time to impose on their manufacture restraints designed to prevent any spirit from escaping the duty. These restraints have the effect of appreciably increasing the cost of manufacture; and in consequence the burden of the duty on the British producer of spirit is not adequately measured by the figure of the duty alone, but must be measured by that figure plus the figure by which the cost of manufacture is increased by the Excise restrictions.

Accordingly if we take x pence per proof gallon for this latter figure, and 11s. per proof gallon as the duty on British spirit, the full burden of the tax on the producer of British spirit per proof gallon is represented by the expression (11s. $+ x$ d.).

It follows that, when the producer of British spirits sends out his goods to compete in neutral markets, he is entitled to relief to the extent of 11s. $+ x$ d. and not of 11s. only per proof gallon; and conversely that foreign goods should not be admitted to the home market at a less charge than 11s. $+ x$ d. per proof gallon.

The values of x have varied from time to time according to the following table.

447

	Surtax.			Allowances.	
	Rum.	Brandy.	Other Sorts.	Plain Spirits.	Compounded Spirits.
From 1860	2d.	5d.	5d.	2d.	3d.
" 1881	4d.	4d.	4d.	2d.	4d.
" 1902	4d.	4d.	5d.	3d.	5d.

The determination of values for x is a matter of extreme difficulty. To arrive at it, it is necessary to take into account—

(a) The tax, if any, on materials of manufacture;
(b) The effect of Excise restrictions on the cost of manufacture.

At the present time (a) is a negligible quantity. For, although there is a tax on sugar and glucose, these materials enter into distillation of spirits to so small an extent that the tax may be left out of acconut. Molasses used for distilling is duty free.

As regards (b), the Excise restrictions that do, or may, affect the cost of manufacture are numerous, but the principal among them are the following:

(1) The prohibition against brewing or distilling simultaneously;
(2) The prohibition against mixing worts during fermentation;
(3) Compulsory stoppage of work between Saturday and Monday;
(4) Restrictions on the manufacture of yeast;
(5) Separation of distillery and rectifying premises and loss of duty on spirits rectified.
(No. 5 hardly affects the cost of manufacture of "plain spirits.")

From this enumeration of the factors which have to be taken into account, it will be obvious that anything like precise accuracy in fixing values for x is unattainable.

The manner in which the rates of Surtax were originally computed in 1860 is shown in the table on page 445, which was first published in the Board of Inland Revenue's Thirteenth Report (1870), and which in the literature of the subject has since been frequently reproduced.

In the period that has elapsed since 1860 appreciable changes have taken place in the conditions of manufacture of spirit and in the rate of duty on spirit, and a computation to-day of the figures at which the rates of Surtax should stand would be based on items and on values that would differ materially from those shown in the original table. Of the composition of the rates as they now stand there is no accepted or authoritative analysis, and all that can be said of them is that they represent the outcome, by way of compromise, of prolonged controversy renewed at frequent intervals, as occasion for question presented itself, during a period extending over more than forty years.

It may, however, be convenient to say a few words as regards the increase by 1d. of the Allowances and of the Surtax on Spirits other than Rum and Brandy, which was made in 1902 at the time when the duty on corn was re-imposed. For the retention of the increase, notwithstanding the repeal of the corn duties in 1903, has been a frequent subject of criticism.

The imposition of the corn duties was the occasion rather than the cause of the addition to the Allowances and the Surtax.

For, taken by themselves, it was calculated that the duties, as first proposed, would not have warranted a larger addition than $\frac{6}{10}$ of a penny, nor, as finally passed, with a reduced duty on maize, a larger addition than $\frac{3}{10}$ of a penny.

	1886. Amount Claimed by		Amount Allowed in 1860.	1866. Considered Admissible by this Department.	
	Scotch Distillers.	English Distillers.		For Uncoloured Spirits.	For Coloured Spirits.
	d.	d.	d.	d.	d.
1st. —Compensation for duty on Foreign grain.	0¾	0¾	0¾	0¾	0¾
2nd.—Prohibition against brewing and distilling at same time	1½	1½	1	1	1
3rd.—Against distillers mixing wort in separate vessels while in process of fermentation	0¼	0¼	0¼	0¼	0¼
4th.—Loss of duty on rectification and flavouring spirits in separate premises.	3	3	1	2¼	2¼
5th.—Colouring matter in Foreign spirits.	2	2	2	Nil	2½
6th.—Increased expense in making malt consequent on Excise restrictions.	0¼	0½	Nil	Nil	Nil
7th.—Difference in mode of charging duty in favour of Foreign spirits.	1 ⎫	1½	Nil	Nil	Nil
8th.—Duty evaded upon Foreign spirits, and by samples drawn in bond.	0¼ ⎭				
	9	9½	5	4¼	6¾

But for some years prior to 1902 the distillers had been urging on the Treasury and the Board of Inland Revenue that the old rates of Allowance and of Surtax were insufficient (notably on the occasion when in March, 1898, a deputation representing the whole trade waited on the then Chancellor of the Exchequer) and the expert officers of the Excise had admitted that they could not dispute the arguments in favour of *some* increase in the rates.

What the amount of increase should be was a matter more difficult to determine, and it was still in question when the revival of the corn duties took place.

That event made action imperative, and an additional penny was agreed to —the addition, however, not to extend to Brandy or Rum, which are not made from grain.

When the duties were repealed in 1903 the question arose as to an adjustment of the rates of Allowance and Surtax. But as the adjustment could not have exceeded $\frac{3}{10}$ of a penny, and as the composition of the remainder of the rates was far from precise, it was decided that no change should be made.

Appendix No. II.

A. REGULATIONS AS REGARDS USE OF SPIRIT FOR INDUSTRIAL, ETC., PURPOSES IN THE UNITED KINGDOM.

The Customs and Excise Taxes on Spirits are:

Customs—11s. 4d. per proof gallon on Rum and Brandy.
    "   11s. 5d. "   "   "   " other Spirits.
Excise—11s. per proof gallon.

DUTY-FREE SPIRIT.

I. Methylated Spirit.

There are two kinds of methylated spirit.

A. "Ordinary" Methylated Spirit for use in manufacturing operations.

This consists of a mixture of 90 parts of ordinary ethylic alcohol of a strength of 60 to 66 o.p. (*i.e.* containing from 91 to 95 per cent. of real alcohol) and 10 parts of wood-naphtha of an approved type.

The official regulations do not require the British or Foreign spirit used to be of a greater strength than 50 o.p. (86 per cent. alcohol), and Colonial rum of a strength of only 20 o.p. (69 per cent. alcohol) may be used; but in practice rum is now never methylated, and the spirit is always over 60 o.p. (91 per cent. alcohol).

No duty is paid on British spirits used for making methylated spirit, and Foreign and Colonial spirits are exempt from the ordinary spirit tax of 11s. per proof gallon; but Foreign spirits have to pay a Customs surtax of 5d. per proof gallon, equivalent to about 8d. per gallon on the spirit as actually methylated. The surtax on Colonial rum is 4d. per proof gallon, equivalent to about 6½d. per gallon at 60 o.p., or less than 5d. per gallon, if rum of 20 o.p. were used for methylating.

Methylated spirit can only be made by—
1. Distillers.
2. Rectifiers, *i.e.*, persons who redistil duty-paid spirit.
3. Licensed methylators.

In practice methylated spirit is, as a rule, made by methylators, who pay an annual license of £10 10s.

All methylators have to provide suitable mixing rooms, vats, locks, fastenings, and appliances for weighing, measuring, and mixing the spirits and wood-naphtha, and the necessary desks for the convenience of the Revenue officials who supervise the operations. Mixing vats must be of a capacity of 550 gallons, and wood-naphtha vats of 100 gallons.

Spirits for methylation come from Customs or Excise duty-free warehouse accompanied by official permits, and are received by a Supervisor and Officer of Inland Revenue, who examine and check the strength and quantity, and see the spirits run into the mixing vats. To the spirit in each vat is then added one-ninth of its bulk of approved wood-naphtha. The contents of the vat have to be thoroughly mixed, and the total quantity and strength again measured by the officials. An official entry of these particulars is made, and the vat and its contents are then handed over to the methylator for disposal in accordance with prescribed regulations. Not less than 500 gallons of methylated spirit must be made at each mixing.

The wood-naphtha used for mixing with the spirit must be approved by the Board of Inland Revenue before it is used. For this purpose a sample is drawn from the naphtha vat and sent to the Government Laboratory for examination, the vat itself being locked up by the Revenue officer until the Principal of the Government Laboratory has certified that the naphtha is fit for methylating purposes. The nature of the examination to which the naphtha is submitted is described below, page 452, and from this the character of the wood-naphtha used for methylating purposes in this country can be gathered.

"Ordinary" or manufacturing methylated spirit can be sold by methylators only to persons authorised by the Board of Inland Revenue to receive this kind of spirit.

A user of this spirit must send to the methylator an official requisition signed by himself, and on which there is a certificate signed by the local Supervisor of Inland Revenue that the applicant is authorised to receive such spirit. Less quantities than five gallons cannot be supplied. The methylator has to enter the particulars of every consignment in an official permit taken from a book supplied to him by the Supervisor, and this permit must accompany the spirit to the premises of the user, and be delivered to the Officer of Inland Revenue when he visits the premises.

When any person wishes to use methylated spirit in any manufacturing process, or for making embrocations, lotions, medicaments or other preparations, written application has to be made to the Board of Inland Revenue. The particular purpose for which the spirit is intended to be used, with some general description of any manufacturing process involved, has to be given, and also a statement of the situation of the premises and of the quantity of spirit likely to be used annually.

After inquiry by the local officials the Board issue their authority for the use of the spirit, and instruct their officers to supply the applicant with a book of Requisition Forms, in order to enable him to obtain a supply of the spirit from a methylator.

Where the quantity of methylated spirit used exceeds 50 gallons per annum a bond, with one or more sureties in sums of £200 to £1,000, for the due observance of any conditions that may be imposed and the proper use of the spirit, is required. Hospitals, infirmaries, colleges, and other public institutions are not usually required to give a bond.

Methylated spirit is not allowed to be used for manufacturing purposes on any premises where ordinary alcoholic beverages are made or sold, nor for the preparation of any article of food or drink, or to be mixed with any medicine capable of being taken internally. With these exceptions methylated spirit may be used in almost any art or manufacture, and is, as a fact, used for a very great variety of manufacturing and technical purposes. For medicinal and pharmaceutical purposes, for instance, the use of methylated spirit has been sanctioned for the extraction, crystallisation and purification of nearly 500 resins, oils, alkaloids, synthetical perfumes and other substances where the finished products contain none of the spirit; for making several hundred embrocations, lotions, liniments, and other medicines for outward application; for most veterinary medicines; and for making collodion, flexible collodion, surgical bandages, iodoform, chloroform, ethyl and methyl chloride and bromide, and other articles used in surgery and medicine.

As a rule the conditions imposed on the users of methylated spirit are very simple, and interfere very little, if at all, with the manufacturing operations. It must not be removed from the premises where its use has been allowed, and the manufacturing operations have to be carried on substantially in the method described in the application. Any material alteration of the process, or those portions of it where the spirit is used, has to be notified to the Revenue officials, and the Board's sanction obtained for the change, but this is merely for the information of the inspecting officers, and permission for any desired alteration is rarely or never refused.

In a great many cases the methylated spirit used in the manufacturing operations is wholly or partially recovered and used over and over again. Where this recovery includes redistillation the Revenue permission has first to be obtained, and in some cases, where the manufacturing operation and the redistillation might so purify portions of the spirit as to render it capable of being used for potable purposes, special conditions are imposed, such as the collection of the whole of the distillate in one receiver and not in fractions, or the immediate mixture of the recovered spirit with fresh methylated spirit, or with some other substance.

As a whole, however, there is very little interference by the Revenue officers. Except for periodical inspections, and the occasional sampling of the recovered spirits and of the intermediate and finished products of the operations, manufacturers are left to carry out their operations in any way they please, provided they supply the Revenue authorities with sufficient information to enable the officers to see where and how the spirit is used.

Neither the methylators nor the manufacturers have to pay anything towards the cost incurred by the Revenue authorities in supervising the making, or the use of the methylated spirit.

B. "Mineralised" Methylated Spirit.

This is the methylated spirit which is sold by retail to the general public for use for burning in spirit lamps, for cleansing and domestic purposes generally, and also to some extent for mixing with paints, stains, varnshes, etc. and for polishing purposes by cabinetmakers, etc.

In making "mineralised" methylated spirit the alcohol is first mixed with the wood-naphtha as in making "ordinary" methylated spirit. After mixing with the wood-naphtha, the whole contents of the vat of "ordinary" methylated spirit, or a portion of the spirit, not less than 100 gallons, removed to another vat, is further mixed with three-eighths of one per cent. (.375 per cent.) of an approved "mineral naphtha." This mineral naphtha is an ordinary light mineral oil having a specific gravity of from 0.800 to 0.830. The addition of this mineral oil does not interfere with the purposes for which this kind of spirit is mainly used, viz., burning in spirit lamps, etc. Its use was introduced some fifteen years ago in order to prevent the drinking of the "ordinary" methylated spirit which was found to be going on to a limited extent among certain classes in the poorer districts of Glasgow and other large cities.

Persons who wish to retail "mineralised" methylated spirit must obtain a licence costing 10s. annually. Anybody except distillers and publicans may obtain this licence. Retailers of "mineralised" methylated spirit are furnished with a book of Requisition Forms to enable them to obtain their supplies of such spirit from the methylators.

Methylators are not allowed to sell the spirit to retailers in greater quantities than fifty gallons, or in less quantities than five gallons, but the smaller retailers are allowed to purchase it in quantities not exceeding a gallon at a time from any other retailer. The stock of "mineralised" methylated spirit which a retailer may keep is limited to fifty gallons, and he is not allowed to sell to any person a greater quantity of such spirit than one gallon at a time.

Retailers are also prohibited from selling the spirit between ten o'clock on Saturday evening and eight o'clock on the following Monday morning; and, in exceptional cases, they have to keep a stock account of all spirit received and sold, and the names of the persons to whom it is sold. These regulations are for the purpose of preventing the illicit drinking of the spirit which still occasionally occurs in some localities, and are required more for police than Revenue purposes.

Any one may buy "mineralised" methylated spirit from a retailer, and may use it for any purpose except in the preparation of beverages or of medicines capable of being taken internally. All attempts to purify or prepare the spirit for use for these purposes are also prohibited; and any one who sells, for use as a beverage or as medicine, or has in his possession any methylated spirit, or any derivative thereof, prepared or purified for such use, incurs a penalty of £100.

THE EXAMINATION OF WOOD-NAPHTHAS.

The wood-naphtha must be sufficiently impure to impart to the methylated spirits, prepared by mixing one part of the wood-naphtha with nine parts of spirits of wine, such an amount of nauseousness as will, in the opinion of the Principal of the Government Laboratory, render such mixture incapable of being used as a beverage, or of being mixed with potable spirits of any kind without rendering them unfit for human consumption.

Wood-naphtha submitted for approval should conform to the following tests:

    (a) Not more than 30 c.c. of the naphtha should be required to decolourise a solution containing 0.5 gram of bromine.

(b) The naphtha, which must be neutral or only slightly alkaline to litmus, should require at least 5 c.c. of decinormal acid to neutralise 25 c.c. of the spirit when methyl orange is used as the indicator.

It should contain:

(a) Not less than 72 per cent. by volume of methyl alcohol.

(b) Not more than 12 grams per 100 c.c. of acetone, aldehydes, and higher ketones, estimated as "acetone" by the formation of iodoform according to Messinger's method.

(c) Not more than 3 grams per 100 c.c. of esters, estimated as methyl acetate by hydrolysis.

The following details of the manner in which the above tests are conducted in the Government Laboratory have been published for the information of the Trade:

Bromine Decolourisation.

A standard bromine solution is made by dissolving 12.406 grams of potassium bromide and 3.481 grams of potassium bromate in a litre of recently boiled distilled water.

50 c.c. of this standard solution (=0.5 gram bromine) are placed in a flask of about 200 c.c. capacity, having a well-ground stopper. To this is added 10 c.c. of dilute sulphuric acid (1 in 4) and the whole shaken gently. After standing for a few minutes the wood-naphtha is slowly run from a burette into the clear brown solution of bromine until the latter is completely decolourised. Not more than 30 c.c. of the wood-naphtha should be required for this purpose.

Methyl Orange Alkalinity Test.

The naphtha should be faintly acid to phenolphthalein, slightly alkaline or neutral, rarely acid to litmus, and always alkaline to methyl orange. 25 c.c. of the wood-naphtha are placed in each of two beakers and titrated with decinormal acid, using in the one case a few drops of litmus solution, and in the other of a solution of methyl oragne, as indicator. With litmus usually 0.1 to 0.2 c.c. of decinormal acid is required to neutralise. With methyl orange the total alkalinity should be greater—at least 5 or 6 c.c. of decinormal acid being required for neutralisation.

The total alkalinity, less that given with litmus, is the "methyl orange alkalinity," and, for the 25 c.c. of wood spirit, should not be less than is required to neutralise 5 c.c. of decinormal acid.

Estimation of Methyl Alcohol.

22 grams of coarsely powdered iodine and 5 c.c. of distilled water are placed in a small flask and cooled by immersion in ice-cold water. Then 5 c.c. of the wood spirit (60.0 o.p.) are added, the flask corked, the contents gently shaken, and allowed to remain in the ice-cold bath for 10-15 minutes.

When well cooled, 2 grams of red phosphorus are added to the mixture of spirit and iodine in the flask, and the latter is immediately attached to a reflux condenser.

The reaction soon commences, and must be moderated by dipping the flask into a cold-water bath. (Spirit may be lost if the reaction is too violent.) After about 15-20 minutes, when all action appears to have ceased, the water bath under the flask is gradually heated to a temperature of about 75° C. (167° F.), and the flask being occasionally shaken is allowed to remain at this temperature for 15-20 minutes. The source of heat is then removed, and the apparatus left for an hour till it has cooled, when the condenser is reversed and the methyl iodide slowly distilled off—first at a low temperature—the bath being allowed to boil towards the end of the operation only. The end of the condenser dips into water in a measuring tube, and the iodide is collected under water and measured at a temperature of 15.5° C. (60° F.).

The percentage (by volume) is found from the formula:

$$\frac{\text{c.c. methyl iodide found} \times .647 \times 100}{\text{c.c. wood spirit taken}} = \text{Percentage by (volume) of methyl alcohol.}$$

Or when 5 c.c. of spirit are taken:

c.c. methyl iodide $\times 12.94$ = percentage (by volume).

Esters, acetals, etc., also yield methyl iodide by this process, and from the percentage of methyl alcohol calculated as above an amount equivalent to the percentage of these substances present must be deducted. Practically, however, methyl acetate is the only compound usually found in quantity sufficient to materially affect the result. The grams of methyl acetate per 100 c.c. of spirit multiplied by .5405 give the equivalent of methyl alcohol to be deducted from the total percentage by volume calculated from the methyl iodide found.

The Acetone Reaction.

25 c.c. of normal soda are placed in a flask similar to those used in the bromine reaction. To this is added 0.5 c.c. of the naphtha. The mixture is well shaken, and allowed to stand 5–10 minutes. Into it from a burette n/5 iodine solution is run slowly, drop by drop, vigorously shaking all the time till the upper portion of the solution, on standing a minute, becomes quite clear. A few c.c. more of n/5 iodine solution are added, as to get concordant results an excess of at least 25 per cent. of the iodine required must be added. After shaking, the mixture is allowed to stand for 10–15 minutes, and then 25 c.c. normal sulphuric are added. The excess of iodine is liberated, titrated with n/10 sodium thiosulphate solution and starch, and half the number of c.c. of thiosulphate solution used are deducted from the total number of c.c. of iodine solution used. The difference gives the amount of acetone by weight in the naphtha by the formula:

c.c. n/5 iodine solution required $\times .3876$ = grams of acetone per 100 c.c. of wood naphtha.

This includes as acetone any aldehydes, etc., capable of yielding iodoform by this reaction.

If the quantity of "acetone" is excessive, a less quantity of the spirit is taken, or 10 c.c. are diluted with 10 c.c. of methyl alcohol free from acetone, and 0.5 c.c. of the mixture is used.

Estimation of Esters.

5 c.c. of the wood-naphtha are run into a silver pressure flask of about 150 c.c. capacity, together with 20 c.c. of recently boiled distilled water. 10 c.c. of normal soda solution are added, the flask securely closed and digested for at least two hours in a water bath at 100° C. (212° F.). The contents are then washed into a beaker, and titrated with normal acid and phenolphthalein. The difference between the number of c.c. of soda taken and of the acid required for neutralisation may be calculated as methyl acetate (weight in volume) from the formula:

$$\frac{.074 \times \text{c.c. soda required} \times 100}{\text{c.c. naphtha taken}} = \text{grams per 100 c.c.}$$

Or if 5 c.c. of spirit are taken as above:

$1.48 \times$ c.c. soda required = grams of methyl acetate per 100 c.c. of spirit.

II. SPIRITS DENATURED WITH OTHER SUBSTANCES THAN WOOD-NAPHTHA.

Under the powers conferred on them by the Spirits Acts, 1880, and Section 8 of the Finance Act of 1902, the Commissioners of Inland Revenue have authorised the use of Ethyl and Methyl alcohol denatured with substances other than wood-naphtha to be used in certain manufacturing operations.

The denaturing substance is, as a rule, one used in the manufacturing operations involved, and there are special conditions as to the mode of working and supervision by the Revenue officials, including in some cases the constant presence of one or more Excise officers on the premises whilst open for work. Traders using these specially denatured spirits have to pay the cost of the Revenue supervision.

Copies of (a) the Commissioners' Minutes on Section 8 of the Finance Act, 1902, and (b) a memorandum indicating the procedure to be observed in connection with the use of Spirits under that section, are subjoined.

(a) MINUTE OF THE BOARD OF INLAND REVENUE ON SECTION 8 OF THE FINANCE ACT, 1902.

The Board take into consideration Section 8 of the Finance Act, 1902, which runs as follows:

1. Where, in the case of any art or manufacture carried on by any person in which the use of spirits is required, it shall be proved to the satisfaction of the Commissioners of Inland Revenue that the use of methylated spirits is unsuitable or detrimental, they may, if they think fit, authorise that person to receive spirits without payment of duty for use in the art or manufacture upon giving security to their satisfaction that he will use the spirits in the art or manufacture, and for no other purpose, and the spirits so used shall be exempt from duty:

Provided that foreign spirits may not be so received or used until the difference between the duty of customs chargeable thereon and the duty of Excise chargeable on British spirits has been paid.

2. The authority shall only be granted subject to a compliance with such regulations as the Commissioners may require the applicant to observe for the security of the revenue, and upon condition that he will, to the satisfaction of the Commissioners if so required by them, render the spirits unpotable before and during use, and will from time to time pay any expenses that may be incurred in placing an officer in charge of his premises.

3. If any person so authorised shall not comply with any regulation which he is required to observe, he shall, in addition to any other fine or liability, incur a fine of fifty pounds.

It is in the first place to be observed that the privilege of using spirit duty free, as contemplated by the section, is to be a personal privilege, entailing personal obligations on the persons or person to whom it is granted; and it follows from this that there can be no question of the Board's granting any general authority under the section to classes of persons, but that each person or body of persons who desires to obtain the benefit of the section must make separate application to the Board, who will consider all the circumstances of each separate application and form their judgment upon them.

At the same time, in laying down some general principles by which they will be governed in dealing with applications submitted to them, it may be possible for the Board to indicate certain classes of cases to which the benefit of the section could not, under any circumstances, be conceded, and so to prevent the multiplication of applications which cannot possibly be entertained favourably.

With this view, and also for the purpose of affording guidance generally to the public and to their own officers with respect to their policy in administering the law, as laid down in the section, the Board proceed to embody in this Minute the following observations on the subject.

The section requires that before the Commissioners can authorise the use of spirits in any "art or manufacture"—terms which they interpret as including the application of spirit to scientific purposes—two main conditions must be fulfilled, viz.:

(a) It must be proved, to the satisfaction of the Commissioners, that the use of methylated spirits is unsuitable or detrimental for the particular purpose; and

(b) The security of the revenue must be guaranteed by such means as the Commissioners may require.

These conditions are cumulative, not alternative—Unless both can be fulfilled there can be no question of a grant of the authority contemplated by the section. In every case therefore it will be necessary to scrutinise in the first instance the objections that may be alleged to the use of methylated spirits, and it is only after the validity of such objections has been admitted, that it will be necessary to proceed to consider whether or by what means the security of the revenue can be guaranteed.

It was explicitly stated in the House of Commons, both by those who promoted legislation in the sense of the section, and by the Chancellor of the Exchequer who assented to it on behalf of H. M. Government, that it was to be understood that the Commissioners should exercise the discretion conferred upon them with great caution, and with a very strict regard to the security of the revenue; and the Board themselves feel strongly that no other attitude would be possible for them.

They intend therefore to insist on a strict observance of the prescribed conditions in every case in which they may grant an authority under the section, and they will not hesitate to reject any application in respect of which it appears to them that the conditions are not, or cannot be, adequately complied with.

Further, as the duty on Spirits is so heavy and of so much importance to the revenue, they consider that they may properly require that the advantage to be obtained by the use of duty-free spirit should be substantial both in character and in weight, and that the benefit of the section should not be accorded in cases of trivial importance or in the purely personal interest of individuals.

In accordance with these principles, the Board will refuse to entertain applications under the section, as follows:

In Respect of Condition (a).

Where in an Art or Manufacture the use of methylated spirit is attended by only slight and immaterial disadvantage.

In Respect of Condition (b).

Where the security of the revenue cannot be guaranteed with reasonable certainty, and at reasonable cost of convenience to the department.

(The cost in money will be a matter always affecting the applicant.)

It is manifest that there must be many cases in which the protection of the revenue would be impossible, if the use of duty-free spirit were permitted, and of these there may be mentioned the following:

(i) The manufacture of articles intended for human consumption, such as Medicines, Essences and Tinctures.

(ii) The manufacture of articles not intended for human consumption, but capable of being so used, if made with pure spirit or with spirit only temporarily rendered unpotable, such as perfumes or spirituous mixtures for purposes of illumination or of generation of heat or motive power.

As regards cases to which the benefit of the section may be extended, the Board may say generally that they will be disposed to entertain favourably applications:

(1) From recognised bodies formed for the advancement of science, or of scientific education, and requiring to use pure spirit in processes of research or of illustration. Applications of this kind from isolated individuals will not commonly be entertained; but might be so on the recommendation and guarantee of a recognised scientific body.

(2) From persons engaged in an industrial enterprise of such magnitude and importance as to give to it a character of public interest in its bearing upon national trade. In any such case the concession will commonly be made subject to an obligation to render the spirit unpotable before and during use, by such means as may be found to be most appropriate to the particular circumstances of the manufacture. Only in very rare instances can the Board contemplate the use of pure spirit in manufacture, and then only subject to close and constant Excise supervision.

In every case of concession, of whatever kind, the persons authorised will be subject to Excise visitation, and to the observance of such regulations as regards receipt, storage, use, or recovery of spirits, and the keeping of accounts of the same, as the Board may prescribe.

H. W. P.

July, 1902.

(b) Procedure to be Observed in Connection with the Use in Manufactures of Spirits on which Duty has not been Paid (Sec. 8 of the Finance Act, 1902).

1. Any person desiring to use spirits without payment of duty in any manufacture carried on by him must make application in writing to the Commissioners of Inland Revenue for authority to receive and use such spirits, and must prove to the satisfaction of the Commissioners that the use of Methylated Spirits would be unsuitable or detrimental.

2. The applicant must give full particulars of the situation of the premises upon which and the purpose for which the spirits are to be used, together with a description of the process of manufacture. He must also state the means by which it is proposed to make the spirits unpotable before and during use, and the quantity likely to be required in the course of a year.

3. Spirits on which duty has not been paid may not be delivered for removal to the premises of any person for use in any manufacture except from a Duty Free Warehouse, and upon production to the Officer of that Warehouse of a Requisition signed by the person authorised to receive the spirits, on which there is a certificate, signed by the Supervisor of the District, that the Applicant is authorised by the Commissioners of Inland Revenue to receive such spirits.

4. The quantity of spirits to be received at one time must not be less than one hundred bulk gallons, and the spirits must be conveyed direct to the premises of the person authorised to receive them, and must there remain without alteration or change in the cask or package in which they were delivered, until an account thereof has been taken by the proper Officer, and they have been rendered unpotable in his presence.

5. Any person authorised to receive spirits on which duty has not been paid must, if so required by the Commissioners of Inland Revenue, provide upon his premises a warehouse, structurally secure to their satisfaction, and all such spirits received must be deposited and retained therein until delivered on proper notice to, and in the presence of, the Officer. He must also, if so required, provide a room approved by the Commissioners in which must be fixed a vat or other vessel of sufficient size to admit of at least one hundred bulk gallons of spirits being rendered unpotable at one time, and must also provide satisfactory accommodation for the Officer of Inland Revenue in attendance at his premises.

6. Security to the satisfaction of the Commissioners of Inland Revenue must be given for the due removal, safe custody, and proper use of the spirits, and the due observance of all regulations and conditions made by the Commissioners.

7. The substance or material to be used for the purpose of rendering spirits unpotable, and the mode in which the spirits are to be rendered unpotable, must be approved by the Commissioners of Inland Revenue, and the person authorised to receive spirits upon which duty has not been paid must, if so required by the Commissioners, provide a store to be approved by them, and used solely for storing and keeping the substance or material so approved.

8. No warehouse, room or store provided in conformity with these Regulations shall be open before 8 o'clock in the morning or after 5 o'clock in the afternoon, but Officers of Inland Revenue shall have access at all times to the premises of any person authorised to use spirits under these Regulations.

9. Notice of the intention to remove spirits from the warehouse on the premises of the person authorised to use them for the purpose of being rendered unpotable or for use under these Regulations must be given to the proper Officer of Inland Revenue on a form of Warrant, on which must be specified the particulars of the spirits as warehoused together with the distinctive marks and numbers of the casks and the date of deposit in the Warehouse, and the spirits must be rendered unpotable in the presence of the proper Officer, who may take an account of such spirits before and on completion of the operation, and may, without payment, take samples at any time of the spirits and of any article in the manufacture of which they are used or which may be on the premises of the user.

10. Spirits which have been rendered unpotable under these regulations shall not thereafter be purified in any manner or be recovered by distillation or any other means, except with the express sanction of the Commissioners of Inland Revenue.

11. A person to whom authority is granted by the Commissioners of Inland Revenue to receive for use in any part or manufacture spirits on which duty has not been paid shall pay to the proper Collector of Inland Revenue, from time to time, such sum or sums as the Commissoners shall determine for the expense incurred for the attendance of an Officer at his premises, and shall also pay duty on any deficiency in the spirits received upon his premises which may arise from abstraction or from any cause which may in the opinion of the Commissioners not be due to natural waste.

Dated this 1st October, 1902.

By Order of the Commissioners of Inland Revenue.

J. B. MEERS, Secretary.

III. UNDENATURED ALCOHOL is allowed to be used by universities, colleges, and other public institutions for research and teaching under certain conditions, a copy of which is subjoined:

1. An Application must be made by the Governing body or their representative, stating the situation of the particular University, College, or Public Institution for Research or Teaching, the number of the Laboratories therein, the purpose or purposes to which the Spirits are to be applied, the bulk quantity likely to be required in the course of a year, and, if it amounts to 50 gallons or upwards, the name or names of one or more Sureties, or a Guarantee Society, to join in a bond that the Spirits will be used solely for the purpose requested and at the place specified.

2. The Spirits received at any one Institution must only be used in the Laboratories of that Institution, and must not be distributed for use in the Laboratories of any other Institution, or used for any other purpose than those authorised.

3. Only plain British Spirits or unsweetened Foreign Spirits of not less strength than 50 degrees overproof (i.e. containing not less than 80 per cent. by weight of absolute alcohol) may be received duty free, and the differential duty must be paid on the Foreign Spirits.

4. The Spirits must be received under Bond either from a distillery or from an Excise or Customs general warehouse and (except with special permission) in quantities of not less than 9 bulk gallons at a time. They will be obtainable only on presentation of a requisition signed by the proper Supervisor.

5. On the arrival of the Spirits at the Institution, the proper Revenue Officer should be informed, and the vessels, casks, or packages containing them are not to be opened until he has taken account of the Spirits.

6. The stock of Spirits in each Institution must be kept under lock in a special compartment under the control of a professor or some responsible Officer of the University, College, or Institution.

7. The Spirits received by the responsible Officer of the Institution may be distributed by him undiluted to any of the Laboratories on the same premises.

8. No distribution of Spirits may be made from the Receiving Laboratory to other Laboratories which are not within the same premises.

9. A Stock Book must be provided and kept at the Receiving Laboratory in which is to be entered on the debit side an account of the bulk and proof gallons of Spirits received with the date of receipt, and on the credit side an account of the bulk and proof gallons distributed to the other Laboratories. A Stock Book must also be kept at each other Laboratory in which must be entered on the day of receipt an account of the bulk and proof gallons of Spirits received from the Receiving Laboratory.

These books must be open at all times to the inspection of the Revenue Officer, and he will be at liberty to make any abstract from them which he may consider necessary.

10. The quantity of Spirits in Stock at any one time must not exceed half the estimated quantity required in a year where that quantity amounts to 20 gallons or upwards.

11. Any contravention of the regulations may involve the withdrawal of the Board's authority to use duty-free Spirits.

12. It must be understood that the Board of Inland Revenue reserve to themselves full discretion to withhold permission for the use of duty-free Spirit in any case in which the circumstances may not seem to them to be such as to warrant the grant of it. They have already decided that the use of duty-free Spirit for the preservation of Natural History or other specimens cannot be allowed.

J. B. MEERS, Secretary.

INLAND REVENUE, SOMERSET HOUSE, W. C., December, 1902.

NOTE.—"Proof Spirit" is defined by law to be such spirit as at the temperature of 51° Fahrenheit shall weigh $\frac{12}{13}$ of an equal measure of distilled water.

Taking water at 51° Fahrenheit as unity, the specific gravity of "proof spirit" at 51° Fahrenheit is .92308. When such spirit is raised to the more usual temperature of 60° Fahrenheit, its specific gravity compared with water at 60° Fahrenheit is .91984.

To calculate the quantity of spirits at proof in a given quantity of spirit over or under proof strength: Multiply the quantity of spirit by the number of degrees of strength of the spirit and divide the product by 100. The number of degrees of strength of any spirit is 100 *plus* the number of degrees overproof, or *minus* the number of degrees underproof.

EXAMPLE: 19.8 gallons of spirits at 64.5 overproof.
$100 + 64.5 = 164.5$ proof strength.
$164.5 \times 19.8 \div 100 = 32.571$,
taken as 32.5 gallons at proof.

APPENDIX No. II.

B. ABSTRACT OF THE APPROXIMATE QUANTITIES OF UNMINERAL-ISED METHYLATED SPIRITS USED IN MANUFACTURING OPERATIONS AND FOR OTHER PURPOSES IN THE UNITED KINGDOM DURING THE YEAR ENDED 31ST MARCH, 1901.

(Prepared from information supplied by Supervisors of Inland Revenue to the Government Laboratory in May, 1901.)

	Nature of Manufacturing Operations or Other Purposes for which the Spirit was Used.	Number of Gallons Used.
1	Making "finish," varnishes, lacquers, stains, paints, enamels, etc.	1,221,013
2	Soap manufacture.	144,384
3	Hat-making.	121,104
4	Celluloid, Xylonite, etc.	106,589
5	Ether, Chloroform, and Iodoform.	97,906
6	Fulminates, smokeless powder, and other explosives (including War Office and Admiralty).	48,052
7	Preparation of solid medicinal extracts, medicaments, fine chemicals, etc.	39,637
8	Dissolving dyes and colours, and for dyeing and cleaning operations, etc.	28,943
9	Making photographic plates, emulsions, films, etc.	24,667
10	Making linoleum, pegamoid, lincrusta walton, and similar goods	21,128
11	Making embrocations, lotions, liniments, cattle and other medicines.	15,410
12	Making filaments, etc., in the incandescent electric-lamp manufacture.	14,964
13	In piano-making	7,510

APPROXIMATE QUANTITIES OF UNMINERALISED METHYLATED SPIRITS USED IN
MANUFACTURING OPERATIONS—*Continued.*

	Nature of Manufacturing Operations or Other Purposes for which the Spirit was Used.	Number of Gallons Used.
14	In silk, crape, and embroidery manufactures, mainly for stiffening.	8,434
15	In the manufacture of aniline and other dyes and colours.	5,657
16	In making fireworks.	2,720
17	Plant washes, insecticides, etc.	1,564
18	In the manufacture of rubber.	1,600
19	For cleaning paint.	1,150
20	In the manufacture of steel pens.	1,669
21	Making blacking and leather dressings.	4,180
22	In "silvering" mirrors, etc.	477
23	In corset-making	590
24	Making sheep dips.	450
25	Preparing surgical dressings.	1,040
26	Adjusting hydrometers, and in making compasses, thermometers, and other instruments.	403
27	In oil-refining.	205
28	Electrotyping.	128
29	Making inks.	197
30	Various miscellaneous manufactures, etc., engraving, brass-founding, watch-making, china-making, printers' rollers, black lead, candle-making, artificial silk, artificial flowers, calico-printing, cotton yarn, ropes, oil gas generators, etc.	1,487
31	Preserving specimens in museums, hospitals, infirmaries, etc., for burning in lamps, washes, lotions, and other purposes in hospitals, infirmaries, and similar institutions, and also for laboratories and educational purposes.	33,780
32	For the War Office and Admiralty requirements, chiefly at Woolwich and Dockyards.	30,624
	Total.	1,987,695

OBSERVATIONS.

The returns from which the Abstract has been prepared are in a very condensed form, and do not give in detail the various purposes for which the spirit is used nor the quantities used for each purpose when there are several. In some cases, therefore, it has been necessary to estimate the probable quantities assigned to each head, and the figures must therefore be taken as approximate only. In the case of the largest users, however, there is no difficulty. The "Ether," "Solid Medicinal Extracts," and "Lotions" are the most doubtful, as most makers use the spirit for all three purposes.

On the whole, however, the figures given are probably very nearly correct.

The "quantities" are the quantities received during the year by the users.

The total, 1,987,665 gallons, compares with 2,075,514 gallons, the estimated quantity of unmineralised methylated spirit made during the year, showing a deficiency of 87,849, or a little over 4 per cent., due partly to waste and partly probably to the imperfections in the returns.

It is not possible to make any separation between "Finish" and "Varnishes," etc., properly so-called, but as "Finish" is itself almost entirely used for making varnishes, or for thinning or manipulating those already made and for polishing purposes, any distinction would not be of much value.

The Mineralised or Retail Methylated Spirit is used mainly for burning in spirit lamps, for cleansing and domestic purposes generally, and also to some extent for mixing with paints, stains, varnishes, etc., and for polishing purposes by cabinet-makers, etc.

APPENDIX No. II.

C.—COMPARISON OF THE QUANTITY OF SPIRITS, ETC., USED IN MAKING METHYLATED SPIRITS, AND OF THE METHYLATED SPIRITS PRODUCED, FOR THE FIVE YEARS ENDING 31st MARCH, 1904.

| Year Ending 31st March. | Proof Gallons of Spirits Delivered for Methylation. | | Total. | Average Strength. | Quantity in Bulk of Spirits Methylated. |
	British.	Foreign.			Gallons.
				o. p.	
1900	4,978,027	6,245	4,984,272	63.7	3,043,485
1901	5,070,713	120,332	5,191,045	64.3	3,158,442
1902	4,640,770	627,410	5,268,180	64.3	3,206.214
1903	4,239,688	1,210,001	5,451,689	64.9	3,305,502
1904	5,054,586	334,140	5,388,726ʳ	63.5	3,295,485

| Year Ending 31st March. | Wood-Naphtha Used. | Ordinary (Unmineralised) Methylated Spirits for Manufacturing Purposes. | Mineral Naphtha. | Mineralised Methylated Spirit for Retail Sale. | Total. |
	Gallons.	Gallons.	Gallons.	Gallons.	Gallons.
1900	338,165	2,058,450	4,962	1,328,162	3,386,612
1901	350,938	2.075,514	5,377	1,439,243	3,514,757
1902	356,246	2,157,127	5,270	1,410,603	3,567,730
1903	367,278	2,213,580	5,472	1,464,672	3,678,252
1904	366,165	2,139,784*	5,707	1,527,573	3,667,357

APPENDIX No. III.

REGULATIONS AS REGARDS USE OF SPIRIT FOR INDUSTRIAL, ETC., PURPOSES IN GERMANY.

TAXES ON SPIRIT.

The spirit taxes in Germany are levied in so many different ways that it is difficult to arrive at any very accurate estimate of the average rate.
CUSTOMS.

On imported spirits of all kinds, including Arrack, Rum, French Brandy, and mixed spirits:

* The decrease in 1903–4 is mainly due to the fact that certain firms, *e.g.*, the British Xylonite Company, Nobels, and Leitch & Company, have been allowed the use of duty-free alcohol denatured by other substances than wood-naphtha.
The total quantity so allowed in 1903–4 was 206,452 proof gallons, which would be 125,885 bulk gallons at 64° o.p. (93.5 per cent. real alcohol).

Liqueurs. . . . . 240 marks
All other Spirits—
    (a) In casks. 160   "
    (b) In bottles, flasks, and other vessels, 240 marks for every 100
        kilograms (220 lbs.), *i.e.,* from about 7¼d. to 1s. 1d. per lb.

But the tax has apparently to be paid on the gross weight of vessel and contents, and no satisfactory comparison with the British system can, therefore, be made. From 5s. to 10s. per proof gallon may be taken as an approximate estimate, according to the character of the spirit and the vessels containing it.

Hamburg, Cuxhaven, Bremerhaven, and Gestemünde, and some other places, are not included in the Spirit Tax Union, and spirits coming from these "free cities" into other parts of the German Empire have to pay the customs taxes.

EXCISE.

Each distillery is allowed to produce a certain fixed quantity of spirit annually, called "The Contingent," on which is paid a "Consumption Tax" ("Verbrauchsabgabe") of 50 marks per hectolitre of pure alcohol. On any excess production over the "Contingent" 70 marks per hectolitre is charged.

The "Contingent" may be increased or decreased for various reasons at any time, and there is a general revision once every five years.

Various other taxes are also levied. For these, German distilleries are divided into three classes:

1. "*Industrial Distilleries*" (Gewerbliche Brennereien) carried on by individuals or companies solely for manufacturing purposes. These Distilleries have to pay per hectolitre of pure alcohol in addition to the "Consumption Tax"
    (a) an "addition" (Zuschlag) of from 16 to 20 marks.
    (b) a "distilling tax" (Brennsteuer) of from 2 to 6½ marks.
Distilleries producing not more than 200 hectolitres of pure alcohol annually (7,700 proof gallons) are exempt from the "Distilling Tax," and the smaller distilleries pay the lower rates according to fixed scales.

2. "*Agricultural Distilleries*" (Landwirthschaftliche Brennereien) are those using as raw materials potatoes or grain grown on the owners' farms, or on the farms of one or more of the owners, if the Distillery belongs to a society or company. These pay modified "additions" of from 10 to 20 marks per hectolitre of pure alcohol, and are exempt from the "Distilling Tax," or pay only from 1 to 3 marks per hectolitre; or instead of these taxes they may elect to pay a "Fermenting vat tax" (Maischbottichsteuer) of from 0.786 mark to 1.31 mark per hectolitre on the fermenting vat capacity for each fermentation.

3. "*Material Distilleries*" (Materialbrennereien) are those using berries, fruits, wine lees, grape pressings, etc.

These appear to be all very small, many of them making no more than 11 to 22 gallons of alcohol annually. In addition to the "Consumption tax" of 50 marks, they pay from 0.10 to 0.85 mark per hectolitre of material used.

The total average tax on spirits produced in "*Industrial Distilleries*" is estimated at not more than 70 marks per hectolitre of pure alcohol, equivalent to about 1s. 9d. per proof gallon, and in the "*Agricultural Distilleries*" at somewhat less—60 to 65 marks per hectolitre—or about 1s. 7d. to 1s. 8d. per proof gallon. By far the greater proportion of the spirit made in Germany is produced by the "Agricultural Distilleries."

DUTY-FREE ALCOHOL.
ABSTRACT OF THE GERMAN REGULATIONS.

Spirit for employment in Industrial operations, vinegar making, cleaning, heating, cooking, or lighting, as well as for educational or scientific purposes, may, after having been denatured according to the regulations, or in special cases without denaturing, on proof of the spirit having been so used, be granted freedom from the spirit taxes on the following conditions:
The freedom from duty includes—
    (a) The release from the "*consumption*" tax and its "*additions*."
    (b) The refunding of the "*fermenting vat*" tax at the rate of 0.16 mark
        per litre of pure alcohol so far as the spirit has been subjected to it.

(c) The return of the *"distilling"* tax at the rate of 0.06 mark per litre of pure alcohol.

Duty-paid spirit and spirit containing more than 1 per cent. of fusel oil are not admitted for denaturing.

The denaturing is either *complete, i.e.*, such as is deemed sufficient to make the spirit undrinkable, or *incomplete, i.e.*, such as requires the employment of other means for the prevention of the improper employment of such spirit.

General denaturing agent for complete denaturing:

4 parts of wood-naphtha, and

1 part pyridine bases,

to each litre of which may be added 50 grams of lavender oil or rosemary oil.

Of this mixture 2½ litres are added to each hectolitre of alcohol.

(German Methylated Spirit therefore contains 2 per cent. wood-naphtha and 0.5 per cent. pyridine bases, with optionally .125 per cent. of a lavender or rosemary oil.)

The mixing of the general denaturing substance can only be carried out by persons who have obtained special authority for the purpose from the chief Inland Revenue Office of the district where the mixing establishments are situated. Authorised methylators have to provide rooms and vessels for storing and mixing the denaturing agents, all materials and implements necessary, and to give the officials the requisite assistance in sampling the denaturing substances and in the mixing them with the spirit. They have also to provide books of an official pattern for entering the particulars of the mixings and of the sale and transport of the denatured spirit.

The denaturing may take place in special vats erected for the purpose, or in the casks or other vessels used to transport the alcohol. Not less than a hectolitre (22 gallons) of alcohol can be denatured at a time. Before denaturing the alcoholic strength and quantity of spirit in each vessel is checked by the Excise Officer, unless such spirit has been sent in vessels under special revenue seals, and which are found intact on examination. The wood-naphtha and pyridine bases used for denaturing must first be examined and approved by official chemists, samples being taken for this purpose from the vessels used for storing these materials, which remain under revenue control from the time the sample is taken until mixed with the spirit. The store vessels must contain not less than 100 litres (22 gallons) of the denaturing agents when sampled. The Excise Officers are directed to see that the denaturing materials are thoroughly mixed with the spirit.

The nature of the official examination of the wood-naphtha is described in the official directions printed on page 256, from which the character of the substance used can be gathered. As compared with the British type of denaturing wood-naphtha the German wood-naphtha is of a more impure character, *i.e.*, it contains a much larger proportion of acetone, and other substances, and less methyl alcohol.

The pyridine bases are used mainly to increase the nauseous character of the methylated spirit, and serve practically the same purpose as the mineral naphtha used in the United Kingdom and in France.

For use in motor-cars and other internal combustion engines, etc., alcohol may also be completely denatured by the addition of 1½ litres of the "general" denaturing agent and ¼ litre of a solution of methyl violet dye, together with from 2 to 20 litres of benzol to every 100 litres of alcohol.

The ordinary completely denatured spirit and the motor-car spirit may be sold by persons who are authorised to do so by the Administration. Written application for a licence has to be made to the superior Excise official, who may exercise his discretion as to whether a licence should be given, and the licence may be withdrawn at any time if it appears advisable to disallow the sale in any particular shop. Before obtaining a licence notification must be given to the police.

The ordinary completely denatured spirit is intended for sale by retail, and may be used for any industrial purpose; for cleansing, heating, lighting and cooking, as well as for educational and medicinal purposes; but must not be present in any substance intended for human consumption, and no attempt must be made to purify such spirit, or to add anything to it to disguise its taste or smell, nor must it be diluted under 85° (49 o.p.). Heavy penalties are imposed for any contravention of the regulations.

The general control over the retail sale of the denatured spirit is very similar to that imposed in this country, but the police appear to be more directly concerned in preventing irregularities than with us.

For general use on a large scale for industrial and manufacturing processes of all kinds, what is called "Wood Spirit denatured" alcohol is allowed to be made and sold under special conditions. This denatured spirit consists of a mixture of 100 litres of alcohol of not less than 90° (58 o.p.) with 5 litres of wood-naphtha.

The denaturing of this spirit may take place either at the works where it is to be used or on the premises of authorised methylators. In the latter case the regulations as to mixing, storing, etc., are the same as in the case of the completely denatured spirit. Permission to sell this "wood spirit denatured" alcohol can only be granted by the Chief Office, and makers who sell this "wood spirit denatured" alcohol have to keep an official "Control Book" in which has to be entered particulars of all spirit denatured, and of every sale of such spirit. A balance is struck annually and duty is charged on any material loss or deficiency that may be shown unless satisfactory explanations can be given. Such spirit can only be sold to factories which can show a licence to buy "wood-spirit denatured" alcohol. Any person wishing to obtain a "buying licence" must apply to the chief office of the province in which the factory where such spirit is to be used is situated. Full particulars of the purposes for which the spirit is required must be given. No person engaged in the spirit trade, or who sells denatured or undenatured spirit, can obtain a licence, and a licence may be refused if any facts are known which render the use of denatured spirit in any factory undesirable. A licence is only given for one year, and the maximum quantity allowed cannot be exceeded without special authority. The "buying licence" must be produced each time any methylated spirit is purchased. The *seller* must enter on the licence the quantity sold, adding his name and the date, and must also enter each sale in an official "Control Book." Not less than 2 litres (½ gallon) may be sold at a time, and the seller must see that the maximum annual quantity shown on the "buying licence" has not already been supplied to the buyer.

The buyer must enter every purchase in a "Control Book" kept at the works. From these entries in the "Control Books" the buying and selling accounts are checked and the annual quantities allowed at each factory are fixed.

The denatured spirit must be stored in a special compartment at the factory, and on each occasion that any of it is removed for use in the works an entry of the quantity and particular purpose for which it is to be used must be made in the "Control Book," and a note must also be entered of the pages of the factory work books and the official business books in which particulars are to be found on the production, storage, and sale of the articles or substances in the manufacture of which the methylated spirit has been used.

On the demand of the superior Officers of the Administration these books and business books must be produced for their inspection.

Where this "wood-naphtha denatured," or the "completely denatured" alcohol is unsuitable for any particular manufacture special denaturing agents may be allowed. Denaturing with special reagents can only be made at the factories where the alcohol is to be used, and permission must first be obtained from the Chief Office of the Province for the use of such spirit.

All the special substances sanctioned for denaturing purposes have to be tested by an official chemist according to officially described methods, and the users of the denatured spirit have to pay for the anlayses as well as to provide the denaturing substances, and proper stores, vessels, etc., for keeping and mixing the approved reagents with the alcohol.

The mixing takes place in the presence of officials, and the quantities of each kind of specially denatured alcohol have to be entered in a separate opening of the "Control Book," kept in separate vessels or compartments at the factory, and used under conditions applicable to the "wood-naphtha denatured" alcohol already described.

A stock account of the amount of all denatured spirit on the premises of users of such spirit is to be taken at least once a year. The entries in the "Control

Book" of the spirit received and used are to be checked, and the result of the comparison submitted to the Chief Office. Payment of duty on any loss of spirit shown by the account may be imposed, but only when there is reason to believe that the spirit has been used in illegal ways.

Denatured spirit may be recovered in any manufacturing operation, but permission must first be obtained. The recovered spirit may be used again for the same purpose as that for which it was previously used. If used for other purposes, or if it is purified, it has to be again denatured and treated as fresh denatured spirit. If exempted from repeated denaturing samples are to be taken and examined, at the cost of the user, by an official chemist in order to determine whether it remains unfit for consumption. Recovered spirit may have to be stored in officially sealed vessels till again denatured. Incompletely denatured spirit must not be removed from the user's premises.

For *incomplete* denaturing the following substances (special denaturing agents) may be used. They are to be added for denaturing purposes in the undernoted quantities per 100 litres of the spirit.

(*a*) For industrial uses of all kinds:
    5 litres of wood spirit,
    or 0.5 " " pyridine bases.

(*b*) For the production of brewers' varnish and similar substances:
    20 litres of a shellac solution, which is made by adding 1 part by weight of shellac in 2 parts by weight of spirit of at least 90° (58 o.p.), are added to the spirit.

In this case the alcohol in the shellac solution if made under official supervision is also allowed exemption from duty.

(*c*) For the production of celluloid and pegamoid:
    1 kilogram of camphor,
    or 2 litres of turpentine,
    or ½ litre " benzol.

(*d*) For the production of the following substances:
    1. Ether, ordinary (with certain limitations and regulations as to sale and use);
    2. Ethyl sulphuric salts;
    3. Agaricin, podophyllin, scammony, guiacum, and jalap resins, as well as other resins and gum resins;
    4. Aldehyde and paraldehyde;
    5. White lead and acetate of lead;
    6. Ethyl chloride, bromide, and iodide;
    7. Photographic paper and dry plates, and emulsions of chloride, bromide and iodide of silver and gelatin, and similar preparations;
    8. Chloral hydrate;
    9. Electrodes for electric storage batteries;
    10. Acetic ether (with certain limitations as to sale and use);
    11. Glucosides;
    12. Rubber preparations;
    13. Collodion, and bromine, chloride and iodide of silver emulsions of collodion;
    14. Pancreatin, alkaloids, santonin, tannin, and salicylic acid and its salts;
    15. Coal-tar colours, including substances used in obtaining them, and intermediate products;
    16. Chemical preparations (not otherwise named) which do not retain any spirit when finished (except formic ether, valerianic ether and butyric ether);
    10 litres of sulphuric ether,
    or 1 litre of benzol,
    or ½ " " turpentine,
    or 0.025 litre of animal oil.

Collodion for sale must contain at least 1/100th of its weight of guncotton.

(e) For the preparation of chloroform:
    300 grams of chloroform.

(f) For the production of vinegar:
    200 litres vinegar containing 3 per cent. acetic acid,
    or 150   "   "   "   4 " " " "
    or 100   "   "   "   6 " " " "
        and 100 litres of water,
  and so on,
    or 50 litres vinegar containing 12 per cent. acetic acid
        and 100 litres of water,
    or 30   "   " containing 6 per cent. acetic acid
        and 70 litres of water,
        and 100 " " "

Any excess of the quantity of acetic acid in the vinegar mixture or of the spirit are to be allowed for, and the water may be replaced entirely or in part by an equal quantity of beer, glattwasser, or natural wine.

(g) For making inks, sealing wax, and stamping inks:
    0.5 litre of turpentine,
    or 0.025 litre of animal oil.

(h) For making bedstead enamels, and brewers varnish, as well as for use in incandescent lamps, for finishing silk ribbons, and for cleansing jewellery, etc.:
    0.5 litre of turpentine.

(i) For making iodoform:
    200 grams iodoform.

The iodoform may be dissolved in part of the spirit, and the solution then added to the remainder of the spirit.

(k) For varnishes and polishes of all kinds:
    2 litres of wood spirit and 2 litres petroleum benzin,
    or 0.5 litre of turpentine.

Polishes and varnishes not for use in the works of the makers, but for sale, must contain at least 1/10th part of their weight of shellac or other resin.

(l) For preparing medical, botanical and zoological preparations for educational purposes:
    1 litre (commercially pure) methyl alcohol,
    and 1   " petroleum benzin.

(m) Soap-making:
    1 kilogram of castor oil and 400 c.c. of soda solution.

The denaturing materials may be dissolved by heating in part of the spirit, and the solution then added to the remainder of the spirit.

(n) For the production of wool fat (lanoline):
    5 litres of petroleum benzin.

Spirit is only allowed duty free for the production of ether and acetic ether under the proviso that they are (under official control) either exported; or else used at home for industrial uses; or for the purpose of testing in scientific and technical trades or professions; or for the production of materials for surgical bandages, but not for ether-containing medicines; or for making fulminates, smokeless powders, and other munitions of war; or for use in certain Public Institutions. So far as the ether and acetic ether are not used by the maker, but are sent to other workshops, or to the named institutions and factories, the regulations as to obtaining a licence for buying, selling and using, as well as to the keeping of a control book by the sellers, are the same as in the case of "wood-naphtha denatured" spirit.

It will be required also that the buyers, by means of their business and manufacturing books, or by special books, shall enter the particulars of the use of the ether and acetic ether.

A buyer's licence for ether made from duty-free spirit can also be given if the ether is to be exported by the buyer, or is to be sent to an authorised industrial user, institution or factory. The intermediate merchant in these cases is under the same control as the maker of ether for sale. The Superintending Officers can permit ether-makers to change ether which has been made from duty-free spirit into taxed ether so that it may be used or sold for the uses excepted in paragraph 1.

In this case the ether is to be notified for taxing, its weight officially taken, and the proper duty, on the basis of 1.6 litre of alcohol for each kilogram of ether, is to be assessed. If the spirit used is subject to any other charges the highest charge is to be taken.

More particular regulations are made by the Chief Office.

The denaturing of spirit with 0.5 litre of turpentine for cleaning bijouterie, and for making polishes and lacquer varnishes which are to be used for lead pencils, toys, and clock-making can also be permitted in the existing districts of the Chief Imperial Finance Ministry even when the spirit is not to be used in the factory of the applicant, but is to be sent to other factories. The regulations as to the sale and use of "turpentine denatured spirit" are the same as for "wood-naphtha denatured" spirit.

PURE DUTY-FREE ALCOHOL.

Pure alcohol without denaturing may be delivered duty free—

(a) *To certain Hospitals, Lying-in Hospitals*, and Lunatic Asylums, as well as to Public Scientific Institutions.

Permission has first to be obtained from the Chief Office of the Province, and an application must be made in writing stating the purposes for which the spirit is to be used, and the extreme annual quantity required. The quantities allowed are fixed by the Chief Office and revised every three years. Not less than 25 litres (5½ gallons) can be received at a time. A stock book has to be kept by some specially designated official of the Institution, in which is to be entered particulars of the receipt and use of the spirit. The spirit may be used only *inside* these Institutions for general scientific and heating purposes and it makes no difference whether the spirit is directly used for the specified purposes or only indirectly so used, *e.g.*, to clean instruments, to disinfect the operators or operating tables, or for heating inhalation apparatus, etc.

Otherwise, the spirit can only be used for the purposes stated. It is specially forbidden to give the spirit to other persons, or to take it outside the Institutions except by special permission of the Chief Office. Duty-free ether and acetic ether are allowed in the Institutions under similar regulations.

(b) *For making smokeless powders, fuses, and fulminates*, as well as for making the varnishes used in finishing these substances.

Permission has to be obtained and the same regulations as are applicable to the buying, storage, and use of "wood-naphtha denatured" spirit, and the keeping of "control books" and other accounts, are enforced. At large works stock is taken at frequent intervals, and there is generally a somewhat more stringent supervision by the Excise Officers. Permission may be granted for recovery of any spirit used in the manufacturing operations. The spirit must only be used *inside* the factories and must not under any circumstances be removed from the works. Duty may be charged on any unexplained loss or deficiency shown at the stock takings. Duty-free ether and acetic ether are allowed in these factories under similar regulations.

Pure undenatured alcohol was formerly allowed to be used by apothecaries, medicine-makers, druggists, doctors, and veterinary surgeons for the preparation of some 80 tinctures, spirits and liquors according to the formulæ of the German pharmacopœia and other authorised formulæ, and also for doctors' prescriptions and for making bandages, etc. This privilege was withdrawn in October, 1902, and all medicines have now to be prepared with duty-paid spirit.

No foreign spirit of any kind, nor any mixtures containing spirit, or substances made from spirit, appear to be allowed to be used duty free in Germany. All imported alcohol, alcoholic mixtures and derivatives have to pay the Customs duties before being delivered for use.

INSTRUCTIONS FOR TESTING WOOD-NAPHTHA.

1. *Colour.* This shall not be darker than that of a solution made by dissolving 2 c.c. of n/10 iodine in 1,000 c.c. of distilled water.

2. *Boiling Point.* 100 c.c. placed in a short-necked copper flask of about 180-200 c.c. capacity is placed on an asbestos plate having a circular hole of 30 mm. diameter. Into the neck of this flask is placed a fractionating tube 12 mm. wide and 170 mm. long, with its side tube connected to a Liebig's condenser at least 400 mm. long. In the fractionating tube, which is provided with a bulb about a centimetre below the side tube, is placed an officially tested thermometer with a scale ranging from 0° C. to 200° C., so that its mercury bulb is in the middle of the bulb. The flask is heated so that the distillation proceeds at about the rate of 5 c.c. per minute. The distillate is collected in a cylinder graduated in c.c., and at 75° C. with a normal barometric pressure of 760 mm. at least 90 c.c. shall be collected. If the barometer is not at 760 mm. during the distillation 1° C. shall be allowed for every variation of 30 mm., *e.g.* at 770 mm. 90 c.c. shall distil at 75°.3 C. and at 750 mm. 90 c.c. at 74°.7 C.

3. *Miscibility with water.* 20 c.c. wood spirit mixed with 40 c.c. water shall give a clear or only slightly opalescent solution.

4. *Acetone Content.*

  (a) *Separation on mixing with soda solution.*

20 c.c. of wood spirit are shaken with 40 c.c. of soda solution of S.G. 1.300. At least 5 c.c. of wood spirit must separate after standing for half an hour.

  (b) *Titration.*

1 c.c. of a mixture of 10 c.c. of wood spirit with 90 c.c. of water is mixed with 10 c.c. of double normal soda solution. Then 50 c.c. of n/10 iodine solution are added with continual shaking and the mixture allowed to remain at least for three minutes. Then excess of dilute sulphuric acid is added, and the excess of iodine titrated with n/10 hypo and starch solution. At least 22 c.c. of n/10 iodine solution shall be required for the acetone.

5. *Bromine Absorption.* 100 c.c. of a solution of $KBrO_3$ and KBr (made up as under) are acidified by the addition of 20 c.c. of dilute H_2SO_4 (S.G. 1.290). To this mixture the spirit is added drop by drop from a burette so long as any colour remains on shaking. The addition shall be so arranged that in one minute 10 c.c. of spirit shall be added. Not more than 30 c.c. shall be required for decolouration, and not less than 20 c.c. This test must be done in full daylight, and the temperature should not exceed 20° C.

Bromine Solution.—After at least two hours' drying at 100° C. and cooling in an exsiccator, 2.447 grams of $KBrO_3$ and 8.719 grams of KBr of tested purity are dissolved in water, and the solution made up to 1 litre.

The following tables [(a) (b) (c)] show, for the three years ended 30th September, 1903, (a) the quantities of duty-free spirits issued for use in Germany, (b) the quantities denatured of the several methods allowed, and (c) the quantities used for particular manufactures, etc.

(a) QUANTITIES OF DUTY-FREE SPIRIT ISSUED DURING 1901, 1902, 1903.

Year Ending 30th September.	Completely Denatured.	Incompletely Denatured.	Undenatured.	Total.
	Hectolitres of Pure Alcohol.			
1901.	782,295	339,754	33,820	1,155,869
1902.	704,729	345,894	59,427	1,110,050
1903.	900,190	360,730	17,792	1,278,712

Year Ending 30th September.	Completely Denatured.	Incompletely Denatured.	Undenatured.	Total.
	Equivalent Bulk Gallons of Pure Alcohol.			
1901.	17,210,490	7,474,588	744,040	25,429,118
1902.	15,504,038	7,609,669	1,307,394 *	24,421,100
1903.	19,804,180	7,936,060	391,424 *	28,131,664

* The use of undenatured duty-free spirit in the preparation of medicinal tinctures and prescriptions was formerly allowed in Germany. This privilege was withdrawn after the 30th September, 1902.

The undenatured alcohol is now only allowed to be used duty free in certain hospitals, asylums. and public scientific institutions, and for making smokeless powders, etc., mainly in government factories

The sudden increase from 33,820 hectolitres in 1901 to 59,427 hectolitres in 1902 was probably connected with the publication of the intention of the government to disallow the use of pure duty-free spirits for medicinal purposes, this intention being published a year in advance of the time that it was to take effect.

(b) METHODS OF DENATURING AND QUANTITIES OF ALCOHOL DENATURED IN THE YEARS ENDING 30TH SEPTEMBER, 1901, 1902, AND 1903.

Denaturing Substance Used per 100 Litres of Alcohol.	Hectolitres of Pure Alcohol.			Equivalent Bulk Gallons of Pure Alcohol.		
	1901.	1902.	1903.	1901.	1902.	1903.
"*Completely denatured.*" *Official Mixture*— 4 parts Wood Naphtha. 1 part Pyridin bases. *For general use*— 2½ litres of Official Mixture.	782,295	704,729	870,735	17,210,490	15,504,038	19,156,170
For m tor engines,etc.— 1¼ litres of Official Mixture, and 2 to 20 litres of Benzol, coloured with Methyl Violet. . . .	—	—	29,455	—	—	648,010
Total "Completely denatured".	782,295	704,729	900,190	17,210,490	15,504,038	19,804,180
"*Incompletely denatured.*" *For sale*— 5 litres Wood Naphtha.	18,689	18,164	20,338	411,158	399,608	447,436
½ litre Turpentine. . .	607	607	639	13,354	13,354	14,058
For use only in the factories, etc., where denatured— Vinegar (various proportions).	166,329	160,287	155,838	3,659,238	3,526,314	3,428,436
.025 litre Animal Oil	66,748	75,831	79,836	1,468,456	1,668,282	1,756,392
½ litre Turpentine. . .	50,334	51,733	54,460	1,107,348	1,138,126	1,198,120
5 litres Wood N'tha.	2,803	2,240	2,379	61,666	49,280	52,338
10 " Ether.	11,495	11,210	14,473	252,890	246,620	318,406
1 kilogram Camphor.	9,396	9,604	11,510	206,712	211,288	253,220
2 litres Turpentine. .	5,001	4,935	7,403	110,022	108,570	162,866
1 li re Benzol	1,879	3,051	4,105	41,338	67,122	90,310
½ " Benzol	1,144	2,356	3,525	25,168	51,832	77,550
1 kg. Castor Oil. . ⎰ 0.4 " Soda Solut. ⎱	1,737	1,710	1,808	38,214	37,620	39,776
20 litres Shellac Sol. .	1,684	1,586	1,795	37,048	34,892	39,409
5 litres Petroleum Benzin.	993	1,052	992	21,846	23,144	21,824
300 gms. Chloroform	296	671	586	6,512	14,762	12,892
½ litre Pyridin bases.	210	509	539	4,620	11,198	11,858
200 gms. Iodoform. .	356	324	322	7,832	7,128	7,084
300 " Ethyl Bromide.	—	—	132	—	—	2,904
1 litre Commercially pure Methyl Alco'l ⎰ 1 litre Petr. Benzin ⎱	6	—	43	132	—	946
2 litres Wood N'tha. ⎰ 2 " Petr. Benzin. ⎱	47	24	7	1,034	528	154
Total Incom. denatured. .	339,754	345,894	360,730	7,474,588	7,609,668	7,936,060

(c) Manufactures, etc., in which "Incompletely Denatured" Alcohol was used in the Years Ending 30th September, 1901, 1902, and 1903.

Manufacture, etc.	Hectolitres of Pure Alcohol.			Equivalent Bulk Gallons of Pure Alcohol.		
	1901.	1902.	1903.	1901.	1902.	1903.
Vinegar.	171,264	164,062	164,754	3,767,808	3,609,364	3,624,588
Polishes, Lacquers and Varnishes.	66,672	65,116	68,095	1,466,784	1,432,552	1,498,090
Ether.	48,265	55,747	51,609	1,061,830	1,226,434	1,135,398
Medicinal Extracts, Alkaloids, Coal Tar Colours, etc.	28,070	32,610	38,637	617,540	717,420	850,014
Celluloid.	15,797	16,684	22,438	347,534	367,048	493,636
Lake Paints and Colours.	2,741	3,460	5,397	60,302	76,120	118,734
Soap.	1,737	1,710	1,808	38,214	37,620	39,776
Fulminates, Percussion Caps, etc.	700	1,650	1,651	15,400	36,300	36,322
Brewers' Glazes	1,447	1,328	1,421	31,834	29,216	31,262
Lanoline Extraction. . . .	1,143	1,052	992	25,146	23,144	21,824
Chloroform.	296	760	586	6,512	16,720	12,892
Iodoform.	369	324	322	8,118	7,128	7,084
Acetic Ether.	245	415	464	5,390	9,130	10,208
Ethyl Bromide.	—	—	132	—	—	2,904
Surgical Dressings	—	—	345	—	—	7,590
Pharmaceutical Remedies and Preparations	425	425	435	9,350	9,350	9,570
Photographic Emulsions, Papers, Plates, etc. . . .	—	—	631	—	—	13,882
Finishing Rubber Goods.	235	258	374	5,170	5,676	8,228
Inks.	112	30	217	2,464	660	4,774
Miscellaneous.	236	263	422	5,192	5,786	9,284
	339,754	345,894	360,730	7,474,588	7,609,668	7,936,060

Appendix No. IV.

REGULATIONS AS REGARDS USE OF SPIRIT FOR INDUSTRIAL, ETC., PURPOSES IN FRANCE.

The Customs and Excise Taxes on Alcohol in France are:

Customs (Importation).

70 francs per hectolitre (equivalent to about 1s. 5d. per proof gallon) and 80 centimes per hectolitre (equivalent to about 1s. 7d. per 100 proof gallons) for control, etc.

These duties are in addition to the Excise duty.

Excise (Internal).

220 francs per hectolitre of pure alcohol (equivalent to about 4s. 6d. per proof gallon).

DUTY-FREE SPIRIT.

Abstract of French Regulations.

Spirits for industrial and domestic use are freed from all taxes on condition that they are denatured, but all medicaments which contain any spirit after their manufacture pay the ordinary spirit duty. Denatured alcohol pays a statistical tax of 0.25 franc per hectolitre of pure alcohol (about 7d. per 100 proof gallons) and also

0.80 franc per hectolitre (about 1s. 10d. per 100 proof gallons) to cover the expense of the examination of the samples and the supervision of the denaturing operations.

Any person who desires to denature spirit must submit a plan of his premises and supply details as to the vats, vessels, etc., and the materials to be used for denaturing.

Denaturing takes place in presence of the Excise officials. The alcohol must be of at least 90° (58 o.p.) and contain not more than 1 per cent. of "fusel oil."

Samples of both the alcohol and of the denaturing substances to be used have to be submitted to analysis as directed by the Ministry of Finance, and all operations are supervised by the Excise officers.

Spirits may be denatured by the "general process" or by "special processes."

Denaturing by the "special" processes is usually carried out at the factories where the spirit is to be used.

General Denaturing Process.

Ten litres of wood spirit of at least 90° (58 o.p.) and containing 25 per cent. acetone and 2.5 per cent of "impurités pyrogénées" for 100 litres of spirit.

Spirit denatured by this reagent is divided into two classes:

1. *For lighting and heating and for making "finish."*—This spirit must contain, in addition to the general denaturing agent, 0.5 per cent. of heavy benzine, distilling between 150° and 200° C., when used for heating and lighting, and 4 per cent. gum resin for "finish."

These spirits are allowed to be sold, under strict regulations and police and excise supervision, both wholesale and by retail to the general public, and correspond to our mineralised methylated spirit and "finish." Since 1st January, 1902, there is allotted to the makers of denatured alcohol for heating, lighting, and motive power a sum of 9 francs per hectolitre of pure alcohol (about 2½d. per proof gallon). This is to reduce the cost of denaturing for the various uses to which this alcohol is applied in competition with petrol.

2. *For manufacturing purposes,* such as varnishes, solid extracts, solidified spirits, plastic substances, alkaloids, fulminate of mercury, transparent soap, insecticides, etc.

Manufacturers wishing to use this spirit must obtain permission. They have to keep an account of spirits received and used, and of the nature and quantity of the products manufactured by its aid.

Excise officers frequently visit the works in order to assure themselves that the products made correspond to the spirit produced.

If the products contain any alcohol they come under the same regulations as to sale, etc., as methylated spirits.

This spirit corresponds to our "Ordinary unmineralised methylated spirit," and the regulations in France are not less but more stringent than in this country.

3. Certain industries cannot use methylated spirit mixed with wood spirit, and the Ministry have authorised the employment of other processes of denaturing specially adapted to the particular necessities of each manufacturer. These are either *special* for each product, and have to be approved by the Minister, or *general* for products or classes of products already approved on the advice of the Consultative Committee.

Of the latter are:

1. *Ethers, simple and compound.*

Alcohol is mixed with 10 per cent. of the residue (of a fixed type) of a previous operation, and 10 per cent. sulphuric acid at 66° B., or 20 per cent. at 54° B. The mixture is heated to a temperature of 80° C. for some time (prolongé) in presence of the Excise Officer.

2. *Ethyl Bromide.*

Seven litres of spirit at 93° with 8½ litres sulphuric acid at 66° and 15 grams bromine.

3. *Ethyl Iodide.*

6 litres of alcohol at 96°, 4 kilograms iodine, and 800 grams amorphous phosphorus.

4. *Ethylate of Soda.*

8 litres absolute alcohol and 500 grams soda.

5. *Nitric Ether.*
    1 part nitric acid at 36° and 4 parts alcohol at 96°.
6. *Ethyl Chloride.*
    1 part hydrochloric acid at 21° and 1 part alcohol at 96°.
7. *Aldehyde.*
    Mix alcohol with 10 per cent. sulphuric acid at 66° B. or 20 per cent. at 54° B., and heat the mixture to a temperature of 80° C. Cool and then pour the mixture on to bichromate of potash.
8. *Chloroform.*
    Mix the alcohol with 5 or 6 kilograms of chloride of lime in solution.
9. *Collodion.*
    Equal volumes of ether and alcohol, and add guncotton. The mixture should represent 2 litres for each litre of alochol, and should contain 6 grams pyroxylin.
10. *Chloral and Chloral Hydrate.*
    A current of chlorine gas is passed through alcohol. Each litre of alcohol of 95° ought to produce 780 grams of chloral hydrate.

In all these cases, as well as those in which the manufacturers are permitted to employ other special formulæ, the denaturing has to be done in presence of an Excise Officer (Agent d'Administration), and the manufacturer has to keep registers of the alcohol used, and of the products made, and to submit to visits from the officials as in the case of those who use the common methylated spirits.

The Administration furnishes the denaturing wood spirit, etc., at the expense of the makers.

The minimum quantity of spirit that can be denatured by the general formula is 20 hectolitres (440 gallons) and by any special formulæ 10 hectolitres (220 gallons).

In all the "special cases" the French regulations appear to involve the presence of an official during at least the initial stages of every manufacturing operation, and in addition a detailed return from the manufacturer of the quantity of the products he obtains and of the spirit used, and the officials have to be satisfied that the correspondence between the spirit used and the products obtained is satisfactory. Manufacturers are charged with duty on any deficiency of spirit shown by the returns or inspections.

There appears to be no provision in France for any remission of the Import (Customs) duty on spirits, and no foreign spirit is denatured.

TABLE SHOWING THE QUANTITIES OF DENATURED SPIRIT USED IN FRANCE FOR VARIOUS MANUFACTURING PURPOSES DURING THE YEARS 1900-1-2-3.

Manufacture, etc., for which Used.	Gallons of Pure Alcohol.			
	1900.	1901.	1902.	1903.
Lighting, heating, motor engines, etc.	2,764,256	3,366,110	4,999,566	5,764,792*
Varnishes, lacquers, and polishes ..	385,264	360,426	312,136	317,834*
Dyeing	3,432	16,346	902	11,704*
Celluloid, etc.	158,356	111,518	87,186	101,090*
Drugs and chemical preparations ..	100,408	60,852	149,886	613,162
Ether and explosives.	1,427,206	1,530,848	1,539,912	1,405,338
Scientific purposes.	8,492	9,438	8,932	11,418
Various.	19,294	78,892	88,000	15,818
Total.	4,866,708	5,534,430	7,186,520	8,241,156

* These spirits, as well as a large proportion of that classed under "chemical preparations" and "explosives," contain 10 per cent of wood-naphtha.

Since January 1, 1902, a drawback of 9 francs per hectolitre (about 2½d. per proof gallon) has been allowed on alcohol used for lighting and heating to compensate for cost of methylating, and to enable this spirit to compete with petrol in motor cars, etc.

There was some alteration of the classification of "drugs," "ether," etc., in 1903.

Appendix No. V.

REGULATIONS AS REGARDS USE OF SPIRIT FOR INDUSTRIAL, ETC., PURPOSES IN SWITZERLAND.

Customs and Excise Duties.

In Switzerland, the manufacture, importation, and the primary sale of alcohol is a monopoly of the Federal Government.

Farmers are permitted to distil small quantities of spirit from grapes, wine, wine lees, wine yeast, fruits, berries, etc., grown on their own lands; but, with this exception, all kinds of distilleries have to work under the supervision of the officials of the Federal Alcohol Department, and all the spirit produced is taken over by this department at prices fixed by agreement made between the distillers and the Federal Finance Minister.

Customs Import Taxes. Brandy, liqueurs, essences, vermouth, tinctures and other special alcoholic liquors may be imported by private persons on payment of an import duty of 80 francs per 100 kilograms gross weight of spirit and vessels, where the strength does not exceed 75° (31 o.p.), and 80 centimes for each degree over that strength (equivalent to about 2s. 6d. to 3s. 6d. per proof gallon).

But all ordinary alcohol, and substances containing alcohol, come ulnder the monopoly, and can only be imported into Switzerland by the Federal Alcohol Department.

Excise (Monopoly) Taxes. All imported alcohol, and all Swiss manufactured alcohol, has to be sent to the warehouses of the Alcohol Department of the Federal Government.

Any one who wishes to buy spirit must order it from the department in quantities of not less than 150 litres. The prices charged are fixed by law at not less than 120 francs or more than 150 francs per hectolitre of pure alcohol.

At present the ordinary "monopoly" prices are as follows:

(a) Wein Sprit, mark A.V.W., or Kahlbaum Sprit (Fein Sprit from Kahlbaum, Berlin).
    142.60 francs per hectolitre at 95° (5s. 2d. per gallon at 66 o.p., 3s. 1½d. per proof gallon).

(b) Prima Sprit, mark A.V.P.
    140.97 francs per hectolitre at 95° (5s. 1d. per gallon at 66 o.p., 3s. 1d. per proof gallon).

(c) Fein Sprit, mark A.V.F.
    138.53 francs per hectolitre at 95° (5s. per gallon at 66 o.p., 3s. per proof gallon).

(d) Raw Potato Spirit, mark A. V. R.
    131.24 francs per hectolitre at 90° (4s. 9d. per gallon at 58 o.p., 3s. per proof gallon).

From these prices the Government profit or tax is equivalent to about 2s. to 2s. 3d. per proof gallon.

Wholesale dealing in spirit or spirituous liquors is not subject to any further licences or taxes, but the retail sale and the regulation of public houses, etc., is under the control of the Cantonal Authorities, who may impose further taxes or licences.

Duty-free Spirit.

ABSTRACT OF THE SWISS REGULATIONS.

The Alcohol Department are authorised to sell denatured spirits in quantities of not less than 150 litres (33 gallons) at cost price for the following purposes:

(a) For cleansing, heating, cooking, lighting, as well as for use in motor engines.

(b) For industrial purposes generally, except the preparation of beverages or of liquid perfumes and cosmetics.

(c) For making vinegar.

(d) For scientific purposes.

(e) For preparing pharmaceutica. products which do not contain any alcohol in their finished condition, and are not mixed with alcohol when used.

The denaturing is either "absolute," *i.e.*, such as is considered sufficient of itself to render the spirit unfit for consumption as a beverage; or it is "relative," *i.e.*, such as requires official supervision in order to prevent such relatively denatured spirit being used for other purposes than those for which it is allowed.

"*Absolutely*" *Denatured Spirit.* The preparation of "absolutely" denatured spirit is exclusively reserved for the Alcohol Department, who prepare it and sell it to users and retailers in quantities of not less than 150 litres at a time, at a price of 50 francs per 100 kilograms at 93° (about 1s. 6d. per gallon at 63 o.p.). On quantities of 10,000 kilograms sent out at one time in boiler tanks a discount of 2 per cent. is allowed off this price, and from 1½ to ½ per cent. when quantities of 10,000 kilograms and 5,000 kilograms are so sent out in large and small casks.

The methods of denaturing and the substances used are regulated by the Alcohol Department.

The "absolutely" denatured spirit is used for cleansing, heating, cooking, lighting, and motor engines, and is for sale by retail. The retail sale is under the control of the Cantonal Authorities.

For "absolutely" denatured spirit the composition of the denaturing mixture is not kept constant, but for various reasons it is changed two or three times per annum. At present (November, 1904) the Department employ a mixture having the following composition:

Acetone Oil	700	parts
Pyridine Bases	100	"
Solvent Naphtha	90	"
Crude Wood Naphtha	110	"
	1,000	parts.

2.7 kilograms of this mixture are added to any 100 kilograms of alcohol at 95° (about 2.7 gallons to 100 gallons of alcohol at 66 o.p.).

This proportion has been kept constant for some time, but cannot be considered as unalterable.

"*Relatively*" denatured spirit. For all manufacturing purposes "relatively" denatured spirit is allowed to be used.

Whoever wishes to use this kind of spirit in his business must make application to the Alcohol Department on a special form.

Persons whose names are not registered in the "Trade List" have to obtain an official certificate as to the character of their establishments, and the kind of business carried on by them. The discretion as to the granting of permission is vested in the Director of the Alcohol Department, who also determines what bonds or guarantees are sufficient to prevent the improper use of such spirit.

Persons who have been allowed to use this spirit must commence operations within three months of the date of their obtaining the permission, otherwise a fresh application has to be made.

Denaturing may take place either in the warehouses of the Alcohol Department or at the premises of the users of such spirit. In the latter case the users of "relatively" denatured spirit have to obtain the pure spirit from the Alcohol Department, and have then to provide the denaturing materials at their own cost, and also premises for mixing the denaturing substances with the spirit in the presence of the officials of the Department.

The officials decide whether the denaturing substances provided comply with the regulations, and if they are not satisfied samples are taken and sent for examination by the technical chemists of the Department at Berne. Traders have also to provide the denaturing substances used at a warehouse.

The following substances have been sanctioned for "relative" denaturing in the undernoted proportions for every 100 litres of alcohol for use for the purposes specified:

(a) *For making Vinegar.*

Five litres of absolute acetic acid dissolved in at least 200 litres of water. The water may be replaced by an equal quantity of beer, wine, yeast, yeast pressings, or similar liquids.

(b) *For preparing Lacquers, Varnishes, and Polishes.*

2 litres of wood spirit and 2 litres of petroleum benzin,

or ½ litre of turpentine,

or 5 litres of wood spirit,

or 2 kilograms of shellac,

or 2 " of copal or resin,

or ½ kilogram of camphor.

The denaturing with camphor will only be allowed to authorised users, who mix varnishes or polishes exclusively for use in their own workshops.

(c) *For preparing Dye Substances.*

10 litres sulphuric ether,

or 1 litre benzol,

or 1 " coal-tar oil,

or ½ " turpentine,

or 25 grams animal oil, and

or 25 " aniline blue or eosin, violet, or fluorescein

or 100 " naphthalene,

or 2 kilograms commercially pure methyl alcohol,

or ½ kilogram camphor.

For the use of other denaturing substances for other purposes special permission has to be obtained from the Federal Council.

In the case of (b) varnishes, etc., and (c) dyes, the Alcohol Department determines, in each case in which permission is granted for the use of "relatively" denatured spirit, which of the different denaturing substances given in the list shall be used.

The authorised users of "relatively" denatured spirit are required (so far as may not be in whole or part dispensed with) to keep prescribed books in which are to be entered the receipt and use of the spirit; the preparation and disposal of the products made with it; and particulars of any sale of the spirit which may be allowed.

They have also to send to the Alcohol Department, immediately after the close of every quarter, certified extracts of these books, giving full particulars of the business done during the preceding quarter, and vouching by signature for the accuracy of these reports.

Officials of the Department may at any time inspect the works, the stock of denatured spirit, and the quantities used, and of the products made with it; and may take samples and inspect any of the business books belonging to the factory.

The trader and his servants must assist the officials of the Department and of the Customs in carrying out the denaturing, and generally in the exercise of their official supervision.

Information must also be immediately given to the officials when there has been any unusual disturbance in the manufacturing operations, or any occurrence which has caused an unusual loss of "relatively" denatured spirit, or of the products made from it.

If more than 10,000 kilograms of relatively denatured spirit are used annually at any factory, iron or other vats with gauge glasses and scales or floats, and means for official locking, must be provided for storing the spirit.

Manufacturers who use both "relatively" and "absolutely" denatured spirit and also undenatured spirit, in their works have to keep separate the processes in which each kind of spirit is used.

No distilling or rectifying apparatus must be used without the special permission of the Department either in the rooms in which "relatively" denatured spirit is being used, or in any adjoining room belonging to the authorised user.

If permission has been given to recover the spirit it must be used again for the same purpose, and the quantities recovered must be entered in the stock books. The permission for the use of the spirit may be withdrawn at any time, and the withdrawal gives no person any claim for compensation. If by death or any other cause a change in the firm occurs, a renewal of the permission must be obtained from the Department by the successors.

When for more than a year no "relatively" denatured spirit has been used, the authorised user must resign his permission, and sell or give over to some other authorised user any unused spirit, or return it to the Alcohol Department, who will pay the market price for it.

The owner of the "relatively" denatured spirit must not sell it, or allow it to leave his manufacturing premises. Permission is given to sell such spirit denatured with—

      (a) 5 litres of Wood Naphtha,
or (b) 3   " of Acetone Oils,
or (c) 2 kilograms of Shellac, per hectolitre.

Such spirit cannot, however, be sold or given to any person who means to sell it again, but only to users of it in their own workshops. Not less than 5 kilograms of such spirit can be sold at a time, and if the person to whom it is sold does not hold a special permission for its use the total quantity he can receive annually must not exceed 150 litres (33 gallons).

Denatured spirit must not be used for any other purposes than those for which permission is given, and more particularly it must not be used in any way for making beverages, and no attempt must be made to remove wholly or partially from such spirit any of the denaturing substances, or to add other substances which would hide either the taste or smell of the denaturing substances. Nor must users of "relatively" denatured spirit in preparing with it articles for sale make so slight a change in the spirit that it practically remains only denatured spirit. In particular all varnishes, etc., must contain at least 6 per cent. of their weight of shellac or similar resin.

The sale of lacquers, varnishes, and polishes containing 6 per cent. of shellac is free. Dealers in all other products containing denatured spirit must obtain permission from the Alcohol Department.

Heavy penalties may be imposed for any breach of the laws or regulations.

The prices at which authorised users of "relatively" denatured alcohol can obtain their spirit from the Alcohol Department are fixed for periods of five years, according to the average prices paid by the Department for spirit during the preceding five years.

The present prices per 100 kilograms net at 95° are as follows:

    (a) Sekunda-Sprit............................... 47.0 francs.
        (about 1s. 4½d. per gallon at 66 o.p.)
    (b) Fein-Sprit or Rohspiritus..................... 48.5   "
        (about 1s. 5d. per gallon at 66 o.p.)
    (c) Prima-Sprit................................. 51.5   "
        (about 1s. 6d. per gallon at 66 o.p.)
    (d) Kahlbaum-Sprit or Wein-Sprit.................. 53.5   "
        (about 1s. 7d. per gallon at 66 o.p.)

The same discounts are given for large orders as in the case of "absolutely" denatured spirit.

The authorised user has to bear the cost of the carriage, and of the denaturing substances in addition. Until recently authorised users were permitted to buy their own alcohol from abroad and to import it through the Department on payment of an import duty of 8 francs per 100 kilograms (about 2½d. per gallon). In future all alcohol must be bought from the Federal Alcohol Department, and the prices for the year 1905 have been fixed as follows:

    (a) Sekunda-Sprit at 41.0 francs per 100 kilograms at 95°.
        (1s. 2½d. per gallon at 66 o.p. = 8½d. per proof gal.)
    (b) Fein-Sprit or Rohspiritus at 42.50 francs per 100 kilograms at 95°.
        (1s. 3d. per gallon at 66 o.p. = 9d. per proof gal.)
    (c) Prima-Sprit at 45.50 francs per 100 kilograms at 95°.
        (1s. 4d. per gallon at 66 o.p. = 9¾d. per proof gal.)
    (d) Wein-Sprit at 47.50 francs per 100 kilograms at 95°.
        (1s. 5d. per gallon at 66 o.p. = 10¼d. per proof gal.)

Authorised users who order at one time one or more tanks of about 10,000 kilograms net content (2,700 gallons) enjoy a discount of 5 per cent. off these prices if

www.KnowledgePublications.com

they give the Alcohol Department a period of 30 days for the execution of their order when foreign kinds of spirit are required.

For all other large orders of over 5,000 kilograms gross weight the usual official discount will be given.

The annexed tables give the quantities of the "absolutely" denatured spirit, and of the different kinds of "relatively" denatured spirit used in 1903, and also the principal purposes for which the latter spirit was used.

QUANTITY OF DENATURED SPIRIT OF ALL KINDS SOLD IN 1903.

	Kilograms at 93° to 95°.	Equivalent Gallons at 63 to 66 o.p.
"Absolutely" Denatured...................	4,758,003	1,284,660
"Relatively" Denatured:		
From Monopoly.........................	110,980	—
" Importations......................	1,567,602	—
	1,678,582	453,217
Total...............................	6,436,585	1,737,877

QUANTITY OF "RELATIVELY" DENATURED SPIRIT USED IN SWITZERLAND IN 1903.

Nature of the Manufacture, etc., in which the Spirit is Used.	Number of Factories or Users.	Quantities of Alcohol Used.	
		Kilograms at 95°.	Equivalent Gallons at 66 o.p.
Vinegar-making.........................	19	225,849	60,980
For lacquers and varnishes................	154	169,767	45,837
Manufacture of dyes......................	8	311,581	84,127
For dissolving dyes for cotton factories......	6	9,150	2,470
For soaps and perfumery..................	11	8,376	2,262
For scientific purposes...................	18	4,048	1,093
Chemical products.......................	27	133,231	35,972
Surgical dressings.......................	3	782	211
Gummed tissues.........................	3	6,049	1,633
Tobacco manufacture.....................	1	17	5
Artificial silk...........................	2	603,730	163,007
Celluloid...............................	1	8,758	2,365
Smokeless powder.......................	1	2,952	797
Fulminate of mercury....................	1	10,932	2,952
Acetic ether............................	1	91,759	24,775
Grafting wax............................	1	258	70
Electrotyping...........................	1	280	76
Preparing cotton goods...................	1	16,069	4,339
Making mixture to prevent freezing of gas-pipes	1	2,536	685
Preserving natural-history specimens........	1	252	68
" botanical specimens..............	3	438	118
In photo-chemical works..................	2	850	230
		1,607,665	434,072

DENATURING SUBSTANCES USED FOR "RELATIVE" DENATURING, AND QUANTITY OF ALCOHOL DENATURED WITH EACH.

Denaturing Substances.	Quantity of Alcohol Denatured.	
	Kilograms at 95°.	Equivalent Gallons at 66 o.p.
1. Shellac, with or without the addition of camphor, turpentine, wood-naphtha, etc.	52,340	14,132
2. Colophony resin.	3,974	1,073
3. Copal resin.	2,455	663
4. Camphor.	22,551	6,089
5. Turpentine.	98,210	26,517
6. Acetic acid.	257,186	69,440
7. Nitric acid.	1,241	335
8. Acetic ether.	3,532	953
9. Ethylic ether.	628,566	169,713
10. Wood-naphtha.	15,751	4,253
11. Pure methyl alcohol.	11,419	3,083
12. Wood-naphtha and pyridine.	352	95
13. Acetone oil.	1,748	472
14. Methyl violet (dye).	132,350	35,734
15. Methylene blue (dye).	524	141
16. Aniline blue (dye).	10,711	2,892
17. Eosin (dye).	133,552	36,059
18. Fluorescein (dye).	87,038	23,500
19. Naphthalein.	9,463	2,555
20. Soap and castor-oil solution.	4,367	1,179
21. Coal-tar oil.	12,670	3,421
22. Benzol.	3,100	837
23. Nitrobenzol.	513	138
24. Phenol.	739	200
25. Pyridin.	87,817	23,710
26. Caustic soda.	15,244	4,116
27. Piperonal.	2,423	654
28. Musk.	8,275	2,234
29. Animal oil.	54,780	14,790
30. Ethyl chloride.	1,243	336
31. Chloroform.	128	34
32. Formalin.	220	59
33. Undenatured (for manufacture of munitions of war)	13,609	3,674
	1,678,091	453,081

Appendix No. VI.

REGULATIONS AS REGARDS USE OF SPIRIT FOR INDUSTRIAL, ETC., PURPOSES IN AUSTRIA-HUNGARY, RUSSIA, HOLLAND, UNITED STATES, BELGIUM.

AUSTRIA-HUNGARY.

The Spirit taxes in Austria and Hungary are:

CUSTOMS (Import).

On Liqueurs, Punch Essence, Sweetened Spirits, Arrack, Rum, French Brandy and Cognac: 150 kronen (£6) per 100 kilograms, equivalent to about 4s. per bulk gallon.

On all other spirits: 110 kronen (£4 8s.) per 100 kilograms, equivalent to about 3s. 3d. per bulk gallon.

These duties are in addition to the highest Excise Duty payable in the country on spirits of the same description.

EXCISE.

Austria.—90 kronen (75s.) per 100 litres pure alcohol, equivalent to 1s. 11d. per proof gallon.

Hungary.—100 kronen (83s. 4d.) per 100 litres of pure alcohol, equivalent to 2s. 2d. per proof gallon.

DUTY-FREE SPIRIT.

Ordinary Methylated Spirit is made by mixing with alcohol of at least 90° (58 o.p.):

2 per cent. Wood Naphtha,
½ per cent. Pyridine Bases, and a
Trace of Phenolphthalein.

A Tax equivalent to about one-third of a penny per gallon is charged for denaturing.

For Varnishes, fulminate of mercury, hat-making, etc.:

½ per cent. of turpentine is the denaturing agent.

For Vinegar the spirit is mixed with "Anhydride."

Very small quantities of pure alcohol are used for scientific purposes under certain conditions free of duty.

RUSSIA.

CUSTOMS AND EXCISE DUTIES ON ALCOHOL.

CUSTOMS (Import).

16 roubles 20 copecks per poud, equivalent to 34s. 6d. per 36 lbs. As in Germany, probably the weight of the vessels is included, and no very exact comparison can be made with the British standard. Approximately, the tax may be taken at 10s. to 12s. per proof gallon.

EXCISE.

The sale of alcohol is a monopoly in Russia, and distillers have to hand over their produce at fixed rates.

DUTY-FREE SPIRIT.

ABSTRACT OF RUSSIAN REGULATIONS.

Persons wishing to use spirit duty free must apply to the Minister of Finance. Permission is generally limited *to one year.* Security for the duty (bond) must be given.

The quantity of spirit allowed is determined each year, and "depends on the productive power of the manufactory, conditions for disposal of manufactured article, scale of annual consumption of spirit," etc. The spirit is issued from distilleries, rectifying works, etc., on production of the order of the Finance Minister. It is received and examined at the factories by Excise Officers, and after *having been denatured*, is placed under revenue seal in a special store and is only issued as required by an Excise Officer. Accounts of receipt and issue are strictly kept, and sent to auditing authorities at the end of each year.

As a general rule a special Excise Controller is attached to each works for constant supervision of the proper use of the duty-free spirit, and the proprietor of the works is bound to provide him with proper dwelling accommodation and with furniture and fuel.

Foreign spirits cannot be imported duty free.

Denaturing Processes employed:

1. *For Varnishes and Polishes.*
    100 parts spirit are mixed with 5 parts wood-naphtha, and 1 part of turpentine, or instead of turpentine resin, shellac, tar, etc., may be used in the proportion of ½ lb. to one vedro (2.7 gallons of spirit).
2. *For the preparation of Wine Vinegar.*
    The spirit is diluted with water and vinegar, so that it shall be of a strength of 12° Tralles (79 u.p.), and contain 1 per cent. of acetic acid.
3. *For the preparation of Ether, Chloroform. Chloral Hydrate and Iodine.*
    20 "lots" of animal oil to 100 vedros (270 gallons) of spirit.
4. *For the preparation of Tannin and Collodion.*
    To 100 parts of spirit 10 parts of sulphuric ether are added.
5. *For the preparation of Santonine.*
    Fresh spirit is mixed with spirit that has already been used in the proportion of 4 parts of fresh spirit to one part of used spirit, or 36 lbs. (1 poud) of crude santonine is mixed with (10 vedros) 27 gallons of spirit.
6. *For the preparation of Phenacetin, Salol, Saligurine and Salicitine-Nitro Salts.*
    5 per cent. of benzol is added to the spirit.
7. *For the preparation of Aniline Dyes.*
    5 parts of wood-naphtha to 100 parts of spirit, or the spirit is mixed with animal oil in the proportion of 20 lots of oil to one vedro of spirit (2.7 gallons).
8. *For the preparation of Artificial Silk.*
    10 per cent. of sulphuric ether is added to the spirit.
9. *For the preparation of Resinite or Ksylite.*
    7 per cent. of ether or acetone.
10. *For Smokeless Powder Manufacture.*
    Spirit is not denatured, but there is strict registration and personal supervision of the Excise Officer.
11. *For Fulminate of Mercury.*
    1/40th of 1 per cent. of animal oil (.025 per cent.), and 5 per cent. of the crude recovered spirit used in the process.
12. *For the Emulsic process, i.e., Extraction of Sugar from Treacle.*
    Fresh spirit is mixed with the spirit that has already been used in the proportion of 1 part of fresh spirit to 1 part of used spirit.
13. *For Preventing Freezing of Gas Pipes.*
    5 parts of wood-naphtha and 1 part of pyridin bases to 100 of spirits.
14. *For Street Lighting in Towns.*
    20 parts of turpentine to 100 parts of spirit; only issued to contractors to town councils, etc.

HOLLAND.

The Spirit Taxes in Holland are:
Excise.
    63 florins per hectolitre of alcohol at 50°, equivalent to about 5s. 6d. per proof gallon.
Customs (Import).
    A Surtax of 350 florins per hectolitre of alcohol at 50°, and in addition the Excise Tax of 63 florins = total 66.50 florins, equivalent to about 5s. 9d. per proof gallon.

DUTY-FREE ALCOHOL.

ABSTRACT OF THE DUTCH REGULATIONS.

Ordinary Methylated Spirits.
1 litre wood spirit.
8 litres alcohol of at least 85° (49 o.p.).
This spirit is free to all who like to use it, on condition that it is not used in articles of human consumption, and that no attempt is made to purify it from methyl alcohol.

Vinegar-making.
1 hectolitre of alcohol at 50° is denatured with
    1 hectolitre vinegar of 4 per cent. strength,
    2 hectolitres water,
or
    20 litres vinegar of 4 per cent.,
    20   "   dried raisin juice,
or
    20 litres vinegar alone if Excise Officers see the mixture added to acidifying vessels.

Permission to receive methylated spirits must be renewed every year.
Wood spirit provided by Government at a fixed price to cover cost of methylating.
Excise keep accounts of quantity used. Vinegar-makers furnish returns of vinegar made.
Specimens in spirit for teaching natural history may be imported duty free, and no Excise duty is charged.
Foreign-made varnishes containing wood naphtha equal to home-made may be imported duty free.

Duties on—

Chloral hydrate	fl 1.30 per kilogram.
(1) Ether, sulphuric	" 2.20 " "
(2) " acetic	" 1.20 " "
(3) Collodion	" 1.90 " "
Chloroform	" 1.50 " "
Nitrous ether	" 1.30 " "
Wood spirit	" 1.15 " litre.

(1) Exempt when required for use in making smokeless powders and glazing porcelain.
(2) Exempt when required for use in making smokeless powders and glazing porcelain.
(3) Exempt when required for incandescent mantles.

Other similar products pay the same Surtax and Excise as 24 litres of alcohol at 50°.

UNITED STATES.

The Customs and Excise duties on Alcohol in the United States are:
CUSTOMS.
    $1.75 (Minimum Reciprocity Tariff),
    $2.25 (General Tariff),
    Per American Proof Gallon; equivalent to 10s. to 12s. 10d. per British Proof Gallon.
EXCISE.
    $1.10 per American Proof Gallon; equivalent to 6s. 3d. per British Proof Gallon.

DUTY-FREE ALCOHOL.

There appears to be nothing equivalent to British methylated spirit or denatured spirit of any kind in the United States.*
The only duty-free alcohol of any kind is that which is supplied in very small quantities to certain schools and colleges for use in Education and research.

---

* Since this report was published, legislation permitting denatured alcohol in the United States has been enacted.

BELGIUM.

The Customs and Excise Taxes on Alcohol in Belgium are:

Customs (Importation).

175 francs per hectolitre at 50°, and 3.50 francs for each degree over 50 for ordinary spirits in bulk (equivalent to 7s. per proof gallon).

In bottles 350 francs per hectolitre. Other alcoholic liqueurs at 350 francs per hectolitre.

Food preparations preserved in alcohol, 175 francs per 100 kilograms.

Wood spirit, methyl and amylic alcohol, and all homologues pay Customs duty.

Excise (Internal).

Excise on home-made spirits is 150 francs per hectolitre at 50° (equivalent to 6s. per proof gallon).

Agricultural Distilleries obtain a rebate of the Excise Duty, equal to 8 to 10 francs per hectolitre at 50° (equivalent to 4d. to 5d. per Proof Gallon).

Duty-free Alcohol.

ABSTRACT OF THE BELGIAN REGULATIONS.

Since 1896 alcohol has been allowed duty free in a few manufactures and in a number of others a proportion of the duty is returned after the alcohol has been mixed with certain denaturing agents. [See table on page 484.]

Duty-free alcohol for heating and lighting has not yet been allowed. In a note to our Ambassador (February, 1902) the Belgian officials say:

"The point is under consideration and the Government are following attentively what is being done in foreign countries, notably in Germany and France. The question, however, has not the same interest in Belgium as in those countries. In France and Germany petrol pays a heavy import duty, while in Belgium it is free from any tax. From an economic point of view it seems probable that it will be always more advantageous to use petrol than alcohol even free of all duty for those purposes in Belgium."

Apparently the only products containing methylated spirits that can be sold are varnishes.

All the other denatured spirits are for use in the factories only, and the denaturing is done under the supervision of officers at the works. Accounts have to be kept at the works of the quantity of methylated spirits used daily. Excise officers frequently take stock of the methylated spirit, and may verify quantities of products made. No stills allowed on works, except when specially authorised under exceptional circumstances.

Two hectolitres at 50° (44 gallons) is the minimum quantity that can be denatured.

Quantity of spirits on which duty remitted in 1901, 21,292 hectolitres (468,424 gallons). Of this

150,000	gallons	were	used	in	making common ether,
121,000	"	"	"	"	" vinegar,
105,000	"	"	"	"	" varnishes,
58,000	"	"	"	"	" artificial silk,

434,000

leaving 14,000 gallons for the other trades.

The conditions under which denatured spirit is allowed in Belgium are evidently less favourable than in this country, as, exclusive of the cost of the denaturing agents, a duty of about 5d. per proof gallon, or 8d. at 60 overproof is charged.

By a law passed in 1902 the Belgian Government is authorised to grant total or partial exemption from the import tax on alcohols intended to be used exclusively for industrial purposes. The alcohol must first be denatured.

The table on page 485 shows the quantity of denatured alcohol used in the various kinds of industry in Belgium since the beginning of 1902.

DUTY REMITTED ON DENATURED ALCOHOL USED IN MANUFACTURES IN BELGIUM.

Manufacture, etc.	Denaturing Agent Used per Hectolitre of Alcohol at 94° or over (64 o.p.).	Duty Remitted per Hectolitre at 50°. (Excise Duty 150 Francs.)
Vinegar	300 litres of water, and 100 litres of vinegar containing 8 per cent. acetic acid	Francs. 120
Varnish	*For use in workshops where made:* 8 litres methyl alcohol (wood spirit) containing 5 per cent. acetone and 25 litres of varnish containing 30 per cent. gum resin. ... *For sale:* 10 litres wood spirit containing 5 per cent. acetone, and 25 litres varnish containing 30 per cent. gum resin	114
Aniline colours	10 litres wood spirit containing 5 per cent. acetone, and 25 grams fuchsine or other aniline colour	140
Hats	10 litres wood spirit containing 5 per cent. acetone, and 25 litres varnish containing 30 per cent. gum resin	140
Artificial flowers.	10 litres wood spirit containing 5 per cent. acetone, and 15 grams aniline colours	140
Frame gilding	20 litres wood spirit containing 5 per cent. acetone, or 3 litres ethyl methyl ketone	114
Fireworks materials	10 litres wood spirit and 5 kilog. gum accroide	140
Refining and washing raw oils	10 litres sulphuric acid at 66° B	140
Transparent soap	5 litres ess. of lavender, aspic of citronella	140
Mercury fulminate	10 litres of crude ethers, recovered in process	140
Collodion for use in workshop where made	50 litres common ether	140
Tannin	50 litres common ether	140
Pegamoids, etc.	5 litres acetone, or 2 litres ethyl-methyl-ketone, or 25 litres ether	140
Smokeless powd.	3 litres ethyl-methyl-ketone	140
Peptones from brewing yeasts	3 " " " "	140
Tineacidine, a disinfectant	3 " " " "	150
Antiseptics and medicaments	3 " " " "	140
Quinoline yellow	3 litres acetone oil	150
Gazage de ficelles	4 " " "	140
Artificial silk	150 litres common ether	150
Soldering metals	3 litres of mixture of equal parts of ethyl methyl ketone and acetone oil	140
Acetic ether	15 litres of acetic ether residues	150
Sulphuric or common ether	10 litres of sulphuric ether residues	150
Anatomical, etc., preparations in superior schools	500 grams nitrobenzol, 500 grams camphor, or 1½ litres methyl ethyl ketone	140

TABLE SHOWING, FOR EACH CLASS OF INDUSTRY, THE QUANTITIES OF DENATURED
ALCOHOL USED IN BELGIUM DURING THE YEARS 1902, 1903, AND THE FIRST
NINE MONTHS OF 1904.

Class of Industry.	Quantity of Denatured Alcohol Used		
	1902.	1903.	Nine Months of 1904.
	Gallons at 50°.	Gallons at 50°.	Gallons at 50°.
Vinegar	174,218	276,760	240,548
Varnish	117,194	123,244	88,462
Aniline Colours	1,628	2,508	2,178
Hats	3,212	2,354	6,160
Fulminate of Mercury	176	3,146	10,230
Collodion	1,122	3,058	2,838
Artificial Flowers	—	—	—
Frame Gilding	308	352	308
Transparent Soap	264	528	792
Refining and Washing Raw Oils	198	—	198
Tannin	—	—	—
Anatomical or Scientific Preparations	638	1,100	550
Antiseptics and Medicaments	3,762	5,962	8,426
Pharmaceutical or Chemical Products	2,508	3,366	3,366
Simili Leather	6,842	462	—
Smokeless Powder	—	—	1,408
Peptones	—	—	—
Acetic Ether	4,268	4,004	—
Sulphuric Ether	308,748	568,194	514,228
Artificial Silk	144,496	325,248	376,816
Alcohol for dissolving Resin used for soldering Metal Boxes	286	660	264
Quinoline Yellow	—	440	330
Tineacidine (disinfectant)	88	154	44
Fireworks Materials	—	—	—
Gazage des ficelles	—	44	—
Total	769,956	1,321,584	1,257,146

ABSTRACT FROM BRITISH REVENUE ACT, 1906, AS TO SPIRITS
USED IN ART, MANUFACTURE, ETC., AND SUPPLEMENTAL
AMENDMENTS OF THE SPIRITS ACT, GRANTING NEW
AND MORE LIBERAL PROVISIONS.

Attention has already been called to these provisions as given in
detail in Chapter IX, and the increased benefits that will thereby accrue
have been explained. We give below a copy of such parts of the British
Revenue Act, 1906, as relate to such new legislation. The author is
indebted to Sir William Crookes, member of the Departmental Committee on Industrial Alcohol, for a copy of their report made to both
Houses of Parliament by Command of His Majesty, and also for a copy
of this Revenue Act, 1906, in which the recommendation of this committee, that for industrial methylated spirit the proportion of wood-
naphtha (wood-alcohol) be reduced from 10 to 5 per cent, was em-
bodied and enacted.

The author also expresses his appreciation of the kindness of the
General Secretary, Charles G. Cresswell, of the Society of Chemical
Industry, for copies of the Statutory Rules and Orders, 1906, No. 622
Excise: Spirits—Regulations, dated August 11, 1906, made by the
Commissoners of Inland Revenue, relating to the Manufacture and Sale
of Spirits and to Spirits received for use in the Arts and Manufactures.
These regulations are given in Chapter IX.

AN ACT to amend the Law relating to Customs and Inland Revenue, and for other
purposes connected with Finance. [4th August, 1906.]

Be it enacted by the King's most Excellent Majesty, by and with the advice
and consent of the Lords Spiritual and Temporal, and Commons, in this present
Parliament assembled, and by the authority of the same, as follows:

PART 1. SPIRITS.

1. (1) Where any spirits are used by an authorised methylator for making
industrial methylated spirits, or are received by any person for use in any art
or manufacture under section eight of the Finance Act, 1902, the like allowance
shall be paid to the authorised methylator or to the person by whom the spirits
are received, as the case may be, in respect of those spirits as is payable on the
exportation of plain British spirits, and the Commissioners may by regulations
prescribe the time and manner of the payment of the allowance and the proof
to be given that the spirits have been or are to be used as aforesaid.

(2) No allowance shall be payable under this section on methylic alcohol,
but foreign methylic alcohol may be received and used under section eight of
the Finance Act, 1902, without payment of the difference of duty mentioned in
that section.

486

(3) One-nineteenth shall, as respects methylated spirits other than mineralised methylated spirits, be substituted for one-ninth as the minimum proportion of the substance or combination of substances to be mixed with spirits under subsection (3) of section one hundred and twenty-three of the Spirits Act, 1880.

(4) Nothwitstanding anything in subsection (2) of section eight of the Finance Act, 1902, an applicant under that section shall not be required to pay any expenses incurred in placing an officer in charge of his premises, except such expenses as, in the opinion of the Commissioners, are incurred for special attendances of the officer, made to meet the convenience of the applicant.

(5) Such quantity as the Commissioners may authorise by regulations in each case shall be substituted for fifty gallons in subsection (c) of section one hundred and twenty-six of the Spirits Act, 1880, as the maximum quantity of methylated spirits that may be received or be in the possession of a retailer at any one time; and for one gallon in subsections (e) and (f) of that section as the maximum quantity of methylated spirit which a retailer may receive from another retailer at a time, and as the maximum quantity which a retailer may sell to or for the use of any one person at a time respectively.

2. (1) Section one hundred and twenty-one of the Spirits Act, 1880 (which forbids the supply of methylated spirits except to the persons mentioned in the section), shall be construed as if, as regards the supply of industrial methylated spirits, a retailer of methylated spirits was not a person excepted under that section.

(2) A retailer of methylated spirits shall not receive or have in his possession any methylated spirits except such as may be authorised by regulations, and if any such retailer contravenes this provision, he shall, for each offence, incur a fine of fifty pounds, and the spirits in respect of which the offence is committed shall be forfeited.

(3) Every vessel in which an authorised methylator stores, keeps, or supplies industrial methylated spirits, or mineralised methylated spirits, must be labelled in such a manner as to show that the methylated spirits are industrial or mineralised, as the case may be, and if an authorised methylator fails to comply with this provision he shall, for each offense, incur a fine of fifty pounds, and the spirits with respect to which the offense is committed shall be forfeited.

(4) In addition to the account required to be kept by the proper officer under subsection (1) of section one hundred and twenty-five of the Spirits Act, 1880, an authorised methylator shall keep distinct accounts in the prescribed forms of any industrial methylated spirits and of any mineralised methylated spirits prepared or received by him and of the sale, use, and delivery thereof, and that section shall apply with reference to each of those accounts and the spirits to which the account relates as it applies with reference to the stock account therein mentioned and to methylated spirits generally.

(5) Section one hundred and thirty of the Spirits Act, 1880, shall apply as if it were an offence under that section without the consent in writing of the Commissioners, or otherwise than in accordance with regulations, to purify or attempt to purify methylated spirits or methylic alcohol, or, after methylated spirits or metyhlic alcohol have once been used, to recover or attempt to recover the spirit or alcohol by distillation or condensation, or in any other manner.

(6) Subsection (2) of section one hundred and thirty of the Spirits Act, 1880, shall apply as respects any article specified in an order of the Commissioners as it applies with respect to sulphuric ether or chloroform.

3. (1) The Commissioners may permit the exportation on drawback of tinctures or of spirits of wine, subject to regulations, direct from the premises of a person licensed to rectify or compound spirits, and the like drawbacks and allowances shall be payable in repsect of tinctures or spirits of wine so exported as would be payable if the tinctures or spirits of wine were exported from an excise or customs warehouse.

(2) In ascertaining the amount of drawback on any tinctures so exported, the Commissioners may make such addition as they think just in respect of waste.

(3) If any person fails to comply with any regulation made under this section, he shall, in addition to any other liability, incur in respect of each offence a fine of fifty pounds and the article in respect of which the offence is committed shall be forfeited.

(4) This section shall apply as respects the shipment of tinctures as stores as it applies with respect to the exportation of tinctures.

4. (1) In this Part of this Act—

The expression "industrial methylated spirits" means any methylated spirits (other than mineralised methylated spirits) which are intended for use in any art or manufacture within the United Kingdom; and

The expression "mineralised methylated spirits" means methylated spirits which, in addition to being methylated as provided by subsection (3) of section one hundred and twenty-three of the Spirits Act, 1880, as amended by this or any other Act, have mixed with or dissolved in them such quantity of such kind of mineral naphtha as may for the time being be prescribed by regulations of the Commissioners . . .

The expression "regulations" means regulations made under section one hundred and fifty-nine of the Spirits Act, 1880.

(2) This Part of this Act shall be construed with the Spirits Act, 1880.

.   .   .   .

13. (1) This Act shall come into operation, save as otherwise expressly provided, on the first day of October, nineteen hundred and six.

(2) This Act may be cited as the Revenue Act, 1906.

AMENDMENTS TO THE ACT OF CONGRESS OF JUNE 7, 1906.*

THIS supplementary legislation was designed to amend and perfect the original denatured alcohol act which was enacted June 7, 1906, and took effect January 1, 1907.

Amendments were enacted in accordance with the Act, a copy of which follows, the purposes of such amendments being to cheapen the cost of the manufacture and transportation of denatured alcohol, and to admit of general competition in its manufacture and sale, thus lessening the cost of the product to the consumer.

This Act will further benefit the American public by permitting the manufacture of ether, chloroform, and other definite chemical substances from tax-free, suitably (specially) denatured alcohol where the alcohol is changed into some other chemical substance and does not appear in the finished product as alcohol.

Among such substances may be mentioned aniline dyes, smokeless powder, ethers, chloroform, chloral hydrate, etc.

This legislation will permit small stills to be operated for producing alcohol from any substance whatever for denaturation only. Such stills to have a daily spirit-producing capacity of not exceeding one hundred proof gallons (about 53 gallons of high-proof alcohol of 95% strength or 190° U. S. proof).

From the Report of the Committee on Ways and Means, submitted by Mr. Hill of Connecticut, accompanying H. R. 24816, the Act containing the legislation to which we refer, it appears that farmers and other small producers can engage in the practical distillation of alcohol, and also that the different sections of the country can be supplied from central points of distribution with alcohol as a cheap source of supply for fuel, light, and power. According to this same report another important benefit which this amending legislation will admit of is the establishment of denaturing plants located in our large manufacturing

---

* Since this book was written supplementary legislation, amending the original denatured alcohol law, has been enacted by our Congress, a copy of which and discussion thereof is here given.

489

centers, where the demand for the product exists and where public convenience and commercial necessities justify their location. This report further states that in England, France, and Germany the denaturing of ethyl alcohol is largely an independent business, like any other manufacturing process, the owner of the plant buying his raw material wherever he pleases and shipping it in bond to the denaturing plant, there to be prepared in accordance with the regulations, released from bond and offered for sale.

Continuing, this report mentions that " judging from the experience of other countries where the right to use denatured alcohol freely has been conceded for twenty-five to fifty years, probably two-thirds of the entire consumption will be of what is known as 'completely denatured' spirit. This is what is used for heating, cooking, lighting, and for all kinds of internal explosion engines and for many manufacturing uses.

" It is purchased and consumed at the will of the buyer, as freely as oil or coal can be, and no records are required to be kept by him and no license needed, except in the case of the manufacturer using an average of more than 50 gallons per month.

" The effect of the denatured alcohol law of last year has been prompt and far reaching. It went into effect on January 1, 1907. Wood alcohol, which the day before was selling at 70 cents per gallon, was at once reduced to 40 cents. Since the law was approved, June 7, 1906, seven new wood-alcohol refineries have been started, and the proprietors announce their intention to enter into a straightforward, uncoddled competition with denatured spirits.

" Denatured alcohol began its new career at 36 cents per gallon at Peoria, Illinois, on January 1, and before January closed was offered at 31 to 32 cents, with the demand far in excess of the supply."

Other interesting statements made by this report are that "in April, 1906, denatured alcohol was selling at wholesale in Berlin at 25.21 cents per gallon" and that " one of the largest locomobile and motor works of Germany has been issuing a trade circular which states that the Central Syndicate of the Alcohol Manufacturer's Interests in Germany with letter dated Berlin, July 23, 1906, have announced that commencing October 1, 1906, the price of 90 per cent motor alcohol (completely denatured) will be reduced to 20 marks per hectolitre. . . . This is equivalent to 18 cents per gallon." From all of these causes mentioned and the data given here, it will be readily appreciated that the field for denatured alcohol in the United States will be very much enlarged by this supplementary legislation to which we have referred and which, together with the U. S. Government Regulations thereon, will go into effect September 1, 1907, in addition to the present law. The use of specially denatured alcohol is increasing and its use will be largely increased by this legislation which we have mentioned. Such special denaturing is done by addition of one or more of the ingredients used in the process of manufacturing the product in question, as the use of castor-oil and caustic soda or lye for specially denaturing alcohol for the manufacture of transparent soap; also the addition of camphor and wood alcohol for specially denaturing alcohol for the manufacture of celluloid and pyralin.

Specially denatured alcohol and the prospect of its greatly extended uses in this country is fully discussed in Chapter X of this book.

The cost of ether should be largely reduced when made from tax-free suitably denatured alcohol (specially denatured), and is only one instance in point.

The field for the manufacture of denatured alcohol, and for the various products mentioned, is thus opened by this Act to general competition, with results that should not only see a low-priced denatured alcohol, but many products that can be made either from it or by its use, either correspondingly cheapened in cost or greatly improved in quality. One great advantage will be the substitution of denatured alcohol for the objectionable and poisonous wood alcohol.

We give here a copy of this Act and the text of the amendments it contains.

AN ACT to amend an Act entitled "An Act for the withdrawal from bond tax free of domestic alcohol when rendered unfit for beverage or liquid medicinal uses by mixture with suitable denaturing materials," approved June seventh, nineteen hundred and six.

Be it enacted by the Senate and House of Representatives of the United States of America in Congress assembled, That notwithstanding anything contained in the Act entitled "An Act for the withdrawal from bond tax free of domestic alcohol when rendered unfit for beverage or liquid medicinal uses by mixture with suitable denaturing materials," approved June seventh, nineteen hundred and six, domestic alcohol when suitably denatured may be withdrawn from bond without the payment of internal-revenue tax and used in the manufacture of ether and chloroform and other definite chemical substances where said alcohol is changed into some other chemical substance and does not appear in the finished product as alcohol: Provided, That rum of not less than one hundred and fifty degrees proof may be withdrawn, for denaturation only, in accordance with the provisions of said Act of June seventh, nineteen hundred and six, and in accordance with the provisions of this Act.

Sec. 2. That the Commissioner of Internal Revenue, with the approval of the Secretary of the Treasury, may authorize the establishment of central denaturing bonded warehouses, other than those at distilleries, to which alcohol of the required proof may be transferred from distilleries or distillery bonded warehouses without the payment of internal-revenue tax, and in which such alcohol may be stored and denatured. The establishment, operation, and custody of such warehouses shall be under such regulations and upon the execution of such bonds as the Commissioner of Internal Revenue, with the approval of the Secretary of the Treasury, may prescribe.

Sec. 3. That alcohol of the required proof may be drawn off, for denaturation only, from receiving cisterns in the cistern room of any distillery for transfer by pipes direct to any denaturing bonded warehouse on the distillery premises or to closed metal storage tanks situated in the distillery bonded warehouse, or from such storage tanks to any denaturing bonded warehouse on the distillery premises, and denatured alcohol may also be transported from the denaturing bonded warehouse, in such manner and by means of such packages, tanks or tank cars, and on the execution of such bonds, and under such regulations as the Commissioner of Internal Revenue, with the approval of the Secretary of the Treasury, may prescribe.   And further, alcohol to be denatured may be withdrawn without the payment of internal-revenue tax from the distillery bonded warehouse for shipment to central denaturing plants in such packages, tanks and tank cars, under such regulations, and on the execution of such bonds as may be prescribed by the Commissioner of Internal Revenue, with the approval of the Secretary of the Treasury.

Sec. 4.   That at distilleries producing alcohol from any substance whatever, for denaturation only, and having a daily spirit-producing capacity of not exceeding one hundred proof gallons, the use of cisterns or tanks of such size and construction as may be deemed expedient may be permitted in lieu of distillery bonded warehouses, and the production, storage, the manner and process of denaturing on the distillery premises the alcohol produced, and transportation of such alcohol, and the operation of such distilleries shall be upon the execution of such bonds and under such regulations as the Commissioner of Internal Revenue, with the approval of the Secretary of the Treasury, may prescribe, and such distilleries may by such regulations be exempted from such provisions of the existing laws relating to distilleries, as may be deemed expedient by said officials.

Sec. 5.   That the provisions of this Act shall take effect on September first, nineteen hundred and seven.

Approved March 2, 1907.

BIBLIOGRAPHY OF DENATURED ALCOHOL AND BOOKS OF REFERENCE.

Maercker's Handbuch der Spiritusfabrikation.   Maercker-Delbruch.

La Rectification de l'Alcool, par Ernest Sorel.

Nouveau Manuel Complet de la Distillation de la Betterave, Pomme de Terre, par E. Hourier.

The Technology of Sugar.   John Geddes M'Intosh.   London: Scott, Greenwood & Co.

Food Inspection and Analysis.   Albert E. Leach.

Études et Recherches sur le Grain de Blé, by Émile Frichot.

A Method for the Identification of Pure Organic Compounds, by Samuel Parsons Mulliken, Ph.D.

Acetylene, by Vivian B. Lewes, F.I.C.

Cellulose, Cellulose Products, and Artificial Rubber, by Dr. Joseph Bersch.

Schweizerisches Alkoholmonopol.   Bern, Buchdruckerei Stämpfli et Cie., 1901.

Jahrbuch des Vereins der Spiritus-Fabrikanten in Deutschland, 1906.

Branntweinsteuer-Ausführungsbestimmung, 8. Theil, betreffend Branntweinsteuer-Befreiungsordnung.   R. von Decker, Berlin.

Principles and Practice of Agricultural Analysis.   Wiley.

Fractional Distillation.   Young.

Provisional Methods for the Analysis of Foods.   Adopted by the A. O. A. C., Nov. 14–16, 1901.

U. S. Department of Agriculture (Composition of Cereals).   See Bulletins 9, 45, 58.

U. S. Internal Revenue Gaugers' Manual, 1900.

Gas-engine Design.   Lucke.

Ministère de l'Agriculture, Concours International de Moteurs et Appareils Utilisant l'Alcool Dénaturé Ayant en Lieu à Paris en mai, 1902.   Rapports des Jurys.   Paris, Imprimerie Nationale, 1902.

The Thermodynamics of Heat Engines.   Reeve, 1903.

The Gas and Oil Engine.   Dugald Clerk.

The Mechanical Engineer's Pocket-book.   Kent.

Combustion Engines, by Guldner; translated by Prof. Diederichs.

Journal of Society of German Engineers.   Tests by Prof. Eugene Meyer, April, May, 1903.

Moteurs à Alcool, par E. Sorel.

Oil Analysis, by Augustus H. Gill.

LIST OF PATENTS RELATING TO THE MANUFACTURE OF ALCOHOL AND ALCOHOL-DISTILLING APPARATUS.

The following list of patents relating to the manufacture of alcohol, improvements in distillation apparatus, by-products of distillation, etc., is added for convenience of reference.

*PROCESSES AND APPARATUS FOR THE MANUFACTURE OF ALCOHOL.

This List Comprises the Important Patents in this Line for the Last Twenty Years.

Patent No. 334222—Horace A. Fitch, New York, Jan. 12, 1886, apparatus for aging spirituous liquors, wines, etc.

370549—John W. Lochner and Nicholas Oester, Aurora, Ind., Sept. 27, 1887, device for aging and purifying liquors.

482018—T. Mason, Jr., Manchester, Eng., Sept. 6, 1892, apparatus for purifying and refining alcoholic liquors and other liquids.

482843—C. Heintz, Buffalo, N. Y., Sept. 20, 1892, apparatus for purifying and aging liquors.

488104—A. L. Wood, Boston, Mass., Dec. 13, 1892, apparatus for aging and purifying liquors.

489363—A. Bornholdt, Brooklyn, N. Y., assignor to The National Vacuum Drying Air Distilling Co., of the same place, Jan. 3, 1893, separating the constituents of liquid bodies.

492542—C. Heintz, Buffalo, N. Y., Feb., 28, 1893, method of and apparatus for purifying and softening liquors.

497033—W. Saint Martin, Paris, France, May 9, 1893, apparatus for maturing and improving fermented alcoholic liquids.

497857—C. Bullock, North Cambridge, Mass., May 23, 1893, method of and apparatus for treating alcoholic liquors.

531718—J. S. Detwiler, Philadelphia, Pa., and M. G. Stevens, Merchantville, N. J., Jan. 1, 1895, apparatus for aging liquors.

582608—M. Whitson, Salina, Kan., May 15, 1897, apparatus for purifying and charging liquids.

748331—J. B. Roche, Louisville, Ky., Dec. 29, 1903, apparatus for heating liquor.

811966—R. A. Stewart, San Francisco, Cal., one-half interest to A. J. Knoblock, of San Francisco, Cal., Feb. 6, 1906, means for aging and purifying liquors.

818478—S. Swayder, Denver, Colo., April 24, 1906, receptacle for storing alcoholic liquors.

608652—A. M. Villon, Lyons, France, Aug. 9, 1898, processes of manufacturing ethylic alcohol.

385625—Wm. L. Horne, Meriden, Conn., to the Horne Vacuum Co., Hartford, Conn., July 3, 1888, alcoholic distillation.

411231—Jokichi Takamine, of Tokio, Japan, processes of manufacture of alcoholic liquids, Sept. 17, 1889.

618207—Johannes Edward Lang, of Berne, Switzerland, Jan. 24, 1899, material for distilling alcohol.

615376—H. W. Wiley, of the District of Columbia, one-half to the Marsden Company, of Philadelphia, Pa., Dec. 6, 1898, manufacture of alcohol.

667359—Geo. Hillard Benjamin, New York, N. Y., Feb. 5, 1901, process of producing alcohol for use in the arts alone.

347441—C. W. Ramsay, of Brooklyn, to the Ramsay Purifying Co., of New York, N. Y., Aug. 17, 1886, process of treating fermented, fermentable and distilled liquids in vacuo.

386748—W. L. Horne, Meriden, Conn., to the Horne Vacuum Co., of Hartford, Conn., July 24, 1888, process of aging liquors.

418792—J. A. H. Hasbrouck, Plainfield, N. J., to the New York and New Jersey Liquor Maturing Co., of the same place, Jan. 7, 1890, process of aging liquors.

471707—J. McKinless, of Manchester, Eng., to the Mechanical Spirit Maturing Syndicate Ltd., of London, Eng., March 29, 1892, apparatus for maturing spirits and other liquors.

485341—I. B. Cushing, Brookline, Mass., Nov. 1, 1892, process of and apparatus for purifying and maturing liquors or distilled spirits.

698184—J. F. Duffy, Chicago, Ill., April 22, 1902, method of refining, mellowing and purifying alcoholic liquors.

489337—E. A. Spink, Chicago, Ill., Jan. 3, process of aging liquors.

508882—Chas. Hornbostel, New York, N. Y., Nov. 14, 1893, preparing fermented and distilled liquids, extracts and solutions.

532399—R. C. Scott, Liverpool, Eng., Jan. 8, 1895, art of aging or treating spirits.

540279—C. A. Oteen, Allegheny, Pa., June 4, 1895, process of aging liquors.

590306—D. J. Etly, Louisville, Ky., Sept. 21, 1897, process of an apparatus for aging liquors artificially.

666242—J. E. Carroll, London, Eng., Jan. 15, 1901, method distillation.

532399—R. C. Scott, Liverpool, Eng., Jan. 8, 1902, art of aging or treating spirits.

390243—J. U. Lloyd, Cincinnati, Ohio, Oct. 2, 1888, condensing apparatus.

407114—L. E. A. Prangey, Paris, France, July 16, 1889, apparatus for separating liquids at different boiling points.

667522—N. H. Hiller, Carbondale, Pa., Feb. 5, 1901, distilling apparatus.

12092—N. H. Hiller, Cardonbale, Pa., March 3, 1903, distilling apparatus.

742697—T. B. Martin, McKee, Ky., to Ad. W. Creekmore and Horatio G. Creekmore, of Lexington, Ky., Oct. 27, 1903.

774824—H. S. Blackmore, Mt. Vernon, N. Y., to Robert C. Mitchell, same place, Nov. 15, 1904, process of making alcohol and aldehyde.

822574—J. J. Brennan, of Louisville, Ky., one-half to Thos. J. Hines, same place, June 5, 1906, apparatus for distillation.

349449—J. C. Peden, Lawrenceburg, Ky., to himself and the Bourbon Copper and Brass Works of Cincinnati, Ohio, Sept 21, 1886, process of and apparatus for distilling.

412407—P. Napoles, Nata, Cal., Oct. 8, 1889, distilling apparatus.

436684—E. A. Barbet, Paris, France, Sept. 16, 1890, apparatus for and process of continuous rectification of spirits, alcohol, etc.

436735—G. Gugnard and A. Hedouin, Paris, France, September 16, 1890, process of and apparatus for manufacturing alcohol.

436764—E. A. Barbet, Paris, France, Sept. 16, 1890, process of and apparatus for rectifying and distilling alcohol.

451679—G. Descamps, Havana, Cuba, one-half to George S. Descamps, of New Orleans, La., May 5, 1891, apparatus for manufacturing alcohol from sugar cane.

504074—Edson Bradley and Edw. N. Dickerson, Jr., New York, N. Y., Aug. 29, 1893, process of making alcoholic distilled liquor.

639979—M. Hickey, Boston, Mass., December 26, 1899, apparatus for recovering waste alcohol for liquor casks.

314340—B. Schumm, New York, N. Y., Feb. 6, 1894, apparatus for preparing and manipulating fermenting mixtures.

733189—W. Griesser, New York, N. Y., July 7, 1903, brewing apparatus.

765549—F. Brogniez, Detroit, Mich., to Pfandler, Vacuum Fermentation Co., of Rochester, N. Y., July 19, 1904, mechanism for regulating the admission of air to liquids.

358615—G. Jordan, New York, March 1, 1887, apparatus for distilling alcohol and other volatile substances.

414936—C. J. T. Burcey, Syracuse, N. Y., apparatus for purifying wood alcohol, Nov. 12, 1889.

484963—M. Hickey, Boston, Mass., apparatus for and method of recovering waste alcohol from liquor casks, Oct. 25, 1892.

639980—M. Hickey, Boston, Mass., apparatus for recovering waste alcohol from casks, Dec. 26, 1899.

636772—C. J. Seltzer, Philadelphia, Pa., process of recovering absorbed alcohol from empty barrels, Nov. 19, 1901.

765148—P. P. Peace, Philadelphia, Pa., process of removing alcoholic liquors from empty casks, July 12, 1904.

815463—T. H. Naughton, Boston, Mass., apparatus for recovering waste alcohol from liquor casks and barrels, March 20, 1906.

815464—T. H. Naughton, Boston, Mass., process for recovering waste alcohol from liquor casks and barrels, March 20, 1906.

285029—A. Deininger, Berlin, Germany, apparatus for manufacture of alcohol, May, 16, 1882.

266925—K. Trobach and A. Cords, process of and apparatus for distilling alcohol, Oct. 31, 1882.

333721—J. Bendix, Berlin, Prussia, Germany, process of filtering alcohol, Jan. 5, 1886.

393057—T. G. Bowick, Harpenden, Eng., apparatus for purifying alcohol, Nov. 20, 1888.

391015—T. G. Bowick, Harpenden, Eng., process of purifying alcohol, Oct. 16, 1888.

408583—Andre Theodore Christoph, Paris, France, rectification of alcohol, Aug. 6, 1889.

412931—Carl Maria Pielsticker, London, Eng., process of purifying alcohol, Oct. 15, 1889.

419332—William L. Horne, of Meriden, assignor to the Horne Vacuum Co., of Hartford, Conn., alcoholic distillation, Jan. 14, 1890.

432198—Gaston Guignard, of Paris, France, process of purifying crude alcohol, July 15, 1890.

457799—Alfred Springer, of Cincinnati, Ohio, method of producing alcohol, Aug. 18, 1891.

470447—Paul Clement Rosseau and Marie Jean De Chauterac, of Paris, and Marie Joseph Denis Alexandre De La Baume, of Tourtour, France, method for the purification of alcoholic liquids, March 8, 1892.

574111—M. Pridham, Philadelphia, Pa., process of and apparatus for purifying, rectifying, and deodorizing alcoholic or other liquids, Dec. 29, 1896.

617400—C. Killing, Düsseldorf, Germany, process of purifying raw alcohol from aldehyde, Jan. 10, 1899.

625650—W. G. Day and T. A. Byran, Baltimore, Md., process of improving alcoholic liquids, May 23, 1899.

645940—Marie Jean De Chauterac, of Paris, and Marie Joseph Denis Alexandre De La Baume, of Tourtour, France, assignors to La Societte Civille Pour L'Exploitation De Brevets D'Invention Concernant L'Industrie De L'Alcool, of Paris, France, purification of alcoholic liquids, March 27, 1900.

736098—Lallah S. Highton, of San Francisco, Cal., administratrix of James Howden, deceased, art of purifying alcoholic liquors, Aug. 11, 1903.

657698—J. A. H. Hasbrouck, Brooklyn, N. Y., process of aging alcoholic liquors, Sept. 11, 1900.

824906—Harry O. Chute, of Cleveland, Ohio, process of making wood alcohol, July 3, 1906.

Fusel oils. Manufacture of E. A. Mirlin, Prague, and L. Lewin, Vienna. Eng. Pat. 10435, May 18, 1905. See Fr. Pat. 354807 of 1905; Jour. S. C. I., 1905,

Distilling apparatus (alcohol, etc.), impts. in. J. H. Covell, Montague, Cape Colony. Eng. Pat. 15371, July 26, 1905.

Distillery "slop" desiccated, and process of making same. G. F. Ahlers, Covington, Ky. U. S. Pat. 821326, May 22, 1906. A dry fodder is prepared from distillery slop by separating the latter into solid and liquid portions. The solid portions are dried to a granular and absorbent condition, while the liquid portions are concentrated to a syrup, which is then incorporated with the absorbent granular portion, and the whole is dried. The product may be mixed with starchy materials to form a properly balanced foodstuff.

Distilling apparatus, new improvements in. No. 731799, patented June 23, 1903. Walter E. Lummus, Lynn, Massachusetts, U. S. A.

Manufacture of alcohol from peat. English Patent applied for, No. 20936. West.

Process of fermentation. English Patent No. 5135 (1906). Vloebergh.

Mash-tuns and infusion decoction and digester vessels. English Patent No. 18837 (1905). House.

Fermenting vats. English Patent 18836 (1905), September 26. House.

Treatment of malt. English Patent 26041 (1905), Oct. 3. Covell.

Conversion of diastatic malt extracts into solid form for rendering same durable. English Patent No. 9886 (1906), Sept. 26. Pollak.

Sterilizing, softening and heating water and other liquids and apparatus therefor. English Patent No. 26527 (1905), Sept. 26. Westrope and Cooper.

GENERAL INDEX.

A

B

C

F

G

H

INDEX TO UNITED STATES REGULATIONS AND INSTRUCTIONS.

PART I.

PART II.

PART III.

PART IV.

PART V.

INDEX TO REPORT OF THE BRITISH DEPARTMENTAL COMMITTEE.

INDEX TO APPENDICES FROM MINUTES OF EVIDENCE TAKEN BEFORE THE BRITISH DEPARTMENTAL COMMITTEE ON INDUSTRIAL ALCOHOL.

KNOWLEDGE PUBLICATIONS
THE WORLDS LARGEST PUBLISHER OF BOOKS ON
HYDROGEN*SOLAR*FUEL CELLS*BIOMASS*ALCOHOL FUEL*WIND

Sunshine To Dollars
Behemoth: The Story of Power
Denatured and Industrial Alcohol
The Mother Earth News Handbook of Homemade Power
How To Save Energy and Cut Costs in Existing Industrial and Commercial Buildings
How to Really Save Money and Energy in Cooling Your Home
Movable Insulation
DOE Chemistry Volumes 1 and 2
DOE Electrical Science Volumes 1-4
DOE Instrumentation and Control Volumes 1 and 2
DOE Material Science Volumes 1 and 2
DOE Mathematics Volumes 1 and 2
DOE Mechanical Science Volumes 1 and 2
DOE Nuclear Physics and Reactor Theory
DOE Classical Physics
DOE Thermodynamics, Heat Transfer and Fluid Flow Volumes 1-3
Effects of Nuclear Weapons
DOE Fuel Cell
Fuel Cells: Power of Tomorrow
Hydraulic Engineering
Hydraulic Motors
Industrial Gases
Industrial Hydrogen
The Complete Handbook of Solar Air Heating Systems
The Solar Cookery Book
Hydrogen Production from Organic Material by Partial Oxidation and Steam Reformation
Mechanical Movements
Hydrogen Generator Gas for Vehicles and Engines: Volumes 1 and 2
Hydrogen Generator Gas for Vehicles and Engines: Volumes 3 and 4
Fabulous Fireball/Experiments With Solar Energy
Construction of Bio-Gas Plants, A Manual
Bio-Gas Volumes 1 and 2
Hydrogen Manufacture by Electrolysis, Thermal Decomposition and Unusual Techniques
Hydrogen Technology for Energy

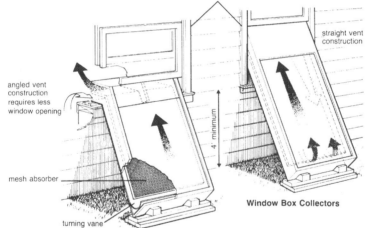

Made in the USA
Charleston, SC
16 August 2011